Major Problems in

AMERICAN DIPLOMATIC HISTORY

MAJOR PROBLEMS IN

American Diplomatic History

DOCUMENTS AND READINGS

Volume II

EDITED BY
Daniel M. Smith, University of Colorado

D. C. HEATH AND COMPANY
LEXINGTON, MASSACHUSETTS

40125

PREFACE

It seemed to the editor, in reflecting on his experiences as student and teacher, that a need existed for readings in American diplomatic history based on a sharply defined problems approach. Much of the interest and value in the study of American foreign relations is found in the asking and answering of the "great questions" of the causes and consequences of decisions for war, peacemaking, and the declaration of major policies.

With the exception of the first introductory chapter, the emphasis has been placed on the debates among historians and statesmen concerning nine specific events or policies. A few selected documents precede the secondary accounts in the chapters, in part because of the conviction that the student should be exposed to the raw material of history, but primarily in order to illustrate the depth and range of the problem under study. It is hoped that this approach will broaden the student's appreciation of American diplomatic history and will not only give him some basis for evaluating the past but will facilitate an understanding of the nature of the historical craft.

Although the editor alone is responsible for the materials in this volume—and is aware that many will ask why certain documents and secondary readings were either included or omitted—he wishes to express gratitude for wisdom and guidance received in the past from Professor Armin Rappaport at the University of California, Berkeley, and Professor Thomas A. Bailey of Stanford University.

MAPS

CONTENTS

PART II:

The Emergence of the United States as a Great World Power, 1890–1963

PART II

Emergence of the United States as a Great World Power

1890-1963

INTRODUCTION

The major themes in American diplomatic history after 1889 are the emergence of the United States as a major world power and the reflection in its foreign policies of the domestic conflict between the "isolationists" and the "internationalists."

From birth, the United States was a world power, as historian T. A. Bailey has pointed out, seriously considered by European states in matters affecting the Western Hemisphere. In the watershed or transitional decade of the 1890's, America clearly became a major or great world power whose wealth, population, and potential military strength made it important in the scales of the global balance of power. The United States began to build a modern navy and to become greatly interested in overseas markets and bases, and in 1898 had a spectacular "coming-out" party in the brief but eminently satisfying Spanish-American War. By 1900 these developments, including acquisition of overseas empire, had inextricably involved America in international politics.

Yet the American people retained a psychological isolationism. In the 19th century, as historian C. Vann Woodward has aptly described it, the United States had enjoyed a long period of "free security," of relative immunity from external threats. This had resulted less from American power and efforts, and more from the existence of a favorable power structure in Europe capped by the generally benevolent sea power of Great Britain. Although this condition ended by 1914, most Americans failed to appreciate the change and remained committed to the older isolationist policies and sentiments. By the turn of the 20th century, the balance of power in Europe and the Far East was shifting and a cycle of incredibly destructive wars was in the offing. The United States henceforth would have to pay a much higher price for security.

By the 1960's, two world wars and a "police action" later, Americans at last were accepting the fact of inescapable involvement and responsibilities in world affairs. Even so, it was for many a most reluctant acceptance—hence the often bitter post-1945 debates over foreign aid and levels of military strength. Isolationism perhaps was dead as a viable policy, but its emotional attitudes have lingered and maturity in foreign affairs is by no means yet achieved.

10 THE SPANISH-AMERICAN WAR: A Popular Crusade?

The United States had attained a high level of agricultural and industrial production by the 1890's and was in the flush of a newly aroused interest in world affairs. Reconstruction was over, the frontier process largely completed, population neared seventy millions, and economic production had achieved such miracles of abundance as apparently to require a more vigorous drive for external markets and raw material sources of supply. Psychologically, the generation of the 1890's was in an expansionist and adventurous mood. Civil War bloodshed and suffering had been dimmed by the passage of time, and nationalism had welled to a new peak of intensity. The result was what historians describe as a revival of Manifest Destiny, a revival of a conviction that America was destined to play a more active role in the world and a renewed interest in overseas colonies and coaling stations. The quickened national tempo was expressed in a number of ways: the launching of the modern Pan American movement in 1889, rivalry with Germany and Great Britain in Samoa, annexation schemes for Hawaii, and clashes with Chile and Great Britain in the Western Hemisphere. The new spirit culminated in the 1898 Spanish-American War over Cuba.

The war in 1898 raises several important questions for students of history. Why did the United States intervene in the Cuban strife, after an earlier abstention during the equally bloody Ten Years' War (1868–1878)? What role did endangered American economic interests in Cuba have in the decision for war? What was the attitude of the big business community within the United States? Was the sensationalist press primarily responsible for the popular demand for intervention? And, finally, why did a war to free Cuba transform the United States into an imperial power?

DOCUMENTS

1. McKinley Decides for War

On March 25 and 27, 1898, Assistant Secretary of State William R. Day instructed the American Minister Stewart L. Woodford to request of the Spanish government the proclamation of an armistice in Cuba until October, the revocation of the reconcentration policy affecting the Cuban population in rebellious areas, and acceptance of American mediation. Although Woodford's reports, on April 9 and 10, indicated that the Madrid regime was beginning to comply, President McKinley in effect asked Congress on April 11 to declare war. Subsequently, historians have roundly condemned him for thus rejecting a peaceful solution and capitulating to popular jingoistic pressures. Yet it should be noted,

283

as his message made clear, the costly patience of the American government in the preceding three years of the civil war. It was by no means probable that the Cuban rebels would accept the armistice and the Spanish authorities were not prepared to consent to an American mediation culminating in Cuban independence.

Congress authorized the use of force on April 19 and war was declared subsequently as of April 21.

McKinley's Address to Congress, April 11, 1898

EXECUTIVE MANSION, April 11, 1898

To the Congress of the United States:

Obedient to that precept of the Constitution which commands the President to give from time to time to the Congress information of the state of the Union and to recommend to their consideration such measures as he shall judge necessary and expedient, it becomes my duty to now address your body with regard to the grave crisis that has arisen in the relations of the United States to Spain by reason of the warfare that for more than three years has raged in the neighboring island of Cuba.

I do so because of the intimate connection of the Cuban question with the state of our own Union and the grave relation the course which it is now incumbent upon the nation to adopt must needs bear to the traditional policy of our Government if it is to accord with the precepts laid down by the founders of the Republic and religiously observed by succeeding Administrations to the present day.

The present revolution is but the successor of other similar insurrections which have occurred in Cuba against the dominion of Spain, extending over a period of nearly half a century, each of which during its progress has subjected the United States to great effort and expense in enforcing its neutrality laws, caused enormous losses to American trade and commerce, caused irritation, annoyance, and disturbance among our citizens, and, by the exercise of cruel, barbarous, and uncivilized practices of warfare, shocked the sensibilities and offended the humane sympathies of our people. . . .

Our people have beheld a once prosperous community reduced to comparative want, its lucrative commerce virtually paralyzed, its exceptional productiveness diminished, its fields laid waste, its mills in ruins, and its people perishing by tens of thousands from hunger and destitution. We have found ourselves constrained, in the observance of that strict neutrality which our laws enjoin and which the law of nations commands, to police our own waters and watch our own seaports in prevention of any unlawful act in aid of the Cubans.

Our trade has suffered, the capital invested by our citizens in Cuba has been largely lost, and the temper and forbearance of our people have been so sorely tried as to beget a perilous unrest among our own citizens, which has inevitably found its expression from time to time in the National Legislature, so that issues wholly external to our own body politic engross attention and stand in the way of that close devotion to domestic advancement that becomes a self-contained commonwealth whose primal maxim has been the avoidance of all foreign entanglements. All this must needs awaken, and has, indeed, aroused, the utmost concern on the part of this Government, as well during my predecessor's term as in my own. . . .

The war in Cuba is of such a nature that, short of subjugation or extermination, a final military victory for either side seems impracticable. The alternative lies in the physical exhaustion of the one or the other party, or perhaps of both—a condition which in effect ended the ten years' war by the truce of Zanjon. The prospect of such a protraction and conclusion of the present strife is a contingency hardly to be contemplated with equanimity by the civilized world, and least of all by the United States, affected and injured as we are, deeply and intimately, by its very existence.

Realizing this, it appeared to be my duty, in a spirit of true friendliness, no less to Spain than to the Cubans, who have so much to lose by the prolongation of the struggle, to seek to bring about an immediate termination of the war. To this end I submitted on the 27th ultimo, as a result of much representation and correspondence, through the United States minister at Madrid, propositions to the Spanish Government looking to an armistice until October 1 for the negotiation of peace with the good offices of the President.

In addition I asked the immediate revocation of the order of reconcentration, so as to permit the people to return to their farms and the needy to be relieved with provisions and supplies from the United States, cooperating with the Spanish authorities, so as to afford full relief.

The reply of the Spanish cabinet was received on the night of the 31st ultimo. It offered, as the means to bring about peace in Cuba, to confide the preparation thereof to the insular parliament, inasmuch as the concurrence of that body would be necessary to reach a final result, it being, however, understood that the powers reserved by the constitution to the central Government are not lessened or diminished. As the Cuban parliament does not meet until the 4th of May next, the Spanish Government would not object for its part to accept at once a suspension of hostilities if asked for by the insurgents from the general in chief, to whom it would pertain in such case to determine the duration and conditions of the armistice. . . .

With this last overture in the direction of immediate peace, and its disappointing reception by Spain, the Executive is brought to the end of his effort. . . .

The grounds for . . . intervention may be briefly summarized as follows:

First. In the cause of humanity and to put an end to the barbarities, bloodshed, starvation, and horrible miseries now existing there, and which the parties to the conflict are either unable or unwilling to stop or mitigate. It is no answer to say this is all in another country, belonging to another nation, and is therefore none of our business. It is specially our duty, for it is right at our door.

Second. We owe it to our citizens in Cuba to afford them that protection and indemnity for life and property which no government there can or will afford, and to that end to terminate the conditions that deprive them of legal protection.

Third. The right to intervene may be justified by the very serious injury to the commerce, trade, and business of our people and by the wanton destruction of property and devastation of the island.

Fourth, and which is of the utmost importance. The present condition of affairs in Cuba is a constant menace to our peace and entails upon this Government an enormous expense. With such a conflict waged for years in an island so near us and with which our people have such trade and business relations; when the lives and liberty of our citizens are in constant danger and their property destroyed and themselves ruined; where our trading vessels are liable to seizure and are seized at our very door by war ships of a foreign nation; the expeditions of filibustering that we are powerless to prevent altogether, and the irritating questions and entanglements thus arising—all these and others that I need not mention, with the resulting strained relations, are a constant menace to our peace and compel us to keep on a semi war footing with a nation with which we are at peace. . . .

In view of these facts and of these considerations I ask the Congress to authorize and empower the President to take measures to secure a full and final termination of hostilities between the Government of Spain and the people of Cuba, and to secure in the island the establishment of a stable government, capable of maintaining order and observing its international obligations, insuring peace and tranquillity and the security of its citizens as well as our own, and to use the military and naval forces of the United States as may be necessary for these purposes.

And in the interest of humanity and to aid in preserving the lives of the starving people of the island I recommend that the distribution of food and supplies be continued and that an appropriation be made out of the public Treasury to supplement the charity of our citizens.

The issue is now with the Congress. It is a solemn responsibility. I have exhausted every effort to relieve the intolerable condition of affairs which is at our doors. Prepared to execute every obligation imposed upon me by the Constitution and the law, I await your action.

Yesterday, and since the preparation of the foregoing message, official information was received by me that the latest decree of the Queen Regent of Spain directs General Blanco, in order to prepare and facilitate peace, to proclaim a suspension of hostilities, the duration and details of which have not yet been communicated to me.

This fact, with every other pertinent consideration, will, I am sure, have your just and careful attention in the solemn deliberations upon which you are about to enter. If this measure attains a successful result, then our aspirations as a Christian, peace-loving people will be realized. If it fails, it will be only another justification for our contemplated action.

2. The March of the Flag

Entering the war to free Cuba, the United States ended it by annexing Puerto Rico, Guam, and the Philippine Islands. Spain was compensated in the peace treaty, signed December 10, 1898, by the sum of 20 million dollars. President McKinley explained to a group of visiting Methodists the mixture of motives— economic, patriotic and missionary—for the decision to acquire the Philippines. Albert J. Beveridge, Republican Senator from Indiana and an ardent expansionist, expressed the same arguments more fully in a flamboyant address known as the "March of the Flag."

McKinley Explains Acquisition of the Philippines

. . . The truth is I didn't want the Philippines, and when they came to us, as a gift from the gods, I did not know what to do with them. When the Spanish War broke out, Dewey was at Hongkong, and I ordered him to go to Manila and to capture or destroy the Spanish fleet, and he had to; because, if defeated, he had no place to refit on that side of the globe, and if the Dons were victorious, they would likely cross the Pacific and ravage our Oregon and California coasts. And so he had to destroy the Spanish fleet, and did it! But that was as far as I thought then.

When next I realized that the Philippines had dropped into our laps I confess I did not know what to do with them. I sought counsel from all sides—Democrats as well as Republicans—but got little help. I thought first we would take only Manila; then Luzon; then other islands, perhaps, also. I walked the floor of the White House night after night until midnight; and I am not ashamed to tell you, gentlemen, that I went down on my knees and prayed Almighty God for light and guidance more than one night. And one night late it came to me this way—I don't know how it was, but it came: (1) That we could not give them back to Spain—that would be cowardly and dishonorable; (2) that we could not turn them over to France or Germany—our commercial rivals in the Orient—that would be bad business and discreditable; (3) that we could not leave them to themselves—they were unfit for self-government—and they would soon have anarchy and misrule over there worse than Spain's was; and (4) that there was nothing left for us to do but to take them all, and to educate the Filipinos, and uplift and civilize and Christianize them, and by God's grace do the very best we could by them, as our fellow-men for whom Christ also died. And then I went to bed, and went to sleep, and slept soundly, and the next morning I sent for the chief engineer of the War Department (our map-maker), and I told him to put the Philippines on the map of the United States [pointing to a large map on the wall of his office], and there they are, and there they will stay while I am President!

Albert J. Beveridge's "March of the Flag" Speech

Fellow citizens, It is a noble land that God has given us; a land that can feed and clothe the world; a land whose coast lines would enclose half the countries of Europe; a land set like a sentinel between the two imperial oceans of the globe, a greater England with a nobler destiny. It is a mighty people that he has planted on this soil; a people sprung from the most masterful blood of history; a people perpetually revitalized by the virile, man-producing workingfolk of all the earth; a people imperial by virtue of their power, by right of their institutions, by authority of their heaven-directed purposes—the propagandists and not the misers of liberty. It is a glorious history our God has bestowed upon his chosen people; a history whose keynote was struck by Liberty Bell; a history heroic with faith in our mission and our future; a history of statesmen who flung the boundaries of the Republic out into unexplored lands and savage wildernesses; a history of soldiers who carried the flag across the blazing deserts and through the ranks of hostile mountains, even to the gates of sunset; a history of a multiplying people who overran a continent in half a century; a history of prophets who saw the consequences of evils inherited from the past and of martyrs who died to save us from them; a history divinely logical, in the process of whose tremendous reasoning we find ourselves today.

. . . Shall the American people continue their resistless march toward the commercial supremacy of the world? Shall free institutions broaden their blessed reign as the children of liberty wax in strength, until the empire of our principles is established over the hearts of all mankind?

Have we no mission to perform, no duty to discharge to our fellowman? Has the Almighty Father endowed us with gifts beyond our deserts and marked us as the people of his peculiar favor, merely to rot in our own selfishness, as men and nations must, who take cowardice for their companion and self for their Deity—as China has, as India has, as Egypt has?

Shall we be as the man who had one talent and hid it, or as he who had ten talents and used them until they grew to riches? And shall we reap the reward that waits on our discharge of our high duty as the sovereign power of earth; shall we occupy new markets for what our farmers raise, new markets for what our factories make, new markets for what our merchants sell—aye, and, please God, new markets for what our ships shall carry?

Shall we avail ourselves of new sources of supply of what we do not raise or make, so that what are luxuries to-day will be necessities to-morrow? Shall our commerce be encouraged until, with Oceanica, the Orient, and the world, American trade shall be the imperial trade of the entire globe? . . .

. . . For William McKinley is continuing the policy that Jefferson began, Monroe continued, Seward advanced, Grant promoted, Harrison championed, and the growth of the republic has demanded. Hawaii is ours; Porto Rico is to be ours; at the prayer of the people Cuba will finally be ours; in the islands of the East, even to the gates of Asia, coaling-stations are to be ours; at the very least the flag of a liberal government is to float over the Philippines, and I pray God it may be the banner that

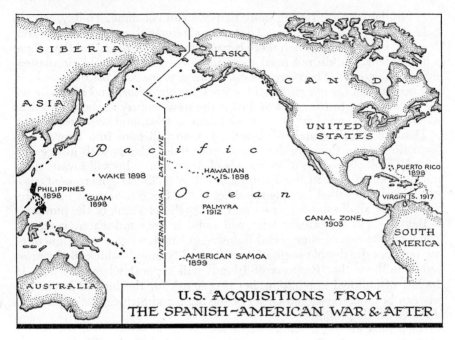

U.S. ACQUISITIONS FROM THE SPANISH–AMERICAN WAR & AFTER

Taylor unfurled in Texas and Fremont carried to the coast—the Stars and Stripes of glory. . . .

The Opposition tells us that we ought not to govern a people without their consent. I answer, The rule of liberty that all just government derives its authority from the consent of the governed, applies only to those who are capable of self-government. I answer, We govern the Indians without their consent, we govern our territories without their consent, we govern our children without their consent. I answer, How do you assume that our government would be without their consent? Would not the people of the Philippines prefer the just, humane, civilizing government of this republic to the savage, bloody rule of pillage and extortion from which we have rescued them?

. . . And, now, obeying the same voice that Jefferson heard and obeyed, that Jackson heard and obeyed, that Monroe heard and obeyed, that Seward heard and obeyed, that Ulysses S. Grant heard and obeyed, that Benjamin Harrison heard and obeyed, William McKinley plants the flag over the islands of the seas, outposts of commerce, citadels of national security, and the march of the flag goes on! . . .

Distance and oceans are no arguments. . . .

Steam joins us; electricity joins us—the very elements are in league with our destiny. Cuba not contiguous! Porto Rico not contiguous! Hawaii and the Philippines not contiguous! Our navy will make them contiguous. Dewey and Sampson and Schley have made them contiguous, and American speed, American guns, American heart and brain and nerve will keep them contiguous forever. . . .

. . . to-day, we are raising more than we can consume. To-day, we are making more than we can use. To-day, our industrial society is congested; there are more workers than there is work; there is more capital than there is investment. We do not need more money—we need more circulation, more employment. Therefore we must find new markets for our produce, new occupation for our capital, new work for our labor. And so, while we did not need the territory taken during the past century at the time it was acquired, we do need what we have taken in 1898, and we need it now.

Think of the thousands of Americans who will pour into Hawaii and Porto Rico when the republic's laws cover those islands with justice and safety! Think of the tens of thousands of Americans who will invade mine and field and forest in the Philippines when a liberal government, protected and controlled by this republic, if not the government of the republic itself, shall establish order and equity there! Think of the hundreds of thousands of Americans who will build a soap-and-water, common-school civilization of energy and industry in Cuba, when a government of law replaces the double reign of anarchy and tyranny!—think of the prosperous millions that Empress of Islands will support when, obedient to the law of political gravitation, her people ask for the highest honor liberty can bestow, the sacred Order of the Stars and Stripes, the citizenship of the Great Republic!

What does all this mean for every one of us? It means opportunity for all the glorious young manhood of the republic—the most virile, ambitious, impatient, militant manhood the world has ever seen. It means that the resources and the commerce of these immensely rich dominions will be increased as much as American energy is greater than Spanish sloth; for Americans henceforth will monopolize those resources and that commerce. . . .

Fellow Americans, we are God's chosen people. Yonder at Bunker Hill and Yorktown his providence was above us. At New Orleans and on ensanguined seas his hand sustained us. Abraham Lincoln was his minister and his was the Altar of Freedom, the boys in blue set on a hundred battlefields. His power directed Dewey in the East and delivered the Spanish fleet into our hands on the eve of Liberty's natal day, as he delivered the elder Armada into the hands of our English sires two centuries ago. His great purposes are revealed in the progress of the flag, which surpasses the intentions of Congresses and Cabinets, and leads us like a holier pillar of cloud by day and pillar of fire by night into situations unforeseen by finite wisdom, and duties unexpected by the unprophetic heart of selfishness. The American people cannot use a dishonest medium of exchange; it is ours to set the world its example of right and honor. We cannot fly from our world duties; it is ours to execute the purpose of a fate that has driven us to be greater than our small intentions. We cannot retreat from any soil where Providence has unfurled our banner; it is ours to save that soil for Liberty and Civilization. For Liberty and Civilization and God's promise fulfilled, the flag must henceforth be the symbol and the sign to all mankind—the flag!—

Flag of the free heart's hope and home,
　　By angel hands to valor given,
Thy stars have lit the welkin dome,
　　And all their hues were born in heaven!
Forever wave that standard sheet,
　　Where breathes the foe but falls before us,
With freedom's soil beneath our feet
　　And freedom's banner streaming o'er us.

READINGS

1. Economics and the Spanish War

Several historians, including Charles A. Beard, have explained American imperialism and the Spanish war on economic grounds: the desire for markets,
and the 150 million American dollars invested in Cuban sugar and trade.
Challenging that interpretation, Julius W. Pratt, in the following selection,
examines the attitude of business groups toward intervention in Cuba and
demonstrates conclusively that powerful economic groups were opposed to war
in 1897 and early 1898. Yet there can be little doubt that economic interests
were to some degree involved in the revival of Manifest Destiny in the 1890's,
and played an even more significant role in the decision to retain the Philippines.

Expansionists of 1898
JULIUS W. PRATT

. . . So reliable a scholar as Professor H. U. Faulkner has asserted that
"the great cause for the war" with Spain is to be found in the fact that by
1898 the United States was "sufficiently advanced for financial imperialism," implying that the war was fought for markets and fields for investment. This interpretation was directly contradicted by the late James Ford
Rhodes, who declared quite as categorically that "the financial and business interests of the country were opposed to the war." We may well
enquire, therefore, what was, in reality, the attitude of American business
both to the war (or to the intervention in Cuba, which brought on the
war) and to the question of territorial expansion.

We may begin with a generalization, the evidence for which will be
presented as the chapter proceeds. American business, in general, had
strongly opposed action that would lead to war with Spain. American
business had been either opposed or indifferent to the expansionist philosophy which had arisen since 1890. But almost at the moment when
the war began, a large section of American business had, for reasons
that will become apparent, been converted to the belief that a program
of territorial expansion would serve its purposes. Hence business, in the
end, welcomed the "large policy" and exerted its share of pressure

Julius W. Pratt, *Expansionists of 1898* (Baltimore: The Johns Hopkins Press, 1936), 232–237,
239–242, 246, 248–252, 266–267, 273–274, 278. Reprinted with permission.

for the retention of the Spanish islands and such related policies as the annexation of Hawaii and the construction of an isthmian canal.

One public man to whom the welfare of American business was of so much concern that he may almost be considered its spokesman in the Senate, was McKinley's friend, Mark Hanna. No one was more unwilling than he to see the United States drift into war with Spain. To Hanna, in the words of his biographer, "the outbreak of war seemed to imperil the whole policy of domestic economic amelioration which he placed before every other object of political action." Hanna's attitude appears to have been identical with that of leading business men. This conclusion is based not only upon the few published biographies of such men, but also upon the study of a large number of financial and trade periodicals, of the proceedings of chambers of commerce and boards of trade, and of material in the *Miscellaneous Files* of the Department of State, containing numerous letters and petitions from business men and organizations.

That business sentiment, especially in the East, was strongly anti-war at the close of 1897 and in the opening months of 1898, is hardly open to doubt. Wall Street stocks turned downward whenever the day's news seemed to presage war and climbed again with information favorable to peace. Bulls and bears on the market were those who anticipated, respectively, a peaceable and a warlike solution of the Cuban question. The "jingo," in Congress or the press, was an object of intense dislike to the editors of business and financial journals, who sought to counteract his influence by anti-war editorials in their columns. Boards of trade and chambers of commerce added their pleas for the maintenance of peace to those of the business newspapers and magazines. So marked, indeed, was the anti-war solidarity of the financial interests and their spokesmen that the jingoes fell to charging Wall Street with want of patriotism. Wall Street, declared the Sacramento *Evening Bee* (March 11, 1898), was "the colossal and aggregate Benedict Arnold of the Union, and the syndicated Judas Iscariot of humanity." Senator Thurston, of Nebraska, charged that opposition to war was found only among the "money-changers," bringing from the editor of *The American Banker* the reply that "there is not an intelligent, self-respecting and civilized American citizen anywhere who would not prefer to have the existing crisis culminate in peaceful negotiations."

This anti-war attitude on the part of several leading financial journals continued up to the very beginning of hostilities. The New York *Journal of Commerce and Commercial Bulletin* declared on February 28 that the only possible excuses for war would be (1) a finding by the naval board investigating the "Maine" disaster that the ship had been destroyed by an official act of the Spanish Government; or (2) a refusal by Spain to make reparation if the board should hold that she had failed to exercise due diligence in safeguarding the vessel. Either of these events it held to be almost inconceivable. The *Commercial and Financial Chronicle* expressed the belief on March 12 that the opposition of the financial interests would yet prevent war; and on April 2 the same journal branded as "monstrous" the proposition to settle the Cuban and "Maine" questions by war while the slightest chance remained for a peaceful solution. On April 16, after the House of Representatives had passed the Cuban resolutions, the Boston *Journal of Commerce* declared: "Sober second thought had but little to do with the deliberations. . . . The members were carried off their feet by the war fever that had been so persistently worked up since the Maine explosion. . . ."

The reasons for this attitude on the part of business are not far to seek. Since the panic of 1893 American business had been in the doldrums. Tendencies toward industrial revival had been checked, first by the Venezuela war scare in December, 1895, and again by the free silver menace in 1896. But in 1897 began a real revival, and before the end of the year signs of prosperity appeared on all sides. The New York *Commercial* conducted a survey of business conditions in a wide variety of trades and industries, from which it concluded that, "after three years of waiting and of false starts, the groundswell of demand has at last begun to rise with a steadiness which leaves little doubt that an era of prosperity has appeared.". . .

To this fair prospect of a great business revival the threat of war was like a spectre at the feast. A foreign complication, thought the *Commercial and Financial Chronicle* in October, 1897, would quickly mar "the trade prosperity which all are enjoying." Six months later (April 2, 1898), after a discussion of the effect of war rumors on the stock exchange, it declared: ". . . Every influence has been, and even now is, tending strongly towards a term of decided prosperity, and that the Cuban disturbance, and it alone, has arrested the movement and checked enterprise." The *Banker and Tradesman* saw in the Cuban complication the threat of a "material setback to the prosperous conditions which had just set in after five years of panic and depression." The same journal summarized a calculation made by the Boston *Transcript* showing that in February, 1898, the wave of prosperity had carried the average price of twenty-five leading stocks within 5½ points of the high for the preceding ten years and 30 points above the low of 1896, and that the Cuban trouble had, in a little over two months, caused a loss of over ten points, or more than one-third of the recent gain. "War would impede the march of prosperity and put the country back many years," said the *New Jersey Trade Review*. The *Railway Age* was of the opinion that the country was coming out of a depression and needed peace to complete its recovery. "From a commercial and mercenary standpoint," it remarked, "it seems peculiarly bitter that this war should have come when the country had already suffered so much and so needed rest and peace.

The idea that war could bring any substantial benefits to business was generally scouted. It would endanger our currency stability, interrupt our trade, and threaten our coasts and our commerce, thought the *Commercial and Financial Chronicle*. It would "incalculably increase the loss to business interests," said the *Banker's Magazine;* while the *United States Investor* held that war was "never beneficial from a material standpoint, that is, in the long run." The *Railroad Gazette* predicted that war would result in "interruption of business enterprise of every kind, stopping new projects and diminution of the output of existing businesses and contraction of trade everywhere." Railroads would lose more than they would gain. Even arms manufacturers were not all agreed that war would be desirable. Journals speaking for the iron and steel industry also argued that war would injure business. It "would injure the iron and steel makers ten times as much as they would be benefited by the prevailing spurt in the manufacture of small arms, projectiles and steel plates for war ships," in the opinion of one of these. The *American Wool and Cotton Reporter* of New York and the *Northwestern Miller* of Minneapolis agreed that war was never materially beneficial in the long run, while trade journals in Atlanta, Chattanooga, and Portland, Oregon, saw as fruits of the approaching conflict only destruction, debt, and depressed industry.

Many conservative interests feared war for the specific reason that it might derange the currency and even revive the free-silver agitation, which had seemed happily dead. The subsistence of that agitation and the prospect of currency reform were among the hopeful factors at the close of 1897. It was not uncommonly charged that the jingoes were animated in part by the expectation that war would lead to inflation in paper or silver. . . .

. . . It remains to examine the attitude of certain American business men and corporations having an immediate stake in Cuba, or otherwise liable to be directly affected by American intervention. Much American capital, as is well known, was invested in the Cuban sugar industry. Upon this industry the civil war fell with peculiarly devastating effect, not only cutting off profits on capital so invested, but also crippling a valuable carrying trade between Cuba and the United States. Naturally enough, some firms suffering under these conditions desired to see the United States intervene to end the war, though such intervention might lead to war between the United States and Spain. In May, 1897, a memorial on the subject bearing over three hundred signatures was presented to John Sherman, Secretary of State. The signers described themselves as "citizens of the United States, doing business as bankers, merchants, manufacturers, steamship owners and agents in the cities of Boston, New York, Philadelphia, Baltimore, Savannah, Charleston, Jacksonville, New Orleans, and other places, and also other citizens of the United States, who have been for many years engaged in the export and import trade with the Island of Cuba." They called attention to the serious losses to which their businesses had been subjected by the hostilities in Cuba and expressed the hope that, in order to prevent further loss, to re-establish American commerce, and also to secure "the blessings of peace for one and a half millions of residents of the Island of Cuba now enduring unspeakable distress and suffering," the United States Government might take steps to bring about an honorable reconciliation between the parties to the conflict.

Another memorial, signed by many of the same subscribers, was presented to President McKinley on February 9, 1898, by a committee of New York business men. It asserted that the Cuban war, which had now continued for three entire years, had caused an average loss of $100,-000,000 a year, or a total loss of $300,000,000 in the import and export trade between Cuba and the United States, to which were to be added "heavy sums irretrievably lost by the destruction of American properties, or properties supported by American capital in the Island itself, such as sugar factories, railways, tobacco plantations, mines and other industrial enterprises; the loss of the United States in trade and capital by means of this war being probably far greater and more serious than that of all the other parties concerned, not excepting Spain herself.". . . .

How much weight such pressure from special interests had with the administration there is no way of knowing. But it is to be noted that the pressure from parties directly interested was not all on one side. Mr. E. F. Atkins, an American citizen who divided his time between Boston and his sugar plantation of Soledad near Cienfuegos, Cuba, which he had developed at a cost of $1,400,000 had been able, through protection received from the Spanish Government and through a corps of guards organized and paid by himself, to continue operations throughout the period of the insurrection. He was frequently in Washington, where he had influential friends, during both the Cleveland and McKinley administrations and worked consistently against the adoption of any measures likely to provoke war.

Unlike some of the sugar plantations, American-owned iron mines in Cuba continued to do active business despite the insurrection. Three American iron and manganese enterprises in the single province of Santiago claimed to have an investment of some $6,000,000 of purely American capital, a large proportion of which was in property which could easily be destroyed. "We are fully advised as to our status in case of war," wrote the representative of one company to the Assistant Secretary of State, "and that this property might be subject to confiscation or destruction by the Spanish Government." War between Spain and the United States, wrote the president of another company, "will very likely mean the destruction of our valuable plant and in any event untold loss to our Company and its American stockholders." An American cork company with large interests in Spain; a New York merchant with trade in the Mediterranean and Black Sea; a Mobile firm which had chartered a Spanish ship to carry a cargo of timber—these are samples of American business interests which saw in war the threat of direct damage to themselves. . . .

It seems safe to conclude, from the evidence available, that the only important business interests (other than the business of sensational journalism) which clamored for intervention in Cuba were those directly or indirectly concerned in the Cuban sugar industry; that opposed to intervention were the influence of other parties (including at least one prominent sugar planter) whose business would suffer direct injury from war and also the overwhelming preponderance of general business opinion. After the middle of March, 1898, some conservative editors came to think intervention inevitable on humanitarian grounds, but many of the most influential business journals opposed it to the end. . . .

In the light of . . . widespread and intense interest in the preservation of the Chinese market, we can perhaps understand why American business, which had been, to all appearances, anti-war and anti-imperialist, was filled with sudden enthusiasm at the news of Dewey's victory at Manila Bay. Not only did the news dissipate all fears of a long and costly war and send stock prices rapidly upward; still more important, it seemed to place in American hands, all unexpectedly, the key to the trade of the Orient. The attack on the Spanish fleet at Manila had been anticipated for months and well advertised by the American press. Some papers had speculated upon the value of the islands as an American colony and had foreseen that a victory there might greatly alter our relation to the imbroglio in China. But for most, this thought did not occur until arrival of the news that the Spanish fleet was destroyed and Dewey safely in possession of Manila Bay. Then, at last, business men joined the jingoes in their acclaim of imperial conquests. Senator Lodge's exclamation—"We hold the other side of the Pacific, and the value to this country is almost beyond recognition"—was matched by many a formerly conservative business journal. It was not the intrinsic value of the Philippines or their trade that most impressed American writers, though this angle of the subject was not overlooked. Rather, their importance appeared to lie in their position as a gateway to the markets of Eastern Asia. . . .

There is no way of measuring accurately the strength of business opinion for and against the retention of the Philippines. Judging opinion as best we can from the available expressions of it, it seems safe to conclude that after the battle of Manila Bay American business became definitely imperialistic—that is, if a wish to retain the Philippines is an evidence of an imperialistic attitude. It seems certain, too, from the prominence given to the Chinese situation in nearly every discussion of the value of the islands, that the conversion of business opinion was accomplished by the combination of a European threat against the freedom of the American market in China, present and prospective, with the dramatic coup of the American fleet in a fine harbor so near the Chinese coast. In one paper, the New York *Journal of Commerce*, there appears with beautiful clarity the shift of position induced by the action of the European Powers in China. In November, 1897, against all schemes of colonial or naval expansion; in December, for a canal, Hawaii annexation, and a big navy; in May and thereafter, for retention of the entire Philippine archipelago and aggressive assertion of American rights in China—the *Journal* reveals a process of thought which perhaps occurred less clearly and consciously in the minds of many business men.

Having concluded that the Philippines were wholesome and digestible, business was disposed to treat itself to more of the same diet. The venture in the Philippines strengthened immeasurably the demand for the annexation of Hawaii. "The battle of Manila Bay," said the *Journal of Commerce*, May 31, "makes it imperative that we should establish permanent arrangements which will make the [Hawaiian] islands a half-way house on the road to the Philippines." But there were other Pacific islands that beckoned. "Bridge the Pacific!" cried the Philadelphia *Press*. "With the Philippines go the Carolines, a Spanish possession, Samoa and the Hawaiian Islands complete the chain." The war in the Pacific, the prospect of new possessions there, and the voyage of the "Oregon" also gave new force to the demand for an isthmian canal. . . .

American business had yielded reluctantly to the necessity of a war with Spain, forced upon the United States by popular reaction to the distressing situation in Cuba. It had not foreseen, or if it foresaw had feared, the colonial responsibilities to which such a war might lead. But when Dewey's dramatic victory on the first of May offered a Far Eastern base from which the threatened markets in China might be defended, it had gladly accepted the result, and long before the conclusion of peace with Spain, it was building high hopes upon the supposed opportunities for trade and exploitation in a string of dependencies stretching from the Philippines to Puerto Rico.

2. The Yellow Press and the Coming of the War

Joseph E. Wisan, an American diplomatic and intellectual historian, agrees with the Pratt view that business groups generally were opposed to involvement in the Cuban imbroglio. He believes the war to have been a people's war, forced on the reluctant McKinley administration by popular emotions and demands. The key to the aroused public feeling was the development of sensation-seeking journalism and above all the circulation war between the New York City press giants, Hearst and Pulitzer.

The Cuban Crisis
JOSEPH E. WISAN

The Press in 1895

The decade of the 1890's which witnessed the final crisis of the long continued friction between Spain and her Cuban colony marked also the appearance of a new type of journalism in New York City. While a number of veteran newspaper men were grimly attempting to maintain conservative standards, a new school in newspaper making with its reckless headlines, "popular" features, and sensational appeals to the masses reached many readers previously impervious to the comparatively staid sheets of the old order. . . .

In 1895 the important metropolitan morning newspapers were the *World*, the *Journal*, the *Sun*, the *Herald*, the *Tribune* and the *Times*; the leading evening sheets were the *Evening Post*, the *Commercial Advertiser*, and the *Mail and Express*. The *Journal of Commerce* represented the financial and commercial elements.

The *World* was owned by Joseph Pulitzer, whose career in the field of journalism had been most unusual. An ambitious immigrant in 1864, Pulitzer had served in many humble occupations. His newspaper ex-

Joseph E. Wisan, *The Cuban Crisis as Reflected in the New York Press, 1895–1898* (New York: Columbia University Press, 1934), 21–26, 187–191, 200–205, 324–332, 389–393, 455–458. Reprinted with permission.

perience began in Carl Schurz's *Westliche Post* in which he later bought an interest. He was employed by the New York *Sun,* purchased the St. Louis *Evening Post* which he transformed into the *Post-Dispatch,* and, in 1883 bought the *World* from Jay Gould. The newspaper was in poor shape when the change in ownership occurred. Pulitzer made a remarkable success of the enterprise. He created a new type of journal, "a journal that is not only cheap but bright, not only bright but large, not only large but truly democratic—dedicated to the cause of the people rather than of purse-potentates—devoted more to the New than the Old World—that will expose all fraud and sham, fight all public evils and abuses—that will serve and battle for the people with earnest sincerity." A week later his platform appeared—taxation of luxuries, of inheritances, of large incomes, of monopolies and privileged corporations, a tariff for revenue, civil service reform, punishment for corruption in office, vote buying and political coercion. Pulitzer employed every device to interest new readers. Screaming headlines, lurid style, profuse illustrations disgusted conservative readers but swelled circulation. Pulitzer outdid the earlier efforts of the Bennetts and the appearance of Hearst as an arch rival for the patronage of the lower classes compelled a reluctant adoption of even more spectacular methods. . . .

A Democrat since 1876, Pulitzer had supported Cleveland in 1884, 1888, and 1892, yet he took sharp issue with the President in several important instances. The *World* believed Cleveland too close to Wall Street; it denounced the sale of bonds to the Morgan-Rothschild syndicate early in 1895 and the failure to prosecute the trusts. It criticized Cleveland's Venezuela message as jingoistic and advocated peace. Olney it detested. . . .

Pulitzer's success with the *World* may be gauged by its increase in circulation. In 1883 the eight-page paper sold about 15,000 copies daily. In 1895 the sixteen page *World,* selling for the same price of two cents, boasted a circulation of 555,570 daily. For the year 1896, the *World* claimed an average week-day circulation of 743,024 and an average Sunday circulation of 562,903. According to its own statement there had been an average increase of 182,934 in the week-day issues and of 176,287 in the Sunday paper. By 1898 the circulation reached over five million copies per week, "the largest of any newspaper printed in any language in any country."

William Randolph Hearst, Pulitzer's chief rival, began his career in New York journalism on September 25, 1895, when, at the age of thirty, he purchased the New York *Morning Journal* from John R. McLean. Hearst's wealthy father had given him control in 1887 of the San Francisco *Examiner,* a newspaper the elder Hearst had taken over for a bad debt some years before. Hearst succeeded in making a financial success of the sheet, raising its circulation from almost nothing to 80,000 in a city of 300,000. This success he achieved by adopting sensational methods copied, generally, from Pulitzer. It was Hearst's ambition to surpass Pulitzer in sensationalism, circulation, and power, and his entrance into New York journalism began an intense rivalry between the two papers.

Hearst reduced the price of the *Journal* to one cent and improved its staff by transfers from his San Francisco *Examiner* and by acquisitions from his New York rivals. Associated with him at various times were Creelman, Grover Flint, Cuban correspondent with Gómez's army for four months, Alfred Henry Lewis, Washington correspondent, Julian Hawthorne, Richard Harding Davis, Karl Decker, Frederic Remington, and George Eugene Bryson. Melodrama, crime, vice, advice to the lovelorn, bizarre treatment of alleged scientific discoveries, became "news"; or as the *Journal* described it, "true stories of the new romances, mystery, pathos and humor caught from the whirl of everyday life." The *Journal* ran theatrical benefits for the city's poor; it offered rewards for the capture of notorious criminals; it interviewed kings; it hired prominent men for special assignments. A favorite trick was to wire statesmen for their views on important questions and to broadcast their replies conspicuously. A special Hoe color press, making possible an eight page comic section for the Sunday *Journal*, was installed. Streamer headlines, introduced in the Sunday *Journal*, were later adopted by the daily.

In international affairs Hearst invariably adopted an anti-foreign attitude. Spain, England, France, Japan, China, were all attacked for purposes of circulation.

In 1897 the *Journal* was increased in size, the regular edition being supplemented by a "magazine" devoted to "science in popular form, news of the week, and human interest," and a 24 page woman's supplement. The Eastern Sunday edition in 1897 reached 116 pages; a special Christmas edition, 112. This was rendered possible by an amazing growth in circulation. Hearst claimed an average daily increase of 1500 new readers during the first year of his proprietorship. The paper advertised an increase from 77,239 to 430,410 for the daily and 54,308 to 408,779 for the Sunday edition. On the day following McKinley's election the *Morning Journal* printed 956,921 copies. This, Hearst declared, was "an achievement not only unparalleled in the history of the world but hitherto undreamed-of in the realm of modern journalism." During each of the three days following the destruction of the *Maine*, the *Journal* printed over a million copies. After Dewey's victory at Manila its circulation exceeded 1,600,000 and it remained well over 1,250,000 during the war. . . .

Weyler and the New Press

The sensational press treatment of the multifarious phases of the Cuban crisis was due only in part to the nature of the events themselves. Much of it resulted from the development of the "new journalism," the roots of which lay in the past, but which reached full development during the years 1897–1898.

The typical new journal was jealous of its power; it was proud of itself and of its circulation, of which it blatantly boasted. It spent money lavishly. It hired special correspondents for important assignments. It "did things" as well as wrote about them. It was contemptuous of its rivals.

The *Journal* offered the most conspicuous example of this attitude and policy. Anxious to wrest circulation leadership from Pulitzer's *World*, it spared no expense to furnish exciting news. To its already costly staff covering the Cuban situation, it added Richard Harding Davis and Frederic Remington for special service. . . .

The *Journal* was the first newspaper to send to Cuba its own dispatch boat, the *Vamoose*. This was done in order to counteract the effects of Weyler's [Spanish commander in Cuba] rigid censorship. It boasted that the *Vamoose* was "the fastest boat in American waters," and that, despite De Lome's [Spanish ambassador in Washington] efforts to delay the progress of her mission to Cuba, she would get the news.

The *Journal* ridiculed the attempts of the other newspapers to keep up with it. It scoffed at "the sneers and snarls of the tired representatives of the old journalism attempting to discredit the *Journal's* exclusive news." The close relationship between the development of the new journalism and the Cuban crisis is well illustrated in an editorial boasting of its priority in reporting the contemplated grant of autonomy. No matter of international discussion interests the people of the United States more than the struggle of the Cubans for liberty. . . . Recognizing the existence of this universal interest, the *Journal* has spared no pains and no expense in its effort to gather and publish every piece of trustworthy information on the subject. It has sent to Cuba from time to time correspondents who represent the highest journalistic, military, political, literary or artistic attainments. It dispatched to Madrid Mr. James Creelman who antedated by sixteen days the *Herald's* instructive 'news' of yesterday. To those eminent exponents of the old journalism, the *Herald*, which copies after sixteen days the news the *Journal* obtained from headquarters at Madrid, and the *World*, which positively contradicted statements of fact which the *Herald* now affirms, the *Journal* presents its compliments and promises to leave them to the uninterrupted practice of their style of newspaper making. The new journalism prints what is new and prints it first."

The *World*, in an attempt to counteract the *Journal's* methods, claimed a series of scoops. In this Scovel was its greatest asset, although Dr. Bowen continued to send extremely good reports from the field. Pulitzer claimed an exclusive Gómez interview obtained at Gómez's camp near Salado, Santa Clara, in which the Cuban general denied his willingness to accept autonomy for the island. Its cruelty-affidavit scoops of early December it considered a real achievement. It prided itself upon an exclusive Weyler statement denying the charge that Maceo had been assassinated. It claimed to have presented "the first authentic news of the movements of the Cuban patriot armies that has reached New York in many weeks.". . .

When subjected to criticism the Pulitzer and Hearst newspapers seemed pleased. A Havana newspaper having published a three-column attack on the American press, charging it with a systematic attempt to deceive, the *World* expressed pleasure that it had been singled out for particular criticism. When Weyler blamed the "pernicious activity" of the newspapers of the United States for his failure to subdue the insurgents earlier, the *Journal* applauded his "tribute to the press," and declared, "it is a grateful compliment. . . . It is true that the press of this country has done what it could to create public sentiment against the infamous cruelty of the Spanish pirate in Cuba and in favor of intervention by this government." The *Evening Post* reported that Spanish officials in Puerto Rico destroyed American newspapers whenever they could find them. . . .

. . . During this period tales of Spanish atrocities increased in frequency. The *World* and *Journal* led, followed by the *Sun* and the *Mail and Express,* while the *Herald, Commercial Advertiser,* and *Times* printed reports occasionally. The stories were similar to those ordinarily believed by a nation at war. One favorite was the tale of political prisoners shot without trial. The *Journal* reported that Spanish officials kept their jails crowded so that they might profit by providing inferior food to the prisoners. The horrors of imprisonment in Spain's African penal settlement were described at great length by the *Mail and Express.* "The butcheries in Cuba would . . . seem almost merciful in comparison. . . . The patriots are . . . buried in a living grave. . . . The true story of the refinement of Spain's bloody cruelty lies hidden in far away Africa, rivaling the Inquisition in horror and surpassing the fastnesses of Siberia in secrecy." Some were reported drowned at night by Havana police; the *Journal's* headline on this was "Feeding Prisoners to Sharks." The *Mail and Express* reported that this practice had continued since September 1, and that sixty-three prisoners had disappeared in this way, officers in Morro Castle complaining because the cries of those doomed disturbed their sleep. Many crimes against non-combatants were reported. Madrid was said to have ordered Weyler to "shoot or bury all those opposed to Spain." Tejeda, "the Dominican Butcher," was reported to be killing peaceful men, women and children in eastern Cuba. The *Sun* asked whether Minister Taylor had received instructions "to invite the attention of the Spanish government to the barbarous manner in which prisoners and non-combatants were being put to death." A drunken Spanish major was reported to have killed fifty Cuban citizens; others, "old men and little boys, were cut down and their bodies fed to the dogs." One Spanish regiment was said to have proudly claimed 140 non-combatant victims. In the opinion of the *Sun,* Spain was "bent on wiping out the whole Cuban population," and officers who killed the most peasants "were decorated and promoted." Eight hundred peaceful inhabitants of the Rubi Hills were reported murdered during Weyler's brief November campaign in that area. Merciless attacks upon hospitals were alleged to be perpetrated by the Spaniards. One such report, describing raids on rebel hospitals at Isabel and Magdalena, declared: "The helpless and wounded were assassinated in their cots and the buildings then burned over their heads to cover up the crime." Another described the butchering of forty wounded prisoners. The poisoning of provisions furnished another type of atrocity story; and the maltreatment of women and the punishment of men attempting to defend women was another usual story.

During June the *World* printed an unusually large number of atrocity stories and also devoted frequent editorials to the subject. It pretended to believe the Spaniards capable of any crime. "Under the impulse of barbaric patriotism the average Spaniard is easily convinced that anyone who, on any account, dares to oppose Spain, is worthy of death in its worst form. Cruelty thus becomes almost a religion with the Spanish soldier." It referred to "the old Spanish habit of fusillading unarmed prisoners." "Genghis Khan and Timour, who made trophies of the skulls of their slaughtered enemies, were no more barbaric than is the Captain-General of Cuba, whose policies are outlined by the corpses of bound prisoners left lying along the march of his troops." Creelman was especially active in writing atrocity stories, and the following quotation is from his pen: "The horrors of the barbarous struggle for the extermination of the native population are witnessed in all parts of the country. Blood on the roadsides, blood in the fields, blood on the doorsteps, blood, blood, blood! The old, the young, the weak, the crippled, all are butchered without mercy. There is scarcely a hamlet that has not witnessed the dreadful work." In a featured article, the *World* presented a fearful record of Spanish atrocities claimed to have been committed in the province of Pinar del Rio under Weyler's command, some 200 victims being catalogued with names and places of residence. The editor claimed to have in his possession a score of affidavits of eye-witnesses sustaining the statements of its correspondent.

Weyler was regarded as the very incarnation of Spanish cruelty. The *Journal* devoted a special Sunday feature "to the prince of all the cruel generals this century has seen." "Spain . . . has at last played her trump card and sent on the field of battle . . . her most ferocious and bloody soldier . . . the fiendish despot whose hand Cuba well knows. . . . A panic has spread over Cuba. . . . Hundreds of Cuban women, maids and matrons, shudder. . . . It is not only Weyler the soldier . . . but Weyler the brute, the devastator of haciendas, the destroyer of families, and the outrager of women. . . . Pitiless, cold, an exterminator of men. . . . There is nothing to prevent his carnal, animal brain from running riot with itself in inventing tortures and infamies of bloody debauchery." The *Sun* said, "He has the ways of a coward"; the *Mail and Express* referred to him as "a menace to Spain"; and the *World* declared him "a barbarian, bred in an atmosphere of medievalism.". . .

. . . Evangelina Cisneros was the daughter of a Cuban insurgent who had been arrested in June, 1895 and imprisoned in Cienfuegos. She had succeeded through an accidental meeting with Martínex Campos's son in securing a commutation of her father's death sentence to one of life imprisonment at Ceuta. Through a personal appeal to Weyler she succeeded in having her father transferred to the penal settlement on the Isle of Pines, to which Miss Cisneros and her sister accompanied him. A moderately pleasant existence on the island was interrupted by the advent of the new military commander, Col. Berriz, nephew of Azcárraga and close friend of Weyler. According to the girl's story, Berriz attempted a brutal assault upon her but received a beating at the hands of a group of fellow-exiles summoned by her cries for help, only the intervention of Spanish soldiers saving him from more severe punishment.

Miss Cisneros was charged with rebellion, removed to Havana and in-
carcerated in the "Recojidas" prison. None of these events had received
newspaper attention when they occurred. On August 17, 1897, some nine
months after the transfer of the girl to Havana, the *Journal* told the
dramatic story of the case, accepting her version in every detail; it reported that Miss Cisneros had been convicted of sedition and warned
that she might be sentenced to twenty years' imprisonment in the African
penal settlement. During the next fortnight, in both the news and editorial
columns, it championed the girl's cause so vociferously that the case assumed international prominence. In its opinion, Spanish viciousness and
cruelty were exemplified in this case. "This tenderly nurtured girl was imprisoned at eighteen among the most depraved negresses of Havana, and
now she is to be sent in mockery to spend twenty years in a servitude
that will kill her in a year." "The unspeakable fate to which Weyler has
doomed an innocent girl whose only crime is that she has defended
her honor against a beast in uniform has sent a shudder of horror
through the American people." "Miss Cisneros is, according to all who
have seen her, the most beautiful girl in the island of Cuba. . . . She was
reared in seclusion and, almost a child in years, is as ignorant of the
world as a cloistered nun." "This girl, delicate, refined, sensitive, unused to
hardship, absolutely ignorant of vice, unconscious of the existence of
such beings as crowd the cells of the Casa de Recojidas, is seized, thrust
into the prison maintained for the vilest class of abandoned women of
Havana, compelled to scrub floors and to sleep on bare boards with
outcast negresses, and shattered in health until she is threatened with an
early death." Berriz was a "lecherous and foiled scoundrel." The *Journal*
sent a telegram to Weyler asking for mercy for the girl. It sent telegrams
to prominent women of the United States, urging them to petition the
Pope and the Queen-Regent of Spain in her behalf. Among those who
responded were Julia Ward Howe, Mrs. Jefferson Davis, Mrs. Mark
Hanna, the mother of President McKinley, Mrs. Julia Dent Grant, widow
of ex-President Grant, Mrs. Sherman, wife of the Secretary of State, Mrs.
Letitia Tyler Semple, daughter of ex-President Tyler, Miss Eugenia Washington, grandniece of George Washington, Mrs. John G. Carlisle, wife of
ex-Secretary of the Treasury Carlisle, Clara Barton, and Mrs. W. C. Whitney. Among many prominent men who publicly congratulated the *Journal*
on its enterprise were Secretary Sherman, Senators Money, Jones, Turner,
Governor Mount of Indiana, and ex-Governor Crittenden of Missouri.

Meanwhile, the *World,* jealous of its rival's exploit, attempted to minimize its importance by publishing a telegram from Weyler denying the
truth of the *Journal's* story. According to Weyler's version, the girl had
"deceitfully lured to her house the military commander of the Isle of
Pines, had men posted secretly who tied him and attempted to assassinate
him." He also denied that the case had been decided and that sentence
had been yet passed. An accompanying *World* editorial bewailed the
Journal's sensationalism. . . .

During the first week in September the case continued to furnish front-
page material. The Queen-Regent's order to Weyler to remove the girl

to a convent pending the completion of the case, the Governor-General's angry refusal to obey the order, the testimony of witnesses to the innocence of the girl and to the shameful jail conditions, the progress of a petition organized by Lady Rothschild and Mrs. Ormiston Chant and widely circulated among the women of England, the reported attempt of Berriz to obtain the girl's freedom in exchange for letters incriminating himself, the Pope's intercession for clemency for the girl, all were fully reported. The *World* continued its sniping tactics. It refuted the *Journal's* claim that the girl was related to the Marquis of Santa Lucía, Cuban President, and was rewarded by a *Journal* editorial directed against the snobbery of "the aristocratic Mr. Pulitzer's *New York World*." It declared that only the Hearst publicity had prevented Weyler from carrying out his original intention to free the girl on Lee's request. It obtained an interview with the girl and described prison conditions as much more satisfactory than those depicted by its rival. It reported fully Lee's criticism of the sensational journalistic misrepresentation of the case.

After a month's absence from the front page, the case entered its second sensational phase with the news that the girl had escaped from jail. The following day some newspapers reported that she had had outside help in effecting her escape. Not until October 10th (Sunday), did the *Journal* make the amazing announcement that it had rescued the prisoner. The first three pages of the issue were devoted to the story. Karl Decker (Charles Duval), a *Journal* reporter replacing the expelled Bryson, had reached Cuba August 28th. Failing in his attempts to bribe the guards, he had, with the help of the prisoner, worked out a plan to free the girl. With two aides, Hernandon and Mallory, he had rented a house next to the prison and, using a ladder to get to the roof, sawed through the cell bars to effect the escape. The other inmates had been drugged. With the girl disguised as a boy, and Decker using a forged visa on his passport, they made their escape on the Ward liner *Seneca*.

For many days the *Journal* reaped a full return of glory for its exploit, which, in its own opinion, was paralleled only by the rescue of Mary Queen of Scots. Congratulatory comments from prominent people were published—Mrs. Grant, Mrs. Sherman, Mrs. Carlisle, Mrs. Governor Bradley, Mrs. Senator Mason, Clara Barton, Senators Money, Jones, Turner, Elkins, Thurston, Governor Mount of Indiana, and many more, including even Secretary Sherman. The Bishop of London congratulated Hearst on his "magnificent journalism." Governor Sadler of Missouri suggested that the *Journal* send five hundred of its reporters to free the island.

There were many columns quoting the congratulatory statements of other newspapers—all from other cities in the United States and in Europe.

A novelized version of the entire case ran as a special Sunday *Journal* feature for three months. In conjunction with the Junta, the newspaper arranged an elaborate dinner at Delmonico's and a monster reception for the girl in Madison Square Garden, at which Henry George spoke. Miss Cisneros's visits to historic New York places were duly chronicled, as was her announced intention to become an American citizen. An interview with President McKinley was arranged, Mrs. Logan presenting the girl and Decker to the President. . . .

. . . The loss of the ship [*Maine*], important in itself, assumed far greater significance in view of the circumstances which surrounded it. It occurred in the harbor of Havana, where loyalist nerves had been frayed by the events of the preceding months and where the *Maine's* presence had been deeply and openly resented. Following closely the January riot and the De Lome letter, it came at a time when Spanish-American relations were highly strained. Suspicion of foul play was inevitable especially among those who for three years had been trained by the pro-Cuban journals to despise the Spanish monarchy and its policies.

An official investigation was inaugurated on February 17th by [Navy] Secretary Long's order that Admiral Sicard select officers from the ships of the North Atlantic Squadron to compose a Court of Inquiry. The Court left for Havana on February 20th. After an investigation of twenty-three days, every effort being made to achieve complete secrecy during its progress, the report of the Court of Inquiry was sent to Congress March 28th.

Those in positions of responsibility acted to prevent the engulfment of the nation in a tide of hysteria. Captain Sigsbee in his first telegraphic report, sent from the *City of Washington,* advised that "public opinion should be suspended until further report." Lee telegraphed a similar request: "Hope our people will repress excitement and calmly await decision." Secretary Long publicly announced his opinion that an explosion in the *Maine's* magazine had caused the accident. President McKinley also expressed his opinion that the catastrophe had resulted from an internal explosion.

However, the sensational newspapers were fully alive to the public's excited interest in the event and to the opportunity offered to themselves and made frantic efforts to get—or manufacture—the news, and to present it in the most lurid fashion. During the week beginning February 17th, the *Journal* devoted a daily average space of 8½ pages to the *Maine* —news, editorials, and pictures. It sent the yachts *Buccaneer* and *Anita* and the tug *Echo* to Havana, and massed at the Cuban capital its group of special correspondents—Hawthorne, Decker, Creelman, Lewis, Bryson, and artists Remington and Bengough. It offered a reward of fifty thousand dollars "for the conviction of the criminals who sent 258 American sailors to their death." Declaring that "the government has set an investigation on foot, and the *Journal* has independently undertaken another," it boasted, "between them the truth will soon be known." It inaugurated a fund to build a monument in memory of the *Maine* victims, associating with itself in this endeavor many names prominent in civil and military life, including Levi P. Morton, General Miles, Rear Admiral Selfridge, O. H. P. Belmont, George Gould, Depew, and General O. O. Howard. The *World* chartered a special tug and engaged divers to investigate the wreck, and was disappointed when refused permission to do so. According to its own figures the *Journal's* circulation for the week of January 9th had averaged 416,885; on February 17th it reached 1,025,624; on February 18th, 1,036,140. For the week beginning February 27th the average figure was 632,217.

The news columns of Hearst's paper seemed deliberately intended to inflame the public. "The warship *Maine* was split in two by an enemy's secret infernal machine"; "Captain Sigsbee practically declares that his ship was blown up by a mine or a torpedo"; "Strong evidence of crime"; "There are many among the Spanish officers and privates who hate Americans to the point of frenzy"; "If this can be proven, the brutal nature of the Spaniards will be shown in that they waited to spring the mine until after all men had retired for the night. The Maltese Cross [referring to an accompanying illustration] shows where the mine may have been fired." One leading headline read, "THE WHOLE COUNTRY THRILLS WITH WAR FEVER." The governors of many states reported the readiness and anxiety of the militia for service. One picture was captioned, "Divers searching for the dead and the evidence that they were murdered under the murky waters of Havana Bay." On February 20th (the day the Court of Inquiry left for Havana to begin its investigation) the *Journal* presented "proof of a submarine mine." Under a headline, "HAVANA POPULACE INSULTS THE MEMORY OF THE MAINE VICTIMS," appeared the statement that Spanish officers had boasted that any other American ship visiting Havana would "follow the *Maine.*" "THE MAINE WAS DESTROYED BY TREACHERY" was another headline. A few days later Karl Decker claimed to have "the secret testimony on which the Court of Inquiry will base its portentous report." The *Journal* quoted authorities (far removed from Havana) to prove its contention that the explosion was external and deliberate—Assistant-Secretary Roosevelt, Chief Constructor Philip Hichborn, Rear Admiral George E. Belknap (retired), and Naval Constructor Bolles. Captain Zalinski (a retired naval officer and "dynamite expert") judged from the *Journal's* photographs that a mine blew up the *Maine.* The Italian ex-Premier Crispi's opinion that the *Maine's* destruction was not accidental was made the subject of a leading editorial.

Though the *World* did not quite match its rival's sensationalism, it adopted similar tactics. Turning from its earlier headline guesses that "The *Maine* explosion was caused by a bomb" and that there was "Suspicion of a torpedo," and emphasizing the work of its own special investigators, it announced on February 20th that the "*World's* discoveries prove the mine theory." Another headline read, "War spirit rising from *World's* evidence." And still another, "Government accepts mine theory of *World.*" It featured a report that Sigsbee had attributed the explosion to external forces. It warned of the damage possible from the guns of the *Vizcaya,* expected to arrive that day. "While lying off the Battery, her shells will explode on the Harlem River and in the suburbs of Brooklyn." A full page streamer announced that the President and Congress were "ready for action." It described the elaborate preparations of the Government to improve the Atlantic Coast defense and insisted that we were fully prepared for war. A large picture representing American cannon pointed at the *Vizcaya* accompanied this article. . . .

Conclusion

The Spanish-American War, so momentous in its consequences, was a popular crusade. Neither the business interests of the nation nor the Government executives desired it. The public, aroused by the press, demanded it.

The leading commercial and financial interests of the nation favored an early restoration of stability in Cuba. They sought not only to avoid war, but to minimize its possibility. Investors in Cuban enterprises, anxious above all else to restore the security of their properties, attributed their losses to the tactics of the insurgents, and opposed all direct or indirect aid to them. Edwin F. Atkins, one of the leading American investors in Cuba, and influential with high officials of both the Cleveland and McKinley Administrations, sought constantly to prevent such aid. Indeed, he was accused of poisoning Olney's mind against the insurgents. General industrial and banking interests, emerging from the serious depression of 1893, and anxious to permit the unhampered operation of McKinley's policies, feared the possible effects of war. Furthermore, the 1896 campaign had not ended the menace of free silver; a war, possibly prolonged and certain to be costly, would strengthen the position of the silverites. It was no mere accident that most of the leading proponents of intervention in Congress represented southern and western states where populism and silver were strongest.

Wall Street served as a sensitive index of the fears of the financial interests. Rumors of increased tension in Spanish-American relations were almost invariably accompanied by a decline in stock prices and by editorial demands for peace from financial organs. Examples of this tendency may be seen in the falling prices which resulted from the Senate's adoption of the belligerency resolutions (Feb. 29, 1896), the conviction of the *Competitor* prisoners (May 12, 1896), a report that the St. Louis convention would demand armed intervention in Cuba (June 18, 1896), the Maceo assassination story (December 15, 1896); the Senate Committee on Foreign Relations' adoption of the Cameron resolution (December 19, 1896), the publicity given to the views of Hannis Taylor (November 5, 1897), the destruction of the *Maine* (February 16, 1898), and the passage of the $50,000,000 defense bill (March 7, 1898). On the other hand, reports of incidents making for peace between the two nations rallied prices. For example, gains were recorded when Cleveland indicated a strong desire to adjust our difficulties amicably (March 10, 1896, April 14, 1896), when Madrid ordered a postponement of the execution of the *Competitor* prisoners (May 13, 1896), and when Olney announced that Cleveland would not be bound by the Congressional Resolution of December, 1896 (December 20, 1896; December 22, 1896). Mark Hanna's determined opposition to the war is typical of the attitude of the nation's leading business men. The *Journal of Commerce* consistently opposed American intervention.

Spain's inability to protect American property in Cuba was annoying, as were the hindrances she imposed upon American commerce during the early part of the insurrection. However, during the later stages of the revolt she did everything possible to offer protection and she removed the curbs on American business in Cuba. American claims for damages could have been settled easily with a nation striving to maintain peace. Spanish historians, such as Maura and Ortega, attach little significance to this aspect of the controversy between the two nations, condemning American Jingoes, not American business men, as the provokers of an unjustifiable war. Indeed, the most bitter complaints of Spain's interferences with American business came from the ranks of the Jingoes thirsting for war, not from among the business men whose financial interests were immediately involved.

Responsible officials of both the Cleveland and McKinley Administrations strove to avoid an open break. Energetic and generally effective steps were taken to prevent filibustering. Cleveland's proclamations of neutrality, his repeated criticism of overzealous Cuban sympathizers in America, his offer of American mediation towards a permanent solution in which Spanish sovereignty would be safeguarded, his anxiety to obtain from the Supreme Court a decision setting clearly defined legal limits to filibustering operations, all bespeak his efforts on behalf of peace. Despite an increasing irritation at Spain's inability to restore peace, he and Olney were a constant bulwark against the Jingoes. McKinley, more responsive to popular and party demands, and willing to add to the prestige of his Administration by minor diplomatic victories, was equally anxious to avoid war, as was his entire cabinet, with the exception of Alger. Despite the presence of bellicose individuals such as Lodge and Roosevelt, the force of Republican leadership was exerted for peace. Woodford's sincere efforts to maintain peace during March and April, 1898, were undertaken to please and help his superiors, not to make their position more awkward. McKinley's problem was made easier by Spain's mounting domestic difficulties and her increasing willingness to accede to American demands, particularly after the accession of the Sagasta Ministry and the removal of Weyler. It was made more difficult by the public's increasing sympathy for Cuba and its growing hatred of Spain. It was made impossible by the high emotional pitch to which the public was raised following the destruction of the *Maine*. Responsibility for this state of mind rests primarily with the press.

In the opinion of the writer, the Spanish-American War would not have occurred had not the appearance of Hearst in New York journalism precipitated a bitter battle for newspaper circulation. The Cuban insurrection and its attendant horrors furnished a unique opportunity to the proprietors of the sensational press to prove their enterprise and provide the type of news that sold papers. Even the conservative journals, irritated by the emphasis the "new journalists" placed upon Cuba, were compelled by that very emphasis to devote considerably more space to Cuban affairs than they otherwise would have done. . . .

3. The Psychic Crisis of the 1890's

Utilizing psychological insights, Richard Hofstadter, the historian of American reform movements and political leaders, suggests that the popular demand for war was not created by the Yellow Press but was the result of a mass sense of frustration and fear, and the seeking of relief through a foreign crusade in Cuba. Acquisition of the Philippines is a separate problem, however, and was the achievement of the plans and actions of a small group of avowed imperialists.

Manifest Destiny and the Philippines
RICHARD HOFSTADTER

The taking of the Philippine Islands from Spain in 1899 marked a major historical departure for the American people. It was a breach in their traditions and a shock to their established values. To be sure, from their national beginnings they had constantly engaged in expansion, but almost entirely into contiguous territory. Now they were extending themselves to distant extra-hemispheric colonies; they were abandoning a strategy of defense hitherto limited to the continent and its appurtenances, in favor of a major strategic commitment in the Far East; and they were now supplementing the spread of a relatively homogeneous population into territories destined from the beginning for self-government with a far different procedure in which control was imposed by force on millions of ethnic aliens. The acquisition of the islands, therefore, was understood by contemporaries on both sides of the debate, as it is readily understood today, to be a turning-point in our history.

To discuss the debate in isolation from other events, however, would be to deprive it of its full significance. American entrance into the Philippine Islands was a by-product of the Spanish-American War. The Philippine crisis is inseparable from the war crisis and the war crisis itself is inseparable from a larger constellation that might be called "the psychic crisis of the 1890's."

Central in the background of the psychic crisis was the great depression that broke in 1893 and was still very acute when the agitation over the war in Cuba began. Severe depression, by itself, does not always generate an emotional crisis as intense as that of the nineties. In the 1870's the country had been swept by a depression of comparable acuteness and duration which, however, did not give rise to all the phenomena that appeared in the 1890's or to very many of them with comparable intensity and impact. It is often said that the 1890's, unlike the 1870's, form some kind of a "watershed" in American history. The difference between the emotional and intellectual impact of these two depressions can be measured, I believe, not by any difference in severity, but rather by reference to a number of singular events that in the 1890's converged with the depression to heighten its impact upon the public mind.

Reprinted from "Manifest Destiny and the Philippines," by Richard Hofstadter, in *America in Crisis* edited by Daniel Aaron, pp. 173–176, 180–187, 189–191, by permission of Alfred A. Knopf, Inc. Copyright, 1952, by Alfred A. Knopf, Inc.

First in importance was the Populist movement, the free-silver agitation, the heated campaign of 1896. For the first time in our history a depression had created an allegedly "radical" movement strong enough to capture a major party and raise the specter, however unreal, of drastic social convulsion. Second was the maturation and bureaucratization of American business, the completion of its essential industrial plant, and the development of trusts on a scale sufficient to stir the anxiety that the old order of competitive opportunities was approaching an eclipse. Third, and of immense symbolic importance, was the apparent filling up of the continent and disappearance of the frontier line. We now know how much land had not yet been taken up and how great were the remaining possibilities of internal expansion both in business and on the land; but to the mind of the 1890's it seemed that the resource that had engaged the energies of the people for three centuries had been used up; the frightening possibility suggested itself that a serious juncture in the nation's history had come. As Frederick Jackson Turner expressed it in his famous paper of 1893: "Now, four centuries from the discovery of America, at the end of one hundred years of life under the Constitution, the frontier has gone, and with its going has closed the first period of American history."

To middle-class citizens who had been brought up to think in terms of the nineteenth-century order, things looked bad. Farmers in the staple-growing region seemed to have gone mad over silver and Bryan; workers were stirring in bloody struggles like the Homestead and Pullman strikes, the supply of new land seemed at an end; the trust threatened the spirit of business enterprise; civic corruption was at a high point in the large cities; great waves of seemingly unassimilable immigrants arrived yearly and settled in hideous slums. To many historically conscious writers, the nation seemed overripe, like an empire ready for collapse through a stroke from outside or through internal upheaval. Acute as the situation was for all those who lived by the symbols of national power—for the governing and thinking classes—it was especially poignant for young people, who would have to make their careers in the dark world that seemed to be emerging.

The symptomatology of the crisis might record several tendencies in popular thought and behavior that had not been observable before or had existed only in pale and tenuous form. These symptoms fall into two basic moods. The key to one of them is an intensification of protest and humanitarian reform. Populism, Utopianism, the rise of the Christian Social gospel, the growing intellectual interest in Socialism, the social settlement movement that appealed so strongly to the college generation of the nineties, the quickening of protest in the realistic novel—all these are expressions of this mood. The other is one of national self-assertion, aggression, expansion. The tone of the first was sympathy, of the second, power. During the 1890's far more patriotic groups were founded than in any other decade of our history; the naval theories of Captain Mahan were gaining in influence; naval construction was booming; there was an immense quickening of the American cult of Napoleon and a vogue of the virile and martial writings of Rudyard Kipling; young Theodore Roosevelt became

the exemplar of the vigorous, masterful, out-of-doors man; the revival of
European imperialism stirred speculation over what America's place
would be in the world of renewed colonial rivalries. But most significant
was the rising tide of jingoism, a matter of constant comment among
observers of American life during the decade.

Jingoism, of course, was not new in American history. But during the
1870's and '80's the American public had been notably quiescent about
foreign relations. There had been expansionist statesmen, but they had
been blocked by popular apathy and statecraft had been restrained. Grant
had failed dismally in his attempt to acquire Santo Domingo; our policy
toward troubled Hawaii had been cautious; in 1877 an offer of two Haitian naval harbors had been spurned. In responding to Haiti, Secretary of
State Frelinghuysen had remarked that "the policy of this Government . . .
has tended toward avoidance of possessions disconnected from the main
continent." Henry Cabot Lodge, in his life of George Washington published in 1889, observed that foreign relations then filled "but a slight
place in American politics, and excite generally only a languid interest."
Within a few years this comment would have seemed absurd; the history
of the 1890's is the history of public agitation over expansionist issues and
of quarrels with other nations.

Historians say that the war was brought on by sensational newspapers.
The press, spurred by the rivalry between Pulitzer and Hearst, aroused
sympathy with the Cubans and hatred of Spain and catered to the belli-
cosity of the public. No one seems to have asked: *Why was the public so
fatally receptive to war propaganda?* I believe the answer must be sought
in the causes of the jingoism that had raged for seven years before the war
actually broke out. The events of the nineties had brought frustration and
anxiety to civically conscious Americans. On one hand, as Mark Sullivan
has commented, the American during this period was disposed "to see
himself as an underdog in economic situations and controversies in his
own country"; but the civic frustrations of the era created also a restless
aggressiveness, a desire to be assured that the power and vitality of the
nation were not waning. The capacity for sympathy and the need for
power existed side by side. That highly typical and symptomatic American, William Allen White, recalls in his *Autobiography* how during the
nineties he was "bound to my idols—Whitman, the great democrat, and
Kipling, the imperialist." In varying stages of solution the democrat and
imperialist existed in the hearts of White's countrymen—the democrat disposed to free Cuba, the imperialist to vent his civic spleen on Spain.

I suspect that the readiness of the public to over-react to the Cuban
situation can be understood in part through the displacement of feelings
of sympathy or social protest generated in domestic affairs; these impulses
found a safe and satisfactory discharge in foreign conflict. Spain was
portrayed in the press as waging a heartless and inhuman war; the Cubans
were portrayed as noble victims of Spanish tyranny, their situation as
analogous to that of Americans in 1776. When one examines the sectional
and political elements that were most enthusiastic about the war, one finds
them not primarily among the wealthy Eastern big-business Republicans

who supported McKinley and read the conservative dignified newspapers, but in the Bryan sections of the country, in the Democratic party, and among the patrons of the yellow journals. During the controversy significant charges were hurled back and forth; conservative peace-advocates claimed that many jingoists were hoping for a costly war over Cuba that could be made the occasion of a return to free silver; in return, the inflammatory press often fell into the pattern of Populist rhetoric, declaiming, for example, about "the eminently respectable porcine citizens who—for dollars in the money-grubbing sty, support 'conservative' newspapers and consider the starvation of . . . inoffensive men, women and children, and the murder of 250 American sailors . . . of less importance than a fall of two points in a price of stocks." Although imputations of base economic motives were made by both sides, it is also significant that the current of sympathy and agitation ran strong where a discontented constituency, politically frustrated by Bryan's defeat, was most numerous. An opportunity to discharge aggressions against "Wall Street interests" coolly indifferent to the fate of both Cuban *insurrectos* and staple farmers may have been more important than the more rationalized and abstract linkage between a war and free silver. The primary significance of the war for the psychic economy of the nineties was that it served as an outlet for aggressive impulses while presenting itself, quite truthfully, as an idealistic and humanitarian crusade. The American public was not interested in the material gains of an intervention in Cuba. It never dreamed that the war would lead to the taking of the Philippines. Starting a war for a high-minded and altruistic purpose and then transmuting it into a war for annexation was unthinkable; it would be, as McKinley put it in a phrase that later came back to haunt him, "criminal aggression."

There is one odd paradox in the evolution of sentiment from a war over freeing Cuba to a peace treaty acquiring the Philippines by conquest. The big-business-conservative-Republican-McKinley element, overwhelmingly hostile to this romantic and sentimental war, quickly became interested in the imperialism that grew out of it. The popular Populist-Democratic-Bryanite element, which had been so keen for the war, became the stronghold—although by no means resolute or unbroken—of opposition to the fruits of war. This much, however, must be said of both the populace and the business community: if the matter had been left either to public clamor or to business interests, there would have been no American entrance into the Philippines in 1898.

The dynamic element in the movement for imperialism was a small group of politicians, intellectuals, and publicists, including Senator Henry Cabot Lodge, Theodore Roosevelt, John Hay, Senator Albert J. Beveridge, Whitelaw Reid, editor of *The New York Tribune*, Albert Shaw, editor of the *Review of Reviews*, Walter Hines Page, editor of the *Atlantic Monthly*, and Henry and Brooks Adams.

Most of these men came from what are known as good families. They were well educated, cultivated, patrician in outlook, Anglo-Saxon in background, noncommercial in personal goals and standards, and conservative reformers in politics. Although living in a commercial world, they could not accept business standards for their own careers nor absorb themselves into the business community. Although they lived in a vulgar democracy, they were not democratic by instinct. They could not and did not care to succeed in politics of the corrupt sort that had become so common in America. They had tried their hands at civic reform, had found it futile, and had become bored with it. When they did not, like Henry Adams, turn away from American life in bitterness, they became interested in some large and statesmanlike theater of action, broader than American domestic policy. Although there were men of this sort in the Democratic ranks, like Walter Hines Page, they were most influential within the Republican Party, which during the mid-nineties had become committed to a policy of expansion.

In general, this group of imperialists was inspired by the navalist theories of Mahan and by the practical example of what they sometimes referred to as Mother England. They saw that a new phase of imperialism had opened in the Western world at large, and they were fearful that if the United States did not adopt a policy of expansion and preparation for military and naval struggle, it would be left behind in what they referred to as the struggle for life or, at other times, as the march of the nations. They were much concerned that the United States expand its army and particularly its navy; that it dig an isthmian canal; that it acquire the naval bases and colonies in the Caribbean and the Pacific necessary to protect such a canal; that it annex Hawaii and Samoa. At their most aggressive, they also called for the annexation of Canada, and the expulsion of European powers from the Western hemisphere. They were much interested in the Far East as a new theater of political conflict and investment possibilities. They were, indeed, more interested than business itself in the Pacific area, particularly in China, as a potential market. As Professor Pratt has observed: "The need of American business for colonial markets and fields for investment was discovered not by businessmen but by historians and other intellectuals, by journalists and politicians."

The central figure in this group was Theodore Roosevelt, who more than any other single man was responsible for our entry into the Philippines. Throughout the 1890's Roosevelt had been eager for a war, whether it be with Chile, Spain, or England. A war with Spain, he felt, would get us "a proper navy and a good system of coast defenses," would free Cuba from Spain, and would help to free America from European domination, would give "our people . . . something to think of that isn't material gain," and would try "both the army and navy in actual practice." Roosevelt feared that the United States would grow heedless of its defense, take insufficient care to develop its power, and become "an easy prey for any people which still retained those most valuable of all qualities, the soldierly virtues." "All the great masterful races have been fighting races," he argued. There were higher virtues than those of peace and material comfort. "No triumph of peace is quite so great as the supreme triumphs of war." Such was the philosophy of the man who secured Commodore Dewey's appointment to the Far Eastern Squadron and alerted him before the actual outbreak of hostilities to be prepared to engage the Spanish fleet at Manila.

Our first step into the Philippines presented itself to us as a "defensive" measure. Dewey's attack on the Spanish fleet in Manila Bay was made on the assumption that the Spanish fleet, if unmolested, might cross the Pacific and bombard the west coast cities of the United States. I do not know whether American officialdom was aware that this fleet was so decrepit that it could hardly have gasped its way across the ocean. Next, Dewey's fleet seemed in danger unless its security were underwritten by the dispatch of American troops to Manila. To be sure, having accomplished his mission, Dewey could have removed his "danger" simply by leaving Manila Bay. However, in war one is always tempted to hold whatever gains have been made, and at Dewey's request American troops were dispatched very promptly after the victory and arrived at Manila in July 1898. Thus our second step into the Philippines was again a "defensive" measure. The third step was the so-called "capture" of Manila, which was actually carried out in co-operation with the Spaniards, who were allowed to make a token resistance, and in exclusion of the Filipino patriots under Aguinaldo. The fourth step was an agreement, incorporated in the protocol suspending hostilities between the United States and Spain, that the United States would occupy the city, bay, and harbor of Manila pending a final settlement in the peace treaty. The fifth step came much later, on December 21, 1898, when McKinley instructed the War Department to extend the military government already in force at Manila to the entire archipelago. This began a fierce revolt by the Filipino patriots, who felt that they had been led to expect a much different policy from the American government. Two days before the vote was taken in the Senate on the ratification of the peace treaty, the patriots and the American forces fought their first battle and American soldiers were killed, a fact that seems to have had an important influence on public discussion. Once again, administrative action had given a sharp bias to the whole process of political decision. Tyler Dennett goes so far as to say that by authorizing a campaign of conquest while the Senate was still dicussing the situation, McKinley "created a situation . . . which had the effect of coercing the Senate." This is a doubtful conclusion, but there is some reason to believe that the hand of expansionists was strengthened by the feeling that opposition to the administration's policy would be unpatriotic.

This much can certainly be said: by the time our policy could be affected by public discussion a great deal had already been accomplished by the annexationists. The tone of the argument was already weighted towards staying in simply because we were there. As McKinley put it: "It is not a question of keeping the islands of the East, but of leaving them." It is not an easy thing to persuade a people or a government during the pitch of war enthusiasm to abandon a potential gain already in hand. Moreover, a great social interest hitherto indifferent to the Philippines, the business community, quickly swung around to an expansionist position. The Protestant clergy, seeing a potential enlargement of missionary enterprise, also threw in its weight. For the first time the group of imperialists and navalists had powerful allies. Business began to talk about the Philippines as a possible gateway to the markets of eastern Asia, the potentialities of which were thought to be very large. The little imperialist group itself was much heartened and, with the help of Navy officers, put increasing pressure upon a rather hesitant administration to follow through. . . .

Who was for and who against annexation? In large measure it was a party issue. The *New York Herald* poll showed that of 241 Republican papers 84.2 per cent were *for* expansion, and of 174 Democratic papers 71.3 per cent were *against* expansion. In some degree it was also a young man's movement. Geographically it extended throughout all sections of the country, and seems to have been favored everywhere but in the South, although even there it was strong. We do not have a clear index of public opinion for the period, but the practical politicians, whose business it was to gauge public sentiment in the best way they knew, concluded that the preponderant feeling was overwhelmingly for annexation.

The debate over the acquisition of the Philippines was perhaps no more than a ceremonial assertion of the values of both sides. The real decisions were made in the office of Theodore Roosevelt, in the Senate cloakroom, in the sanctums of those naval officers from whom the McKinley administration got its primary information about the Philippines during its period of doubt over annexation, and, by McKinley's own testimony, in the privacy of his chambers late at night. The public was, by and large, faced with a *fait accompli* that, although theoretically reversible, had the initial impetus of its very existence to carry it along. The intensity of the public discussion, at any rate, showed that the American conscience had really been shocked. No type of argument was neglected on either side. Those who wanted to take the Philippines pointed to the potential markets of the East, the White Man's Burden, the struggle for existence, "racial" destiny, American traditions of expansion, the dangers of a general war if the Philippines were left open to a European scramble, the almost parental duty of assuming responsibility for the allegedly childlike Filipinos, the incapacity of the Filipinos for self-government, and so on. The anti-imperialists based their essential appeal on political principle. They pointed out that the United States had come into existence pledged to the idea that man should not be governed without his consent. They suggested that the violation of these political traditions (under which the nation had prospered) was not only a gross injustice to others, of which we should feel deeply ashamed, but also a way of tempting Providence and risking degeneration and disintegration as a sort of punishment for the atrophy of one's own principles. They pointed also to the expense of overseas dominions, standing armies, and navalism, and the danger of being embroiled in imperialist wars.

Many leading anti-imperialists were men of great distinction; their ranks included by far the greater part of the eminent figures of the literary and intellectual world. Most of them were, however, in the unfortunate position of opposing the fruits of a war that they had either favored or failed to oppose. Unlike the expansionists, they did not have complete control of a major party (there were more expansionists among the Democrats than there were anti-expansionists among the Republicans). They were hopelessly heterogeneous: Gold Democrats, Bryan Democrats, New-England-conscience Republicans, and a scattering of reformers and intellectuals.

They organized late—the Anti-Imperialist League grew up in the months after November 1898—and their political leadership, however ardent in sentiment, pursued a hesitant and uncertain course. Their most eminent political leaders were chiefly old men, and the strongest appeal of the anti-imperialist movement seems to have been to the old, high-principled elements in the country, while the imagination of the young was fired far more by the rhetoric of expansionism. It seems clear that the main chance of this minority was to use its position in the Senate to deny the necessary two-thirds approval to the peace treaty acquiring the islands from Spain. Here the opponents of annexation might have delayed it long enough to give themselves a chance to reach the public. But William Jennings Bryan, for reasons that are not altogether clear, persuaded enough members of his party to vote for the treaty to lose the case. Bryan hoped to continue the fight, of course, and grant independence later, but over his conduct and his explanations there hangs a heavy sense of inevitable defeat, stemming from his recognition that the voice of the majority demanded the bold and aggressive policy. . . .

Additional Reading

G. W. Auxier, "Middle Western Newspapers and the Spanish-American War, 1895–1898," *Mississippi Valley Historical Review*, XXVI (1940), 523–534.

E. J. Benton, *International Law and Diplomacy of the Spanish-American War* (1908).

F. E. Chadwick, *The Relations of the United States and Spain: Diplomacy* (1909).

Foster Rhea Dulles, *The Imperial Years* (1956).

Margaret Leech, *In the Days of McKinley* (1959).

Ernest R. May, *Imperial Democracy: Emergence of America as a Great Power* (1961).

Walter Millis, *The Martial Spirit* (1931).

M. M. Wilkerson, *Public Opinion and the Spanish-American War* (1932).

II THE "OPEN-DOOR" POLICY:
Markets and Morality

The traditional trading policy of the United States in China was an insistence on commercial equality with other powers, expressed in treaty form as "the most favored nation" principle. When Great Britain, at the conclusion of the Opium War, compelled the Chinese imperial government to open five ports to British trade, the United States secured similar privileges in the 1844 Treaty of Wanghia. Other nations interested in the China trade obtained the same rights. The principle of commercial equality in China was thus the first phase of the "Open-Door" policy: equal privileges, uniform tariff rates, port charges, and transportation fees.

In the last years of the 19th century, the economic situation began to change. Western interests in the Celestial Empire had heretofore been commercial; now, the emphasis began to be placed on mining concessions, railroad construction, and financial investments. The major powers scrambled for leased ports and spheres of influence in China, within which discrimination was usually practiced against all other foreign competitors. The weak Chinese government was unable to resist successfully these demands and China appeared to be on the verge of dismemberment and partition. Russia was driving southward from maritime Siberia into Manchuria and northern Korea; Germany acquired leaseholds in 1897 in Shantung province; France pushed northward from Indo-China; and Japan made substantial gains after victory in the 1894–95 Sino-Japanese War.

British trading interests had been predominant in China in the past and were obviously endangered by these threats to the principle of commercial equality. Alarmed at the danger and seeking closer Anglo-American relations, the British government in 1898 and early 1899 proposed to the United States joint action in behalf of the preservation of commercial equality in China. The McKinley administration, aware of the small American interest in China and because of traditional isolationist policies, declined. A reversal, however, took place after the Spanish-American War. Secretary of State John Hay enunciated in two notes to the major powers what came to be known as the "Open-Door" policy. Though the two statements were unilateral declarations, scholars have asked if they were not undertaken at the British initiative and in the British behalf, and in an area of little real concern to the United States. Or, if the notes represented concrete American interests in China, what were those interests and to what extent were they exaggerated as the basis for action?

DOCUMENTS

1. Commercial Equality of Opportunity

The first "open-door" note has often been misunderstood. Secretary of State John Hay did not object to spheres of influence but merely requested that within leased ports and spheres discrimination should not be practiced against other foreign commerce. The September 6 note here reprinted was sent to Germany, Britain, Russia, France, Japan and other powers. The replies generally were evasive, contingent upon acceptance by other governments and exempting certain areas from observance of the commercial open door. The Russian response, of December 18–30, was the most evasive and reluctant of all. Yet Secretary Hay blandly announced that the replies had been satisfactory. His statement of March 20, 1900, has been praised by some as a masterpiece of diplomatic maneuver, and by others as an unfortunate bluff falsely giving the American people the impression that moral platitudes and pronouncements suffice in a power-system world.

Secretary of State John Hay's "Open-Door" Note

DEPARTMENT OF STATE,
Washington, September 6, 1899.

At the time when the Government of the United States was informed by that of Germany that it had leased from His Majesty the Emperor of China the port of Kiao-chao and the adjacent territory in the province of Shantung, assurances were given to the ambassador of the United States at Berlin by the Imperial German minister for foreign affairs that the rights and privileges insured by treaties with China to citizens of the United States would not thereby suffer or be in anywise impaired within the area over which Germany had thus obtained control.

More recently, however, the British Government recognized by a formal agreement with Germany the exclusive right of the latter country to enjoy in said leased area and the contiguous "sphere of influence or interest" certain privileges, more especially those relating to railroads and mining enterprises; but as the exact nature and extent of the rights thus recognized have not been clearly defined, it is possible that serious conflicts of interest may at any time arise not only between British and German subjects within said area, but that the interests of our citizens may also be jeopardized thereby.

Earnestly desirous to remove any cause of irritation and to insure at the same time to the commerce of all nations in China the undoubted benefits which should accrue from a formal recognition by the various powers claiming "spheres of interest" that they shall enjoy perfect equality of treatment for their commerce and navigation within such "spheres," the Government of the United States would be pleased to see His German Majesty's Government give formal assurances, and lend its cooperation in securing like assurances from the other interested powers, that each, within its respective sphere of whatever influence—

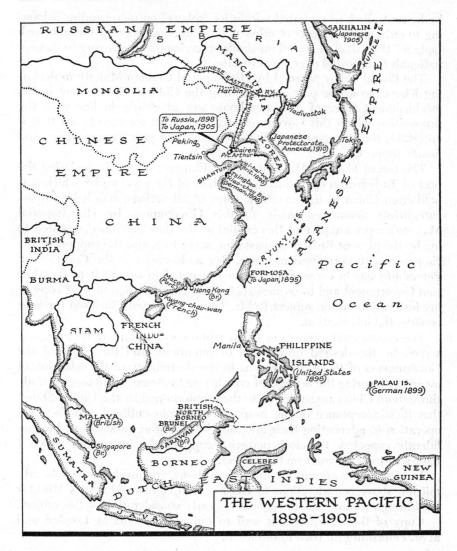

THE WESTERN PACIFIC
1898-1905

First. Will in no way interfere with any treaty port or any vested interest within any so-called "sphere of interest" or leased territory it may have in China.

Second. That the Chinese treaty tariff of the time being shall apply to all merchandise landed or shipped to all such ports as are within said "sphere of interest" (unless they be "free ports"), no matter to what nationality it may belong, and that duties so leviable shall be collected by the Chinese Government.

Third. That it will levy no higher harbor dues on vessels of another nationality frequenting any port in such "sphere" than shall be levied on vessels of its own nationality, and no higher railroad charges over lines built, controlled, or operated within its "sphere" on merchandise belonging to citizens or subjects of other nationalities transported through such "sphere" than shall be levied on similar merchandise belonging to its own nationals transported over equal distances.

The liberal policy pursued by His Imperial German Majesty in declaring Kiao-chao a free port and in aiding the Chinese Government in the establishment there of a custom-house are so clearly in line with the proposition which this Government is anxious to see recognized that it entertains the strongest hope that Germany will give its acceptance and hearty support.

The recent ukase of His Majesty the Emperor of Russia declaring the port of Ta-lien-wan open during the whole of the lease under which it is held from China to the merchant ships of all nations, coupled with the categorical assurances made to this Government by His Imperial Majesty's representative at this capital at the time and since repeated to me by the present Russian ambassador, seem to insure the support of the Emperor to the proposed measure. Our ambassador at the Court of St. Petersburg has in consequence been instructed to submit it to the Russian Government and to request their early consideration of it. A copy of my instruction on the subject to Mr. Tower is herewith inclosed for your confidential information.

The commercial interests of Great Britain and Japan will be so clearly served by the desired declaration of intentions, and the views of the Governments of these countries as to the desirability of the adoption of measures insuring the benefits of equality of treatment of all foreign trade throughout China are so similar to those entertained by the United States, that their acceptance of the propositions herein outlined and their cooperation in advocating their adoption by the other powers can be confidently expected. I inclose herewith copy of the instruction which I have sent to Mr. Choate on the subject.

In view of the present favorable conditions, you are instructed to submit the above considerations to His Imperial German Majesty's Minister for Foreign Affairs, and to request his early consideration of the subject.

Copy of this instruction is sent to our ambassadors at London and at St. Petersburg for their information.

The Russian Reply to the American Ambassador

MINISTRY OF FOREIGN AFFAIRS,
December 18–30, 1899.

Mr. Ambassador: I had the honor to receive your excellency's note dated the 8th–20th of September last, relating to the principles which the Government of the United States would like to see adopted in commercial matters by the powers which have interests in China.

In so far as the territory leased by China to Russia is concerned, the Imperial Government has already demonstrated its firm intention to follow the policy of "the open door" by creating Dalny (Ta-lien-wan) a free port; and if at some future time that port, although remaining free itself, should be separated by a customs limit from other portions of the territory in question, the customs duties would be levied, in the zone subject to the tariff, upon all foreign merchandise without distinction as to nationality.

As to the ports now opened or hereafter to be opened to foreign commerce by the Chinese Government, and which lie beyond the territory leased to Russia, the settlement of the question of the customs duties belongs to China herself, and the Imperial Government has no intention whatever of claiming any privileges for its own subjects to the exclusion of other foreigners. It is to be understood, however, that this assurance of the Imperial Government is given upon condition that a similar declaration shall be made by other powers having interests in China.

With the conviction that this reply is such as to satisfy the inquiry made in the aforementioned note, the Imperial Government is happy to have complied with the wishes of the American Government, especially as it attaches the highest value to anything that may strengthen and consolidate the traditional relations of friendship existing between the two countries.

Hay's Instructions to the United States Ambassadors at London, Paris, Berlin, St. Petersburg, and Rome, and to the United States Minister at Tokyo

DEPARTMENT OF STATE,
Washington, March 20, 1900.

The —— Government having accepted the declaration suggested by the United States concerning foreign trade in China, the terms of which I transmitted to you in my instruction No. —— of ——, and like action having been taken by all the various powers having leased territory or so-called "spheres of interest" in the Chinese Empire, as shown by the notes which I herewith transmit to you, you will please inform the Government to which you are accredited that the condition originally attached to its acceptance—that all other powers concerned should likewise accept the proposals of the United States—having been complied with, this Government will therefore consider the assent given to it by —— as final and definitive.

You will also transmit to the minister for foreign affairs copies of the present inclosures, and by the same occasion convey to him the expression of the sincere gratification which the President feels at the successful termination of these negotiations, in which he sees proof of the friendly spirit which animates the various powers interested in the untrammeled development of commerce and industry in the Chinese Empire, and a source of vast benefit to the whole commercial world.

2. Chinese Territorial Integrity

The July 3, 1900, circular from Hay to the great powers was occasioned by the Boxer Rebellion in China and the resultant threat of an imminent partition of the empire. It did not request formal replies and was intended to avert the danger without unduly affecting the presidential campaign under way in the United States. Probably Hay did not intend to inaugurate a new policy, binding on subsequent administrations, yet such was to result from his vague commitment of the United States to the preservation of Chinese independence and integrity. American policy in the past had been to observe that principle itself, but Hay now seemed to imply that the United States would try to protect China against all other powers.

Hay's Note of 1900 to the Great Powers

DEPARTMENT OF STATE,
Washington, July 3, 1900.

In this critical posture of affairs in China it is deemed appropriate to define the attitude of the United States as far as present circumstances permit this to be done. We adhere to the policy initiated by us in 1857, of peace with the Chinese nation, of furtherance of lawful commerce, and of protection of lives and property of our citizens by all means guaranteed under extraterritorial treaty rights and by the law of nations. If wrong be done to our citizens we propose to hold the responsible authors to the uttermost accountability. We regard the condition at Pekin as one of virtual anarchy, whereby power and responsibility are practically devolved upon the local provincial authorities. So long as they are not in overt collusion with rebellion and use their power to protect foreign life and property we regard them as representing the Chinese people, with whom we seek to remain in peace and friendship. The purpose of the President is, as it has been heretofore, to act concurrently with the other powers, first, in opening up communication with Pekin and rescuing the American officials, missionaries, and other Americans who are in danger; secondly, in affording all possible protection everywhere in China to American life and property; thirdly, in guarding and protecting all legitimate American interests; and fourthly, in aiding to prevent a spread of the disorders to the other provinces of the Empire and a recurrence of such disasters. It is, of course, too early to forecast the means of attaining this last result; but the policy of the Government of the United States is to seek a solution which may bring about permanent safety and peace to China, preserve Chinese territorial and administrative entity, protect all rights guaranteed to friendly powers by treaty and international law, and safeguard for the world the principle of equal and impartial trade with all parts of the Chinese Empire.

You will communicate the purport of this instruction to the minister for foreign affairs.

READINGS

1. The Open Door: an Altruistic Policy

The journalist Mark Sullivan expresses in the following excerpt the popular view held by most Americans of the Hay "Open-Door" notes. Detecting the selfish plans of the other great powers, the American government on its own initiative acted to uphold commercial equality in China and to prevent the dismemberment of the empire. Far-visioned statesmanship and vigorous, imaginative, diplomacy averted the peril.

Our Times
MARK SULLIVAN

On January 2, 1900, Hay announced to the Cabinet that he had completed negotiations for the "open door" in China. The negotiations consisted of securing assurances from the various Powers, Great Britain, France, Germany, Russia, Japan, and Italy, who then had or looked to acquiring interests in China, that in whatever influence they might exercise over China or any part of it, the treaty rights of the United States, and of all other nations, with China, would be respected; that neither our citizens and commerce, nor those of any other nation, would be placed at a disadvantage by any discriminating tariff laws or other conditions.

The "open door" policy in China was an American idea. It was set up in contrast to the "spheres-of-influence" policy practised by other nations. "Spheres of influence" was really a euphemism for the "partition of China," which in 1900 was looked upon as well under way. Since her defeat by Japan in 1894, it had been realized that China was not a fighting nation, and could not defend herself against modern armies and navies. She lay like a stranded whale.

While Hay put his negotiations on the ground of maintaining the existing status of the interests of the United States in territory grabbed by other Powers (which was the only aspect he had a clear right to discuss), its effect was to take away some of the motive of the Powers for aggrandizement, and ultimately to save the territorial and national integrity of China.

The "open door" is one of the most creditable episodes in American diplomacy, an example of benevolent impulse accompanied by energy and shrewd skill in negotiation. Not one of the statesmen and nations that agreed to Hay's policy wanted to. It was like asking every man who believes in truth to stand up—the liars are obliged to be the first to rise. Hay saw through them perfectly; his insight into human nature was one of his strongest qualities. Doubtless he had his own moments of indignation, but he had learned something of patience and long-suffering self-restraint from Lincoln, although even in his mellow maturity he never

Reprinted with the permission of Charles Scribner's Sons from *Our Times: The United States* Vol. I by Mark Sullivan. Copyright 1926 Charles Scribner's Sons; renewal copyright 1954 Mark Sullivan. Pp. 508–512.

quite ceased to be what his college mates described: "A fellow who would never do a mean act, nor tolerate one."

Every aspect of Hay's achievement excites enthusiasm. His vision and idealism were the more remarkable, since he was going against the current of the age, as only a scholar, a man who knew the world and history, would. The atmosphere of the time took the dismemberment of China for granted. The air was full of a hypocritical cant which put greed in words of benevolence—everybody not a White Man was regarded as a White Man's Burden. It was Europe, mainly, that was grabbing, but we were in it too, and there were plenty who would have counselled that our policy should be to join the scramble, take our share and take it in time. There was much talk about using the Philippines as a foothold for further expansion in the Orient. Hay took his course without any appearance of doing a daring thing; even in his own mind he did not seem to set it up as anything dramatic—it was just the natural expression of honesty and wisdom, the ordinary day's work of a gentleman in high office.

The "open-door" policy survived, and despite some setbacks, grew so that in 1925 the integrity of China was far more secure than had seemed likely in 1900.

Less than a month after the announcement of success in the "open-door" negotiations, Hay's altruistic course was made more difficult by the necessity of uniting with Great Britain, France, and Germany, in a joint note to the Chinese Government demanding protection for missionaries who, with other foreigners, were being subjected more and more to threats by the natives. The anti-foreign movement came to a head in June, 1900, when the foreign legations in Pekin were attacked. . . .

Troops of all the Great Powers were sent to relieve their legations, and to put down the uprising, for the Chinese Government was not only too feeble to resist foreign aggression, but even to put down internal conflict. The conditions seemed not only to tempt but almost to justify seizure of Chinese territory. The German Von Waldersee, as the highest in rank among the foreign commanders, was made commander-in-chief. Leaving Berlin, he wore the uniform presented to him by Emperor William, which the latter had worn on his voyage to Jerusalem. The German troops before leaving for China were harangued by the War Lord, who instructed them to so comport themselves in China that "no Chinese shall ever again dare even to look at a German askance." As it turned out, the Germans were no more ruthless than the troops of some other nations.

While the American Government participated energetically with troops and otherwise in rescuing foreigners and suppressing the outbreak, President McKinley and Secretary Hay maintained an attitude of sympathetic understanding of the cause, and controlled the situation in such a way as to avoid its being used as an occasion for the disruption of China's national and territorial entity. Hay persuaded the Powers to agree to joint occupation until the issues were settled, shrewdly assuming that in a joint occupation mutual jealousies would prevent any one Power from seizing any portion of the empire. He then persuaded England and

Germany not to demand territory, and to oppose such a demand from the others. Thereafter it was agreed that the reparations should be in the form of money.

2. The British Influence

A. Whitney Griswold, a respected authority on American policies in the Orient, emphasized the role of Great Britain in triggering the "Open-Door" notes. Hay's two declarations were not mere reiterations of traditional American policies in the Far East, but instead were major forays into world politics. China was saved from further partition, he concludes, not by the American actions—for these were not backed by force—but by the precarious balance of power prevailing in Europe and the Far East. Yet Hay had helped frame policies which were subsequently viewed as permanent American commitments and which eventually were to result in conflict with Japan.

Writing the Open-Door Notes
A. WHITNEY GRISWOLD

. . . Business and diplomacy were not the only forces impelling Hay toward his fateful decision. American missionaries in the Far East had also been thrilled by the conquest of the Philippines. In 1899 there were between one thousand and fifteen hundred of them in China where they, and their predecessors, had early assumed a political importance out of all proportion to their numbers. Now their situation was very comparable to that of American businessmen in China. Just as they were rejoicing in the annexation of the Philippines for the aid and comfort they thought it would give their cause, they found themselves confronted by an anti-foreign movement stirred up partly by the concessions-scramble, partly by their own proselytizing, that was to culminate in the Boxer Rebellion. In 1899 they, too, wished the United States to show a strong hand in China.

So far the McKinley Administration had adhered strictly to precedent in the Far East. It had kept free of alliances or understandings with foreign powers. It had called the attention of Europe to the long-established interest of the United States in the open door and the preservation of existing treaty rights. From the two particular nations that caused it most alarm it had obtained assurances. The President had declared himself satisfied with these, and proved it by rejecting Pauncefote for the second time within a year. In spite of the concessions-scramble, American trade with China, small though it was, was actually increasing. If it appeared likely to certain business groups that Russia would some day close them out of Northern China, others comtemplated great profit in the sale of products essential to Russia in the development of that region. As yet Germany had been no less hospitable to American trade and capital in Shantung than England had been in the Yangtse Valley. American fears of exclusion, like American hopes of gain, were all in the future. Up to the summer of 1899 neither had been strong enough to cause a departure from the diplomatic traditions and precedents of the past hundred years.

Then, in July and August, through informal, personal channels, the British influence was once more turned on Hay, this time with success.

Like most Secretaries of State, John Hay had only a superficial knowledge of conditions in the Far East. To advise him on this complicated subject he had chosen a friend and, as it happened, one of the best-informed authorities on China of his generation, William W. Rockhill. Born in Philadelphia in 1854, Rockhill's early youth was spent in France, where he completed his education at the military school at Saint Cyr, and where he acquired an interest in the Chinese language and literature. After three years of service as lieutenant in the French Foreign Legion in Algeria, he returned to the United States, and in 1884 procured an appointment as Second Secretary of the Peking Legation. The next year he was promoted to First Secretary. During the winter of 1886–1887 he served as Chargé d'Affaires at Seoul, Korea. He had entered the diplomatic service as a means of pursuing his Chinese studies. He resigned because of personal incompatibility with Denby. After two famous journeys of exploration through Mongolia and Tibet (1888–1889 and 1891–1892) he returned to the diplomatic service as Chief Clerk of the State Department in 1893. From February 14, 1896, to May 10, 1897, he served as Assistant Secretary of State under Olney, during part of which period (March 4 to May 10, 1897) he filled the gap between Olney and Sherman as Acting Secretary.

By this time Rockhill's scholarly writings and explorations had brought him membership in learned Oriental societies and scientific institutes all over the world. His wide experience in the Far East and in the Department of State had established his reputation as an expert on China and earned him the friendship and admiration of influential Republicans including Roosevelt, Lodge and Hay. When it became evident that Denby was to be replaced, Rockhill's friends urged McKinley to appoint him Minister to China, a post his training pre-eminently qualified him to fill. They were disappointed. Rockhill was sent to Athens as Minister to Greece, Roumania and Servia. It was from this post that Adee and Hay rescued him in April, 1899, by helping to secure his appointment as Director of the Bureau of American Republics in Washington, presumably in order to have the benefit of his counsel on affairs in Eastern Asia. In any event, Rockhill had no sooner assumed his new office (May 22) than the Secretary of State began to solicit his advice.

Rockhill, too, had his confidential adviser in Alfred E. Hippisley, a British subject and a member of the Chinese Imperial Maritime Customs Service. Hippisley was an old China hand. It should be recalled that the Chinese customs service was administered by the British, a privilege ultimately sanctioned by treaty in 1898 for as long as England's share of China's foreign trade should exceed that of any other nation. A member of this service since 1867, Hippisley had long followed political affairs in China with a sharp, intelligent eye. His acquaintance with Rockhill dated from the autumn of 1884 when the latter first joined the staff of the American legation in Peking. "In a small community such as that of Peking," wrote Hippisley many years later, "acquaintance quickly ripens into intimacy between persons who have similar tastes, and both Rockhill and I were deeply interested in China and Chinese politics, and in my case the intimacy was made the closer by my marriage in the following year with Miss Howard, a friend of long standing of Mrs. Rockhill's, who had accompanied the latter and her husband from Baltimore." What Rockhill was to Hay, Hippisley was to Rockhill: an old friend and trusted adviser on the Far East.

Mutual friendship—and fate—drew the three men together in the early summer of 1899. Simultaneously with Rockhill's inauguration as Director General of the Bureau of American Republics, a periodic leave of absence brought Hippisley to the United States on his way home to England. From about the middle of June to the end of July the Englishman visited his wife's family in Baltimore. He was pleased to renew his acquaintance with Rockhill, whom he had not seen for over ten years. "Naturally," he remembers, "I went over as frequently as I could to Washington to discuss the conditions in China with him and especially what could be done to maintain the 'open door' or equality of opportunity for all nations in that country." On one of these occasions Rockhill, deeply impressed by his friend's ideas, introduced him to the Secretary of State. Hay heard him expound, in outline, the scheme ultimately comprehended by the open door notes.

Throughout the informal negotiations of that summer, Hippisley was clearly the prime mover. Hay, though disposed to cooperate with England, was waiting for Rockhill to find a way to do it. Rockhill, who had been absent from China for seven years, was rusty on China. Hippisley came fresh from the scene, his mind brimming with images and theories of the concessions-scramble and how to deal with it. It was he who took the initiative, who supplied the concrete plans; nor did he lack encouragement. "China is, and will remain, the one absorbing subject," Rockhill told him, "so I am awfully anxious to have all the data you can give me on the subject, that I may not make any mistake, and that my conclusions shall be practicable."

When, about August first, Hay left Washington for his summer home in New Hampshire, and Hippisley departed Baltimore on a leisurely journey, *via* Lenox and Bar Harbor to Quebec (whence he would sail for England September seventh), Hippisley opened an active correspondence with Rockhill. "As I shall not now have an opportunity of seeing you before we start for Europe," he wrote July 25, "I write these lines to ask you to use your influence towards, if possible, inducing the govt. to do what it can to maintain the open door for ordinary commerce in China."

. . . Rockhill passed Hippisley's recommendations on to Hay after adding to their weight his own authoritative *imprimatur*. The same day he replied to Hippisley:

You know what my views are about the position the United States should take in China; I would like to see it make a declaration in some form or other, which would be understood by China as a pledge on our part to assist in maintaining the integrity of the Empire. I fear, however, that home politics and next year's elections will interfere with this, for it might be interpreted by a large part of the voting population of the United States, especially the Irish and the Germans, as an adoption of the policy advocated by England, and any leaning towards England on the part of the administration would, at this time and for the next year to come, be dangerous, and might lose the President his nomination. I consequently fear that he will do absolutely nothing either on the lines you indicate, and which are clearly those most beneficial to our interests in China, or in any other which will commit us. We will simply continue drifting along.

Hay confirmed these doubts. "I thank you for your letter inclosing Mr. Hippisley's," he wrote, August 7. "I am fully awake to the great importance of what you say, and am more than ready to act. But the senseless prejudices in certain sections of the 'Senate and people' compel us to move with great caution."

Hippisley did not give up hope. His reason for "urging *prompt* action" along the lines of his last note was, he explained, "precisely to forestall any suggestion likely to prove injurious to the Administration that it was following the lead of or leaning towards England by inducing it to take the initiative itself; then if England took similar action, she would follow America's lead." The Englishman had developed a remarkable solicitude for the welfare of the United States. "I think it would be suicidal for America to drift and do nothing for another year," he warned.

My latest advices from Peking say: "the activity of the Russians in Manchuria is simply wonderful. . . . The Russification of Peking and of North China will proceed as rapidly as has that of Manchuria." These are precisely the districts which are the great consumers of American textile fabrics, and I don't for a moment believe that American manufacturers will sit by with folded hands and see these districts closed without making an effort to retain them. Pressure will therefore be brought to bear upon the Administration and it may then have no option but to take such action as I have suggested, with possibly however the difference of following instead of leading England.

This time Rockhill's response was more encouraging. He had received "today," he wrote on the eighteenth, "pretty clear assurances from the State Department that it may take some action sooner than could be anticipated from the position it held until within a few weeks and which I gave you in my last letter." But Rockhill was not over-sanguine. Once more he showed himself to be in advance of Hippisley: he favored securing "tangible" assurances from the powers "as to their desire to maintain and insure the integrity of the Chinese Empire. . . ." This, he still believed the Administration was unwilling to consider; the best he and Hippisley could do was to "keep pegging away at it." The next day he submitted to Adee long extracts from Hippisley's last two letters.

Meanwhile two things had come to Hippisley's support. Almost simultaneously came the news of the return to the United States of Dr. Jacob Gould Schurman, Chairman of the President's Philippine Commission, and the Czar's ukase of August 15 declaring Talienwan a free port. All that restrained Hay from embarking on the policy advocated by Hippisley, apparently, was the opposition to it of the President himself. Whatever the true source of this opposition—respect for tradition, the lingering influence of Sherman, sincere conviction or mere partisan expediency—it had tied the Secretary's hands since his assumption of office. Undoubtedly Hay had been converted as early as June, 1898, when he had written McKinley a personal letter from the London embassy, urging him to reconsider the first Pauncefote overture. More lately he had professed to be "more than ready to act" and lamented the "senseless prejudices" that restrained him. It is probable that, for the past year, whenever the occasion had offered, he had urged on the President some such policy as that now in the making. Dr. Schurman and the Czar seem to have knocked the last props from under McKinley's resistance. . . .

The Rockhill memorandum (dated August 28, 1899) appears to have been the final instrument of McKinley's conversion. For, on September 5, Rockhill composed the actual drafts of the open door notes themselves, which, after a few corrections by Adee, were despatched the following day, over the signature of the Secretary of State, to the American ambassadors in London, Berlin and St. Petersburg. The notes, like the memoranda from which they were written, and as their authors had privately agreed, eschewed the subject of China's territorial integrity. This Rockhill felt to be "still such a complex question that I do not think we have it in anything like a shape to discuss it advantageously . . . so awfully big, that I think for the time being we had better not broach it over here." But, he believed, the notes would have the desired effect of giving China breathing space, of promoting "a general line of policy which may be favorable to the maintenance and the strengthening of the Peking Government."

The notes were carefully worded. Their authors were aware of the exigencies of American politics that restrained their own personal desires. Accordingly they recognized the spheres of influence as existing facts, omitted any reference to mining and railway concessions, and the whole perplexing problem of capital investment, and specifically asked only for equal commercial opportunity within each sphere. Each power addressed was requested to give its formal assurances that it would observe the regulations presented by the notes *mutatis mutandis*. But that is not all the notes requested. In addition to its own assurances, each power was urged to co-operate with the United States in obtaining the assurances of all the other powers concerned. Thus the notes invoked not only the time-honored American principle of the open door, but also the so-called "co-operative policy." The combination of the two, applied to the current situation in China, made the notes something more than a mere iteration of the traditional Far Eastern policy of the United States. It made them a foray into

World politics, an attempt to influence the foreign policies of the European powers in such a way as to establish free commercial competition in the region of Eastern Asia. It was an unusual thing for the United States to seek to influence the dispensations of international politics in regions outside its own hemisphere. . . .

A careful perusal of the replies to the open door notes shows Rockhill's assumptions, both as to the influence of the United States in the Far East and the effectiveness of the notes themselves, to have been unfounded. The replies to the notes were uniformly evasive and non-committal. The first and most satisfactory reply was the British, but even this left much to be desired. Though Lord Salisbury professed his enthusiasm for the open door principle, he was loath to apply it either to Hongkong or to Weihaiwei, contending that the former was a colony, the latter a leased territory, and opposing the application of the principle to areas in either of these categories.

The Prime Minister's attitude was "rather disappointing in view of his first reception of your proposition," Ambassador Choate wrote Hay. Moreover, Salisbury was of the opinion that "we are a little too sanguine in our expectations of obtaining Declarations from the other Powers." Nearly three months elapsed before Salisbury was willing to compromise, which he did grudgingly. Great Britain agreed to the application of the open door principle to Weihaiwei, and to all British leased territory and spheres of interest in China, present or future, the United States acquiesced in the exemption of Hongkong from this rule. The entire British declaration was then emasculated by the proviso that it was "to be considered as dependent on similar assent by the other Powers in like circumstances."

The replies of the other powers were full of loopholes, Russia's amounting to a thinly disguised rejection of the whole proposition. Each of them, like the British, made its acceptance contingent upon the acceptance of all the others, which reduced everyone to the least common denominator, the Russian. Rockhill and Hay realized the situation perfectly and tried to meet it with bluff. Rockhill privately admitted to Hippisley that the Russian reply "has what we call in America a string attached to it"; but he thought it "prudent" to accept it none the less. "Our object," Hay wrote Tower, "is now to give the widest significance to the Russian reply of which it is capable. Without running the risk of bringing upon ourselves a contradiction of our assumptions, we want to take it for granted that Russia has acceded to our proposals without much qualification." At length, on March 20, the Secretary of State cavalierly announced that he had received satisfactory assurances from all the powers addressed, and that he regarded each as "final and definitive."

Hay had not long to wait to discover just how "final and definitive" they were. In June, not three months after his expression of satisfaction, a Chinese patriotic society known to the West as the "Boxers" stirred up an armed rebellion against foreign missionaries and concession-hunters and the Manchu Government that had truckled with them. Ripping up portions of the Tientsin-Peking Railway and destroying telegraph lines, the rebels cut off Peking from the outside world, murdered the secretary of the Japanese legation, and the German minister, and besieged the foreign legations in the city. An allied military force was hastily despatched to the relief of the legations. From June 20 until August 14, the day the siege was lifted, the foreigners in Peking lived under fire in the legation compound, menaced by starvation and disease, their fate unknown either to their governments or to the troops marching to their rescue.

It was apparent to Hay from the outset that the disorders had provided certain of the powers not unwelcome pretexts for enlarging their spheres and extending their influence in China. Russia and Germany were on the march. Hay sensed the need—or opportunity—for more extensive measures than mere participation in the allied relief expedition. "We have no policy in China except to protect with energy American interests, and especially American citizens, and the legation," he had wired Conger, June 10. "There must be nothing done which would commit us to future action inconsistent with your standing instructions. There must be no alliances." When the Boxers moved on Peking he showed his hand more fully. On July 3, with the approval of McKinley, he despatched to the powers another circular defining American policy. Unlike the notes of the previous September, this circular asked for no assurances and, indeed, elicited none; it was merely submitted to the consideration of each of the powers addressed. Taking cognizance of the "virtual anarchy" existing in China it set forth the purpose of the United States to "act concurrently with the other powers" in restoring order and protecting the lives and property of its nationals and "all legitimate American interests." In its concluding sentence, however, it added to this purpose a momentous new objective, namely, "to seek a solution which may bring about permanent safety and peace to China, *preserve Chinese territorial and administrative entity,* protect all rights guaranteed to friendly powers by treaty and international law, and safeguard for the world the principle of equal and impartial trade with all parts of the Chinese Empire."

The United States had always stood for the "territorial and administrative entity" of China but in a purely subjective way. It had observed the principle itself; it had not assumed the function of persuading others to observe it. The notes of September 6, as we have seen, had accepted the impairment of China's territorial integrity as a *fait accompli.* They had taken it for granted that foreign spheres of influence and territorial concessions in China would continue to exist, and even to expand, as is proved by the fact that the notes asked for most-favored-nation treatment for American commerce in all future as well as present spheres and leased territories. But the circumstances attending the Boxer Rebellion, following the unfavorable reception of the September notes, led Hay to the conclusion that the maintenance of the open door in China depended on the maintenance of China's complete sovereignty over her own territories. In his circular of July 3, 1900, therefore, he went further than reiterating America's traditional policy of respect for China's integrity, further than asking the powers to observe the principle of equal commercial opportunity. He suggested a collective guarantee of both these conditions. To "preserve" Chinese integrity was something different from merely respecting it. Assuming, as did Hay himself, that the chief end of America's Far Eastern policy remained commercial, the circular of July 3 and the subsequent adherence of the United States to the principles it contained, appreciably altered the means to that end. He had committed the United States to the policy of striving to deter its competitors for the Chinese market from violating the territorial and administrative integrity of the Chinese nation.

Only Great Britain made response to Hay's circular, and this in the most casual manner. The other powers proceeded with their independent plans for obtaining satisfaction from, or taking advantage of, China. Russia continued to pour troops into Manchuria. That England had no faith in the Hay policy, and had decided to reply on means other than American note-writing to defend her interests in China, seems obvious. She had never banked wholly on American co-operation in the Far East, but had used this only as one of three instruments, the other two being outright participation in the concessions-scramble, and bilateral agreements with her rivals.

Hay need not have been puzzled (as he was) by Pauncefote's uncommunicative attitude during the summer of 1900; by Salisbury's intrigues with the other powers to permit Japan to send an expeditionary force into northern China; by the Anglo-German declaration of October 16, 1900, in favor of the open door and the territorial integrity of China. What these signs indicated was that Great Britain had turned to Japan as her partner in the Far East, her ally against Russia, and had resorted to bilateral negotiations to stay the advance of Germany.

It was in this manner that the partitioning of China was halted, temporarily, in 1900. The Boer War, the German navy, the maneuverings of the hostile European coalitions, the Czar, the Kaiser, Delcassé and Salisbury—these were the factors and agents that called the halt, not the diplomacy of John Hay. It was a case of political stalemate rather than conversion to principle. No power dared move further for fear of precipitating the universal *débâcle* that was destined to come a decade later, and so China was granted a brief respite.

Experience was disillusioning to the authors of the open door notes, as it was to Roosevelt in the case of the Philippines. No sooner had the rescue of the legations been effected than McKinley began to press for the withdrawal of the American troops from China. He feared their continued residence there as a political liability at home. Rockhill, who had done so much to launch the United States on its new policy, and who, in July, 1900, was sent to China as special commissioner to investigate the rebellion and represent his country at the peace settlement, readily confessed his discouragement. So did Hippisley. The excessive indemnities demanded of China, the latter wrote, after a long silence, in March, 1901, would have to be "liquidated by territorial concessions leading to partition and so ultimately to war among the Powers.

The soldiers have committed atrocities horrible beyond description, and the Ministers of their nationals are all engaged in looting. While [sic] Russia working independently on her own account places Manchuria, Mongolia and Turkestan under a protectorate, and throws the treaty rights of other nations into the dustbin. Right and reason disappear, and we return to the ethics of the Dark Ages. To an outsider it is all very sad and shows utter demoralisation."

Rockhill replied in the same gloomy vein. He was, he said, "sick and tired of the whole business and heartily glad to get away from it.

I have been able to do something for commercial interests, and in a number of points have been able to carry out the Secretary's views, but have been practically alone in the negotiations. England has her agreement with Germany, Russia has her alliance with France, the Triple Alliance comes in here, and every other combination you know of is working here just as it is in Europe. I trust it may be a long time before the United States gets into another muddle of this description."

Hay's disillusionment, though less outspoken, was if anything more complete. For in November, 1900, under pressure from the War and Navy Departments, he executed the surprising *volte face* of instructing Conger to endeavor to obtain for the United States a naval base and territorial concession at Samsah Bay in the Chinese maritime province of Fukien. The erstwhile champion of Chinese integrity, still outwardly loyal to the policy of his notes, had actually forsaken that policy and tried to enter the concessions-scramble. As it happened Fukien had already been pre-empted as a sphere of influence by Japan, whose treaty right in the province would be infringed by the American venture. Japan had to be consulted. It must have been embarrassing for Hay to read the Japanese reply, reminding him of his own admonitions against using the Boxer Rebellion as the opportunity for territorial aggrandizement, and reaffirming the Imperial Government's adherence to that principle.

Thereafter the Secretary of State trimmed the sails of his Far Eastern policy ever more closely to the wind. As Russia strengthened her hold on Manchuria, he gradually retreated to the position of his first open door notes, accepting the fact that Manchuria was no longer an integral part of the Chinese Empire, but rather a Russian province, in which open door treatment was to be bargained for with the Czar. "I take it for granted," he told Roosevelt in April, 1903, "that Russia knows as we do that we will not fight over Manchuria, for the simple reason that we cannot. . . . If our rights and interests in opposition to Russia in the Far East were as clear as noonday, we could never get a treaty through the Senate, the object of which was to check Russian aggression." To all intents and purposes Hay had abandoned the doctrine of the territorial integrity of China, at least to the extent of recognizing Manchuria as beyond the Chinese pale.

What, then, had the open door notes accomplished? They had not invented, or even promoted, a "co-operative" policy. There never had been a co-operative policy in Eastern Asia that rose above joint military expeditions, such as the Shimonoseki and Boxer, or identic notes of protest at anti-foreign riots. Only in common defense of their nationals did the powers stand together. As for co-operating among themselves, in the interest of collective security, fair play, free competition, equal opportunity, there was none of that; there never had been any. Japanese, Russian, British, German, French and American soldiers could all march together to Peking. But once the siege was raised and the diplomats had taken charge, every semblance of co-operation vanished.

It has been suggested that the Hay notes were part of a diplomatic trade by which the United States gained supremacy in the Caribbean, in return for co-operating with England in the Far East. But, in spite of intensive search, no evidence has been discovered that would remove the idea from the realm of conjecture. Chronology alone makes it plausible. By the Hay-Pauncefote Treaty of 1900 the United States gained from England the right to construct and maintain a canal across the Isthmus of Panama. At approximately the same time, America came to England's assistance in China. History abounds, however, with examples of the *post hoc* fallacy. Rockhill and Hippisley, at pains to exhaust every possible argument that might further their designs, never mentioned the connection between the Caribbean and the Far East, which Hippisley has since called "the product of lively but ill-balanced imagination."

England was scarcely in a position to exact any such price as that supposed to have been paid by Hay for her strategic retreat from the Caribbean. The Boer War, the growing power of the United States, not to recapitulate more of the many international factors already reviewed, were sufficient to account for that. Months before the open door notes were written, Salisbury had informed Hay (through Henry White) in so many words that he realized the United States would build the canal, that he approved, and that "the canal is of comparatively little importance to England now that they have the Suez Canal. . . ." Pauncefote and Salisbury did not receive the open door notes or the circular on China's territorial integrity as if they were collecting payment for value received.

Hay's claim that he had "accomplished a good deal in the East, but thus far without the expense of a single commitment or promise" is no less difficult to validate. Hay was technically correct: nothing had been "put in writing." Legally the United States was no more bound to pursue the policy of the notes than the powers which had, in varying degrees, evaded their demands. It was the style of the notes, the fact that they were promulgated in a manner deliberately contrived to mobilize public opinion and create the impression of an international commitment, and most important of all, the way Hay's successors practiced what he preached that molded American policy. It may be conceded that the Secretaries of State who followed John Hay did not adhere to the principles of the open door and the preservation of China's territorial integrity solely because he had done so, and at the same time, that tradition and precedent exert a powerful influence on foreign policy.

One thing is clear: Hay had not secured anything approaching an international guarantee of the open door or the "territorial and administra-

tive entity" of China. He had merely oriented American policy toward a
more active participation in Far Eastern politics in support of those
principles. In so doing he had kept pace with the expansionist forces (of
which he was as much product as cause) that had propelled the United
States into the conquest and annexation of the Philippines.

3. *"China's Illimitable Markets"*

The following article does not deny the role of altruism in the Hay "Open-
Door" policy but does reveal that powerful economic groups in America were
involved in China and were partly responsible for the two notes. Many in the
United States believed that unless foreign markets could be found for the ever-
increasing surplus of American agricultural and industrial goods, the results
would be contraction and economic depression. China's hundreds of millions
of people offered a most attractive market solution to the "Bogey of the Surplus." Charles S. Campbell, Jr., is the author of a major study on Anglo-
American relations at the turn of the 20th century.

American Business Interests and the Open Door in China
CHARLES S. CAMPBELL, JR.

One of the basic aims of American foreign policy has been to maintain the
right of all countries to trade with China on an equal basis. The first
formal declaration of this aim came with the sending of the Open Door
notes in September, 1899. The origin of these notes has received much
attention from historians in recent years, and certain aspects of their
origin, particularly the part played by W. W. Rockhill and the Englishman, Alfred Hippisley, have become very well known. At least one
aspect, however, has been entirely overlooked: namely, that special business interests in the United States were concerned over the possible loss
of the Chinese market; were eager to have the government take just the
sort of action which it did take; and were active in bringing pressure
to bear on the government. It is the thesis of this article that they were
partly responsible for the sending of the notes and, consequently, for
America's Open Door policy.

It should be emphatically stated, however, that this article does not pretend to give a complete account of the origins of the Open Door policy.
Not only does the author not believe that such an account can be given
merely in terms of business pressure on Washington, but the article does
not even consider business in general; it is limited almost exclusively to
two groups of special interests, which might, indeed, be called one, so
closely did they overlap. The almost complete absence of reference to
many of the well-known aspects of the origin of the policy does not mean
that the author considers these factors unimportant, but simply that he is
confining himself to what has not been elaborated elsewhere. Numerous
writers have attempted to give a rounded account of the matter; a very

Charles S. Campbell, Jr., "American Business Interests and the Open Door in China," *The
Far Eastern Quarterly*, I (1941), 43–58. Reprinted with permission.

few have gone deeply into the part played by business; but no writer has dealt specifically with the special interests here under consideration. Yet the influence of these interests appears to have been so great that any complete history of the origins of the Open Door policy should include some mention of them.

One of these special interests was the American-China Development Company, a corporation founded in 1895 for the purpose of getting railroad concessions in China. Its sixty shares of stock were held by forty-nine shareholders, of whom the best known were the following: the Carnegie Steel Company; Thomas C. Platt, Senator from New York; Levi P. Morton, vice-president of the United States under President Harrison; Frederick P. Olcott, president of the Central Trust Company of New York; John I. Waterbury, president of the Manhattan Trust Company; James Stillman, president of the National City Bank; George F. Baker, president of the First National Bank of New York; Charles Coster, member of J. P. Morgan and Company; Jacob Schiff, member of Kuhn, Loeb, and Company; E. H. Harriman, chairman of the executive committee of the Union Pacific Railway; and G. R. Hegeman, president of the Metropolitan Life Insurance Company. Three officials of the Development Company were also important shareholders: A. W. Bash, its representative in China; General William Barclay Parsons, its chief engineer; and Clarence Cary, its legal adviser. With seven shares of stock, Cary was the company's chief shareholder.

Shortly after the formation of the American-China Development Company, Bash was sent to China to try to get a concession. In May, 1895, he called on Charles Denby, the American minister in Peking, and asked for his assistance. Since Denby had for years been trying to persuade Americans to do business in China, he was anxious to do what he could for Bash; but in view of the State Department's traditional caution about supporting private business interests, he thought it prudent to ask for instructions from Washington.

About this time Richard Olney became Secretary of State. As an advocate of more vigorous support for American enterprise in foreign countries than most of his predecessors, it is not surprising to find him advising Denby "to employ all proper methods for the extension of American commercial interests." It was perhaps as a result of this note that Bash secured shortly afterwards a preliminary contract for a railway concession between Peking and Hankow. But Bash was not empowered to conclude the contract; it was, therefore, necessary to wait until authorized agents of the company should arrive in China. When the agents, one of whom was Clarence Cary, did arrive, they found the Chinese refusing to continue negotiations. Accordingly, they complained to Denby. The minister called on the Chinese foreign office and told the officials that it would be "a breach of good faith" not to go through with the contract. Taking a strong line, he succeeded in persuading the Chinese to resume negotiations.

Meanwhile Olney had been succeeded by John Sherman, a man who did not believe in government support for such ventures as the Development Company. When the new Secretary of State read Denby's official report about the above incident, he was not pleased. "You should be cautious," he warned the minister, "in giving what might be understood as this Government's indorsement of the financial standing of the persons seeking contracts with that of China." It is not wholly surprising, therefore, that two months later a Belgian syndicate, instead of the American-China Development Company, was awarded the contract.

Despite the turn of events the Americans continued their efforts to obtain a concession somewhere in China; but the year closed with no success to report. Did the officials and the powerful shareholders of the Development Company know of Sherman's warning to Denby? Whether they did or not, they must have found little to their liking in the negative policy of the State Department under its new Secretary; and some of them took part in the organized attempt, as will be noted in what follows, to persuade the government to adopt a different policy.

A second group of special interests was the American exporters of cotton goods. Cotton goods were America's chief export to China, and that country provided by far the largest market for American cotton mills. In 1899 this country exported $24,852,691 worth of cotton goods, of which almost half, $10,290,981, went to China alone. No other country came close to this, the second largest importer taking only about one-fourth as much.

At that time England was the leading exporter of cotton goods to China, the United States was second, and far in the rear were Japan and the Netherlands. Although the annual value of the American exports was only about half that of the English, it had increased over 120 per cent from 1887 to 1897; while English exports had declined almost 14 per cent. Americans attached considerable importance to this rapid growth of exports. They believed that the United States was capturing the Chinese market and that it was a market well worth acquiring. Even those with little or no business in China were impressed, for they had great hopes for the future. In those times, as still today, China was considered in wide circles to be potentially the greatest market in the world.

We have, then, in the case of cotton, an American industry vitally concerned with the Chinese market. As many members of the industry were almost altogether dependent on that market, anything which the government might do to preserve it would be to their direct interest. The same, of course, was true of the American-China Development Company. The men connected with this company, along with the cotton exporters, were those who had the greatest financial interest in China, and it was they who were most active in bringing pressure to bear on the American government. Of course, business anxiety over the Chinese market was by no means limited to these two groups, but as they had so much more at stake than any other group, it would be misleading not to give them special treatment.

The first step taken by these special interests occurred at the beginning of 1898. At that time considerable anxiety arose out of developments in China. The previous March, France had made the island of Hainan a sphere of influence; in November, German troops had landed at Kiaochow; and shortly afterwards a Russian fleet had dropped anchor at Port Arthur. It looked to many businessmen as though something which they had been fearing for several years—the partition of China—might be on the verge of realization. The threat to Port Arthur was particularly disturbing to Americans, for it was a key city of Manchuria, which, together with the adjoining provinces of China proper, was the chief market for American cotton goods. It was widely expected that, should Russia get control, discriminatory tariffs would be introduced, and an important market would be lost to the United States.

Business opinion was also aroused by the attitude of the State Department. Despite what seemed to be so obviously a dangerous situation in China, responsible officials were giving no sign of alarm; in fact, they seemed almost to welcome the situation. Interviewed by the Philadelphia *Press*, Secretary Sherman stated that he did not see any likelihood of partition—at least, not for some time. Even if China should be partitioned, he said, "the powers would gladly seize the opportunity to trade with us. Our commercial interests would not suffer, as far as I can see, in the least —quite the contrary."

This expression of opinion was most disturbing to those with financial interests in China. In an article which he wrote apparently just after Sherman's statement, Clarence Cary, back from his unsuccessful trip to China in behalf of the American-China Development Company, denounced what he termed the Secretary's "quaint and dangerous view that the interests of the citizens of the United States are not threatened by a possible partition of China." In a similar vein, the New York *Journal of commerce and commercial bulletin,* a newspaper which often expressed the point of view of many cotton exporters, spoke in a strongly worded editorial of the "generally admitted necessity of prompting the Administration to give notice to the world that the United States will suffer no interference with the commercial rights it now possesses in China."

This combination of encroachment on Chinese soil and evidence of what they took to be disinterestedness on the part of the State Department so alarmed some of those with financial interests in China that they determined to take action. On January 6, 1898, three days after Sherman's statement to the *Press,* they held a meeting in the office of Clarence Cary in New York City. At the meeting a "Committee on American Interests in China" was founded. It was instructed to confer, first with the New York Chamber of Commerce, and then, if it should seem desirable, with other commercial organizations throughout the country, regarding "the methods to be adopted to conserve the rights of citizens of the United States in the Chinese Empire."

There were five members of the Committee: Clarence Cary, Everett Frazer, S. D. Brewster, John Foord, and E. L. Zalinski. Cary has been mentioned before; Frazer was the head of an American firm in Shanghai; Brewster, a partner in one of the large firms handling the export of cotton to China; Foord, a contributing editor of the *Journal of commerce and commercial bulletin;* and Zalinski, a member of the Bethlehem Iron Company. It should be noted that men connected with both the American-China

Development Company and with the cotton interests were on the committee. The committee became the channel through which men like Cary, interested in China as a field of investment, and others, anxious to preserve a market for their cotton, could and did attempt to divert the government from the negative attitude characteristic of it while Sherman was Secretary of State. Through it they were able to organize and co-ordinate their efforts to bring about a new policy.

Just a week after its founding the committee submitted to the New York Chamber of Commerce a petition signed by a large number of important firms. The petition urged the chamber to take such action as would direct the attention of the government to the threatening situation in China and would ensure "that the important commercial interests of the United States" be safeguarded. As a result of the petition the chamber adopted the following memorial on February 3 and forwarded it to President McKinley the same day:

> That there are important changes now going on in the relations of European powers to the Empire of China . . . affecting the privileges enjoyed under existing treaty rights by American citizens trading in and with China. That the trade of the United States to China is now rapidly increasing, and is destined, with the further opening of that country, to assume large proportions unless arbitrarily debarred by the action of foreign governments. . . . That, in view of the changes threatening to future trade development of the United States in China, the Chamber of Commerce . . . respectfully and earnestly urge that such proper steps be taken as will commend themselves to your wisdom for the prompt and energetic defence of the existing treaty rights of our citizens in China, and for the preservation and protection of their important commercial interests in that Empire.

Secretary Sherman, to whom the President had referred the memorial, informed the New York Chamber that the matter was being given the "most careful consideration." As a matter of fact, the same day that he wrote to the chamber he instructed the ambassador in Berlin to inform the authorities in that country of "the interest which this Government must necessarily feel in conserving and expanding the volume of trade which it has built up with China." If, as seems probable, this step was in part the result of the above memorial, it was the first success of the special interests in influencing the policy of the government.

During the first four months of 1898 there were several further developments which originated in the Committee on American Interests in China. The committee had communicated with the commercial organizations of Philadelphia, Boston, San Francisco, and Cleveland, as well as with that of New York, and during this period all except the Cleveland Chamber sent to Washington memorials similar to the one quoted above. Not quite so directly attributable to the committee were memorials received by the government from the Chambers of Commerce of Baltimore and Seattle. That they were inspired, at least indirectly, by the Committee on American Interests is evident in the fact that they were almost identical in wording with the memorial from the New York Chamber. It might also be

mentioned that a number of American businessmen in China sent a telegram to the New York body, endorsing its memorial and stating that
"immediate action" was necessary for the protection of American interests.
This message was forwarded to the State Department.

The adoption of these memorials of early 1898 is doubtless to be
attributed not only to the Committee on American Interests but also to
events taking place in China during these same months. In February,
China was forced to promise Great Britain that the rich Yangtze provinces
would never be alienated to another power. This came as something of a
shock to Americans, for Britain was commonly regarded as one of the bul-
warks of the Open Door in China. Two months later a similar agreement
regarding some of the southern provinces was made with France. Most
alarming of all were the settlements with Germany and Russia in March—
settlements which wound up the Kiaochow and Port Arthur affairs, the
beginnings of which have been referred to. Germany succeeded in obtaining a ninety-nine-year lease of the land around Kiaochow Bay, along
with extensive economic rights in Shantung province. Russia, after an
acute crisis which almost led to war with Great Britain, secured a twenty-
five-year lease of the southern tip of the Liaotung peninsula, with the
right of building a railway to its principal city, Port Arthur. A more direct
threat to the North China market could hardly have been imagined.

Despite both the ominous developments in the Far East and the memorials urging action, the State Department was not pursuing a forceful
line. Apart from the mild warning to Germany mentioned above, the only
positive step taken during the first part of 1898 was the sending of a
telegram by the Secretary of State to Ambassador Hitchcock in St. Petersburg. Hitchcock was instructed to sound out Russia's intentions and to
inform the Russian government that the United States was anxious to
"maintain open trade in China." Although it was not at all the strong kind
of move desired by the special interests, this *démarche* represented a
further step in the evolution of the State Department away from the extreme indifference of Sherman earlier in the year. Together with the telegram to Germany it suggests that the memorials originating in the Committee on American Interests were having some effect in Washington.

Not only the government, but also the public in general, was becoming
more conscious of the China market; and here too, part of the change
must be attributed to the Committee on American Interests in China.
Since the memorials inspired by it had been widely discussed in the press,
they had reached a larger audience than government circles, and they had
not been without effect on public opinion. Evidence for this is to be found
in an article by John Foord, stating that because of the memorials the
whole question of American business interests in China "began to assume
a position of national prominence." As a member of the Committee on
American Interests and as an editor of the *Journal of commerce*, Foord, it
would seem, was in a position to assess the situation accurately.

The war with Spain, which began in April, 1898, brought with it a rising
tide of imperialistic sentiment in the United States. Caught up in this tide
and modified by it was the American attitude toward the complex situa-

tion in China. To be sure, there was no widespread thought of China as a possible colony, or even of a sphere-of-influence there, but, as Professor Pratt has shown, the foothold which the triumph at Manila Bay gave us in the Philippines was considered by many to be important chiefly because it might help us to hold open the door in the Far East. Then too the fact that America seemed to be suddenly growing up into a great power probably had the effect of making Americans more insistent that treaty rights, including those in China, be upheld.

During the war one of the most important developments in the history of the origins of the Open Door policy took place. The Committee on American Interests had come to the decision that a more permanent form of organization was needed, and to meet that need the committee was transformed in June, 1898, into the American Asiatic Association. The association had the same general aim as its predecessor. As stated in its constitution, this was "to secure the advantage of sustained watchfulness and readiness for action . . . in respect of . . . Asiatic trade, as well as in matters of legislation, or treaties affecting the same." All the members of the original committee became members of the Asiatic Association, and four of them became leading officials. Everett Frazer was the president; S. D. Brewster, the vice-president; John Foord, the secretary; and Clarence Cary, a member of the executive committee.

The reader will have noticed how often the names of two of these officials, Clarence Cary and John Foord, have occurred in the above pages. Both of them were intimately associated with the campaign to influence the policy of the government. Consider the strategic position of each: Cary, counsel for the American-China Development Company and member of the executive committee of the American Asiatic Association; Foord, secretary of the Asiatic Association, editor of its magazine, *Asia,* and contributing editor of the *Journal of commerce.* Although these men were influential only in indirect ways, it is entirely possible that they had as much to do with the sending of the September notes as had such well-known figures as W. W. Rockhill and Alfred Hippisley.

Four days after its founding the Association had just under fifty members. Among them were the General Electric Company; the Guaranty Trust Company; the New York Central and Hudson River Railroad Company; Charles Denby; W. W. Rockhill; Calvin Brice and W. D. Washburn, both officials of the American-China Development Company; and a large number of men in the cotton business.

In order to reach as wide an audience as possible, the association undertook the publication of a periodical entitled *Asia: journal of the American Asiatic association,* the editor of which, as has been said, was John Foord. But propaganda by the association did not become particularly widespread at this time; for, like its predecessor, the association devoted its attention chiefly to the State Department.

The American Asiatic Association was the principal channel through which the special interests made their influence felt in Washington and in the country at large. It was strongly supported by the *Journal of commerce and commercial bulletin,* which devoted an extraordinary amount

of editorial and news space to questions of the Chinese market and consistently advocated energetic action by the government to safeguard that
market. Co-operation between the association and the journal was doubtless facilitated by the fact that John Foord occupied an important position
in each of these guardians of American interests in the Far East.

The founding of the Asiatic Association was the chief event concerned
with the origins of the Open Door policy which took place during the war
with Spain. However, a few other developments of the same time, though
of comparatively minor importance, may also be mentioned.

Perhaps the outstanding of these was a recommendation to Congress by
Sherman's successor in the State Department, William R. Day, that a
trade commission be sent to China to investigate possibilities for greater
exports to that part of the world. Although Congress took no action at the
time, the incident has some significance as marking a further step in the
evolution of the government toward the point of view of the special interests.

Also of significance was the appointment of John Hay to the position of
Secretary of State. In view of the memorials of the early part of the year
and such a further indication of the opinion of influential businessmen as
the establishment of the Asiatic Association, it is quite possible that Hay's
well-known propensity for the Open Door in China was one of the reasons
for his appointment. Hardly had he assumed office when the new Secretary showed that his Far Eastern policy was going to be stronger than
that of his two predecessors. Perhaps as a result of a memorial from one
of the American establishments in China, stating that there was a "probability of serious interference [by Russia] with America's important trade
in cotton . . . unless immediate steps are taken in Pekin to insist that our
treaty rights with China be maintained," Hay ordered two gunboats to
proceed to North China. The New York Chamber of Commerce, incidentally, expressed its "high appreciation" of the act. For the time being,
however, nothing further came of the Russian threat.

The last event we need mention which occurred during the war was
the annual message to Congress of President McKinley. Repeating Day's
recommendation of a trade commission, the President stated that the
United States was not an "indifferent spectator" of what was going on in
China but that it would preserve its "large interests in that quarter by all
means appropriate to the constant policy of our Government." This strong
declaration was naturally hailed with delight by those with business interests in China.

When the war with Spain formally came to an end early in 1899 with
the ratification of the peace treaty by the Senate, the government was able
to turn its attention from military matters to such peacetime considerations as trade with China. In January it received an important memorial.
Coming from a large number of cotton manufacturers, the memorial
stated that the Chinese market would be lost to American cotton exporters "unless a vigorous policy is pursued on the part of the . . . Government"; it requested that the American diplomatic representatives at
Peking and St. Petersburg "be instructed to give special attention to the

subject." This memorial seems to have impressed Secretary Hay even more than the memorial of the preceding January had impressed Sherman. Referring to the "high character and standing of the signers," he ordered the envoys to give the "special attention" requested of them; and about a month later, apparently afraid he had not been sufficiently emphatic, he wrote a second time to the ambassador to Russia, asking him to continue "to act energetically in the sense desired by the numerous and influential signers of the petition."

Another episode of early 1899 worth mentioning was the Asiatic Association's strong support of a protest by the United States against an attempt by France to extend her concession in Shanghai. The association wrote to McKinley and Hay, urging that "all available means" be used "towards preserving for the world's commerce an 'open door' in the Far East." In sharp contrast with this was the association's viewpoint regarding an attempt to obtain an extension of the combined British and American concession. Negotiations with China had been going on for some time but without success. Angered and alarmed, the association informed Secretary Hay of "the necessity of . . . vigorous action . . . in order to obtain a definite solution." Sending a copy of this letter to the minister to China, Hay instructed him to devote his efforts to obtaining the extension. Two months later China gave way.

In March the campaign for the Open Door took a more decisive turn. It became known at that time that Italy was endeavoring to secure from the Chinese government a lease of Sanmen Bay, a bay located not far from Shanghai, the center of foreign business in China. Fears of partition once again rose quickly to the surface. There was widespread suspicion that Italy had the backing of Great Britain; if true, it would mean that the only remaining great power opposed to the partition of China was the United States.

The situation disturbed the American Asiatic Association to an extent which might seem surprising today. Today we know that the Sanmen Bay affair turned out to be a comparatively insignificant incident. But to those who lived at the time of the crisis itself this knowledge was lacking, and to them, fearful as they were that it would take very little indeed to start off the process of dismembering China, the spring of 1899 was a time of grave anxiety. So disturbing was the situation to the officials of the Asiatic Association that they held a series of meetings in order to discuss the possibility of a fundamental modification of the policy they had been pursuing.

As has been shown, this policy was to concentrate on the Department of State. True, there had been a certain amount of propaganda directed at the public in general through the periodical, *Asia: journal of the American Asiatic association,* and true it is also that this propaganda had been meeting with some success. As early as January the *Journal of commerce,* that close observer of anything pertaining to the Open Door, had pointed to the "new attitude of this country towards its commercial interests in China" and had stated that it was "partly the result of the American Asiatic Association." Nevertheless, greater success had been gained with the State Department. Secretary Sherman and Secretary Day had moved closer to the viewpoint of businessmen who were eager to see the Chinese market safeguarded. John Hay had not once failed to carry out any formal request regarding Far Eastern policy, and, indeed, the department under Hay had shown itself so willing to co-operate that there could be no doubt about its desire to maintain the Open Door in China.

Because of these facts the *Journal of commerce* and the Asiatic Association appear to have realized that pressure upon the State Department had become much less necessary than before. But this did not suggest to them that their usefulness was at an end. For although it was clear that many of the high officials in Washington were convinced that the Chinese market was of considerable value to the United States, it was equally clear that the general public was not convinced. Consequently, what had become desirable in place of so much attention to the State Department was, as the journal said, "education of the people, the press, and the politicians by those who see the vital necessity of the Chinese market"—in short, "active propaganda in the country at large." The Asiatic Association, as a faithful ally of the journal, came to the same conclusion. At the series of meetings which its officials were holding it was decided to embark upon "a campaign of public education in regard to the magnitude of the commercial interests of the United States in China." A committee to take charge of the campaign was appointed.

The writer has not been able to discover many details about the ensuing campaign. It is known that it was carried on in the press—the *Journal of commerce* presumably being the chief organ—and in publications of the association itself. It is also known that by the end of 1899 the association had at its disposal a fund for propaganda purposes amounting to several thousand dollars and that among the contributors to this fund were many of the exporters of cotton goods. Not much additional material, however, is available.

Did the campaign have any success in persuading the public of the importance of the market in China? No conclusive answer can be given to this question; for not only is it foolish to make too definite claims about the effects of any bit of propaganda, no matter how much one may know its nature, but also we have here a propaganda compaign concerning which relatively little is known.

It is worth while, however, to point out that both the American Asiatic Association and the *Journal of commerce* were convinced that their propaganda did have very considerable success. The statement of the journal in January, 1899, regarding the influence of the Asiatic Association in moulding public opinion has been mentioned above. Ten months later, in November, the propaganda of the Association had had more time to make itself felt. At that time the *Journal of commerce* reported that "there has never been a more remarkable advance of public sentiment in this country than that which has taken place . . . in regard to the responsibilities to be faced by our Government in the Far East." The journal boasted that "to the stage of public education which has been reached on this subject [the necessity of the Open Door to the United States] this journal may fairly claim to have largely contributed." The vice-president of the Asiatic Association said that the work of his organization would "take its place in history as part of one of the most memorable chapters in the annals of the American people. . . . You have only to compare," he said, "the state of public sentiment which we found existing in regard to the responsibilities of our country in Eastern Asia with the feeling which exists on that subject to-day to appreciate what the influence of the Association has been."

Moreover, at least one contemporary observer supported their claims. James S. Fearon, one of the leading exporters of cotton to China and for years chairman of the Shanghai Municipal Council—presumably a man whose opinions regarding American relations with China are worthy of respect—stated that much of the credit for the changed attitude of the American people toward the Chinese market was due to the American Asiatic Association and to the *Journal of commerce*.

The propaganda compaign was the outstanding feature of the months just before the sending of the Open Door notes, but this period was also marked by further pressure brought to bear on the State Department by the special interests. Although they initiated no more memorials at this time, the officials of the Asiatic Association are known to have corresponded with Secretary Hay and to have called upon him frequently regarding the country's Far Eastern policy.

The activity of the special interests during these months of 1899 was of such a nature as to make it extremely difficult to evaluate its significance. It is, of course, quite understandable that no records exist stating explicitly whether or not the administration was influenced by the propaganda campaign, and it is equally understandable that Secretary Hay never wrote down anything which would enable us to judge whether or not his thinking was affected by the letters from the officials of the Asiatic Association and by the visits these men paid him. It is far easier to trace the effects of the memorials of 1898 than of the propaganda and informal contacts of 1899.

But it would be a great mistake to overlook the possibility that these later activities too were of considerable importance. It may well have been that the *Journal of commerce* and the Asiatic Association were quite correct in their belief that the propaganda campaign was successful. If it was successful, if it did in fact make the public more conscious of America's stake in the Far East, it doubtless made it easier for the administration to take action designed to preserve the Chinese market. As for the letters and visits from the Asiatic Association to Hay, it is highly probable that such frequent reminders of the desires of certain businessmen had at least the effect of bolstering up the Secretary's own inclinations with respect to China. At any rate, it is clear that these activities of the special interests during the spring and summer of 1899 must have, along with the memorials of 1898, a place in any complete history of the origins of the Open Door policy.

On September 6, 1899, the first group of Open Door notes was dispatched. This was just the kind of step for which the special interests had been hoping and for which they had been working. To the cotton exporters the notes meant that their market appeared to be far more secure; and to the American-China Development Company they meant that there was much to be hoped for from a grateful China—and, indeed, a few months later the company at last secured the contract which it had so long been seeking.

The sending of these notes resulted from a great many factors, one of which was the organized attempt of certain business interests, particularly the men connected with the American China Development Company and the cotton exporters, to persuade the government to take just such a step. It has been shown how these interests, fearful lest the turn of events in China should result in financial loss to themselves, took measures designed to persuade the government to safeguard the Chinese market. First of all, they established the Committee on American Interests in China; later on, when this proved to be too weak an organization, they transformed it into the American Asiatic Association. This association, consistently supported by the *Journal of commerce and commercial bulletin,* was influential in persuading the administration (and very possibly the general public as well) that a particular line of policy would be of benefit to the nation as a whole. In these facts lies part of the explanation for the formulation of America's Open Door policy.

Additional Reading

Charles S. Campbell, Jr., *Anglo-American Understanding, 1898–1903* (1957).
————, *Special Business Interests and the Open Door Policy* (1951).
Tyler Dennett, *John Hay* (1933).
A. L. P. Dennis, *Adventures in American Diplomacy, 1896–1906* (1928).
L. M. Gelber, *The Rise of Anglo-American Friendship* (1938).
Pauline Tompkins, *American-Russian Relations in the Far East* (1949).
Paul A. Varg, *Open Door Diplomat: The Life of W. W. Rockhill* (1952).
E. H. Zabriskie, *American-Russian Rivalry in the Far East, 1895–1914* (1946).

12 CARIBBEAN POLICY: Dollars or Security?

As the year 1898 began, the United States was without naval bases and influence in the vital Caribbean area. Yet by 1917, the Caribbean Sea had been transformed into an American-controlled "lake." A canal route through the Central American isthmus had been acquired, five protectorates had been established (Cuba, Panama, Santo Domingo, Nicaragua, Haiti), the Danish West Indies were purchased, and European influence had been largely supplanted. Theodore Roosevelt made great strides by incorporating the Platt Amendment in a treaty with Cuba, leasing a canal zone from Panama, and proclaiming an international policeman's role for the United States in the Caribbean. President Taft assumed a financial protectorate in Nicaragua and launched a small-scale armed intervention there as well. The Wilson administration, although entering office pledged to end the alleged "dollar imperialism" of the past, was soon constrained by national exigencies and by benevolent impulses to undertake extensive armed interventions in Haiti and Santo Domingo.

In the aftermath of World War I, with its disillusionment with noble crusades and the revelation of unpleasant details in the armed occupations of Santo Domingo and Haiti, it became fashionable in "liberal" circles to denounce the Caribbean policies of the United States as dollar imperalism. American actions were viewed as undertaken primarily for crass economic reasons, to protect and promote private investments in the republics in the Central American area. The approach of World War II, however, with its external dangers to the Western Hemisphere, caused a reappraisal of past American policies in the Caribbean in terms of security requirements and benevolent impulses.

DOCUMENTS

1. Cuba and Panama: American Protectorates

Although Cuba obtained independence as a result of the Spanish-American War, it was kept under the tutelage of the United States. The Platt Amendment to the army appropriation bill in 1901 provided for a protectorate arrangement and the substance of this measure was subsequently incorporated in the 1903 treaty with Cuba. American troops withdrew from the island in 1902, but returned briefly in 1906–09 and 1917–22 to help preserve order in the republic. The 1903 Treaty with Panama in effect also made that state a satellite and illustrates the process of converting the Caribbean into an American sphere of control and influence.

347

Treaty between the United States and Cuba, signed, 1903

Article I. The Government of Cuba shall never enter into any treaty or other compact with any foreign power or powers which will impair or tend to impair the independence of Cuba, nor in any manner authorize or permit any foreign power or powers to obtain by colonization or for military or naval purposes, or otherwise, lodgment in or control over any portion of said island.

The Government of Cuba shall not assume or contract any public debt to pay the interest upon which, and to make reasonable sinking-fund provision for the ultimate discharge of which, the ordinary revenues of the Island of Cuba, after defraying the current expenses of the Government, shall be inadequate.

Article III. The Government of Cuba consents that the United States may exercise the right to intervene for the preservation of Cuban independence, the maintenance of a government adequate for the protection of life, property, and individual liberty, and for discharging the obligations with respect to Cuba imposed by the Treaty of Paris on the United States, now to be assumed and undertaken by the Government of Cuba.

Article V. The Government of Cuba will execute, and, as far as necessary, extend the plans already devised, or other plans to be mutually agreed upon, for the sanitation of the cities of the island, to the end that a recurrence of epidemic and infectious diseases may be prevented, thereby assuring protection to the people and commerce of Cuba, as well as to the commerce of the Southern ports of the United States and the people residing therein.

Article VII. To enable the United States to maintain the independence of Cuba, and to protect the people thereof, as well as for its own defense, the Government of Cuba will sell or lease to the United States lands necessary for coaling or naval stations, at certain specified points, to be agreed upon with the President of the United States. . . .

Convention between the United States and Panama, signed 1903

Article I. The United States guarantees and will maintain the independence of the Republic of Panama.

Article II. The Republic of Panama grants to the United States in perpetuity the use, occupation and control of a zone of land and land under water for the construction, maintenance, operation, sanitation and protection of said Canal of the width of ten miles extending to the distance of five miles on each side of the center line of the route of the Canal to be constructed. . . .

Article III. The Republic of Panama grants to the United States all the rights, power and authority within the zone mentioned and described in

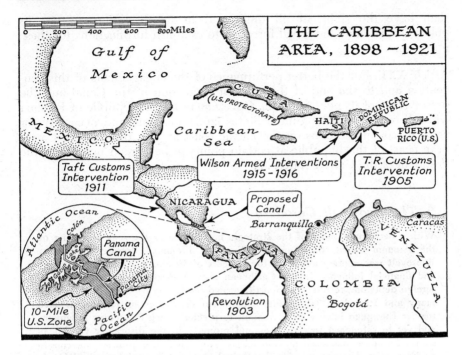

Article II of this agreement and within the limits of all auxiliary lands and waters mentioned and described in said Article II which the United States would possess and exercise if it were the sovereign of the territory within which said lands and waters are located to the entire exclusion of the exercise by the Republic of Panama of any such sovereign rights, power or authority.

Article XIV. As the price or compensation for the rights, powers and privileges granted in this convention by the Republic of Panama to the United States, the Government of the United States agrees to pay to the Republic of Panama the sum of ten million dollars ($10,000,000) in gold coin of the United States on the exchange of the ratification of this convention and also an annual payment during the life of this convention of two hundred and fifty thousand dollars ($250,000) in like gold coin, beginning nine years after the date aforesaid. . . .

Article XVIII. The Canal, when constructed, and the entrances thereto shall be neutral in perpetuity, and shall be opened upon the terms provided for by Section I of Article three of, and in conformity with all the stipulations of, the treaty entered into by the Governments of the United States and Great Britain on November 18, 1901. . . .

Article XXIII. If it should become necessary at any time to employ armed forces for the safety or protection of the Canal, or of the ships that make use of the same, or the railways and auxiliary works, the United States shall have the right, at all times and in its discretion, to use its police and its land and naval forces or to establish fortifications for these purposes. . . .

Article XXV. For the better performance of the engagements of this convention and to the end of the efficient protection of the Canal and the preservation of its neutrality, the Government of the Republic of Panama will sell or lease to the United States lands adequate and necessary for naval or coaling stations on the Pacific coast and on the western Caribbean coast of the Republic at certain points to be agreed upon with the President of the United States. . . .

2. The Roosevelt Corollary

With a new-found sense of the strategic importance of the seas bordering on the Panama Canal, the American "imperial life-line," President Theodore Roosevelt was acutely aware of the dangers of European armed intervention and financial influence in the Caribbean area. Venezuelan defaulting on its foreign debts had resulted in tripartite armed retaliation by Great Britain, Germany and Italy in 1902. Similar Dominican difficulties in 1904 threatened further European intervention. Anxious to preclude such dangerous lodgments and yet to safeguard foreign lives and property in the disorderly Caribbean states, President Roosevelt announced an extension of the Monroe Doctrine to an international police role for the United States. A financial overlordship in Santo Domingo ensued in 1905 and set the pattern for comparable arrangements later in Nicaragua, Santo Domingo, and Haiti.

Roosevelt's Annual Message to Congress, December 1904

. . . It is not true that the United States feels any land hunger or entertains any projects as regards the other nations of the Western Hemisphere save such as are for their welfare. All that this country desires is to see the neighboring countries stable, orderly, and prosperous. Any country whose people conduct themselves well can count upon our hearty friendship. If a nation shows that it knows how to act with reasonable efficiency and decency in social and political matters, if it keeps order and pays its obligations, it need fear no interference from the United States. Chronic wrongdoing, or an impotence which results in a general loosening of the ties of civilized society, may in America, as elsewhere, ultimately require intervention by some civilized nation, and in the Western Hemisphere the adherence of the United States to the Monroe Doctrine may force the United States, however reluctantly, in flagrant cases of such wrongdoing or impotence, to the exercise of an international police power. If every country washed by the Caribbean Sea would show the progress in stable and just civilization which with the aid of the Platt amendment Cuba has shown since our troops left the island, and which so many of the republics in both Americas are constantly and brilliantly showing, all question of interference by this Nation with their affairs would be at an end. Our

interests and those of our southern neighbors are in reality identical. They
have great natural riches, and if within their borders the reign of law and
justice obtains, prosperity is sure to come to them. While they thus obey
the primary laws of civilized society they may rest assured that they will
be treated by us in a spirit of cordial and helpful sympathy. We would
interfere with them only in the last resort, and then only if it became evident that their inability or unwillingness to do justice at home and abroad
had violated the rights of the United States or had invited foreign aggression to the detriment of the entire body of American nations. It is a mere
truism to say that every nation, whether in America or anywhere else,
which desires to maintain its freedom, its independence, must ultimately
realize that the right of such independence can not be separated from the
responsibility of making good use of it. . . .

3. Wilsonian Caribbean Diplomacy

Although repeatedly proclaiming a new approach to Latin America, which disavowed imperialism and advocated harmonious and cooperative relations,
President Woodrow Wilson approved more armed interventions than had his
two predecessors in office. The reasons were in part the security requirements
of defending the Panama Canal but also involved his determination to incul-
cate habits of good government in the Caribbean. Secretary of State William
Jennings Bryan's instructions to the American minister in Santo Domingo, on
September 9, 1913, reveal these purposes.

Wilson's Declaration of Policy with
Regard to Latin America

One of the chief objects of my administration will be to cultivate the
friendship and deserve the confidence of our sister republics of Central
and South America, and to promote in every proper and honorable way
the interests which are common to the peoples of the two continents. I
earnestly desire the most cordial understanding and cooperation between
the peoples and leaders of America and, therefore, deem it my duty to
make this brief statement.

Cooperation is possible only when supported at every turn by the
orderly processes of just government based upon law, not upon arbitrary
or irregular force. We hold, as I am sure all thoughtful leaders of republican government everywhere hold, that just government rests always upon
the consent of the governed, and that there can be no freedom without
order based upon law and upon the public conscience and approval. We
shall look to make these principles the basis of mutual intercourse, respect,
and helpfulness between our sister republics and ourselves. We shall lend
our influence of every kind to the realization of these principles in fact
and practice, knowing that disorder, personal intrigues, and defiance of
constitutional rights weaken and discredit government and injure none so
much as the people who are unfortunate enough to have their common

life and their common affairs so tainted and disturbed. We can have no sympathy with those who seek to seize the power of government to advance their own personal interests or ambition. We are the friends of peace, but we know that there can be no lasting or stable peace in such circumstances. As friends, therefore, we shall prefer those who act in the interest of peace and honor, who protect private rights, and respect the restraints of constitutional provision. Mutual respect seems to us the indispensable foundation of friendship between states, as between individuals.

The United States has nothing to seek in Central and South America except the lasting interest of the peoples of the two continents, the security of governments intended for the people and for no special group or interest, and the development of personal and trade relationships between the two continents which shall redound to the profit and advantage of both and interfere with the rights and liberties of neither.

From these principles may be read so much of the future policy of this Government as it is necessary now to forecast, and in the spirit of these principles I may, I hope, be permitted with as much confidence as earnestness to extend to the Governments of all the Republics of America the hand of genuine disinterested friendship, and to pledge my own honor and the honor of my colleagues to every enterprise of peace and amity that a fortunate future may disclose.

Secretary of State William Jennings Bryan's Instructions to the American Minister in Santo Domingo

DEPARTMENT OF STATE,
Washington, September 9, 1913

The President directs me to say for your instruction that the influence of this Government will be exerted for the support of lawful authorities in Santo Domingo, and for the discouragement of any and all insurrectionary methods. You will carry with you a copy of the President's statement of last March which sets forth fully, and in such a way as to leave no doubt, his position on two important points, namely: First, that we can have no sympathy with those who seek to seize the power of government to advance their own personal interests or ambition; and, second, that the test of a republican form of government is to be found in its responsiveness to the will of the people, its just powers being derived from the consent of the governed.

It is not to be expected that those in power will be able to avoid mistakes but mistakes should be corrected by constitutional means. Neither is it to be supposed that reforms will in all cases be brought about as soon as they ought to be, but the remedy for this is agitation—not insurrection.

Say to any who may feel aggrieved or who may be disposed to resort to violence that the good offices of this Government can be counted upon at all times to assist in the establishment of justice, in the remedying of abuses, and in the promotion of the welfare of the people. We must depend, therefore, upon all the people of Santo Domingo, of whatever party or faction, to join together in securing justice through law and in the election by free and fair ballot of officials whom the people desire. You will make it known to those now in insurrection that this Government will employ every legitimate means to assist in the restoration of order and in the prevention of further insurrections, holding itself open at all times to advise with the government in behalf of those who feel that they have a grievance.

I am sure that when the disinterestedness of our Government is fully understood, its friendship will be appreciated and its advice sought.

READINGS

1. Dollar Diplomacy in the Caribbean

Charles A. Beard, noted in American historiography for an economic interpretation of history, explains the Caribbean policies of the United States from 1901 through World War I as an example of economic and political imperialism. Most diplomatic historians view his explanation as too sweeping and oversimplified in the emphasis on economic motives as the main cause of interventions.

Imperial America
CHARLES AND MARY BEARD

The annexation of Porto Rico and absorption of Cuba under Republican auspices had been merely a prelude to the transformation of the Gulf of Mexico and the Caribbean into an inland sea of the United States. In the nature of things, to use the language of diplomacy, the region was a part of the American empire; for a lion's share of the commerce with nearly all the islands scattered between the Bahamas and Trinidad had been readily gathered into American hands. Even British and French traders could not resist the pull of the powerful market in the United States; while the combined efforts of Britain and Canada could not make water run up hill. On the mainland also, in Mexico, Central America, Colombia, and Venezuela, American business enterprise marched from one victory to another.

Political as well as economic processes favored the development of American hegemony. In those places where European powers did not keep order, there were periodic uprisings against the titular governments, revolts often purely factious, sometimes the efforts of honest men to oust corrupt and tyrannical adventurers, occasionally the outcome of a failure to appreciate the merits of foreign investors. Regardless of their source, they were always disturbing to business interests, particularly to the holders of local bonds. As a rule the outstanding obligations of Latin-American republics were large for the pertinent revenues. In fact they

were generally inflated to a high pressure; for each uprising the debts of
the defeated party were added to those of the victors, thereby preventing
any such magnificent repudiation as had occurred when the government
of Abraham Lincoln triumphed over that of Jefferson Davis in the Second
American Revolution. It required, accordingly, no sweeping derangement
of the social order in a Latin-American country to fetch down a high
structure of finance.

In every crisis the government of the United States was involved, and
given new occasions for assimilation. Besides being pledged under the
Monroe Doctrine to prevent European powers from occupying more territory in the western hemisphere, even in the honest performance of collecting debts, it was continually besieged by American bankers and business men to help them save endangered revenues. At no time did it feel
inclined to say that it would neither allow European governments to succor
their nationals among the bondholders nor make any movement itself on
their behalf. If the duties imposed by the necessity for action were slight,
the mere presence of American battleships in the offing might enable
bankers to take possession of customs houses and effect amicable settlements of debts by negotiations. If, however, local leaders refused to listen
to the voice of warning and forced the landing of American marines, a
limited warfare sometimes had to be waged on the basis of presidential
orders to the Navy Department. And yet in no case did the parties of interest feel constrained to invoke the constitutional provision vesting the
power to declare war in the Congress of the United States. As things
turned out, American economic and political sovereignty was steadily advanced in the Caribbean without breaking the legal peace of the western
hemisphere or disturbing the party of pacific intentions in the domestic
hinterland.

A brief illustrative chronology hints at the process. In 1903, Germany
was compelled by a threat of force from President Roosevelt to withdraw
from Venezuela and submit certain financial claims to arbitration. In
1905, Roosevelt, by executive action, took over the customs houses of
Santo Domingo and stationed war vessels in Dominican waters to give
point to the argument. Under the Platt amendment, he interfered in
Cuba in 1906, giving the natives a convincing proof that American warnings against disorder were to be respected. By a formal treaty ratified by
the Senate of the United States, the pecuniary protectorate over Santo
Domingo was made regular in 1907. The next year Secretary Knox broke
off relations with the President of Nicaragua; a little later an American
warship served notice on local contestants for power that there was to be
no fighting in Bluefields—"thus protecting the preponderating American
and other foreign interests," as the State Department in Washington put
it. In 1911, on the suggestion of New York bankers, a treaty was negotiated with Honduras, extending American authority over that republic;
though ratified by the United States Senate, it was rejected by the native
authorities.

During the same year an American warship was sent to Nicaragua, a loan arranged, and a treaty drawn, reciting "the benevolent intentions" of the United States and putting the customs into the hands of a presidential appointee. When, in spite of three urgent messages from President Taft, the Senate declined to ratify the agreement, marines were landed in Nicaragua and business was restored to a normal course. In 1914–16, a treaty with Nicaragua was at last adopted ceding a canal strip and naval bases to the United States in return for three million dollars in cash to be expended largely for American goods in coöperation with American authorities. In 1915, the marines carried the flag into Haiti and established American suzerainty there after killing more than two thousand natives who, for one reason or another, got in the way of the operation. In 1916, Admiral Knapp—"to maintain domestic tranquillity"—took possession of Santo Domingo and declared that "republic" subject to the military government of the United States. In 1917, the Virgin Islands were purchased from Denmark. In 1920, the American navy was employed in helping to stabilize Guatemala. In 1921, after some American marines had smashed the office of the *Tribuna* in Managua, for printing critical articles, the minister of the United States requested the local Nicaraguan government to set apart adequate space outside the capital for drill grounds, a dance hall, and a moving picture theater to be used by American forces and also to designate special liquor saloons for their convenience. In 1923, the national assembly of Panama approved a large loan for highway construction to be secured by investments correctly placed in New York City. In 1924, the American marines once more came to the aid of public order in Honduras. In 1927, the marines were again in Nicaragua. Such was in brief a partial chronicle of what Secretary Knox called "dollar diplomacy."

The series of events here recited were accompanied by no expressions of ill-will on the part of the American government. On the contrary, Roosevelt, Taft, Wilson, Harding, and Coolidge all agreed that, in this connection, there was nothing either sinister or ungenerous in the purposes of the United States. Wilson was especially emphatic on this point. Speaking cordially of the Latin-American countries, he said: "We must prove ourselves their friends and champions upon terms of equality and honor. . . . We must show ourselves friends by comprehending their interests whether it squares with our interests or not." . . .

In fact, each of the numerous incidents in the extension of American authority over the Caribbean was marked by colors and episodes peculiar to the occasion. For that reason, the bare chronicle of the forward movement as a whole fails to give a correct impression of the higher law in its specific application. To gain an insight into that phase it is necessary to examine somewhat minutely an entire chapter of contingencies, and for the purpose of illustration the case of Haiti offers a sufficient revelation. That little island republic became the scene of revolutions and assassinations as soon as it cast off the yoke of France in 1803 and at all times thereafter showed an evident need for law, order, good roads, sanitation, education, and industrial progress. But the southern planters who ruled the United States in the middle period of national expansion, although they were ready to raise the flag over good land fit for cotton culture, shrank from relations too cordial with a spot where slaves had made a successful revolution and were trying to govern themselves. Moreover, their successors at Washington, the masters of business, were also largely indifferent to the requirements of Haiti as long as domestic enterprise—even farm mortgages—yielded ten or fifteen per cent or happy negotiations with the federal land office brought larger returns on smaller risks. But at the end of the century, when the southern slavocracy had moldered in its grave and the pecuniary equipment of the United States had been well rounded out, there arose a marked solicitude about the welfare of Haiti.

In 1902, one of the periodical rebellions that had plagued that small republic sent it swimming within the range of American kinetics. Turning for aid to the United States, the Haitian government floated a loan in New York at twelve per cent and invested large sums in ammunition at two or three times the usual price. Unabashed by these commitments, American munition makers showed an equal interest in the revolutionary forces fighting for "liberty" and sold them instruments of destruction, also on profitable terms. Observing the scrimmage from afar, European capitalists tendered their good offices with the same devotion to both parties, everyone of them knowing, as the American minister on the spot remarked with casual directness, that the civilized powers concerned would make the Haitians pay all bills no matter which side won in the civil war. Now, among the countries involved in this crisis, none was more anxious than the German Empire. German merchants controlled about nine-tenths of Haiti's foreign trade and showed a concern in local affairs that was artistically proportioned to the flow of goods. In the press of things, they were able to place a loan of half a million at thirty-five per cent interest and later they managed to float a smaller issue of three hundred thousand dollars which yielded a net sum of about half that amount to the Haitian treasury.

Naturally vexed by this precocity on the part of the Germans and fearing utter discomfiture at the hands of their rivals, American business men began to display great consternation, the State Department sharing their fear. Although an American company had got important railway and land concessions and although the National City Bank of New York had gathered in much of the Haitian debt on terms presumably not adverse, it was thought that the American share of the local proceeds was entirely too small. Moreover, there were irritations connected with an affront to national honor; open discrimination was shown by Haitians against some American citizens of Syrian origin who had been very active in bringing local trade into American hands. And this annoyance was augmented by an untoward incident, arising from an attempt of the Haitian president to seize the gold reserve in the local national bank, a design foiled by the intervention of American marines, and the transfer of the treasure on an American war vessel to New York, where it was safely deposited at a low rate of interest, leaving the Government of Haiti to clamor loudly for a return of the funds.

Since it was now evident that the friendly concern of the State Department in Washington must take a more practical form, President Wilson sent commissioners to Haiti charged with the task of persuading Vilbrun Guillaume Sam, president of the republic, to accept the benevolent protection of the United States. At the same time American bankers served notice on him that no more loans were to be expected without adequate guarantees, placing him in a real dilemma. Procuring aid from Berlin was out of the question, for Germany, in the toils of war, was blockaded by an invincible sea power. Neither was assistance from France forthcoming; that country, far from indicating a desire to help President Sam out of his pinch, dispatched a naval force to his republic to protect French lives and property.

Given this signal for action, the government of the United States, in the summer of 1915, ordered Admiral Caperton, in command of the good ship, *Washington,* to Haitian waters, just in time to learn that President Sam, enraged by the turn of events, had ordered the murder of more than a hundred prisoners and had been himself assassinated in retaliation. Visibly disturbed by such cruel deeds, the Admiral directed his marines to seize the local political theater and some blood was shed in the operation, but not enough to cause a declaration of war by Congress. Competent directors now being in charge, martial law was instituted under American auspices and the Haitian national assembly was permitted to elect as president, General Dartiguenave, a candidate acceptable to Admiral Caperton and apparently disposed to cooperate with American representatives on the ground.

At all events, as soon as he was installed, the General signed a treaty with his new friends. In the preamble, the document stated that it was the desire of the "High contracting parties . . . to confirm and strengthen the amity existing between them by the most cordial cooperation in measures for their common advantage." According to the terms of the bond the United States was to use its good offices in developing the agricultural, mineral, and commercial resources of the little republic, to name engineers whose advice was to be binding in the management of the said resources, to take over and administer the customs of the republic, and to select the financial adviser charged with directing the fiscal affairs of the local government.

Thus, in a single stroke, the United States undertook to promote private enterprise and safeguard the public finances upon which large bond issues afloat in the United States rested for security. With the restraint that characterized Clive's course in India, the American administration refrained from annexing Haiti; indeed this would have been inconsistent with Wilson's lofty declaration of two years before to the effect that this country would "never again seek one additional foot of territory by conquest." In this spirit the Senate ratified the Haitian treaty of amity in the spring of 1916.

2. Securing the Approaches to the Panama Canal

Samuel F. Bemis rejects economic explanations and, correctly in the view of the majority of American historians, assigns great weight to strategic factors in the Caribbean. Dangerous foreign interpositions to protect their nationals and property could not be permitted in the zone of the vital Panama Canal. The only alternative envisioned by Roosevelt and Taft was to have the United States itself intervene to preserve order and encourage stability in the area.

The Roosevelt Corollary and Dollar Diplomacy
SAMUEL FLAGG BEMIS

. . .The day before the Senate of the United States advised the ratification of the Hay-Bunau-Varilla Treaty with the new republic of Panama, a most significant juridical verdict was announced on the other side of the Atlantic. The Hague Court of Permanent Arbitration on February 22, 1904, rendered its decision on the issue of preferential rights of the intervening powers to the designated Venezuelan assets for satisfaction of the adjudicated claims of foreign nationals. Unequivocally it decided that Germany, Great Britain, and Italy, the powers which had resorted to force to secure justice, had a right to payment ahead of the powers who had been content with a peaceful solution.

There is no question but that this decision placed a premium, in international law, upon forceful intervention against a delinquent state. In so doing, it put to American diplomacy a very serious dilemma. Within the strategic radius of the Panama Canal there were other Latin American republics, in the Caribbean and in Central America, whose irresponsibility toward their just obligations to foreigners was almost as confirmed as in Venezuela, and whose political stability was continually uncertain. Either the United States must recognize this sanctioned right of European intervention—now juridically sanctioned—and the contingent possibilities of foreign danger to the Monroe Doctrine in the neighborhood of the Panama Canal or it must itself vicariously assume responsibility for justice to the foreign nationals so that their governments would not have to intervene. The assumption of such responsibility entailed intervention by the United States itself. This was the dilemma, then: should the United States stand by with folded arms while non-American powers, backed in principle by a Hague Court decision, intervened and perhaps ensconced themselves in strategic positions from which in the future they might cut the Panama life-line and the security of the Continental Republic; or should it intervene itself to guarantee justice and responsibility in strategically located countries whose condition invited foreign intervention, and thereby run the risk of incurring by its own intervention the misunderstanding and animosity of the neighboring republics?

These questions were not new. Before the Civil War, Senator Sam Houston of Texas had advocated a protectorate over Mexico which would

From *The Latin American Policy of the United States*, copyright, 1943 by Samuel Flagg Bemis. Reprinted by permission of Harcourt, Brace & World, Inc. Pp. 151–158, 161–166.

include a service on her foreign bonds. He urged it as a means of extricating Mexico from the British lion's mouth, and thought that Great Britain might even welcome it. John Forsyth, United States minister to Mexico, had negotiated a treaty in 1857, by which the United States would have loaned money to Mexico to pay off British bondholders, the loan to be secured by a portion of that republic's customs revenues. Secretary of State Seward, in an effort to stave off European intervention, had negotiated a loan with the Juarez Government to enable it to pay the interest—at only 3 per cent—on its foreign debt for five years at least, but he never ventured to submit it to the Senate. The French intervention in Mexico was an historic example of how such European loans could lead to political and military intervention, to loss of independence itself. Secretary Hamilton Fish in 1869 favored collection of Venezuelan customs by United States officials in order to service that nation's defaulted foreign bonds—with a priority in payment to United States nationals. Except for this last condition, Fish's proposal anticipated the "dollar diplomacy" of the twentieth century. Again in 1881 Secretary of State James G. Blaine had suggested that the United States might place an agent in charge of the pledged customs of Venezuela to pay off foreign creditors pro rata in a secure and orderly way.

On all these occasions since the Civil War, British creditors, at least, expressed themselves favorable to such a collection by the United States. After the Venezuelan boundary controversy the British Government frequently hinted that if the United States expected to assume authority in the Caribbean region, it ought also to assume responsibility for the foreign debts of those states. Before the intervention in Venezuela in 1902 the German *chargé* in Caracas had asked the United States Minister there whether his Government would participate in a joint intervention. The latter, Herbert W. Bowen, said no: his Government could scarcely join in any forceful measures with European powers against an American republic; if any policing were to take place it ought to be by the United States alone, who could take care competently of the concerns of the European powers. As the Venezuela crisis of December, 1902, eased off, by the agreement in principle to arbitrate, the British Prime Minister, A. J. Balfour, had intimated that his government would be glad to see the United States take the troublesome republics of South America in hand; it had no objection to the Monroe Doctrine—on the contrary. "If the United States could see their way," declared a government spokesman in the debates on the Venezuelan affair in the House of Commons, "to the adoption of some effective course by which these almost periodical difficulties arising between the great powers and some of the states of South America could be prevented, I think I may say it would meet with cordial concurrence in this country." The London press chimed in with the same note. It was a welcome contrast to Great Britain's attitude at the beginning of the American Civil War. Then on the occasion of threatened Spanish invasion of the Dominican Republic, the British Ambassador at Washington had told Secretary Seward that he could not "allow" him to assert the Monroe Doctrine without reminding him that Great Britain repudiated it altogether!

Thus there was adequate reason to believe that Great Britain would welcome intervention by the United States alone, to clean up the bad finances of these shaky republics in case of another lapse of justice, and that Germany would not object to it. It proved that France and Belgium, too, were ready to acquiesce in such a procedure. To the United States such a course was preferable to participation in a joint receivership as proposed at various times by representatives of the European powers, which would have meant an "ottomanization" of the strategic Caribbean area. The events of the previous five years, together with the European situation, had induced—we will not say reconciled, unless in the case of Great Britain—the powers tacitly to accept the hegemony of the United States in that region.

The decision of the Hague Tribunal had hardly been announced when the Venezuela claims situation with all its implications for the Monroe Doctrine, implications so sharpened by that decision, repeated itself in the Dominican Republic. Anarchy, confusion and disaster had there become the order of the day. In April, 1904, the United States Minister in Santo Domingo reported—what was subsequently denied to the American Ambassador at Rome by the Italian Minister for Foreign Affairs— that Italy was about to intervene with naval forces to secure the rights of Italian nationals, fixed by a protocol of 1903. "I understand," he said, "that the action of the Italian Government is based upon the recent decision at the Hague."

The total Dominican debt in default was $32,000,000. Various national revenues had been hypothecated to Belgian, French, German, Italian, and Spanish creditors. Amidst alternating dictatorships and revolutions, the Santo Domingo Improvement Company, a New York corporation, had refunded some of the older defaulted foreign loans and floated new ones for public construction work. The United States Government was unwilling to intervene diplomatically to support this American corporation or importunate individual citizens until it became evident that it was more than a question of securing justice for the financial contracts of a national: it was a matter of defending by diplomatic arrangements the independent status of the island republic against *justifiable* forceful interventions *à la* Venezuela, justifiable interventions that might grow into more or less permanent occupations for other purposes, as in Egypt; that would menace the safety of the canal, the security of the two-ocean republic.

During the Venezuelan imbroglio the Department of State in 1903 peaceably arranged a diplomatic settlement by which the Santo Domingo Improvement Company ceded to the Dominican Government its holdings in the National Bank and the Central Dominican Railway, and accepted $4,500,000 in acquittal of a total credit claimed of $11,000,000. By this agreement a mixed commission of arbitration laid down (July 14, 1904) a schedule of payments, secured by stipulated customs revenues, to be made to an agent appointed by the United States Government and paid over to the creditor. At the first default the agent should have full power and authority to step in and to fix and collect customs and port dues of Puerto Plata, Sánchez, Samaná, and Montecristi, and apply them, after expenses of collection, to the scheduled liquidation of the debt.

Straightway the Dominican Government defaulted, and the agent took over collection (October, November, 1904). To this the other foreign creditors, with their colliding special hypothecations, quite naturally objected. They clamored for the support of their governments. President Roosevelt had to look forward to a foreign intervention or take the responsibility for intervention by the United States. He had little choice other than to intervene to secure justice for all the foreign creditors. Public opinion, as evidenced by the recent Venezuelan imbroglio, would not have tolerated an European intervention, nor would it have accepted participation by the United States in a joint intervention in an island that dominated so strategically the Caribbean Sea and the Atlantic approaches to the Panama Canal.

The Hague Court decision of February 22, 1904, significant as it was, was not necessary to convince President Roosevelt of the need of intervention by the United States. "San Domingo is drifting into chaos," he wrote to his eldest son, at the outbreak of the Russo-Japanese war, "for after a hundred years of freedom it shows itself utterly incompetent for governmental work. Most reluctantly I have been obliged to take the initial step of interference there. I hope it will be a good while before I will have to go further. But sooner or later it seems to me inevitable that the United States should assume an attitude of protection and regulation in regard to all these little states in the neighborhood of the Caribbean. I hope it will be deferred as long as possible but I think it is inevitable."

The first step in dealing with this dangerous Dominican dilemma had been to send Admiral Dewey and Assistant Secretary of State F. B. Loomis to investigate conditions in the Dominican Republic. Loomis's confidential report of March, 1904, stressed the chaotic situation there and the cross-claims of the foreign governments, and suggested an American receivership. Despite repeated importunities of successive Dominican Governments, and none more insistent than that which was temporarily and precariously in power in 1904, Theodore Roosevelt had no idea of annexing the island republic, or its neighbor Haiti, or even of establishing a naval base there. None was necessary between the United States naval base at Guantánamo, on the eastern tip of Cuba, and the United States island of Puerto Rico to the east of Hispaniola. The President went out of his way to repudiate in the most explicit manner, by personal statements, and by a note from the Secretary of State to the Haitian Minister in Washington, any thought of annexation. What he wanted was to accept, with the implied mandate of the European creditor powers, and at the request of the tottering Dominican Government, responsibility for the efficient and honest collection of the customs— pledged and cross-pledged as they already were—and a pro rata payment by an United States receivership of the foreign debt within the capacity of the island government. The reason for this, we cannot repeat too emphatically, was to remove any justification for intervention by foreign powers, after the fashion of Venezuela, within this strategic area so vitally related to the new Atlantic-Pacific life-line of the United States.

Diplomacy sealed the arrangement in the form of a protocol with the Dominican Government calling for a receivership in the hands of an agent appointed by the President of the United States, who would collect the customs under the protection of the United States Government if necessary, and pay out 45 per cent of the proceeds to the creditors pro rata, after satisfying the expenses of the receivership, and turn the remaining funds over to the Dominican Government. It does not seem, from the manner in which the negotiations were carried on, that the President had intended any more than an executive agreement; but apparently on mature consideration he decided that it was his duty to submit the document to the Senate for advice and consent as to formal ratification. At first the protocol contained a guaranty of the territorial integrity of the Dominican Republic. Since the Senate might stick at a guaranty, there was substituted in the final treaty a pledge to respect the territorial integrity of the Dominican Republic. Even so, the Senate postponed for two years its acceptance of the arrangement. A partisan minority resented Roosevelt's original intention not to consult it at all. But the strategic significance of the island was too vital to be neglected. In 1907 the Senate approved a new treaty, somewhat modified by dropping the territorial pledge and all references to the danger of foreign intervention, retaining the essential financial provisions. Meanwhile President Roosevelt had been executing its terms under a *modus vivendi* based on executive agreement. Controlling forces of the United States navy hovered in Dominican waters, if only to overawe the presence of Italian, French, and German units, but there was no occupation of the island, no interference (before 1912) with its internal affairs beyond the receivership of customs. An expert appointed by President Roosevelt was able in 1905 to scale down the debt, with the agreement of the creditors, from $32,000,000 to $17,000,000, and start a scheduled payment of new 50-year 5 per cent bonds issued, at the request of the Department of State, by New York banks to refund the adjusted debt. The result was a novel prosperity for the republic accompanied by a frustration of revolutionary habits hitherto confirmed.

Theodore Roosevelt confused the Latin American policy of the United States by identifying intervention in the Dominican Republic with the Monroe Doctrine, thus making that Doctrine, which had said "hands off" to Europe, seem to say "hands on" for the United States. Actually, as many a responsible statesman has pointed out since Woodrow Wilson's time, the Monroe Doctrine did not give to, nor did it withhold from the United States a right or policy of intervention. But President Roosevelt honestly and resolutely thought that because the Monroe Doctrine prohibited European intervention to secure justice, it ought to follow as a logical corollary that it sanctioned intervention by the United States in order to prevent it by Europe. In presenting the "protocol" to the Senate (February 15, 1905), he said:

> An aggrieved nation can without interfering with the Monroe Doctrine take what action it sees fit in the adjustment of its disputes with American States, provided that action does not take the shape of interference with their form of government or of the despoilment of their territory under any disguise. But, short of this, when the question is one of a money claim, the only way which remains, finally, to collect it is a blockade, or bombardment, or the seizure of the customhouses, and this means what is in effect a possession, even though only a temporary possession, of territory. The United States then becomes a party in interest, because under the Monroe doctrine it can not see any European power seize and permanently occupy the territory of one of these republics; and yet such seizure of territory, disguised or undisguised, may eventually offer the only way in which the power in question can collect any debts, unless there is interference on the part of the United States.

This was the well-intended but withal portentous "Roosevelt Corollary" to the Monroe Doctrine, the so-called policy of the "Big Stick": benevolent United States intervention to prevent non-American intervention, a bit of necessary diplomacy—at that time—but bad logic, which has required a generation to cast off.

Thoughtful scholars, like Professor Rippy, have wondered why it never occurred to Roosevelt to let all alien investors shift for themselves in the Dominican Republic. As a matter of fact, Roosevelt did announce in 1905 that his Government had always refused resort to the use of force for the collection of contract debts, and Secretary of State Root later repeated this in South America. Indeed, the United States had just ratified the inter-American convention of 1902 for the arbitration of pecuniary claims, and was preparing to support the Drago Doctrine at the coming Hague Peace Conference.

The obvious answer to the question just noted is that the other great powers would not renounce the right of intervention to secure justice, including contract debts; it had proven impossible in Venezuela a year previously for the United States to leave alien investors to shift for themselves. The European powers had intervened, and the Hague Court had just put an impressive sanction of international law on the justice of their use of force. If Roosevelt had stood aside in 1904, another intervention would almost certainly have followed and the control of the United States over the Panama Canal might have been checkmated at the very start of construction. Certainly the danger of this was sufficiently imminent to cause grave concern. Roosevelt was acting upon the traditional motive of security for the Continental Republic as he, and his compatriots, sensed it at the time. Not until the menace of European intervention had temporarily disappeared as a result of the First World War could a President of the United States safely think of liquidating the protective imperialism that had been established in the vital Caribbean area at the beginning of the century; not until then could there be a reasonable expectation, during the period between the two great wars, that the non-American powers would refrain from intervention in the New World to secure justice denied to their nationals.

This Dominican receivership does not appear to have awakened contemporaneously any appreciable resentment or distrust of other governments, even of the Latin American republics, although the press of France and Germany was caustic. The Latin American literary Yankeephobia that flamed up later was fanned to life in the intellectual foyers of the very European nations whose governments, under the circumstances of 1904–1907, had been so willing, even anxious, to have the rights of their nationals secured by the United States. . . .

Discerning students have blamed Taft and more particularly his Secretary of State, Philander C. Knox, for carrying the Roosevelt Corollary toward a more active and less disinterested intervention, notably in Nicaragua. They have stigmatized this action with the derogatory phrase of "dollar diplomacy," taking their cue from some frank avowals of the President that he considered it a most useful function of government to advance and protect the legitimate trade and investments of United States citizens in foreign countries, particularly in areas of competition like China, where they served to chaperon or neutralize imperialistic designs. In the course of this study we shall have more to say of dollar diplomacy. It was not designed to profit private interests. It was intended rather to support the foreign policy of the United States; in the instance of Latin America to support the Roosevelt Corollary to the Monroe Doctrine. In these interventions in Central America and the Caribbean there was also a certain characteristic missionary impulse to help the people themselves, willy-nilly, by stabilizing their governments and economies.

Zelaya resented the diplomatic intrusion of the United States and Mexico because it interfered with his own ambition to unify all Central America under his mastery by overturning governments in the neighboring states and putting in his puppets. He had consistently opposed the whole movement toward Central American solidarity by diplomatic and by constitutional processes. In his resentment he had also been very hostile to American private capital legally invested in Nicaragua. For example, he wished to cancel the United States-Nicaragua Concession, a mining property owned by a Pittsburgh corporation which represented the principal American private capital in the Isthmian republic. He wanted to take back this concession and sell it over again to somebody else for better terms. As a Pennsylvania lawyer and counsel to the corporation, Philander C. Knox, before he became Secretary of State, had himself passed upon the validity of the contract. It became clear that the Nicaraguan dictator was the greatest single menace to the whole treaty structure, as well as to American private contracts; that the Washington conventions would have little effect in stabilizing and uniting the five republics as long as Zelaya remained President of Nicaragua. There is no evidence to show that President Taft and Secretary Knox were more charitable toward the ambitious Isthmian general because of the latter's high-handed violation of these concessions, like Castro in Venezuela; on the contrary! Nor did reports of Zelaya's plans to make secret advances to Japan for a canal treaty ingratiate the dictator with the United States Government.

United States intervention in Nicaragua followed a revolution which broke out in 1909 against Zelaya in Bluefields and had at least the sympathy of the company which operated the United States-Nicaragua Concession. Zelaya's forces captured two United States citizens, named Cannon and Groce, professional dynamiters, who were laying mines in the San Juan River for the revolutionists, and executed them after court martial. They held commissions in the revolutionary army and considered themselves prisoners of war. President Taft made this the occasion for dismissing Zelaya's representative at Washington and landing marines to protect foreign nationals and property at Bluefields. Secretary Knox declared that the United States was convinced "that the revolution represented the ideals and will of a majority of the Nicaraguan people more truthfully than does the government of President Zelaya." As a result of this intervention Zelaya was overthrown. President Porfirio Díaz of Mexico, who had cooperated throughout with the United States to bring stability to Central America, advised Zelaya to quit. Soon a revolution in Mexico dethroned Díaz himself and left the United States as the sole sponsor of the precarious regional peace structure.

After a confusing interlude of shifting personnel in the revolutionary Nicaraguan government, Adolfo Díaz, who had been secretary of the United States-Nicaragua Concession emerged in 1911 with the assistance of American diplomacy as "constitutional" President, recognized by the United States. Secretary Knox negotiated with the new Government a treaty (the Knox-Castrillo convention), signed June 6, 1911, generally similar to the treaty of 1907 with the Dominican Republic, and identical to one that had just been signed with Honduras (January 10, 1911), for the purpose of refunding the debt of Nicaragua through new loans from New York bankers (Brown Brothers, J. and W. Seligman & Co.). This would have taken the old debt entirely out of the hands of an English syndicate, and put the new loan in a schedule of payment under an American receivership like that in the Dominican Republic. A separate executive agreement provided for a mixed commission to arbitrate the claims of American citizens against Nicaragua.

The Senate of the United States rejected both of these treaties, but the bankers, at the request of the Department of State and with its assistance, put through private contracts with Nicaragua which set up much the same sort of regime without treaty guaranties. On this basis they made a much smaller loan, $1,500,000 instead of $15,000,000, upon condition of securing control of the contemporaneously established National Bank of Nicaragua and the Nicaraguan state railways. Knox may have felt that he had the precedent behind him of Theodore Roosevelt's *modus vivendi* with the Dominican Republic after the Senate had first rejected the "protocol" of 1905; but unlike the Dominican example, the Senate never ratified the Knox treaties.

A new revolution against Adolfo Díaz's regime threatened to drift into the control of Zelaya's followers. If they should have gained control of the government, "all of the efforts of the State Department [says an historian of Central America] to place Nicaragua on her feet politically and financially would have been useless, and the interests of the New York bankers, who had undertaken their operations in the country at the express request of the United States Government, would be seriously imperiled." Accordingly, at the request of the Díaz Government the United States landed some 2,700 marines in 1912 and occupied the principal cities of the interior after a sharp engagement at Leon. From 1912 to 1933 (except for a brief interval following a trial withdrawal in 1925) a small force of United States marines maintained the Government of Nicaragua in office, supervised and policed elections, and trained up a Nicaraguan constabulary.

Thus fortified the government kept up payments on the old loans by the London bankers and the new loans of the New York bankers. Meanwhile, continued political agitation, crime, periodic revolts, disease, grasshopper plagues, and earthquakes worried, robbed, harassed, ravaged, devoured, and shook the already impoverished country and its people. The intervention of the United States was barely adequate to maintain elected governments in power and thus keep the pledged finances in order; it was not enough to regenerate Nicaragua as an effective protectorate had done in Cuba. Light as the intervention was, it was sufficient to arouse the animosity of other Latin American countries to whom Nicaraguan dissidents made their appeal. A full protectorate would not have been more hateful, and could have benefited the people much more.

After the failure of his financial treaties, Secretary Knox, alarmed at rumors of German interest in the Nicaraguan waterway, signed another treaty agreeing to pay Nicaragua $3,000,000 for an exclusive right of way for a canal, a naval base on the Gulf of Fonseca, and a ninety-nine-year lease of Great Corn and Little Corn Islands in the Caribbean near the Atlantic terminus of the route. This treaty was submitted to the Senate too late to get ratification before the end of the Taft Administration, but President Wilson took up the idea, with some modifications, and put it through, as we shall see in a later chapter.

It was one thing to build up, by cooperative measures short of actual military intervention, a structure of preventive diplomacy, designed to remove any justification for intervention by a non-American power in the Caribbean region. So Roosevelt and Root had done in Cuba and the Dominican Republic, in the latter instance with the implied mandate of the European powers, and this Roosevelt had rested on his famous Corollary. It was another step that Taft had taken under Knox's legal guidance: outright military intervention to safeguard the strategical interest of the United States in the Isthmian region. This smacked more of Roosevelt's intervention in Panama than it did of his diplomatic intervention in the Dominican Republic carried through under Root's guidance. By the same token, and other appearances (that of serving private interests), it created greater resentment both in Latin America and at home than did the Dominican receivership.

Intervention in Nicaragua and the occupation of that republic were certainly high-handed, uncalled for by any immediate exigency of foreign policy or national security, and actually contrary to the principles of the Washington conventions of 1907. Its effect, after the Senate rejected the Knox treaties of 1911, was to place the finances of that Isthmian country in the hands of private bankers for the next eight years. Their strict measures, alleviated by the Bryan-Chamorro Treaty ratified in 1916, and terminated by the Financial Plan of 1917, achieved the fiscal redemption of the country, but it is doubtful whether the local governments thus supported by United States marines furthered the concept of Central American confederation and union.

Knox would have imposed financial receiverships on Honduras and Guatemala too, if the Senate would have stood for it.

The Taft Administration took great pains to justify the Nicaraguan intervention constitutionally before Congress. Mr. J. Reuben Clark, Jr., Solicitor of the Department of State, compiled a long memorandum on *The Right to Protect Citizens in Foreign Countries by Landing Forces,* as established in international law and by United States precedent. Even after these arguments, the candid historian may be critical of the whole episode, but it certainly would be most unjust to attribute even the occupation of Nicaragua—cited so profusely as the standard illustration of the evils of dollar diplomacy—to the controlling power of private vested interests over the United States Government. Back of that intervention was an honest intent, at least, to stabilize and strengthen the international relations of Central America by substituting for Zelaya's focus of revolution and wars a truly representative and independent government and to further a union of all the Central American states on the foundation of the Washington conventions. The United States was interested in promoting this regional peace structure principally in order to remove any conceivable danger, even a remote one, of ultimate foreign intervention that might give military lodgment in the neighborhood of the Panama Canal, then advancing toward completion, or any possibility of a rival canal route falling under non-American influence.

Unfriendly foreign critics used the phrase "dollar diplomacy" to suggest a deliberate design by the United States to dominate the nearest Latin American republics, even the whole Western Hemisphere, for the private profit of "Wall Street." While not losing sight for one moment of the mistakes of foreign policy in the hands of the blundering Knox and Taft —and it is fortunate that the United Sates did not have to confront under their leadership any major crisis of diplomacy during the years 1909–1913—it is only fair to say that dollar diplomacy was more an easily misusable journalistic alliteration, alliterative unfortunately in all the principal languages of the New World and western Europe, that easily lent itelf to hateful propaganda and exaggerated Yankeephobia, than it was a truthful characterization of the protective foreign policy of the United States.

In their own uniquely inept way Taft and Knox were also following the instinct and traditions of continental security rather than the lead of selfish private interests. Nicaragua, like the Dominican Republic, like

Panama, like Haiti (where Woodrow Wilson was soon to send marines as well as to Santo Domingo), was one of the states of the New World, indeed of the entire world, where the least American capital was invested. It is a well-known fact that before the First World War indigenous capital found more lucrative employment in the United States than outside of its boundaries, that it was only with difficulty that the Department of State was able to persuade bankers to invest their funds for political purposes in foreign countries. The larger holdings of capital invested abroad in the New World were in Cuba, where "big business" had opposed intervention in 1898, in Mexico, where the United States Government and public opinion have certainly been averse to intervention for nearly a century; in Canada, and in the larger and more stable republics of South America.

It seems to be an historical fact that the more capital a country of the New World has accepted from private investors in the United States the less danger there has been of intervention. Such investments have brought a wealth of good to Latin American countries, but in the large it is doubtful whether they have been profitable to the economy of the United States, not to mention the investors. This is because they have not been wholly safe. They represented an overflow of luxury that the United States, unlike the great powers of the Old World, had not been willing, with its deep continental instincts of nonintervention, to guarantee and to secure by the use of force. But American diplomacy has always been sensitive to the strategical requirements of continental security. This, and not selfish private interests, really explained both the Roosevelt Corollary and the dollar diplomacy of Taft. It also explains in large measure the Latin American policy of Woodrow Wilson.

Additional Reading

W. H. Callcott, *The Caribbean Policy of the United States, 1890–1920* (1942).
H. C. Hill, *Roosevelt and the Caribbean* (1927).
Arthur S. Link, *Woodrow Wilson and the Progressive Era, 1910–1917* (1954).
———, *Wilson: the New Freedom* (1956).
Dana G. Munro, *The United States and the Caribbean Area* (1934).
E. T. Parks, *Colombia and the United States, 1765–1934* (1935).
J. Fred Rippy, *The Caribbean Danger Zone* (1940).
Charles C. Tansill, *The Purchase of the Danish West Indies* (1932).

13 *THE GREAT CRUSADE:*
American Involvement in World War I

Much heat and some light have resulted from the controversy over the causes of the American entry into World War I. That this event should have occasioned an often impassioned debate is not surprising, in view of the psychological shock which the war dealt to older popular assumptions and beliefs.

The outbreak of the European war in August of 1914 came as a disheartening surprise to most Americans. Nurtured on the belief that the world was becoming economically interdependent and more civilized, educated Americans assumed that Western society had outgrown the barbaric warfare of the unhappy past. Peace societies flourished here and in Europe—both President Woodrow Wilson and William Jennings Bryan, his first secretary of state, had joined the American Peace Society—and two Hague conferences had attempted to humanize warfare through codifications of so-called international law. In this condition of shock, and despite the initial tendency to sympathize with the cause of the Entente Powers led by Great Britain and France, the people heartily approved President Wilson's proclamation of neutrality. The United States need not and should not become involved in the holocaust in Europe. The American tradition of isolation, stemming from Washington's Farewell Address and adhered to during the 19th century, assured citizens that the nation should remain aloof from the quarrels of the Old World.

A few realistic students of world affairs realized that isolation was no longer possible for a great power in the 20th century—indeed, that it had not really worked before, for the peace and prosperity of 19th century America was less the result of its deliberate policy of abstention and more the fortuitous and unearned security made possible by a century of general peace in Europe (1815–1914) and the benevolent role of Great Britain, the unchallenged mistress of the seas. Such persons were, as a consequence, greatly alarmed at the possibility of a German victory over British sea power, which might redouble Teutonic competition in Latin America and threaten the security of the United States in the Western Hemisphere.

Most Americans were not accustomed to realistic appraisals of the national interests, however, and reacted to the war largely on emotional and traditional grounds. Consequently, when events did pull the United States actively into the conflict in April, 1917, it was generally understood to be simply on the grounds of German violations of American neutral rights and honor. To justify the war, both to the nation and to himself, Wilson turned it into a crusade for universal democracy and perpetual peace. Inevitably there was an emotional letdown after the war, which was worsened by the Allied haggling over the spoils at the Paris Peace Conference and the subsequent Senate rejection of the treaty of peace and League of Nations. The disillusionment of the 1920's with crusades deepened into a resurgence of isolationist feeling as the rise of aggressive totalitarian states in Europe and the Far East in the 1930's threatened another world conflict. It was in this atmosphere that the historical debate over the origins of the first world war occurred.

DOCUMENTS

1. Belligerent Threats to Freedom of the Seas

In the agony of war, both sides undertook measures which affected American neutral rights on the presumably "free" seas. The British mining of the North Sea threatened neutral shipping and lives in that area—yet the United States declined to join other neutrals in protest. On the other hand, when Germany subsequently proclaimed a submarine zone around the British Isles, the American response was to enter a firm and vigorous unilateral protest.

The British North Sea Mining Zone, November 3, 1914

. . . During the last week the Germans have scattered mines indiscriminately in the open sea on the main trade route from America to Liverpool via north of Ireland. Peaceful merchant ships have already been blown up with loss of life by this agency. . . .

These mines can not have been laid by any German ship of war. They have been laid by some merchant vessels flying neutral flags which have come along the trade route as if for purposes of peaceful commerce and while profiting to the full by immunity enjoyed by neutral merchant ships have wantonly and recklessly endangered the lives of all who travel on the sea regardless of whether they are friend or foe, civilian or military in character.

Mine laying under neutral flag and reconnaissance conducted by trawlers, hospital ships, and neutral vessels are the ordinary features of German naval warfare.

In these circumstances, having regard to the great interests entrusted to the British Navy, to the safety of peaceful commerce on high seas, and to the maintenance within limits of international law of trade between neutral countries, the Admiralty feel it necessary to adopt exceptional measures appropriate to the novel conditions under which this war is being waged.

They therefore give notice that the whole of the North Sea must be considered a military area. Within this area merchant shipping of all kinds, traders of all countries, fishing craft, and all other vessels will be exposed to the gravest dangers from mines which it has been necessary to lay and from warships searching vigilantly by night and day for suspicious craft.

All merchant and fishing vessels of every description are hereby warned of the dangers they encounter by entering this area except in strict accordance with Admiralty directions. Every effort will be made to convey this warning to neutral countries and to vessels on the sea, but from the 5th of November onwards the Admiralty announce that all ships passing a line drawn from the northern point of the Hebrides through Faroe Islands to Iceland do so at their own peril. . . .

The United States Declines to Protest the Mining Zone
The Secretary of State to Minister in Norway

WASHINGTON, *November 10, 1914*

You may inform the Minister for Foreign Affairs that this Government does not see its way at the present time to joining other governments in protesting to the British Government against their announcement that ships entering the North Sea after November 5 do so at their own peril.

"Strict Accountability" Toward German Submarine Warfare
The Secretary of State to the Ambassador in Germany

WASHINGTON, *February 10, 1915*

Please address a note immediately to the Imperial German Government to the following effect:

The Government of the United States, having had its attention directed to the proclamation of the German Admiralty issued on the 4th of February, that the waters surrounding Great Britain and Ireland, including the whole of the English Channel, are to be considered as comprised within the seat of war; that all enemy merchant vessels found in those waters after the eighteenth instant will be destroyed, although it may not always be possible to save crews and passengers; and that neutral vessels expose themselves to danger within this zone of war because, in view of the misuse of neutral flags said to have been ordered by the British Government on the thirty-first of January and of the contingencies of maritime warfare, it may not be possible always to exempt neutral vessels from attacks intended to strike enemy ships, feels it to be its duty to call the attention of the Imperial German Government, with sincere respect and the most friendly sentiments but very candidly and earnestly, to the very serious possibilities of the course of action apparently contemplated under that proclamation.

The Government of the United States views those possibilities with such grave concern that it feels it to be its privilege, and indeed its duty in the circumstances, to request the Imperial German Government to consider before action is taken the critical situation in respect of the relations between this country and Germany which might arise were the German naval forces, in carrying out the policy foreshadowed in the Admiralty's proclamation, to destroy any merchant vessel of the United States or cause the death of American citizens.

It is of course not necessary to remind the German Government that the sole right of a belligerent in dealing with neutral vessels on the high seas is limited to visit and search, unless a blockade is proclaimed and effectively maintained, which this Government does not understand to be proposed in this case. To declare or exercise a right to attack and destroy any vessel entering a prescribed area of the high seas without first certainly determining its belligerent nationality and the contraband character of its cargo would be an act so unprecedented in naval warfare that

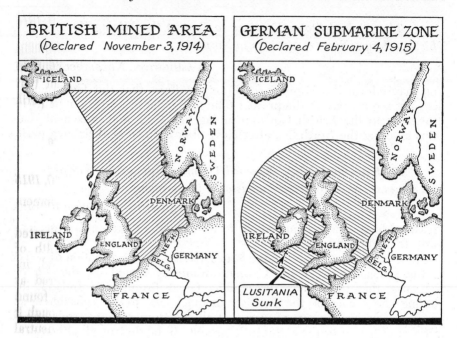

this Government is reluctant to believe that the Imperial Government of Germany in this case contemplates it as possible. The suspicion that enemy ships are using neutral flags improperly can create no just presumption that all ships traversing a prescribed area are subject to the same suspicion. . . .

If the commanders of German vessels of war should act upon the presumption that the flag of the United States was not being used in good faith and should destroy on the high seas an American vessel or the lives of American citizens, it would be difficult for the Government of the United States to view the act in any other light than as an indefensible violation of neutral rights which it would be very hard indeed to reconcile with the friendly relations now so happily subsisting between the two Governments.

If such a deplorable situation should arise, the Imperial German Government can readily appreciate that the Government of the United States would be constrained to hold the Imperial German Government to a strict accountability for such acts of their naval authorities and to take any steps it might be necessary to take to safeguard American lives and property and to secure to American citizens the full enjoyment of their acknowledged rights on the high seas. . . .

2. The British "Blockade" and American Acquiescence

In contrast to the insistence that Germany adhere strictly to the demands of international law, the British "blockade" of March, 1915 received only a long but mild protest.

The British "Blockade," March 11, 1915

WHEREAS the German Government has issued certain orders which, in violation of the usages of war, purport to declare the waters surrounding the United Kingdom a military area, in which all British and allied merchant vessels will be destroyed irrespective of the safety of the lives of passengers and crew, and in which neutral shipping will be exposed to similar danger in view of the uncertainties of naval warfare; and . . .

WHEREAS such attempts on the part of the enemy give to His Majesty an unquestionable right of retaliation; . . .

His Majesty is therefore pleased, by and with the advice of his Privy Council, to order and it is hereby ordered as follows:

1. No merchant vessel which sailed from her port of departure after the 1st March 1915 shall be allowed to proceed on her voyage to any German port. . . .

2. No merchant vessel which sailed from any German port after the 1st March 1915 shall be allowed to proceed on her voyage with any goods on board laden at such port. . . .

3. Every merchant vessel which sailed from her port of departure after the 1st March 1915 on her way to a port other than a German port, carrying goods with an enemy destination, or which are enemy property, may be required to discharge such goods in a British or allied port. Any goods so discharged in a British port shall be placed in the custody of the marshal of the Prize Court, and, unless they are contraband of war, shall, if not requisitioned for the use of His Majesty, be restored by order of the Court, upon such terms as the Court may in the circumstances deem to be just to the person entitled thereto. . . .

4. Every merchant vessel which sailed from a port other than a German port after the 1st March 1915 having on board goods which are of enemy origin or are enemy property may be required to discharge such goods in a British or allied port. Goods so discharged in a British port shall be placed in the custody of the marshal of the Prize Court, and, if not requisitioned for the use of His Majesty, shall be detained or sold under the direction of the Prize Court. The proceeds of goods so sold shall be paid into Court and dealt with in such manner as the Court may in the circumstances deem to be just. . . .

The American Reaction to the Blockade

The Secretary of State to the Ambassador in Great Britain

WASHINGTON, *March 30, 1915*

You are instructed to deliver the following to His Majesty's Government. . . .

The Government of the United States has given careful consideration to the subjects treated in the British notes of March 13 and March 15, and to the British order in council of the latter date.

These communications contain matters of grave importance to neutral nations. They appear to menace their rights of trade and intercourse not only with belligerents but also with one another. They call for frank comment in order that misunderstandings may be avoided. The Government of the United States deems it its duty, therefore, speaking in the sincerest spirit of friendship, to make its own view and position with regard to them unmistakably clear.

The order in council of the 15th of March would constitute, were its provisions to be actually carried into effect as they stand, a practical assertion of unlimited belligerent rights over neutral commerce within the whole European area, and an almost unqualified denial of the sovereign rights of the nations now at peace. . . .

A belligerent nation has been conceded the right of visit and search, and the right of capture and condemnation, if upon examination a neutral vessel is found to be engaged in unneutral service or to be carrying contraband of war intended for the enemy's government or armed forces. It has been conceded the right to establish and maintain a blockade of an enemy's ports and coasts and to capture and condemn any vessel taken in trying to break the blockade. It is even conceded the right to detain and take to its own ports for judicial examination all vessels which it suspects for substantial reasons to be engaged in unneutral or contraband service and to condemn them if the suspicion is sustained. But such rights, long clearly defined both in doctrine and practice, have hitherto been held to be the only permissible exceptions to the principle of universal equality of sovereignty on the high seas as between belligerents and nations not engaged in war.

It is confidently assumed that His Majesty's Government will not deny that it is a rule sanctioned by general practice that, even though a blockade should exist and the doctrine of contraband as to unblockaded territory be rigidly enforced, innocent shipments may be freely transported to and from the United States through neutral countries to belligerent territory without being subject to the penalties of contraband traffic or breach of blockade, much less to detention, requisition, or confiscation. . . .

The note of His Majesty's Principal Secretary of State for Foreign Affairs which accompanies the order in council, and which bears the same date, notifies the Government of the United States of the establishment of a blockade which is, if defined by the terms of the order in council, to include all the coasts and ports of Germany and every port of possible access to enemy territory. But the novel and quite unprecedented feature of that blockade, if we are to assume it to be properly so defined, is that it embraces many neutral ports and coasts, bars access to them, and subjects all neutral ships seeking to approach them to the same suspicion that would attach to them were they bound for the ports of the enemies of Great Britain, and to unusual risks and penalties.

It is manifest that such limitations, risks, and liabilities placed upon the ships of a neutral power on the high seas, beyond the right of visit and search and the right to prevent the shipment of contraband already referred to, are a distinct invasion of the sovereign rights of the nation whose ships, trade, or commerce are interfered with.

The Government of the United States is, of course, not oblivious to the great changes which have occurred in the conditions and means of naval warfare since the rules hitherto governing legal blockade were formulated. . . .

The possibilities of serious interruption of American trade under the order in council are so many, and the methods proposed are so unusual and seem liable to constitute so great an impediment and embarrassment to neutral commerce that the Government of the United States, if the order in council is strictly enforced, apprehends many interferences with its legitimate trade which will impose upon His Majesty's Government heavy responsibilities for acts of the British authorities clearly subversive of the rights of neutral nations on the high seas. It is, therefore, expected that His Majesty's Government, having considered these possibilities, will take the steps necessary to avoid them, and, in the event that they should unhappily occur, will be prepared to make full reparation for every act, which under the rules of international law constitutes a violation of neutral rights.

As stated in its communication of October 22, 1914, "This Government will insist that the rights and duties of the United States and its citizens in the present war be defined by the existing rules of international law and the treaties of the United States, irrespective of the provisions of the Declaration of London, and that this Government reserves to itself the right to enter a protest or demand in each case in which those rights and duties so defined are violated, or their free exercise interfered with, by the authorities of the British Government."

In conclusion you will reiterate to His Majesty's Government that this statement of the views of the Government of the United States is made in the most friendly spirit, and in accordance with the uniform candor which has characterized the relations of the two Governments in the past, and which has been in large measure the foundation of the peace and amity existing between the two nations without interruption for a century.

READINGS

1. Unneutrality and American Involvement

Critics of the American involvement in the great 1914–1918 conflict styled themselves "revisionists," meaning those who sought to probe behind the official explanations to the actual underlying causes of the war.* These writers challenged the generally accepted view that hostilities had resulted in 1917 only because of ruthless German submarine warfare affecting neutral trade and lives. Revisionist writers not only reflected the postwar mood of cynicism toward the war but also revealed strong inclinations toward an economic interpretation of history and a Freudian-produced awareness of mass psychology and the role of propaganda. The revisionists generally have agreed that the country had not really been neutral in thought or deed in 1914–1917. Instead,

* For an excellent historiographical article, consult Richard W. Leopold, "The Problem of American Intervention, 1917: An Historical Retrospect," World Politics, II (1950), 405–425.

most citizens had been pro-Ally from the beginning, a sentiment shared by President Wilson and most of his top officials. American policies toward the belligerents were benevolent toward the Allies and grudgingly strict toward Germany. Economically and financially, the nation through the one-sided war trade and private loans became virtually a silent partner of the Entente. Astute British propaganda capitalized on the situation to promote widespread condemnation of Germany as autocratic, militaristic and aggressive. A combination of pro-Ally policies and economic ties eventually pulled the United States into the war. The submarine, therefore, was not the basic cause of hostilities but simply the excuse. Harry Elmer Barnes was a pioneer revisionist and this selection has the virtue of being a bold and concise statement of that point of view.

The Entry of the United States into the World War

HARRY ELMER BARNES

... The approach to any interpretation of the entry of the United States into the World War must rest upon a review of the relations between Germany and the United States in the generation before the World War. The change in our sentiment towards Germany between 1870 and 1914 has been made the subject of an illuminating book by Dr. Clara E. Schieber. In 1870 we were overwhelmingly on the side of Prussia in the Franco-Prussian War, and were very friendly with the German states. Prussia was also the first European country to accept the sacrifices involved in the Bancroft treaties recognizing American naturalization as a renunciation of German citizenship. By 1914 there was more adverse sentiment towards Germany in this country than was directed against any other European state. The reasons for this transformation are numerous.

There was unquestionably some development of antipathy on account of the Bismarckian autocracy and militarism. The Kaiser's utterances on these and other matters were of striking character, much like those of Mr. [Theodore] Roosevelt in this country, and hence made good copy for the newspapers. Very important was the growth of trade rivalry. Both Germany and the United States underwent a tremendous economic and commercial development prior to the World War, and this led to competition for the markets of the world. Many believe this to be the most important and deep-seated cause of the growing coolness between the two countries. The imperialism associated with this commercial expansion brought numerous clashes in foreign policy. There was some trouble over Samoa between 1872 and 1889. The conduct of Admiral von Diederichs in the Philippines in 1898 was distinctly unfriendly to this country, and in marked contrast to that of the commander of the British fleet in these waters at the time. The procedure of Germany in China at the time of the occupation of the Shantung peninsula and in the Boxer Revolt alarmed the representatives of American interests in China. Germany was also making a notable economic conquest of Latin American markets in

Reprinted from *The Genesis of the World War* by Harry Elmer Barnes, by permission of Alfred A. Knopf, Inc. Copyright, 1926 by Alfred A. Knopf, Inc. Renewed, 1954 by Harry Elmer Barnes. Pp. 587–589, 593–596, 598–600, 600–601, 604–607, 607–612, 614–615, 632–633, 634.

the decade before the War, and stirred the envy of American merchants and investors. Then there was a definite clash over Venezuela during Roosevelt's administration.

Another very important factor lay in the fact that few American papers had competent foreign correspondents in Germany, and, hence, relied for most of their material on German affairs upon the Harmsworth papers in England which were even notoriously anti-German. By the opening of the present century the anti-German current was definitely setting in in this country, and the various efforts to counteract it through the visit of Prince Henry in 1902, the gift of the statue of Frederick the Great in 1905, the exchange professorships, and the interpretation of German culture by Hugo Münsterberg were inadequate to the task. In other words, we were already very strongly pro-Entente before Printsip began his target-practice in the spring of 1914. . . .

The alleged reason why the United States entered the War was, of course, the resumption of unlimited German submarine warfare, but to have any understanding of the deeper causes we must get at the causes for the German submarine warfare in general, as well as its resumption in January, 1917. Here we are on firm ground. There is no doubt that the German submarine warfare was developed as a counter movement against the English violation of international law in regard to blockade, contraband and continuous voyage. By practically destroying, in these respects, the rights of neutrals, which had been worked out in a century of the development of international law, Great Britain was virtually able to shut off all imports into Germany from foreign countries, not only directly but also through neutral ports. It was to retaliate against this that Germany initiated her submarine warfare, which certainly cannot be regarded as in any sense more atrocious in fact or law than those English violations of neutral rights which had produced the submarine campaign. By practically acquiescing in these British violations of international law we not only lost most of what we had gained in the past in the way of establishing neutral rights on the seas, but also set a precedent which will prove an extremely nasty and embarrassing stumbling-block in the course of future negotiations in the event of war.

In addition to these English violations of international law which vitally affected Germany as well as neutrals, there were many other examples of British lawlessness, such as the interception of our mails, the use of the American flag on British ships, the seizure and search of United States officials below the rank of minister while traveling to and from their continental posts, and the capture of ships like the Dacia (by the French at the instigation of Page and the British), which had been legally transferred from enemy countries to American owners. If the United States had held England strictly to international law upon the threat of severance of diplomatic relations or even war, as we did in the case of Germany and as we unquestionably should have done in the case of England, the German submarine warfare would not have been necessary and probably would not have been utilized. So we may say with absolute certainty that it was the unneutrality, lack of courage, or maladroitness of the Washington authorities in regard to English violations of international law which produced the German submarine warfare that actually led us into war. It must be remembered, however, that the resumption of German submarine warfare, like the Belgian question in England, was the excuse and not the real reason for our entering the War. President Wilson and Colonel House had decided that we would come in at least a year before the submarine warfare was resumed by Germany.

The gist of the whole matter, then, appears to be that Mr. Wilson failed himself to observe the neutrality he enjoined upon his country at the outbreak of the War. By permitting England but not Germany to violate international law promiscuously he inevitably invited those reprisals which occurred. He then found in the action which he thus stimulated those ostensible causes for the war which he idealized after April, 1917. . . .

On the point that the failure of the United States to deal with both belligerents in identical fashion helped to bring on the War, Germany stated her position in the note of February 18, 1915, in which she said that "They (the Germans) rely on the neutrals who have hitherto tacitly or under protest submitted to the consequences, detrimental to themselves, of England's war of famine to display no less tolerance toward Germany, even if the German measures constitute new forms of maritime war, as has hitherto been the case with the English measures." This demand for impartiality of treatment was proper, but that the State Department did not consider it so is evident from Secretary Lansing's note to the German Government on May 8, 1916, as follows: "In order, however, to avoid any possible misunderstanding the Government of the United States notifies the Imperial Government that it cannot for a moment entertain, much less discuss, a suggestion that respect by German naval authorities for the rights of citizens of the United States upon the high seas should in any way or in the slightest degree be made contingent upon the conduct of any other Government affecting the rights of neutrals and non-combatants. Responsibility in such matters is single, not joint; absolute, not relative." This position of Secretary Lansing was unsound and improper. He could hardly demand that one belligerent obey the laws of war and tolerate repeated violations by the other. The toleration of British violation induced and made necessary the German departure. At an earlier stage in the war, our State Department seems to have admitted some such doctrine, but as we gradually departed from neutrality, the view changed and it was deemed proper to hold one belligerent to strict compliance with the laws governing neutrality and to permit the other widely to depart therefrom. At one time Lansing denounced the British measures as "illegal and indefensible" but he did nothing to support the use of these harsh words.

In considering the problem as to why Mr. Wilson and his associates were unwilling to intervene to coerce England and restrict her lawlessness on the seas, we can be sure that there were many and varied factors involved. Unquestionably the most powerful influence was the virulent pro-English attitude of Ambassador [Walter Hines] Page, who persistently and openly fought against Mr. Bryan and Mr. Lansing in the efforts of the latter to protect American rights against the arrogance and maritime anarchy of Great Britain. . . .

The following is a fair sample of Mr. Page's "patriotic" procedure as the accredited representative of the United States at the Court of St. James, entrusted with the responsibility of protecting the rights of his country. Our government had mildly protested against the flagrant violation of international law by the English, but Page, instead of presenting a forceful case to Sir Edward Grey, went through the form of reading it to Grey and then asked Grey to cooperate with him in formulating an effective reply *to our own State Department.* The offense of Benedict Arnold seems highly comparable. Both worked earnestly and directly to promote the cause of Anglo-American unity. This astonishing conduct of Page is revealed by Sir Edward Grey in his recently published memoirs. . . .

Added to Page's primary responsibility were the Anglo-mania of Secretary [of Agriculture, David F.] Houston, who had great influence with Mr. Wilson as an individual and as a member of his cabinet, and finally the very real pro-British sentiments of Mr. Wilson. Though Mr. Wilson's Anglo-mania was relatively slight and benign as compared with that of Mr. Page, it was unquestionably robust, and all of his writings from his youth onward reveal the fact that Mr. Wilson knew little or cared little about the culture of any other European country save that of England. All of his great heroes in literature and political science were English authors. These diverse facts and influences prevented Mr. Wilson from ever sending the strong note he had drafted in protest against English violations of our rights, and also prevented him from thoroughly backing up Mr. Lansing in his struggle against Mr. Page and the British authorities in the vain effort to defend American rights against Great Britain.

Our attitude as to the settlement of claims against the Entente and against Germany has been as lacking in impartiality as our conduct in enforcing the recognition of international law as between these two groups. Mr. Lansing announced in April, 1917, that our claims against Germany demanded immediate intervention and reprisal, and he added that our claims against the Allies for property losses in violation of American neutrality would be settled immediately after the close of the War. The claims against Germany, even when judged by standards entirely outside of international law, boil down to $180,000,000. In part to vindicate these claims we entered a war that cost us about $30,000,000,000. The claims against the Entente, even when based strictly on international law, greatly exceed $180,000,000. Nevertheless, though eight years have passed since the termination of hostilities, our Department of State has never made the slightest move to bring about a settlement of these large claims against the Entente.

Next we should note the powerful pressure of the great American financial interests and their subsidized press. From the beginning the international banking houses of the United States had taken a distinctly unneutral attitude, favoring investment in the bonds of the Allied countries, and discouraging or refusing investment in the paper of the Central

Powers. This immediately gave us a strong financial stake in the cause of the Entente, and this stake grew larger with each year of the war. Likewise, American industry inevitably became violently pro-Ally. This was due to the fact that the British illegal blockade unlawfully cut off our sales of war materials to the Central Powers and made our enormous war profits dependent upon the purchases made by Great Britain, France, Russia and Italy. Upon the prospects of their success in the War and their ability to prolong the conflict depended the relative amount of American profits and the probability of our receiving payment for the goods we sold to these Entente powers.

The writer is no fervent believer in the universal validity of the economic interpretation of history or in the correctness of the attempts which have been made to demonstrate that the United States went into the World War solely because of our investments in and sales to the Allied countries, but unquestionably from 1915–1918 the enormous power of American finance and industry was directed wholly toward the defense of the Allied powers and the support of their subtle propaganda. In most cases this did not rest upon any original sympathy with these countries, but upon the actual nature of the economic realities of the moment. Had we invested primarily in the bonds of the Central Powers, and had we been selling most of our goods to these same powers, there is no doubt that American finance and industry would have been as flagrantly pro-German as it was pro English and pro French in 1915, 1916 and 1917. . . .

The problem of the American bankers in regard to Allied credit became acute at the close of 1916. The ability to raise further loans for the Entente countries from private credit was practically at an end by January, 1917, and the Wall Street bankers were in despair. Their only hope of relief lay in the possibility of shifting the burden from their own shoulders to the back of the United States treasury. This feat could only be achieved by having the United States abandon the pretense of technical and formal neutrality and enter the conflict as a co-belligerent. The German submarine note of January 31, 1917, was therefore a veritable god-send to the international bankers of this country. It crowned with success their earlier efforts to bring about American intervention. One does not have to adopt the theory of diabolic possession in interpreting this aspiration or this conduct on the part of the leading bankers, many of whom were high-minded and pacifically inclined individuals. They had simply become very heavily involved in a complex net of international finance which seemed likely to disintegrate with disastrous results to themselves and their clients if we did not enter the World War. As is usual in the business world, they put their professional interests and commitments ahead of their personal opinions, preferences and convictions. It should be pointed out in passing that in one important way the entry of the United States proved a disaster to the bankers. By prolonging the War it brought on the Russian Revolution and the consequent loss of the loans to Russia.

One does not have to follow Upton Sinclair in every phase of his argument to be aware that American newspapers follow the dictates of American finance and industry very closely and very faithfully. Hence, the

American press had become by 1915 and 1916 almost uniformly and intolerantly pro-Ally, and in its editorials and its handling of the news scathingly attacked Mr. Wilson's neutral efforts. The favoritism of the press went so far that in some cases Englishmen actually took over the control of some of the leading dailies. Northcliffe spent vast sums of money to secure extensive control over the sentiment of the American press. In the case of the Providence *Journal,* the propaganda efforts of the editor were so extreme and flagrant, that in the case of faked material prepared for *World's Work,* the government had to intervene, and force moderation.

This favorable attitude of the American press toward the Entente Powers was an enormous advantage to them as compared with Germany in regard to the spreading of propaganda before the American people. We had no means of knowing that Germany would not have invaded Belgium or attacked the French Channel ports if England had agreed to remain neutral, or that Grey had made the decision for war before Belgium was invaded. We were ignorant of the fact that England had repudiated the cause of Serbia, and that France and Russia had been on the lookout for a Balkan dispute of an appropriate sort to be utilized as the basis for provoking a European war. Hence we felt that the Entente was fighting the cause of the small and weak nations against the ruthlessness of a great bully. We, of course, were led to believe that the war had been started through the deliberate determination of Germany to initiate her alleged long cherished plan to dominate the planet, while the Entente had proposed diplomatic settlement from the beginning and had only taken up arms in self-defense with the utmost reluctance. This theory of the German provocation of the War and the German lust for world dominion was played up in the newspapers and distributed in pamphlets of the National Security League and the American Defense Society until the danger from Germany struck terror into the hearts of Americans, and citizens of Peoria, Illinois, and Council Bluffs, Iowa, lived in daily dread of a German submarine attack; as a few years later they searched under their beds nightly for the Bolshevik there secreted.

Then, the United States was peculiarly at the mercy of the falsified atrocity pictures and other propaganda poured into this country by the Allies, who were at the same time able to keep from public knowledge the German counter-propaganda as well as German proofs of the falsity of these atrocity pictures, recently so conclusively demonstrated by Ferdinand Avenarius. These circumstances made it much easier for the pro-Ally groups to inflame American opinion and swing the country for war.

Further, the Germans were singularly awkward and unhappy in their utterances. The more exuberant among them openly voiced their aspirations as to territorial aggression and aggrandizement, while the Allies carefully restricted their similar plans to closely hidden secret treaties, and concentrated their publicity upon their unselfish and disinterested struggle for ideals and the peace of the world.

Finally there is the question of the *Lusitania,* one of the matters most exploited by friends of the Entente in their efforts to drive Mr. Wilson into the War. We now know that the *Lusitania* was carrying munitions of war—5400 cases of ammunition—as well as passengers, mail and express. It is a debatable point as to whether the *Lusitania* was violating international law by carrying these munitions of war. But it is beyond question that as a naval auxiliary, as a British ship warned of her danger in the war zone, and as a warship carrying munitions, she lost about all of her immunities as a merchant ship. Her passengers likewise assumed the risks inherent to their danger in accepting passage on the boat. If, in addition, she was armed she unquestionably lost all of her privileges as a peaceful merchant ship, and was not even entitled to a warning before being attacked. While any humane person would naturally deplore the loss of life incidental to the sinking of the *Lusitania*, it is necessary to insist here that the sinking of a score of ships such as the *Lusitania* in no way compared as an inhuman atrocity to the illegally produced British blockade of Germany which brought disease or starvation to tens of thousands of innocent German non-combatants. . . .

The case of Woodrow Wilson is singularly like that of Sir Edward Grey [British Foreign Secretary], namely, that of a man who loved peace but was drawn into war by a false conception of the facts and issues involved. There is no doubt that he was a pacifist at heart, but he viewed the conflict as one in which England was upholding the cause of civilization. This led to his determination to enter the conflict if the entry of the United States should become essential to a British victory and it was possible to put the country in as a unit. His policy, then, was one of combining a hope for an Entente victory with the preparation of the country for war in the event that England could not win without our assistance. There is no doubt that Wilson was as determined to enter the conflict as was Roosevelt, but he was far more subtle and adroit in his method of getting the country ready to support him in that move. When Wilson put the country into the War he had given the impression of having been a long-suffering and much abused pacifist who had resolutely stood out against war until no other alternative presented itself. This made the country convinced that it was really fighting in self-defense, something far different from what would have been the case if we had followed Roosevelt's advice and jumped headlong into the conflict after the sinking of the *Lusitania*. . . .

After the [1916] election, Germany, convinced, quite correctly, that the United States had in practice given up the pose of neutrality and intended to get into the War as soon as possible, decided to resort to a revival of unrestricted submarine warfare as a last hope and expedient. This decision was taken quite as much through a popular demand for such action in Germany as through any sinister and secret plotting of von Tirpitz [Navy Minister] or other officials. A starving people were demanding an early release from their suffering and despair through a rapid termination of the War. Having been the victims of illegal starvation and cut off from even neutral foodstuffs, they assented to the necessity of unrestricted submarine warfare which Tirpitz and others had assured them would bring the War to a speedy close. The United States had helped along this step in that our unwillingness to restrain Allied illegality forced Germany to seek reprisal and relief through the pursuit of desperate methods. Many believe that joy reigned in the White House when the German note of January 31, 1917, announcing the resumption of submarine warfare, reached this country. Whether this is true or not, there can be no doubt of the universal and complete rejoicing in Wall Street. . . .

Some have held that a powerful factor affecting Mr. Wilson's decision was his conviction by 1916 that he could not lead world policy through pacific methods but might assume world leadership if he threw the United States into the War and was thereby able to dominate the war aims of the Allied powers and the United States. Many of the facts in his conduct in the spring of 1916 and thereafter lend much plausibility to this hypothesis. The writer believes, however, that it was his pro-British sympathy more than anything else which led Mr. Wilson into his decision by the close of 1915 that we must enter the World War unless the English objectives could be realized through a negotiated peace. . . .

2. "The War Was Made in Berlin"

Opposed to the revisionists is the school of interpretation most fittingly described as the "submarine thesis." Adhering to the wartime explanations, this group of writers has maintained that hostilities resulted primarily from Germany's practice of underseas warfare. The American government had proclaimed official neutrality in 1914 and thereafter pursued impartial policies toward both belligerent sides. Neutral rights were diligently defended against the infractions of Great Britain and Germany, although the fact that the submarine threatened not merely property but lives as well made the deeds of the Berlin government far more serious than those of London. Wilson would not abandon the right of neutral citizens to travel the high seas subject only to the normal challenges of belligerents, a right which the U-boat violated by the sinking of merchant ships without warning and without providing for the safety of passengers and crew. As for the one-sided war trade with the Allies, this merely reflected the fact of British control of the seas and hence of access to the American market. Sentiment and economic ties no doubt helped explain why war with the Allies over their actions was improbable but they did not explain satisfactorily why the nation went to war with Germany. Only the ruthless use of the submarine against neutral lives and property forced a reluctant America to abandon its peaceful course and enter the war. Charles Seymour, a Wilsonian supporter during the war and professor of history at Yale University, in the following selection vigorously counters revisionist arguments and charges resulting from the then current Nye Committee congressional investigation into the activities of the bankers and munitions makers during the neutrality period 1914–17.

The Experience of 1914–1917
CHARLES SEYMOUR

Recent discussions of the causes of American intervention in the World War have stirred emotions; but they have failed to suggest conclusively measures that might have served to keep us at peace. There is talk of

Charles Seymour, *American Neutrality 1914–1917* (New Haven: Yale University Press, 1935), 1–26. Reprinted with permission.

the intrigues of munitions makers and the greed of capitalists. Less fantastic is the revival of the thesis that if we had treated Germany and the Allies with an even hand in meeting their attacks upon American neutral rights, we might have avoided intervention. A popular outline of the years 1914–17, by Mr. Walter Millis, implies that as we had permitted infractions of our rights by the Allies we had no right to protest to the point of war against Germany's use of the submarine. But he suggests no practicable alternatives to the policy followed by President Wilson. The country slithered into war, he evidently feels, much as Lloyd George once remarked that Europe had slithered into war in 1914. "Among them all," Mr. Millis writes of the Americans of 1917, "none quite knew how it had happened, nor why. . . ."

There was at least one American who was acutely aware of why the United States was brought into the World War. This was the President of the United States, who for nearly three years struggled to maintain neutrality in the face of difficulties that finally proved uncontrollable. Whether as a basis for future policy, or merely to set the historical record straight, it is worth while to review Woodrow Wilson's fight to avoid intervention.

Any inquiry into the causes of American participation in the war must begin with the personality of Wilson. His office conferred upon him a determining influence in foreign policy which was heightened by the troubled state of affairs abroad. His character was such that he never let this influence slip into other hands. He was his own foreign secretary. Conscious of the power and character of public opinion, "under bonds," as he put it, to public sentiment, he nevertheless made the major decisions on his own responsibility. He delivered his "too proud to fight" speech and he sent Bernstorff home without stopping to ask what the man in the street would say. Dominant sentiment in the United States was certainly pro-Ally. American economic prosperity, furthermore, depended upon the maintenance of our trade with the Allies. But it is a far cry from these facts to the assumption that because of them we adopted a policy that pointed toward intervention. It would be necessary to show that emotional sympathy and material interests overcame the strong pacifistic sentiment of Congress and people. It would especially be necessary to show that because of them Wilson first adopted a discriminatory attitude toward Germany and then surrendered his determination to keep the country out of war.

Ample evidence is now available regarding Wilson's sentiments toward the belligerents. If it reveals an underlying personal sympathy with the Allies, it also reveals a studied insistence not to permit that feeling to affect national policy. He was so far successful that he was attacked in turn by each belligerent group as being favorable to the other. There can be no question that he regarded the maintenance of peace as his first duty. Always he held to the double principle he formulated at the moment he was smarting under the news of the *Arabic's* sinking in August, 1915: "1. The people of this country count on me to keep them out of the war; 2. It would be a calamity to the world at large if we should be actively drawn into the conflict and so deprived of all disinterested influence over the settlement." He maintained this attitude in the face of what he regarded as gross affronts by Germany. "The country is undoubtedly back of me in the whole matter," he wrote privately in September, 1915, "and I feel myself under bonds to it to show patience to the utmost. My chief puzzle is to determine where patience ceases to be a virtue."

But across the determination to preserve peace ran the equally strong determination to preserve the neutral rights of the country. There was a higher principle which the President placed above peace: the honor of the United States. The outcome of this contradiction would be determined not by Wilson's policy but by that of the belligerents. . . .

Against both groups of belligerents Wilson steadily maintained American neutral rights. It is by no means a fact that he accepted British and Allied infractions of what he described as "hitherto fixed international law." The notes of protest which he sponsored and which so greatly annoyed those who, like Ambassador Page, frankly favored the Allied cause, made clear that the United States did not, and would not, recognize the legality of the Allied pseudo-blockade. In the late summer of 1916 the President secured from Congress wide powers permitting him to prohibit loans and to impose embargoes if retaliatory measures appeared advisable. A few weeks later he asked House to warn Sir Edward Grey "in the strongest terms" that the American people were "growing more and more impatient with the intolerable conditions of neutrality, their feeling as hot against Great Britain as it was first against Germany. . . ."

That he did not actually exercise the pressure of embargoes against the British and French resulted from two factors. The first was that the conflict over Allied interference with neutral trade was pushed into the background at critical moments by the more immediate and intense conflict with Germany over the submarine campaign. "If Germany had not alienated American sympathies," wrote Colonel House, "by her mode of warfare, the United States would not have put up with Allied control of American trade on the high seas." The fact has been emphasized by Winston Churchill: "The first German U-boat campaign," he writes, "gave us our greatest assistance. It altered the whole position of our controversies with America. A great relief became immediately apparent."

The second reason for not pushing the diplomatic conflict with the Allies to the point of retaliatory measures lay in the economic interests of America. Any practicable measures designed to enforce our interpretation of international law would have ruined the interests they meant to safeguard. By our formal protests we protected our ultimate property rights and built up a case for future damages to be proved before an international tribunal. Through private negotiations we secured in large measure the protection of immediate commercial interests. Whatever the inconvenience and delays experienced in our trade with the northern European neutrals, American foreign commerce was deriving rich profits. Allied command of the sea did not touch our pockets so much as our pride. As [British] Ambassador Spring Rice cabled to Grey, it seemed "objectionable not because it is what it is, but because it is so all-pervading." Thus, if Wilson had destroyed the basis of our prosperity in order to compel immediate acceptance of the American interpretation of international law, which very few Americans understood and which even now is not entirely clear, he would have provoked something like a revolt against his administration. "If it came to the last analysis," wrote House to Wilson in the summer of 1915, "and we placed an embargo upon munitions of war and foodstuffs to please the cotton men, our whole industrial and agricultural machinery would cry out against it." Wilson's policy was designed not to favor the Allies but to protect the immediate interests of the nation and at the same time to preserve our ulimate legal rights. He yielded no principle and surrendered no claim.

The German attack upon American rights Wilson believed to be of an entirely different nature and one that must be met by different methods. The intensive submarine campaign was the answer to the system of Allied maritime control; logically, an excuse might be found for it. But its effects upon neutral rights were far more disastrous. For technical reasons and to operate effectively, the submarines must make their attack without warning, destroy blindly, escape as speedily as possible, leaving the sinking merchant ship, which might be neutral or belligerent, which might or might not carry contraband, with no assurance of what would happen to passengers and crew. To Wilson and to dominant American opinion, such wholesale methods of destroying enemy and neutral commerce were shocking. This was no question of "juridical niceties." The submarine campaign, unlike the Allied blockade, involved undiscriminating destruction of American property rights. It permitted no distinction between contraband and free goods. The Allied system gave to the American shipper reasonable assurance of safe passage after he had complied with certain formalities. Under the threat of the submarine the shipper faced the risk of losing his entire cargo. The Allied system did not involve the loss of American ships; if held in a British prize court the owner could find protection for them in legal procedure. The German submarine threatened the loss of the ship and the death of the crew and passengers as well.

Thus, from the point of view of material interests, there could be no comparison between the damage resulting to Americans from the Allied blockade and that from the intensive submarine campaign. If the latter were permitted, under protests comparable to those sent to the Allies, the result would be an almost complete blockade of American commerce, since shippers would not dare send cargoes and crew out to destruction. A clear illustration of the effect of the submarine campaign on American commercial, industrial, and agricultural interests was given by the congestion of our ports that followed the threat of submarine attacks in February and March, 1917. Freights were snarled, goods were spoiled, business was menaced with a complete tie-up.

Even so, Wilson might not have taken his firm stand against the submarine if merely property rights had been threatened. He was always careful not to interpret national policy in terms of purely material interests. Despite the difficulties involved, the economic aspects of the diplomatic conflict with Germany might have been adjudicated. But the submarine warfare involved attacks upon American lives, whether sailors on merchant ships or passengers. To Wilson it seemed a war on humanity. Between property interests and human rights there lay a clear distinction. It was brought home to all America when, on May 7, 1915, the *Lusitania* was sunk without warning, over eleven hundred persons drowned, men, women, and children, among them more than one hundred and twenty Americans. . . .

It has been frequently suggested that since the submarine campaign was designed to interrupt the flow of munitions from the United States to the Allies, Wilson might have imposed embargoes upon the export of munitions as a diplomatic bribe to Germany to give up the intensive use of the submarine. There is no indication that the President ever seriously considered this course. He was willing to utilize embargoes, if necessary as measures of retaliation against the Allies in the defense of American rights. But he was not willing to penalize ourselves in order to redress the inherent disadvantage of Germany resulting from Allied command of the seas. He agreed with Lansing that such a policy ran counter to the neutral duties of the United States. It would certainly have ruined not merely the "war babies" of industry, but the cotton and wheat growers, the copper producers, the iron and steel workers, and have thrown the country back into the bleak depression and unemployment from which it had just emerged.

There is no evidence that even the broadest sort of American embargo would have induced the Germans to forego the intensive use of the submarine. They meant to stop British imports of all raw materials, especially foodstuffs, not merely from the United States but from South America, India, and the Dominions. The purpose of the submarine campaign was far wider than the interruption of the Allied "munitions" trade with America; it was, according to the testimony given to the Reichstag investigating committee, designed to throw over the British the deadly fear of complete starvation and thus to compel them to sue for peace on German terms. [Field Marshal] Hindenburg and Ludendorff made quite plain that, in the winter of 1916–17, nothing but the prospect of immediate peace on such terms could have prevented the resumption of the submarine campaign.

Wilson, of course, might have avoided a break with Germany by surrendering the right to send American ships and citizens out on the high seas. Thus they would not be sunk by submarines. Such a policy was suggested by Mr. Bryan and was later embodied in the Gore-McLemore resolutions brought before Congress. The President believed that no government was justified in making this surrender. Through his protests to the Allies he had secured, without yielding any principle, a working arrangement that gave reasonable protection to American commercial interests. Now if, under the threat of the German submarine, he withdrew protection on the seas from American goods, sailors, and pas-

sengers, he would sacrifice interests that no protests could compensate
and yield principles that nothing in the future could make good. . . .

It was all very well, Wilson pointed out, to argue that the material
value of these rights could not be compared with the cost of a war.
But if you begin to surrender accepted rights, where do you stop?

> If in this instance we allowed expediency to take the place of principle,
> the door would inevitably be opened to still further concessions. Once
> accept a single abatement of right, and many other humiliations would
> certainly follow. . . . What we are contending for in this matter is of the
> very essence of the things that have made America a sovereign nation.
> She cannot yield them without conceding her own impotency as a
> Nation and making virtual surrender of her independent position among
> the nations of the world.

Such was Wilson's position, written for all the world and especially for
Germany to read. He maintained it consistently from the first declaration
of submarine warfare in February, 1915, two years before the final break,
when he warned the German Government that it would be held to "a
strict accountability" for acts endangering American lives and property,
and that the American Government would take any necessary steps to
"secure to American citizens the full enjoyment of their acknowledged
rights on the high seas." This warning was translated into specific terms
a year later, after the sinking of the *Sussex*, taking the form of an ultimatum which left no further room for negotiation. . . .

The Germans yielded, if only for the moment, as a result of this definite
warning. During the course of 1915 they had taken [Ambassador] Von
Bernstorff's warnings not too seriously, and heeded them largely because
they had not yet themselves realized what a powerful weapon they possessed in the submarine. After Wilson's *Sussex* note they were under
no illusions. "There was no longer any doubt in Berlin," wrote the German Ambassador, "that persistence in the point of view they had hitherto
adopted would bring about a break with the United States." But in the
early autumn Hindenburg and Ludendorff threw their influence in favor
of a resumption of the submarine campaign. The discussions in Berlin
were clearly based upon the assumption of war with the United States. . . .

The one chance of preventing the resumption of the submarine campaign, and thus keeping the United States out of war, lay in peace
negotiations. Bernstorff judged correctly that neither Wilson nor public
opinion would permit America to enter the war on any issue other than
the submarine, and that it was vital to secure a postponement of the
intensive campaign. . . . Hence the eagerness with which he pressed
upon Colonel House the importance of peace action by Wilson before it
was too late. Hence also the determination with which Wilson, who
realized the approaching danger, prepared his peace note of December
18, 1916. He wanted to make it, he wrote House, "the strongest and
most convincing thing I ever penned."

In the circumstances the effort was bound to fail. Its effect was confused by the issuance of Bethmann's peace statement on December 12,
which made Wilson's note appear to the Allies as part of a plan to rescue

the Central Powers from defeat. The Allies were quite unwilling to negotiate with an unbeaten Germany. The Germans were determined to insist upon terms which the Allies would not have accepted until all hope of victory had faded. Neither side wished the mediation of Wilson. The British, according to Sir William Wiseman, felt that Wilson merely talked about ideals for which the Allies were dying. "We entertain but little hope," [Foreign Minister] von Jagow had written to Bernstorff, "for the result of the exercise of good offices by one whose instincts are all in favor of the English point of view, and who in addition to this, is so naïve a statesman as President Wilson." The new German Foreign Secretary, Zimmermann, said to the budget committee of the Reichstag: "The good thing about the break with the United States is that we have finally gotten rid of this person as peace mediator."

Wilson was not discouraged by the failure of the December peace notes. He worked all through January to secure a private statement of German terms, equipped with which he could start negotiations with the Allies. He was determined to save American neutrality. On January 4, 1917, in reply to House's suggestion of the need of military preparation "in the event of war," the President insisted: "There will be no war. This country does not intend to become involved in this war. We are the only one of the great white nations that is free from war today, and it would be a crime against civilization for us to go in." On January 22 he delivered before the Senate the address which he hoped would serve as a general basis for a negotiated peace, a settlement that would leave neither the one side nor the other crushed and revengeful, "a peace without victory." It opened, as British writers later insisted, the "last opportunity of ending the war with a real peace. For America was still pacific and impartial. . . . But unhappily for mankind, the British and Prussian war machines had by then taken charge."

It is possible that if Germany had then held her hand Wilson might have been able to force negotiations. The Allies were beginning to scrape the bottom of the money chest and the time was approaching when they would be dependent upon American credits. He could soon have exercised strong pressure upon them. On the other side the Kaiser, Bethmann, and Bernstorff had no profound confidence in the submarine and were inclined toward compromise. But the decision had already been taken in Germany. On January 9 Hindenburg and [Admiral] Holtzendorf insisted that all chance of peace had disappeared and forced approval of the intensive submarine campaign. On January 31 Bernstorff gave notice that from the following day the engagements of the pledge given after the sinking of the *Sussex* would no longer be observed.

Thus ended Wilson's last effort to achieve a compromise peace, and the rupture between Germany and the United States became inevitable. The President saw no escape from the fulfilment of the warning he had given the previous April. The shock was the worse for Wilson inasmuch as it came just as he hoped to initiate mediation. He said "he felt as if the world had suddenly reversed itself: that after going from east to west, it had begun to go from west to east and he could not get his balance."

Resentment against Germany, with whom he had been working for peace, was strong. He felt with House that Germany "desires some justification for her submarine warfare and thought she could get it by declaring her willingness to make peace." Bernstorff himself insists that it was the German declaration of submarine warfare and nothing else that mattered with Wilson. . . .

Even after the diplomatic rupture Wilson waited long weeks, to give every opportunity to the Germans to avoid war. Only actual overt acts would persuade him that they would carry their policy into effect. He was willing to negotiate everything except the sinking of passenger and merchant ships without warning. The Germans showed no sign of weakening. When it was suggested that America might be kept neutral if the submarines "overlooked" American boats, the Kaiser wrote on the margin of the memorandum which disapproved the suggestion on technical grounds: "Agreed, reject. . . . Now, once for all, an *end* to negotiations with America. If Wilson wants war, let him make it, and let him then have it." On March 27, following the sinking of four American ships, the President took the decision, and on April 2 he asked Congress to declare the existence of a state of war with Germany.

So far as tests can be applied, Wilson's position was approved by the American people. Like him they were determined to stay at peace so far as the exercise of their acknowledged rights could keep them at peace, but they regarded the submarine attacks as acts of war. They were by no means prepared to sacrifice American rights on the seas and adopt a policy of nonintercourse with European belligerents and neutrals which would have resulted in economic depression or disaster in the United States. So much is indicated by the votes in Congress on the Gore-McLemore resolutions and the armed shipping bill which gave overwhelming endorsement to Wilson's policy. On the other hand, whatever the emotional sympathy for the Allied cause in the United States and however close Allied and American commercial interests, the prevailing sentiment of the people was indelibly for peace until the submarines sank American ships. They rewarded the patience with which Wilson carried on long negotiations over the *Lusitania* as well as the firmness with which he issued the *Sussex* ultimatum by reëlecting him President in the autumn of 1916. He owed his victory to the pacifists. So far from being accused of chauvinism because of the stand he had taken against the submarine campaign, he was presented and elected on the basis of having "kept us out of war." But when on April 2, following the destruction of American ships, he declared that peace was no longer consistent with honor, Congress voted for war by tremendous majorities.

It frequently happens that the occasion for an event is mistaken for its cause. Sometimes, however, the occasion and the cause are the same. There is every evidence that the sole factor that could have driven Wilson from neutrality in the spring of 1917 was the resumption of the submarine campaign. On the very eve of his war speech he was seized by his hunger for peace.

For nights, he said, he'd been lying awake over the whole situation . . .
He said he couldn't see any alternative, that he had tried every way he
knew to avoid war . . . had considered every loophole of escape, and as
fast as they were discovered Germany deliberately blocked them with
some new outrage.

In the circumstances there was no escape, for the point had been reached
which he had long foreseen and dreaded, where he could not preserve
both the peace and honor of the United States. "There is one choice we
cannot make, we are incapable of making," he told Congress on April 2.
"We will not choose the path of submission."

3. The National Interests and the War

A new trend in interpretation began to emerge during and after World War II.
Denoting it, for lack of a better title, as the "national interest" school, this
point of view reflected the increasing consciousness by Americans of their in-
extricable involvement in international politics. The journalists Walter Lippmann and Forest Davis advanced the provocative view that the United States
had gone to war in 1917 primarily to protect the national security against a
threatened German victory over the Allies. Since 1945 scholars have further
explored this thesis and have found some supporting evidence. Edward H.
Buehrig, a political scientist, in the next selection very subtly denotes the
elements of realistic thinking behind Wilsonian policies and evaluates the
President as not lacking in an awareness of balance of power considerations
but as moving beyond that by 1917 to espouse the idealistic plan of perpetual
peace through a league of nations organization.

Wilson and the Balance of Power
E. H. BUEHRIG

Foreword

The central theme of American foreign relations in the nineteenth century
was the mutual accommodation progressively achieved between ourselves
and Great Britain. The main theme in the present century is quite different, offering a melancholy contrast. At the turn of the century Germany
and the United States had already emerged as great powers, and Japan
was in process of attaining that status. Presently Russia took on new form
and vigor, and Italy was to entertain high political ambition. Later still,
India began to emerge, as did China. Coincident with this revolutionary
change in the old order, the United States has come to blows twice with
Germany and once each with Japan and Italy. Moreover, we have fought
China and must consider the danger of war with the Soviet Union. At the
halfway mark, the new century has witnessed serious conflict between
ourselves and all our rising contemporaries save India.

Such a vast change of fortune suggests the presence of general causes,
overshadowing the specific causes attending each of the successive crises.

Edward H. Buehrig, *Woodrow Wilson and the Balance of Power* (Bloomington: Indiana University Press, 1955), vii–ix, 268–275. Reprinted with permission.

How shall we characterize these broad movements of history, and what is the connection between them and our involvement in the first World War?

We can see today, what was much less clearly visible at the time, that the first World War signalized the decline of Europe from its former pre-eminence in world politics. With it, indeed, the Columbian era, that brilliant period of European expansion of which we ourselves are lasting evidence, was drawing to a close. Sooner or later such a decline was bound to occur. But the manner of its occurrence is a matter of particular interest. In the actual event, Europe did not succumb to superior alien forces but to her own internecine strife. German ambition, beyond the capacity of Continental Europe to cope with, engaged the energies of Great Britain. In fact, Anglo-German rivalry became a major point of tension, and Britain was no longer able to remain detached from Continental politics. Absorbed in the compelling necessities of European politics, Britain also ceased to serve effectively as a buffer between Europe and the United States.

Had it been accustomed to acting on power considerations, the United States might have based a policy forthrightly on Germany's attempt to supplant Great Britain. But the United States was not habituated to viewing international politics in such harsh terms. Moreover, it did not desire a future different from the past, nor was it covetous of either the glory or the responsibilities of world power. There was, consequently, no head-on collision with Germany. Rather German-American relations entered a legalistic maze in the perplexing intricacies of which the two countries eventually came to blows. It seems unlikely that the lawyers, by taking paths other than those actually chosen, might have significantly altered the outcome. Nor was commercial, any more than legal policy, the truly basic factor. The United States and Germany became embroiled because of their differing attitudes toward British control of the seas. Germany felt that she must challenge that control in the interest of her own future freedom of action. The United States, for its part, regarded British power benevolently, as a factor contributing to American security.

This is the state of affairs which the probing of the submarine revealed. Unwittingly, it was the instrument which laid bare the political connection with Europe which most Americans had ceased to believe existed, and which they were disposed to act on instinctively, rather than face the full implications of what was disclosed. . . .

A New Mold for American Policy

Our earliest experiences with foreign relations, in the period beginning with the American Revolution, required hard decisions and provided for the nation only a narrow margin of safety. In this respect the diplomacy of the Founding Fathers was not unlike today's. What came to be regarded as the traditional pattern of American policy, however, is of nineteenth-century origin. The announcement of the Monroe Doctrine in

1823 coincided with the beginning of an extraordinary period for the United States, in which the demands of security progressively relaxed. The Doctrine was a carefully considered response to a situation containing some elements of menace; but, oddly enough, the subsequent security of the nation was not attributable to its enforcement. For, as things turned out, there was no need to enforce it. This lack of serious occasion (except for the French intervention in Mexico during the American Civil War) for invoking the Doctrine, rather than the fact of its existence, underlay the unprecedented freedom of action of the United States in the nineteenth century; and this in turn gave rise to the isolationist tradition.

If we look for an explanation of so extraordinary a situation, we will find it in a circumstance not fully appreciated at the time, the character of our relations with Great Britain. Britain was herself a North American power—indeed at the end of the Napoleonic wars the dominant power in the Western Hemisphere. It followed that Great Britain was the main factor in our nineteenth-century situation, and the New World was the testing ground of Anglo-American relations. Fortunately accommodation rather than rivalry emerged as the dominant feature of Anglo-American relations. The achievement of this harmony between the two great English-speaking peoples is a lesson in statesmanship. Yet, because of its very completeness, accommodation exacted a price. In the United States it fostered indifference toward foreign policy which hampered the nation in responding with alert realism to the vastly altered conditions of world politics confronting it in the present century.

The first half of the twentieth century has been a transitional period in American history marking the end of one era and beginning of another. We had on the eve of the new century engaged in a small war of our own choosing. The imperial fruits of the ensuing peace treaty with Spain were regarded with considerable uneasiness. Events, however, soon pushed us into the main stream of international politics quite without regard to our own desires in the matter. Unwilling voyagers, we steered an erratic course. It required a second World War, the postwar pressure of Soviet Communism, and the new weapons of mass destruction to make us begin to exert our full influence in world affairs.

The war of 1914–18 presented the first major challenge to the pattern of our foreign relations as established in the nineteenth century; it also produced a response which even today continues to condition American policy. Already fully fashioned by April 1917, the response consisted of a league of nations with a universal guarantee of territorial integrity and political independence. This was a far cry indeed from adherence to the law of neutrality which in 1914 had been the automatic policy of the United States.

By what path did Woodrow Wilson arrive at the position of 1917, based on assumptions so radically different from those of traditional American policy? Speaking before the Senate in January 1917, Wilson contended that the United States, if it joined other nations in "guaranteeing the permanence of peace," would not break with tradition but actually fulfill "all that we have professed or striven for." He said he was proposing

that the nations should with one accord adopt the doctrine of President
Monroe as the doctrine of the world: that no nation should seek to extend
its polity over any other nation or people, but that every people should
be free to determine its own polity, its own way of development, un-
hindered, unthreatened, unafraid, the little along with the great and
powerful. . . . There is no entangling alliance in a concert of power.
When all unite to act in the same sense and with the same purpose all
act in the common interest and are free to live their own lives under a
common protection.

But we must judge this attempt to relate the new policy to the old a
failure, for actually the historical record does not support the suggestion
of an unbroken line of development from the Monroe Doctrine to the
League of Nations. To be sure the Monroe Doctrine was designed to
preserve the territorial integrity and political independence of the nations
of the Western Hemisphere, but it had an obverse side: an attitude of
aloofness toward Europe which had crystallized into a sort of permanent
neutrality toward European politics. Essentially the United States, without full awareness, had in the nineteenth century sought a relationship
to Europe not unlike that of neutralization attained by Switzerland. However, less undemanding than Switzerland, we had staked out a vast
hemispheric area of primary interest. Moreover, much of the Western
Hemisphere was economically underdeveloped and politically unstable,
and it could not, therefore, escape the consequences of a major shift in
the European balance of power. It was inevitable that with the first disturbance of such a nature the United States would drop its indifference
toward European politics. The first World War was that occasion, and
American policy responded in the halting, devious way that we have
described.

We have seen that neutrality in 1914 was no mere personal preference
of Wilson's. Its adoption was determined by history, whose molds are not
easily broken and never so by intellectual processes alone. In fact, until
the character and course of the war had emerged, it was unclear whether
neutrality was the right or wrong policy. But as the war's true nature
unfolded, American policy, adapting to the fact of a cataclysmic European
and world struggle for power, early became a policy of benevolent neutrality strongly favoring the Allies. Yet, though the spirit of American
neutrality departed increasingly from the letter until the discrepancy was
wide indeed, Wilson steadfastly refused to acknowledge the divergence.
Undoubtedly Wilson entertained a lingering regard for neutrality, the
more so as a base from which to seek mediation, but his failure to
characterize his policy openly for what it was—in such terms as House,
for instance, employed privately—was due above all to a divided and
clamorous public opinion, always on the verge of paralyzing disunity. No
longer a private citizen in 1914–17, Wilson was the head of a great
Government, and frankness appeared not a simple virtue and not always
expedient.

Seeking the flexibility denied to a policy tied to the tactics of the submarine, Wilson endeavored to deemphasize the rules of maritime warfare and

to take the ultimate political effects of the European struggle as the gauge of American action. It was in consequence of this endeavor that the league of nations became the dominant feature of his policy. The idea had been much abroad in the public mind, but as official policy the league emerged laboriously out of Anglo-American diplomacy, stemming from the efforts of House and Wilson on behalf of a negotiated peace. The initial attempts to mediate studiously avoided any commitment concerning future use of American power. Yet, as one observer expressed it, England was fighting for the nursery; as indeed was Germany also—with the difference that the latter was seeking to overturn the *status quo* which the former was determined to maintain. The war was not a mere quarrel over relative advantage but a struggle in which the future of great nations was at stake. Any attempt to mediate, therefore, had to take into account the dominating passion for security. In keeping with this characteristic of the war, Sir Edward Grey reacted to American proposals for mediation by advancing an idea of future concerted action against aggression. The foreign secretary was looking at the European situation, and saw the league as a device for bringing American power to bear in a Europe no longer capable of controlling itself. In a manner even more direct than that employed by George Canning in 1823, Grey was endeavoring through the New World to redress the balance of the Old.

Wilson's incorporation of the league idea into American policy was in response to Grey's initiative, but the idea did not have the same connotation for both men. Grey's thinking was empirical, in terms of the European problem; Wilson's idealistic, and of universal application. Grey saw the league as an elaboration of the traditional pattern of diplomacy; Wilson saw it as a new and independent force in the world capable of overriding the animosities and conflicts. To Grey the league was a means of channeling American power; to Wilson it was more the rallying point of world opinion.

Such in any event was the guise in which Wilson eventually depicted the league, though we have noted occasions when the President assessed the problem of American foreign policy in different terms. Not always had he regarded justice as a goal directly accessible through good will and rationality. In the debate with Lansing over the implications for American policy of the ideological aspect of the war, in the candid expression of misgivings to Frank I. Cobb on the eve of the War Message, and concealed in the January 22, 1917 address to the Senate—indeed underlying Wilson's whole policy of peace without victory—was an appreciation of the balance of power point of view: namely, that stability is to be found in an equilibrium of forces no less than in moral excellence.

Recognizing that these points of view are logically incompatible but that neither is exclusive of the other, we must ask why the idealistic element in Wilson's policy was finally so preponderant. To answer that this outcome accorded with Wilson's philosophical and temperamental leanings would not seem to cover the whole ground. Wilson, whether consciously or not, adapted his arguments to the requirements of public opinion, and nostalgic for the nineteenth century, the American nation wished to minimize the very exertion which Sir Edward Grey deemed the essential thing. Unaccustomed to the risk and burden of international responsibility, Americans were above all responsive to expressions of hope, pride, and sentiment. Thus the league was depicted in a fashion reflecting the very isolationism to which it was the supposed antithesis.

Additional Reading

Edwin Borchard and W. P. Lage, *Neutrality for the United States* (1937).
C. H. Grattan, *Why We Fought* (1929).
A. S. Link, *Woodrow Wilson and the Progressive Era, 1910–1917* (1954).
———, *Wilson: The Struggle for Neutrality, 1914–1915* (1960).
———, *Wilson the Diplomatist* (1957).
Ernest R. May, *The World War and American Isolation, 1914–1917* (1959).
Walter Millis, *Road to War: America, 1914–1917* (1935).
Alice M. Morrissey, *The American Defense of Neutral Rights, 1914–1917* (1939).
Harley Notter, *The Origins of the Foreign Policy of Woodrow Wilson* (1937).
H. C. Peterson, *Propaganda for War* (1939).
Daniel M. Smith, *Robert Lansing and American Neutrality, 1914–1917* (1958).
Charles C. Tansill, *America Goes to War* (1938).

14 *THE DEFEAT IN THE SENATE OF THE VERSAILLES TREATY*

As President Wilson in Paris was completing the fastening of the Covenant of the League of Nations to the treaty of peace with Germany, he received from America indications of mounting criticism of his handiwork. The Republican party had captured control of both houses of Congress in the 1918 elections and Henry Cabot Lodge of Massachusetts became chairman of the powerful Foreign Relations Committee in the new Senate. Under Lodge's direction, the committee was organized with a large number of opponents of the league concept. Made aware of growing political criticism during a quick return to the United States in February, 1919, Wilson upon resuming his labors in Paris secured a number of changes in the league charter which he hoped would allay the fears of critics. His efforts were to prove of little avail.

After the formal signing of the peace treaty at Versailles, the triumphant President bore the document with its precious covenant back to the United States and on July 10, 1919, formally laid the treaty before the Senate for its approval. Referred to the Lodge committee, there ensued a delaying process of protracted hearings and often irrelevant testimony before the treaty was reported back to the Senate burdened with 45 amendments and 4 reservations. These Republican-sponsored changes were subsequently reduced to the 14 "Lodge reservations," to be attached to the treaty as conditions of ratification.

Opposed to encumbering modifications of the treaty, President Wilson undertook an extensive speaking tour in September in the hope of bringing popular pressures to bear on recalcitrant senators. Never in robust health and now weakened by the tensions of war-waging and peace-making, the exhausted President was compelled to cancel the tour in late September and to return to the White House for rest. There, early in the following month, he suffered a severe stroke which rendered him partially paralyzed. Isolated in his sickroom, the seriously-ill Wilson was not active politically until November and in fact he made only a very limited recovery during the remainder of his term of office.

It was under these circumstances that the peace treaty came to a vote before the Senate on November 19, 1919, and was defeated. The feeble President continued to oppose the Lodge reservations and he urged loyal Democratic senators to vote against the treaty with reservations. Yet because of the Republican majority and the nature of the opposition in the Senate, the only hope for approval of the treaty was with the reservations. Consequently, the vote was 41 ayes to 50 nayes for the treaty with reservations, and 38 ayes to 53 nayes without. Revived for another vote on March 19, 1920, the treaty with the Lodge reservations—now 15 in number, after the addition of a clause advocating Irish independence—was again rejected by the vote of 49 ayes to 35 nayes. As the final tabulation was only 7 votes short of the necessary two-thirds majority, it was clear that Wilson himself had defeated the treaty by persuading 23 Democratic senators to join 12 "irreconcilables" in voting negatively.

Though Wilson hoped to make the treaty the key issue in the 1920 presidential campaign, the March vote in fact signified the death of the League in so far as American participation was concerned.

Questions raised by scholars about the defeat of the peace treaty and league have centered around the motives and actions of Lodge and Wilson. How seriously would the Lodge Reservations have affected the treaty and the operations of the league? If very little, and this has been the conclusion of most students of the period, why did the two antagonists attach so much importance to the reservations that Lodge and his supporters would not approve the treaty without the reservations and Wilson would not accept it with the changes? Was the Massachusetts senator motivated in his course by high principle, or was he following an obstructionist course merely for narrow partisan and personal purposes? Why did not Wilson, presumably aware of the innocuous if personally objectionable character of the reservations, rise above petty considerations to accept the treaty in the only way it could pass the Senate?

DOCUMENTS

1. The Capstone of the Versailles Treaty: the League Covenant

The focus of the public debate on the Treaty of Versailles was on Part I, the Covenant of the League of Nations. Within the Covenant, the key articles were numbers 10 through 16, involving the mutual guarantee and containing provisions for settlement of disputes and punishment of aggressors.

From the Covenant of the League of Nations

Article 1 [3]. Any Member of the League may, after two years' notice of its intention so to do, withdraw from the League, provided that all its international obligations and all its obligations under this Covenant shall have been fulfilled at the time of its withdrawal.

Article 2 The action of the League under this Covenant shall be effected through the instrumentality of an Assembly and of a Council, with a permanent Secretariat.

Article 3 [3]. The Assembly may deal at its meetings with any matter within the sphere of action of the League or affecting the peace of the world.

[4]. At meetings of the Assembly each Member of the League shall have one vote, and may have not more than three Representatives.

Article 4 [1]. The Council shall consist of Representatives of the Principal Allied and Associated Powers, together with Representatives of four other Members of the League. These four Members of the League shall be selected by the Assembly from time to time in its discretion. . . .

Article 5 [1]. Except where otherwise expressly provided in this Covenant or by the terms of the present Treaty, decisions at any meeting of the Assembly or of the Council shall require the agreement of all the Members of the League represented at the meeting.

Article 6 [1]. The permanent Secretariat shall be established at the Seat of the League. The Secretariat shall comprise a Secretary General and such secretaries and staff as may be required.

[2]. The first Secretary General shall be the person named in the Annex; thereafter the Secretary General shall be appointed by the Council with the approval of the majority of the Assembly.

Article 8 [1]. The Members of the League recognise that the maintenance of peace requires the reduction of national armaments to the lowest point consistent with national safety and the enforcement by common action of international obligations.

[2]. The Council, taking account of the geographical situation and circumstances of each State, shall formulate plans for such reduction for the consideration and action of the several Governments.

[6]. The Members of the League undertake to interchange full and frank information as to the scale of their armaments, their military, naval and air programmes and the condition of such of their industries as are adaptable to war-like purposes.

Article 10 The Members of the League undertake to respect and preserve as against external aggression the territorial integrity and existing political independence of all Members of the League. In case of any such aggression or in case of any threat or danger of such aggression the Council shall advise upon the means by which this obligation shall be fulfilled.

Article 11 [1]. Any war or threat of war, whether immediately affecting any of the Members of the League or not, is hereby declared a matter of concern to the whole League, and the League shall take any action that may be deemed wise and effectual to safeguard the peace of nations. In case any such emergency should arise the Secretary General shall on the request of any Member of the League forthwith summon a meeting of the Council.

[2]. It is also declared to be the friendly right of each Member of the League to bring to the attention of the Assembly or of the Council any circumstance whatever affecting international relations which threatens to disturb international peace or the good understanding between nations upon which peace depends.

Article 12 [1]. The Members of the League agree that, if there should arise between them any dispute likely to lead to a rupture, they will submit the matter either to arbitration or judicial settlement or to inquiry by the Council, and they agree in no case to resort to war until three months after the award by the arbitrators or the judicial decision, or the report by the Council.

Article 13 [1]. The Members of the League agree that, whenever any dispute shall arise between them which they recognize to be suitable for submission to arbitration or judicial settlement, and which cannot be satisfactorily settled by diplomacy, they will submit the whole subject matter to arbitration or judicial settlement.

[2]. Disputes as to the interpretation of a treaty, as to any question of international law, as to the existence of any fact which, if established, would constitute a breach of any international obligation, or as to the extent and nature of the reparation to be made for any such breach, are declared to be among those which are generally suitable for submission to arbitration or judicial settlement. . . .

[4]. The Members of the League agree that they will carry out in full good faith any award or decision that may be rendered, and that they will not resort to war against a Member of the League which complies therewith. In the event of any failure to carry out such an award or decision, the Council shall propose what steps should be taken to give effect thereto.

Article 14 The Council shall formulate and submit to the Members of the League for adoption plans for the establishment of a Permanent Court of International Justice. The Court shall be competent to hear and determine any dispute of an international character which the parties thereto submit to it. The Court may also give an advisory opinion upon any dispute or question referred to it by the Council or by the Assembly.

Article 15 [1]. If there should arise between Members of the League any dispute likely to lead to a rupture, which is not submitted to arbitration or judicial settlement in accordance with Article 13, the Members of the League agree that they will submit the matter to the Council. Any party to the dispute may effect such submission by giving notice of the existence of the dispute to the Secretary General, who will make all necessary arrangements for a full investigation and consideration thereof.

[8]. If the dispute between the parties is claimed by one of them, and is found by the Council, to arise out of a matter which by international law is solely within the domestic jurisdiction of that party, the Council shall so report, and shall make no recommendation as to its settlement.

Article 16 [1]. Should any Member of the League resort to war in disregard of its covenants under Articles 12, 13 or 15, it shall *ipso facto* be deemed to have committed an act of war against all other Members of the League, which hereby undertake immediately to subject it to the severance of all trade or financial relations, the prohibition of all intercourse between their nationals and the nationals of the covenant-breaking State, and the prevention of all financial, commercial or personal intercourse between the nationals of the covenant-breaking State and the nationals of any other State, whether a Member of the League or not.

[2]. It shall be the duty of the Council in such case to recommend to the several Governments concerned what effective military, naval or air force the Members of the League shall severally contribute to the armed forces to be used to protect the covenants of the League.

[3]. The Members of the League agree, further, that they will mutually support one another in the financial and economic measures which are taken under this Article, in order to minimise the loss and inconvenience resulting from the above measures, and that they will mutually support one another in resisting any special measures aimed at one of their number by the covenant-breaking State, and that they will take the necessary steps to afford passage through their territory to the forces of any of the Members of the League which are co-operating to protect the covenants of the League. . . .

Article 21 Nothing in this Covenant shall be deemed to affect the validity of international engagements, such as treaties of arbitration or regional understandings like the Monroe doctrine, for securing the maintenance of peace.

Article 22 [*1*]. To those colonies and territories which as a consequence of the late war have ceased to be under the sovereignty of the States which formerly governed them and which are inhabited by peoples not yet able to stand by themselves under the strenuous conditions of the modern world, there should be applied the principle that the well-being and development of such peoples form a sacred trust of civilisation and that securities for the performance of this trust should be embodied in this Covenant.

[2]. The best method of giving practical effect to this principle is that the tutelage of such peoples should be entrusted to advanced nations who by reason of their resources, their experience or their geographical position can best undertake this responsibility, and who are willing to accept it, and that this tutelage should be exercised by them as Mandatories on behalf of the League.

2. Republican Objections: the Case for a "Little" America

The Lodge Reservations to the Treaty of Peace, in the view of many Republicans and critics of the Covenant, were designed merely to safeguard legitimate American interests and rights. In his speeches, Senator Lodge disclaimed hostility to the idea of a league as such, but obviously he wanted one which was safe for the United States to join.

The Lodge Resolution of Ratification of the Treaty of Peace, November 19, 1919

Resolved . . . That the Senate advise and consent to the ratification of the treaty of peace with Germany . . . subject to the following reservations and understandings . . . which ratification is not to take effect or bind the United States until the said reservations and understandings . . . have been accepted by . . . at least three of the four principal allied and associated powers. . . .

1. . . . in case of notice of withdrawal from the league of nations, as provided in said article [Article 1], the United States shall be the sole

judge as to whether all its international obligations . . . have been fulfilled, and notice of withdrawal . . . may be given by a concurrent resolution of the Congress of the United States.

2. The United States assumes no obligation to preserve the territorial integrity or political independence of any other country . . . under the provisions of article 10, or to employ the military or naval forces of the United States under any article of the treaty for any purpose, unless in any particular case the Congress, which . . . has the sole power to declare war . . . shall . . . so provide.

3. No mandate shall be accepted by the United States under article 22 . . . except by action of the Congress of the United States.

4. The United States reserves to itself exclusively the right to decide what questions are within its domestic jurisdiction. . . .

5. The United States will not submit to arbitration or to inquiry by the assembly or by the council of the league of nations . . . any questions which in the judgment of the United States depend upon or relate to . . . the Monroe doctrine; said doctrine is to be interpreted by the United States alone and is . . . wholly outside the jurisdiction of said league of nations. . . .

6. The United States withholds its assent to articles 156, 157, and 158 [Shantung clauses]. . . .

7. The Congress of the United States will provide by law for the appointment of the representatives of the United States in the assembly and the council of the league of nations, and may in its discretion provide for the participation of the United States in any commission. . . . no person shall represent the United States under either said league of nations or the treaty of peace . . . except with the approval of the Senate of the United States.

9. The United States shall not be obligated to contribute to any expenses of the league of nations . . . unless and until an appropriation of funds . . . shall have been made by the Congress of the United States.

10. If the United States shall at any time adopt any plan for the limitation of armaments proposed by the council of the league . . . it reserves the right to increase such armaments without the consent of the council whenever the United States is threatened with invasion or engaged in war.

14. The United States assumes no obligation to be bound by any election, decision, report, or finding of the council or assembly in which any member of the league and its self-governing dominions, colonies, or parts of empire, in the aggregate have cast more than one vote. . . .

From a Speech by Henry Cabot Lodge in the Senate, August 12, 1919

. . . In article 10 the United States is bound on the appeal of any member of the league not only to respect but to preserve its independence and its boundaries, and that pledge if we give it, must be fulfilled.

There is to me no distinction whatever in a treaty between what some persons are pleased to call legal and moral obligations. A treaty rests and must rest . . . upon moral obligations. No doubt a great power impossible of coercion can cast aside a moral obligation if it sees fit and escape from the performance of the duty which it promises. The pathway of dishonor is always open. I, for one, however, cannot conceive of voting for a clause of which I disapprove because I know it can be escaped in that way. Whatever the United States agrees to, by that agreement she must abide. . . .

If China should rise up and attack Japan in an effort to undo the great wrong of the cession of the control of Shantung to that power, we should be bound under the terms of article 10 to sustain Japan against China. . . . I do not like the prospect. It shall not come into existence by any vote of mine. . . .

Let me now briefly point out the insuperable difficulty which I find in article 15. It begins: "If there should arise between members of the league any dispute likely to lead to a rupture." "Any dispute" covers every possible dispute. It therefore covers a dispute over tariff duties and over immigration. . . .

Immigration . . . cannot escape the action of the league by any claim of domestic jurisdiction; it has too many international aspects.

. . . So far as immigration is concerned, and also so far as tariff duties . . . are concerned, I deny the jurisdiction. There should be no possibility of other nations deciding who shall come into the United States, or under what conditions they shall enter. The right to say who shall come into a country is one of the very highest attributes of sovereignty. If a nation cannot say without appeal who shall come within its gates and become a part of its citizenship it has ceased to be a sovereign nation. . . .

If other nations are willing to subject themselves to such a domination, the United States, to which many immigrants have come and many more will come, ought never to submit to it for a moment. . . .

Let me now deal with the article [21] itself. . . . the Monroe doctrine is no more a regional understanding than it is an "international engagement." The Monroe doctrine was a policy declared by President Monroe. . . . It rested firmly on the great law of self-preservation, which is the basic principle of every independent State. . . .

The instant that the United States . . . ceases to be the sole judge of what it means, that instant the Monroe doctrine ceases and disappears from history and from the face of the earth. I think it is just as undesirable to have Europe interfere in American affairs now as Mr. Monroe thought it was in 1823, and equally undesirable that we should be compelled to involve ourselves in all the wars and brawls of Europe. . . .

Article 10 I have already discussed. There is no question that the preservation of a State against external aggression can contemplate nothing but war. In article 11, again, the league is authorized to take any action which may be necessary to safeguard the peace of the world. "Any action" includes war. . . . Article 16 embodies the boycott and also, in the last paragraph, provides explicitly for war. . . . Taken altogether, these provisions for war present what to my mind is the gravest objection to this league in its present form. We are told that of course nothing will be done . . . without the assent of Congress. If this is true, let us say so in the covenant. But as it stands there is no doubt whatever in my mind that American troops and American ships may be ordered to any part of the world by nations other than the United States, and that is a proposition to which I for one can never assent. It must be made perfectly clear that no American soldiers, not even a corporal's guard . . . can ever be engaged in war or ordered anywhere except by the constitutional authorities of the United States.

3. Wilson Appeals to the People

To President Wilson, on the other hand, the Lodge reservation strategy revealed doubts and hesitations unworthy of America and indicated a less than enthusiastic shouldering of the obligations of a great power. In addition, he asserted that the suggested alterations actually weakened the League and would cause other powers to insist on further changes.

Speech of President Wilson, Auditorium, San Francisco, September 17, 1919

. . . It is my purpose, fellow citizens, to analyze the objections which are made to this great League, and I shall be very brief. In the first place, you know that one of the difficulties which have been experienced by those who are objecting to this League is that they do not think that there is a wide enough door open for us to get out. For my own part, I am not one of those who, when they go into a generous enterprise, think first of all how they are going to turn away from those with whom they are associated. I am not one of those who, when they go into a concert for the peace of the world, want to sit close to the door with their hand on the knob and constantly trying the door to be sure that it is not locked. If we want to go into this thing—and we do want to go into it—we will go in it with our whole hearts and settled purpose to stand by the great enterprise to the end. Nevertheless, you will remember—some of you, I dare say—that when I came home in March for an all too brief visit to this country, which seems to me the fairest and dearest in the world, I brought back with me the first draft of the Covenant of the League of Nations. I called into consultation the Committees on Foreign Affairs and on Foreign Relations of the House and Senate of the United States, and I laid the draft of the Covenant before them. One of the things that they proposed was that it should be explicitly stated that any member of the League should have the right to withdraw. I carried that suggestion back to Paris, and without the slightest hesitation it was accepted and acted upon; and every suggestion which was made in that conference at the White House was accepted by the conference of peace in Paris. There is not a feature of the Covenant, except one, now under debate upon which suggestions were not made at that time, and there is not one of those suggestions that was not adopted by the conference of peace.

The gentlemen say, "You have laid a limitation upon the right to withdraw. You have said that we can withdraw upon two years' notice, if at that time we shall have fulfilled all our international obligations and all our obligations under the Covenant." "Yes," I reply; "is it characteristic of the United States not to fulfill her international obligations? Is there any fear that we shall wish to withdraw dishonorably? Are gentlemen willing to stand up and say that they want to get out whether they have the moral right to get out or not?" I for one am too proud as an American to debate that subject on that basis. The United States has always fulfilled its international obligations, and, God helping her, she always will. There is nothing in the Covenant to prevent her acting upon her own judgment with regard to that matter. The only thing she has to fear, the only thing she has to regard, is the public opinion of mankind, and inasmuch as we have always scrupulously satisfied the public opinion of mankind with regard to justice and right, I for my part am not afraid at any time to go before that jury. It is a jury that might condemn us if we did wrong, but it is not a jury that could oblige us to stay in the League, so that there is absolutely no limitation upon our right to withdraw.

One of the other suggestions I carried to Paris was that the committees of the two Houses did not find the Monroe Doctrine safeguarded in the Covenant of the League of Nations. I suggested that to the conference in Paris, and they at once inserted the provision which is now there that nothing in the Covenant shall be construed as affecting the validity of the Monroe Doctrine. What is the validity of the Monroe Doctrine? The Monroe Doctrine means that if any outside power, any power outside this hemisphere, tries to impose its will upon any portion of the Western Hemisphere the United States is at liberty to act independently and alone in repelling the aggression; that it does not have to wait for the action of the League of Nations; that it does not have to wait for anything but the action of its own administration and its own Congress. This is the first time in the history of international diplomacy that any great government has acknowledged the validity of the Monroe Doctrine. Now for the first time all the great fighting powers of the world except Germany, which for the time being has ceased to be a great fighting power, acknowledge the validity of the Monroe Doctrine and acknowledge it as part of the international practice of the world.

They are nervous about domestic questions. They say, "It is intolerable to think that the League of Nations should interfere with domestic questions," and whenever they begin to specify they speak of the question of immigration, of the question of naturalization, of the question of the tariff. My fellow citizens, no competent or authoritative student of international law would dream of maintaining that these were anything but exclusively domestic questions, and the Covenant of the League expressly provides that the League can take no action whatever about matters which are in the practice of international law regarded as domestic questions. We did not undertake to enumerate samples of domestic questions for the very good reason, which will occur to any lawyer, that if you made a list it would be inferred that what you left out was not included. Nobody with a thoughtful knowledge of international practice has the least doubt as to what are domestic questions, and there is no obscurity whatever in this Covenant with regard to the safeguarding of the United States, along with other sovereign countries, in the control of domestic questions. I beg that you will not fancy, my fellow citizens, that the United States is the only country that is jealous of its sovereignty. Throughout these conferences it was necessary at every turn to safeguard the sovereign independence of the several governments who were taking part in the conference, and they were just as keen to protect themselves against outside intervention in domestic matters as we were. Therefore the whole heartiness of their concurrent opinion runs with this safeguarding of domestic questions.

It is objected that the British Empire has six votes and we have one. The answer to that is that it is most carefully arranged that our one vote equals the six votes of the British Empire. Anybody who will take the pains to read the Covenant of the League of Nations will find out that the assembly—and it is only in the assembly that the British Empire has six votes—is not a voting body. . . .

Not a single affirmative act or negative decision upon a matter of action taken by the League of Nations can be validated without the vote of the United States of America. We can dismiss from our dreams the six votes of the British Empire, for the real underlying conception of the assembly of the League of Nations is that it is the forum of opinion, not of action. It is the debating body; it is the body where the thought of the little nation along with the thought of the big nation is brought to bear upon those matters which affect the peace of the world, is brought to bear upon those matters which affect the good understanding between nations upon which the peace of the world depends; where this stifled voice of humanity is at last to be heard, where nations that have borne the unspeakable sufferings of the ages that must have seemed to them like æons will find voice and expression, where the moral judgment of mankind can sway the opinion of the world. That is the function of the assembly. The assembly is the voice of mankind. The council, where unanimous action is necessary, is the only means through which that voice can accomplish action.

You say, "We have heard a great deal about Article X." I just now said that the only substitute for the League of Nations which is offered by the opponents is a return to the old system. What was the old system? That the strong had all the rights and need pay no attention to the rights of the weak; that if a great powerful nation saw what it wanted, it had the right to go and take it; that the weak nations could cry out and cry out as they pleased and there would be no hearkening ear anywhere to their rights. . . .

READINGS

1. The Case against Lodge

Some scholars have answered the question of who killed the treaty by attaching primary responsibility to Senator Lodge. The mastermind of Republican senatorial strategy, Lodge is depicted as motivated by an intense personal dislike of President Wilson and by a desire to embarrass the Democrats and win political advantages for the Republican party. Representative of this point of view is the following selection, utilizing psychological insights, by historians A. L. and J. L. George.

Battle with the Senate
A. L. AND J. L. GEORGE

All the time President Wilson was in Paris spending himself to the utmost first to secure the League Covenant and then to amend it, his enemies at home, led by Senator Lodge, plotted his defeat. When Lodge read the revised Covenant in the newspapers on April 28, 1919, he immediately concluded that Wilson's Herculean effort to amend the Covenant satisfactorily had been in vain. ". . . It is obvious," he stated to the press the next day, "that it will require further amendments . . ." Thereafter, he took the position that, so far from being an improvement over the original, the revised Covenant was "much worse than it was before." The Senate, he indicated, would have to save the country from the perils into which the President's feckless leadership, unless checked, would lead it.

Lodge, indeed, did not even have to examine the Covenant to be certain that it was a dangerous proposition. He had long since decided that while it would be "a mistake" to reject the *idea* of a league of nations—everyone, after all, favored the preservation of world peace—it would be possible to confound any practical plan, no matter what its terms. . . .

Throughout the battle over Senate ratification of the Treaty of Versailles, Lodge piously maintained that his position was dictated by an overriding concern for safeguarding the interests of the United States, and that he favored American entry into the League of Nations if only the Covenant could be so changed that basic American interests would be protected. It was widely suspected at the time, and frequently has been suggested since, that Lodge was out first and foremost to humiliate President Wilson, and that he had no use whatever for Wilson's League in any form. Since a policy of outright rejection would surely fail because of widespread public endorsement of the League, Lodge shrewdly feigned a more moderate position. He did so, according to this theory, the better ultimately to kill Wilson's creation or, at the very least, to change it and force the proud President to bow to the Republican-controlled Senate, thus yielding prestige, both personal and political.

In the light of Lodge's maneuvers throughout the Treaty fight, this interpretation is persuasive. It gains all but irresistible plausibility from the fact that when at last the Senate rejected the Treaty, League and all, Lodge felt, as he declared in a letter, that he and his colleagues had done very well. To one of his Senate colleagues, he referred to the outcome of the controversy as a "victory." Further, at the Republican Convention of 1920, Lodge refused to urge ratification of the Treaty with the reservations he had so vociferously advocated but preferred, instead, to leave the way open for a complete repudiation of the League. And when, indeed, the Republicans won the election of 1920, Lodge exultantly declared that so far as the United States was concerned, the League of Nations was dead.

Lodge personally detested Wilson, a fact to which his letters and papers eloquently testify. Quite apart from this highly personal consideration, however, as a Republican political leader Lodge had his eye upon the next presidential election, an event which has seldom failed to magnify the partisan component of issues before Congress for long months before its occurrence.

Whatever complex combination of personal, partisan and patriotic motives animated Lodge, certain it is that as soon as the Germans sued for peace in October, 1918, he turned all the resources of a cunning mind to the task of publicly embarrassing Wilson at every turn. He who had once proclaimed that where questions of foreign policy were concerned his politics always stopped at the water's edge, attempted, via Henry White,* to furnish Allied diplomats at the Peace Conference a memorandum suggesting that the President's ideas misrepresented the real sentiments of the people and Senate of the United States. His purpose, he stated frankly, was to strengthen the hands of these foreign diplomats in their dealings with Wilson. Lodge organized the Round Robin, which struck Wilson's prestige a mighty blow at just the moment the President needed all his authority to induce the Allies to moderate some of their demands. At the height of the Italian crisis, while Wilson was standing foursquare against the Italian claim to Fiume, Lodge issued a statement to the Italians of Boston upholding the Italian position. The Shantung settlement, the justice of which was indeed debatable, provided Lodge and his cohorts with a splendid excuse to heap further abuse upon their favorite villain.

As the *George Washington* bearing the President home from the Peace Conference coursed toward American shores, Senator Lodge was deep in plans to bring to his knees the man he hated more, he once confessed, than he had ever expected to hate anyone in politics, the man whom, James Buchanan perhaps excepted, he judged to be the worst President in the nation's history. The great alarm which he and his friends were spreading the length and breadth of the land was that Wilson's League was fraught with dire danger for the United States and that the Senate must now change the Covenant to make it safe.

Almost any man who was confronted with opponents as intelligent and resourceful as Lodge and his cohorts would be distressed and angered. A more detached leader than Wilson, however, might have been capable of

* A member of the American Peace Commission to Paris.

dispassionately countering Lodge's tactical maneuvers and of taking practical steps to mobilize all possible Senate support for the Treaty. Wilson's particular anxieties rendered him incapable of meeting Lodge's challenge with such equanimity. Because he was so peculiarly vulnerable to them, Lodge's barbs affected him as the proverbial red flag affects the proverbial bull.

Wilson had deep-seated doubts, which originated in his early years, of his intellectual competence, his moral worth and his strength. He had tried to overcome these self-doubts by rigorous training and ceaseless self-vindicating demonstrations through accomplishment that he was indeed of superior intelligence, of good and "unselfish" character, and of sufficient strength to escape the degradation of capitulating to anybody. With an unerring sense of where his adversary's weak points lay and with an air of patronizing superiority, Lodge peppered him with just those personal attacks which intensified Wilson's inner anxieties.

Did Wilson, after suffering much mortification for his "slowness" as a child, joyfully discover in his adolescence that he "had a mind" and thereafter take especial pride in his intellectual attainments? Lodge was not at pains to conceal his contempt for Wilson's "mind." In a Senate speech on February 28, 1919, it will be recalled, Lodge had derided Wilson as one whose intellect and position in the world he found something less than overpowering. As for being the "scholar in politics"—until Wilson's star eclipsed his own, Lodge had enjoyed that popular appellation—why, Wilson was no scholar at all, Lodge maintained. (As evidence of this, in a book he subsequently wrote, the learned Senator cited the fact that in making a classical allusion, Wilson had once confused Hercules with Antaeus, a blunder which Lodge considered "incredible.")

Did Wilson, trained by a father obsessed with the importance of proper use of the English language, take great pains with his style and inordinately value mellifluous phrases and graceful expression? "As an English production," Lodge once remarked of the Covenant, "it does not rank high. It might get by at Princeton but certainly not at Harvard."

Did Wilson secretly fear his "selfish" motives in exercising leadership and continually proclaim his own disinterestedness and, by extension, the disinterestedness of the nation in dealing with other nations? Lodge thought Wilson self-seeking, unprincipled, egotistical, timid, narrow-minded, a demagogue interested exclusively in his own aggrandizement —and he made no secret of his opinion.

Did Wilson, desperately eager to undercut Lodge's position, make the most painful compromises during the latter half of the Peace Conference in order to obtain amendments to the Covenant which would meet the major objections which had been raised against it? Lodge, so far from being nonplussed by Wilson's coup, summarily dismissed the revisions as worthless and served notice that the Senate would have to make further changes. Unless the President accepted these changes, he warned repeatedly, the Treaty would be defeated.

Not only was the substance of Lodge's thrusts unbearable to Wilson: the Senator's manner stung him to the quick. Even one of Lodge's life-long friends, William Lawrence, in summing up Lodge's career regretfully noted that "Cabot" had "a certain quality of voice in making his brightest and most penetrating remarks" which could mortally offend. . . .

Lodge trained all this capacity for sneering sarcasm against Wilson. There was something contemptuous in the very calmness of the man: it was as though he felt the objects of his scorn unworthy even of his enmity.

Once before, long ago, Wilson had had to endure barbed criticism. Once before, long ago, he had been sent in humiliation to revise and re-revise some carefully wrought composition. And long ago, overwhelmed by his masterful father, he had submitted to sarcastically made demands and to aspersions on his moral and intellectual worth. He had submitted in seeming docility. Perhaps the rage that he had suppressed then emerged in full force against those he encountered in later years who re-awakened the disagreeable sensations of half a century and more before.

Wilson's emotional commitment to the League was, as we have seen, of surpassing intensity. Even in connection with projects of far less personal significance to him, he habitually experienced any interference in his exercise of power as an intolerable threat. Small wonder, given the very real menace Lodge presented both to the League and to Wilson's inner equilibrium, that the mere mention of the Senator's name caused Wilson to clench his teeth in rage.

President Wilson arrived home from Europe on July 8, 1919. Two days later he appeared before the Senate to lay the Treaty before it for ratification. Shortly before leaving the White House to address the Senate, Wilson held a press conference. One of the reporters inquired whether the Treaty would pass if the Senate attached reservations to it. "I do not think hypothetical questions are concerned," Wilson flashed back. *The Senate is going to ratify the treaty.*

If his address to the Senate had a somewhat less peremptory tone, its plain implication was the same: the Senate *must* ratify the Treaty—it was God's will. It was not a perfect instrument, the President conceded. Many "minor compromises" had been made but, he declared euphemistically, the settlement "squares, as a whole, with the principles agreed upon as the basis of the peace. . . ." The Treaty's most important accomplishment was the creation of the League of Nations. "Dare we reject it and break the heart of the world?" Rejection was unthinkable. America, as had been universally recognized, "entered the war to promote no private or peculiar interest of her own but only as the champion of rights which she was glad to share with free men and lovers of justice everywhere." Now the world looked to America for moral leadership, and it was our duty to accept the responsibility of providing it. "The stage is set, the destiny disclosed," the President concluded. "It has come about by no plan of our conceiving, but by the hand of God who led us into this way. We cannot turn back. We can only go forward, with lifted eyes and freshened spirit, to follow the vision. It was of this that we dreamed at our birth. America shall in truth show the way. The light streams upon the path ahead, and nowhere else."

Unfortunately, as their immediate comments disclosed, many of the Senators saw "the light" streaming upon a number of alternative paths that the zealous President did not espy; and they regarded the destiny for America which Wilson envisaged more as a product of the plans of Woodrow Wilson than as a manifestation of the "hand of God." What about reservations, a number of them demanded. The President had not even mentioned the subject, which was uppermost in the minds of the Senators. Instead he had treated them to, as Senator Brandegee (R., Conn.) put it, "soap bubbles of oratory and soufflé of phrases."

The Treaty having been formally placed before the Senate, it was immediately referred to the Senate Foreign Relations Committee. The chairman of this Committee, of course, was Henry Cabot Lodge.

Though chairman of the Foreign Relations Committee and leader of the majority party in the Senate—there were 49 Republicans and 47 Democrats in the Senate newly organized in accordance with the results of the 1918 elections—Lodge was in an extremely difficult position. The nub of his dilemma was that public opinion overwhelmingly favored *a* league and, after Wilson succeeded in amending the Covenant in Paris to eliminate most of the dangers its opponents professed to see in it, the public plainly favored *the* League. Several polls testified to that fact. So did the tidal wave of favorable comment in the press and in lecture halls and pulpits throughout the land, of resolutions of endorsement by farm and labor organizations and by state legislatures.

Senator Lodge was greatly concerned over this state of affairs. He was shrewd enough to realize that, given the temper of the country and even of a goodly number of his Republican colleagues in the Senate, any immediate showdown between the supporters of the League and its opponents would result in a rout of the latter. To A. J. Beveridge he wrote in February, 1919:

> The situation . . . practically must be treated with great care. I have no doubt that a large majority of the people of the country are very naturally fascinated by the idea of eternal preservation of the world's peace. . . . Now I do not think it would be wise for us at this stage to make it a party issue, nor to confront it with a blank negative. I think what is necessary for us to do is to begin to discuss it and try to get what it involves and what it means before the American people. . . . I think the second thought is going to be with us, but the first thought is probably against us. Therefore, we must proceed with caution . . .

Lodge accordingly felt that it was necessary to gain time to influence opinion against the Treaty as it stood. The thing to do, Lodge thought, was to proclaim the supposed dangers inherent in Wilson's League from the Atlantic to the Pacific, from Canada to Mexico. Money aplenty was available for this enterprise. Speeches by Lodge and other critics of the League were printed and distributed by the hundreds of thousands. Meetings were held at which speakers warned that Wilson's League impaired American sovereignty, surrendered the Monroe Doctrine, entangled us in European and Asiatic intrigues, thus flouting George Washington's time-honored advice, and subjected American boys to the authority of a foreign agency which might at any time order them into battle for remote causes in remote parts of the world. Worse still, our boys might be ordered to fight in causes which would be plainly repugnant to any freedom-loving American, such as the quelling of Irish revolutionists for the benefit of their English oppressors.

Several minority groups were highly susceptible to these arguments. First, there were the Irish-Americans, bitterly resentful of Wilson because he had not fought for Irish self-determination at the Peace Conference. Then there were the German-Americans, some seven million strong, and in varying degrees incensed at Wilson for his role in the ignominious defeat of the Fatherland. Too, there were the Italian-Americans, up in arms against Wilson for his implacable opposition to awarding Fiume to Italy.

Other groups, based on mutually shared viewpoints rather than national origins, opposed the Treaty. There were, for example, the liberals, who were deeply disillusioned at what they considered Wilson's betrayal of his own principles at the Peace Conference. One of the leading liberal weeklies, *The Nation,* referred to the League of Nations as, to quote the title of one of its articles on the subject, "A Colossal Humbug," and analyzed one of the President's attempts to depict the disadvantages of rejecting the Treaty under the heading, "Mr. Wilson Rants."

More numerous and an even greater stumbling block to the League were the isolationists—those who still thought America could be a land unto herself and exist without sullying her hands in the endless broils of the rest of the world. To them, the League represented a dangerous departure from the principle, which had served so well in the past, of avoiding foreign entanglements. Once enter the League, they cried, and the United States would find that she had surrendered her sovereignty to a mongrel superstate. The isolationists drew strength from the fact that theirs was the hallowed national tradition. Their predictions of the dire consequences of venturing into new international relationships gave their more forward-looking compatriots many sober second thoughts.

All of these groups were natural targets for anti-League propaganda. Lodge and his political friends tirelessly fanned the flames of their various fears and resentments. The resultant cacophony of anti-League and anti-Wilson invective made many a citizen, not associated with any special group, wonder whether there must not be a kernel of truth in all the criticisms of the League; whether, after all, it would not be wise to "Americanize" the Treaty as so many people so loudly and so urgently recommended. By the time Wilson returned from Paris, there was still a widespread disposition to accept the Treaty and enter the League, but it was qualified by the growing feeling that perhaps the Treaty ought to be changed to further protect American interests.

If opinion throughout the country was growing more confused by the day as the result of the anti-League campaign, opinions in the Senate were in confusion twice compounded. For not only were the Senators prey to all the intellectual cross-currents abroad in the land: in addition, they were swayed by two other factors. First, it was in the nature of the case that the Senators, as politicians, should have politics on their minds—and the 1920 presidential election was little over a year away. Second, many a

Senator, on both sides of the aisle, welcomed the opportunity to settle old personal scores with Wilson, now that the war was over and they no longer felt obliged to suppress their antagonism. They would give Wilson an object lesson in respect for the legislative branch of government, using his beloved Treaty as the text. . . .

From a strictly partisan point of view, it would never do to allow Wilson, singlehanded, the great accomplishment of which he dreamed. On the heels of such a success, the Republicans feared, he might seek a third term—and might even win it. From the Republican point of view, Wilson's League must either be defeated or, at the very least, so "Republicanized" that the GOP could claim credit for some of its good features. That the Treaty would be ratified and the United States would enter the League, however, seemed a foregone conclusion. A large proportion of Republican Senators were willing to content themselves with making only minor changes in the Treaty. They, together with the Democrats, constituted a majority of the Senate and could probably attract sufficient additional votes to make up the necessary two-thirds for ratification.

It was into this complex situation that Lodge entered as majority leader of the Senate. It was a situation which filled the enemies of the Treaty with despair, for it seemed inevitable that, with some minor alterations, the Treaty would pass. One evening, Senator James E. Watson of Indiana dined with Lodge to discuss means for meeting the challenge posed by the Treaty. "Senator," Watson declared, "I don't see how we are ever going to defeat this proposition. It appears to me that eighty percent of the people are for it."

Lodge replied, "Ah, my dear James, I do not propose to try to beat it by direct frontal attack, but by the indirect method of reservations."

Watson was puzzled and asked Lodge to elaborate. Lodge did so, for two hours, until Watson, as he later wrote, "became thoroughly satisfied that the Treaty could be beaten in that way." For sheer brilliance of conception Lodge's strategy stands without parallel in American history. For the finesse with which he applied it, Lodge stands without peer as a master tactician and psychologist.

Lodge's whole plan of action was based upon his estimate that Wilson would never consent to accepting Senate reservations to the Treaty. To Lodge, as he later wrote, Wilson "was simply an element to be calmly and coolly considered in a great problem of international politics." It was the Senator's "calm" and "cool" judgment that Wilson would do all he could to "prevent the acceptance of the treaty with reservations. . . ."

Given this conviction and the intrepidity to stake his whole strategy on it, Lodge was able to map out a plan of action at once beautifully simple and subtle. All he had to do was tack reservations onto the Treaty, and most particularly onto the League Covenant, which Wilson held so dear. Then, if his theory was correct, Wilson could be counted on himself to destroy what he had invested his lifeblood to create. Lodge's first problem, therefore, was to make certain that a majority vote could be commanded for his reservations.

Of the forty-nine Republican Senators, fifteen, who came to be known as "irreconcilables" and "bitter-enders," were opposed to the Treaty in any way, shape or form. Led by William Borah of Idaho, a man of incorrupt- ible conviction so fiercely determined to keep this nation out of the League that it was commonly believed he would bolt the Party in 1920 if dissatisfied with Republican leadership on the Treaty issue, the "irrecon- cilables" had unequivocally announced their intention of voting against the Treaty, amended or unamended, with reservations or without.

On April 29, 1919, three weeks before the new Congress was to con- vene, Lodge conferred with Borah for the purpose of enlisting his support for amendments and reservations. Lodge told Borah that in his judgment "the great mass of the people, the man in the street, to use a common expression" favored Wilson's League, and that "the vocal classes of the community"—clergymen, educators, newspaper editors, and opinion lead- ers generally—were also advocating the League as it stood. "With these conditions existing, I said to Senator Borah, it seemed perfectly obvious to me that any attempt to defeat the treaty of Versailles with the League by a straight vote in the Senate, if taken immediately, would be hopeless, even if it were desirable." There was only one thing to do, Lodge argued, and that was to attach amendments and reservations to the Treaty. If the Treaty then failed of ratification, Borah and his colleagues would be satis- fied. If it passed, it would at least bear Republican improvements. Borah agreed with Lodge's analysis of the situation and pledged himself to vote for amendments and reservations with the understanding, of course, that on the final vote he would vote against ratification of the Treaty. Lodge was greatly pleased with this outcome—it "confirmed me in the opinions which I had formed as to the proper way of dealing with the treaty when it came before us."

Next, Lodge turned his attention to the organization of the Committee on Foreign Relations, the composition of which would be, as he later wrote, of unusual consequence. Lodge loaded the Committee with "ir- reconcilables," deliberately rejecting such middle-grounders as Senator Kellogg, because Kellogg declined to commit himself blindly to Lodge's leadership. Of the ten Republicans on the Committee, six were "irrecon- cilables" and three were strong reservationists. The Republican "mild reservationists" were appalled. It could be seen immediately, Lodge later blandly recorded, that it was a "strong" committee of the kind the situation required.

The dozen or so "mild reservationists" in the Senate, as their name im- plies, favored reservations, though of a generally minor character. Lodge could count on them to support *some* program of reservations. He would have to feel his way along to see how broad a one they would swallow. He could also count for support on three or four Democrats, who stood ready to defy Wilson and work for the interment of the Treaty.

By the time Wilson returned to Washington in July, 1919, Lodge could be certain that the one condition upon which his hopes rested—that Wilson would be confronted with the necessity of accepting reservations on pain of seeing the whole Treaty go down in defeat—would be ful- filled.

The arithmetic of the problem was inescapable. No matter what he did, Wilson was caught by it. There was only one exit from the trap: compromise on reservations. The possibility that the President would bow to the realities of the situation and accept reservations, either those of the "mild reservationists" or, if need be, Lodge's own, was the great vulnerability of the anti-Treaty strategy, the waking nightmare of those interested in defeating the Treaty during the nine months that it was before the Senate. Lodge remained imperturbable.

On one occasion, Senator Watson said to him, "Senator, suppose that the President accepts the Treaty with your reservations. Then we are in the League, and once in, our reservations become purely fiction."

Lodge smiled. "But, my dear James, you do not take into consideration the hatred that Woodrow Wilson has for me personally. Never under any set of circumstances in this world could he be induced to accept a treaty with Lodge reservations appended to it."

"But that seems to me to be rather a slender thread on which to hang so great a cause," Watson replied.

"A slender thread!" exclaimed Lodge. "Why, it is as strong as any cable with its strands wired and twisted together."

In later years, Lodge was able to write with some satisfaction that he had made no mistake in his estimate of what President Wilson would do under certain conditions.

Once in the hands of the Foreign Relations Committee, the Treaty was at the mercy of Lodge and the "strong" colleagues he had so carefully selected to assist in the contemplated operation upon Wilson's brain child. First, however, the patient had to be very, very carefully examined—and no one could hurry Dr. Lodge, for he and his fellow Republicans controlled the Committee.

Lodge began by reading the entire Treaty aloud—all two hundred sixty-eight pages of it. It took him two weeks. Much of his performance was witnessed only by the Committee clerk. On one occasion, even this captive audience departed. Undaunted, Lodge soliloquized. The reading finally completed, the Committee began hearings. Representatives of numerous groups which had failed to satisfy their aspirations at Paris gave vent to their spleen before the sympathetic Senators. Their complaints furnished excellent publicity for the alleged inequities of the Treaty. The hearings also served to give the Treaty's opponents, both in and out of the Senate, further time in which to educate public opinion to the dangers which they claimed would envelop the United States were the League Covenant to be allowed to stand unchanged.

Critics of the Covenant heaped abuse on it from its first word to its last, but major fire was concentrated on four points. First it was alleged that the Covenant as it stood gave the League the right to meddle in the domestic affairs of its members. Did we want to authorize a foreign superstate to interfere with our immigration policies, to tell us, for example, that we must admit Orientals into this country on an unrestricted basis? Or, to take another example, to authorize the League to dictate our tariff policy? Wilson's supporters pointed out that it was to meet this very criticism that the President, when he had returned to Paris in March, had secured an amendment to the Covenant providing that if a dispute between contending parties "is claimed by one of them, and is found by the Council, to arise out of a matter which by international law is solely within the domestic jurisdiction of that party, the Council shall so report, and shall make no recommendation as to its settlement." This formulation, Wilson's critics retorted, left it to the Council of the League to decide whether or not a dispute fell within the domestic jurisdiction of one of the parties. The United States should have this decision in its own hands where any question involving this country arose.

Second, it was alleged that the Covenant endangered the Monroe Doctrine. Wilson's supporters drew attention to a second amendment to the Covenant he had obtained while still in Paris stipulating that "nothing in this Covenant shall be deemed to affect the validity of international engagements, such as treaties of arbitration or regional understandings like the Monroe Doctrine, for securing the maintenance of peace." To this Wilson's critics replied that the Monroe Doctrine was *not* an "international engagement" or a "regional understanding." It was a unilateral policy of the United States, and must be expressly exempted from interpretation by foreign powers.

Third, it was alleged that the provision for withdrawal from the League was unsatisfactory. A third amendment to the Covenant which Wilson had secured in Paris in response to criticism at home provided that "any Member of the League may, after two years' notice of its intention so to do, withdraw from the League, provided that all its international obligations and all its obligations under this Covenant shall have been fulfilled at the time of its withdrawal." But who would decide whether a withdrawing nation had fulfilled all its obligations, it was demanded. Obviously, declared Wilson's supporters, the withdrawing nation would, since the League was nowhere empowered to decide such a question. This answer failed to satisfy Wilson's detractors. To them, the provision was, at best, ambiguous, and there must be no ambiguity in such a matter: the world must know that the United States alone would decide whether or not her obligations had been fulfilled and would expect the unconditional right to withdraw.

Fourth, having been uncertain for a time whether to regard Wilson's League as a powerless debating society or a dangerous superstate, Lodge and his friends took the latter position and fell upon Article X of the Covenant. Article X read:

> The Members of the League undertake to respect and preserve as against external aggression the territorial integrity and existing political independence of all Members of the League. In case of any such aggression or in case of any threat or danger of such aggression the Council shall advise upon the means by which this obligation shall be fulfilled.

This provision plainly overrode the United States Constitution, Wilson's critics charged. Under it, the League could order American boys into battle, or order the United States to impose economic boycotts on other nations. The Constitution, however, provides that only Congress can declare war, and all bills to raise revenue or affecting revenue must be passed by Congress and signed by the President. Wilson's defenders pointed out that since the Council's decisions required unanimity, it could not act without the assent of its United States delegate. This would prevent the Council from taking actions obnoxious to the United States. Further, the Council's action in any case was only *advisory*. It had no power to issue a legally binding order. Its advice created a moral, rather than a legal obligation, the point being that a moral obligation left room for the exercise of discretion and judgment. It would be up to Congress to decide whether to accept the Council's advice, and to determine what action to take in any particular case. If there were only a moral obligation, the anti-Wilsonites retorted, then what avail Article X? Every nation could construe the Council's advice as it pleased and the Council would then amount to nothing more than a toothless forum, after all. Wilson and his supporters replied that in such matters, there is a national good conscience. Nations generally attempt to fulfill solemn obligations, moral as well as legal. The mere acceptance of a moral obligation by nations toward each other was an excellent step forward in international relations.

There had been a time, not so many years before, when Lodge had cordially endorsed this very idea. . . .

In May, 1916, speaking at a meeting of the League to Enforce Peace, Lodge had reiterated the view that the only hope for future world peace lay in the creation of an international league with force at its disposal. "I know the obstacles," Lodge then had said:

> I know how quickly we shall be met with the statement that this is a dangerous question which you are putting into your agreement, that no nation can submit to the judgment of other nations, and we must be careful at the beginning not to attempt too much. I know the difficulties that arise when we speak of anything which seems to involve an alliance. But I do not believe that when Washington warned us against permanent alliances he meant for one moment that we should not join with the other civilized nations of the world if a method could be found to diminish war and encourage peace.

A man can change his opinions, however, and when his earlier views materialized in Wilson's Covenant, Lodge invoked the Founding Fathers to vindicate his opposition to Wilson's League in general and Article X in particular.

Wilson's adherents complained that the League's critics spoke as though the Covenant's provisions applied exclusively to the United States; as though the League were nothing but a gigantic conspiracy against the sovereignty of the United States. Britain, France, Italy and other nations were as concerned as we were to preserve their freedom of action and to keep control of their domestic problems in their own hands. All members would be bound by the same rules, these Wilsonians asserted. That being the case, and the other nations being as jealous of their prerogatives as the United States, in practice no great sacrifice of sovereignty would be required. Therefore, the safeguards which so many people were demanding in the form of changes in the Covenant were unnecessary because they were already clearly implicit and tacitly accepted by the other powers.

It will be obvious to the reader, even from this abbreviated account of some of the points of contention, that many arguments could be mustered to support a variety of views concerning each of them. Many were. The newspapers carried column after column of intricate legal discussions, with opinions and counteropinions, with accounts of complicated parliamentary maneuvers in the Senate and of a dizzying variety of views on a dizzying number of the Treaty's provisions. The public was rapidly becoming thoroughly confused, though through it all it remained clear that most people and most Senators wanted the League and the Treaty in some form. Why not, then, attach reservations, even if only to still groundless fears, and get the whole bothersome business out of the way once and for all? This feeling grew, both in and out of the Senate, as the dispute wore on.

Faced with this tangled situation, President Wilson struck an attitude which is as simple to describe as it is difficult to analyze. He would not consent to the embodiment of reservations or amendments of the Treaty in the resolution of ratification. He would consider, however, the possibility of issuing a separate statement of "reasonable interpretation(s)" simultaneously with the resolution of ratification. He took this position on the day he presented the Treaty to the Senate. He reaffirmed it when he met with the Senate Foreign Relations Committee on August 19. From start to finish, he did not deviate one jot from this position. It was on this issue of the *form* of the reservations, as well as of the content of the final version of the reservation to Article X, that the whole Treaty foundered. . . .

2. Wilson Dooms His Own Handiwork

Although aware of Lodge's motives and role, other historians have attributed the defeat of the Versailles Treaty largely to the stubborn pride and uncompromising course of President Wilson. By his failure to conciliate moderate critics of the League and his refusal to accept the Lodge Reservations, Wilson doomed his own creation to senatorial rejection. Professor Bailey concludes that Wilson must bear the major onus for the killing of the treaty in the United States.

The Supreme Infanticide

T. A. BAILEY

. . . Is it true that the invalid in the White House really strangled the treaty to death with his own enfeebled hands?

It is seldom that statesmen have a second chance—a second guess. They

Reprinted with permission of The Macmillan Company from *Woodrow Wilson and the Great Betrayal* by Thomas A. Bailey. Copyright 1945 by Thomas A. Bailey. Pp. 275–282.

decide on a course of action, and the swift current of events beats them downstream from the starting point. Only rarely does the stream reverse itself and carry them back.

In November, Wilson had decided that he wanted deadlock, because he reasoned that deadlock would arouse public opinion and force the Senate to do his bidding. The tidal wave of public opinion did surge in, and Wilson got his second chance. But he threw it away, first by spurning compromise (except on his terms), and then by spurning the Lodge reservations.

There had been much more justification for Wilson's course in November than in March. In November [1919] he was sick, secluded, was fed censored news, and was convinced by Hitchcock that the strategy of deadlock was sound. In March, [1920] he was much improved in health, far less secluded, more in touch with the press and with the currents of opinion, though probably still not enough. He consulted even less with the Senate, presumably because he had made up his mind in advance to oppose the Lodge reservations. In November, there was a fair possibility of reconsideration; in March, it was clear that the only possibility lay in making the League an issue in the coming campaign. Wilson, with his broad knowledge of government and politics, should have seen that this hope was largely if not completely illusory. Perhaps he would have seen it had he not been blinded by his feeling for Lodge.

The evidence is convincing that Wilson wanted this issue cast into the hurly-burly of politics. He could not accept Lodge's terms; Lodge would not accept his terms. The only possible chance of beating the senator—and this was slim indeed—was to win a resounding mandate in 1920.

Yet this strategy, as already noted, meant further delay. At Paris, the feeling at times had been, "Better a bad treaty today than a good treaty four months hence." Europe was still in chaos, and increasingly in need of America's helping hand. Well might the Europeans cry, "Better a treaty with the Lodge reservations today than a probable treaty without reservations after the election." Or as Dr. Frank Crane wrote in *Current Opinion*, "It is vastly more needful that some sort of League be formed, *any sort*, than that it be formed *perfectly*." (Italics Crane's.)

Yet Wilson, for the reasons indicated, could not see all this clearly. Four days after the fatal vote he wrote Hitchcock, praising him for having done all in his power to protect the honor of the nation and the peace of the world against the Republican majority.

Mrs. Wilson, no doubt reflecting her husband's views, later wrote, "My conviction is that Mr. Lodge put the world back fifty years, and that at his door lies the wreckage of human hopes and the peril to human lives that afflict mankind today."

To the very end Wilson was a fighter. When the Scotch-Irish in him became aroused, he would nail his colors to the mast. He said in 1916 that he was "playing for the verdict of mankind." His conception of duty as he saw it was overpowering. He once remarked that if he were a judge, and it became his duty to sentence his own brother to the gallows, he would do so—and afterwards die of a broken heart.

It is well to have principles; it is well to have a noble conception of duty. But Wilson, as he became warmed up in a fight, tended to get things out of focus and to lose a proper sense of values.

The basic issue in 1920 was the Hitchcock reservations or the Lodge reservations. Wilson accepted those of Hitchcock while rejecting those of Lodge, which, he said, completely nullified the treaty and betrayed his promises to the Allies and to the American dead.

This, as we have seen, was a gross exaggeration. Minds no less acute than Wilson's, and less clouded with sickness and pride, denied that the Lodge reservations completely nullified the treaty. To the man in the street—in so far as he gave the dispute thought—there was little discernible difference between the two sets of reservations. How could one decry statements which merely reaffirmed the basic principles of the Constitution and of our foreign policy? To a vast number of Americans the Lodge reservations, far from nullifying the treaty, actually improved it. This was so apparent to even the most loyal Democrats in the Senate that Wilson could barely keep them in line.

In the final analysis the treaty was slain in the house of its friends rather than in the house of its enemies. In the final analysis it was not the two-thirds rule, or the "irreconcilables," or Lodge, or the "strong" and "mild reservationists," but Wilson and his docile following who delivered the fatal stab. If the President had been permitted to vote he would have sided with Borah, Brandegee, Johnson, and the other "bitter-enders"—though for entirely different reasons.

Wilson had said that the reservation to Article X was a knife thrust at the heart of the Covenant. Ironically, he parried this knife thrust, and stuck his own dagger, not into the heart of the Covenant, but into the entire treaty.

This was the supreme act of infanticide. With his own sickly hands Wilson slew his own brain child—or the one to which he had contributed so much.

This was the supreme paradox. He who had forced the Allies to write the League into the treaty, unwrote it; he who had done more than any other man to make the Covenant, unmade it—at least so far as America was concerned. And by his action, he contributed powerfully to the ultimate undoing of the League, and with it the high hopes of himself and mankind for an organization to prevent World War II.

The preceding dogmatic observations are of course qualified by the phrase, "in the last analysis."

Many elements enter into a log jam. Among them are the width of the stream, the depth of the stream, the swiftness of the current, the presence of boulders, the size of the logs, and the absence of enough lumberjacks. No one of these factors can be solely responsible for the pile-up.

Many elements entered into the legislative log jam of March, 1920.

Among them were isolationism, partisanship, senatorial prerogative, confusion, apathy, personal pride, and private feuds. No one of them was solely responsible for the pile-up. *But as the pile-up finally developed, there was only one lumberjack who could break it, and that was Woodrow Wilson.* If at any time before the final vote he had told the Senate Democrats to support the treaty with the Lodge reservations, or even if he had merely told them that they were on their own, the pact would almost certainly have been approved. So "in the last analysis" the primary responsibility for the failure in March rested with Wilson.

What about Lodge? If the treaty would have passed by Wilson's surrendering, it is not equally true that it would have passed by Lodge's surrendering?

The answer is probably "Yes," but the important point is that Lodge had far less responsibility for getting the treaty through than Wilson. If Lodge had yielded, he probably would have created a schism within his ranks. His ultimate responsibility was to keep the party from breaking to pieces, and in this he succeeded. Wilson's ultimate responsibility was to get the treaty ratified, and in this he failed. With Lodge, as with any truly partisan leader, the party comes before country; with the President the country should come before party, though unhappily it often does not.

It is possible that Wilson saw all this—but not clearly enough. He might have been willing to compromise if his adversary had been any other than Lodge. But so bitter was the feeling between the two men that Wilson, rather than give way, grasped at the straw of the election of 1920.

Lodge did not like Wilson either, but he made more of a show of compromising than the President. He actually supported and drove through amendments to his original reservations which were in line with Wilson's wishes, and he probably would have gone further had the "irreconcilables" not been on his back. He fought the crippling Irish reservation, as well as others supported by the "bitter-enders." Finally, he gave the Democrats a fair chance to reconsider their vote and get on the bandwagon, but they spurned it.

If Lodge's words mean anything, and if his actions were not those of a monstrous hypocrite, he actually tried to get the treaty through with his reservations. When he found that he could not, he washed his hands of the whole business in disgust.

The charge is frequently made that, if Wilson had yielded to his adversary, Lodge would have gleefully piled on more reservations until Wilson, further humiliated, would have had to throw out the whole thing.

The strongest evidence for this view is a circumstantial story which Secretary [of Agriculture] Houston relates. During a Cabinet meeting Wilson was called to the telephone, and agreed to make certain concessions agreeable to Lodge. Before adjournment the telephone rang again, and word came that Lodge would not adhere to his original proposal.

This story is highly improbable, because Wilson attended no Cabinet meetings between September 2, 1919, and April 13, 1920. By the latter date, all serious attempts at compromise had been dropped; by the earlier date the treaty was still before the Senate committee, and the Lodge reservations, though in an embryonic stage, were yet unborn. But, even if the story is true, it merely proves that Lodge veered about, as he frequently did under "irreconcilable" pressure.

In March, as in November, all Wilson had to do was to send over Postmaster General Burleson to the Senate a few minutes before the final vote with the quiet word that the Democrats were to vote "Yea." The treaty would then have passed with the Lodge reservations, and Lodge could hardly have dared incur for himself or his party the odium of moving to reconsider for the purpose of screwing on more reservations. Had he tried to do so, the "mild reservationists" almost certainly would have blocked him.

A few days after the disastrous final vote, Wilson's only comment to Tumulty was, "They have shamed us in the eyes of the world." If his previous words said what he really meant, he was hardly more shamed by the defeat of the treaty than by the addition of the Lodge reservations. In his eyes it all amounted to the same thing.

If the treaty had passed, would the President have been willing to go through with the exchange of ratifications? Would he not have pocketed it, as he threatened to do prior to the November vote?

Again, if Wilson's words may be taken at their face value, this is what he would have done. He had not backed down from his pre-November position. His Jackson Day message and his letter to Hitchcock made it unmistakably clear that he preferred the uncertainties of a political campaign to the certainties of ratification with the Lodge reservations. The addition of the indefensible Irish reservation provided even stronger justification for pocketing the entire pact.

It is probable that some of the loyal Democrats voted as they did partly because they were convinced that Wilson was going to pigeonhole the treaty anyhow. From their point of view it was better that the odium for defeat should seemingly rest on Lodge rather than on their President. It also seems clear that Wilson preferred, as in November, to have the blood of the treaty on the Senate doorstep rather than on his. As he wrote to Secretary [of State] Colby, on April 2, 1920, the slain pact lay heavily on the consciences of those who had stabbed it, and he was quite willing to have it lie there until those consciences were either awakened or crushed.

Yet it is one thing to say, just before Senate action, "I will pocket the treaty." It is another, after the pact is approved and sent to the White House, to assume this tremendous responsibility. The eyes of the world are upon the President; he is the only man keeping the nation out of the peace which it so urgently needs; he is the one man standing in the way of the rehabilitation which the world so desperately demands. Public pressure to ratify in such a case would be enormous—probably irresistible.

Some years later Senator Hitchcock said that in the event of senatorial approval Wilson would possibly have waited for the November election. If he had won, he would have worked for the removal of the Lodge reservations; if he had lost, then the compulsion to go through with ratification would have become overpowering. By November more than six months would have passed, and by that time Wilson might have developed a saner perspective.

But this is all speculation. Wilson gave orders that the treaty was to be killed in the Senate chamber. And there it died.

One other line of inquiry must be briefly pursued. Is it true, as some writers allege, that the thirty-odd Allied signatories of the original treaty would have rejected the Lodge reservations when officially presented? We recall that under the terms of the preamble these nations were privileged to acquiesce silently or file objections.

One will never know the answer to this question, because Wilson denied the other signatories a chance to act. But it seems proper to point to certain probabilities.

One or more of the Latin American nations might have objected to the reservation regarding the then hated Monroe Doctrine. Yet the Monroe Doctrine would have continued to exist anyhow; it was already in the Covenant; and these neighboring republics might well have swallowed their pride in the interest of world peace.

Italy probably would have acquiesced, and the evidence is strong that France would have done likewise. The Japanese could not completely overlook the Shantung reservation, but it was generally recognized in their press as meaningless, and for this reason it might have been tolerated, though not without some loss of face. It is noteworthy that the most important Japanese newspapers regretted the Senate stalemate as an encouragement to world instability, particularly in China.

Great Britain probably would have been the chief objector. The reservation on Ireland was highly offensive but completely innocuous, for the British lion had long endured Irish-American tail-twistings in pained but dignified silence. The reservation on six-to-one was a slap at the loyal and sacrificing Dominions, but it did not mean that their vote was to be taken away. Moreover, the contingency envisaged by this proviso was unlikely to arise very often, and in the long run would doubtless have proved inconsequential.

In sum, there were only two or three reservations to which the outside powers could seriously object. If they had objected, it is probable that a satisfactory adjustment could have been threshed out through diplomatic channels. For when it became clear that only a few phrases stood between the United States and peace, the dictates of common sense and the pressure of public opinion probably would have led to an acceptable compromise. If the Senate had refused to give ground in such a case, then the onus would have been clearly on it and not on Wilson. . . .

3. Wilson Defended

Arthur S. Link, author of a multi-volume biography of Wilson, recognizes the President's mistakes and defects but points out that Wilson had serious and defensible objections on high policy grounds to many of the Lodge Reservations.

Wilson the Diplomatist

ARTHUR S. LINK

. . . Virtually all historians now agree that Wilson's refusal to permit his followers in the Senate to approve the treaty with the Lodge reservations was an error of tragic magnitude. Having built so grandly at Paris, having fought so magnificently at home for his creation, he then proceeded by his own hand to remove the cornerstone of his edifice of peace. Why? Were there inner demons of pride and arrogance driving him to what one historian has called "the supreme infanticide"? Did his illness and seclusion prevent him from obtaining a realistic view of the parliamentary situation, or so disarrange him emotionally that he became incompetent in the tasks of statesmanship? Or was he simply an idealist who would make no compromises on what he thought were fundamental principles?

The historian, who sees through a glass darkly when probing the recesses of the mind, is not able to give final answers to questions like these. Wilson, for all his high-mindedness and nobility of character, was headstrong and not much given to dealing graciously or to compromising with men whom he distrusted and disliked. Once before, in a violent dispute at Princeton over control of the graduate school, he had revealed these same traits and suffered defeat because he could not work with men whom he did not trust. The sympathetic biographer would like to believe that it was his illness, which aggravated his bitterness and his sense of self-righteousness, that drove Wilson to his fatal choice. Perhaps this is true. He had not always been incapable of compromise; perhaps he would have yielded in the end if disease had not dethroned his reason.

These attempts to extenuate ignore the fact that there were fundamental and vital issues at stake in the controversy over the treaty— whether the United States would take leadership in the League of Nations without hesitations and reservations, or whether it would join the League grudgingly and with no promises to help maintain universal collective security. To Wilson the difference between what he fought for and what Lodge and the Republicans would agree to was the difference between the success or failure and the life or death of man's best hope for peace. This he had said on his western tour, at a time when his health and reasoning faculties were unimpaired. This he believed with his heart and soul. It is, therefore, possible, even probable, that Wilson would have acted as he did even had he not suffered his breakdown, for it was not in his nature to compromise away the principles in which he believed.

If this is true, then in this, the last and greatest effort of his life, Wilson spurned the role of statesman for what he must have thought was the nobler role of prophet. The truth is that the American people were not prepared in 1920 to assume the world leadership that Wilson offered them, and that the powers of the world were not yet ready to enforce the worldwide, universal system of collective security that the President had created.

Arthur S. Link, *Wilson the Diplomatist* (Baltimore: the Johns Hopkins Press, 1957), 153–156. Reprinted with permission.

Collective security failed in the portentous tests of the 1930's, not because the League's machinery was defective, but because the people of the world, not merely the American people alone, were unwilling to confront aggressors with the threat of war. As a result a second and more terrible world conflict came, as Wilson prophesied it would, and at its end the United States helped to build a new and different league of nations and took the kind of international leadership that Wilson had called for. But events of the past decade have not fully justified Wilson's confidence in international organization; the only really promising systems of collective security, the regional ones like NATO, have been of a kind that Wilson fervently denounced; and only the future can reveal whether his dream of a universal system can ever be made a reality.

And so it was Wilson the prophet, demanding greater commitment, sacrifice, and idealism than the people could give, who was defeated in 1920. It is also Wilson the prophet who survives in history, in the hopes and aspirations of mankind and in whatever ideals of international service that the American people still cherish. One thing is certain, now that men have the power to sear virtually the entire face of the earth: The prophet of 1919 was right in his larger vision; the challenge that he raised then is today no less real and no less urgent than it was in his own time.

Additional Reading

Selig Adler, *The Isolationist Impulse: Its Twentieth Century Reaction* (1957).

R. J. Bartlett, *The League to Enforce Peace* (1944).

Dana F. Fleming, *The United States and the League of Nations, 1918–1920* (1942).

John A. Garraty, *Henry Cabot Lodge* (1953).

W. Stull Holt, *Treaties Defeated by the Senate* (1933).

Rayford W. Logan, *The Senate and the Versailles Mandate System* (1945).

15 *THE TWENTIES:* *Isolationist?*

Senatorial rejection of the Versailles Peace Treaty and the subsequent Republican victory in the 1920 presidential election has usually been interpreted by historians as the beginning of a long period of isolationist foreign policies by the United States. Some have drawn graphic pictures of Uncle Sam, ostrich-like, burying his head in the sand and turning his back on world affairs in order to concentrate on the feverish boom of domestic prosperity. The period 1920–1933 thus seemed almost a disgraceful interlude between the earlier internationalism of Wilson and the later era of Franklin D. Roosevelt.

Yet study of the decade after 1920 reveals contradictory phenomena. On the one hand, the United States refused to join the League of Nations, raised its tariff rates to astronomical heights, refused to recognize a connection between German reparations and Allied ability to repay the war debts, and attached reservations disavowing any enforcement responsibility to most of the international agreements it approved. Conversely, the American government participated in several arms limitation conferences, cooperated increasingly in various League specialized functions and projects, helped launch the multilateral Pact of Paris denouncing aggressive warfare, and proclaimed during the depression a moratorium on collection of intergovernmental debts.

Perhaps the most satisfying interpretation of this rather confused period has been offered by Selig Adler, *The Isolationist Impulse* (1957). He sees the decade as neither isolationist by 19th-century standards nor as fully internationalist as were the eras of Wilson and F.D.R. Instead, it was characterized by "neo-isolationism," marked on the governmental level by limited international participation and the avoidance of binding political-military obligations. On the public level, most Americans were increasingly disillusioned and determined to avoid embroilments abroad, while a minority of devoted Wilsonians continued to struggle for the assumption of a larger role in international affairs.

DOCUMENTS

1. Economic Isolationism

The mixed character of the period is indicated by the following two documents. Wilson vetoed in 1921 the first of the high postwar tariffs, on the grounds that it would make repayment of the war debts difficult and would adversely affect world free trade. After his departure from office, and despite the warnings of many economists, the tariff was successfully raised in 1922 and again in 1930. Yet in 1931, as the world depression was deepening, President Herbert Hoover recognized a degree of American economic responsibility in proposing a "holiday" on payments of intergovernmental debts.

Wilson's Tariff Veto Message, March 3, 1921

I return herewith without my approval H. R. 15275, an act imposing temporary duties upon certain agricultural products to meet present emergencies, to provide revenue, and for other purposes. . . .

One does not pay a compliment to the American farmer who attempts to alarm him by dangers from foreign competition. The American farmers are the most effective agricultural producers in the world. Their production is several times as great for each worker as that of their principal foreign rivals. This grows out of the intelligence of the American farmer, the nature of his agricultural practices and economy, and the fact that he has the assistance of scientific and practical agencies which in respect to variety of activity, of personnel, and of financial support exceed those of any other two or three nations in the world combined. There is little doubt that the farmers of this Nation will not only continue mainly to supply the home demand but will be increasingly called upon to supply a large part of the needs of the rest of the world.

What the farmer now needs is not only a better system of domestic marketing and credit, but especially larger foreign markets for his surplus products. Clearly measures of this sort will not conduce to an expansion of the foreign market. . . .

I imagine there is little doubt that while this measure is temporary it is intended as a foundation for action of a similar nature of a very general and permanent character. It would seem to be designed to pave the way for such action. If there ever was a time when America had anything to fear from foreign competition, that time has passed. I can not believe that American producers, who in most respects are the most effective in the world, can have any dread of competition when they view the fact that their country has come through the great struggle of the last few years, relatively speaking, untouched, while their principal competitors are in varying degrees sadly stricken and laboring under adverse conditions from which they will not recover for many years. Changes of a very radical character have taken place. The United States has become a great creditor Nation. She has lent certain Governments of Europe more than $9,000,000,000, and as a result of the enormous excess of our exports there is an additional commercial indebtedness of foreign nations to our own of perhaps not less than $4,000,000,000. There are only three ways in which Europe can meet her part of her indebtedness, namely, by the establishment of private credits, by the shipment of gold, or of commodities. It is difficult for Europe to discover the requisite securities as a basis for the necessary credits. Europe is not in a position at the present time to send us the amount of gold which would be needed, and we could not view further large imports of gold into this country without concern. The result, to say the least, would be a larger disarrangement of international exchange and disturbance of international trade. If we wish to have Europe settle her debts, governmental or commercial, we must be prepared to buy from her, and if we wish to assist Europe and ourselves by the export either of food, of raw materials, or finished products, we must be prepared to welcome commodities which we need and which Europe will be prepared, with no little pain, to send us.

Clearly, this is no time for the erection here of high-tariff barriers. It would strike a blow at the large and successful efforts which have been made by many of our great industries to place themselves on an export basis. It would stand in the way of the normal readjustment of business conditions throughout the world, which is as vital to the welfare of this country as to that of all the other nations. The United States has a duty to itself as well as to the world, and it can discharge this duty by widening, not by contracting, its world markets. . . .

The Hoover Debt Moratorium, 1931

The American Government proposes the postponement during one year of all payments on intergovernmental debts, reparations and relief debts, both principal and interest, of course, not including obligations of governments held by private parties. Subject to confirmation by Congress, the American Government will postpone all payments upon the debts of foreign governments to the American Government payable during the fiscal year beginning July 1 next, conditional on a like postponement for one year of all payments on intergovernmental debts owing the important creditor powers. . . .

The purpose of this action is to give the forthcoming year to the economic recovery of the world and to help free the recuperative forces already in motion in the United States from retarding influences from abroad.

The world-wide depression has affected the countries of Europe more severely than our own. Some of these countries are feeling to a serious extent the drain of this depression on national economy. The fabric of intergovernmental debts, supportable in normal times, weighs heavily in the midst of this depression.

From a variety of causes arising out of the depression such as the fall in the price of foreign commodities and the lack of confidence in economic and political stability abroad there is an abnormal movement of gold into the United States which is lowering the credit stability of many foreign countries. These and the other difficulties abroad diminish buying power for our exports and in a measure are the cause of our continued unemployment and continued lower prices to our farmers.

Wise and timely action should contribute to relieve the pressure of these adverse forces in foreign countries and should assist in the reestablishment of confidence, thus forwarding political peace and economic stability in the world. . . .

I wish to take this occasion also to frankly state my views upon our relations to German reparations and the debts owed to us by the allied Governments of Europe. Our government has not been a party to, or exerted any voice in determination of reparation obligations. We purposely did not participate in either general reparations or the division of colonies or property. The repayment of debts due to us from the Allies for the advance for war and reconstruction were settled upon a basis not contingent upon German reparations or related thereto. Therefore, reparations is necessarily wholly a European problem with which we have no relation.

I do not approve in any remote sense of the cancellation of the debts to us. World confidence would not be enhanced by such action. None of our debtor nations has ever suggested it. But as the basis of the settlement of these debts was the capacity under normal conditions of the debtor to pay, we should be consistent with our own policies and principles if we take into account the abnormal situation now existing in the world. I am sure the American people have no desire to attempt to extract any sum beyond the capacity of any debtor to pay and it is our view that broad vision requires that our government should recognize the situation as it exists. . . .

2. Limited Participation

Internationalists did win a limited victory in the 1920's in persuading a majority of Americans that it was safe to join the World Court. Yet the Senate attached reservations to its approval in 1926 which other signatories would not accept, particularly the fifth reservation concerning advisory opinions. Presidents Hoover and Roosevelt also failed in attempts to get favorable senatorial action, despite indications that a majority of citizens and members of the Senate were in approval. The Kellogg-Briand Pact or Treaty of Paris of 1928, condemning aggressive warfare but containing no enforcement provisions, thus represented the outer limits of participation in world affairs and the assumption of international responsibilities in the 1920's. Even so, in granting its approval the Senate Foreign Relations Committee attached interpretations safeguarding the right of self-defense and disavowing any obligation to enforce the pact against transgressors.

Reservations by the Senate to Joining the World Court, January 27, 1926

Resolved (*two-thirds of the Senators present concurring*), That the Senate advise and consent to the adherence on the part of the United States to the said protocol of December 16, 1920, and the adjoined statute for the Permanent Court of International Justice (without accepting or agreeing to the optional clause for compulsory jurisdiction contained in said statute), and that the signature of the United States be affixed to the said protocol, subject to the following reservations and understandings, which are hereby made a part and condition of this resolution, namely:

1. That such adherence shall not be taken to involve any legal relation on the part of the United States to the League of Nations or the assumption of any obligations by the United States under the treaty of Versailles. . . .

4. That the United States may at any time withdraw its adherence to the said protocol and that the statute for the Permanent Court of Inter-

national Justice adjoined to the protocol shall not be amended without the consent of the United States.

5. That the court shall not render any advisory opinion except publicly after due notice to all states adhering to the court and to all interested states and after public hearing or opportunity for hearing given to any state concerned; nor shall it, without the consent of the United States, entertain any request for an advisory opinion touching any dispute or question in which the United States has or claims an interest.

The signature of the United States to the said protocol shall not be affixed until the powers signatory to such protocol shall have indicated, through an exchange of notes, their acceptance of the foregoing reservations and understandings as a part and a condition of adherence by the United States to the said protocol.

Resolved further, As a part of this act of ratification that the United States approve the protocol and statute hereinabove mentioned, with the understanding that recourse to the Permanent Court of International Justice for the settlement of differences between the United States and any other state or states can be had only by agreement thereto through general or special treaties concluded between the parties in dispute; and

Resolved further, That adherence to the said protocol and statute hereby approved shall not be so construed as to require the United States to depart from its traditional policy of not intruding upon, interfering with, or entangling itself in the political questions of policy or internal administration of any foreign state; nor shall adherence to the said protocol and statute be construed to imply a relinquishment by the United States of its traditional attitude toward purely American questions.

The Kellogg-Briand Pact, August 27, 1928

Article I. The High Contracting Parties solemnly declare in the names of their respective peoples that they condemn recourse to war for the solution of international controversies, and renounce it as an instrument of national policy in their relations with one another.

Article II. The High Contracting Parties agree that the settlement or solution of all disputes or conflicts of whatever nature or of whatever origin they may be, which may arise among them, shall never be sought except by pacific means.

Article III. The present Treaty shall be ratified by the High Contracting Parties named in the Preamble in accordance with their respective constitutional requirements, and shall take effect as between them as soon as all their several instruments of ratification shall have been deposited at Washington. . . .

READINGS

1. The Return to Normalcy: Isolationism

John D. Hicks, a respected authority on Populism and recent American history, portrays the diplomacy of prosperous and isolationist America as ranging from restrictive immigration laws and an insistence on full repayment of the war debts to conclusion of that innocuous international gesture of good-will, the Pact of Paris.

The Diplomacy of Isolation

JOHN D. HICKS

Coolidge prosperity and American isolationism were in a sense two sides of the same coin. Whatever the American people might have thought about the subject during the debate on the Treaty of Versailles, most of them as the years wore on tended to accept as right and proper a minimum of American involvement in foreign affairs. American prosperity seemed to vindicate Harding's decision to turn his back on the League and the world, and Coolidge was not the man to embark upon any dangerous changes of direction.

There is reason to believe that Secretary Hughes accepted the return to isolation with considerable misgivings, but he was wise enough to know that the President, whatever his shortcomings, makes American foreign policy, not the Secretary of State. At first Hughes even failed to acknowledge the communications the United States received from the League of Nations, but when he saw that this gave offense, he corrected the error. Also, he arranged that the United States, through unofficial observers, should keep in touch with League affairs. When the American Bar Association met in London in July, 1924, as guests of the British bar, Hughes, who attended as president of the visiting group, took advantage of the opportunity to spell out American foreign policy, as he saw it, in precise detail. The United States, he said in a public address, was a nonaggressor nation devoted to peace; it would co-operate fully with other nations in the promotion of public health and other humanitarian enterprises, such as checking the trade of narcotics; it would give its support to institutions of international justice; and it would help with the economic rehabilitation of Europe, but by means other than direct governmental aid. Hughes's efforts to maintain international good manners worried some of the extreme isolationists, among them Senator Hiram Johnson of California, who privately questioned the Secretary's good faith, and as a member of the Senate Committee on Foreign Relations gloomily expressed his hope to delay, even if he could not prevent, "our going into Europe in one form or another."

The new immigration policy of the postwar years served to emphasize the wish of the American people to cut as completely as possible the ties that bound them to the Old World. During the war the double loyalties

Pp. 130–146, 149–152 Republican Ascendancy, 1921–1933, by John D. Hicks. Copyright © 1960 by John D. Hicks. Reprinted with the permission of Harper & Row, Publishers, Incorporated.

of certain "hyphenate" groups had aroused much criticism, and after the war the "red hysteria" undoubtedly contributed further to the conviction that the American nation had taken in about as many foreigners as it could digest. Organized labor had long expressed disapproval of letting in immigrants to compete in the American job market, and industry, with a steady backlog of unemployed from which to draw, offered little more than token objection to restriction. One of the first acts of the Harding administration was the Emergency Quota Act, signed May 19, 1921, which limited the number of aliens of any nationality who might be admitted in any fiscal year "to 3 per centum of the number of foreign-born persons of such nationality resident in the United States as determined by the United States census of 1910." The Act was originally designed to last for one year only, but it was later extended until 1924.

By that time experience had shown that the assigned quotas were permitting far more immigrants to enter the United States than Congress had intended—the total for 1924 exceeded 700,000; also, the law failed to discriminate as much as its proponents had hoped against immigrants from southern and eastern Europe. The Immigration Act of 1924, therefore, reduced the annual quota of each nationality to 2 per cent, and for the next three years shifted the computation of quotas to the census of 1890. The law stated that after 1927, however, the annual quota for each nationality was no longer to be computed from the number of foreign-born in the United States at any given time, but from "the number of inhabitants in 1920 whose origin by birth *or ancestry*" could be attributed to a given national area. And the annual quota of any nationality was to be a number which would bear "the same relationship to 150,000 as the number of inhabitants in continental United States in 1920 having that national origin" bore to the total number of inhabitants for the same year. To the Secretaries of State, Commerce, and Labor fell the thankless task of fixing quotas, but they found "national origins" so difficult to determine that the application of this aspect of the law was postponed from 1927 to 1929. The effect of the Act of 1924 was to hold immigration from 1925 to 1930 down to an annual average of about 300,000; and for the next ten years after that, with the help of the depression, to an annual average of about 50,000. The new Immigration Act thus marked the end of an era. The United States was no longer the refuge of the world's poor and oppressed; the Statue of Liberty now lifted her lamp only for a favored few.

The Act of 1924 made certain other innovations. Quotas established under the Act of 1921 applied only to Europe, the Near East, Africa, and Australia; for the Western Hemisphere there were no restrictions, and for certain Asiatic countries, notably Japan, other and special arrangements provided for virtual exclusion. The new law still permitted free access to the United States for immigrants from Canada, Newfoundland, and all the independent American republics, but it extended the quota system to the rest of the world, allowing to each nation a minimum of 100 immigrants, with this notable exception, that "No alien ineligible to citizenship shall be admitted to the United States." It was obvious that this clause was aimed directly at Japan, although the Gentlemen's Agreement of Theodore Roosevelt's administration was accomplishing the same end without a direct prohibition. But anti-Japanese sentiment on the Pacific Coast was strong, and Congress yielded to it the more readily when the Japanese ambassador announced that such a direct affront would have grave consequences. Japan, some congressmen implied, was threatening the United States. Secretary Hughes did his best to persuade Congress that this wanton insult to a supersensitive nation would destroy much of the good will achieved by the Washington Conference and by the generous American response to Japan's needs after the great earthquake of 1923. But Congress was not to be deterred, and Coolidge weakly signed the bill into law. Since the Supreme Court in *Ozawa* v. *the United States* (1922) had already decided that persons of Japanese birth were ineligible for naturalization, the effect of the law was crystal clear, and the reaction in Japan was extremely unfavorable. Congress by its thoughtless action had handed another weapon—popular hatred of the United States—to the Japanese militarists who plotted expansion in the Far East, even at the cost of war.

The Immigration Act of 1924 aroused much resentment also in Europe, particularly in Italy, where under the new quotas emigration to the United States dropped off by about nine-tenths. Because of the increased population pressure from which Italy suffered, Mussolini, whose attainment of power showed how unsafe the world was becoming for democracy, felt the freer to proceed with his program of colonial empire. Not only in Italy, but in many other countries also, the United States lost friends as the cruelties implicit in the law began to make themselves felt—wives denied permission to join their husbands in America, children separated from their parents, long quota waits for those who could go, detention and return for the ill-advised. Furthermore, the void left by the drop in European immigration tended to be filled in part by entrance into the United States of equally alien peoples from the Western Hemisphere, especially from Mexico, French Canada, and Puerto Rico. Also, there was a serious problem of enforcement, and the "bootlegging" of ineligibles into the United States, together with their occasional enforced return to their own country, added further to the international strain. Yet for the great majority of Americans there was no sign of regret over the policy of exclusion; the inequities in the law, most people agreed, should be ironed out, but the United States must never again open its portals to the Old World's "huddled masses yearning to breathe free."

There was something of this same spirit in the refusal of the United States to recognize the new government of Soviet Russia; if the actions of a given nation varied too much from what Americans regarded as proper, then its existence could simply be ignored. This policy, which the Harding administration inherited from its predecessor was by no means universally approved in the United States. Two senators, William E. Borah of Idaho and Joseph I. France of Maryland, took a particularly firm stand in favor of recognition. Borah was much influenced by Raymond Robins and other outstanding liberals, who believed that as long as the Russian problem remained unsettled the peace of Europe would remain unsettled, while France had visited Russia in the summer of 1921, had met the Bolshevik leaders, and had returned to the United States convinced that American recognition would help advance the conservative trend he thought he had seen in the Soviet Union. But Borah's Senate resolution favoring recognition was merely laid on the table, while France was ridiculed in the press as an "innocent abroad," or worse. On behalf of the administration, Secretary Hughes denied that the form of government adopted by Soviet Russia had anything to do with the official American attitude. The trouble, he said, was that the Soviet government had refused in three ways to accept its international obligations: (1) it had repudiated the debt it owed to the government of the United States, (2) it had confiscated the private property of American nationals, and (3) it had promoted propaganda in the United States that had as its object the overthrow of the American government. Borah, France, and others returned to the attack time after time, but Russian recognition was delayed until after the Roosevelt administration took office in 1933.

Nor was the American government disposed to promote in any way the resumption of normal trade relations between the United States and Soviet Russia. It had no objection to the mobilizing of American charity to help battle starvation during the Russian famine of 1921; according to Secretary Hoover the American Relief Administration spent $50 million for this purpose, and for the purchase of seed to be used in the 1922 planting. Nor was there any prohibition against individuals risking their property in trade with Russia, or even lending money to Russia if they so desired. But all Russian overtures for assistance from the United States government in reviving trade between the two nations were sternly discountenanced. The power of Russia to buy, Hughes maintained, depended on its ability to produce something to sell, and both he and Secretary Hoover implied in public statements that Russia could not hope to revive production until the Soviet government was ready to recognize the rights of private property.

Senator France argued for an American loan to Russia, the proceeds of which would enable the Soviets to pay claims against them and to buy American goods. But Hughes was adamant in his insistence that the Soviet government must demonstrate its willingness to guarantee within its borders the safety of life and property, the sanctity of contracts, and the rights of free labor before the United States would negotiate. The Russians made some effort to satisfy these conditions. At the Genoa Conference, which the nations of Europe held in the spring of 1922, a Russian representative told the American ambassador to Italy that, while Russia was unwilling to admit any such obligations as Hughes stipulated, it would in fact observe them with reference to Americans, if only the United States would recognize Russia. But again the United States was unresponsive. Whatever else the Department of State may have had in mind, it is obvious that it had no intention of doing anything that might in any way serve to perpetuate the Soviet system of government.

The United States also pursued an uncompromising policy, as long as it could, in its attempt to collect the intergovernmental debts due it from its former associates in the war, and from the succession states that the Peace of Paris had created in central and eastern Europe. Of the more than $10.3 billion so lent, only about $7 billion net was actually borrowed during the war, and not less than nine-tenths of this sum was used to pay for American goods purchased in the United States by the Allies. After the war was over the American government lent the war-torn nations of Europe an additional $3.3 billion in money and supplies for use in rehabilitation and relief. The American public should have distinguished between the war debts and these "peace debts," but it seldom did so; most Americans assumed that the European nations had borrowed the entire $10.3 billion for war purposes, and that ultimately they would repay these sums with interest—the rate, pending a postwar settlement, being set at 5 per cent.

The war was not long over before European nations began to take a very different view of debt repayment. To Americans the problem seemed simple: the United States had lent vast sums; the nations that had borrowed the money should pay back their loans. In Coolidge's words, "They hired the money, didn't they?" But to Europeans it was not that easy. In their view the war was fought for a common objective, and the victory was as essential for the safety of the United States as for their own. The United States had entered the struggle late, and had poured forth no such contribution in lives and losses as the Allies had made. It had paid in dollars, not in death and destruction, and now it wanted its dollars back— Uncle Shylock. Many Americans saw in this attitude only an attempt to defraud. A correspondent who had toured Europe wrote to Senator Johnson: "All of the peoples abroad look upon us as an international sucker from whom should be obtained by wheedling or otherwise part of our ill-gotten gains, but whom, during the process of relieving us of our funds, they regard with contempt, and about whom they laugh among themselves."

The real trouble was that the European nations had not the means with which to pay. Their gold had flowed in great quantity to the United States during the period of neutrality in payment for American goods; they could not send more without completely wrecking their currencies. Equally distressing was the American tariff policy; European nations could never hope to sell enough to the United States over its high tariff wall to enable them to build up the American balances they would need to liquidate their debts. The problem was further complicated by the debts that European nations owed each other, debts mainly due to loans the stronger Allies had made to the weaker before the United States became the chief banker for them all. Indeed, the British government had made loans comparable in face value to those made by the United States, and had actually lent more to the other Allies by many billions of dollars than it had borrowed from the United States. Protected by these mitigating circumstances, Great Britain took the lead as early as February, 1920, in broaching to the American government the subject of a general cancellation of war debts, pointing out the political and economic advantages that the adoption of such a policy would ensure.

Whatever the merits of the case, the American government showed no slightest disposition to accept the British overtures. Nor would it ever concede that the capacity of the Allies to repay the United States depended upon their ability to collect corresponding reparations from Germany. During the campaign of 1920, the Republicans denounced the Wilson administration for its failure to begin collections, and promised that as soon as they took office they would do better. When Secretary Mellon attempted to deliver on this promise, he found existing legislation inadequate to authorize the funding policy he had in mind, and asked Congress for plenary powers to deal with the problem. But Congress thought the matter too important for the Secretary of the Treasury to handle alone, and by an act of February 9, 1922, set up instead a World War Debt Funding Commission, consisting at first of five and by a later amendment of eight members, with the Secretary of the Treasury as chairman and the other members to be appointed by the President and confirmed by the Senate. (Among the appointive members, Harding chose Secretaries Hughes and Hoover.) The law also stipulated that loans should be repaid in twenty-five years, that the rate of interest charged should not be less than 4.25 per cent, and that there should be no cancellation of debts "except through payment thereof."

Smarting under the necessity, but consoled by the hope of collecting reparations from Germany, all the major debtors and most of the others—thirteen in all—eventually negotiated agreements with the Commission. In the negotiations the American representatives departed considerably from the instructions Congress had given them. While in each case they required ultimate payment in full of the principal, they spread the amortization over a period of sixty-two years instead of twenty-five, and they disregarded at will the high interest rate set by Congress. This policy meant that each agreement would have to be submitted to Congress for approval, but the commissioners realized, even if Congress did not, that the alternative would be no agreements at all. Throughout the negotiations the commissioners kept one eye on the capacity of each debtor nation to pay and the other on what minimum terms Congress would be willing to accept. They reached their first settlement with Great Britain in July, 1923, after six months of negotiation. The British representatives were shocked at the interest rates the American negotiators demanded, for the prewar borrowing rates in England had been much lower, and the American ambassador to Great Britain, Colonel George Harvey, had given them reason to expect a 2 per cent rate instead of the 3.3 per cent that the American commissioners demanded. Eventually the British government accepted the sixty-two year, 3.3 per cent terms as the best it could get.

The British agreement served as a model for the others, but Great Britain was the only wartime borrower to be charged so high a rate of interest. The other nations that agreed to pay 3.3 per cent on their loans were Czechoslovakia, Estonia, Finland, Hungary, Latvia, Lithuania, Poland, and Rumania, none of whom had borrowed from the United States until after the signing of the armistice, and all of whom owed comparatively small sums. For the remaining borrowers there were greatly reduced interest rates, for Belgium 1.8 per cent, for France 1.6 per cent, for

Italy 0.4 per cent, and for Yugoslavia 1 per cent. The terms of payment also differed considerably from country to country—Belgium, for example, was charged no interest on her pre-armistice debt, while France and Italy were not required to pay interest for the first five years of their indebtedness. But had the debts been paid in accordance with the agreements, the interest rates would have averaged out about as indicated. The life of the Commission expired by law on February 9, 1927; thereafter the Treasury Department worked out such agreements with other borrowers as were deemed necessary and possible. Among the impossible was the settlement of the Russian debt to the United States, which, however, was only $192 million, a small sum in comparison with Russia's debt to Great Britain of $4.3 billion.

Whatever the United States chose to pretend regarding the divorcement of war debts and reparations, in actual practice the two subjects were closely intertwined. By the much-debated war guilt clause, the Treaty of Versailles had required Germany to accept for herself and her allies the responsibility "for causing all the loss and damage to which the Allied and Associated Governments and their nationals have been subjected as a consequence of the war imposed upon them by the aggression of Germany and her allies." This clause in itself aroused great resentment, for few Germans believed that the Central Powers alone were responsible for the outbreak of war in 1914. Allied reliance upon the war-guilt thesis as the sole reason tor demanding reparations made matters even worse. Had the victors merely assumed that they had the right to make the vanquished pay because they had lost the war, there would have been less room for argument. As it was, Germans could maintain with reason that the demand for reparations had no more validity than the charge of war guilt. Partly on this account neither the German government nor the German people ever really accepted the obligation of reparations payments; lacking any will to pay, their goal became instead the avoidance of payment. As Germans saw it, the Treaty of Versailles, by trimming Germany's borders at many vital spots, and by dividing her colonies among the victors, had gone far enough; the demand for reparations in addition was both unjust and unrealistic. Some Americans agreed. "I should like to see the 'sole guilt' fallacy rejected once and for all," wrote Senator Borah a few years later. "It is to the benefit of no one to maintain a false contention which serves only to keep alive resentment and retard the good faith and amity which we ought in every way to seek to foster and maintain. There was no 'sole guilt' as to that war."

Since the negotiators at Paris were unable to agree upon the total reparations bill, they put off for a period of two years the determination of the final figure; during this interval, however, they required Germany to pay nearly $5 billion in cash or in goods. The rest of the debt was to be determined by a Reparations Commission consisting of representatives from Great Britain, the United States, France, Italy, and, in alternation, Japan and Belgium. Failure of the United States to ratify the treaty cost Germany its only possible friend on the Commission; the other members differed only as to how much they thought they could get. When the

Commission reported in the spring of 1921, it proposed the colossal sum of $33 billion to be paid during a period of still undetermined length, but with an expectation of about $375 million each year from 1921 to 1925, and about $900 million each year thereafter. The Commission might reduce either the debt or the interest charges, but the Allied governments could punish by the armed invasion of German territory any willful defaults. Efforts to collect the huge sums expected proved to be singularly fruitless, but such payments as were made, together with the disruptions that the war had bequeathed to the German economy, led to a runaway inflation in Germany that virtually destroyed the middle class and undermined the authority of the new Weimar Republic. In January, 1923, over the opposition of Great Britain, the Reparations Commission declared Germany in willful default, and the troops of France and Belgium occupied the Ruhr Valley, the greatest industrial district left to Germany. But the military demonstration solved no problems, and made more; passive resistance in the Ruhr cut down on German production, while in France inflation began to mount ominously.

However much the United States might wish to remain isolated from Europe, there was no escaping the fact that the economic collapse of Germany would be a matter of almost as grave concern to Americans as to Europeans. Not only were the problems of war debts and reparations involved but also the economic health of Europe as a whole. American trade with Europe was vital to American prosperity; with the reparations problem unsolved that trade could not follow its natural lines. Secretary Hughes, who well understood that American isolation was a myth, began even before the invasion of the Ruhr to take a hand in the diplomatic game. Speaking before the American Historical Association in New Haven, Connecticut, he suggested on December 29, 1922, the creation of an international commission of experts to determine how much Germany was able to pay, and how the payments were to be made. "I have no doubt," he added, "that distinguished Americans would be willing to serve in such a commission." But the French were unwilling to accept this arrangement until the fall of 1923, when it became evident that the Ruhr invasion would accomplish nothing. They then joined with the other Allies in devising a plan whereby the Reparations Commission should appoint two committees, one to concentrate principally on problems of the German currency and budget, and the other on the recovery of German holdings from abroad. To head the first committee the choice fell upon an American, Charles Gates Dawes, and the agreements the committees reached became known as the Dawes Plan. Most Americans acquiesced readily in this limited degree of American participation in European affairs, but to a few extreme isolationists anything of the kind remained a base betrayal.

Whether Hughes was "the real author and spiritual father of the Dawes Plan," as a German journalist claimed, or Dawes himself, the program that the experts devised seemed to make sense. It recognized that there were two separate problems involved, (1) the attainment of solvency by the German government, with an annual excess of receipts over expendi-

tures, and (2) the actual transfer to the Allies of surplus sums so accumulated. First of all Germany had to have a stable currency. To this end the
Dawes Plan proposed an international loan of $200 million in gold, the
reorganization of the Reichsbank under Allied supervision, and the issuance of a new monetary unit, the reichsmark, with a gold value of 23.8
U.S. cents. As for reparations, the plan set no precise figure, but, on the
basis of careful study of Germany's capacity to pay, it proposed a gradu-
ated schedule of annuities, beginning at $250 million the first year and
rising over a period of five years to a normal expectation of $625 million;
this sum, however, could be increased or reduced as German prosperity
rose or fell. During the first two years the German government might meet
its obligations in part from the international loan, but it was also required
to bond and mortgage its railways and principal industries, and to use the
proceeds along with taxes to make the stipulated payments. The Dawes
Plan also provided safeguards to prevent reparations payments from
"threatening the stability of the German currency." While the German
government must make all payments as scheduled, these funds would remain in Germany until such a time as the exchange market justified their
transfer. An Agent General for Reparations Payments, to be appointed by
the Reparations Commission, was to co-ordinate and supervise these activities.

The Dawes Plan, after acceptance by both Germany and the Allies,
went into effect September 1, 1924, and for a time seemed to work reason-
ably well. It carried with it a separate agreement for the withdrawal of
foreign troops from the Ruhr, a process that began at once and ended on
July 31, 1925. The international loan was readily subscribed, with over
half the money coming from American investors, and other measures that
the Plan called for were gradually effected. For a time the revival of the
German economy seemed assured. The choice of S. Parker Gilbert of
Morgan and Company as Agent General proved to be singularly felicitous,
and the German government profited greatly from his advice. It was Gilbert's opinion, however, that Germany must eventually be left "to perform
on her own responsibility," while with the fulfillment of the German disarmament program it also seemed reasonable that the foreign troops still
stationed in the Rhineland should be removed.

Eventually another committee of experts, headed by another American,
Owen D. Young, produced a new set of agreements even more favorable
to Germany than those of the Dawes Plan. The representatives of fifteen
nations, including Germany, signed the preliminary terms at The Hague,
August 31, 1929, in the presence of an American observer. This time Germany's total liability was set definitely at a little more than $8 billion, with
interest at 5.5 per cent, the payments to be distributed over a period of
58.5 years. The new plan required "unconditional" annuities of only $153
million, much less than the payments required by the Dawes Plan, but,
oddly enough, about equal to the total sums the Allied nations had agreed
to pay each year on their war debts to the United States. "Conditional"
payments, which depended on German prosperity, and ran much higher,
were secured by a mortgage on the German railways. The problem of

turning German marks into foreign currencies now became the responsibility of the German government, which would work through a new Bank of International Settlements set up by the Allies at Basel, Switzerland. Whereas the Dawes Plan was meant to be merely temporary, the Young Plan was regarded as "final and definitive." As further evidence that the Allies now regarded Germany as trustworthy, they withdrew the rest of their troops from German soil.

During the five years of the Dawes Plan and the first two of the Young Plan the German government met its reparations payments regularly, although it was usually forced to borrow in order to balance its budget. But confidence in German recovery was high, and there were plenty of investors who were ready to purchase German securities, both within and without Germany. It was the outside borrowing that enabled Germany to keep up with its reparations payments. Not only the various German governmental units, federal state and municipal, borrowed heavily from foreign investors, but German business firms, banks, and public utilities also followed this course. Precise figures on the amount of outside capital that flowed into Germany during these years are hard to get, but undoubtedly the American loans alone were not less than the $2.6 billion that the United States collected from the Allies prior to July 1, 1931, on their war debts. The direct relation between German reparations and Allied payments to the United States on war debts could hardly have been more obvious. What happened in effect was that Germany used the credits provided by outside investors, at least in part, to pay its reparations bills, while the Allies used that portion of these credits furnished by American investors to meet their war-debt payments to the United States. Thus the sums that the American Treasury collected from European debtor nations came in reality from the American people. More than that, the export of American capital to foreign borrowers, regardless of nationality, did much to support the business boom of the 1920's in the United States. Few people seemed to realize that the American nation was not only sending American goods abroad in gratifying volume, but that it was also sending along the money with which to pay for them. When finally American investors cut down on their foreign loans, the resulting decline in foreign purchases added materially to the economic gloom that settled down over the United States in the early 1930's.

American participation in the settlement with Germany indicated that the involvement of the United States in world affairs ran far deeper than many Americans realized. The United States, try as it might, could not simply concentrate on its own prosperity, and let the rest of the world "stew in its own juice"; it could not even permit Germany to collapse. Above all, the American nation must somehow share in the task of preserving world peace, for war anywhere in the world was certain to affect the United States, however determined its neutrality. A convinced minority of the American people still adhered to the conviction that the United States should have entered the League of Nations, and hoped that eventually this end might be achieved.

Numerous societies made this their goal, among them the League of

Nations Non-Partisan Association, headed by John H. Clarke, a former
Justice of the United States Supreme Court, whose book on *America and
World Power* (1925) well summarized the pro-League position. The
World Peace Foundation, generously endowed many years before by Ed-
win Ginn, the Boston publisher; the Carnegie Endowment for Interna-
tional Peace, headed by the indefatigable Nicholas Murray Butler; and
the Institute of International Relations, operating from Geneva with both
British and American backing, all undertook the wide distribution of pro-
League literature.

Such prominent individuals as Walter Lippmann, William Allen White,
Hamilton Holt, Manley O. Hudson, and Raymond B. Fosdick gave the
cause their earnest support. The Woodrow Wilson Foundation presented
in 1924 the first of a series of $2,500 awards to individuals who had in
some outstanding way contributed to world peace; Elihu Root, recipient
of the second such award, rebuked the United States in his acceptance
statement for its faithlessness in failing to enter the League. But the implacable opposition of the Republican party to the League, coupled with
the indifference toward it of too many leading Democrats, foredoomed the
pro-League advocates to failure. By the end of the 1920's they tacitly accepted as a substitute goal the greater co-operation of the United States
with the League, pointed with pride to the important parts that American
observers took in League meetings, and noted pleasurably the numerous
League agreements that the United States had accepted. According to
Charles A. Beard, the United States was in actual fact a member of the
League, whatever its pretenses.

But Beard was wrong; the United States was not only not a member of
the League, it refused so much as to give its adherence to the World
Court, although during the Roosevelt and Taft administrations Republicans and Democrats alike had regarded the creation of such a body as a
matter of primary importance. In accordance with Article 14 of the
League Covenant, plans for the establishment of a Permanent Court of
International Justice began to take form as early as June, 1920, and by
January, 1922, the Court was able to hold its first session. Among the distinguished jurists who had framed the protocol under which it was to
operate was Elihu Root, elder statesman of the Republican party, and
during the deliberations he had had as his legal adviser James Brown
Scott, a distinguished American authority on international law. The protocol left the way open for American adherence to the World Court, as it
was commonly called, and undoubtedly the overwhelming majority of the
American people favored such a course. But the extreme isolationists in
the Senate had driven themselves into such a frenzy of opposition to anything that savored of "Wilsonism" or the League that the Harding administration moved cautiously on the subject. Finally Hughes, who
strongly favored American adherence, persuaded the President to advocate such a course in a message to the Senate, February 24, 1923. Four
reservations drawn by Hughes were designed to protect the United States
against any slightest League involvement. But the Senate Committee on

Foreign Relations was still dominated by the intransigents, Harding's support proved to be only lukewarm, and the Senate failed to act.

President Coolidge in his first annual message, December, 1923, also commended the Court to the favorable consideration of the Senate, and the evidence that public opinion still favored adherence could hardly have been stronger. The Senate obstructionists, lacking any real arguments to justify their position, finally hit upon the right of the Court to give "advisory opinions" as somehow dangerous to the independence of signatory powers. The result, arrived at after a maximum of delay and debate, was a fifth reservation, insisting that the Court should not render any such opinion without giving due notice in advance to all interested states and providing them an opportunity for public hearings if they so desired; also, that it should not, "without the consent of the United States, entertain any request for an advisory opinion touching any dispute or question in which the United States has an interest." Finally on January 27, 1926, nearly three years after Harding's original message on the subject, the Senate voted for adherence to the Court, 76 to 17, conditioned upon acceptance of the reservations it had adopted. But the end was not yet. When the Council of the League of Nations sought to clarify the meaning of the American reservations, President Coolidge took the position that they had been rejected. Under the circumstances, he said, he could see "no prospect of this country adhering to the Court." Twice later, once during Hoover's administration and once during Roosevelt's, the Senate had a chance to ratify the World Court protocol on terms carefully drawn to meet American objections, but twice more the Senate failed to approve. . . .

Before his term of office ended, Coolidge consented to one more effort on behalf of world peace. Two Americans, a Chicago lawyer named Salmon O. Levinson and a Columbia University professor, James T. Shotwell, had for several years advocated, quite separately from each other, that the true approach to world peace was through an international agreement that would officially condemn war. As matters stood, international law accepted war as legal; why should war not be made to bear instead the stigma of illegality? Levinson believed that if the nations of the world would only outlaw war formally, that might be enough, but Shotwell regarded sanctions as a necessity; there must be force behind the agreement. Among the many Americans who took up with the "outlawry of war" idea, as the concept came generally to be called, was William E. Borah, chairman of the Senate Committee on Foreign Relations. The notion that some positive action should be taken toward the abolition of war also crossed the Atlantic, where it was deliberately planted in the mind of Aristide Briand, French Foreign Minister, by Professor Shotwell himself. And Briand, a master politician, used it in an address to the American people, April 6, 1927, which announced that "France would be ready publicly to subscribe, with the United States, to any mutual engagement tending, as between those two countries, to outlaw war." Since France did not see eye to eye with the United States on such important matters as the Geneva Conference and war debts, Briand perhaps thought this gesture of good will might not be amiss. Secretary Frank B. Kellogg, who had succeeded Hughes in 1925, was at first annoyed at Briand's move, while President Coolidge was piqued that the French Foreign Minister had gone over the head of the American government to the American people directly. Just at this juncture, Charles A. Lindbergh flew the Atlantic in his *Spirit of St. Louis* and landed at Paris; the general enthusiasm that this exploit awakened seemed somehow to call for appropriate action. Both the Levinson and the Shotwell groups made the most of this situation, public opinion soon began to veer strongly their way, and Kellogg at length invited Briand to submit his proposal through normal diplomatic channels, which was done.

Both Borah and the American State Department were quick to see the hazards of the Briand proposal in its original form. It would not do for the United States to sign a special treaty outlawing war between the United States and France without signing similar treaties with many other powers. A bilateral treaty might, by itself, even imply an alliance; for if France went to war with some other nation, then the United States would be bound in advance not to fight against France, come what might. The only tolerable procedure would be to expand the Briand proposal into a general agreement. Finally on December 28, 1927, Kellogg wrote Briand that the United States would favor, instead of the two-power treaty, "an effort to obtain the adherence of all the principal powers of the world to a declaration renouncing war as an instrument of national policy." This was more than Briand had bargained on, and for a time he stalled. Could such a treaty, he questioned, be reconciled with the commitments to other powers that France had already made? But Kellogg's enthusiasm for the idea grew; he even circulated a draft agreement among the great powers that was accepted without hesitation by Germany, Italy, and Japan. Great Britain and France, after the best American tradition, insisted on wordy reservations, but at length they also agreed. Kellogg would have preferred to sign the treaty in Washington, but as part of the price necessary to win French approval, he yielded to Briand's desire that it be signed in Paris. There on August 27, 1928, fifteen nations affixed their signatures to a pact renouncing war "as an instrument of national policy," and promising to solve all disputes of "whatever nature or whatever origin" by "pacific means." Thereafter the pact remained open "for adherence by all the other powers of the world." The first such adherent was the Soviet Union, whose presence at Paris the United States had not desired, lest it might imply recognition.

By the time the Pact of Paris reached the United States Senate, public opinion throughout the nation had so firmly endorsed the document that ratification came easily. Instead of the customary reservations, the Committee on Foreign Relations provided the Senate with an interpretative report. The pact, declared the committee, did not in any way curtail the right of the United States to self-defense, of which the Monroe Doctrine was an essential part; nor did it provide for sanctions, either express or implied, which would in any way oblige the United States to take action against a violator of the pact; nor did it in any respect change or qualify "our present position or relation to any pact or treaty existing between other nations or governments." So interpreted, the Pact of Paris received the approval of the Senate by a vote of 85 to 1, the lone objector being Senator John J. Blaine of Wisconsin. Not every senator who voted for it, however, believed in its value. Senator Carter Glass of Virginia, for example, pointed out that unless the signatory powers stood behind the treaty with force it could never amount to anything, and voted for it as "worthless, but perfectly harmless." Senator Hiram Johnson of California asserted that, like the characters in a Henry James novel, it had been "analyzed by its proponents practically into disintegration." "The explanations and interpretations," he wrote to his sons, "have made its nothingness complete." But Borah noted in rebuttal that treaties with sanctions had usually only led to war, and that the mobilization of world opinion against war was in itself a considerable victory. By the time the treaty was officially declared in force at Washington, July 24, 1929, thirty-one nations, in addition to the original fifteen, had adhered to it, and they were later followed by eighteen others, a total of sixty-four. Only four nations, all Latin American (Argentina, Bolivia, El Salvador, and Uruguay), failed to adhere. Mere gesture that it was, the Kellogg-Briand Peace Pact expressed eloquently the earnest hope of the world for peace.

2. Economic Internationalism

In a provocative essay, William A. Williams dissents from the accepted version of the 1920's and instead depicts it as a decade of forceful American economic international expansion and of vigorous diplomacy. Sweeping aside what he describes as stereotyped definitions of "internationalists" and "isolationists," Williams asserts that the foreign policies of the Harding-Coolidge era were aimed at promoting a world-wide community of interest by persuading other powers to accept the internationalizing of business methods and techniques: by limiting the Soviet Russian influence, preventing colonial clashes and rebellion, integrating Japan and Germany into the new system, and persuading Great Britain to accept American leadership.

The Legend of Isolationism in the 1920's

W. A. WILLIAMS

The widely accepted assumption that the United States was isolationist from 1920 through 1932 is no more than a legend. Sir Francis Bacon might have classed this myth of isolation as one of his Idols of the Market-Place. An "ill and unfit choice of words," he cautioned, "leads men away into innumerable and inane controversies and fancies." And certainly the application of the terms *isolation* and *isolationism* to a period and a policy that were characterized by vigorous involvement in the affairs of the world with consciousness of purpose qualifies as an "ill and unfit choice of words." Thus the purpose of this essay: on the basis of an investiga-

William Appleman Williams, "The Legend of Isolationism in the 1920's" *Science & Society,* XVIII (1954), 1–20. Reprinted with permission.

tion of the record to suggest that, far from isolation, the foreign relations
of the United States from 1920 through 1932 were marked by express and
extended involvement with—and intervention in the affairs of—other nations of the world.

It is both more accurate and more helpful to consider the twenties as
contiguous with the present instead of viewing those years as a quixotic
interlude of low-down jazz and lower-grade gin, fluttering flappers and
Faulkner's fiction, and bootlegging millionaires and millionaire bootleg-
gers. For in foreign policy there is far less of a sharp break between 1923
and 1953 than generally is acknowledged. A closer examination of the so-
called isolationists of the twenties reveals that many of them were in fact
busily engaged in extending American power. Those individuals and
groups have not dramatically changed their outlook on foreign affairs.
Their policies and objectives may differ with those of others (including
professors), but they have never sought to isolate the United States.

This interpretation runs counter to the folklore of American foreign
relations. Harvard places isolationism "in the saddle." Columbia sees
"Americans retiring within their own shell." Yale judges that policy "degenerated" into isolation—among other things. Others, less picturesque
but equally positive, refer to a "marked increase of isolationist sentiment"
and to "those years of isolationism." Another group diagnoses the populace as having "ingrained isolationism," analyzes it as "sullen and selfish"
in consequence, and characterizes it as doing "its best to forget international subjects." Related verdicts describe the Republican party as "predominantly isolationist" and as an organization that "fostered a policy of
deliberate isolation."

Most pointed of these specifications is a terse two-word summary of
the diplomacy of the period: "Isolation Perfected." Popularizers have
transcribed this theme into a burlesque. Their articles and books convey
the impression that the Secretaries of State were in semi-retirement and
that the citizenry wished to do away with the Department itself. Colum-
nists and commentators have made the concept an eerie example of
George Orwell's double-think. They label as isolationists the most vigorous interventionists.

The case would seem to be closed and judgment given if it were not
for the ambivalence of some observers and the brief dissents filed by a
few others. The scholar who used the phrase "those years of isolationism,"
for example, remarks elsewhere in the same book that "expansionism . . .
really was long a major expression of isolationism." Another writes of the
"return to an earlier policy of isolation," and on the next page notes a
"shift in policy during the twenties amounting almost to a 'diplomatic
revolution.'" A recent biographer states that Henry Cabot Lodge "did not
propose . . . an isolationist attitude," but then proceeds to characterize the
Monroe Doctrine—upon which Lodge stood in his fight against the
League of Nations treaty—as a philosophy of "isolation." And in the last
volume of his trilogy, the late Professor Frederick L. Paxton summed up
a long review of the many diplomatic activities of the years 1919–1923

with the remark that this was a foreign policy of "avoidance rather than of action."

But a few scholars, toying with the Idol of the Market-Place, have made bold to rock the image. Yet Professor Richard Van Alstyne was doing more than playing the iconoclast when he observed that the "militant manifest destiny men were the isolationists of the nineteenth century." For with this insight we can translate those who maintain that Lodge "led the movement to perpetuate the traditional policy of isolation." Perhaps William G. Carleton was even more forthright. In 1946 he pointed out that the fight over the League treaty was not between isolationists and internationalists, and added that many of the mislabeled isolationists were actually "nationalists and imperialists." Equally discerning was Charles Beard's comment in 1933 that the twenties were marked by a "return to the more aggressive ways . . . [used] to protect and advance the claims of American business enterprise." All these interpretations were based on facts that prompted another scholar to change his earlier conclusion and declare in 1953 that "the thought was all of keeping American freedom of action."

These are perceptive comments. Additional help has recently been supplied by two other students of the period. One of these is Robert E. Osgood, who approached the problem in terms of *Ideals and Self-Interest in American Foreign Relations*. Though primarily concerned with the argument that Americans should cease being naive, Osgood suggests that certain stereotypes are misleading. One might differ with his analysis of the struggle over the Treaty of Versailles, but not with his insistence that there were fundamental differences between Senators Lodge and William E. Borah—as well as between those two and President Woodrow Wilson. Osgood likewise raises questions about the reputed withdrawal of the American public. Over a thousand organizations for the study of international relations existed in 1926, to say nothing of the groups that sought constantly to make or modify foreign policy.

Osgood gives little attention to this latter aspect of foreign relations, a surprising omission on the part of a realist. But the underlying assumption of his inquiry cannot be challenged. The foreign policy issue of the twenties was never isolationism. The controversy and competition were waged between those who entertained different concepts of the national interest and disagreed over the means to be employed to secure that objective. Secretary of State Charles Evans Hughes was merely more eloquent, not less explicit. "Foreign policies," he explained in 1923, "are not built upon abstractions. They are the result of practical conceptions of national interest arising from some immediate exigency or standing out vividly in historical perspective."

Historian George L. Grassmuck used this old-fashioned premise of the politician as a tool with which to probe the *Sectional Biases in Congress on Foreign Policy*. Disciplining himself more rigorously in the search for primary facts than did Osgood, Grassmuck's findings prompted him to conclude that "the 'sheep and goats' technique" of historical research is eminently unproductive. From 1921 to 1933, for example, the Republicans in both houses of Congress were "more favorable to both Army and Navy measures than . . . Democrats." Eighty-five percent of the same Republicans supported international economic measures and agreements. As for the Middle West, that much condemned section did not reveal any "extraordinary indication of a . . . tendency to withdraw." Nor was there "an intense 'isolationism' on the part of [its] legislators with regard to membership in a world organization." And what opposition there was seems to have been as much the consequence of dust bowls and depression as the product of disillusioned scholars in ivory towers.

These investigations and correlations have two implications. First, the United States was neither isolated nor did it pursue a policy of isolationism from 1920 to 1933. Second, if the policy of that era, so generally accepted as the product of traditional isolationist sentiment, proves nonisolationist, then the validity and usefulness of the concept when applied to earlier or later periods may seriously be challenged.

Indeed, it would seem more probable that the central theme of American foreign relations has been the expansion of the United States. Alexander Hamilton made astute use of the phrase "no entangling alliances" during the negotiation of Jay's Treaty in 1794, but his object was a *de facto* affiliation with the British Fleet—not isolation. Nor was Thomas Jefferson seeking to withdraw when he made of Monticello a counselling center for those seeking to emulate the success of the American Revolution. A century later Senator Lodge sought to revise the Treaty of Versailles and the Covenant of the League of Nations with reservations that seemed no more than a restatement of Hamilton's remarks. Yet the maneuvers of Lodge were no more isolationist in character and purpose than Hamilton's earlier action. And while surely no latter-day Jefferson, Senator Borah was anything but an isolationist in his concept of the power of economics and ideas. Borah not only favored the recognition of the Soviet Union in order to influence the development of the Bolshevik Revolution and as a check against Japanese expansion in Asia, but also argued that American economic policies were intimately connected with foreign political crises. All those men were concerned with the extension of one or more aspects of American influence, power, and authority.

Approached in this manner, the record of American foreign policy in the twenties verifies the judgments of two remarkably dissimilar students: historian Richard W. Leopold and Senator Lodge. The professor warns that the era was "more complex than most glib generalizations . . . would suggest"; and the scholastic politician concludes that, excepting wars, there "never [was] a period when the United States [was] more active and its influence more felt internationally than between 1921 and 1924." The admonition about perplexity was offered as helpful advice, not as an invitation to anti-intellectualism. For, as the remarks of the Senator implied, recognition that a problem is involved does not mean that it cannot be resolved.

Paradox and complexity can often be clarified by rearranging the data around a new focal point that is common to all aspects of the apparent contradiction. The confusion of certainty and ambiguity that characterizes most accounts of American foreign policy in the twenties stems from the fact that they are centered on the issue of membership in the League of Nations. Those Americans who wanted to join are called internationalists. Opponents of that move became isolationists. But the subsequent action of most of those who fought participation in the League belies this simple classification. And the later policies of many who favored adherence to the League casts serious doubts upon the assumption that they were willing to negotiate or arbitrate questions that they defined as involving the national interest. More pertinent is an examination of why certain groups and individuals favored or disapproved of the League, coupled with a review of the programs they supported after that question was decided.

Yet such a re-study of the League fight is in itself insufficient. Equally important is a close analysis of the American reaction to the Bolshevik Revolution. Both the League Covenant and the Treaty of Versailles were written on a table shaken by that upheaval. The argument over the ratification of the combined documents was waged in a context determined as much by Nikolai Lenin's *Appeal to the Toiling, Oppressed, and Exhausted Peoples of Europe* and the Soviet *Declaration to the Chinese People* as by George Washington's Farewell Address.

Considered within the setting of the Bolshevik Revolution, the basic question was far greater than whether or not to enter the League. At issue was what response was to be made to the domestic and international division of labor that had accompanied the Industrial Revolution. Challenges from organized urban labor, dissatisfied farmers, frightened men of property, searching intellectual critics, and colonial peoples rudely interrupted almost every meeting of the Big Four in Paris and were echoed in many Senate debates over the treaty. And those who determined American policy through the decade of the twenties were consciously concerned with the same problem.

An inquiry into this controversy over the broad question of how to end the war reveals certain divisions within American society. These groupings were composed of individuals and organizations whose position on the League of Nations was coincident with and part of their response to the Bosheviks; or, in a wider sense, with their answer to that general unrest, described by Woodrow Wilson as a "feeling of revolt against the large vested interests which influenced the world both in the economic and the political sphere." Once this breakdown has been made it is then possible to follow the ideas and actions of these various associations of influence and power through the years 1920 to 1933.

At the core of the American reaction to the League and the Bolshevik Revolution was the quandary between fidelity to ideals and the urge to power. Jefferson faced a less acute version of the same predicament in terms of whether to force citizenship on settlers west of the Mississippi who were reluctant to be absorbed in the Louisiana Purchase. A century later the anti-imperialists posed the same issue in the more sharply defined circumstances of the Spanish-American War. The League and the Bolsheviks raised the question in its most dramatic context and in unavoidable terms.

There were four broad responses to this reopening of the age-old dilemma. At one pole stood the pure idealists and pacifists, led by William Jennings Bryan. A tiny minority in themselves, they were joined, in terms of general consequences if not in action, by those Americans who were preoccupied with their own solutions to the problem. Many American business men, for example, were concerned primarily with the expansion of trade and were apathetic toward or impatient with the hullabaloo over the League. Diametrically opposed to the idealists were the vigorous expansionists. All these exponents of the main chance did not insist upon an overt crusade to run the world, but they were united on Senator Lodge's proposition that the United States should dominate world politics. Association with other nations they accepted, but not equality of membership or mutuality of decision.

Caught in the middle were those Americans who declined to support either extreme. A large number of these people clustered around Woodrow Wilson, and can be called the Wilsonites. Though aware of the dangers and temptations involved, Wilson declared his intention to extend American power for the purpose of strengthening the ideals. However noble that effort, it failed for two reasons. Wilson delegated power and initiative to men and organizations that did not share his objectives, and on his own part the president ultimately "cast in his lot" with the defenders of the status quo.

Led by the Sons of the Wild Jackass, the remaining group usually followed Senator Borah in foreign relations. These men had few illusions about the importance of power in human affairs or concerning the authority of the United States in international politics. Prior to the world war they supported—either positively or passively—such vigorous expansionists as Theodore Roosevelt, who led their Progressive Party. But the war and the Bolshevik Revolution jarred some of these Progressives into a closer examination of their assumptions. These reflections and new conclusions widened the breach with those of their old comrades who had moved toward a conservative position on domestic issues. Some of those earlier allies, like Senator Albert J. Beveridge, continued to agitate for an American century. Others, such as Bainbridge Colby, sided with Wilson in 1916 and went along with the president on foreign policy.

But a handful had become firm anti-expansionists by 1919. No attempt was made by these men to deny the power of the United States. Nor did they think that the nation could become self-sufficient and impregnable in its strength. Borah, for example, insisted that America must stand with Russia if Japan and Germany were to be checked. And Johnson constantly pointed out that the question was not whether to withdraw, but at what time and under what circumstances to use the country's influence. What these men did maintain was that any effort to run the world by establishing an American system comparable to the British Empire was both futile and un-American.

In this they agreed with Henry Adams, who debated the same issue with his brother Brooks Adams, Theodore Roosevelt, and Henry Cabot Lodge in the years after 1898. "I incline now to anti-imperialism, and very strongly to anti-militarism," Henry warned. "If we try to rule politically, we take the chances against us." By the end of the first world war another generation of expansionists tended to agree with Henry Adams about ruling politically, but planned to build and maintain a similar pattern of control through the use of America's economic might. Replying to these later expansionists, Borah and other anti-expansionists of the nineteen-twenties argued that if Washington's influence was to be effective it would have to be used to support the movements of reform and colonial nationalism rather than deployed in an effort to dam up and dominate those forces.

For these reasons they opposed Wilson's reorganization of the international banking consortium, fearing that the financiers would either influence strongly or veto—as they did—American foreign policies. With Senator Albert B. Cummins of Iowa they voted against the Wilson-approved Webb-Pomerene Act, which repealed the anti-trust laws for export associations. In the same vein they tried to prevent passage of the Edge Act, an amendment to the Federal Reserve Act that authorized foreign banking corporations. Led by Borah, they bitterly attacked the Versailles Treaty because, in their view, it committed the United States to oppose colonial movements for self-government and to support an unjust and indefensible status quo. From the same perspective they criticized and fought to end intervention in Russia and the suppression of civil liberties at home.

Contrary to the standard criticism of their actions, however, these anti-expansionists were not just negative die-hards. Senator Cummins maintained from the first that American loans to the allies should be considered gifts. Borah spoke out on the same issue, hammered away against armed intervention in Latin America, played a key role in securing the appointment of Dwight Morrow as Ambassador to Mexico, and sought to align the United States with, instead of against, the Chinese Revolution. On these and other issues the anti-expansionists were not always of one mind, but as in the case of the Washington Conference Treaties the majority of them were far more positive in their actions than has been acknowledged.

Within this framework the key to the defeat of the League treaty was the defection from the Wilsonites of a group who declined to accept the restrictions that Article X of the League Covenant threatened to impose upon the United States. A morally binding guarantee of the "territorial integrity and existing political integrity of all members of the League" was too much for these men. First they tried to modify that limitation. Failing there, they followed Elihu Root and William Howard Taft, both old time expansionists, to a new position behind Senator Lodge. Among those who abandoned Wilson on this issue were Herbert Hoover, Calvin Coolidge, Charles Evans Hughes, and Henry L. Stimson.

Not all these men were at ease with the vigorous expansionists. Stimson, for one, thought the Lodge reservations "harsh and unpleasant," and later adjusted other of his views. Hoover and Hughes tried to revive their version of the League after the Republicans returned to power in 1920. But at the time all of them were more uneasy about what one writer has termed Wilson's "moral imperialism." They were not eager to identfy themselves with the memories of that blatant imperialism of the years 1895 to 1905, but neither did they like Article X. That proviso caught them from both sides, it illegalized changes initiated by the United States, and obligated America to restore a status quo to some aspects of which they were either indifferent or antagonistic. But least of all were they anxious to run the risk that the Wilsonian rhetoric of freedom and liberty might be taken seriously in an age of revolution. Either by choice or default they supported the idea of a community of interest among the industrialized powers of the world led by an American-British entente as against the colonial areas and the Soviet Union.

This postwar concept of the community of interest was the first generation intellectual off-spring of Herbert Croly's *Promise of American Life* and Herbert Hoover's *American Individualism*. Croly's opportunistic nationalism provided direction for Hoover's "greater mutuality of interest." The latter was to be expressed in an alliance between the government and the "great trade associations and the powerful corporations." Pushed by the Croly-Hoover wing of the old Progressive Party, the idea enjoyed great prestige during the twenties. Among its most ardent exponents were Samuel Gompers and Matthew Woll of the labor movement, Owen D. Young of management, and Bernard Baruch of finance.

What emerged was an American corporatism. The avowed goals were order, stability, and social peace. The means to those objectives were labor-management co-operation, arbitration, and the elimination of waste and inefficiency by closing out unrestrained competition. State intervention was to be firm, but moderated through the cultivation and legalization of trade associations which would, in turn, advise the national government and supply leaders for the federal bureaucracy. The ideal was union in place of diversity and conflict.

Other than Hoover, the chief spokesmen of this new community of interest as applied to foreign affairs were Secretaries of State Hughes and Stimson. In the late months of 1931 Stimson was to shift his ground, but until that time he supported the principle. All three men agreed that American economic power should be used to build, strengthen, and maintain the co-operation they sought. As a condition for his entry into the cabinet, Hoover demanded—and received—a major voice in "all important economic policies of the administration." With the energetic assistance of Julius Klein, lauded by the National Foreign Trade Council as the "international business go-getter of Uncle Sam," Hoover changed the Department of Commerce from an agency primarily concerned with interstate commerce to one that concentrated on foreign markets and loans, and control of import sources. Hughes and Stimson handled the political aspects of establishing a "community of ideals, interests and purposes."

These men were not imperialists in the traditional sense of that much abused term. All agreed with Klein that the object was to eliminate "the old imperialistic trappings of politico-economic exploitation." They sought instead the "internationalization of business." Through the use of economic power they wanted to establish a common bond, forged of similar assumptions and purposes, with both the industrialized nations and the native business community in the colonial areas of the world. Their deployment of America's material strength is unquestioned. President Calvin Coolidge reviewed their success, and indicated the political implications thereof, on Memorial Day, 1928. "Our investments and trade relations are such," he summarized, "that it is almost impossible to conceive of any conflict anywhere on earth which would not affect us injuriously."

Internationalization through the avoidance of conflict was the key objective. This did not mean a negative foreign policy. Positive action was the basic theme. The transposition of corporatist principles to the area of foreign relations produced a parallel policy. American leadership and intervention would build a world community regulated by agreement among the industrialized nations. The prevention of revolution and the preservation of the sanctity of private property were vital objectives. Hughes was very clear when he formulated the idea for Latin America. "We are seeking to establish a *Pax Americana* maintained not by arms but by mutual respect and good will and the tranquillizing processes of reason." There would be, he admitted, "interpositions of a temporary character"—the Secretary did not like the connotations of the word intervention—but only to facilitate the establishment of the United States as the "exemplar of justice."

Extension to the world of this pattern developed in Latin America was more involved. There were five main difficulties, four in the realm of foreign relations and one in domestic affairs. The internal problem was to establish and integrate a concert of decision between the government and private economic groups. Abroad the objectives were more sharply defined: circumscribe the impact of the Soviet Union, forestall and control potential resistance of colonial areas, pamper and cajole Germany and Japan into acceptance of the basic proposition, and secure from Great Britain practical recognition of the fact that Washington had become the center of Anglo-Saxon collaboration. Several examples will serve to illustrate the general outline of this diplomacy, and to indicate the friction between the office holders and the office dwellers.

Wilson's Administration left the incoming Republicans a plurality of tools designed for the purpose of extending American power. The Webb-Pomerene Law, the Edge Act, and the banking consortium were but three of the more obvious and important of these. Certain polishing and sharpening remained to be done, as exemplified by Hoover's generous interpretation of the Webb-Pomerene legislation, but this was a minor problem. Hoover and Hughes added to these implements with such laws as the one designed to give American customs officials diplomatic immunity so that they could do cost accounting surveys of foreign firms. This procedure was part of the plan to provide equal opportunity abroad, under which circumstances Secretary Hughes was confident that "American business men would take care of themselves."

It was harder to deal with the British, who persisted in annoying indications that they considered themselves equal partners in the enterprise. Bainbridge Colby, Wilson's last Secretary of State, ran into the same trouble. Unless England came "to our way of thinking," Colby feared that "agreement [would] be impossible." A bit later Hughes told the British Ambassador that the time had come for London's expressions of cordial sentiment to be "translated into something definite." After many harangues about oil, access to mandated areas, and trade with Russia, it was with great relief that Stimson spoke of the United States and Great Britain "working together like two old shoes."

Deep concern over revolutionary ferment produced great anxiety. Hughes quite agreed with Colby that the problem was to prevent revolutions without making martyrs of the leaders of colonial or other dissident movements. The despatches of the period are filled with such expressions as "very grave concern," "further depressed," and "deeply regret," in connection with revolutionary activity in China, Latin America, and Europe. American foreign service personnel abroad were constantly reminded to report all indications of such unrest. This sensitivity reached a high point when one representative telegraphed as "an example of the failure to assure public safety . . . the throwing of a rock yesterday into the state hospital here." Quite in keeping with this pattern was Washington's conclusion that it would support "any provisional government which gave satisfactory evidence of an intention to re-establish constitutional order."

Central to American diplomacy of the twenties was the issue of Germany and Japan. And it was in this area that the government ran into trouble with its partners, the large associations of capital. The snag was to convince the bankers of the validity of the long range view. Hoover, Hughes and Stimson all agreed that it was vital to integrate Germany and Japan into the American community. Thus Hughes opposed the French diplomacy of force on the Rhine, and for his own part initiated the Dawes Plan. But the delegation of so much authority to the financiers backfired in 1931. The depression scared the House of Morgan and it refused to extend further credits to Germany. Stimson "blew up." He angrily told the Morgan representative in Paris that this strengthened France and thereby undercut the American program. Interrupted in the midst of this argument by a trans-Atlantic phone call from Hoover, Stimson explained to the president that "if you want to help the cause you are speaking of you will not do it by calling me up, but by calling Tom Lamont." Stimson then turned back to Lamont's agent in Europe and, using "unregulated language," told the man to abandon his "narrow banking axioms."

Similar difficulties faced the government in dealing with Japan and China. The main problem was to convince Japan, by persuasion, concession, and the delicate use of diplomatic force, to join the United States in an application of its Latin American policy to China. Washington argued that the era of the crude exploitation of, and the exercise of direct political sovereignty over, backward peoples was past. Instead, the interested powers should agree to develop and exercise a system of absentee authority while increasing the productive capacity and administrative efficiency of China. Japan seemed amenable to the proposal, and at the Washington Conference, Secretary Hughes went a great distance to convince Tokyo of American sincerity. Some writers, such as George Frost Kennan and Adolf A. Berle, claim that the United States did not go far enough. This is something of a mystery. For in his efforts to establish "cooperation in the Far East," as Hughes termed it, the Secretary consciously gave Japan "an extraordinarily favorable position."

Perhaps what Kennan and Berle have in mind is the attitude of Thomas Lamont. In contrast to their perspective on Europe, the bankers took an extremely long range view of Asia. Accepting the implications of the Four and Nine Power Treaties, Lamont began to finance Japan's penetration of the mainland. Hughes and Stimson were trapped. They continued to think in terms of American business men taking care of themselves if given an opportunity, and thus strengthening Washington's position in the world community. Hughes wrote Morgan that he hoped the consortium would become an "important instrumentality of our 'open door' policy." But the American members of the banking group refused to antagonize their Japanese and British colleagues, and so vetoed Washington's hope to finance the Chinese Eastern Railway and its efforts to support the Federal Telegraph Company in China.

In this context it is easy to sympathize with Stimson's discomfort when the Japanese Army roared across Manchuria. As he constantly reiterated to the Japanese Ambassador in Washington, Tokyo had come far along the road "of bringing itself into alignment with the methods and opinion of the Western World." Stimson not only wanted to, but did in fact give Japan every chance to continue along that path. So too did President Hoover, whose concern with revolution was so great that he was inclined to view Japanese sovereignty in Manchuria as the best solution. Key men in the State Department shared the president's conclusion.

Stimson's insight was not so limited. He realized that his predecessor, Secretary of State Frank B. Kellogg, had been right: the community of interest that America should seek was with the Chinese. The Secretary acknowledged his error to Senator Borah, who had argued just such a thesis since 1917. Stimson's letter to Borah of February 23, 1932, did not say that America should abandon her isolationism, but rather that she had gone too far with the wrong friends. The long and painful process of America's great awakening had begun. But in the meantime President Hoover's insistence that no move should be made toward the Soviet Union, and that the non-recognition of Manchuko should be considered as a formula looking toward conciliation, had opened the door to appeasement.

Additional Reading

Selig Adler, *The Isolationist Impulse* (1957).
Joseph Brandes, *Herbert Hoover and Economic Diplomacy: Department of Commerce Policy, 1921–1928* (1962).

Robert P. Browder, *The Origins of Soviet-American Diplomacy* (1953).

Richard W. Current, *Secretary Stimson: A Study in Statecraft* (1954).

L. Ethan Ellis, *Frank B. Kellogg and American Foreign Relations, 1925–1929* (1961).

Herbert Feis, *The Diplomacy of the Dollar: First Era, 1919–1932* (1950).

Robert H. Ferrell, *American Diplomacy in the Great Depression: Hoover-Stimson Foreign Policy, 1929–1933* (1957).

———, *Peace in Their Time: The Origins of the Kellogg-Briand Pact* (1952).

E. E. Morison, *Turmoil and Tradition: A Study of the Life and Times of Henry L. Stimson* (1960).

Dexter Perkins, *Charles Evans Hughes and American Democratic Statesmanship* (1956).

J. Chalmers Vinson, *William E. Borah and the Outlawry of War* (1957).

B. H. Williams, *Economic Foreign Policy of the United States* (1929).

16 THE WASHINGTON ARMS CONFERENCE:
Statesmanship or Illusion?

The 1920's have been described as the era of the disarmament illusion. Optimism then seemed justified as the civilized world voiced a realization of the destructive futility of war and significant progress apparently was made toward large-scale arms reductions and the pacific settlement of international disputes. Peace societies in Europe and America redoubled efforts in behalf of peace and disarmament and carried on extensive educational and lobbying activities. A series of naval arms conferences were held, the Pact of Paris condemning war as an instrument of national policy was adopted by most nations of the world, and in 1932, after years of preparation, the League of Nations sponsored a World Disarmament Conference in Geneva attended by 60 countries. Alas, it was destined for failure, as the rise of Adolf Hitler to power in Germany and the march of an expansionist Japan in the Far East ushered in a decade of crises and another global war.

The American people in the hopeful twenties were proud that their government was playing a vigorous role in the great movement for world peace. For in addition to a vital part in initiating the "outlawry of war" in the Pact of Paris, the United States sponsored a series of apparently epochal naval arms limitation conferences. The Harding Administration began in 1921 when, anxious to avert an expensive arms race and to balance rejection of the League with a positive gesture at international cooperation and peace, a conference of major naval powers and states interested in the problems of the Pacific was called at Washington. The resultant Washington treaties ostensibly stabilized the Far East and curtailed naval establishments. It was hailed as a great achievement for the United States, the Republican administration, and world peace. Later efforts to extend limitations to naval craft below the capital warship class, after suffering a check at the Geneva Conference in 1927, scored a victory at the London Conference in 1930. The structure collapsed shortly thereafter, however, as Japan demanded parity with Great Britain and the United States in all warship categories. The Japanese government denounced the naval agreements in 1934 and the second London Conference of 1935 failed to bridge the disagreement. The United States once more found itself in a naval construction race, woefully lagging behind a now aggressive Japan.

The value of the Washington agreements was questioned even at the time by some sceptical Americans. Later, the whole movement seemed to many to have been a costly illusion. The questions raised by the many efforts at arms limitations in the 1920's, which no doubt have applicability in the present Cold War period as well, are several: What causes wars—arms races *per se* or underlying political tensions and conflicting goals? Can there be successful arms reductions without adequate prior provisions for the security of the involved

456

nations? Are limited efforts at stabilization of an area, such as the Washington conference undertook, more feasible than the large-scale efforts sponsored by the League of Nations and later by the United Nations?

DOCUMENTS

"The Parchment Peace"

In the pretentious and vague rhetoric for which he was renowned, President Warren G. Harding in an annual message hailed the successes of the recent Washington Conference. Besides confidently predicting that the pacts had ended all chance of war in the Pacific, he made clear that the United States would not assume any binding obligations in world affairs but would confine its role to "moral influence." To underscore that point, the Senate in approving the consultative Four Power Pact, attached a reservation disavowing any commitment to support the agreement by use of force. The Five Power Pact compensated Japan for the short end of the capital ship ratio by prohibiting further naval fortifications by Great Britain and the United States in the western Pacific while Japan was left free to strengthen bases in its home islands. The Nine Power Pact gave the Open Door in China international treaty status for the first time but contained no enforcement provisions. Little wonder that a later historian has aptly described the achievements as "The Parchment Peace."

President Harding's Annual Message, December 8, 1922

. . . I bring you no apprehension of war. The world is abhorrent of it, and our own relations are not only free from every threatening cloud, but we have contributed our larger influence toward making armed conflict less likely.

Those who assume that we played our part in the World War and later took ourselves aloof and apart, unmindful of world obligations, give scant credit to the helpful part we assume in international relationships.

Whether all nations signatory ratify all the treaties growing out of the Washington Conference on Limitation of Armament or some withhold approval, the underlying policy of limiting naval armament has the sanction of the larger naval powers, and naval competition is suspended. Of course, unanimous ratification is much to be desired.

The four-power pact, which abolishes every probability of war on the Pacific, has brought new confidence in a maintained peace, and I can well believe it might be made a model for like assurances wherever in the world any common interests are concerned.

We have had expressed the hostility of the American people to a supergovernment or to any commitment where either a council or an assembly of leagued powers may chart our course. Treaties of armed alliance can have no likelihood of American sanction, but we believe in respecting the rights of nations, in the value of conference and consultation, in the effectiveness of leaders of nations looking each other in the face before resorting to the arbitrament of arms. . . .

After all there is less difference about the part this great Republic shall play in furthering peace and advancing humanity than in the manner of playing it. We ask no one to assume responsibility for us; we assume no responsibility which others must bear for themselves, unless nationality is hopelessly swallowed up in internationalism. . . .

The Four Power Pact between the United States of America, the British Empire, France, and Japan, Signed December 13, 1921

I

The High Contracting Parties agree as between themselves to respect their rights in relation to their insular possessions and insular dominions in the region of the Pacific Ocean.

If there should develop between any of the High Contracting Parties a controversy arising out of any Pacific question and involving their said rights which is not satisfactorily settled by diplomacy and is likely to affect the harmonious accord now happily subsisting between them, they shall invite the other High Contracting Parties to a joint conference to which the whole subject will be referred for consideration and adjustment.

II

If the said rights are threatened by the aggressive action of any other Power, the High Contracting Parties shall communicate with one another fully and frankly in order to arrive at an understanding as to the most efficient measures to be taken, jointly or separately, to meet the exigencies of the particular situation.

III

This Treaty shall remain in force for ten years from the time it shall take effect, and after the expiration of said period it shall continue to be in force subject to the right of any of the High Contracting Parties to terminate it upon twelve months' notice. . . .

The Five Power Pact between the United States of America, the British Empire, France, Italy, and Japan, Signed February 6, 1922

Article II. The Contracting Powers may retain respectively the capital ships which are specified in Chapter II, Part 1. On the coming into force of the present Treaty, but subject to the following provisions of this Article, all other capital ships, built or building, of the United States, the British Empire and Japan shall be disposed of as prescribed in Chapter II, Part 2. . . .

Article III. Subject to the provisions of Article II, the Contracting Powers shall abandon their respective capital ship building programs, and no new capital ships shall be constructed or acquired by any of the Contracting Powers except replacement tonnage which may be constructed or acquired as specified in Chapter II, Part 3. . . .

Article IV. The total capital ship replacement tonnage of each of the Contracting Powers shall not exceed in standard displacement, for the United States 525,000 tons (533,400 metric tons); for the British Empire 525,000 tons (533,400 metric tons); for France 175,000 tons (177,800 metric tons); for Italy 175,000 tons (177,800 metric tons); for Japan 315,000 tons (320,040 metric tons).

Article V. No capital ship exceeding 35,000 tons (35,560 metric tons) standard displacement shall be acquired by, or constructed by, for, or within the jurisdiction of, any of the Contracting Powers.

Article VI. No capital ship of any of the Contracting Powers shall carry a gun with a calibre in excess of 16 inches (406 millimetres).

Article VII. The total tonnage for aircraft carriers of each of the Contracting Powers shall not exceed in standard displacement, for the United States 135,000 tons (137,160 metric tons); for the British Empire 135,000 tons (137,160 metric tons); for France 60,000 tons (60,960 metric tons); for Italy 60,000 tons (60,960 metric tons); for Japan 81,000 tons (82,296 metric tons).

Article IX. No aircraft carrier exceeding 27,000 tons (27,432 metric tons) standard displacement shall be acquired by, or constructed by, for or within the jurisdiction of, any of the Contracting Powers.

However, any of the Contracting Powers may, provided that its total tonnage allowance of aircraft carriers is not thereby exceeded, build not more than two aircraft carriers, each of a tonnage of not more than 33,000 tons (33,528 metric tons) standard displacement, and in order to effect economy any of the Contracting Powers may use for this purpose any two of their ships, whether constructed or in course of construction, which would otherwise be scrapped under the provisions of Article II. . . .

Article XII. No vessel of war of any of the Contracting Powers, hereafter laid down, other than a capital ship, shall carry a gun with a calibre in excess of 8 inches (203 millimetres).

Article XIX. The United States, the British Empire and Japan agree that the *status quo* at the time of the signing of the present Treaty, with regard to fortifications and naval bases, shall be maintained in their respective territories and possessions specified hereunder:

(1) The insular possessions which the United States now holds or may hereafter acquire in the Pacific Ocean, except (*a*) those adjacent to the

coast of the United States, Alaska and the Panama Canal Zone, not including the Aleutian Islands, and (*b*) the Hawaiian Islands;

(2) Hongkong and the insular possessions which the British Empire now holds or may hereafter acquire in the Pacific Ocean, east of the meridian of 110° east longitude, except (*a*) those adjacent to the coast of Canada, (*b*) the Commonwealth of Australia and its Territories, and (*c*) New Zealand;

(3) The following insular territories and possessions of Japan in the Pacific Ocean to wit: the Kurile Islands, the Bonin Islands, Amami-Oshima, the Loochoo Islands, Formosa and the Pescadores, and any insular territories or possessions in the Pacific Ocean which Japan may hereafter acquire.

The maintenance of the *status quo* under the foregoing provisions implies that no new fortifications or naval bases shall be established in the territories and possessions specified; that no measures shall be taken to increase the existing naval facilities for the repair and maintenance of naval forces, and that no increase shall be made in the coast defenses of the territories and possessions above specified. This restriction, however, does not preclude such repair and replacement of worn-out weapons and equipment as is customary in naval and military establishments in time of peace. . . .

The Nine Power Pact between the United States of America, Belgium, the British Empire, China, France, Italy, Japan, the Netherlands, and Portugal, February 6, 1922

Article I. The Contracting Powers, other than China, agree:

(1) To respect the sovereignty, the independence, and the territorial and administrative integrity of China;

(2) To provide the fullest and most unembarrassed opportunity to China to develop and maintain for herself an effective and stable government;

(3) To use their influence for the purpose of effectually establishing and maintaining the principle of equal opportunity for the commerce and industry of all nations throughout the territory of China;

(4) To refrain from taking advantage of conditions in China in order to seek special rights or privileges which would abridge the rights of subjects or citizens of friendly States, and from countenancing action inimical to the security of such States.

Article II. The Contracting Powers agree not to enter into any treaty, agreement, arrangement, or understanding, either with one another, or, individually or collectively, with any Power or Powers, which would infringe or impair the principles stated in Article I.

Article VII. The Contracting Powers agree that, whenever a situation arises which in the opinion of any one of them involves the application of the stipulations of the present Treaty, and renders desirable discussion of such application, there shall be full and frank communication between the Contracting Powers concerned. . . .

READINGS

1. A Victory for Peace and Trade

In 1931 it was still possible to be optimistic about the prospects for further arms reductions and the maintenance of peace. Benjamin H. Williams, a political scientist and author of a treatise on American economic foreign policies, concluded that substantial progress had been made in the Twenties and at the American initiative, and he confidently anticipated further gains at the World Disarmament Conference scheduled for 1932. He noted the close alliance between American business groups interested in foreign trade and the State Department, manifested in the calling of the Washington Conference to halt a costly naval race and thereby to allay world tensions and rivalries harmful to the international business community.

The Washington Conference
BENJAMIN H. WILLIAMS

The conference method of dealing with international questions has almost unlimited possibilities. In the solution of problems of mutual interest among nations it represents the substitution of intelligent direction for disorganization and chance. The use of this method in attempting to bring rational order into world affairs has been given great stimulus in the years following the war, and in no field has it been used more strikingly than in that of naval limitation. Before 1914, as has been shown, the efforts to stop the growth of armaments were sporadic and ineffectual. Since the war there has been hardly a year in which there has not been a notable meeting of an international conference or commission to give serious and prolonged consideration to the matter. And a continuation of the series of important gatherings to grapple with the question is definitely upon the program for the future. Some of these meetings have accomplished real gains and others have been unable to achieve any concrete or immediate results. Practically every discussion has, however, helped to clarify the subject, and has made a later solution easier. The whole movement bears unmistakable marks of progress. Only by comparison with the past can we judge the trend of the movement. The present situation is certainly far more encouraging than was that at the time of the Second Hague Conference in 1907 when the subject could not be placed on the agenda for fear of breaking up the conference. . . .

The Washington Conference was an epochal event in international politics, for it reached the first important agreement among the great powers for the limitation and reduction of armaments. It established the method and set the standard for practically all the immediately effective work on this subject for a decade, and its precedent will probably influence the movement for many years to come.

From the beginning the Washington Conference was dominated by the personality of Secretary of State Charles Evans Hughes. Mr. Hughes was fairly well in tune with the sentiments of the large business groups

Benjamin H. Williams, *The United States and Disarmament* (New York & London: McGraw-Hill, 1931, 140–160, 304–310. Reprinted with permission.

centered in New York City. As has been said, one of the guiding principles of the international bankers is friendship between the United States and the greater powers. . . .

At Washington, Mr. Hughes was desirous of removing certain particular causes of friction which were pregnant with danger, and he wished, in general, to build up the intangible asset of good will. To do this he was willing to sacrifice the large capital ships which were in the process of construction, for he felt that because of the bitterness which they were certain to promote they were a liability to the expanding American economy. Realistic thinking was necessary to grasp this proposition which runs decidedly counter to the older systems of thought.

Doubtless the great climax of Mr. Hughes' successful career came at the opening of the Washington Conference. In a speech delivered on November 12, 1921, he outlined in detail practically all that was to be accomplished in the way of naval tonnage limitation. He offered to abandon the American program of capital ship construction in return for concessions from Great Britain and Japan on a somewhat smaller scale. . . .

Secretary Hughes then presented a specific and practical program for reduction, the main points of which were as follows:

1. That all capital ship building programs, either actual or projected should be abandoned;
2. That further reduction should be made through the scrapping of certain of the older ships;
3. That, in general, regard should be had to the existing naval strength of the powers concerned;
4. That the capital ship tonnage should be used as the measurement of strength for navies and a proportionate allowance of auxiliary combatant craft prescribed.

Becoming more concrete, he detailed a program for the scrapping of American, British, and Japanese capital ships and further specified which ships each of the three powers should retain. The limitations on the French and Italian navies were reserved for later consideration. Here, indeed, was a departure from the grandiose generalities and meaningless professions of good will which had been the bane of previous disarmament discussions. Nor was there the resort to bickerings over minor technicalities in guns and characteristics of ships which is often the defense of the unwilling technician. The method of disarmament was free-handed and sweeping. The British writers, Kenworthy and Young, said about it: "He was sinking in a few sentences more tonnage in battleships than all the battles of the world had sunk in a century." Ichihashi, who was present and attached to the Japanese delegation, wrote: "It electrified the calm session; some were shocked, some were even alarmed, but others were pleased. It made the day a memorable one in history." Seasoned journalists, whose lives have been devoted to dramatizing political events for their newspaper readers, have sought to depict the effect of the speech. Mark Sullivan in his book, *The Great Adventure at Washington*, has devoted many pages to describing the reaction to "that inspired moment" of various personalities in the plenary session. According to his description, Admiral Beatty of the British Navy "came forward in his chair with the manner of a bulldog, sleeping on a sunny porch, who has been kicked in the stomach by the foot of an itinerant soap-canvasser." Lord Lee reached around excitedly for pencil and paper. Miss Tarbell testifies that the Japanese "took it without a flicker of an eyelash," while Louis Seibold wrote: "There was no discounting the surprise of Prince Tokugawa, Baron Kato, and Ambassador Shidehara. The Italian, Portuguese, and Belgian envoys appeared to be greatly pleased if a trifle startled." Well might these veteran writers wax enthusiastic, if slightly at variance, for they had lived through a climax in the drama of history.

The Hughes plan for reducing the capital ships of the three powers to the ratios of 5 : 5 : 3 was adopted. The tonnage figures which were first suggested by the Secretary of State were scaled slightly upwards to make it possible for the Japanese to retain the newly completed *Mutsu*, a ship which, it was stated, had been constructed partially from contributions of Japanese school children. Japanese naval officers had taken great pride in this modern 16-inch gun battleship. Accordingly, the *Mutsu* was retained and the feelings of the Japanese school children were spared, but the other powers were given compensation in additional tonnage.

The ratios for France and Italy, after some heavy pressure upon the French delegates, were finally set at 1.67 each as compared with 5 : 5 : 3 for the United States, Great Britain, and Japan. Hereafter, for convenience, the ratios of the five powers will be referred to as 10 : 10 : 6 :- 3.33 : 3.33. The numbers and tonnage of capital ships to be retained by each of the powers were eventually fixed as follows:

Country	No.	Tonnage
United States	18	525,850
Great Britain	20	558,950
Japan	10	301,320
France	10	221,170
Italy	10	182,800

It will be noted that the tonnage left to the powers did not correspond entirely to the ratios agreed upon. Thus the American tonnage was 33,-100 tons below that of Great Britain. The reason for this discrepancy was that the British vessels retained were slightly older than those left to the United States. With the larger tonnage given to Great Britain it was estimated that the two fleets of capital ships were of about the same strength.

The tons in which the fleets were measured were not the same but varied somewhat according to systems in use in the different navies. The treaty included a definition of standard displacement as that of the ship complete, fully manned, engined and equipped ready for sea, including all armament and ammunition, equipment, outfit, provisions and fresh water for crew, miscellaneous stores and implements of every description that are intended to be carried in war, but without fuel or reserve feed water on board. The ton agreed upon was the long ton of 2,240 pounds.

When this standard ton was later applied to measure the existing fleet it was found that the older British method of measurement had included fewer items than the treaty definition of displacement while the American method had included more. The British ships, when translated into standard tonnage, accordingly ran somewhat higher than the treaty figures and the American ships ran somewhat lower. The revised figures as of December 31, 1929, which were accepted as correct by the American delegates to the London Conference, showed 532,400 tons of capital ships for the United States. This included some 30,000 tons that had been added through the modernization of ten American ships since the Washington Conference. The British capital ship strength was set down as 608,650 tons. Thus, even with the increase from modernization, the American ships were 76,250 tons behind the British.

The discrepancy, however, was of only temporary importance. After the year 1931, when replacements of capital ships were to be permitted, the tonnage of the various powers was expected to fall in line with their respective ratios until in 1942 they would be exactly in accord with their allotments. Measured in treaty tons the 1942 strength would be as follows:

Country	No.	Tonnage
United States	15	525,000
Great Britain	15	525,000
Japan	9	315,000
France	5	175,000
Italy	5	175,000

All of this reduction required the destruction of many capital ships. American critics of the Washington Conference have pointed out that the United States gave up much more than did the other powers. This is true. A comparison of the tonnage destroyed is difficult to reduce to exact mathematical terms because of the variation in the definition of displacement which then existed in the different navies, and because of other variable factors such as the age and gun power of the existing vessels which were destroyed and the percentage of completion of the doomed ships which were in process of construction. The following figures set forth the number of the scrapped ships and their tonnage, but, because of the difference in definition of tons involved, the statistics are only approximately accurate.

Country	No. of capital ships destroyed	Tonnage
United States	28	845,740
Great Britain	24	583,000
Japan	16	435,328
Total	68	1,864,068

Of the sixteen powerful capital ships of the 1916 program, eleven were scrapped, or, if you include the *Lexington* and *Saratoga*, battle cruisers which were not destroyed but were converted into aircraft carriers, the number is thirteen. Senator Hale, chairman of the Senate Committee on Naval Affairs, estimated that of these ships, which were all in process of construction, the battleships were 43 per cent and the battle cruisers were 16 per cent complete. This is what is referred to when critics of the Washington Conference speak of the sinking by the United States of the most powerful fleet afloat.

In addition to limitations upon capital ships, the tonnage for aircraft carriers was restricted as follows:

United States	135,000
Great Britain	135,000
Japan	81,000
France	60,000
Italy	60,000

Auxiliary combat craft, including cruisers, destroyers, submarines, and other smaller types of ships, were not limited at the Washington Conference. In his opening speech, Secretary Hughes had suggested figures of limitations for auxiliary vessels as well as for capital ships, but this part of the program met with little enthusiasm from the other powers. The most apparent reason for the failure of this proposal was the inability to agree regarding the submarine.

The people of Great Britain, remembering the lessons of the World War, were desirous of abolishing the submarine. The prospect of starvation in a future war, because of the blocking of trade routes and the stoppage of food importation, had created a bitter antagonism in the British Isles against this instrument of commerce destruction. Seeking to capitalize the great moral indignation against the U-boat which continued as a hang-over from the days of the war, the British delegation asked that the submarine be abolished. Lord Lee, the principal spokesman of the delegation on the subject, advanced an elaborate argument to prove that the submarine was not of much value in coastal defense or in attack against naval vessels. The destruction of commerce was the only use to which it could be put, he alleged, and in this work it could not be employed except in violation of the rules of international law. The only solution to the problem, according to his reasoning, was to do away with the nefarious craft altogether. His argument fell upon deaf ears, for all of the four other powers were able to see great possibilities for the submarine outside of the field of commerce destruction. They, accordingly, refused to agree to abolition.

Another conflict arose over the tonnage in submarines which was to be allotted under the treaty. Mr. Hughes had proposed 90,000 tons for Great Britain and the United States, 54,000 tons for Japan, and it was his intention that the French and Italian submarine quotas should be fixed in accordance with their capital ship ratios, which would have given them 30,000 tons each. When the British protested that the tonnage figures were too large, Mr. Hughes suggested that the United States and Great Britain should reduce their strength to 60,000 tons and that Japan, France, and Italy should retain their existing tonnage which he understood to be 31,452 for Japan, 31,391 for France, and about 21,000 tons for Italy.

The French, who are the chief admirers of the submarine, now came forth to block further progress in this direction. They had been displeased with the low ratio awarded to them in capital ships and were not disposed to yield further ground. After receiving instruction from Paris, M. Sarraut of the French delegation announced that the cabinet and Supreme Council of National Defense had fixed 90,000 tons as the absolute minimum below which France could not go in submarines "without imperiling the vital interests of the country and of its colonies and the safety of their naval life." Mr. Balfour, the cold and cynical leader of the British delegation, replied bitingly to the effect that

> this constituted a somewhat singular contribution to the labors of a conference called for the diminution of armament . . . It was perfectly obvious that the proposed 90,000 tons of submarines were intended to destroy commerce. They could not be intended for any other purpose . . . It was perfectly clear that if at Great Britain's gates a fleet of 90,000 tons of submarines (60,000 tons of which were to be of the newest type) was to be constructed, no limitation of any kind of auxiliary vessels capable of dealing with submarines could be admitted by the Government which he represented.

The British thereupon refused to accept limitations as to destroyers, which are the swift surface vessels used to hunt down and annihilate the submarine. The limitation of cruisers, which are the nemesis of the destroyer, was in turn impossible. Perhaps the British delegates were secretly glad that there was to be no limitation of auxiliary combat craft; but it was far better for their purposes that the breakdown should be laid to the French submarine program rather than to the needs of the British for commerce destroyers. The latter necessity might have been difficult to defend in the atmosphere of Washington. It may be that similar sentiments were held by Italy and Japan, but their delegates openly regretted that auxiliary craft were not included in the restricted classes. At any rate the failure to limit these vessels, as will be seen, left an opening for another naval race.

The conference made one final attempt to restrict the submarine. The sentiment on the part of the British delegation against that vessel was too strong to be utterly ignored. Accordingly, a draft treaty was drawn up which prohibited the employment of submarines as commerce destroyers by the five powers and invited all other nations to adhere to the prohibition. The treaty failed, however, owing to the fact that France neglected to ratify it. The French are much like other people, and when it comes to naval bickerings they are very reluctant to give up any prospective advantages. Furthermore, their moral indignation, as in other countries, runs strangely enough along the lines of self-interest. During the war the use of the submarine by the Germans against commercial vessels was widely deprecated as inhuman and barbarous. But when it came to ratifying an agreement denying themselves the right to do the same thing, the French were negligent. And so, in the final result, the submarine was not limited at Washington.

Another matter as serious as the competition in capital ships was the growing menace of fortifications in the Pacific. The lines of attack in a conflict between the United States and Japan were gradually moving closer. Prior to the conference there had been much talk of increasing the American fortifications in Guam and the Philippines. Japan had rather hurriedly completed the naval works at the Bonin Islands and Amami-Oshima. Hector Bywater, who has studied the Far Eastern situation carefully, says that the evidence of these serious naval preparations had led many observers in the Far East to believe that Japan would have made the beginning of work on the American bases in Guam and Manila a cause for war. Few people in the United States realized that American peace was thus threatened. These minor policies in the Far East which were comparatively unimportant to the American people, so far as prospective benefits were concerned, were of immence importance to Japan, who regarded her very existence as in jeopardy.

When Japan came to the conference, therefore, her delegates were firmly prepared to seek a *status quo* limitation on fortifications in the Pacific. In fact, if such limitation had not been forthcoming it is very doubtful if the Japanese would have been willing to agree to capital ship limitation on the 10 : 10 : 6 basis. On the other hand American naval officers who had long laid plans for the extension of the fortifications and fleet facilities in both Guam and the Philippines raised objections to the Japanese demand for limitation. Secretary Hughes was in a difficult situation. If he listened to the Japanese demand he would offend the American naval group. If he listened to the American naval advice he would wreck the conference. He chose to give success to the conference through an agreement to the *status quo* on naval bases.

The treaty finally provided for the maintenance of the *status quo* with regard to the following Pacific fortifications and naval bases:

Those of the United States: The insular possessions in the Pacific except (a) those adjacent to the coast of the United States, Alaska, and the Panama Canal Zone (not including the Aleutian Islands), and (b) the Hawaiian Islands. The possessions to which the restriction applies are the Philippines, Guam, American Samoa, and the Aleutian Islands. Henceforth the United States must depend upon Hawaii for its furthest fortified western base.

Those of Great Britain: Hongkong and the insular possessions in the Pacific, east of the meridian of 110 degrees east longitude, except (a) those adjacent to the coast of Canada, (b) the Commonwealth of Australia and its territories, and (c) New Zealand. The line drawn at 110 degrees east longitude excluded Singapore from the operation of the treaty.

Those of Japan: The following insular possessions in the Pacific: the Kurile Islands, the Bonin Islands, Amami-Oshima, the Loochoo Islands, Formosa and the Pescadores, and any insular territories or possessions in the Pacific Ocean which Japan may hereafter acquire. This leaves the Japanese free to fortify Japan proper.

The effect of this limitation is admirably summarized by Bywater who states that before the conference the possible bases of war between Japan and the United States were about to be extended to within easy striking distance of each other. If the United States had carried out its plans to fortify Guam and the Philippines, the distance between the base at Cavite and the Japanese coast would have been 1,700 miles while the American stronghold at Guam would have been but 1,360 miles from Japan and 800 miles from the Bonin Islands. The wide waste of water which had served so well to isolate the United States in the past was to be eliminated. Now with the *status quo* decided upon at Washington the ocean barrier has been maintained. The distance from the Hawaiian Islands to Yokosuka, the most easterly base in Japan proper, is 3,375 miles; and thus a great stretch of ocean continues to intervene between the American base of naval operations and that of a prospective foe. . . .

One of the major results of the conference, which helped to clear the air of international suspicion, was the termination of the Anglo-Japanese Alliance. The alliance had been first formed in 1902, and in the original form it related to the questions of equal opportunity and territorial integrity in China and Korea. If either party to the alliance should engage in war with another power regarding its interests in these questions and should be attacked by a third power, then the other party to the alliance would come to the assistance of its doubly beleaguered ally. Thus, in the Russo-Japanese War, if either France or Germany had entered the war on the side of Russia, Great Britain would have been obligated to come to the assistance of Japan. The purpose of the Japanese in entering the alliance was to secure support against Russia, which country was at that time bearing down upon Manchuria. The Japanese also realized that an alliance with Great Britain would greatly enhance their prestige. On the part of Great Britain the alliance was intended to secure the benevolent neutrality of Japan in case of trouble with either Russia or Germany, and the assistance of Japan in case of war with both over the eastern question. . . .

In 1911 the alliance was again renewed with an amendment to the effect that it should not be operative as against a third power which should conclude a general arbitration treaty with one of the parties to the alliance. By this amendment Great Britain hoped to allay the fears of the United States, for a general arbitration treaty had just been negotiated between the two Anglo-Saxon powers. Later, however, the arbitration treaty received the customary death blow in the Senate.

In 1921, the treaty, which was to run for ten years, would have been terminated if denounced by either party. If neither party took action, it was to continue indefinitely. There was at that time much speculation as to the fate of the alliance. Germany had disappeared from the scene even more completely than Russia. The only common danger which faced the two countries in the Far East was the United States with its expanding fleet. The menace of American battleships and prospective bases in the Philippines and Guam gave Japan a strong reason for desiring the continuation of the alliance. British interests were divided. A war with the United States, even with Japan as an ally, would have been exceedingly disastrous to British commerce; and it might likewise have divided the empire. The Pacific dominions regarded the United States as a lesser evil than Japan, and definitely showed their hostility to the alliance in the Imperial conference of 1921. On the other hand, a ruthless and crushing competition in shipbuilding on the part of the United States which would have compelled the British to accept naval inferiority would not have left them in a satisfactory position to terminate the alliance. Baffled for financial reasons in maintaining her position on the sea, Great Britain might conceivably have felt such indignation that she would have been moved to combine her naval strength with that of Japan. When, however, the United States at the opening of the Washington Conference showed a willingness to scrap her mammoth capital ship program, the last important reason from the standpoint of Great Britain for continuing the compact with Japan was gone. Great Britain took the initiative in the abandonment of the alliance. Mr. Balfour submitted to Mr. Hughes a tentative suggestion for a triple or quadruple entente in the Pacific. The Japanese were then bluntly told of this action which meant the passing of the alliance.

In place of the alliance the Four-power Pacific Treaty was signed by the United States, Great Britain, Japan, and France. The treaty obliges the four parties to respect the rights of one another relating to their insular possessions and insular dominions in the Pacific. The obligation of consultation in a conference in case of disputes arising from any Pacific question which cannot be diplomatically adjusted is imposed. If the rights of the parties in the Pacific are threatened by the aggressive action of any outside power, the parties have agreed to communicate with one another as to the best measures to be taken.

The treaty marks a departure from the separate policy of the United States in the Pacific. If Great Britain and Japan should have a dispute over Japanese economic claims in Manchuria, the United States would be bound to meet with the treaty powers to consult as to a solution of the matter. The consultation agreement is the mildest form of joint action for the prevention of war. The slender obligations imposed upon the United States under it are, after all, to the best interests of this country, as a war in the Pacific region could not but prove a danger to all of the larger powers in that area. Furthermore, an exceedingly valuable consideration which the United States received for signing the treaty was the cancellation of the Anglo-Japanese Alliance.

The Four-power Treaty together with the other acts of the conference went far to make the great ocean off our western coast pacific in fact as well as in name.

The conference marks a turning point in international relations. By 1921, the western world had at last been convinced that heavy naval armaments were unprofitable and dangerous. At that point the United States, because of its wealth and on account of the building program already under way, held the key position in much the same way as did Germany in 1899. For certain understandable reasons the United States was willing to forego its leadership in naval building. These reasons were a lack of strong militarist tradition and the fact that business leaders in this country were not convinced of the economic necessity of sea supremacy. Fortunately at that moment there was in the office of Secretary of State a clear-headed man who could see with realistic vision the true self-interest of his country and who was competent to enact that interest into policy. The Washington Conference deservedly stands as one of the most commendable achievements in post-war diplomacy.

2. Naval Arms Limitations in the Twenties: Immediate Successes and Eventual Failures

From the perspective of another world war and the beginnings of the Cold War with Russia, Dr. Merze Tate, an historian of disarmament diplomacy, sketches the movement for arms limitations and thoughtfully evaluates the successes and failures of the 1920's and 1930's. She carefully relates arms proposals to national policies and security requirements, and concludes that while the Washington Conference was a notable achievement for the times, it later proved to have been a costly failure. The entire structure of naval limitations, so painfully erected at the Washington Conference in 1921 and the London Conference in 1930, was destroyed by 1935 because underlying assumptions of continuing stability in Europe and the Far East proved erroneous.

Naval Conferences between the Wars

MERZE TATE

. . . The Washington Conference of 1921, despite its failure to limit auxiliary naval craft and land and air forces, was a memorable occasion, for it was the first successful attempt to restrict and reduce armaments. All earlier parleys had failed because concrete plans had been avoided and only general views had been exchanged. In this conference the United States had proposed a definite program for the limitation of naval armaments. The nature of the plan and the source from which it came arrested the attention of the war-weary world. No ulterior motives, such as those attributed to the Czar and his ministers in 1898, and to the British Liberal Government in 1907, could be ascribed to the United States government. Our country with its enormous financial and natural resources occupied a position of commanding advantage in any armament race; therefore, as initiator of the conference, the United States was in a peculiarly strong and unassailable position to take the lead. While asking others to make some sacrifices, Washington seemed ready to make even larger ones. In a sense the United States was practicing self-denial in accepting a position of theoretical parity with her closest rival.

At the conference, the naval limitation provisions were avowedly aimed at giving Great Britain, the United States, and Japan maritime superiority in their own waters. But Japanese control of the Far East was buttressed by the nonfortification agreement. This removed the chance of England's and America's having the use of either Corregidor or Hong Kong as naval

Reprinted by permission of the publishers from Merze Tate, *The United States and Armaments.* Cambridge, Mass.: Harvard University Press, Copyright, 1948, by The President and Fellows of Harvard College. Pp. 138–140, 254–265.

bases in the event of war in the Pacific. Under the established 5–5–3 ratio, Japan, in addition, was given an absolute naval mystery in all Asiatic waters between the Aleutian Islands and Indo-China, because distance more than counterbalanced the numerical advantage of the Anglo-American fleets. Raymond Leslie Buell summarized the Pacific situation created at Washington as follows:

As a result of the Naval Treaty, adopting the 5–5–3 ratio and the non-fortification agreement, it is now impossible for any power to intervene successfully in the Orient by force, if acting alone. By the Four-Power Treaty, it is now impossible for Great Britain and the United States to combine their fleets in order to intervene jointly. Moreover, by the Four-Power Treaty the freedom of the United States and Great Britain to bring diplomatic pressure against Japan is also probably limited. Consequently, as long as these Treaties are adhered to, Japan is absolutely supreme in the eastern Pacific and over Asia.

At the same time, the Naval Treaty has made a successful Japanese attack on the Pacific Coast impossible, because Japan, as far as capital ships are concerned, will have a fleet forty per cent inferior to the American fleet; because Japan has no real bases or fortifications in the Pacific this side of the Bonins; and because the United States retains the right to increase the fortifications in Hawaii. As a result of this Treaty, it has become a physical impossibility for the United States successfully to attack Japan and Japan to attack the United States.

Concerning the other points that were treated at the Washington Con-ference, the territorial integrity and the independence of China were guaranteed. This guarantee was in the form of the Nine-Power Treaty, signed by all the Pacific powers except the Soviet Union.

The Washington settlement, through the abrogation of the Anglo-Japanese Alliance, resulted in a sweeping adjustment of the political alignment in the Pacific region; it freed the United States, especially the west coast area, from apprehension of a Japanese attack; it also relieved the Japanese of uneasiness about naval bases in the Pacific, and so, temporarily, reduced the tension in the Far East. No action, however, was taken to revise American immigration and tariff policies, both deep sources of irritation to the Japanese.

Today, considering in retrospect the history of the intervening twenty-six years since the Washington Treaties were signed, it is difficult to hail the conference as a diplomatic victory for the United States. Instead of securing our national interest vis-á-vis Great Britain and Japan, we made a double surrender. In consenting in advance to scrap our excess tonnage in capital ships, the United States relinquished the most effective means of obtaining British consent to parity in all other categories. Likewise, in pledging ourselves not to add to the existing fortifications on Guam, Tutuila, the Aleutians, and the Philippines, we surrendered our power to act in the Far East not only to preserve the "open door" and the territorial integrity of China but to protect our own outlying possessions. When war with Japan came, the Philippines, Guam, and Wake were hers. Even Hawaii was at her mercy had Japan realized it. Air power, which has profoundly altered the strategy and use of naval strength, was left out of consideration. Nor was real progress in limitation or reduction of naval armaments achieved, for the restrictions in the treaty extended only to dreadnoughts and aircraft carriers. As a consequence, the naval race was transferred from capital ships to big crusiers, and in this category a new competition ensued.

. . . The Washington, Geneva, and two London naval conferences brought into bold relief the clash in national policies of the parties concerned, and illustrated that arms can be limited only when states feel secure. Thus, deliberations at Washington were dominated by the conviction that the greatest threat to world peace lay in the disturbed conditions and international rivalries in the Pacific. The United States, in calling that conference, was anxious to stabilize the Far Eastern situation in a way favorable to American interests. In persuading Great Britain and Japan to give up their alliance we eliminated a powerful combination which might have thwarted or frustrated American policies in the Orient.

Limitation of battleships and aircraft carriers was realized at Washington because of a combination of several circumstances. These were:

1. The policies of the three great naval powers apparently were not in conflict. Not one appeared to covet the territory of the other or to have any political reason for establishing naval superiority over others in their homewaters. At the same time, all had an economic interest in stabilizing armament.

2. The initiator of the conference was in a superior economic position and under a system of unbridled competition could easily outstrip its rivals.

3. The same country, nevertheless, was willing to make the greatest sacrifices to achieve a satisfactory understanding at a level which would represent economy and security for all.

4. This potentially superior state was at the same time satisfied with its territorial and political position, and enjoyed the greatest national security.

5. There were no political disputes outstanding between the English-speaking powers, so Anglo-American agreement on naval parity was possible. Thus the conference established the psychological—but not the technical—basis for a future understanding.

6. The agreement was restricted to two types of vessels—capital ships and aircraft carriers. Thus the conference did not have to consider the defense of the lines of communication of the British Empire and the naval forces of the minor powers, or to raise the question of the interdependence of armaments generally. An attempted solution of any one of these problems would have wrecked the conference. Moreover, quantitative and qualitative limitations of battleships were achieved, perhaps, not only because this type of ship was extremely costly but also because certain technical experts doubted its fighting value.

7. The American proposal was an attempt to apply the total or "global" tonnage method of limitation; consequently, France and Italy could adhere to some features of it, thus making a five-power agreement possible.

8. The Washington Treaty provided for a limitation of capital ships based on the approximate *status quo*. Acceptance of this principle, unfortunatly, led to competition in other categories of vessels.

9. Japan accepted a position of capital ship inferiority in accordance with the 5–5–3 ratio on condition that Great Britain and the United States agree not to build new fortifications in the Pacific during the life of the treaty. Thus Japan temporarily abandoned naval equality with her most powerful competitors in exchange for security, indeed supremacy, in her home waters and the seas of the Far East. But in return for that naval supremacy in the western Pacific, she promised to evacuate Siberia, restore Shantung, and respect the sovereignty of China.

10. Finally, no attempt was made to provide machinery for the prevention or settlement of international disputes in the Pacific. Both Great Britain and the United States were willing to accept and trust Japan's word, which was the only sanction of the agreements.

The Washington treaties, taken together, were based on certain assumptions which in the long run proved fallacious. Thus, according to George E. Taylor:

> They assumed that there would not be any serious changes in Europe; this was correct enough for a decade but not for two decades. They assumed that China would put her house in order without the aid of Soviet Russia, without a strong anti imperialist movement, and without popular revolution. They assumed that constitutional government would prosper in Japan, and that expansive tendencies would get weaker rather than stronger. The Washington Treaties, if these assumptions had been at all correct, would have written into international law the structure of a stable Pacific. There was every reason to think that the balance of power had been restored in America's favor.

These Washington agreements concerned, in their substantive effect, the three great sea powers, and the negative results of this lack of a real basis of accord between the ocean powers and the naval powers of Europe were seen in the succeeding conferences. Although no understanding was reached with regard to land and air armaments, submarines, and auxiliary craft, the limitation of capital ships produced a favorable psychological effect, and led members of the Congress and the House of Commons to request another conference to deal with those categories of vessels left unlimited at Washington.

Accordingly, in 1927 President Coolidge invited the naval powers to consider the extension of the Washington ratios to auxiliary craft. At the Geneva Three-Power Naval Conference, although Great Britain and the United States were agreed on accepting parity, no formula could be found to achieve it. At Washington the plan of Charles Evans Hughes had provided for a flat tonnage system of measurement. American and British fleets were to be equal, or approximately so, ship for ship and ton for ton. But this method was too inflexible to meet the problems of cruiser limitation. Great Britain could not see why the United States should want parity in 6-inch-gun cruisers, since our defense needs were far less than hers. Consequently England decided that if our country desired equality for its prestige value, the American fleet would have to be expanded to match Great Britain's, since reduction to the American level would have endangered the safety of the Empire.

On the other hand, the United States could not understand why Great Britain should object to American construction of 10,000-ton cruisers so long as the total mathematical tonnage did not exceed that of the British. We contended that parity in all classes had been agreed upon at Washington, while the British insisted that they had accepted the principle of equality only in battle fleets—not in those vessels required for trade route protection. Each side argued for a definition of "equality" or "parity" which, if accepted, would give it superiority.

The reason for the special difficulties in applying the principle of mutual limitation to cruisers could, however, be traced further back than the Washington Conference. One was the peculiarly unbalanced composition of the American fleet. For fifteen years prior to the conference, speed had been of secondary consideration in planning our battle fleet. We had not constructed enough cruisers to perform the duties of advance guards, outposts, or eyes of the battleships. Money appropriated by Congress had gone mainly into the construction of capital ships. Moreover, the undiscussed problems of capture at sea and the convertibility of merchant ships into cruisers were other underlying difficulties which prevented an understanding.

The Three-Power Conference approach to disarmament was purely technical, and naval experts were in charge of the proceedings. No proposal was advanced like that Secretary Hughes made at Washington, which went beyond numerical calculations of ratios of tons and guns, which translated idealism into practical propositions. At Geneva the United States had no concessions to make, no offering of vessels as in the conference of 1921. There was a difference between the actual scrapping of ships built and building and the threat to construct if agreement were not reached. Even the ordinary layman could see the dramatic sacrifices made at Washington. But the British proposition to limit the 8-inch-gun cruiser at the Geneva Conference was viewed with skepticism and could not be interpreted as a concession. Great Britain had been the first to initiate extensive construction of these super-cruisers and had, therefore, set the pace in a new, dangerous, and expensive form of competition. Her action could be interpreted in a fashion similar to her proposal to limit dreadnoughts at the second Hague Conference—a desire to force a halt in competition at the moment of her own great preponderance.

Failure of the British and Americans to reach an agreement in 1927 was more unfortunate than was realized at the time and of greater import for its effects on the Far Eastern situation than the temporary misunderstanding between the two nations. Viscount Cecil observes:

> In fact, it was even more serious than we knew, for up to that time Japanese policy had been essentially pacific and accommodating. A very few years later it changed its character and became unscrupulously adventurous, resulting in the Manchurian policy which began the series of international aggressions leading ultimately to the Polish war. It is at

least possible that, if we had settled the cruiser question, as Japan was most anxious to do, we should have helped to strengthen the peace party in that country and the invasion of Manchuria might never have taken place. The fact that the break arose from Anglo-American differences was another serious feature, not only because any injury to our relations with the United States is to be deplored, but because such a difference is especially harmful in the Far East. It was the want of hearty co-operation between the two countries which encouraged Japan to attack Manchuria, and added greatly to the difficulty of stopping her.

With the American invention of a flexible yardstick, an agreement was possible which would permit Great Britain and the United States to have the type of fleet each required. The adoption of such a criterion, the change of governments in both countries with the resultant willingness of each nation to make concessions to the other's point of view, and the signing of the Kellogg-Briand Pact created an atmosphere in which discussions of naval limitation could be resumed. If that agreement was to help maintain international peace, armaments could not longer be employed for the furtherance of national policies. If the United States and Great Britain were sincere in their adherence to the Pact, the principle of "offensive power parity" or "combat parity" had lost its meaning. With political differences settled, the problems of the "offensive" 8-inch-gun cruiser versus the "defensive" 6-inch-gun cruiser, and the arming of merchant ships—problems which had been insoluble at Geneva in 1927—were easily resolved at London. The London Conference of 1930 demonstrated that all classes of naval vessels could be limited by diplomacy.

In the years following the Washington settlement, and especially after the Geneva Three-Power Conference, when attention was focused on the Anglo-American controversy over equality, Japan was regarded of secondary importance in naval considerations. She made no impossible demands and was ready to accept almost any arrangement on which Great Britain and the United States would agree so long as she secured about the same ratios as at Washington. Nevertheless, during the twenties Japan quietly engaged in a building program which gave her, in both cruisers and submarines, an actual ratio somewhat in excess of 5-3. Thus, when the first London Conference met she had achieved virtual parity in cruisers with the United States and tonnage superiority in submarines. While the United States and Great Britain debated the problem of naval "equality," the conflict between our country and Japan arose from the endeavor on the part of the United States to extend the 5-3 ratio to auxiliary categories, which the oriental power countered with an increasingly persistent effort to gain recognition of a higher ratio. At London, Japan secured a slightly higher ratio in cruisers and parity in submarines. But far more portentous was her announcement that five years later she might demand parity in all categories.

Between the signing of the London Treaty of 1930 and the London Conference of 1935, there were increased political tension in the Mediterranean and undeclared wars in Ethiopia and Asia. Japan's conquest of Manchuria and her threat of hegemony in the Far East conflicted with

both American and British interests. Fearing that the United States and
Great Britain might some day challenge her imperialistic ventures, Japan
demanded parity, for equality from her point of view would only mean a
10–5 ratio in the face of a combined Anglo-American force.

In such a charged international atmosphere, the conference of 1935
seemed doomed to failure. The chief difficulty arose over the question
whether disarmament should rest on the principle of equality of armament or equality of security. Japanese demands for a so-called "upper
limit" amounted to changing the 5–5–3 ratio to 5–5–5. Neither English-
speaking power was willing to accede to this proposal, for it would have
given their rival more than equality of security, which she already had in
the China Sea and the Pacific Ocean. Thereupon Japan withdrew from the
conference, and the system of combined quantitative and qualitative
limitation of naval armaments ended. Although the United States preferred a combination of the two methods, she was forced to the conclusion that qualitative even without quantitative restriction would offer distinct advantages, and would certainly be better than no limitation at all.
Thus the London Treaty of 1936 differed from its predecessors by giving
more prominence to restrictions upon the size of ships and the caliber of
their guns.

By 1936 the United States and Great Britain were firmly resolved they
should have no competitive building. Those two powers, which had maintained an unbroken peace for over a century, were able to agree because
their national policies coincided. On this point Simonds and Emeny write:

> If American policy envisaged the annexation of Canada or of the cor-
> ridor separating Alaska from the United States, or if British policy con-
> templated the seizure of Alaska to anticipate such annexation, no Anglo-
> American agreement in the matter of naval strength would have been
> possible. For parity would have conferred such decisive superiority upon
> the United States in American waters that Canada would be completely
> cut off from British aid, while the superiority Great Britain would demand
> for the defense of Canada would constitute a threat to the security of the
> United States.

Why should Anglo-American relations have been disturbed for a
decade over "parity," and for what reason was that term ever applied to
naval limitation? So far as the United States was concerned, equality with
Great Britain was not based upon any potential danger, but was a matter
of national pride and prestige. If parity with Great Britain required a
naval tonnage far in excess of what our country wanted to construct and
greater than it needed for national security, why should this nation have
insisted upon it? Why could we not accept British superiority? On the
other hand, what danger did Great Britain face in granting superiority in
8-inch-gun cruisers to the United States if the total British tonnage guaranteed the security of the Empire? If war between the two English-
speaking countries was out of the question, should one of them have worried whether the other built 8-inch-gun or 6-inch-gun cruisers? The
answer to this question was complicated by the fact that Britain was most
directly concerned with the navies of other powers. The effect of the in-

crease of American naval strength on the relations of Great Britain with other states worried British statesmen. Although Britain might not notice what ships were constructed on this side of the Atlantic, other nations would; with these countries Great Britain was concerned.

Furthermore, why were the two great sea powers able to agree upon parity in 1929? Finally, why were they firmly opposed to granting parity to Japan? And why did Japan insist upon it when parity meant an unassailable supremacy in the Far East? The answers to the foregoing questions are to be found in the national policies of the states concerned. The arguments over parity, equality, minimum requirements, "offensive" 8-inch-gun cruisers, submarines, etc., were simply political difficulties dressed in technical garb.

The approach to disarmament based on purely technical grounds, on an attempt to fix a ratio of the relative military and naval strengths to be allotted the different states, was bound to fail because it presupposed that nations would still go on fighting each other. The technical justification of military and naval requirements rested upon the experience of past battles and upon the anticipation of future wars. And every nation defined "requirements" to suit its own particular situation. So long as the approach to the problem was based upon old fears and old suspicions there could be little hope of disarmament. No country could obtain security for itself by a fixed minimum or maximum of armaments which it might create.

Hence the Washington, Geneva, and London naval conferences taken together achieved no general limitation of armaments and thus contributed little to permanent peace. The Washington Treaty ensured Great Britain, the United States, and Japan absolute superiority in the regions of primary interest to each of them. Of the three powers, Japan made the greatest gains in security for herself, and at the same time removed all possibility of interference with her national policies. When, in pursuance of an aggressive nationalism and in total disregard of the Nine-Power Treaty to respect Chinese territory, that oriental power invaded Manchuria, Britain and America lacked the means to make an effective protest. At Washington they had surrendered the right to maintain adequate naval bases in the Far East and had agreed to a naval ratio that rendered successful intervention impossible. Even more disastrous for them, as subsequent events demonstrated, the two English-speaking nations underestimated the overwhelming significance and striking power of airplanes, and they neglected to prepare an adequate defense against that weapon for their treaty fleets.

Twentieth century development of aircraft has presented the world with a revolutionary means of transportation, communication, and destruction. The invention of Wilbur and Orville Wright should have operated to improve the distribution of resources and to increase goodwill among peoples. Actually, it has operated principally to make war most efficient and more devastating.

Representatives at the postwar naval conferences, however, practically ignored this new weapon. They argued and debated for days and weeks over naval ratios, parity, caliber of guns, and tonnage of ships, thinking and scheming in terms of Jutland or Skagerrak. Within two decades after the Washington Conference, and only five years after the second London Conference, sea power had been shorn of much of its effectiveness when used without air support. In World War II the battleship had to face as an adversary the airplane, which had lifted "striking force into a third dimension, into a medium which the surface vessel cannot penetrate." In the battle for Crete, where there was a "clear-cut confrontation of overwhelming sea power and overwhelming air power," air power triumphed. At the outbreak of the Pacific war the United States was particularly deficient in modern land-based fighters and in carriers. In the first phase of that war, therefore, the Japanese, because of their initial air superiority, won one success after another in the Philippines, Malaya, the Netherlands East Indies, the Islands of the Pacific, Burma, and in the Bay of Bengal.

The officials of the United States Strategic Bombing Survey were of the opinion that "one thousand planes in the Philippines, at least equal in performance to the best then available to the Japanese, including types effective against shipping, well-manned, equipped and supplied, and dispersed on some 50 airfields, would have seriously impeded the original Japanese advance if knowledge of their existence had not entirely dissuaded the Japanese from making the attempt."

The destructive aërial blows Japan dealt Pearl Harbor on December 7, 1941, put out of commission 18 vessels, 177 planes, and a large floating dry-dock, as well as other essential piers and dockyards. That attack crippled the United States Pacific air and naval forces for the first year of the war, and prevented them from operating to save the Philippines. The supremacy of the air arm was again clearly demonstrated by the fact that airplanes sank the *Prince of Wales*, the *Repulse*, the *Haruna*, and the *Arizona*. Naval experts had given assurance that the first-named vessel was unsinkable. Moreover, in the decisive Battle of the Bismarck Sea, March 3–5, 1943, United Nations' land-based air power scored such a complete victory that to the Japanese it assumed the proportion of a major disaster.

Upon entering the war, the United States was deficient not only in the numbers but in the quality of many of its aircraft types. We were forced thereafter into hasty and costly modification and technical development programs to raise the performance of our aircraft to acceptable standards. These programs could have been conducted more efficiently and economically during prewar years. But, "in the actual conduct of the war we more quickly grasped the strategic revolution brought about by the capabilities of air power than did the Japanese. By the end of 1943 we had achieved through combat and the augmentation of our forces, such clear-cut superiority over the Japanese in all elements of air power that eventual victory was assured."

Japan, more than any other ocean power, watched the growth of air armaments with ill-concealed alarm, and made concessions on naval ratios only after having prevented the further construction of naval and air bases within striking distance of her shores. In the conversations preliminary to the London Conference of 1935 Admiral Yamamoto contended that developments in aviation had upset the equilibrium established in the

Pacific by the Washington Treaty, to the advantage of an attacking fleet. At this second London Conference the Japanese delegates proposed the abolition of what they termed the "aggressive" aircraft carrier, realizing, of course, its potential menace to their teeming, lightly-built cities, all of which were within bombing range of planes from large carriers. With few British and American bastions in the Far East, with Singapore and Pearl Harbor 3000 and 3400 miles respectively from Japan, the aircraft carrier has served as a floating base from which planes have operated directly against the Japanese cities and fleet.

The Japanese contention of the increased danger to their Empire from air power was certainly justifiable and their fears of modern aviation were realized in World War II. During that war American naval aviation in the Pacific won both success and distinction in its basic purpose of destroying hostile air and naval forces, in amphibious warfare involving attacks in support of landing operations, in reconnaisance over the sea, and in challenging and defeating land-based planes over positions held in force by the Japanese. Moreover, because of its mobility and the striking power and long range of its weapons, the aircraft carrier proved itself a major and vital element of naval strength. The epic Battle of the Coral Sea demonstrated how devastating a modern carrier could be. Within a period of eleven hours, on May 4, 1942, American pilots, gunners, and carrier crews damaged or destroyed more warships, transport, and auxiliary vessels than ever before had been wrecked by airplanes in a single sustained bombardment. Finally, the first bombs to fall on Tokyo were launched from carrier-based planes, while Japan's dramatic capitulation followed the dropping from the air of two small atomic bombs on Hiroshima and Nagasaki.

This study has emphasized and reiterated that armies, navies, and air fleets are the most important instruments of national policy. A country's armaments must, therefore, be adequate to sustain its commitments, and its preparedness must coincide with and be sufficient to support its foreign policies. To this simple and cardinal principle the United States government failed to adhere throughout the twenties and thirties and the American people have paid dearly for the mistake.

Certain of our foreign policies, namely, the maintenance of the Open Door and the territorial integrity and political entity of China, could not be enforced by our warships and airplanes. An attempt by Great Britain and the United States to stabilize and protect China and to police the Orient was bound to lead to a war with Japan, a struggle which the English-speaking powers would find difficult to win.

Therefore, the questions naturally arise: If our treaty fleet and bases were inadequate to enforce certain of our Far Eastern policies, should not those policies have been revised or abandoned? Or should we have built more battleships and airplanes and fortified more bases?

Building overwhelming navies and air fleets and maintaining large imperial forces would not have proved a satisfactory solution of the Far Eastern question. Nor was conceding ships and granting security ratios the proper approach. The concessions that Great Britain and the United States should have made would have cost little and would have held no danger for anyone. Only two years after the Washington Conference, the American Congress in 1923 largely undid the work and destroyed the spirit created there by terminating the Gentlemen's Agreement, and by passing an "unwise, impolitic and dangerous" exclusion law, which for thirty years the United States and Japanese governments had tried to avoid. In 1925 the United States declined Japan's offer of a draft treaty which would have given American authorities complete control over Japanese immigration upon a basis of reciprocity. Thus the first blow at the spirit of the Washington treaties was struck, not by Japan, but by the United States. Also irritating to the leading oriental power was the British Commonwealth policy of prohibiting immigration to Australia, New Zealand, and Canada to all but Caucasians. As though these acts were not sufficient, the Smoot-Hawley tariff of 1930 and the British imperial preference policy did further damage.

Actually, what was needed in the twenties and thirties was not a series of disarmament conferences to palaver over such terms and questions as war potential, budgetary limitation versus limitation of material, displacement and replacement of ships, caliber of guns, parity, and naval ratios among nations—problems which will never be resolved permanently so long as primary sources of friction are not removed. Instead of carrying on discussions about the foregoing subjects, the states should have established a system of collective security against aggression, and then proceeded to the gradual removal of the causes of war, peaceful reconsideration of treaties which had become inapplicable, recognition of the right of defeated countries to equality in armaments, readjustment of distorted boundary lines, liberalization of immigration and tariff policies, redefinition or abrogation of the Open Door policy, redistribution of colonial territories and raw materials, and reëxamination and revision of imperialism.

Military preparations are the visible signs of national passions and international unrest, and so long as the utility of armaments as instruments of policy is not reduced, limitation will not be achieved. Disarmament, both by the direct method of restriction and by the indirect process of organizing collective security, has failed tragically because all peoples have coveted national security but have envisioned different means of achieving it. The supreme desire of Great Britain was peace—that peace in Europe and throughout the world which would bring prosperity to the British Empire. To attain that end the United Kingdom advocated land disarmament, for large standing armies were not essential to her security. Moreover, they might disturb the peace of Europe and involve England in another Continental war. Britain was determined, however, to maintain naval superiority in all regions vital to her. At the same time, the primary concern of the United States was peace and noninvolvement in European quarrels. Security for the homeland had long since been attained and was no grave problem. No population pressures disturbed the country, and self-sufficiency in the economic field, which removed the menace of blockade, reconciled the American people to the *status quo*. Great Britain and the United States, although satisfied with their territorial possessions and sincere in their acceptance of the world *status quo*, were not prepared to defend it in regions where their interests were not vital. France, too, desired peace, but peace based upon either Anglo-American guarantees of French security or an effective League of Nations. The Soviet Union, likewise, was ready to respect the *status quo* and the territorial integrity of other nations. Each of these powers was fairly satisfied with its geographic boundaries. On the other hand, Germany, Italy, and Japan found the *status quo* intolerable because it restricted them to limits they considered incompatible with their future national development.

The post-World War I peoples were therefore divided into two classes: those satisfied and those dissatisfied with the *status quo*. The French, British, and Americans were in the first group. They had already secured what they wanted, did not intend to expand further, and consequently believed expansion to be generally wrong. The Germans, Japanese, and Italians sought security through the revision of the existing frontiers; they intended to expand because some important principle seemed to make it right in their particular cases. The determination of the dissatisfied or "renovating" states to expand endangered the peace of the world even more than did the imperialism of those powers of the nineteenth century which believed that expansion was the "white man's burden," the "*mission civilisatrice*," or "manifest destiny.". . .

Additional Reading

R. L. Buell, *The Washington Conference* (1922).

R. H. Ferrell, *American Diplomacy in the Great Depression* (1957).

D. F. Fleming, *The United States and World Organization, 1920–1933* (1938).

A. W. Griswold, *The Far Eastern Policy of the United States* (1938).

Y. Ichihashi, *The Washington Conference and After* (1928).

Raymond G. O'Connor, *Perilous Equilibrium: The United States and the London Naval Conference of 1930* (1962).

Harold and Margaret Sprout, *Toward a New Order of Sea Power* (1940).

J. Chalmers Vinson, *The Parchment Peace: the United States Senate and the Washington Conference, 1921–1922* (1955).

17 PEARL HARBOR: F.D.R., War Monger or Statesman?

The 1930's were years of deepening isolationist sentiment in America. Disillusionment with the 1917 Great Crusade, the menace of new aggression in the Far East and Europe, and the problems of depression at home made the majority of citizens increasingly determined not to become involved again in an overseas war. The Nye Committee investigations of the connection between munitions makers, bankers, and war in 1917 suggested means of avoiding another unnecessary entanglement. The result of these factors was passage of neutrality legislation in 1935–1937, designed to prevent a future involvement by abandoning much of America's traditional defense of neutral rights. In future wars, American citizens would be prohibited from loaning money or selling arms to belligerents, and from traveling on belligerent passenger ships.

President Franklin D. Roosevelt and a growing number of influential citizens became convinced that isolationist policies would not adequately safeguard the nation's interests against the Axis threat in Europe and the Japanese expansionist drive in the Far East. Efforts were made to re-educate the American public and to use American influence on the side of the resistors of aggression. After the European War began in September, 1939, the Roosevelt administration moved from making the American market available to Great Britain and her allies to the extension of material aid and a posture just short of formal hostilities with Germany. In the Pacific, efforts to check Japan's drives in China and in southeastern Asia took the form of repeated warnings and moral condemnations and tightening economic coercion: the restrictive licensing of exports of petroleum and scrap metals in July, 1940, and the embargoing of the exportation of aviation gasoline outside the Western Hemisphere; in September, 1940, in reaction to the signing of the Rome-Berlin-Tokyo Tripartite Alliance, exports of scrap iron and steel were also prohibited; and in July, 1941, in response to the ominous Japanese occupation of southern Indo-China, all Japanese assets in the United States were frozen, which meant that all trade including vital oil shipments was halted. War came in December, 1941, as the result of Japanese attacks in the Pacific; Germany and Italy responded to their ally's actions by also declaring war on the United States.

Since 1945, both political and scholarly debate has raged about the causes and wisdom of the American involvement in World War II. In a very real sense, this was merely a continuation of the pre-Pearl Harbor political controversies on foreign policy, temporarily silenced by the need for wartime unity, and of the historical dialogue on the Great Crusade in World War I. Historians naturally sought to relate as fully as possible the events culminating in the second global holocaust in the 20th century. In addition, many Americans were soon dismayed at the shape of the postwar world, in which the United States and its friends seemed even more insecure than in 1939–1941, in the face of a worldwide Communist drive for empire. Frustration, disillusionment, and

482

weariness with the costs of the Cold War intermingled with domestic politics to lead to a frantic search of the historical record for convenient scapegoats on which to blame the nation's plight. Among scholars, critics of F.D.R.'s foreign policies and the war entry have again been styled "revisionists," while defenders are best described as "internationalists." Although the exchanges have been marked by impassioned charges of blunders and plots, some accomplishments have resulted from the academic battle. Official and private papers have become available more rapidly than after the First World War; the story has therefore been more completely related, and several noteworthy scholarly volumes have been published.*

DOCUMENTS

1. Steps toward a "Shooting War" in the Atlantic

With the Nazi attack on Poland and the formal beginning of World War II in September, 1939, President Roosevelt successfully sought to amend the neutrality laws to permit Allied arms purchases. The Fourth Neutrality Act on November 4, 1939, repealed the arms embargo and permitted "cash and carry" sales to the belligerents. The fall of France in June of 1940 indicated that more had to be done if Great Britain was to survive, which Roosevelt believed American interests required. In response to urgent British requests, fifty World War I destroyers were exchanged, on executive authority only, for defense bases from Newfoundland to the Caribbean. Following the presidential election, Roosevelt reluctantly decided that even more aid was mandatory, and after a fireside chat urging that the United States should be an "arsenal of democracy," he proposed the Lend-Lease scheme to Congress. It was approved on March 11, 1941. These measures, although patently unneutral and scathingly condemned by non-interventionists, received the support of the majority of Americans. Patrolling and then convoying followed passage of Lend-Lease and eventually clashes resulted between American naval vessels and German submarines. In justifying "shoot on sight" orders because of German U-boat attacks, Roosevelt neglected to tell the American people that the destroyer *Greer* had been trailing the underseas craft before being fired upon.

The Destroyer-Bases Swap: Message of President Roosevelt to the Congress, September 3, 1940

I transmit herewith for the information of the Congress notes exchanged between the British Ambassador at Washington and the Secretary of State on September 2, 1940, under which this Government has acquired the right to lease naval and air bases in Newfoundland, and in the islands of Bermuda, the Bahamas, Jamaica, St. Lucia, Trinidad, and Antigua, and in British Guiana; also a copy of an opinion of the Attorney General dated August 27, 1940, regarding my authority to consummate this arrangement.

The right to bases in Newfoundland and Bermuda are gifts—generously given and gladly received. The other bases mentioned have been acquired in exchange for fifty of our over-age destroyers.

* See Wayne S. Cole, "American Entry in World War II: A Historiographical Appraisal," *Mississippi Valley Historical Review*, XLIII (1957), 595–617.

This is not inconsistent in any sense with our status of peace. Still less is it a threat against any nation. It is an epochal and far-reaching act of preparation for continental defense in the face of grave danger.

Preparation for defense is an inalienable prerogative of a sovereign state. Under present circumstances this exercise of sovereign right is essential to the maintenance of our peace and safety. This is the most important action in the reinforcement of our national defense that has been taken since the Louisiana Purchase. Then as now, considerations of safety from overseas attack were fundamental.

The value to the Western Hemisphere of these outposts of security is beyond calculation. Their need has long been recognized by our country, and especially by those primarily charged with the duty of charting and organizing our own naval and military defense. They are essential to the protection of the Panama Canal, Central America, the Northern portion of South America, The Antilles, Canada, Mexico, and our own Eastern and Gulf Seaboards. Their consequent importance in hemispheric defense is obvious. For these reasons I have taken advantage of the present opportunity to acquire them.

Lend-Lease Aid to the Allies: Speech by President Roosevelt to the Congress, January 6, 1941

I address you, the Members of the Seventy-seventh Congress, at a moment unprecedented in the history of the Union. I use the word "unprecedented," because at no previous time has American security been as seriously threatened from without as it is today.

Our national policy is this:

First, by an impressive expression of the public will and without regard to partisanship, we are committed to all-inclusive national defense.

Second, by an impressive expression of the public will and without regard to partisanship, we are committed to full support of all those resolute peoples, everywhere, who are resisting aggression and are thereby keeping war away from our hemisphere. By this support, we express our determination that the democratic cause shall prevail; and we strengthen the defense and security of our own Nation.

Third, by an impressive expression of the public will and without regard to partisanship, we are committed to the proposition that principles of morality and considerations for our own security will never permit us to acquiesce in a peace dictated by aggressors and sponsored by appeasers. We know that enduring peace cannot be bought at the cost of other people's freedom.

In the recent national election there was no substantial difference between the two great parties in respect to that national policy. No issue was fought out on this line before the American electorate. Today, it is abundantly evident that American citizens everywhere are demanding and supporting speedy and complete action in recognition of obvious danger.

Therefore, the immediate need is a swift and driving increase in our armament production.

To change a whole nation from a basis of peacetime production of implements of peace to a basis of wartime production of implements of war is no small task. And the greatest difficulty comes at the beginning of the program, when new tools and plant facilities and new assembly lines and shipways must first be constructed before the actual matériel begins to flow steadily and speedily from them.

The Congress, of course, must rightly keep itself informed at all times of the progress of the program. However, there is certain information, as the Congress itself will readily recognize, which, in the interests of our own security and those of the nations we are supporting, must of needs be kept in confidence.

New circumstances are constantly begetting new needs for our safety. I shall ask this Congress for greatly increased new appropriations and authorizations to carry on what we have begun.

I also ask this Congress for authority and for funds sufficient to manufacture additional munitions and war supplies of many kinds, to be turned over to those nations which are now in actual war with aggressor nations.

Our most useful and immediate role is to act as an arsenal for them as well as for ourselves. They do not need man power. They do need billions of dollars worth of the weapons of defense.

The time is near when they will not be able to pay for them in ready cash. We cannot, and will not, tell them they must surrender, merely because of present inability to pay for the weapons which we know they must have.

I do not recommend that we make them a loan of dollars with which to pay for these weapons—a loan to be repaid in dollars.

I recommend that we make it possible for those nations to continue to obtain war materials in the United States, fitting their orders into our own program. Nearly all of their matériel would, if the time ever came, be useful for our own defense.

Taking counsel of expert military and naval authorities, considering what is best for our own security, we are free to decide how much should be kept here and how much should be sent abroad to our friends who by their determined and heroic resistance are giving us time in which to make ready our own defense.

For what we send abroad, we shall be repaid, with a reasonable time following the close of hostilities, in similar materials, or, at our option, in other goods of many kinds which they can produce and which we need.

Let us say to the democracies: "We Americans are vitally concerned in your defense of freedom. We are putting forth our energies, our resources, and our organizing powers to give you the strength to regain and maintain a free world. We shall send you, in ever-increasing numbers, ships, planes, tanks, guns. This is our purpose and our pledge."

In fulfillment of this purpose we will not be intimidated by the threats of dictators that they will regard as a breach of international law and as an act of war our aid to the democracies which dare to resist their aggression. Such aid is not an act of war, even if a dictator should unilaterally proclaim it so to be.

When the dictators are ready to make war upon us, they will not wait for an act of war on our part. They did not wait for Norway or Belgium or the Netherlands to commit an act of war.

Their only interest is in a new one-way international law, which lacks mutuality in its observance, and, therefore, becomes an instrument of oppression.

The happiness of future generations of Americans may well depend upon how effective and how immediate we can make our aid felt. No one can tell the exact character of the emergency situations that we may be called upon to meet. The Nation's hands must not be tied when the Nation's life is in danger.

We must all prepare to make the sacrifices that the emergency—as serious as war itself—demands. Whatever stands in the way of speed and efficiency in defense preparations must give way to the national need. . . .

In the future days, which we seek to make secure, we look forward to a world founded upon four essential human freedoms.

The first is freedom of speech and expression—everywhere in the world.

The second is freedom of every person to worship God in his own way —everywhere in the world.

The third is freedom from want—which, translated into world terms, means economic understandings which will secure to every nation a healthy peacetime life for its inhabitants—everywhere in the world.

The fourth is freedom from fear—which, translated into world terms, means a world-wide reduction of armaments to such a point and in such a thorough fashion that no nation will be in a position to commit an act of physical aggression against any neighbor—anywhere in the world.

That is no vision of a distant millennium. It is a definite basis for a kind of world attainable in our own time and generation. That kind of world is the very antithesis of the so-called new order of tyranny which the dictators seek to create with the crash of a bomb.

To that new order we oppose the great conception—the moral order. A good society is able to face schemes of world domination and foreign revolutions alike without fear. . . .

Roosevelt's "Shoot on Sight" Address,
September 11, 1941

The Navy Department of the United States has reported to me that on the morning of September fourth the United States destroyer *Greer*, proceeding in full daylight towards Iceland, had reached a point southeast of Greenland. She was carrying American mail to Iceland. She was flying the American flag. Her identity as an American ship was unmistakable.

She was then and there attacked by a submarine. Germany admits that it was a German submarine. The submarine deliberately fired a torpedo at the *Greer*, followed later by another torpedo attack. In spite of what Hitler's propaganda bureau has invented, and in spite of what any American obstructionist organization may prefer to believe, I tell you the blunt

THE
NORTH
ATLANTIC
1941

GREENLAND

German
Blockade
Zone

ICELAND

SCOTLAND
ENGLAND
IRELAND

GREER
attacked
Sept. 4

KEARNY
torpedoed
Oct. 17

REUBEN
JAMES
Sunk
Oct. 31

CANADA

NEWFOUNDLAND

NOVA
SCOTIA

Roosevelt–Churchill
Meeting, Aug. 9–12

fact that the German submarine fired first upon this American destroyer without warning, and with deliberate design to sink her.

Our destroyer, at the time, was in waters which the Government of the United States had declared to be waters of self-defense—surrounding outposts of American protection in the Atlantic. . . .

This was piracy—legally and morally. It was not the first nor the last act of piracy which the Nazi Government has committed against the American flag in this war. Attack has followed attack. . . .

The important truth is that these acts of international lawlessness are a manifestation of a design which has been made clear to the American people for a long time. It is the Nazi design to abolish the freedom of the seas and to acquire absolute control and domination of the seas for themselves.

For with control of the seas in their own hands, the way can become clear for their next step—domination of the United States and the Western Hemisphere by force. Under Nazi control of the seas, no merchant ship of the United States or of any other American republic would be free to carry on any peaceful commerce, except by the condescending grace of this foreign and tyrannical power. The Atlantic Ocean which has been, and which should always be, a free and friendly highway for us would then become a deadly menace to the commerce of the United States, to the coasts of the United States, and to the inland cities of the United States.

The Hitler Government, in defiance of the laws of the sea and of the recognized rights of all other nations, has presumed to declare, on paper, that great areas of the seas—even including a vast expanse lying in the Western Hemisphere—are to be closed, and that no ships may enter them for any purpose, except at peril of being sunk. Actually they are sinking ships at will and without warning in widely separated areas both within and far outside of these far-flung pretended zones.

This Nazi attempt to seize control of the oceans is but a counterpart of the Nazi plots now being carried on throughout the Western Hemisphere —all designed toward the same end. For Hitler's advance guards—not only his avowed agents but also his dupes among us—have sought to make ready for him footholds and bridgeheads in the New World, to be used as soon as he has gained control of the oceans.

His intrigues, his plots, his machinations, his sabotage in this New World are all known to the Government of the United States. Conspiracy has followed conspiracy. . . .

To be ultimately successful in world-mastery, Hitler knows that he must get control of the seas. He must first destroy the bridge of ships which we are building across the Atlantic, over which we shall continue to roll the implements of war to help destroy him and all his works in the end. He must wipe out our patrol on sea and in the air. He must silence the British Navy.

It must be explained again and again to people who like to think of the United States Navy as an invincible protection, that this can be true only if the British Navy survives. That is simple arithmetic.

For if the world outside the Americas falls under Axis domination, the shipbuilding facilities which the Axis powers would then possess in all of Europe, in the British Isles, and in the Far East would be much greater than all the shipbuilding facilities and potentialities of all the Americas— not only greater but two or three times greater. Even if the United States threw all its resources into such a situation, seeking to double and even redouble the size of our Navy, the Axis powers, in control of the rest of the world, would have the man-power and the physical resources to outbuild us several times over.

It is time for all Americans of all the Americas to stop being deluded by the romantic notion that the Americas can go on living happily and peacefully in a Nazi-dominated world. . . .

We have sought no shooting war with Hitler. We do not seek it now. But neither do we want peace so much that we are willing to pay for it by permitting him to attack our naval and merchant ships while they are on legitimate business.

I assume that the German leaders are not deeply concerned by what we Americans say or publish about them. We cannot bring about the downfall of Nazism by the use of long-range invective.

But when you see a rattlesnake poised to strike, you do not wait until he has struck before you crush him.

These Nazi submarines and raiders are the rattlesnakes of the Atlantic. They are a menace to the free pathways of the high seas. They are a challenge to our sovereignty. They hammer at our most precious rights when they attack ships of the American flag—symbols of our independence, our freedom, our very life. . . .

It is no act of war on our part when we decide to protect the seas which are vital to American defense. The aggression is not ours. Ours is solely defense.

But let this warning be clear. From now on, if German or Italian vessels of war enter the waters the protection of which is necessary for American defense they do so at their own peril.

The orders which I have given as Commander-in-Chief to the United States Army and Navy are to carry out that policy—at once.

The sole responsibility rests upon Germany. There will be no shooting unless Germany continues to seek it. . . .

2. Who Served an Ultimatum, Japan or the United States?

Revisionists have emphasized that the American government knew through the Magic code intercepts that the Japanese offer of the *modus vivendi* on November 20, 1941, was final and if it failed would be followed by hostilities. The Hull reply six days later, therefore, has been described by these writers as an ultimatum. Secretary Hull later stated that he and the President believed that to accept the Japanese plan would have been an abandonment of Nationalist China; they viewed the American reply of November 26 as merely a formal restating of the American position for the sake of the historical record.

Draft Proposal Handed by the Japanese Ambassador (Nomura) to the Secretary of State, November 20, 1941

1. Both the Governments of Japan and the United States undertake not to make any armed advancement into any of the regions in the Southeastern Asia and the Southern Pacific area excepting the part of French Indo-China where the Japanese troops are stationed at present.

2. The Japanese Government undertakes to withdraw its troops now stationed in French Indo-China upon either the restoration of peace between Japan and China or the establishment of an equitable peace in the Pacific area.

In the meantime the Government of Japan declares that it is prepared to remove its troops now stationed in the southern part of French Indo-China to the northern part of the said territory upon the conclusion of the present arrangement which shall later be embodied in the final agreement.

3. The Governments of Japan and the United States shall cooperate with a view to securing the acquisition of those goods and commodities which the two countries need in Netherlands East Indies.

4. The Governments of Japan and the United States mutually undertake to restore their commercial relations to those prevailing prior to the freezing of the assets.

The Government of the United States shall supply Japan a required quantity of oil.

5. The Government of the United States undertakes to refrain from such measures and actions as will be prejudicial to the endeavors for the restoration of general peace between Japan and China.

**Document Handed by the Secretary of State to the
Japanese Ambassador (Nomura)**

WASHINGTON, NOVEMBER 26, 1941

OUTLINE OF PROPOSED BASIS FOR AGREEMENT BETWEEN
THE UNITED STATES AND JAPAN

SECTION I

Draft Mutual Declaration of Policy

The Government of the United States and the Government of Japan both being solicitous for the peace of the Pacific affirm that their national policies are directed toward lasting and extensive peace throughout the Pacific area, that they have no territorial designs in that area, that they have no intention of threatening other countries or of using military force aggressively against any neighboring nation, and that, accordingly, in their national policies they will actively support and give practical application to the following fundamental principles upon which their relations with each other and with all other governments are based:

(1) The principle of inviolability of territorial integrity and sovereignty of each and all nations.
(2) The principle of non-interference in the internal affairs of other countries.
(3) The principle of equality, including equality of commercial opportunity and treatment.
(4) The principle of reliance upon international cooperation and conciliation for the prevention and pacific settlement of controversies and for improvement of international conditions by peaceful methods and processes.

The Government of Japan and the Government of the United States have agreed that toward eliminating chronic political instability, preventing recurrent economic collapse, and providing a basis for peace, they will actively support and practically apply the following principles in their economic relations with each other and with other nations and peoples:

(1) The principle of non-discrimination in international commercial relations.
(2) The principle of international economic cooperation and abolition of extreme nationalism as expressed in excessive trade restrictions.
(3) The principle of non-discriminatory access by all nations to raw material supplies.
(4) The principle of full protection of the interests of consuming countries and populations as regards the operation of international commodity agreements.
(5) The principle of establishment of such institutions and arrangements of international finance as may lend aid to the essential enterprises

and the continuous development of all countries and may permit payments through processes of trade consonant with the welfare of all countries.

SECTION II

Steps to Be Taken by the Government of the United States and by the Government of Japan

The Government of the United States and the Government of Japan propose to take steps as follows:

1. The Government of the United States and the Government of Japan will endeavor to conclude a multilateral non-aggression pact among the British Empire, China, Japan, the Netherlands, the Soviet Union, Thailand and the United States.

2. Both Governments will endeavor to conclude among the American, British, Chinese, Japanese, the Netherland and Thai Governments an agreement whereunder each of the Governments would pledge itself to respect the territorial integrity of French Indochina and, in the event that there should develop a threat to the territorial integrity of Indochina, to enter into immediate consultation with a view to taking such measures as may be deemed necessary and advisable to meet the threat in question. Such agreement would provide also that each of the Governments party to the agreement would not seek or accept preferential treatment in its trade or economic relations with Indochina and would use its influence to obtain for each of the signatories equality of treatment in trade and commerce with French Indochina.

3. The Government of Japan will withdraw all military, naval, air and police forces from China and from Indochina.

4. The Government of the United States and the Government of Japan will not support—militarily, politically, economically—any government or regime in China other than the National Government of the Republic of China with capital temporarily at Chungking.

5. Both Governments will give up all extraterritorial rights in China, including rights and interests in and with regard to international settlements and concessions, and rights under the Boxer Protocol of 1901.

Both Governments will endeavor to obtain the agreement of the British and other governments to give up extraterritorial rights in China, including rights in international settlements and in concessions and under the Boxer Protocol of 1901.

6. The Government of the United States and the Government of Japan will enter into negotiations for the conclusion between the United States and Japan of a trade agreement, based upon reciprocal most-favored-nation treatment and reduction of trade barriers by both countries, including an undertaking by the United States to bind raw silk on the free list.

7. The Government of the United States and the Government of Japan

THE JAPANESE EMPIRE, 1941

Japanese Expansion in Asia to Dec. 7, 1941

will, respectively, remove the freezing restrictions on Japanese funds in the United States and on American funds in Japan.

8. Both Governments will agree upon a plan for the stabilization of the dollar-yen rate, with the allocation of funds adequate for this purpose, half to be supplied by Japan and half by the United States.

9. Both Governments will agree that no agreement which either has concluded with any third power or powers shall be interpreted by it in such a way as to conflict with the fundamental purpose of this agreement, the establishment and preservation of peace throughout the Pacific area.

10. Both Governments will use their influence to cause other governments to adhere to and to give practical application to the basic political and economic principles set forth in this agreement.

READINGS

1. F.D.R.: War Monger

Charles C. Tansill has written for World War II, as earlier for World War I, the most scholarly account from the revisionist point of view. The revisionists are agreed that the Axis was not a threat to the United States and that there was no imperative need for America to enter the conflict. Yet for reasons of his own—perhaps ambition or love of the British—President Roosevelt deliberately embarked on a course which he knew would probably lead to war. At the same time, he carefully concealed his true purposes from the American people and justified his policies on the grounds that they would keep the nation at peace. When Adolf Hitler refused to be baited into declaring war in the Atlantic, the United States entered via the "backdoor," by provoking Japan into the Pearl Harbor assault. Most historians decline to accept as valid such revisionist views.

Backdoor to War
CHARLES C. TANSILL

Roosevelt Regards Neutrality as an Outmoded Concept

While the President was pleading with Mussolini to remain neutral in the great conflict that was wrecking Europe, he himself was pushing America down the road to war. On April 16 it was reported that the Anglo-French Purchasing Commission could obtain planes of almost any type then being produced for the armed forces of the United States. This news encouraged the French Premier, Paul Reynaud, to send to Washington (May 14) the startling request that the American Government arrange for the "sale or lease of old destroyers." On the following day Winston Churchill, who displaced Chamberlain as Prime Minister on May 10, sent a more ambitious request that was quite breath-taking:

> All I ask now is that you [President Roosevelt] should proclaim non-belligerency, which would mean that you would help us with everything short of actually engaging armed forces. Immediate needs are: First of all, the loan of forty or fifty of your older destroyers; . . . Secondly, we want several hundred of the latest types of aircraft; . . . Thirdly, anti-aircraft equipment and ammunition. . . . Fourthly, the fact that our ore supply is being compromised from Sweden, from North Africa and perhaps from Northern Spain, makes it necessary to purchase steel in the United States. . . . I should like to feel reasonably sure that when we can pay no more, you will give us the stuff all the same. Fifthly, . . . the visit of a United States Squadron to Irish ports . . . would be invaluable.

The President replied that he could not make a deal concerning the destroyers "without authorization from Congress." Moreover, America "needed the destroyers" for its "own defences." Churchill greatly regretted this negative answer but he still hoped to get "at the earliest possible date" the "largest possible number of Curtiss P-40 fighters." In conclusion he

Charles Callan Tansill, *Backdoor to War: The Roosevelt Foreign Policy, 1933–1941.* Copyright, 1952. Henry Regnery Company. Reprinted with permission of the publisher. Pp. 586–589, 595–599, 602–606, 611–615, 616, 639–642, 645–652.

sounded a loud note of alarm that he knew would profoundly affect the
President. If Britain were "left by the United States to its fate," there was
a definite danger that the British fleet might be turned over to the Germans as a bargaining point.

We have already noted that in 1939, while Chamberlain was still Prime
Minister, Churchill began his momentous personal correspondence with
President Roosevelt. It has been stated that one of the first cablegrams sent
by Churchill to Roosevelt was phrased in a most grandiloquent manner.
The gist of it has been given as follows: "I am half American and the
natural person to work with you. It is evident we see eye to eye. Were I
to become Prime Minister of Britain we could control the world."

Churchill states that he sent "nine hundred and fifty" of these cablegrams to the President and received "about eight hundred in reply." His
relations with the American Chief Executive "gradually became so close
that the chief business between our two countries was virtually conducted
by these personal interchanges between him and me. . . . As head of
the State as well as Head of the Government, Roosevelt spoke and acted
with authority in every sphere."

It is obvious that Churchill regarded Roosevelt as an American dictator
who had little concern for the opinions of Congress and the American
people. With reference to the matter of war the Churchill cablegrams reveal that he believed that Roosevelt could plunge America into the conflict
in Europe at any time he desired. The French Cabinet apparently had the
same viewpoint.

The urgency of Churchill was translated into hysteria by Premier Reynaud. On May 18, Bullitt was informed by Alexis Léger, Secretary-General
of the French Foreign Office, that Reynaud was about to request President Roosevelt to ask Congress for a declaration of war against Germany.
Bullitt frankly informed Léger that such a request would be worse than
useless: Congress would almost unanimously vote against such a declaration. The President then talked to Bullitt over the telephone and instructed him to say that "anything of this nature was out of the question."
But Reynaud continued to press for the impossible. On May 22 he told
Bullitt that the German tide was growing more menacing every minute.
There was grave danger that the French public would insist upon a
separate peace with Germany. In that event a German victory over
Britain "would follow in a few weeks." After this dire event the Panama
Canal would be destroyed by air bombardment and the "American Army
would be able to offer little resistance." Prompt action by the American
Government was "the only real guarantee that Hitler would not some day
be in the White House."

A week later the Reynaud appeals grew more frantic. On May 28 he
warned Bullitt that he had convincing evidence that "if France and England were conquered, Hitler would move almost immediately against the
United States." The American fleet should be sent at once to the Mediterranean so as to exert pressure upon Mussolini to stay out of the war.

The President did not send the fleet to the Mediterranean but he decided to permit American pilots to fly planes, ordered by the Allies, to

Halifax and other ports in the Canadian maritime provinces. Before this decision the Dominion had been designated as a combat area and American nationals had not been allowed to enter it in aircraft belonging to belligerent nations. The President then urged Churchill to send additional planes to France but he was told that Britain needed all available aircraft for defense against expected German attack. Ambassador Bullitt became furious over this negative reply from Britain and he confided to Secretary Hull his belief that the British Cabinet "might be conserving their air force and fleet so as to use them as bargaining points in negotiations with Hitler."

Both the President and Secretary Hull discounted these observations of Bullitt. They were certain that while France "was finished," Britain, with the aid of American supplies, could withstand a German assault. It was imperative, therefore, that these supplies be rushed at once to British ports. Joseph C. Green, chief of the Division of Controls, brought to Secretary Hull's attention an old statute of May 12, 1917. The language of this statute could be interpreted so as to authorize the exchange of army and navy aircraft for new models of a more advanced type. Arrangements were made with a Buffalo concern to deliver to them fifty planes belonging to the Naval Reserve squadrons in exchange for planes of a "superior type." These planes were then rushed to Britain. But Churchill wanted more than planes. In order to meet his importunate requests, the President turned to the Acting Attorney General, Francis Biddle, who conveniently ruled that the Secretary of War had the right to sell surplus war supplies to "any corporation or individual upon such terms as may be deemed best."

General George C. Marshall, as Chief of Staff, now came to the front and directed his chief of Ordnance and his Assistant Chief of Staff to survey the entire list of American reserve ordnance and munitions stocks. On June 3 he approved these lists. The first list was a lengthy one. . . .

The Destroyer Deal

The fall of France imparted a sense of urgency to the Administration's program for aiding Britain by the sale or lease of war matériel. The President's qualms about constitutional limitations slowly disappeared under the drumfire of repeated requests from Churchill. Moreover, he brought into his Cabinet certain new members who were not averse to a prowar inclination. This was particularly true of the new Secretary of War, Henry L. Stimson, who was a notorious war hawk. It is apparent that after June 1940 the Administration embarked upon a phony bipartisan policy that pointed directly to American intervention in the European conflict.

This policy was given a green light on June 10 when Senator Sheppard offered an amendment to a pending defense bill authorizing the War Department to exchange unserviceable or surplus materials for others of which there was a scarcity. Senator Clark, of Missouri, declared that the purpose of the amendment was "an evasion of international law and of the Neutrality Act." But the amendment was adopted by a large majority and the measure finally became law on July 2, 1940.

In the meantime Senator David I. Walsh had sponsored legislation that would provide against any "limitation or reduction in the size of our Navy." The Act of June 28, 1940, embodied the ideas of Senator Walsh. It was not long, however, before the fertile mind of Benjamin Cohen, special assistant to the Attorney General, found several loopholes in this act. The President still had wide powers he could use without previous consultations with Congress. This opinion of Mr. Cohen was shrewdly argued but the Chief Executive "frankly doubted" if it would "stand up." He also feared that Congress was "in no mood at the present time to allow any form of sale."

These doubts were dissolved under the impact of pressure from Churchill. On June 24 he wrote to Mackenzie King and once more emphasized the danger that if England fell there was the possibility that Hitler would get the British fleet. Four days later, in a letter to Lord Lothian in Washington, he repeated this disturbing thought which should be repeated to Roosevelt. He also complained that Britain had "really not had any help worth speaking of from the United States so far." After more than a month of silence he wrote again to the President (July 31) to inform him that the need for destroyers had "become most urgent." The whole fate of the war might rest upon the speed with which these destroyers were delivered. He was confident that the President would not "let this crux of the battle go wrong" for want of the much-needed warships. When Lord Lothian spoke of an exchange of naval bases for destroyers, Churchill indicated his preference was for an indefinite lease and not an outright sale.

Churchill's cablegram to the President (July 31) had led to a Cabinet meeting in the White House on August 2. There was immediate agreement that "the survival of the British Isles under German attack might very possibly depend on their getting these destroyers," but there was also recognition that legislation would be "necessary" to authorize any deal concerning the destroyers. If the British Government would give positive assurances that the British fleet "would not under any conceivable circumstances fall into the hands of the Germans," the opposition in Congress would be "greatly lessened." Perhaps William Allen White would work upon Wendell Willkie, Joseph Martin, and Charles McNary and thus divide the Republican ranks! When the President talked with White over the telephone he elicited a promise from the famous editor to get in touch with Willkie at once.

There was no doubt in Churchill's mind that any transfer of American destroyers to Britain would be a "decidedly unneutral act by the United States." It would justify a declaration of war by Hitler. Such action would be eminently agreeable to Churchill who would ardently welcome American help in the struggle against the dictatorships. But the situation had to be handled carefully. When Lord Lothian (August 6) cabled that the President was exceedingly anxious for a pledge that the British fleet would not be turned over to the Germans in the event that Britain fell, Churchill refused to give one. The British nation would "not tolerate any discussion of what we should do if our island were overrun." It would be best to couple the transfer of destroyers with the lease of naval and air bases in Newfoundland and on some British islands in the Caribbean.

On August 13 the essential paragraphs in this agreement were worked out during a conference between the President, Secretaries Knox, Morgenthau, and Stimson, and Sumner Welles. In the meantime William Allen White had received assurances from Wendell Willkie that he would "not make a campaign issue of the transfer." The services of General Pershing were next enlisted. The old warrior warned the American public in a broadcast that Britain needed immediate aid. This could best be given by placing at the disposal of the British and Canadian governments "at least fifty over-age destroyers which are left from the days of the World War." Admirals Yarnell, Standley, and Stirling supported this viewpoint.

On August 16, President Roosevelt issued a statement that he was negotiating with the British Government for the acquisition of naval and air bases. Nothing was said about a deal for destroyers. Senator David I. Walsh was still showing strong opposition to such a transaction. With the hope of changing the Senator's opinion in this regard the President wrote him a letter with the familiar salutation, "Dear Dave." He assured the Senator that the British islands were "of the utmost importance to our national defence as naval and operating bases." After reminding him that Jefferson in 1803 had purchased Louisiana "without even consulting Congress," the President then expressed the hope that there would be no further opposition to a deal that would be the "finest thing for the nation that has been done in your lifetime and mine."

"Dear Dave" did not fall for this bait so he was later smeared as a loose character. But even so staunch a New Dealer as Secretary Hull had doubts about a destroyer deal and he regretfully informed Lord Lothian that in order "to meet the wishes of your Government an amendment to these provisions of law [the United States Code and the Act of June 28, 1940] may be necessary." But this would take time and Britain's need was immediate. In the meantime Churchill on August 20 had announced in Parliament that negotiations were in progress for leasing air and naval bases in Newfoundland and on British islands in the Caribbean to the United States. Two days later he explained to President Roosevelt the difficulties that would attend any exchange of letters that would admit "in any way that the munitions which you send us are a payment for the facilities." The dispatch of war matériel to Britain should seem to be "a separate spontaneous act on the part of the United States, arising out of their view of the world struggle." But Sumner Welles informed Lord Lothian that under existing legislation it was "utterly impossible" for the President to send destroyers to Britain as a spontaneous gift; they could be sent only as a *quid pro quo*.

On August 23 the President confessed to Secretary Hull that the negotiations with Britain "on the bases and destroyers have bogged down. Please see what you can do." In an extended conference among the President, Secretary Hull, and Lord Lothian the matter was further explored. Secretary Hull made it clear to the British Ambassador that the President "had no authority whatever to make a gift of public property to any Government or individual." But Attorney General Jackson had no trouble finding convenient loopholes in existing legislation. His assistant, Ben Cohen, had also discovered them some months previously. The Act of June 15, 1917, made it unlawful to send any ship out of the United States that was "built, armed or equipped as a vessel of war, with any intent or under any agreement or contract . . . that such vessel shall be delivered to a belligerent nation." This restriction did not apply "to vessels like the over-age destroyers which were not built, armed, equipped as, or converted into, vessels of war with the intent that they should enter the service of a belligerent."

Mr. Jackson blandly pushed aside the pertinent provisions of the Treaty of Washington (May 8, 1871) and Article 8 of the Hague Convention XIII of 1907 which required that a neutral government take measures to prevent the departure from its jurisdiction of any vessel intended to engage in belligerent operations, if the vessel was specially adapted within the neutral's jurisdiction to warlike use. The one precedent that Mr. Jackson adduced to support his contention concerning the transfer of destroyers was a most dubious one. Indeed, the opinion of the Attorney General was distinctly "phony" and was based upon the familiar dictum: "What's the Constitution between friends."

The way was now prepared for the destroyer deal. On September 2 notes were exchanged between Secretary Hull and Lord Lothian which first recited that the British Government, freely and without consideration, granted to the United States a lease for the "immediate establishment and use of naval and air bases and facilities" on the Avalon Peninsula and on the southern coast of Newfoundland, and on the east coast and on the Great Bay of Bermuda. The second item dealt with the establishment by the United States of air and naval bases on certain British territory in the Caribbean (Bahamas, Jamaica, Saint Lucia, Trinidad, Antigua, and British Guiana) in exchange "for naval and military equipment and material which the United States Government will transfer to His Majesty's Government." The leases would run for a period of 99 years. At the same time Churchill also gave an assurance that the British fleet would not be scuttled or surrendered. This assurance was not to be published.

From the viewpoint of international law the destroyer deal was definitely illegal. As Professor Herbert Briggs correctly remarks: "The supplying of these vessels by the United States Government to a belligerent is a violation of our neutral status, a violation of our national law, and a violation of international law." Professor Edwin Borchard expressed a similar opinion: "To the writer there is no possibility of reconciling the destroyer deal with neutrality, with the United States statutes, or with international law." The whole matter was correctly described by the *St. Louis Post-Dispatch* in a pertinent headline: "Dictator Roosevelt Commits an Act of War."

Lend-Lease—Back Door to Intervention in World War II

It was entirely fitting that lend-lease legislation should have a prelude
of promises by the President that American boys would not be sent abroad
to die along far-flung frontiers. It had been evident to the President in the
summer of 1940 that American involvement in World War II might be
just around the corner of the next year. Senator Wheeler had read between the lines of the President's pronouncements and when he saw the
word *war* written in bold letters he tried to block such a contingency by
a strongly-worded plank in the Democratic platform. But the pledge to
keep out of "foreign wars" was nullified by the pregnant phrase—"except
in case of attack." It would not be difficult for an Administration seeking
war to push one of the Axis powers to the point where an attack was
inevitable.

But the American people, like William Allen White, had to be fooled
by pacific phrases. When the election currents in the fall of 1940 appeared
to be making a turn towards Wendell Willkie, the President made some
new pledges at Philadelphia on October 23: "To every man, woman and
child in the nation I say this: Your President and your Secretary of State
are following the road to peace. . . . We are arming ourselves not for
any purpose of conquest or intervention in foreign disputes." A week later,
in Boston, his pledge became more specific: "While I am talking to you
mothers and fathers, I give you one more assurance. I have said this before, but I shall say it again and again and again: Your boys are not going
to be sent into any foreign wars."

Robert Sherwood who helped to prepare this Boston speech had some
qualms of conscience in later years: "For my own part, I think it was a
mistake for him [the President] to go so far in yielding to the hysterical
demands for sweeping reassurance, but, unfortunately for my own conscience, I happened at the time to be one of those who urged him to go
the limit on this. . . . I burn inwardly whenever I think of those words
'again—and again—and again.'"

In the spring of 1941 these fires of conscience were burning very low
in the President's entourage. Under the impact of appeals from Churchill
in England the entire structure of American neutrality was finally de-
molished by the legislative bomb of lend-lease. This bomb was many
months in the making. On November 6, 1940, Churchill wrote to Roosevelt to express his profound relief at the election results: "I feel you will
not mind my saying that I prayed for your success and that I am truly
thankful for it. . . . I must avow my sure faith that the lights by which
we steer will bring us all safely to anchor." Those lights would lead America into the war.

On December 8, 1940, Churchill sent another long letter in which he
outlined in great detail the pressing needs of Britain. In Churchill's eyes
these needs were also America's needs because Britain was fighting our
war as well as hers. The safety of the United States was "bound up with
the survival and independence of the British Commonwealth of Nations."
Therefore, America should rush to Britain war matériel of specified kinds

together with the gift or loan "of a large number of American vessels of war." It was useless to expect Britain to pay for these loans. The moment was approaching when the British Government would "no longer be able to pay cash for shipping and other supplies." The few dollars Britain had left were badly needed for domestic requirements. It would be wrong "in principle" for Britain to be "divested of all saleable assets, so that after the victory was won with our blood, civilisation saved, and the time gained for the United States to be fully armed against all eventualities, we should stand stripped to the bone." America should bear a large part of the financial burden for a new crusade in Europe.

Roosevelt received this communication while he was cruising in the Caribbean. When he returned on December 16 he signified his ardent approval of aid to Britain at America's expense. On the following day, at a press conference, he recited an interesting parable:

> Suppose my neighbor's house catches fire and I have a length of garden hose four or five hundred feet away. If he can take my garden hose and connect it up with his hydrant, I may help him to put out the fire. Now what do I do? I don't say to him before that operation, "Neighbor, my garden hose cost me fifteen dollars; you have to pay me fifteen dollars for it." No! What is the transaction that goes on? I don't want fifteen dollars— I want my garden hose back after the fire is over. . . . What I am trying to do is to eliminate the dollar sign.

What he really meant to say was that he was trying to eliminate the dollar sign so far as Britain was concerned. The American taxpayers would have it before their anxious eyes for the next generation. But before they had time to make any estimates, a lend-lease bill was introduced in the House of Representatives. It bore the significant number H.R. 1776. In that year we declared our independence from Britain; in 1941 we put it into grave peril by giving Britain a blank check which Churchill filled in with great gusto and then sent back to Washington for Roosevelt's indorsement. Harry Hopkins was the contact man in this regard and while still in Britain he heard Churchill's famous broadcast in which the following dangerous nonsense was beamed to rapt American listeners:

> It seems now to be certain that the Government and the people of the United States intend to supply us with all that is necessary for victory. In the last war the United States sent two million men across the Atlantic. But this is not a war of vast armies, firing immense masses of shells at one another. We do not need the gallant armies which are forming throughout the American Union. We do not need them this year, nor next year, nor any year that I can foresee.

These assurances of Churchill were of the same stripe as the Roosevelt assurances during the last days of his campaign for re-election. He probably remembered Lord Northcliffe's sharp indictment of the American masses during the World War: "What sheep!" They could be sheared once more for British benefit by constant repetition of the old propaganda line about Britain fighting America's fight. Roosevelt repeated this line on December 29 in a "fireside chat" to the American people. Aid to Britain was now a question of "national security." If Britain were conquered, "all of us in the Americas would be living at the point of a gun."

On the following day the President summoned to the White House, Secretary Morgenthau and Arthur Purvis, head of the Anglo-French Purchasing Commission, to discuss the details of lend-lease legislation. On January 2, 1941, Edward Foley, Morgenthau's general counsel, and his assistant, Oscar Cox, began the arduous task of drafting the bill. When opposition to the bill developed in certain circles in the State Department, Secretary Knox remarked to Morgenthau in his best serio-comic manner: "Let's organize a hanging bee over there someday and hang the ones that you and I pick out." Some of the clique around the President probably would have regarded the matter of a hanging bee very seriously when Senator Wheeler began a series of blasts against lend-lease legislation. On January 4, 1941, he asked some very pertinent questions: "If it is our war, how can we justify lending them stuff and asking them to pay us back? If it is our war, we ought to have the courage to go over and fight it, but it is not our war." A week later, in a radio broadcast, he feathered a shaft that evoked an immediate cry of pain from the sensitive President. He regarded the lend-lease program as "the New Deal's 'triple A' foreign policy—to plow under every fourth American boy." The President deeply resented these prophetic words and denounced the Wheeler comment upon lend-lease as the "rottenest thing that has been said in public life in my generation."

Although Admiral Stark expressed on January 13 the opinion that "we are heading straight for this war," the lend-lease program was sold to the American people as a form of peace insurance. On March 11, 1941, the lend-lease bill was signed by the President. . . .

In the meantime the Führer was showing a strong determination to adhere to his policy of keeping out of war with the United States. In May 1941 the German attitude was summed up at a meeting between Hitler and his naval advisers:

> Whereas up to now the situation confronting submarines and naval forces on operations was perfectly clear, naval warfare in the North Atlantic is becoming increasingly complicated as the result of the measures taken by the U.S.A. In order to help Britain, the American neutrality patrol, which was hitherto confined to the area within the American neutrality zone, has been reinforced and considerably extended toward the east to about 38° W., i.e. as far as the middle of the Atlantic. The true character of the American neutrality patrol is shown by the fact that vessels on patrol have also been instructed to report by radio any battleships encountered. . . .
>
> We have laid down the following rules for naval warfare in order to comply with German political aims with regard to the U.S.A.:
>
> No attack should be made on U.S. naval forces and merchant vessels.
>
> Prize regulations are not to be applied to U.S. merchant ships.
>
> Weapons are not to be used, even if American vessels conduct themselves in a definitely unneutral manner.
>
> Weapons are to be used *only if U.S. ships fire the first shot.*
>
> As a result of these instructions and of the constant endeavors on the

part of Germany not to react to provocation, incidents with the U.S.A. have been avoided up to the present time.

It is unmistakable that the U.S. Government is disappointed about this cautious attitude on the part of Germany, since one of the most important factors in preparing the American people for entry into the war is thus eliminated. The U.S. is therefore continuing its attempt to obliterate more and more the boundary line between neutrality and belligerency, and to stretch the "short of war" policy further by constantly introducing fresh measures contrary to international law.

The next naval incident involving German-American relations was the sinking of the American merchant ship (May 21, 1941) *Robin Moor*, New York to Cape Town, by a German submarine. There was no visit or search but the crew and passengers were allowed to take to open lifeboats. As the sinking occurred outside the blockade zone it is evident that the submarine commander disregarded orders concerning American ships. Admiral Raeder immediately issued orders to prevent further incidents of this nature, and Hitler, after confirming these instructions, remarked that he wished to "avoid any incident with the U.S.A." On June 20 the President sent a message to Congress in which he bitterly criticized Germany as an international outlaw. He followed this message with another move in the direction of war. On July 7 he ordered American occupation of Iceland. Two days later Secretary Knox gave a statement to the press which implied that the American patrol force in the North Atlantic had the right to use its guns when the occasion arose.

This occasion arose on September 4, 1941, when the destroyer *Greer*, bound for Iceland, was informed by a British plane that a submerged U-boat lay athwart her course some ten miles ahead. The *Greer* at once laid a course for the reported submarine, and after having made sound contact with it, kept it on her bow for more than three hours. During this period a British plane dropped four depth charges in the vicinity of the submarine without effect. Finally, the submarine commander grew tired of this game of hide-and-seek and launched a torpedo which the *Greer* was able to dodge. When the *Greer* counterattacked with depth charges, the submarine launched another torpedo which was avoided. When sound contact with the submarine could not be reestablished, the *Greer* resumed course for Iceland.

On September 11 the President gave a broadcast which presented a distorted version of the *Greer* incident. He conveniently forgot to tell that the initiative had been taken by the *Greer*: "She [the *Greer*] was flying the American flag. Her identity as an American ship was unmistakable. She was then and there attacked by a submarine. Germany admits that it was a German submarine. . . . We have sought no shooting war with Hitler. . . . The aggression is not ours. Ours is solely defense." American vessels would now shoot at sight.

In the face of this serious incident that clearly showed the aggressive character of American naval patrolling, Hitler maintained his policy of avoiding difficulties with the United States. On September 17 orders concerning American merchant vessels exempted them from attack, even when in convoy, in all zones except that immediately surrounding the British Isles. In the Pan-American safety belt "no warlike acts" were to be carried out on German initiative.

The American answer to these pacific gestures was to authorize escort duty for American destroyers. It was arranged that an American escort group, based on Argentia, should take over from a Royal Canadian Navy escort at a designated place off Newfoundland and hand over the convoy to a Royal Navy escort at an agreed mid-ocean meeting place. Convoying was now an established practice, and it should be kept in mind that Secretary Knox, during the lend-lease hearings, had frankly admitted that he regarded convoying as an "act of war."

This *de facto* war in the Atlantic soon produced another incident. On October 16 five American destroyers rushed from Reykjavik, Iceland, to the help of a convoy that was being attacked by submarines. On the following day, while in the midst of the fighting, the destroyer *Kearny* was struck by a torpedo and slowly made its way back to Iceland. It had deliberately moved into the center of a pitched battle between German submarines and British and Canadian warships and had taken the consequences. It was not long before President Roosevelt gave to the American people a twisted account of the incident. On October 27 he recounted the happenings on October 16 and 17 and asserted that he had "wished to avoid shooting," America had "been attacked. The U.S.S. *Kearny* is not just a Navy ship. She belongs to every man, woman, and child in this Nation. . . . Hitler's torpedo was directed at every American." In order to give additional overtones of villainy to his description of Nazi wickedness he then stated that he had a secret map made in Germany which disclosed Hitler's plan to put all the continent of South America under his domination. But that was not all. He had in his possession another document made in Germany that revealed Hitler's intention, if he was victorious, to "abolish all existing religions." It should be evident that the "forward march of Hitlerism" should be stopped. . . . We are pledged to pull our own oar in the destruction of Hitlerism." The American Navy had been given orders to "shoot on sight." The Nazi "rattlesnakes of the sea" would have to be destroyed.

This declaration of war was confirmed by the *Reuben James* incident. On October 31, while the *Reuben James* was escorting a convoy to Iceland, some German submarines were encountered about 600 miles west of that island. The American destroyer was struck by a torpedo and rapidly sank. Only 45, out of a crew of about 160, were saved. When the news of the sinking of the *Reuben James* reached Germany, Hitler remarked: "President Roosevelt has ordered his ships to shoot the moment they sight German ships. I have ordered German ships not to shoot when they sight American vessels but to defend themselves when attacked." On November 13, 1941, the directives for conduct of German warships when encountering American naval vessels remained pacific: "Engagements with American naval or air forces are not to be sought deliberately; they are to be avoided as far as possible. . . . If it is observed before a convoy is attacked that it is being escorted by American forces, the attack is not to be carried out."

Germany was trying desperately to stay out of war with the United States. America's attitude was clearly stated by Sumner Welles at Arlington on November 11: "Beyond the Atlantic a sinister and pitiless conqueror has reduced more than half of Europe to abject serfdom. It is his boast that his system shall prevail even unto the ends of the earth. . . . The American people after full debate . . . have determined upon their policy. They are pledged . . . to spare no effort and no sacrifice in bringing to pass the final defeat of Hitlerism and all that which that evil term implies. . . . We cannot know, we cannot yet foresee, how long and how hard the road may be which leads to that new day when another armistice will be signed."

To the mind of Welles and to others in the White House group it was obvious that America was really in the war. But the American people did not realize that momentous fact, nor did they know that they were pledged "to spare no effort and no sacrifice in bringing to pass the final defeat of Hitlerism." It was easy for Mr. Welles to speak glibly of sacrifice. He had long enjoyed wealth and high social position. The word "sacrifice" had always been excluded from his dictionary. As the spokesman for the President he was suddenly breaking to the American people the dread news that they had become involved in a war they had ardently wished to avoid. The war hawks of 1941 were never tired of sneering at the majority of Americans as benighted isolationists who had tried to build a Chinese wall around the United States and thus cut it off from all foreign contacts. They knew their sneers were patent lies. America had never been isolated from the social, economic, religious, and cultural forces that shaped the modern world. Thanks to its geographical position it had escaped the recurring tides of conflict that had crumbled the walls of ancient civilizations and washed away the heritage men had earned through dauntless courage and high endeavor. Americans had been isolationists only against war and its evident evils, and their country had grown prosperous beyond the dreams of the founding fathers. But in 1915, President Wilson began to nurse the thought of sharing America's ideals and wealth with the rest of the world, and two years later he led us into a foreign war that he hoped would make the world safe for democracy. But this theme song turned sour in American ears when it led to the great parade of 1917 which ended for many men in the vast cemeteries in France. It gained new popularity after 1933, and with Roosevelt as maestro, the old macabre accents began to haunt every home. In 1941 his orchestra of death was anxiously waiting for the signal to begin the new symphony. He had hoped for a German motif but Hitler had refused to assist with a few opening martial notes. Perhaps some Japanese statesman would prove more accommodating. At any rate, after the *Reuben James* incident had fallen flat he turned his eyes towards the Orient and sought new inspiration from the inscrutable East. He found it at Pearl Harbor when Japanese planes sounded the first awesome notes in a chorus of war that is still vibrating throughout the world. The story of how the first notes in the script of that chorus were written in by President Roosevelt is told in the next chapter.

When the President perceived that Hitler would not furnish the pretext for a war with Germany, he turned to the Far East and increased his pressure upon Japan. The path to Pearl Harbor had already been pointed out by Mr. Hornbeck in February 1939. After discussing how the American Government had tried to restrain the Japanese advance in North China by "moral and economic opposition," he stated his belief that in the long run the situation would so "develop that military opposition by this country will have to be offered."

But Herbert Feis, the adviser on International Economic Affairs, still favored economic pressure, so on July 26, 1939, Secretary Hull sent a note to Ambassador Horinouchi informing him that the Treaty of February 21, 1911, would terminate on January 26, 1940. The way was thus prepared for an all out economic offensive against Japan. . . .

The Atlantic Conference Pushes America Closer to a Break with Japan, 1941

For Japan there were very dark clouds along the Newfoundland horizon. On the evening of August 9, in the Newfoundland harbor of Argentia, Roosevelt and Churchill had their first conference. The British were particularly concerned about the danger of a Japanese thrust into the southwest Pacific area, and Sir Alexander Cadogan had drafted parallel Anglo-American declarations designed to halt this possible advance. America was to state very frankly that "any further encroachment by Japan in the Southwestern Pacific" would compel the United States to take measures that might lead to war. In order to implement this declaration the President was to "seek authority from Congress" to employ American armed forces as he thought best. The President at once rejected any thought of consulting with Congress. On his own initiative and responsibility he would let the Japanese Government know that if her armed forces moved southward, "various steps would have to be taken by the United States notwithstanding the President's realization that the taking of such further measures might result in war between the United States and Japan." But Sumner Welles thought that the United States should play the role of policeman in a much wider area than the southwest Pacific. America should be ready to repel any Japanese thrust whether it was directed "against China, against the Soviet Union or against the British Dominions or British colonies, or the colonies of the Netherlands in the Southern Pacific area." Churchill and Roosevelt were in hearty agreement with this wider formula, but the President was too cautious to broadcast it to the American public. It had better remain a secret understanding.

Churchill had failed to secure a parallel declaration that pointed straight to war, but the Roosevelt pledges of support relieved most of his fears. This fact was revealed in his speech to Parliament on January 27, 1942: "The probability, since the Atlantic Conference . . . that the United States, even if not herself attacked, would come into a war in the Far East, and thus make final victory sure, seemed to allay some of these anxieties. . . . As time went on, one had greater assurance that if Japan ran amok in the Pacific, we should not fight alone."

Roosevelt Refuses to Meet Prince Konoye

In a statement he handed to the Japanese Ambassador on August 17, Roosevelt carried out his pledge to Churchill. It was phrased in language that was not unduly provocative, but its meaning was very clear:

> If the Japanese Government takes any further steps in pursuance of a policy or program of military domination by force or threat of force of neighboring countries, the Government of the United States will be compelled to take immediately any and all steps which it may deem necessary toward safeguarding the legitimate rights and interests of the United States and American nationals and toward insuring the safety and security of the United States.

With reference to a meeting between Prince Konoye and President Roosevelt, the Japanese Ambassador was informed that if his Government was ready "to suspend its expansionist activities" and embark upon a "peaceful program for the Pacific," the government of the United States "would be glad to endeavor to arrange a suitable time and place to exchange views."

Before this Roosevelt statement could reach Tokyo, Foreign Minister Toyoda had a conference with Ambassador Grew and once more strongly pushed the idea of a meeting at Honolulu between Konoye and Roosevelt. He ardently hoped that at such a meeting it would be possible "to reach a just and equitable agreement." Grew was so deeply impressed with the sincerity of Toyoda's plea that he immediately sent a dispatch to Secretary Hull and urged, "with all the force at his command, for the sake of avoiding the obviously growing possibility of an utterly futile war between Japan and the United States, that this Japanese proposal not be turned aside without very prayerful consideration. . . . The opportunity is here presented . . . for an act of the highest statesmanship . . . with the possible overcoming thereby of apparently insurmountable obstacles to peace hereafter in the Pacific."

On August 28, Ambassador Nomura delivered to President Roosevelt a personal message from Konoye pleading for a meeting which could "explore the possibility of saving the situation." In his remarks to Nomura with reference to a possible meeting with Konoye, the President appeared to think that it would be difficult for him to go as far as Hawaii. Possibly Juneau, Alaska, would be more suitable.

As the President vacillated as to what course to pursue about this proposed meeting with Konoye, an Imperial conference was held on September 6. It was finally decided that Japanese preparations for war would have to be continued so "that they be completed approximately toward the end of October." At the same time, the Foreign Office should "endeavor by every possible diplomatic means to have our demands agreed to by America and England." If these negotiations did not lead to favorable results by the early part of October, then the government should "get ready for war against America."

The position of Japan was very clear. It was insisting upon American recognition of Japan's dominance in the Far East. In the Root-Takahira Agreement of November 30, 1908, we had given Japan a green light to move ahead in Manchuria. Japan had taken advantage of President Theodore Roosevelt's friendly suggestions and had strongly intrenched herself in large areas in North China. In the face of rapidly expanding Russian power in the Far East, this action had been regarded as a national imperative. In the Far East the future belonged either to Japan or Russia, not to a China that had been exhausted by an endless cycle of war, revolution, and war. The policy of President Franklin D. Roosevelt and Secretary Hull in giving strong support to a gravely weakened China was highly unrealistic, and the later collapse of the American position in China stems straight back to the decisions taken in September and October 1941.

During the eventful weeks of September, President Roosevelt seemed unable to make up his mind concerning a meeting with Konoye. In order to dispel this sense of uncertainty, the Division of Far Eastern Affairs (Mr. Ballantine) prepared a long memorandum which was highly critical of Japan. In conclusion, Mr. Ballantine remarked: "The holding of the meeting between the President and the Japanese Prime Minister on the basis of the present status of the discussions between this country and Japan would result in more of disadvantage than of advantage as regards this country's interests and policies." From Tokyo, Ambassador Grew spoke from an entirely different angle. He would not stand inflexibly upon certain principles and demand that Japan agree to accept every one of them. Political differences can be expressed in subtle shades that need not affront nations involved in serious controversy; one does not have to insist upon the conventional pattern of black and white. If America would show some slight spirit of compromise, this concession might evoke concessions on the part of Japan and some path to understanding might be found. There was no real point in insisting that Konoye agree in advance to a long agenda which would awaken instant opposition in Japan. During the sessions of a conference between Konoye and Roosevelt it was highly possible that a spirit of reciprocity might arise which would turn thoughts from war to peace. The situation required statesmanship of the highest order. There seemed no reason to doubt that it could be found in Washington.

Unfortunately, at this time of national crisis, President Roosevelt did not measure up to the demands of the hour. Without the courage to make a decision in the matter of meeting Konoye, he pushed the responsibility upon the shoulders of Secretary Hull. Hull did not hesitate. He was always "wound-up" for such occasions. On October 2 he handed to Ambassador Nomura a statement that contained all the Hull clichés about high moral principles being the directing force in international relations. Dubious American practices in the Caribbean were not mentioned. After a long rehearsal of the reasons why the Hull-Nomura conversations had been a flat failure, he sonorously remarked that before there could be a meeting between the President and Prince Konoye, there would first have to be an agreement upon basic principles of policy. He knew that such an agreement was not possible. He had cleared the decks of the American ship of state for war at any time. It would not be long in coming. . . .

Japan Is Maneuvered into Firing the First Shot at Pearl Harbor

In the second week in November 1941 tension began to mount in Tokyo. On November 10 the Japanese Foreign Minister expressed to Grew the opinion that the "preliminary and exploratory conversations" in Washington had proceeded long enough. It was time for both countries to "enter into formal and official negotiations." The Japanese Government had "repeatedly made proposals calculated to approach the American point of view, but the American Government . . . had taken no step toward meeting the Japanese position." On this same day (November 10), Ambassador Nomura presented to President Roosevelt a further explanation of his Government's proposals. In the meantime the Japanese Foreign Office instructed Nomura that November 25 was the deadline. All negotiations would have to be concluded by that date. This deadline was repeated from Tokyo on November 11. Under pressure from the Foreign Office, Nomura was extremely anxious to secure an early answer to the Japanese proposals of November 7 and 10. While he was awaiting this answer, he noted the military preparations that were being rushed by the Roosevelt Administration: "They are contriving by every possible means to prepare for actual warfare." Tokyo replied to this cablegram by insisting that the deadline of November 25 was "an absolutely immovable one."

Secretary Hull knew of this deadline through intercepted Japanese instructions to Nomura, so on November 15 he handed to Nomura a long oral statement setting forth the bases of an agreement. He knew they would not be acceptable to Japan. Complete control over "its economic, financial and monetary affairs" should be restored to China, and Japan should abandon any thought of preserving in China, or anywhere else in the Pacific area, a "preferential position."

The abrupt tone of this note was a challenge that could easily lead to a break in diplomatic relations. Japan had long feared that such a break was inevitable, but in a final attempt to stave off such an emergency it had been decided to send to Washington another diplomat who would assist Nomura in the delicate negotiations that were hanging by a very slender thread. The new appointee, Saburo Kurusu, had served as consul in Chicago and New York and had recently been in Berlin as ambassador. His happy marriage to an American girl gave him a personal interest in maintaining friendly relations between Japan and the United States.

On November 17, Nomura and Kurusu had a talk with President Roosevelt, and then long, inconclusive conversations with Hull were carried on. To Kurusu it seemed that the President was "very much in earnest in regard to effecting an understanding between Japan and the United States." With Hull, little progress was made. This was particularly true with reference to a solution of the difficulties between China and Japan. Roosevelt seemed to have taken a liking to his old naval acquaintance, Nomura, and was not ready to push things. One day Lowell Mellett and Max Lowenthal paid a visit to the office of Senator Burton K. Wheeler to convey the information that "the President does not want to push America into the war." The Senator took this statement with a large grain of salt, but he remembered that at times Secretary Hull had been more belligerent than the President. This fact had been particularly evident during the sessions of the Democratic National Convention in 1940. When Wheeler was putting up a strong fight to write an antiwar plank in such specific terms that the President could not disregard it, "Jimmy" Byrnes confided to him that Hull was strongly against such a plank. It would prevent him from exerting maximum pressure upon Japan.

In November 1941 the Hull policy of pressure upon Japan was being implemented at full strength. On November 20, Kurusu discussed with Hull the matter of bringing to a close the hostilities between China and Japan. The Japanese Foreign Office believed this could be arranged if the United States would stop sending supplies to China. After stressing this point, Nomura then remarked: "If the tension between Japan and the United States can be relaxed, be it ever so little, particularly in the southwestern Pacific, and quickly clear the atmosphere, then I think we could go on and settle everything else." Kurusu pushed the idea of a *modus vivendi*, and President Roosevelt responded by outlining one that might be accepted. The fourth item in this Presidential proposal read as follows: "U.S. to *introduce* Japs to Chinese to talk things over but U.S. to take no part in their conversations. Later on Pacific agreements."

Japan met this show of conciliation with a concession of her own. The deadline in the negotiations was now extended from November 25 to November 29. But this was the final concession: "This time we mean it, that the deadline absolutely cannot be changed. After that things are automatically going to happen."

On the same day that this deadline was extended (November 22), Nomura and Kurusu once more met Hull in conference. It was soon apparent from his tone that there was small chance that Japanese conditions for a truce would be accepted: (1) a revocation of the American order of July 26 freezing Japanese credits in the United States and thereby stopping all shipments of oil from American ports; (2) American consent to a program aimed at increasing the export of oil and other commodities from the Netherlands East Indies to Japan; (3) American mediation between China and Japan so as to initiate negotiations between the two powers and the cessation of American assistance to Chiang Kai-shek. American consent to these conditions was out of the question even if Japan made far-reaching concessions in return.

During the conference on November 22, Hull acidly complained of the "threatening tone" of the Japanese press and then asked why some Japanese statesman did not start "preaching peace?" When Nomura remarked that he "did not have the slightest doubt that Japan desired peace," Hull scoffed at this statement and lamented that it was a pity that Japan "could not do just a few small things to help tide over the situation." He was particularly critical of the Japanese attitude towards Chiang Kai-shek.

Two days later (November 24), Hull had a conference with the diplomatic representatives of Australia, Britain, China, and the Netherlands. He quickly discovered that the Chinese Ambassador, Dr. Hu Shih, was not enthusiastic about a three months' truce with Japan. But Hull went ahead and drafted a *modus vivendi* which President Roosevelt regarded as a "fair proposition" but he was "not very hopeful" and thought there might be "real trouble very soon."

On the following morning (November 25), Hull showed to Secretaries Knox and Stimson this draft that provided for a three months' truce with Japan. But its terms were so drastic that Stimson believed that Japan would not accept it. That afternoon Secretaries Hull, Knox, and Stimson, along with General Marshall and Admiral Stark, went to the White House for a long conference with the President. From intercepted Japanese cablegrams to Nomura, the President knew that the Japanese deadline for an end to the current negotiations was on November 29. He expressed a fear that Japanese armed forces might make an attack "as soon as next Monday." The main question was "how we should maneuver them into the position of firing the first shot without allowing too much danger to ourselves.

When Hull returned to the Department of State he had a long talk with the Chinese Ambassador who handed him a telegram from Chungking: "After reading your [Hu Shih's] telegram the Generalissimo showed rather strong reaction. He got the impression that the United States Government has put aside the Chinese question in its conversations with Japan instead of seeking a solution and is still inclined to appease Japan at the expense of China." This impudent telegram placed Hull on the defensive. He frankly admitted that the conversations he had been carrying on with the Japanese envoys were merely a delaying action: "The official heads of our Army and Navy for some weeks have been most earnestly urging that we not get into war with Japan until they have an opportunity to increase further their plans and methods and means of defense in the Pacific area."

On the afternoon of November 25 there were more cablegrams from China. Mr. T. V. Soong handed Secretary Stimson another cablegram from Chiang Kai-shek in which the Generalissimo urged the United States to be "uncompromising" in its attitude towards Japan. This pressure was increased by a communication from Owen Lattimore, the American adviser of Chiang Kai-shek, to Lauchlin Currie, administrative assistant to President Roosevelt: Any *"modus vivendi"* arrived at with

Japan "would be disastrous to Chinese belief in America." For a week Currie was "terribly anxious" because he feared that "Hull was in danger of selling China and America and Britain down the river." In Chungking, Madame Chiang Kai-shek became "unrestrainedly critical" of the American Government for its failure to "plunge into the war" and thus aid China.

On the morning of November 26, Hull saw a telegram from Churchill to the President: "There is only one point that disquiets us. What about Chiang Kai-shek? Is he not having a very thin diet?" It was not long before Hull was nearly hysterical. During a telephone conversation with Secretary Stimson he remarked that he had just about made up his mind about the *modus vivendi*—he "would kick the whole thing over." A few moments later Stimson phoned to the President and informed him that a Japanese expeditionary force was moving south from Shanghai. The President promptly "blew up" and exclaimed that this fact "changed the whole situation because it was an evidence of bad faith on the part of the Japanese." But the leading officers of the American armed forces still counseled caution. On this same morning (November 26) there was a meeting of the Army-Navy Joint Board and Admiral Ingersoll presented a series of arguments "why we should not precipitate a war."

But Hull was tired of carrying on negotiations with Japan. He was not a master of diplomatic double talk and he squirmed under the direct questions of the Japanese envoys. As far back as January 23, 1941, he had listened without any real interest to the proposals that Bishop Walsh and Father Drought had brought from Matsuoka: "(1) an agreement to nullify their [Japanese] participation in the Axis Pact; (2) a guarantee to recall all military forces from China and to restore to China its geographical and political integrity." If he had rejected these unusually conciliatory proposals why should he be deeply concerned about recent ones that did not go nearly so far!

On the afternoon of November 26 he abandoned all thought of a truce with Japan and put into final shape a ten-point proposal. Both he and the President knew this program would be rejected by Japan. There was no thought of compromise or conciliation: "The Government of Japan will withdraw all military, naval, air and police forces from China and from Indochina." When Kurusu read the ten-point proposal of Secretary Hull he immediately inquired if this was the American answer to the Japanese request for a *modus vivendi* or truce. Was not the American Government interested in a truce? Hull merely replied that "we have explored that" but had arrived at no real decision. Kurusu could only reply that the Secretary's attitude "could be interpreted as tantamount to meaning the end." It was obvious that the next step was war.

On the morning of December 4, the Navy radio receiving station at Cheltenham, Maryland, intercepted a Japanese overseas news broadcast from Station JAP in Tokyo, in which there was inserted a false weather report, "east wind rain." On November 19 the Japanese Government had instructed its ambassador in Washington that such a weather forecast would indicate imminence of war with the United States. After intercepting this Japanese instruction the radio receiving stations of the American armed forces were on the alert for the "east wind rain" message. As soon as it was translated, Lieutenant Commander Kramer handed it to Commander Safford with the exclamation: "This is *it*." Safford got in touch immediately with Rear Admiral Noyes who telephoned the substance of the intercepted message "to the naval aide to the President."

According to the testimony of Captain Safford [in 1941 a Commander], the

> "winds" message and the change of the [Japanese] naval operations code came in the middle of the week: two days to Saturday and three days to Sunday. It was unthinkable that the Japanese would surrender their hopes of surprise by delaying until the week-end of December 13–14. This was not crystal-gazing or "intuition"—it was just the plain, common sense acceptance of a self-evident proposition. Col. Sadtler saw it, and so did Capt. Joseph R. Redman, U.S.N., according to Col. Sadtler's testimony in 1944. . . . The Japanese were going to start the war on Saturday, December 6, 1941, or Sunday, December 7, 1941.

For the next three days Commander Safford and Lieutenant Commander Kramer tried in vain to get some action out of their superior officers with regard to the implications of the "east wind rain" message. When they induced Captain McCollum to exert some pressure upon Admiral Stark he was given a sharp rebuke which so infuriated him that he later poured the whole story into the receptive ears of Admiral Kimmel. This disclosure led Kimmel to press for the Pearl Harbor investigations.

The unaccountable failure of high naval officers to convey a warning to Honolulu about the imminence of war was given additional highlights on the evening of December 6 when the Japanese reply to the American note of November 26 was sent secretly to Ambassador Nomura. It was intercepted by Navy receiving stations and decoded. When the President read this message to Nomura he at once exclaimed: "This means war!" He tried to get in touch with Admiral Stark but was informed that the chief of naval operations was at the National Theatre enjoying the delightful strains of *The Student Prince*. The next day the Admiral's ears would be assailed by the crashing echoes of the attack upon Pearl Harbor.

It would ordinarily be assumed that the President, after reading this intercepted Japanese message, would hurriedly call a conference of the more important Army and Navy officers to concert plans to meet the anticipated attack. The testimony of General Marshall and Admiral Stark would indicate that the Chief Executive took the ominous news so calmly that he made no effort to consult with them. Did he deliberately seek the Pearl Harbor attack in order to get America into the war? What is the real answer to this riddle of Presidential composure in the face of a threatened attack upon some American outpost in the faraway Pacific? This problem grows more complicated as we watch the approach of zero hour. At 9:00 A.M. on December 7, Lieutenant Commander Kramer delivered to Admiral Stark the final installment of the Japanese instruction to Nomura. Its meaning was now so obvious that Stark cried out in great alarm: "My God! This means war. I must get word to Kimmel at once." But he made no effort to contact Honolulu. Instead he tried to get in touch with General Marshall, who, for some strange reason, suddenly decided to go on a long horseback ride. It was a history-making ride. In the early hours of the American Revolution, Paul Revere went on a famous ride to warn his countrymen of the enemy's approach and thus save American lives. In the early hours of World War II, General Marshall took a ride that helped prevent an alert from reaching Pearl Harbor in time to save an American fleet from serious disaster and an American garrison from a bombing that cost more than two thousand lives. Was there an important purpose behind this ride? This question looms constantly larger as we look further into the Pearl Harbor hearings.

When Colonel Bratton, on the morning of December 7, saw the last part of the Japanese instruction to Nomura he realized at once that "Japan planned to attack the United States at some point at or near 1 o'clock that day." To Lieutenant Commander Kramer the message meant "a surprise attack at Pearl Harbor today." This information was in the hands of Secretary Knox by 10:00 A.M., and he must have passed it on to the President immediately.

It was 11:25 A.M. when General Marshall returned to his office. If he carefully read the reports on the threatened Japanese attack (on Pearl Harbor) he still had plenty of time to contact Honolulu by means of the scrambler telephone on his desk, or by the Navy radio or the FBI radio. For some reason best known to himself he chose to send the alert to Honolulu by RCA and did not even take the precaution to have it stamped, "priority." As the Army Pearl Harbor Board significantly remarked: "We find no justification for a failure to send this message by multiple secret means either through the Navy radio or the FBI radio or the scrambler telephone or all three." Was the General under Presidential orders to break military regulations with regard to the transmission of important military information? Did he think that the President's political objectives outweighed considerations of national safety? Was the preservation of the British Empire worth the blood, sweat, and tears not only of the men who would die in the agony of Pearl Harbor but also of the long roll of heroes who perished in the epic encounters in the Pacific, in the Mediterranean area, and in the famous offensive that rolled at high tide across the war-torn fields of France? New cemeteries all over the world would confirm to stricken American parents the melancholy fact that the paths of military glory lead but to the grave.

But the President and Harry Hopkins viewed these dread contingencies with amazing equanimity. In the quiet atmosphere of the oval study in the White House, with all incoming telephone calls shut off, the Chief Executive calmly studied his well-filled stamp albums while Hopkins fondled Fala, the White House scottie. At one o'clock, Death stood in the doorway. The Japanese had bombed Pearl Harbor. America had suddenly been thrust into a war she is still fighting.

2. F.D.R. and the Axis Threat

Rooseveltian foreign policy was defended against revisionist charges by Basil Rauch of Columbia University, author of an early study of the New Deal. With other historians in the "internationalist school," he believes that Roosevelt correctly viewed Hitlerite Germany as a threat to American security and values. Consequently, F.D.R. rendered aid short of war to Britain and the other states resisting Hitler. He long believed, however, that the Axis could be checked without direct American involvement. As for Japan, although the Roosevelt administration condemned the Japanese invasion of China, dating from 1937, it was hoped that peace could be preserved, especially since Europe had top priority. The tortuous negotiations and the slowly tightening economic pressures were intended to check Japan without war; even when code intercepts indicated that the Japanese leaders were determined on hostilities unless America acquiesced in the Nipponese conquests, it was still hoped that the conflict could be delayed. The Pearl Harbor attack came as a complete surprise. (The Beard and Morgenstern volumes referred to by Rauch in the following selection are: Charles A. Beard, *President Roosevelt and the Coming of the War* [1948]; and George Morgenstern, *Pearl Harbor: The Story of the Secret War* [1947].)

From Munich to Pearl Harbor

BASIL RAUCH

During the decade 1933–1942, world events and President Franklin D. Roosevelt led the American people and their government to adopt collective security as the foreign policy of the United States. The late Dr. Charles A. Beard is the only historian who has written on the process by which the nation abandoned isolationism and turned to internationalism. His two books, *American Foreign Policy in the Making: 1932–1940: A Study in Responsibilities*, and *President Roosevelt and the Coming of the War: 1941. A Study in Appearances and Realities* frankly aim to destroy the faith of Americans in the honesty of President Roosevelt in planning the new foreign policy.

These books propose a revisionist interpretation of the causes of American entry into the Second World War. After the First World War, revisionist historians won over the American public to their view that the United States had entered that war not because Germany committed aggression against it, but because American bankers and munitions manufacturers plotted entry for their own profit. The thesis provided justification for the return to isolationism. Beard's purpose was to create a similar disillusionment regarding the reasons for American entry into the recent war, and a similar revulsion against the foreign policy of internationalism.

The villain in Beard's plot is not an economic group with a vested interest in war, but the President of the United States acting for motives which are not defined. The picture of President Roosevelt engaged in a colossal and profoundly immoral plot to deceive the American people into

Basil Rauch, *Roosevelt: From Munich to Pearl Harbor.* New York: Farrar, Straus and Cudahy, Inc. (Creative Age Press), 1950. Reprinted with permission. Pp. 1–6, 376, 388–390, 392–393, 455, 458–459, 460–461, 462–467, 468–472, 475–477 participating in the war unnecessarily and contrary to their interests might be thought so overdrawn as to be unconvincing. But Beard relies upon the effects of the twelve and more years of widely publicized hatred of Roosevelt by a minority of the public and the majority of the press to make the familiarity of his characterization overcome its implausibility.

An indication of Beard's desire to capitalize on anti-Roosevelt feeling is that in his two books he almost completely ignores the part Secretary of State Hull played in the making of administration foreign policy. Hull's work was certainly second in importance only to that of the President himself, and in details it was more revealing than Roosevelt's. But, because Hull was generally regarded as an honest and safe leader, his presence on Beard's stage as Roosevelt's partner would have been an inartistic contradiction of Beard's image of Roosevelt pursuing a sinister plot.

This is only one of the many artful exclusions Beard practices. More important is his exclusion of any data on the objective course of world events which might suggest that the United States, confronted by rising Axis power, did actually face danger to its own security. In Beard's books, not policies of Hitler or Japan but the policies of Roosevelt created first the danger and then the fact of United States participation in the Second World War. In the early pages of *American Foreign Policy in the Making,* Beard shows admirable, perhaps even excessive, respect for the complexities of problems of historical causation, but only in order to justify his own failure to assess the part of the aggressor nations in causing the Second World War. Thereafter Beard proceeds in the remainder of that book and throughout his second one to make a masterpiece of oversimplification in order to lay responsibility for war upon Roosevelt.

Besides excluding material essential for the understanding of Roosevelt's foreign policy, Beard violently distorts the material he does use. His principal distortions are two: that internationalists, led by Roosevelt during the thirties, wanted the United States to go to war; and that Roosevelt practiced deception on the American people regarding the nature and aims of his foreign policy.

The first of these distortions depends upon a perverse definition of internationalism. Beard lifts his definition from the lexicon of isolationism and uses it in both his books as axiomatic truth. His complete definition follows:

> Here and in the following pages the term *internationalism* is used as meaning: World peace is desirable and possible; it is indivisible and can be secured for the United States only by entering into a positive connection with a league, or association, of nations, empowered to make pacific adjustments of international conflicts and to impose peace, by effective sanctions or by force, on aggressors or peace breakers; the United States cannot maintain neutrality in case of any major war among European and Asiatic powers.

This definition is fair enough up to the word "only," which, strengthened as it is by the word "positive," falsifies the program of American internationalists, especially of the time when President Roosevelt came to

office, as if the *ultimate* step by the United States in the direction of collective security, that is, "a positive connection with a league, or association,
of nations," was the "only" and therefore the *first* step they advocated. The
Roosevelt administration never advocated United States entry into the
League of Nations. It did advocate parallel action with the League in
particular cases, after the United States should have first decided independently in each case that the action of the League corresponded to the
interests and policy of the United States. Whether independent and
parallel action with the League of Nations may be termed a "positive connection with a league" is debatable, but it is also beside the point.

The heart of the argument was that isolationists during the period between the two World Wars asserted the impossibility of the United States
taking part in collective action against an aggressor without forming "entangling alliances" and making "prior commitments" which would destroy
the sovereignty of the United States and permit other nations to determine
its policy and even plunge it into war against its will. This was the chief
argument against joining the League after the First World War. Henry L.
Stimson, President Hoover's Secretary of State, President Roosevelt, and
Secretary Hull were, nonetheless, internationalists even though they conceded to the power of this argument. Their statesmanship consisted in
devising techniques which would permit the United States to take part in
international action for collective security without forming entangling
alliances or making prior commitments. One such was the technique of
"parallel action"; another was "consultation," whereby the United States
promised to consult with other nations when aggression occurred, but reserved the right to judge for itself in each case whether it should take
action against the aggressor; a third was a discriminatory arms embargo
against aggressors; a fourth was Lend Lease; a fifth was the "veto power"
of the United States in the Security Council of the United Nations, which
not only avoids prior commitment by the United States to take action in
any particular case, but enables the United States to prevent the Security
Council itself from taking action.

The development of such techniques is of supreme importance in the
history of collective security as an American policy. It is sometimes argued
that these techniques compromised the policy of collective security to the
point of obliteration. In this view, the effective policy of the United States
under Roosevelt shifted not from isolation to collective security but from
isolation to participation in world politics to protect the United States and
increase its power at the expense of other powers. Whether this is indeed
a fair statement of the "inner meaning" or Roosevelt's policy will be discussed hereafter. In either case, Roosevelt's method was cooperation with
some powers against others; the method was supported by internationalists and the development certainly marked a change in United States
foreign policy. Whatever the "inner meaning" of this development, isolationists denied that national sovereignty could be preserved by any
method except abstinence from cooperation with other governments; they
asserted that the object of the new policy was not peace but war, and
Beard perpetuates their distortions as "truths of history."

The new techniques enabled Roosevelt and other leaders to go before the country and plead for collective security, and at the same time promise in good faith that they did not contemplate entangling alliances or prior commitments and that they had as their greatest purpose avoidance of United States participation in war. Throughout his two books, Beard calls such promises "retreats" from the policy of collective security or "denials" of that policy and examples of how Roosevelt "misled" the people. Evidently parallel action, consultation, and a discriminatory arms embargo do not constitute for Beard a "positive connection with a league." Positive or not, these techniques constituted the program of American internationalism during the thirties, and Beard's definition of that word evades, as isolationists generally evaded, that fact, in order to make the false charge that internationalism did involve entangling alliances and prior commitments—and war.

Collective security, the isolationists charged, would involve the United States in war. It would be a most evil war because entangling alliances and prior commitments would make it an "offensive" war, one that was "none of our business," fought by the United States "against our will," "to pull other people's chestnuts out of the fire." The President was accused of advocating internationalism *because* it would involve the United States in war. Beard arranges his definition of internationalism to lead his readers into acceptance of the charge as truth. The central argument of internationalists, that collective security is precisely the only means whereby the United States can *avoid* war, he distorts into a charge that they believe in using force, not solely as a last recourse *after* peaceful moral, diplomatic, economic, and political sanctions have failed to halt an aggressor, but at the outset, as an *alternative* to other sanctions. The word "or" in Beard's definition ". . . impose peace, by effective sanctions or by force, . . ." mashes into one lump the series of measures, carefully graded from less to more coercive, with which internationalists believe an aggressor should be faced—those measures to be applied successively, with the hope and reasonable expectation that the threat of stronger measures would, at a stage short of war, stop the aggressor. No reasonable observer is likely to argue that, if all the allied and associated powers that ultimately combined to win the First and Second World Wars had combined before those wars began and faced Germany and its allies with the certainty of their collective action, those wars would have occurred.

A fair definition of internationalism must specify that the policy involves a series of collective measures, graded from less to more coercive, by a group of nations having a large share of world power, and the reasoned conviction of internationalists that the threat of these measures will stop aggression before the last one, force, is reached. Thus the central, simple fact may be understood: internationalists support collective measures against aggression as the best means of securing world peace.

Beard's other chief distortion—that Roosevelt practiced deception on the American people regarding the nature and aims of his foreign policy —depends upon his distorted definition of internationalism. Beard proves in great detail that Roosevelt repeatedly assured the American people that his policy was to avoid entangling alliances, prior commitments, and war. He finds deception in these assurances because an internationalist policy, in Beard's view, could not avoid entangling alliances, prior commitments, and war.

His thesis is maintained by butchering the record and throwing out its most vital parts. Roosevelt, from his first to his last days in office, not only repeatedly assured the American people that his policy was to avoid entangling alliances, prior commitments and war, but he devised and repeatedly urged upon the public and Congress techniques of collective security which, while avoiding entangling alliances and prior commitments, he as an internationalist was convinced were the best means of preventing United States involvement in war. . . .

Japan's Secret Program

[Japanese Foreign Minister] Matsuoka's statement afforded a public glimpse of the secret program of the Japanese government, which was fully exposed after the war by the International Military Tribunal for the Far East. It was adopted in October, 1940, and designated three objectives: early successful settlement of the China Incident; a nonaggression pact with Russia; and incorporation of the countries of southeast Asia and the southwest Pacific, including Malaya, India, Australia, and New Zealand, in the Greater East Asia Co-Prosperity Sphere. Singapore and the Philippines were regarded as the keys. If they were won, all the rest would fall easily to Japan.

Action to achieve the third objective was planned on two fronts: diplomatic and military. Britain would be offered Japanese mediation in the European war in return for recognition of the Co-Prosperity Sphere, including surrender of Singapore. In February, 1941, the Japanese leaders told the Germans that a military attack against Singapore was planned. Military bases were to be secured in Indo-China and Thailand. The United States was to be offered Japanese recognition of "Philippine independence" in return for American recognition of the Co-Prosperity Sphere. In January, 1941, the Japanese Commander of the Combined Fleets approved and transmitted to Imperial General Headquarters a plan for a surprise attack on Pearl Harbor while the two countries were at peace. In May, 1941, the Japanese Navy began training for the attack.

Thus it is now clear that when Matsuoka told the Japanese Diet in January, 1941, that he wanted the United States to agree to Japanese supremacy in the western Pacific, he actually demanded American cooperation with Japan to achieve its conquests as the price of American immunity from Japanese attack against the United States.

In the innumerable American-Japanese conversations of 1941, the Roosevelt administration never refused to discuss a Japanese proposal, it never issued an ultimatum, and it never offered or agreed to proposals which signified appeasement, that is, which gave consent or support to Japanese conquests of territories of third countries. . . .

Roosevelt and Hull Call a Halt

The Japanese-American conversations had all but broken down when Hitler invaded the Soviet Union on June 22. The Roosevelt administration became concerned that the Japanese would attack Russia or take advantage of Russia's preoccupation to launch the long-expected southward movement. The President sent a message to Premier Konoye on July 6 stating the earnest hope of the United States government that reports of Japan's decision to enter the war against the Soviet Union were not based on fact, because it would destroy the possibility of strenthening the peace of the Pacific area. Konoye answered with a copy of an oral statement Matsuoka had made to the Soviet Ambassador on July 2, declaring that Japan, in its present "awkward" position, hoped to preserve the spirit of mutual trust among the Axis allies while maintaining good relations with the Soviet Union. And Konoye turned about to ask the United States whether reports were true that the United States intended to intervene in the European war. The American answer to this was that United States policy was based solely on self-defense against the Germans, who were the chief threat to the security of the Western Hemisphere, and that American aid to Russia would "in no manner threaten the security of nations which have not joined the conflict on Hitler's side."

At the same time, the Roosevelt administration received alarming information of Japanese preparations for a major war. Ominous movements were made publicly, and Magic intercepts contained such signals as the following, in a message from Tokyo to Berlin on July 2, the day of an Imperial Conference:

> The Imperial Government shall continue its endeavor to dispose of the China incident, and shall take measures with a view to advancing southward in order to establish firmly a basis for her self-existence and self-protection.

Other intercepts named French Indo-China and Thailand as immediate targets. Matsuoka instructed Nomura:

> In the meantime, diplomatic negotiations shall be carried on with extreme care. Although every means available shall be resorted to in order to prevent the United States from joining the war, if need be Japan shall act in accordance with the three-Power pact and shall decide when and how force will be employed.

Matsuoka was not quite frank with Nomura. The Far East Tribunal later learned that the Imperial Conference of July 2 had decided to continue conversations with the United States as a cover while final preparations for military action were completed. Troops that later landed in Malaya and the Philippines now began practicing.

On July 18, Admiral Teijiro Toyoda replaced Matsuoka as Foreign Minister of Japan. This shift is called by Morgenstern proof that Japan was amenable to American criticisms of Matsuoka. But promptly after the change, on July 21, Japanese troops invaded southern Indo-China, and it is doubtful whether Roosevelt and Hull could, in the light of that act, sensibly interpret the fall of Matsuoka as a sign of a Japanese turn against the policy of aggression. In southern Indo-China the Japanese occupied and built up bases which gave them a strategic position pointing inexorably towards the Philippines, Malaya, Singapore, and the NEI. In short, the new aggression was proof that the program of southward advance was underway.

It made a farce of Nomura's pretense that his government wished a "peaceful settlement," that Matsuoka's belligerence was a matter of "politics" only for "home consumption." The conversations were broken off by the United States on July 23. It was Japan's new aggression, in contradiction of its professions in Washington, that led Roosevelt and Hull to call a halt. Morgenstern distorts the incident by avoiding mention of the crucial sequence of dates and by giving Japanese unwillingness to sign a blank check for the United States in Europe as the reason why negotiations "stalled." The Japanese, in Morgenstern's account, gave ample proof of good faith by dismissing Matsuoka from power. The Roosevelt administration was unreasonable in its demands and sought excuses to break off conversations in order to invoke economic sanctions with "clear understanding" that they "might easily precipitate war."

The possibility that Japanese invasion of southern Indo-China may have influenced the administration is carefully ignored by Morgenstern. On July 23, two days after that invasion, Sumner Welles told Nomura that Secretary Hull could see no basis for continuation of their conversations. He asserted that agreement with the United States would have given Japan an "infinitely greater amount of security, both military and economic," than it could obtain by conquest. He said the United States had to assume that the Japanese government was taking "the last step" before proceeding on a campaign of totalitarian expansion in the South Seas. Nomura pleaded for "patience" and against "hasty conclusions." He said an embargo on oil exports to Japan would undoubtedly "inflame Japanese public opinion." Welles assured him that Hull would wish to talk again with him. . . .

Economic Sanctions

On July 25 [1941] the administration froze Japanese assets in the United States to prevent their use in trade between the United States and Japan "in ways harmful to national defense and American interests." It also froze Chinese assets at the request of the Chinese government to prevent liquidation of those which were obtained by "duress or conquest." The purpose of the latter action was underlined in a statement of the President that the administration of the licensing system with respect to Chinese assets would be conducted with a view to strengthening the Chinese government and was "a continuation of this Government's policy of assisting China." Synchronization of British policy was apparent the next day when Britain froze Japanese assets and denounced its commercial agreements with Japan. Also on July 26, President Roosevelt nationalized the armed forces of the Philippines.

On the day the United States froze Japanese assets, Colonel Iwakuro told Joseph W. Ballantine, of the State Department, that if the United States took such action, he believed Japan would have no alternative but to go south to Malaya and the NEI to obtain essential supplies. He said such action would also prevent another attempt to reach an "understanding," which his government otherwise urged. Iwakuro said Nomura was too "gentle" to express these views as he did. Ballantine received the impression that the Japanese had no real expectation that conversations would be resumed and that no reply was called for beyond the statements of Welles and Roosevelt to Nomura.

In Tokyo, Ambassador Grew asked Toyoda to consider well how the President's offer to neutralize Indo-China met Japanese contentions. He said that if it were accepted it might establish a new basis for continuation of the Hull-Nomura talks looking towards a general agreement. Grew and Welles both told the Japanese the freezing order, like the earlier abrogation of the American-Japanese commercial treaty, would at first be interpreted liberally by the United States.

Thus doors were again left open by the Roosevelt administration for the Japanese government to achieve peacefully its legitimate ambitions. But immediately reports were received that the Japanese were making demands on Thailand of the same sort which had preceded invasion of southern Indo-China.

Roosevelt promptly on July 31 told the Japanese government through Welles and Nomura that in the judgment of the United States government "there was not the remotest threat of danger to Japan nor the slightest justification for Japan alleging" that concessions by Thailand were necessary as a means of assuring a Japanese source of raw materials or as a military precaution. But Roosevelt again offered Japan a constructive alternative: he said his offer to neutralize Indo-China should now be regarded as embracing Thailand in order to give Japan the same guarantees and security in that area.

Just as the offer regarding Indo-China had been backed up by the freezing order, so now the President's offer regarding Thailand was backed up on August 1 by an embargo against the export of aviation gasoline. The stated purpose was "in the interest of national defense," and merely on that ground the order was long overdue. In the opinion of most Americans it was also long overdue as an economic sanction against Japanese aggression, and the order was greeted with very wide public satisfaction. . . .

Roosevelt and Pearl Harbor

The fall of the Konoye government led Admiral Stark to send a war warning on October 16, 1941, to Admiral Husband E. Kimmel in command of the Pacific fleet and to Admiral Thomas C. Hart in Command of the Asiatic fleet. The first inference in this warning was that war between Japan and Russia was "a strong possibility." But, the warning continued:

Since the United States and Britain are held responsible by Japan for her present desperate situation, there is also a possibility that Japan may attack these two powers. In view of these possibilities, you will take due precautions, including such preparatory deployments as will not disclose strategic intention nor constitute provocative actions against Japan.

This reflected the estimate of Washington authorities that Japan was most likely to attack Russia at the penultimate moment of Hitler's conquest, in like manner as Mussolini had attacked France. The Pacific commanders were given enough information regarding diplomatic developments to lead them to believe that they knew the situation, but not enough to judge it as effectively as the leaders in Washington. Magic intercepts, the best source of information regarding Japanese intentions, were not transmitted to the commanders. Copies went to only nine persons in Washington, including President Roosevelt, Secretaries Hull, Stimson and Knox, General Marshall and Admiral Stark. General Marshall later said this was necessary to guard a military secret of incalculable value. . . .

Foreign Minister Togo on November 3 sent Saburo Kurusu, former Japanese Ambassador to Germany, to Washington to "assist" Nomura. He had signed the Axis alliance in Berlin. In spite of this, Ambassador Grew saw no reason to believe that Kurusu was "any more friendly to the Nazis than to us."

Grew sent a report to Hull and Welles on November 3 which, as he wrote in his diary, he hoped history would not overlook if war occurred. He did not renew his September 29 proposal that "constructive conciliation" be the policy of the United States. Once more he ruled out appeasement of Japan. But he did give full credit to the sincerity of the Tojo government in "seeking conciliation with the United States." He reasoned that Japanese pro-Axis elements had gained power following the Fall of France. But after the signing of the Axis alliance, Germany's failure to invade Britain and its attack against the Soviet Union, coupled with the strong policy of the United States, had strengthened moderate elements and led the Japanese government to seek conciliation with the United States. If this effort failed, Grew wrote that he foresaw:

a probable swing of the pendulum in Japan once more back to the former Japanese position or even farther. This would lead to what he has described as an all-out, do-or-die attempt, actually risking national hara-kiri, to make Japan impervious to economic embargoes abroad rather than to yield to foreign pressure. It is realized by observers who feel Japanese national temper and psychology from day to day that, beyond peradventure, this contingency not only is possible but is probable.

This turned out to be a correct prediction. But Grew offered no advice as to how the United States might fend off Japan's "do-or-die attempt." It was his opinion that strengthening economic sanctions would not avert war. But he believed the primary question was whether American national interests justified war in case the first line of national defense, diplomacy, failed.

Since appeasement of Japan, including the relaxation of economic sanctions, was ruled out, the only possibility Grew saw for a peaceful solution is found in his assertions that Japanese "moderate elements" were still in power, that the Japanese government actually sought conciliation with the United States.

If Hull could agree with this on November 3, his belief vanished two days later. A Magic intercept of Togo to Nomura read:

> "Because of various circumstances, it is absolutely necessary that all arrangements for the signing of this agreement be completed by the 25th of this month. I realize that this is a difficult order, but under the circumstances it is an unavoidable one. Please understand this thoroughly and tackle the problem of saving the Japanese-American relations from falling into a chaotic condition."

Secretary Hull observes in his *Memoirs* that this meant Japan had "already set in motion the wheels of her war machine. . . ." This and other signs Hull read as proof that Japan was turning to new aggressive advances in the South Seas, "including war with the United States if we did not sign the agreement she required."

Grew himself saw similar evidence in the Japanese press. On November 5 he noted in his diary a list of seven demands which the *Japan Times and Advertiser* said the United States should adopt to make "restitution" to Japan. Besides bald versions of demands already made officially by the Japanese government, this one was laid down:

> Acknowledge Japan's Co-Prosperity Sphere and leadership of the western Pacific, letting Manchuria, China, Indo-China, Thailand, the Netherlands Indies and other states and protectorates establish their own political and economic relations with Japan without interference of any kind.

This newspaper was known to be the organ of the Japanese Foreign Office. . . .

To Gain Time

To keep the door open in order to seize the last chance of tiding things over became the purpose of the Roosevelt administration in the last round of conversations with Japan. Hull warned the President and Cabinet on November 7 that "we should be on the lookout for a military attack by Japan anywhere at any time." This led to warning speeches to the public by Secretary Knox and Under Secretary Welles.

But Hull's warning to the Cabinet did not lead to a new warning by authorities in Washington to commanders in the Pacific for two more weeks. Secretary of War Stimson has written that since August, 1941, the General Staff had been developing an important new strategic concept regarding the Philippine Islands. Formerly the Islands had been regarded as an "unprotected pawn" certain to fall easily to Japan early in a war. But General Douglas MacArthur had been recalled in July to active duty in the United States Army after building up the Philippine Army for the Commonwealth, and he was highly optimistic that his forces could hold the Islands. Also, proponents of air power believed that if a force of the new B-17 heavy bombers, the Flying Fortresses, could be sent to the Philippines, the Islands could be defended and the Japanese could be prevented from moving south through the China Sea. Stimson on October 6 told Hull the Army needed three months to build up the Philippines.

Concentration on the task of building up defenses of the Philippines, as the point where the United States was most likely to be attacked by Japan, evidently preoccupied Washington authorities during the weeks following Hull's warning to the Cabinet. The Secretary of State set out to provide the commodity his colleagues demanded of him—time. . . .

Kurusu

Kurusu arrived in Washington on November 17 and was immediately presented to Hull and Roosevelt. Hull distrusted him and was convinced that he knew the plans of his government and played a double role of trying to press the United States to accept Japan's terms or, failing that, would try to lull the administration with talk until Japan was ready to strike. An oral statement to Hull by Nomura ignored the request that Wakasugi's October 13 statements be confirmed. An "explanation" declared that the escape clauses in the Japanese draft proposals for an agreement were used

> only in order to express the qualification which is due to and necessary for a sovereign state and were not intended to limit or narrow down in any way the peaceful intentions of the Japanese Government.

This was very different from Wakasugi's offer to withdraw the clauses.

The President told Kurusu that the policy of the United States in relation to Germany was one of self-defense. Kurusu said Germany had not "up to this time" asked Japan to fight; that Japan was serving "a desirable purpose" without fighting. This evidently meant that Japan was keeping large bodies of Soviet troops and large portions of the British and American Navies diverted from Europe and the Atlantic. The President and Hull found it necessary to explain that not the United States but Japan was the aggressor in the Pacific. Kurusu said he was not familiar with commercial policy and had not examined Hull's proposal on that issue. He repeated the perennial Japanese complaint that troops could not be withdrawn from China "at once." The President in turn repeated the American answer that "the question ought to be worked out in a fair way considering all of the circumstances. . . ." And he promised that "at a suitable stage," after Pacific questions had been determined, the United States might bring Japan and China together to settle remaining questions or details.

"East Wind Rain"

Secretary Hull wrote in his *Memoirs* that the situation now "could not have been more tense." The day before Kurusu arrived, a Magic intercept from Togo to Nomura rejected Nomura's suggestion that the Japanese government ought to "wait and see what turn the war takes and remain patient." Togo replied that he was "awfully sorry to say that the situation renders this out of the question. I set the deadline for the solution of these negotiations . . . and there will be no change." That deadline, November 25, was a week off. Nomura grasped at the President's mention on November 10 of a *modus vivendi* between Japan and the United States. In an intercepted message to Tokyo on November 19, Nomura stated: "I think that it would be better to fix up a temporary 'truce' now in the spirit of 'give and take' and make this the prelude to greater achievements to come later." Tokyo answered on November 20: "Under the circumstances here, we regret that the plan suggested by you . . . would not suffice for saving the present situation."

This interchange demonstrated two things about the *modus vivendi,* which was presently discussed in Washington: that even the "moderate" Nomura meant it to be preliminary not to peace but to "greater achievements," that is, conquest; and that his government was not interested in a truce which would require postponement of the attacks it had planned. If one speaks of the realities of the situation, as they were exposed to Roosevelt and Hull in the intercepted Japanese messages, it was Japan that issued an ultimatum, including demands, a deadline, and threat of aggression if the demands were not met in the specified time; and for the United States it was, in Hull's words, "a case of signing on the dotted line or taking the consequences."

Ambassador Grew, on the same day that Kurusu arrived in Washington, sent Hull another warning of "the need to guard against sudden Japanese naval or military actions in such areas as are not now involved in the Chinese theater of operations." He said that the intelligence activities of his Embassy were practically restricted to "what could be seen with the naked eye," and that Washington must not depend upon him for any advance information. Troop dispositions, however, indicated new operations either in the southwest Pacific, or Siberia, or both. Actually of course the Japanese were organizing the raiding force that attacked Pearl Harbor, as well as the other forces designated for points in the southwest Pacific, including the Philippines. But it is notable that Grew in Tokyo evidently saw no reason to warn Washington against more than the "normal" targets of Japan: the southwest Pacific and Siberia.

Nor did Magic intercepts give the administration leaders a more accurate picture of Japanese intentions. The most specific intercept was the famous "east wind rain" message of November 19 from Tokyo to the Japanese Embassy in Washington. In it a complete breakdown of the conversations was foreseen, and a code for future use was designated:

In case of emergency (*danger of cutting off our diplomatic relations*), and the cutting off of international communications, the following warning will be added in the middle of the daily Japanese language short wave news broadcast:
(1) In case of Japan-U.S. relations *in danger:* Higashi No Kazeame [east wind rain].
(2) Japan-U.S.S.R. relations: Kitanokaze Kumori [north wind cloudy].
(3) Japan-British relations: Nishi No Kaze Hare [west wind clear].

The prevailing expectation in Washington was that the Japanese would move into Thailand and southward towards Malaya and the NEI, with a possible attack against the Philippines to protect their flank; or, less likely than the southward move, they might move against Siberia. The words italicized in the message quoted above indicate that the code was to be used in a situation amounting to less than a Japanese surprise attack against one or more of the three great powers, that is, *danger,* not certainty, that *diplomatic relations* would end. In another message on the same day, Tokyo warned that if relations with the United States were "*becoming dangerous,*" the word "Higashi" would be used at the beginning and end of Japan's intelligence broadcast."

It may be conjectured that the Japanese government used such "mild" terms out of caution, not wishing to reveal its actual plans in any message sent abroad. Furthermore, Admiral T. S. Wilkinson, Director of Naval Intelligence, believed that the Germans knew in October, 1941, that the United States had solved the Japanese code and had warned the Japanese government. It would be an obvious ruse of the Japanese to send plausible but misleading information in the useless code. If Washington officials were suspicious that the Japanese knew their code was broken, they would not accept intercepts at face value.

It seems doubtful that one may fairly base judgments of the actions of the Roosevelt administration upon the premise that the Magic intercepts gave leading officials accurate foreknowledge of Japanese actions. Not only was there no reference in the intercepts to an impending Japanese attack upon any American territory, but the intercepts were probably read with considerable skepticism. Responsible officials in Washington could be expected to rely chiefly on known Japanese military and naval movements and an estimate of "logical" probabilities. Both pointed to Japanese attack upon the Philippines as the most extreme probability, and Magic intercepts did not contradict this estimate.

The chief item used by Morgenstern to support the isolationist thesis that Washington officials knew beforehand Pearl Harbor would be attacked is a series of intercepts beginning September 24, 1941, of messages between Tokyo and the Japanese Consul General in Honolulu. These messages conveyed the anxiety of Tokyo for data regarding the exact locations of warships in Pearl Harbor, and the reports of the Consul General containing full information. Morgenstern neglects to mention that such information was well within the requirements of a Japanese plan of sabotage by Japanese agents. The authorities at Pearl Harbor were prepared against that danger. But Morgenstern himself does not claim to find in any message prior to one dated 7:22 P.M., December 6, and another of a few hours later, 12:42 A.M., December 7, material that "gave away" the secret of a bombing raid. In these messages the Consul General *for the first time* spoke of air defenses at Hawaii and observed: "I imagine that in all probability there is considerable opportunity left to take advantage for a surprise attack. . . ." Morgenstern then comments that after a December 4 intercept of an "east wind rain" execute message, and the long series of Japanese messages from Honolulu to Tokyo, "there could be no question where the attack would come."

This slurs over his own admission that, not the "long series of messages," but only those sent within the last twelve hours before the Japanese planes appeared over Pearl Harbor at dawn on December 7 actually pointed to raiding planes rather than sabotage. The fact that the two messages which did expose the secret were not decoded until December 8, Morgenstern calls "Washington's excuse. . . ." But Morgenstern himself makes this excuse seem extremely plausible. He describes how the "give-away" messages were intercepted in San Francisco and copies mailed to Washington. Hearing of this, Army Signal Intelligence Service ordered the messages to be sent to Washington on a new teletype machine which had been installed that day. When the messages arrived in Washington, translators were called to night duty. But the final and very lengthy Japanese diplomatic message was then being intercepted, and the translators worked on it instead. Other messages less indicative of Japanese attack were processed even more slowly.

Such is the best evidence Morgenstern can find that for Washington officials "there could be no question where the attack would come," with its implication that commanders at Pearl Harbor were not ordered to shift from preparations against sabotage to preparations against air attack because Roosevelt, Hull, Stimson, Knox, Marshall, and Stark preferred the more serious loss of life and damage to the fleet that would result from mistaken preparations. For such a terrible implication, Morgenstern at the crucial point can do no better than verify the plain reason why Washington officials did not receive the "give-away" messages in time, and call the reason an "excuse." . . .

The Modus Vivendi

The Japanese on November 20 offered a draft proposal for a "temporary agreement." In the light of the rejection by the Japanese government, on November 19, of Nomura's suggestion in favor of such an agreement, this proposal must be regarded as the sheerest of hypocrisies designed to occupy the time while the Japanese task force proceeded to Hawaii. Two of the chief issues on which the United States desired settlement, namely, Japan's obligation under the Axis alliance, and economic policy in China and the Pacific regions, were left for later consideration. On remaining issues, Japan offered to make one concession, withdrawal of Japanese troops from southern to northern Indo-China, in return for United States cooperation with Japan in securing the fruits of aggression in China. Japan asked the United States to stop giving aid to China and to restore economic relations with Japan, including delivery to Japan of a required quantity of oil, while Japan made "peace" with China. Kurusu had admitted to Hull that "peace" with China would involve the stationing of Japanese troops there for an indefinite period. Besides providing Japan with American oil to help it impose its will on China, the United States was asked to "cooperate" with Japan in obtaining for it oil and other materials in the NEI. Japan would promise to make no armed movement southward, but offered no guaranty against aggression northward.

Hull considered that the proposals called for "virtually a surrender" by the United States. He asked Kurusu and Nomura, as he later wrote:

> what they thought would be the public reaction in the United States if we were to announce tomorrow that we had decided to discontinue aid to Great Britain. There was no reply. "In the minds of the American people," I continued, "the purposes underlying our aid to China are the same as the purposes underlying aid to Great Britain. . . ."

Hull regarded the situation as virtually hopeless. But the military leaders pleaded with him for more time, and therefore Hull and State Department officials sought desperately to work out some counterproposal to keep the conversations going. For a few days a three-months' *modus vivendi* was considered. It is noteworthy that it was while Hull worked on this scheme, that the Japanese task force was ordered on November 22 to proceed eastward through the north Pacific to reach Hawaii by December 7. No inkling of this reached American observers or officials in Washington, but ominous movements of Japanese forces into positions where they were poised for attacks against Thailand, Malaya, the NEI, and possibly the Philippines or Guam, were known in detail. On November 24, Army and Navy commanders in the Pacific were warned that a Japanese "surprise aggressive movement in any direction including an attack on the Philippines or Guam is a possibility." This was interpreted in Hawaii to require no change in preparations against sabotage as the chief danger.

President Roosevelt, Secretary of the Treasury Morgenthau, and other officials helped Hull explore the possibility of a *modus vivendi*, and he consulted the representatives of Great Britain, China, the Netherlands, and Australia. A Magic intercept from Tokyo to Kurusu and Nomura on November 22 extended the deadline from November 25 to 29. One phrase in it provides the first reason why Hull in the end decided not to make a counterproposal for a *modus vivendi*. The Japanese Ambassadors were instructed: "Stick to our fixed policy. . . ." This could only mean that nothing but complete American surrender to the Japanese proposals would satisfy Tojo. It confirmed Hull's belief that no arrangement that the United States could accept would be acceptable to Japan. The intercepted message ended: "This time we mean it, that the dead line absolutely cannot be changed. After that things are automatically going to happen."

The second reason why Hull decided against the *modus vivendi* is that the government of China objected to it and obtained wide support for its objection, including that of Churchill. The final American draft of the *modus vivendi* called for mutual pledges that the United States and Japan would not advance in the Pacific area by force or threat of force; Japan would withdraw its troops from southern Indo-China, and also reduce its forces in northern Indo-China to 25,000—a number thought to preclude a campaign to close the Burma Road; the United States would allow limited quantities of American oil, cotton, and other commodities to go to Japan and it would buy Japanese goods; the United States would urge Britain, Australia, and the Netherlands to resume trade similarly with Japan; and the United States affirmed its fundamental position that any settlement between Japan and China must be based upon the principles of "peace, law, order, and justice." Attached to this three-months' *modus vivendi* was a ten-point proposal for a permanent agreement.

The *modus vivendi* drawn up by Hull meant temporary appeasement of Japan insofar as it would give temporary United States approval to Japanese conquests and relax the economic sanctions which the United States, Britain, Australia and the Netherlands had imposed against Japan during preceding months. The plan must be regarded as a product of the desperation of the Roosevelt administration in its fight for time. Had it been offered to Japan, it would have been a violation of the administration's principle of no compromise with aggression.

Only agreement by China, the government which would be the chief victim of this appeasement, that the time which might be gained would be worth the sacrifice, would have justified such an offer to Japan. China refused to agree. Churchill supported the Chinese view. After hectic discussions, the decision was reached on the night of November 25 to make no counterproposal of a *modus vivendi* but to answer the Japanese only with the ten-point proposal for a permanent settlement.

On the Rock of Principle

In this decision the Roosevelt administration met the supreme test of its statesmanship in service of the policy of collective security against aggression. Beard's statement that the decision was made "for reasons which are nowhere explicit" is nonsense; Beard himself recites the evidence that the Chinese government violently opposed the *modus vivendi*. He ignores another contributing factor, that is, the futility of offering to Japan, in the face of the intercepted instructions to the Ambassadors to "stick to our fixed policy," an American *modus vivendi* which would have required Japan to retreat from its "fixed policy," especially in the matter of the number of troops to be left in northern Indo-China. Beard does not wish to admit that the one thing which might have justified temporary appeasement of Japan was the consent of China. The Roosevelt administration refused to make a deal with Japan affecting China's fate without its consent. It refused to ignore the rights of China as Chamberlain had ignored those of Czechoslovakia at Munich.

On the rock of this principle, the last possibility of Roosevelt and Hull attempting to postpone the deadline in Japan's ultimatum collapsed. Actually, no such possibility existed. But the administration believed that a possibility still existed that Japan would only attack non-American territory, leaving room for a choice by the United States whether it should enter the war.

No one but an absolute pacifist would argue that the danger of war is a greater evil than violation of principle. It must be concluded that the isolationist thesis involves denunciation of the Roosevelt-Hull decision against the *modus vivendi* because of the nature of the principle involved. The isolationist believes that appeasement of Japan without China's consent violated no principle worth a risk of war. The internationalist must believe that the principle did justify a risk of war. In short, subjective and *a priori* attitudes ultimately determine judgment of the Roosevelt-Hull policy. If an observer can be imagined to exist who is "neutral" as between the attitudes of isolationists and internationalists, he might conclude that it did not matter whether or not the Roosevelt administration offered the *modus vivendi* because the Japanese government was certain to reject it. . . .

The Message of November 26

Hull's answer on November 26 was a refusal to surrender to the Japanese ultimatum. This was implicit in his rejection of the Japanese proposal for a *modus vivendi*. But he did not entirely reject that proposal, and he offered Japan a draft plan for an agreement on all points at issue as a basis for continued negotiations. This took away from his answer all character of a challenge to Japan to carry out its threat of war. Hull did not expect the Japanese government to accept his constructive proposal for an agreement, and he warned the armed service chiefs that Japan could be expected now to attack, but this was not, as the isolationists charge, proof that he regarded his answer as an "ultimatum." It was proof that he judged correctly that Japan would attack if the United States did not entirely surrender to Japan's ultimatum.

Hull's draft proposal for an American-Japanese agreement contained ten points. None of them was unacceptable or disadvantageous to a Japanese government mindful of the real interests of Japan: 1) a multilateral nonaggression pact among the governments principally concerned in the Pacific; 2) an agreement among the governments principally interested to respect the territorial integrity of Indo-China and equality of economic opportunity in that country; 3) no support of any Chinese government except the national government of Chiang Kai-shek; 4) relinquishment of extraterritorial rights in China by the United States as well as all other powers; 5) a liberal trade agreement between the United States and Japan; 6) mutual removal of freezing measures; 7) stabilization of currency values between the dollar and the yen; 8) an agreement that neither country would interpret an agreement with a third country in a way that would conflict with the fundamental purpose of establishing peace; 9) both governments would use their influence to lead other governments to accept and carry out the principles of this American-Japanese agreement; 10) Japan would withdraw its forces from China and Indo-China.

This draft proposal was accompanied by an explanation that the United States government regarded "some" but not all of the points in the Japanese *modus vivendi* of November 20 as in conflict with the fundamental principles to which each government had committed itself. The American draft proposal was not offered as the only terms of agreement the United States was willing to accept. Hull explained to Nomura and Kurusu that it was offered as *"one practical exemplification of a program which this Government envisages as something to be worked out during our further conversations."*

To sum up: the American answer to Japan on November 26 did not reject *all* of the terms of Japan's proposed *modus vivendi;* the American draft proposal was not offered as the *only* terms of agreement the United States would accept; the United States made *no demands* upon Japan; the American draft proposal contained many offers that the Japanese had often admitted were advantageous to Japan because they would satisfy Japanese demands for security and prosperity—most significantly, an offer to end United States economic sanctions against Japan; it named *no deadline* for an answer by Japan; it contained *no threat of force or war* or other penalty if Japan refused to accept the American proposal; it specifically *invited* Japan to *continue negotiations;* it *promised to consider* new Japanese proposals, in the usual manner of a peaceful power, in the course of further negotiations.

To call such a proposal an "ultimatum" or an "ultimative notice" is to murder the meaning of the word. If, as the Minority Report asserts, the Japanese war lords "treated" this answer "as an ultimatum," evidence is available, in Togo's description of the Japanese terms of November 20 as an ultimatum, which proves that he, at least, had for some days already accepted the fact which American isolationists reject: that to the Japanese government belonged the responsibility for war that accrues to a government guilty of issuing an ultimatum. When the Japanese Foreign Minister admits responsibility, it seems excessive for Americans to find the Japanese innocent and their own government guilty. . . .

Additional Reading

Harry Elmer Barnes, ed., *Perpetual War for Perpetual Peace* (1953).
Charles A. Beard, *President Roosevelt and the Coming of the War, 1941* (1948).
Robert J. C. Butow, *Tojo and the Coming of the War* (1961).
W. H. Chamberlin, *America's Second Crusade* (1950).
Wayne S. Cole, *America First: The Battle Against Intervention, 1940–1941* (1953).
Robert A. Divine, *The Illusion of Neutrality* (1962).
Donald F. Drummond, *The Passing of American Neutrality, 1937–1941* (1955).
Herbert Feis, *The Road to Pearl Harbor* (1950).
William L. Langer and S. E. Gleason, *The Challenge to Isolation, 1937–1940* (1952).
———, *The Undeclared War, 1940–1941* (1953).
Walter Millis, *This Is Pearl!* (1947).
Paul W. Schroeder, *The Axis Alliance and Japanese-American Relations, 1941* (1958).
R. A. Theobald, *The Final Secret of Pearl Harbor* (1954).
Gerald E. Wheeler, *Prelude to Pearl Harbor: The United States Navy and the Far East, 1921–1931* (1963).
Roberta Wohlstetter, *Pearl Harbor: Warning and Decision* (1962).

18 THE YALTA CONFERENCE:
Unnecessary Concessions or the Price
of Coalition Diplomacy?

When Soviet Russia was suddenly attacked by its erstwhile ally Nazi Germany, on June 22, 1941, the American government promptly decided to extend Lend-Lease aid to the new recruit against the Axis. The flow of war supplies was substantially increased after the United States actively entered the war and by 1945 totaled approximately $11 billions. Roosevelt and Winston Churchill, the British Prime Minister, also made repeated efforts to assuage Soviet suspicions of the West and thus not only to facilitate the waging of war but to lay the basis for an enduring postwar collaboration and peace.

Russia seemed to undergo a fundamental change during the war, presaging Big Three cooperation in the post-Hitler world. The Communist International, instrument of world revolution, was disbanded; a measure of religious freedom was permitted within the Soviet Union; and the Declaration of the United Nations, a statement of liberal war goals, was subscribed to by Moscow. A series of major conferences among the Big Three powers appeared to have solidified cooperation and alliance: the Moscow Foreign Ministers' Conference in October, 1943; the Roosevelt-Churchill meeting with Premier Joseph Stalin at Teheran in December, 1943; and the summit conference at Yalta in the Crimea, February, 1945.

The Yalta Conference marked the apex of Big Three collaboration and was probably the most important of the conferences in its far-ranging decisions. The final stages of the war against Hitler were determined and Russia agreed to enter the Far Eastern phase against Japan. Important decisions affecting the map of postwar Europe were adopted and concessions were made in the Far East to Russia as the price of cooperation.

Even during the war, there were some vocal critics of the alliance with Soviet Russia. In the years of Cold War from 1947 on, this criticism mounted and often became bitter and hysterical in tone. The Cold War struggle was so different from the expected postwar world, so costly in money, manpower, and foreign commitments, that it caused a searching re-examination of wartime diplomacy and agreements. Domestic politics also were involved, as many Republicans were eager to belabor the Democratic New Deal–Fair Deal administration with charges of blunders at home and abroad. The Yalta Conference and agreements were especially singled out for scathing attacks and even for charges of treason and betrayals to the Communists.

DOCUMENTS

The Yalta Conference

The Big Three leaders, with their aides, met February 4–11, 1945 to make final military arrangements and begin the planning of the postwar world. Besides the public agreements, several secret accords were concluded regarding the kinds of reparations to be secured from defeated Germany, three votes for Russia in the projected United Nations, and the entry of the Soviet Union into the struggle with Japan. The following selections include extracts from the Protocol of the Proceedings of the conference, which was then a secret document.

Report of the Crimea Conference

For the past eight days, Winston S. Churchill, Prime Minister of Great Britain, Franklin D. Roosevelt, President of the United States of America, and Marshal J. V. Stalin, Chairman of the Council of Peoples' Commissars of the Union of Soviet Socialist Republics have met with the Foreign Secretaries, Chiefs of Staff and other advisors in the Crimea. . . .

The following statement is made by the Prime Minister of Great Britain, the President of the United States of America, and the Chairman of the Council of Peoples' Commissars of the Union of Soviet Socialist Republics on the results of the Crimean Conference:

I

The Defeat of Germany

We have considered and determined the military plans of the three allied powers for the final defeat of the common enemy. The military staffs of the three allied nations have met in daily meetings throughout the Conference. These meetings have been most satisfactory from every point of view and have resulted in closer coordination of the military effort of the three Allies than ever before. . . .

Nazi Germany is doomed. The German people will only make the cost of their defeat heavier to themselves by attempting to continue a hopeless resistance.

II

The Occupation and Control of Germany

We have agreed on common policies and plans for enforcing the unconditional surrender terms which we shall impose together on Nazi Germany after German armed resistance has been finally crushed. These terms will not be made known until the final defeat of Germany has been accomplished. Under the agreed plan, the forces of the Three Powers will each occupy a separate zone of Germany. Coordinated administration and control has been provided for under the plan through a central Control

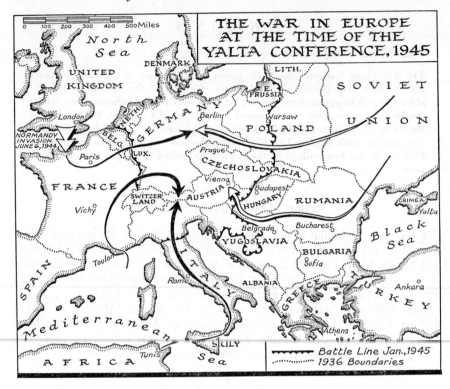

Commission consisting of the Supreme Commanders of the Three Powers
with headquarters in Berlin. It has been agreed that France should be
invited by the Three Powers, if she should so desire, to take over a zone of
occupation, and to participate as a fourth member of the Control Commission. The limits of the French zone will be agreed by the four governments concerned through their representatives on the European Advisory
Commission.

It is our inflexible purpose to destroy German militarism and Nazism
and to ensure that Germany will never again be able to disturb the peace
of the world. We are determined to disarm and disband all German
armed forces; break up for all time the German General Staff that has
repeatedly contrived the resurgence of German militarism; remove or
destroy all German military equipment; eliminate or control all German
industry that could be used for military production; bring all war criminals to just and swift punishment and exact reparation in kind for the
destruction wrought by the Germans; wipe out the Nazi party, Nazi laws,
organizations and institutions, remove all Nazi and militarist influences
from public office and from the cultural and economic life of the German
people; and take in harmony such other measures in Germany as may be
necessary to the future peace and safety of the world. It is not our purpose to destroy the people of Germany, but only when Nazism and Mili-

tarism have been extirpated will there be hope for a decent life for Germans, and a place for them in the comity of nations.

III

Reparation by Germany

We have considered the question of the damage caused by Germany to the Allied Nations in this war and recognized it as just that Germany be obliged to make compensation for this damage in kind to the greatest extent possible. A Commission for the Compensation of Damage will be established. . . .

IV

United Nations Conference

We are resolved upon the earliest possible establishment with our allies of a general international organization to maintain peace and security. We believe that this is essential, both to prevent aggression and to remove the political, economic and social causes of war through the close and continuing collaboration of all peace-loving peoples. . . .

We have agreed that a Conference of United Nations should be called to meet at San Francisco in the United States on April 25th, 1945, to prepare the charter of such an organization, along the lines proposed in the informal conversations at Dumbarton Oaks. . . .

V

Declaration on Liberated Europe

We have drawn up and subscribed to a Declaration on liberated Europe. This Declaration provides for concerting the policies of the three Powers and for joint action by them in meeting the political and economic problems of liberated Europe in accordance with democratic principles. The text of the Declaration is as follows:

The Premier of the Union of Soviet Socialist Republics, the Prime Minister of the United Kingdom, and the President of the United States of America have consulted with each other in the common interests of the peoples of their countries and those of liberated Europe. They jointly declare their mutual agreement to concert during the temporary period of instability in liberated Europe the policies of their three governments in assisting the peoples liberated from the domination of Nazi Germany and the peoples of the former Axis satellite states of Europe to solve by democratic means their pressing political and economic problems.

The establishment of order in Europe and the rebuilding of national economic life must be achieved by processes which will enable the liberated peoples to destroy the last vestiges of Nazism and Fascism and to creat[e] democratic institutions of their own choice. This is a principle of the Atlantic Charter—the right of all peoples to choose the form of government under which they will live—the restoration of sovereign rights and self-government to those peoples who have been forcibly deprived of them by the aggressor nations.

To foster the conditions in which the liberated peoples may exercise these rights, the three governments will jointly assist the people in any European liberated state or former Axis satellite state in Europe where in their judgment conditions require (a) to establish conditions of internal peace; (b) to carry out emergency measures for the relief of distressed people; (c) to form interim governmental authorities broadly representative of all democratic elements in the population and pledged to the earliest possible establishment through free elections of governments responsive to the will of the people; and (d) to facilitate where necessary the holding of such elections. . . .

VI

Poland

We came to the Crimea Conference resolved to settle our differences about Poland. We discussed fully all aspects of the question. We reaffirm our common desire to see established a strong, free, independent and democratic Poland. As a result of our discussions we have agreed on the conditions in which a new Poland Provisional Government of National Unity may be formed in such a manner as to command recognition by the three major powers.

The agreement reached is as follows:

A new situation has been created in Poland as a result of her complete liberation by the Red Army. This calls for the establishment of a Polish Provisional Government which can be more broadly based than was possible before the recent liberation of western Poland. The Provisional government ["Lublin" regime] which is now functioning in Poland should therefore be recognized on a broader democratic basis with the inclusion of democratic leaders from Poland itself and from Poles abroad. This new Government should then be called the Polish Provisional Government of National Unity.

M. Molotov, Mr. Harriman and Sir A. Clark Kerr are authorized as a Commission to consult in the first instance in Moscow with members of the present Provisional Government and with other Polish democratic leaders from within Poland and from abroad, with a view to the reorganization of the present Government along the above lines. This Polish Provisional Government of National Unity shall be pledged to the holding of free and unfettered elections as soon as possible on the basis of universal suffrage and secret ballot. In these elections all democratic and anti-Nazi parties shall have the right to take part and to put forward candidates.

When a Polish Provisional Government of National Unity has been properly formed in conformity with the above, the Government of the U.S.S.R., which now maintains diplomatic relations with the present Provisional Government of Poland, and the Government of the United Kingdom and the Government of the United States will establish diplo-

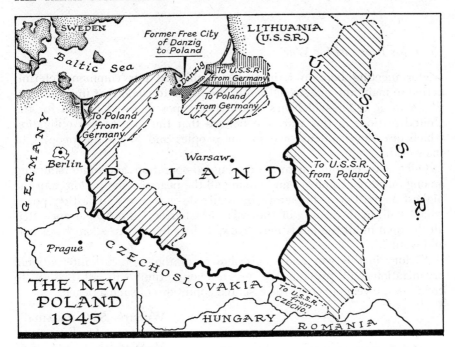

matic relations with the new Polish Provisional Government of National Unity, and will exchange Ambassadors by whose reports the respective Governments will be kept informed about the situation in Poland.

The three Heads of Government consider that the eastern frontier of Poland should follow the Curzon Line with digressions from it in some regions of five to eight kilometres in favor of Poland. They recognize that Poland must receive substantial accessions of territory in the north and west. They feel that the opinion of the new Polish Provisional Government of National Unity should be sought in due course on the extent of these accessions and that the final delimitation of the western frontier of Poland should thereafter await the Peace Conference. . . .

VIII

Meetings of Foreign Secretaries

Throughout the Conference, besides the daily meetings of the Heads of Governments and the Foreign Secretaries, separate meetings of the three Foreign Secretaries, and their advisers have also been held daily.

These meetings have proved of the utmost value and the Conference agreed that permanent machinery should be set up for regular consultation between the three Foreign Secretaries. They will, therefore, meet as often as may be necessary, probably about every three or four months. These meetings will be held in rotation in the three Capitals, the first meeting being held in London, after the United Nations Conference on world organization.

IX

Unity for Peace as for War

Our meeting here in Crimea has reaffirmed our common determination to maintain and strengthen in the peace to come that unity of purpose and of action which has made victory possible and certain for the United Nations in this war. We believe that this is a sacred obligation which our Governments owe to our peoples and to all the peoples of the world.

Only with continuing and growing co-operation and understanding among our three countries and among all the peace-loving nations can the highest aspiration of humanity be realized—a secure and lasting peace which will, in the words of the Atlantic Charter, "afford assurance that all the men in all the lands may live out their lives in freedom from fear and want."

Victory in this war and establishment of the proposed international organization will provide the greatest opportunity in all history to create in the years to come the essential conditions of such a peace.

WINSTON S. CHURCHILL
FRANKLIN D. ROOSEVELT
[I. STALIN]

FEBRUARY 11, 1945 [Released to the press February 12, 1945]

Protocol of the Proceedings of the Crimea Conference

The Crimea Conference of the Heads of the Governments of the United States of America, the United Kingdom, and the Union of Soviet Socialist Republics which took place from February 4th to 11th came to the following conclusions.

I. World Organization

It was decided:

(1) that a United Nations Conference on the proposed world organization should be summoned for Wednesday, 25th April, 1945, and should be held in the United States of America.

(2) the Nations to be invited to this Conference should be:

(a) the United Nations as they existed on the 8th February, 1945 and

(b) such of the Associated Nations as have declared war on the common enemy by 1st March, 1945. (For this purpose by the term "Associated Nation" was meant the eight Associated Nations and Turkey). When the Conference on World Organization is held, the delegates of the United Kingdom and the United States of America will support a proposal to admit to original membership two Soviet Socialist Republics, i.e., the Ukraine and White Russia. . . .

III. *Dismemberment of Germany*

It was agreed that Article 12 (*a*) of the Surrender Terms for Germany should be amended to read as follows:

"The United Kingdom, the United States of America and the Union of Soviet Socialist Republics shall possess supreme authority with respect to Germany. In the exercise of such authority they will take such steps, including the complete disarmament, demilitarisation and the dismemberment of Germany as they deem requisite for future peace and security."

The study of the procedure for the dismemberment of Germany was referred to a Committee. . . .

V. *Reparation*

The following protocol has been approved:

1. Germany must pay in kind for the losses caused by her to the Allied nations in the course of the war. Reparations are to be received in the first instance by those countries which have borne the main burden of the war, have suffered the heaviest losses and have organised victory over the enemy.

2. Reparation in kind is to be exacted from Germany in three following forms:

a) Removals within 2 years from the surrender of Germany or the cessation of organised resistance from the national wealth of Germany located on the territory of Germany herself as well as outside her territory (equipment, machine-tools, ships, rolling stock, German investments abroad, shares of industrial, transport and other enterprises in Germany etc.), these removals to be carried out chiefly for purpose of destroying the war potential of Germany.

b) Annual deliveries of goods from current production for a period to be fixed.

c) Use of German labour.

3. For the working out on the above principles of a detailed plan for exaction of reparation from Germany an Allied Reparation Commission will be set up in Moscow. It will consist of three representatives—one from the Union of Soviet Socialist Republics, one from the United Kingdom and one from the United States of America.

4. With regard to the fixing of the total sum of the reparation as well as the distribution of it among the countries which suffered from the German aggression the Soviet and American delegations agreed as follows:

The Moscow Reparation Commission should take in its initial studies as a basis for discussion the suggestion of the Soviet Government that the total sum of the reparation in accordance with the points (*a*) and (*b*) of the paragraph 2 should be 20 billion dollars and that 50% of it should go to the Union of Soviet Socialist Republics.

The British delegation was of the opinion that pending consideration of the reparation question by the Moscow Reparation Commission no figures of reparation should be mentioned.

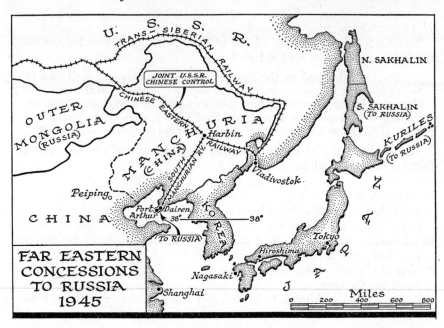

FAR EASTERN
CONCESSIONS
TO RUSSIA
1945

The above Soviet-American proposal has been passed to the Moscow Reparation Commission as one of the proposals to be considered by the Commission.

VI. Major War Criminals

The conference agreed that the question of the major war criminals should be the subject of enquiry by the three Foreign Secretaries for report in due course after the close of the Conference. . . .

[Released to the press by the State Department, March 24, 1947]

Agreement Regarding Entry of the Soviet Union into the War Against Japan

TOP SECRET

Agreement

The leaders of the three Great Powers—the Soviet Union, the United States of America and Great Britain—have agreed that in two or three months after Germany has surrendered and the war in Europe has terminated the Soviet Union shall enter into the war against Japan on the side of the Allies on condition that:

1. The *status quo* in Outer-Mongolia (The Mongolian People's Republic) shall be preserved;

2. The former rights of Russia violated by the treacherous attack of Japan in 1904 shall be restored, viz:

(*a*) the southern part of Sakhalin as well as all the islands adjacent to it shall be returned to the Soviet Union,

(*b*) the commercial port of Dairen shall be internationalized, the preeminent interests of the Soviet Union in this port being safeguarded and the lease of Port Arthur as a naval base of the USSR restored,

(*c*) the Chinese-Eastern Railroad and the South-Manchurian Railroad which provides an outlet to Dairen shall be jointly operated by the establishment of a joint Soviet-Chinese Company it being understood that the preeminent interests of the Soviet Union shall be safeguarded and that China shall retain full sovereignty in Manchuria;

3. The Kuril islands shall be handed over to the Soviet Union.

It is understood, that the agreement concerning Outer-Mongolia and the ports and railroads referred to above will require concurrence of Generalissimo Chiang Kai-Shek. The President will take measures in order to obtain this concurrence on advice from Marshal Stalin.

The Heads of the three Great Powers have agreed that these claims of the Soviet Union shall be unquestionably fulfilled after Japan has been defeated.

For its part the Soviet Union expresses its readiness to conclude with the National Government of China a pact of friendship and alliance between the USSR and China in order to render assistance to China with its armed forces for the purpose of liberating China from the Japanese yoke.

[I. STALIN]

FRANKLIN D. ROOSEVELT

WINSTON S. CHURCHILL

FEBRUARY 11, 1945 [Released to the press by the State Department, February 11, 1946]

READINGS

1. *"Stalin's Greatest Victory"*

Although the Yalta Conference occurred in the recent past, a number of pertinent public and private records have already been opened to scholarly use and several important studies have appeared. Among critics of Yalta, the outpouring ranges from hysterical charges of treason and conspiracy to balanced but critical evaluations. Chester Wilmot's account, written by an English writer close to British officials during the war, falls into the latter category. Wilmot is critical of Roosevelt's suspicions of alleged British imperialism, which he claims prevented closer Anglo-American diplomatic collaboration, and of the American President's naive belief that he could win Stalin's friendship through conciliation and concessions. The Far Eastern concessions to Russia gave Stalin a "moral cloak" for aggression in China.

The Struggle for Europe
CHESTER WILMOT

. . . Three days before he set out for Malta and the Crimea, Roosevelt took the oath for the fourth time as President of the United States, and, in the course of his inaugural address, declared, "We have learned to be citizens of the world, members of the human community. We have learned the simple truth, as Emerson said, 'the only way to have a friend is to be one.'"

This was the creed that Roosevelt carried to Yalta. There was, in his view, no fundamental conflict of national interest between the Soviet Union and the United States; the Russian and American peoples had so much in common that they would readily co-operate in the cause of peace and freedom if only there could be a real meeting of minds between their leaders. His trust in Stalin and his faith in his own ability to win the Soviet Union's lasting co-operation were still high, although the unhappy course of Russo-Polish relations during the past year might well have given him reason to doubt both his own personal influence and Russia's post-war intentions.

Three times since Teheran, Roosevelt had made a direct approach to Stalin in the hope of inducing him to reach a reasonable agreement with the Polish Government in London; each time he had been rebuffed and Stalin had shown no inclination whatever to allow the principles of the Atlantic Charter to apply to Poland. Nevertheless, Mikolajczyk [Premier of the Polish Government in Exile] reports—and there is no reason to disbelieve him—that, when he was in Washington in June 1944, Roosevelt told him, "Stalin is a realist, and we mustn't forget, when we judge Russian actions, that the Soviet régime has had only two years of experience in international relations. But of one thing I am certain, Stalin is not an Imperialist." Roosevelt explained to Mikolajczyk that he had not been able to take a public stand on the Polish question because it was election year, but "eventually," he said, "I will act as moderator in this problem and effect a settlement." Believing, as he had said after Teheran, that Stalin was "getatable," Roosevelt felt sure that when they met again across the conference table there would be no problem they could not solve on a "man-to-man" basis.

Roosevelt was not alone in thinking that Diplomacy by Friendship would bring a sympathetic response from Stalin. The most influential of his advisers—military and political alike—were agreed, as Hull says, that they "must and could get along with the Soviet Government," and that this would be possible if they were "patient and forbearing." The idea that they could "get along with" the Russians came more easily to the American leaders than to the British, for the United States is the great melting pot and the American people have shown an unparalleled capacity for absorbing into their own society a multitude of nationalities.

Perhaps the best exposition of Roosevelt's idea is to be found in a memorandum which Hopkins [Harry Hopkins, Roosevelt's personal adviser] wrote six months after Yalta. "We know or believe," he said, "that Russia's interests, so far as we can anticipate them, do not afford an opportunity for a major difference with us in foreign affairs. We believe we are mutually dependent upon each other for economic reasons. We find the Russians as individuals easy to deal with. The Russians undoubtedly like the American people. They like the United States. They trust the United States more than they trust any other power in the world . . . above all, they want to maintain friendly relations with us. . . . They are a tenacious, determined people who think and act just like you and I do."

Eisenhower endorsed this view of the Russian people when he wrote, "In his generous instincts, in his love of laughter, in his devotion to a comrade, and in his healthy, direct outlook on the affairs of workaday life, the ordinary Russian seems to me to bear a marked similarity to what we call an 'average American.'" Eisenhower believed too that there was a special bond between the United States and the Soviet Union, a bond that was inevitably lacking in the Anglo-American association. He felt, he says, that "in the past relations of America and Russia there was no cause to regard the future with pessimism." On the one hand, "the two peoples had maintained an unbroken friendship that dated back to the birth of the United States as an independent republic"; on the other, "both were free from the stigma of colonial empire building by force."

This remarkable statement stems straight from the Founding Fathers. It was the American way of saying that politically both peoples were free from original sin. That this was not true of either was irrelevant; it was believed, not merely by Eisenhower but also by many Americans who should have been better acquainted with their own history. This belief was implicit in Roosevelt's approach to the problems which were to be discussed at Yalta. In his eyes, Britain was an Imperial Power, bearing the "colonial stigma"; Russia was not. That assessment of his allies was a decisive factor in Roosevelt's readiness to make concessions to the Soviet Union both in Europe and Asia in order to ensure Stalin's entry into the Pacific War.

Roosevelt's intimates give two reasons for his determination to enlist the aid of Russia against Japan. His personal Chief of Staff, Admiral Leahy, says that the President was actuated by the belief that "Soviet participation in the Far East operation would insure Russia's sincere co-operation in his dream of a united, peaceful world." On the other hand, his Secretary of State, Stettinius, reports that "immense pressure [was] put on the President by our military leaders to bring Russia into the Far Eastern War. At this time the atomic bomb was still an unknown quantity and our setback in the Battle of the Bulge was fresh in the minds of all. We had not as yet crossed the Rhine. No one knew how long the European War would last nor how great the casualties would be." Stettinius adds that the American Chiefs of Staff had warned Roosevelt that "without Russia it might cost the United States a million casualties to conquer Japan" and that the Pacific War might not end until 1947.

The chief advocate of this view was Marshall [Army Chief of Staff], but Roosevelt's military advisers were by no means unanimous in the belief that it would be necessary to invade the Japanese home islands. Leahy says that at Pearl Harbour, in July 1944, both MacArthur and Nimitz (the two commanders directly concerned) had told the President that "Japan could be forced to accept our terms of surrender by the use of sea and air powers without the invasion of the Japanese homeland." Since then, at the Battle for Leyte Gulf in October, the Japanese Navy had suffered such a crushing defeat that well before Yalta Leahy considered that the war against Japan "had progressed to the point where her defeat was only a matter of time and attrition." This was also the opinion of Arnold, the Chief of the Air Staff, whose Super-Fortresses were already bombing Japan from island airfields. There was no longer any great need for air bases in the Maritime Provinces of the Soviet Union, and, after the unhappy experiment of "shuttle-bombing" in Europe, Arnold did not set much store by any facilities he might be granted in Asia. Nevertheless, the advice of Marshall and King prevailed.

The supporters of Russian intervention were considerably influenced by their estimate of the amount of help the United States would receive, or should accept, from Britain in the war against Japan. Here the colonial issue again entered American calculations. Virtually all the British and Imperial forces in the Far East were deployed in Admiral Lord Louis Mountbatten's South-East Asia Command (SEAC) for operations in Burma, and in due course Malaya and Sumatra. This deployment was dictated as much by geographical as political factors, but it was presumed in Washington that Churchill was more interested in regaining Britain's lost colonies than in bringing about the early defeat of Japan. Consequently, it came as a great surprise—to the British as much as to the American Chiefs of Staff—when at Quebec in September 1944 the Prime Minister suddenly offered to send a large part of R.A.F. Bomber Command and the main British Battle Fleet into the Central Pacific. This offer was promptly accepted by Roosevelt, but, when it was raised at the next meeting of the Combined Chiefs of Staff, "all hell broke loose"—Arnold's phrase—and King "hotly refused to have anything to do with it." Cunningham, the First Sea Lord, reports that King was sharply called to order by Leahy and "eventually gave way; but with a very bad grace."

Although there was no trace of King's Anglophobia in Marshall or Arnold, the American Chiefs of Staff had never allowed their British colleagues any voice in the conduct of the Pacific War, nor were they eager to have British forces play a major part in it lest this should give Britain the right to claim possession or trusteeship of some of the Japanese Empire. Further, they believed—and they so advised the President— that "in the interests of national defence, the Japanese mandated islands in the Pacific captured by our forces should be retained under the sovereignty of the United States and not delivered to the trusteeship of the United Nations." True to his principles, Roosevelt rejected this pro-

posal, but those same principles made him distrustful of the activities
and intentions of the British and French in South-East Asia.

Roosevelt was determined that Indo-China should not go back to
France and he had refused to agree to any French military mission being
accredited to SEAC. He was prepared to allow the Dutch to return to the
Netherlands East Indies, because Queen Wilhelmina had promised to
give them self-government, but he intended that these islands should
be liberated by American forces so that he would be in a position to
enforce fulfilment of this promise. Accordingly, the sole Dutch possession
placed within the sphere of prospective British operations was Sumatra
and this island only because of its geographical relation to Malaya.
Moreover, the American Chiefs of Staff, on MacArthur's recommendation, decided that the British should not be allowed to take over the
military control of the East Indies after their recapture. "The exact
British intentions were not known," says Leahy, "but past experience
indicated that if they did get control of some Dutch territory, it might
be difficult to pry them loose." This view appears to have been shared
by Roosevelt, for he told Stettinius that "the British would take land
anywhere in the world even if it were only rock or a sandbar."

Roosevelt's eagerness to buy Stalin's aid in the war against Japan
was principally due to his desire to save lives, but in the light of all the
evidence it seems fair to say that he was also actuated by the hope that
Russia's intervention would enable the United States to strike the
decisive blow at Japan, and compel her surrender, before the British,
French or Dutch could regain possession of their colonies. The United
States would thus be able to demand that the colonies which had been
liberated from the Japanese should now be liberated from the dominion
of their original owners.

In due course, as it turned out, the Americans were able to achieve this
purpose without the intervention of Russia. When the Japanese announced their readiness to capitulate, MacArthur, who was acting as
co-ordinator of all the surrender arrangements, forbade Mountbatten to
accept any local surrender in South-East Asia or to send any relief or
reoccupation forces into Japanese-held areas until the overall surrender
had been signed in Tokyo. Since this ceremony was not to take place for
another twelve days, Mountbatten ignored his orders so far as missions
of mercy were concerned, because, as he says in his dispatch, "if relief
stores and personnel had not been sent in at once, the delay of twelve
days imposed on me would have resulted in many more deaths each day
among the prisoners [of war]."

The instructions regarding the movement of naval and military forces
were observed, though these were already at sea, and the British were
thus placed in the humiliating position of not being permitted to re-
occupy their own colonies, until the Japanese High Command had
formally acknowledged defeat to an American general on an American
battleship in Tokyo Bay.

Although this particular manifestation of American anti-colonialism was not revealed until six months after Yalta, the attitude which inspired it was implicit in the policy Roosevelt pursued throughout the war.

The plenary sessions of the Yalta Conference were held at Livadia Palace overlooking the Black Sea. The ownership of this palace had changed since it was built by the Romanoffs, but the aims and ambitions of the new owners differed little from those of its former masters. The only significant difference was that the men who now sought to fulfil Russia's imperial destiny were more ruthless and more powerful.

At the opening session on Sunday, February 4th, Stalin made a gesture which was both tactful and tactical. He proposed, as he had at Teheran, that Roosevelt should take the chair, and thus once again he brought the President half-way to his side. Yet Stalin showed no early inclination to follow the chairman's lead, least of all with regard to the President's cherished plan for creating a world peace organisation based on the recognition of the sovereign rights of all nations. The first time the subject was raised, "Stalin made it quite plain," says Stettinius, "that the three Great Powers which had borne the brunt of the war should be the ones to preserve the peace." He declared, moreover, that he would "never agree to having any action of any of the Great Powers submitted to the judgment of the small powers." In reply to this argument Churchill spoke for all the Western World in saying, "The eagle should permit the small birds to sing and care not wherefor they sang." That evening, when Stettinius and Eden discussed the outlook, they agreed that "the trend . . . seemed to be more towards a three-power alliance than anything else."

Evidently sensing that the time was not opportune to pursue the question of the world peace organisation, Roosevelt, at the start of the second plenary meeting, turned the discussion to the future of Germany. At the Moscow Conference of Foreign Ministers in November 1943 it had been decided that Germany should be completely disarmed and should pay reparations for the physical damage she had inflicted on the Soviet Union and other Allied countries. Then, and at Teheran, the question of partitioning Germany had been debated without any conclusions being reached, but it had been assumed that in any case the three powers would occupy the country, and by November 1944 they had agreed upon the actual zones of occupation and upon their joint responsibility for Berlin. At Yalta the "Big Three" confirmed their determination to demand the "Unconditional Surrender" of Germany and, for the first time, there was detailed consideration by the Russian and Anglo-American Chiefs of Staff on the military measures necessary to bring about Hitler's final defeat. On the question of post-war Germany, however, there was no such unanimity and it was soon evident that there was a considerable divergence between the British and Russian attitudes, especially with regard to the principle of partition, the extent of reparations and the right of France to share in the occupation.

The Russian view was that there should be only three occupying powers; that they should decide at Yalta to partition the Reich into a number of separate states and to include a declaration to this effect in the surrender terms; and that Germany should be deprived of eighty per cent of her heavy industry and should pay reparations in kind to the value of twenty billion dollars, half of which should go to the Soviet Union.

Churchill was not slow to realise that, if these proposals were adopted, Germany would be rendered politically impotent and economically impoverished. Although determined to ensure that Germany should not again disturb the peace of Europe, he did not wish to see her entirely neutralised as a factor in the balance of power. Accordingly, he doubted the wisdom of partitioning the Reich unless the Soviet Union would agree to the creation of a strong Danubian Confederation—and this had already been rejected by both Stalin and Roosevelt. Moreover, he did not wish to make Germany pay such severe reparations that her economy would collapse unless it were sustained by the Western Powers as it had been after the First World War. Finally, the Prime Minister wanted the French to have an equal share in both the occupation and administration of Germany so that there would be a second European voice to support Britain's in the Allied Control Commission. He was the more emphatic on this point, for the President said that the American troops would be withdrawn from Europe in "two years at the outside." Whereupon Churchill commented, without indicating what threat he feared, "Great Britain alone will not be strong enough to guard the Western approaches to the Channel."

As the discussion developed—both in the plenary sessions and at meetings of the Foreign Ministers—Roosevelt and Stettinius endeavoured to take an intermediate stand on these issues. The result was that three distinct viewpoints emerged. With regard to partition, Stalin wanted a definite commitment both now and in the surrender terms; Churchill wished to make no commitments either way; and Roosevelt suggested that they should mention dismemberment in the terms without binding themselves to this policy. On the matter of reparations, Stalin demanded explicit acceptance in the Protocol of the overall figure of twenty billion dollars; Churchill opposed any mention of any figure even in a secret document; and Roosevelt inclined to the view that the Russian figure might be taken as "a basis for discussion." As for the occupation of Germany, Churchill insisted that France should have a seat on the Control Commission as well as a zone; Stalin argued against both suggestions; and Roosevelt proposed that France should have a zone but no seat.

On each of these questions the President was in fundamental agreement with the Prime Minister's stand (though not with all his reasons), but in public discussion Roosevelt played the mediator. He was not interested in upholding the balance of power concept, nor was he deeply concerned with the intrinsic merits of the German problem. To him Germany was not an issue in itself, but a bargaining point in the wider issue that was uppermost in his mind—the winning of Stalin's cooperation in the international peace organisation, and in the war against Japan.

To some extent the role of arbiter was thrust upon Roosevelt when he became chairman, but there is no doubt that he preferred it since he was thus able to preserve greater freedom of action and to avoid committing himself until he had heard the rival views. The results of the President's determination to act as mediator were twofold. On the one hand, the assertion of what were in reality Anglo-American views and principles was frequently left to the British alone—much to Churchill's annoyance; and on the other, as one of Roosevelt's closest advisers says, "the Soviet leaders did over-estimate the ultimate extent of the President's generosity and his willingness to compromise on principles."

The problem of Germany's future was still undecided when—at the third plenary session on February 6th—Roosevelt returned to the question of post-war peace and asked Stettinius to review the questions which had been in dispute at the Dumbarton Oaks Conference. There the Americans, British, Chinese and Russians had agreed on the principles and purposes of what was to become the United Nations, and had decided there should be a General Assembly, a Security Council and various other instrumentalities. The area of agreement had ended, however, when the Soviet Delegate, Gromyko, had proposed that all sixteen republics of the Soviet Union should have seats in the Assembly (a proposal which "left Stettinius and Cadogan breathless"), and had demanded that in the Security Council the Great Powers should have the right to veto any proposals, except those which related to points of procedure.

It has been alleged by some of Roosevelt's critics that the establishment of the veto power in the Security Council was a concession made by him at Yalta to induce Stalin to join the United Nations. This is not so. The basic principle of the veto was never in dispute. None of the Great Powers was prepared to submit itself and its interests unreservedly to the jurisdiction of an international security organisation. All were agreed that there must be "unqualified unanimity of the permanent members of the Council on all major decisions relating to the preservation of peace, including all economic and military enforcement measures." This was inevitable. The President, haunted by the ghost of Wilson, insisted on the veto power because he knew that the United States Senate would not surrender to an international body the right to commit American forces to military action. Churchill was equally insistent on this point because, as he said at Yalta, he would "never consent to the fumbling fingers of forty or fifty nations prying into the life's existence of the British Empire."

Although both Britain and America felt obliged to retain the right to veto any international "police action," they had no desire to curtail discussion or to prevent any small power bringing a cause of grievance to the notice of the Security Council. At Dumbarton Oaks, however, Gromyko had refused to accept this view and had told Stettinius, "The Russian position on voting in the Council will never be departed from!" Nevertheless, on December 5th, 1944, Roosevelt had sent to Stalin and

Churchill a compromise formula which, while recognising the need for unanimity on matters involving the application of sanctions, provided that on questions relating to the peaceful settlement of any dispute no member of the Council would cast its vote, or exercise its veto, if it were a party to that dispute.

Now, at Yalta, after Stettinius had re-stated this formula, Churchill declared Britain's acceptance of it, and added, "We see great advantage in the three Great Powers not assuming the position of rulers of all the rest of the world without even allowing them to state their case." When Stalin spoke, however, he again emphasised the importance of unanimity, declaring that the real problem was to preserve the unity of the Great Powers and to work out a covenant that would achieve this purpose. "The danger in the future," he said, "is the possibility of conflicts among ourselves." Apologising to the President, Stalin said that he was not yet ready to pass judgment on the voting formula, because he had had "no chance to study this question in detail." Yet he proceeded to give such a concise analysis of its implications that it was obvious he must have studied it rather carefully at some time during the two months since he had received Roosevelt's draft!

After this exchange Stettinius was more confident, believing that for the first time Stalin really understood the American point of view. Byrnes, on the other hand, felt that the Russians "could not be greatly interested in the United Nations organisation," and Leahy thought it "difficult to foresee on what grounds an agreement could be reached." This impression seemed to be confirmed when, at the next meeting of the Foreign Ministers, Molotov refused even to discuss the Security Council voting procedure.

Leaving this matter for the moment, Roosevelt brought up the Polish question. He announced his readiness to accept the Curzon Line, but proposed that Stalin might agree to leave within Poland the city of Lwow and the nearby oilfields. "He pointed out," says Stettinius, "that he was merely suggesting this for consideration rather than insisting on it." In fact, the main argument he advanced in its support was that "it would have a salutary effect on American public opinion," a consideration which was hardly likely to carry much weight with the Soviet dictator. Thus, although the President's expert advisers had warned him that these oilfields were essential to the Polish economy, he did not make an issue of it, so anxious was he to preserve the role of mediator, not only on the frontier question but also in the establishment of a new Polish government.

Churchill was already committed to the Curzon Line, but he declared that if Stalin were to accept the President's Lwow plan, it would be "a magnanimous gesture" which Britain would "admire and acclaim." The Prime Minister said, however, that he was more interested in the sovereignty and independence of Poland than in the matter of frontiers, and that he, like the President, wished to see established in Warsaw a "fully representative Polish government," pledged to the holding of free elections. For Britain, having risked so much in Poland's cause, this was a question of honour.

In reply, Stalin delivered an impassioned speech. "For the Russian people," he said, "Poland is not only a question of honour but also a question of security. Throughout history Poland has been the corridor through which the enemy has passed into Russia . . . It is in Russia's interests that Poland should be strong and powerful, in a position to shut the door of this corridor by her own force." Turning to the problem of frontiers, he said that the Soviet Union must have Lwow and could not accept anything but "the line of Curzon and Clemenceau." Stalin declared: "You would drive us into shame! What will be said by the White Russians and the Ukrainians? They will say that Stalin and Molotov are far less reliable defenders of Russia than are Curzon and Clemenceau . . . I prefer the war should continue a little longer . . . to give Poland compensation in the West at the expense of the Germans. . . . I am in favour of extending the Polish Western frontier to the Neisse River.

Stalin was equally unresponsive to Roosevelt's suggestion that a new Polish Government should be formed from members of the five main political parties, including representatives of the Government in London. He stated that he did not trust the London Poles and would not recognise any administration except that already established in Lublin. "We demand order," he said, "and we do not want to be shot in the back."

Churchill joined issue vigorously with Stalin, declaring that Britain could not accept the Lublin Committee, since it did not represent more than a third of the nation; nor could he agree to extend Poland's western frontier to the River Neisse, thus giving her virtually all Silesia. "It would be a pity," he said, "to stuff the Polish goose so full of German food that he will die of indigestion." On that discordant note the meeting adjourned.

That evening Roosevelt sent Stalin a conciliatory letter, in which he reaffirmed the American opposition to the Lublin Committee, but added the assurance, "The United States will never lend its support in any way to any provisional government in Poland which would be inimical to your interests." Although he regarded this letter as an act of mediation, Roosevelt compromised his own independence by telling Stalin, "I am determined there shall be no breach between ourselves and the Soviet Union." With that statement he admitted that, if Stalin made an issue of Poland, the United States would give way.

When the Big Three met again next afternoon (February 7th) Stalin acknowledged receipt of the President's letter, but stated that his own reply was not yet ready as it was being typed; in the meantime he would like to discuss the international peace organisation. Roosevelt agreed, and Molotov proceeded to say that the Soviet Union was "happy to accept the entire American proposal" about voting in the Security Council, and would not press for all sixteen Soviet Republics to be members of the United Nations. It would be satisfactory if seats were granted to the Ukraine and White Russia. As it had already been agreed that Britain, the four Dominions and India should have individual representation in the General Assembly, Churchill could not oppose this request, and, although Roosevelt did not give his consent immediately, he told Stettinius that he "did not believe there was anything preposterous about the Russian proposal." Indeed, he regarded it as a small price to pay for Soviet co-operation.

The President and the Prime Minister were delighted at this manifestation of Stalin's willingness to join the United Nations and they felt he had made substantial concessions on two vital issues about which he had previously been intractable. They had feared that Stalin was interested only in securing a Three-Power Alliance, but now Roosevelt, at any rate, believed he had persuaded Stalin not only to recognise the sovereign rights of small nations, but also to act in friendly concert with the other great Powers in maintaining peace and extending the frontiers of freedom.

This belief was confirmed when Stalin agreed that the Soviet Union would take part in the United Nations Conference to be held in San Francisco in April, and would support there the right of the United States to have three votes in the General Assembly, if the President desired to make such a claim. It seemed to Roosevelt that these concessions were an earnest of Stalin's good faith, for it could not be foreseen then that the Soviet Union would abuse the veto power, as it was to do in the years after the war, employing it to prevent discussion as well as decision and endeavouring to exercise it even on questions of procedure. That afternoon at Yalta it appeared that Anglo-American diplomacy had gained a considerable victory, and the President felt that the long and arduous journey had not been in vain.

During the brief adjournment which followed this discussion about the United Nations the prevailing opinion among the Western delegates was that the concessions Stalin had made represented a decided change of heart. Considered in relation to what followed, however, these concessions appear as a tactical manœuvre designed to make the Western delegations more receptive to the Soviet plan for Poland which Molotov put forward while the meeting still glowed with goodwill. This plan did little more than set out in formal terms the attitude Stalin had so forcibly proclaimed the day before. The only hint of any readiness to meet the Western view was contained in the statement that the present Provisional Government (i.e. the Lublin Committee) might be enlarged to include "some democratic leaders from Polish émigré circles." Since the Russians refused to regard even Mikolajczyk, the leader of the Peasant Party, as a "democrat," that concession meant nothing. The moral of this day's proceedings was that, while Russia was willing to join the United Nations, she was not prepared to rely on it entirely. She intended to safeguard her own security in any event by ensuring that she had subservient neighbours in Europe and a commanding position in Asia.

Stalin's Asiatic ambitions were revealed on the following afternoon during a private discussion with Roosevelt about the Soviet Union's entry into the Japanese War. This discussion was conducted on a strictly

Russo-American basis and in conditions of great secrecy. The only other persons present, apart from the two interpreters, were Molotov and Averell Harriman, the American Ambassador to the Soviet Union.

At the President's request, Churchill was not there and, when the negotiations were continued on the technical level by the Chiefs of Staff, the British did not take part. Even within his own entourage Roosevelt was most uncommunicative. Stettinius, though Secretary of State, was merely notified that talks were in progress. When he asked if the State Department should not be represented, Roosevelt replied that the problem was "primarily a military matter . . . and had best remain on a purely military level." This was a specious answer, for Stalin had long since committed himself on the basic military issue; the main point to be decided at Yalta was the political price of his participation.

It was in October 1943 that Stalin had first promised to join in the war against Japan after the defeat of Germany. He had made this offer to Cordell Hull, who says that it was "entirely unsolicited . . . and had no strings attached to it." At Teheran a month later, Stalin had repeated this promise virtually as a *quid pro quo* for the Second Front and for Lend-Lease. Nevertheless, Roosevelt had then volunteered to restore Russia's rights in the Manchurian port of Dairen and to ensure her free access to warm waters. Finding that the President was a "soft touch," Stalin proceeded to make this gesture his price with the paradoxical result that Soviet demands grew as the American need for Russian assistance in the Eastern War declined. During Churchill's visit to Moscow in October 1944, the Marshal said that "the Soviet Union would take the offensive against Japan three months after Germany's defeat, provided the United States would assist in building up the necessary reserve supplies and *provided the political aspects of Russia's participation had been clarified.*" During this Moscow meeting, as on five other separate occasions in 1944, Stalin gave an assurance that Russian air and naval bases in the Maritime Provinces would be made available to American forces. In December, however, this assurance was withdrawn, presumably with a view to strengthening the bargaining position of the Soviet Union at Yalta.

The course of the fateful discussions which took place behind closed doors in Livadia Palace on the afternoon of February 8th is not known in detail, for none of those who took part have publicly revealed what was said and the accounts given by Leahy, Sherwood and Stettinius, though authoritative, are second-hand. What was decided, however, is revealed only too clearly in the terms of the agreement which was subsequently signed by Stalin, Roosevelt and Churchill. This provided that "in two or three months after Germany has surrendered . . . the Soviet Union shall enter the war against Japan" on certain conditions: that "the status quo in Outer Mongolia" was to be preserved; that the Kurile Islands, north of Japan, were to be "handed over to the Soviet Union"; and that the rights Russia had lost after her defeat by Japan in 1904 were to be restored. Russia was thus to regain possession of Southern Sakhalin, the "international port" of Dairen and the naval base of Port Arthur. In addition, although China was to "retain full sovereignty in Manchuria," the principal Manchurian railways were to be "jointly operated by . . . a Soviet-Chinese Company" which was to safeguard "the pre-eminent interests of the Soviet Union." Apart from agreeing to enter the Pacific War, Stalin conceded nothing in writing. He promised Roosevelt that the United States could have bases in the Maritime Provinces, but this was not mentioned in the agreement, nor was there any reference to the one million tons of additional supplies that were to be provided by the Americans. These supplies were duly delivered, but the Russians made sure that the establishment of the bases never proceeded beyond discussions in Moscow.

The President's Chief of Staff (Admiral Leahy) says that, when the Russian terms were mentioned at a subsequent plenary session, there was "little discussion and no argument." It appears that Stalin blandly explained, "I only want to have returned to Russia what the Japanese have taken from my country"; and that Roosevelt replied, "That seems like a very reasonable suggestion from our ally. They only want to get back that which has been taken from them." Churchill must have listened a little incredulously to this exchange for he cannot have forgotten that Roosevelt had once said to him: "Winston . . . you have four hundred years of acquisitive instinct in your blood and you just don't understand how a country might not want to acquire land somewhere if they can get it. A new period has opened in the world's history and you will have to adjust yourself to it."

The British should have known, if the Americans did not, that Stalin's justification could not by any means cover all the Soviet claims. The Kuriles had never formally belonged to Russia. The reclaimed "rights" in Manchuria were those which in the nineteenth century had enabled Russia to exercise in this province a degree of dominion which seriously impinged upon Chinese sovereignty. These "rights" rested on no more substantial foundations than those extra-territorial privileges which the United States, Britain and other countries had given up in 1943 at Roosevelt's own instigation and in fulfilment of his pledge to restore and respect the independence of China. To accept the "status quo" in Outer Mongolia, which Moscow had been sedulously luring away from its allegiance to Chungking, was to acknowledge that the Soviet Union, not China, should enjoy political supremacy in that country. In short, by this agreement Russia was to become, with Anglo-American consent, the political heir of Japan in Manchuria, and thereby in North China.

No arrangement was made at Yalta with regard to the occupation of Korea and the post-war fate of that unhappy country appears to have been mentioned only incidentally. Stalin inquired whether it was to be occupied by any foreign troops. When Roosevelt replied that this was not intended, Stalin, no doubt thinking far into the future, "expressed his approval."

Upon learning the full extent of the Soviet terms, some of Churchill's advisers were deeply concerned, for they discovered that, although Stalin had made no further commitments whatever and although the

most important of his claims had to be met by their ally, China, not by
Japan, the President and the Prime Minister were required to declare that
"these claims of the Soviet Union shall be unquestionably fulfilled after
Japan has been defeated." Moreover, Stalin was insisting that for security
reasons the Chinese Government should not even be informed until
the Soviet Union was ready to attack. Roosevelt had undertaken to secure
Chiang Kai-Shek's compliance in due course but, as Sherwood says, "if
China had refused to agree to any of the Soviet claims, presumably the
U.S. and Britain would have been compelled to join in enforcing them."
To some of the British delegation it seemed rather incongruous that, while
urging Churchill to hand Hong Kong over to China as "a gesture of good-
will," Roosevelt was prepared to promise Stalin substantial concessions
in Manchuria, and to do this without so much as consulting the Chinese.
This point was appreciated by at least one of his staff, for Leahy reports
that he warned Roosevelt, "Mr. President, you are going to lose out on
Hong Kong if you agree to give the Russians half of Dairen"; and that
Roosevelt replied, "Well, Bill, I can't help it."

Eden did all he could to dissuade the Prime Minister from setting his
signature to the terms agreed upon by Roosevelt and Stalin. Churchill
replied that he must sign, because he felt that "the whole position of the
British Empire in the Far East might be at stake." The Prime Minister
had good reason to fear that, since he had been excluded from the
negotiations about the Japanese War, Britain might well be excluded
from future discussions about the Far East if she did not stand by the
United States now. Like Leahy, he may also have foreseen that, if these
territorial concessions were made to Russia, Roosevelt would not be in a
strong moral position to enforce his oft-repeated "threat" to reform the
British Empire.

Of all the agreements reached at Yalta, this is the most controversial
and would seem to be the least defensible. Yet it does not appear that
the concessions, which Stalin obtained, were wrung from a reluctant
Roosevelt. Sherwood records that the President had been "prepared even
before the Teheran Conference . . . to agree to the legitimacy of most
if not all of the Soviet claims in the Far East," although he expresses
the opinion that "Roosevelt would not have agreed to the final firm
commitment," if he had not been "tired and anxious to avoid further
argument." Stettinius disagrees with this opinion and explains that "the
Far Eastern agreement was carefully worked out and was not a snap
decision made at Yalta." He endeavours to defend the concessions by asking: "What, with the possible exception of the Kuriles, did the Soviet
Union receive at Yalta which she might not have taken without any
agreement?"

That question does not pose the real issue which surely was: What did
the Soviet Union receive at Yalta which she could not have taken without
flagrantly violating the fundamental principles of the Atlantic Charter and
the United Nations to which she had subscribed? The real issue for the
world and for the future was not what Stalin would or could have taken
but what he was given the right to take. This agreement provided Stalin

with a moral cloak for his aggressive designs in Asia, and, more important, with almost a legal title enforceable at the Peace Conference to the territories and privileges which he demanded.

The President's surrender on this question is the more remarkable because it involved the sacrifice of those very principles which he had striven to uphold throughout his dealings with Churchill and Stalin. He had always insisted that he would not make any post-war commitments which would prejudice the peace treaties; he would recognise no spheres of influence, no territorial changes except those arrived at by mutual agreement, and no transfers of colonial territory except under conditions of international trusteeship. By making this agreement about the Japanese War, however, Roosevelt weakened both his mediating influence and his bargaining position in relation to problems arising out of the German War. He was not well placed to defend the sovereignty of Poland, once he had agreed to the infringement of China's sovereignty without her consent and in breach of the promise he had given to Chiang Kai-Shek at Cairo in 1943. He could not make any effective protest against the Russians' creating a sphere of influence in the Balkans, when he had acknowledged their sphere of influence in Mongolia and Manchuria. Having departed from his principles in Asia, he could not expect to be allowed to apply them in Europe; not against a realist like Stalin. Consequently, the President was now in a less favourable position than he had been at the start of the conference. Stalin's appetite had been whetted, not satisfied.

The records kept by those who were present at Yalta give the impression that the negotiations about Russia's part in the Pacific War on the Thursday afternoon marked the turning point in the week's discussions. If this was not realised by the Western delegations at the time, it seems to have been fully appreciated by Stalin. Thereafter, having gained the concessions which were to enable him to dominate China, he proceeded to consolidate politically the strategic advantages his armies had already secured in Europe. Stalin was better able to press his demands now, for he could play upon the sense of gratitude and co-operation he had built up in the Americans, and to a lesser extent in the British, by his agreement to help in the defeat of Japan and the creation of the international security organisation. The remaining negotiations were to prove the truth of the warning which had been sent to Washington two months earlier by the Head of the American Military Mission in Moscow (General Deane), an astute and not unsympathetic observer of the Soviet scene. In a letter to Marshall in December Deane had written, "We never make a request or proposal to the Soviets that is not viewed with suspicion. They simply cannot understand giving without taking, and as a result even our giving is viewed with suspicion. Gratitude cannot be banked in the Soviet Union. Each transaction is complete in itself without regard to past favours."

When the discussions about Poland were continued, as they were at each session on the last four days, the Russians gained their way on almost every point. Nothing more was heard of the President's suggestion that Poland should keep the Lwow region. The Curzon Line was accepted and this fact was duly recorded in the Protocol. With regard to Poland's

western frontier, however, Stalin did not press for the formal recognition
of a specific line, since he realised that neither Roosevelt nor Churchill
were prepared to go beyond the Oder. He readily consented to the suggestion that "the final delimitation of the western frontier should await
the Peace Conference," for in the meantime that left him free to make his
own arrangements about the German territory between the Oder and the
Neisse.

The negotiations about the future government of Poland were very
much more protracted and involved. The essence of the argument was
that the Western Powers advocated the formation of an entirely new
administration representing "all democratic and anti-Fascist forces,"
whereas the Russians proposed merely to enlarge the Lublin Committee,
and to do this in such a way that the Polish Communists could retain
control. Churchill and Eden fought for four days against this proposal,
insisting that Great Britain could not withdraw her recognition of the
London Government unless there was "a completely new start . . . on
both sides on equal terms." The British also demanded that the new government should be provisional and should be pledged to hold "free and
unfettered elections as soon as possible on the basis of universal suffrage
and secret ballot," and that these elections should be conducted under
the supervision of the American, British and Soviet Ambassadors.

The Russians consented to the holding of free elections and Molotov
told Roosevelt that these could be held "within a month." On the other
hand, he bluntly rejected the supervision proposal, arguing that this
would be "an affront to the pride and sovereignty of the independent
people"! Eden endeavoured to insist on this safeguard, for he feared that
any unsupervised elections would be a mockery, but at the final meeting
of the Foreign Ministers Stettinius announced that "the President was
anxious to reach agreement and that to expedite matters he was willing to
make this concession." With regard to the setting up of a new administration, the three Ministers eventually decided upon a compromise formula
which read: "The Provisional Government which is now functioning in
Poland should be reorganised on a broader democratic basis with the
inclusion of democratic leaders from Poland itself and from Poles abroad."
To this end various Polish leaders from all non-Fascist parties were to be
brought together in Moscow for consultations with Molotov and the
British and American Ambassadors.

When this formula was adopted at the plenary session on February
10th the Western delegates, with few exceptions, believed that they had
reached, as Sherwood says, "an honourable and equitable solution." They
were acting in good faith and they presumed that Stalin was equally sincere, for he also set his hand to a "Declaration on Liberated Europe"
which reaffirmed the principles of the Atlantic Charter. By this Declaration the three Powers bound themselves "to build . . . a world order
under law, dedicated to peace, security and freedom and the general well-
being of all mankind," and agreed to act in concert "in assisting the
peoples liberated from the dominion of Nazi Germany and the peoples of

the former Axis satellite states of Europe . . . to create democratic institutions of their own choice."

These fine phrases were to prove less important than the terms of the Polish formula, which was so loosely worded that it left the Russians ample room to manœuvre. Roosevelt certainly entertained some doubts on this score, for he concurred when Leahy said to him, "Mr. President, this is so elastic that the Russians can stretch it all the way from Yalta to Washington without ever technically breaking it." The essential fact was that, while the British and Americans started by refusing to accord any recognition whatever to the Lublin Committee, they ended by allowing it to be described in the communiqué as "the present Provisional Government of Poland." Moreover, although they had originally insisted that an entirely fresh administration should be formed, they finally agreed to the words "the Provisional Government now functioning in Poland should be reorganised." The only real difference between that formula and what Stalin had initially demanded was a change in verb; "enlarged" had become "reorganized."

Having secured virtually all he wanted in Poland, Stalin made a conciliatory gesture with regard to the occupation of Germany. When the President announced that he now believed France should have a seat on the Control Commission as well as a zone of occupation, Stalin replied simply, "I agree." So far as he was concerned, this was a minor concession, for it did not require any material sacrifice on the part of the Soviet Union. Where her interests and assets were directly concerned, however, as in the matter of reparations, he was both stubborn and persistent. On the one hand, he refused altogether to discuss the Soviet Union's right to use German manpower; on the other, he demanded that a firm agreement should be reached at Yalta on the amount of "reparations in kind" that Germany should be required to pay. Again and again, one or other of the Soviet delegates returned to their original figure of "20 billion dollars" arguing that, if this amount were accepted as "a basis for discussion," it "would not commit the Allies to that exact sum."

The Americans were inclined to accept that assurance, especially when it was repeated by Stalin, and to allow the figure to be mentioned in the Protocol. On this question, however, the British were absolutely adamant. Eden pointed out that they could not tell what Germany could afford to pay until they had discovered how much of the German economy survived the bombing and the general destruction of war. The settlement of the actual amount should be left to the Reparations Commission, which they had agreed to create. The Yalta Protocol should merely lay down principles to guide the Commission and should state that, "In establishing the amount of reparations account should be taken of arrangements made for the partitioning of Germany, the requirements of the occupying forces and Germany's need from time to time to acquire sufficient foreign currency from her export trade to pay for current imports." The British wanted it expressly stated that "Germany's industrial capacity would not be reduced to a point which would endanger the economic existence of the country." Eden argued that the Russians could not expect Germany to make large annual payments out of current production over a period of ten years, if German manufacturing capacity were reduced to the extent the Soviet Union demanded. These two objectives, he declared, were irreconcilable, as indeed they were to prove to be. "The British objective," said Eden, with marked prescience, "is to avoid a situation in which as a result of reparations we will have to finance and feed Germany." The logic of Eden's arguments was overwhelming and both Roosevelt and Stettinius agreed with it, but they did not think that the Soviet figure was unreasonable and they were strongly moved by sympathy for the terrible sufferings of the Russian people.

At the penultimate plenary session Stalin spoke with great emotion of the vast and wanton destruction which the Germans had caused in Russia and pleaded for due compensation. Churchill read a telegram from the British War Cabinet protesting that reparations to the value of 20 billion dollars was far more than Germany could afford. It seemed that a deadlock had been reached. The Russians would not accept the British principles, and the British would not accept the Russian figure, not even as "a basis for discussion." Thereupon, Roosevelt suggested that the whole problem should be left to the Reparations Commission in Moscow. Churchill and Stalin agreed, but that was not the end of the matter.

During this session Hopkins scribbled a note to Roosevelt saying, "Mr. President, the Russians have given in so much at this Conference that I do not think we should let them down. Let the British disagree if they want to—and continue their disagreement at Moscow." That night at a dinner given by the Prime Minister, Stalin tackled Churchill again, saying that he did not like to have to go back to Moscow and tell the Soviet people that owing to British opposition they would not receive adequate reparations. The combined effect of Stalin's persistence and Hopkins's intervention was that when the Protocol was signed next morning it contained the statement that "the Soviet and American delegations agreed" that the Reparations Commission "should take in its initial studies as a basis for discussion the suggestion of the Soviet Government that the total sum should be 20 billion dollars and that 50 per cent of it should go to the U.S.S.R." The British view that "no figure should be mentioned" was also recorded, but this was of little account. The figure was there—however hedged around with qualifying phrases—and it was linked to the names of the Soviet Union and the United States.

Although the very persistence of the Russians on this point might well have served as a warning, it is doubtful whether any member of the Western delegations foresaw then that, in spite of Stalin's repeated assurances, the Russians would soon be claiming that to "take as a basis for discussion" meant to "accept in principle." From this it was a short step to the claim subsequently made by Molotov that "President Roosevelt had agreed at Yalta that Soviet reparations should total at least ten billion dollars."

On that final Sunday morning at Livadia Palace neither the Americans nor the British suspected that the public communiqué and the secret protocol, so solemnly signed and endorsed with such expressions of mutual trust and good-will, would soon be distorted and violated by their Soviet Allies, and that this process of distortion and violation would begin before the Prime Minister and the President had been able to report to their respective legislatures on the conference at which, they both asserted, the Great Powers were "more closely united than ever before."

In the House of Commons on February 27th, the Prime Minister declared: "The impression I brought back from the Crimea . . . is that Marshal Stalin and the Soviet leaders wish to live in honourable friendship and equality with the Western democracies. I feel also that their word is their bond. I decline absolutely to embark here on a discussion about Russian good faith." That evening in Bucharest—despite the Yalta Declaration on Liberated Europe—Molotov's deputy (Andrei Vishinsky) issued to King Michael a two-hour ultimatum, demanding the dismissal of the Rumanian Prime Minister, General Radescu, the leader of an all-party Government.

Four days later, addressing a joint session of Congress, the President said: "The Crimea Conference . . . spells—and it ought to spell—the end of the system of unilateral action, exclusive alliances, and spheres of influence, and balances of power and all the other expedients which have been tried for centuries and have always failed. . . . I am sure that—under the agreement reached at Yalta—there will be a more stable political Europe than ever before." That evening in Bucharest, without any reference whatever to the Allied Control Commission, Vishinsky issued to King Michael a second ultimatum, demanding that he should appoint as Prime Minister Petru Groza, the leader of the Rumanian Communists.

2. Yalta in Historical Perspective

John L. Snell, an authority on recent European diplomatic history, has edited a stimulating volume on various aspects of the Yalta agreements. The following selection by Forrest C. Pogue concludes that Yalta was a defensible attempt to insure continued Soviet cooperation through minimum concessions to Russian desires. Even the Far Eastern terms, perhaps indefensible on strictly moral grounds, were understandable from a military and political point of view. Yalta was the supreme effort at wartime and postwar cooperation; it also was an attempt to set outer limits to Soviet expansion. Its chief defect, therefore, was that Russia did not observe in the future the commitments made at the Crimea meeting.

Yalta in Retrospect
FORREST C. POGUE

The Yalta conference ended on February 11 on notes of friendship and good will. At the final banquet the evening before, Churchill declared hopefully in his toast to Stalin that the "fire of war had burnt up the misunderstandings of the past." But he more accurately summarized the

John L. Snell, editor, *The Meaning of Yalta* (Baton Rouge: Louisiana State University Press, 1956), 188–208. Reprinted with permission.

general meaning of Yalta later when, in writing of the agreements reached at the meeting, he concluded: "All now depended upon the spirit in which they were carried out."

PRAISE AND HOPE

Roosevelt and Churchill returned home by easy stages while communiqués summarizing some of their agreements were circulated throughout the world. The Far Eastern agreements could not be made known, of course, until after Russia actually entered the war against Japan. Similarly, the agreements to consider the dismemberment of Germany and the detailed statement on reparations for the Soviet Union could not be published, lest they give Nazi propagandists ammunition and thereby prolong the war in Europe. But the communiqué did make known all the Yalta agreements concerning Poland and summarized the essence of the Yalta agreements concerning the United Nations.

In the United States and Great Britain, the political leaders, press and public, on the basis of the Yalta communiqué, gave high praise to the work of the Crimea conference. *Time,* largest news magazine of the United States, spoke for many segments of public opinion in reporting that Yalta might turn out to be the most important conference of the century. It praised the special recognition by the conferees of the principle of free and unfettered elections in liberated territories and the reaffirmation of the Dumbarton Oaks principles, which would "reassure many a citizen that World War II was not being fought in vain." The magazine reported that Congress, in its first, informal reaction, "overwhelmingly" approved the results of the conference. *Time* drew attention to the special statement of the former isolationist leader, Senator Arthur H. Vandenberg, that Yalta reaffirmed "basic principles of justice to which we are deeply attached, and it undertakes for the first time to implement these principles by direct action." Herbert Hoover was quoted as saying that the conference offered "a great hope to the world," and Senator Alben W. Barkley, the majority leader of the Senate, declared that he regarded it "as one of the most important steps ever taken to promote peace and happiness in the world." These opinions, delivered before some of the Yalta agreements were known, emphasized those achievements which Roosevelt had put first at the Crimea conference, the effort to make effective the organization of the U.N. in accordance with the principles outlined at Dumbarton Oaks.

At first most of the western world rejoiced at Big Three agreement on the important issues of war and peace. Germany and Japan were to be defeated, peace to be restored, and Good was to reign in the world. The first protests were raised by the Polish leaders abroad. The Polish government in exile received the Yalta communiqué on the evening of February 12 and denounced it next morning as a violation of the principles of the Atlantic Charter and the right of every nation to protect itself. And when Prime Minister Churchill asked the House of Commons on February 27 to approve his actions at Yalta, he was attacked because of his conces-

sions to the Russians on the Polish question. To his critics he spoke of
Stalin's solemn pledges and declined "absolutely" to embark on a discussion of Russian good faith. He admitted that many imponderables lay
ahead, but cautioned that it was a mistake to look too far into the future.
"Only one link in the chain of destiny," he added, "can be handled at a
time." A great majority in the House of Commons approved the Yalta decisions, but twenty-five members, most of them Conservatives, voted
against Churchill, and eleven members of the government abstained.

Roosevelt on March 2 made his report on Yalta to a joint session of
Congress. Sitting to avoid the use of heavy braces on his legs, he showed
the exhaustion of his long trip and the exertions of twelve years in the
Presidency in his haggard face, his almost unique reference to his in-
firmity, and in the thickness of his speech. He asked the support of Congress and the American people in carrying out the Yalta decisions, saying
that without their backing the meeting would have produced no lasting
results.

THE ONSET OF DISILLUSIONMENT

The initial praise for those Yalta agreements which were known in
February, 1945, soon gave way to criticism of Russia in the American
press. In the United Nations Conference for World Organization at San
Francisco in April, 1945, and in pre-armistice negotiations in March and
April, the U.S.S.R. began to empty the reservoir of good will which it had
built up in the West in the last years of the war. At San Francisco in
April, 1945, Molotov began the tactics of negation which were to make
nyet a dirty word in Western lexicons. Before the war ended in Europe
in May, Soviet activities in the Baltic states, Rumania, Hungary, and
Poland caused uneasiness among the western Allies. By the end of 1945 it
was apparent that Red Army occupation forces intended to despoil their
area of Germany, reform its society in the Soviet image, and integrate it
into the Soviet orbit. But for a time American soldiers who had seen their
friends killed by German arms and who regretted their years spent in a
war they had not wanted actually welcomed Russian occupation of Germany on the grounds that the Red forces would punish the Nazis as they
deserved. Despite some alarm over Soviet activities in eastern and central
Europe, the American people in the latter half of 1945 and the early part
of 1946 were intent on getting the troops home as soon as possible.

Expansion of Russian Influence in Europe

Even before the German surrender was signed at Reims in May, 1945,
the Soviet Union began the policy of creating satellite states on its borders. Old-time Communist agitators, deserters, expatriates, exiles, escaped
prisoners, and apprentice conspirators began to find their way to power.
Some emerged from resistance ranks, where they had served courageously
during part of the war years, or were sent back from the Soviet Union to
their former homes to organize or strengthen Communist cadres in key

government ministries. In some cases they reached power directly; often they infiltrated labor or agrarian regimes and ultimately eliminated or won over those who initially opposed them. Some of the Communist-controlled countries invited Soviet military missions, which virtually ran the armed forces of the countries concerned and gave backing to the police forces of such states. In Hungary, Rumania, Yugoslavia, and the Russian zone of Austria, the Russians gained a strong foothold.

The China Deal Falls Through

The treaty agreements of August, 1945, between Nationalist China and the U.S.S.R. soon proved disappointing. Part of the troubles arose, however, because of the weakness and unfavorable location of Nationalist Chinese troops. At the war's end Chiang Kai-shek's troops were concentrated in southwest China, pushed there by the Japanese or sent there for possible use in Burma. Forces of Red China were in a better position to co-operate with the Soviet forces in the north and northeast. . . .

SUSPICION BEGINS AT HOME

In the five years between the end of World War II and the beginning of war in Korea, American distrust and fear of Soviet Russia increased as the Chinese Communists mastered all of continental China, Communist parties made election gains in France and Italy, and the U.S.S.R. imposed an "Iron Curtain" over most of central and eastern Europe. Greece, Turkey, and Iran were threatened and the western sector of Berlin was menaced with starvation by a Soviet blockade. Russian benediction was given to the North Korean attack in 1950 and to the later Chinese entry into the battle against the United Nations forces. The calling up of American troops for service in Korea intensified the sense of betrayal and frustration which had been created by the earlier aggression. To all Americans it was a forcible and sickening reminder that the war against totalitarianism had merely reached the intermission period in 1945, not the final curtain. Realization that years of war had brought only the briefest of respites from conflict created a mass anger which reached the point of hysteria when it was found that the Russians had the secret of that monstrous invention and "ultimate" weapon, the A-bomb.

Suspicion grew rapidly in the atmosphere of fear and anger and defeat, generated in the years 1945–50. When Whittaker Chambers, self-confessed former Russian agent, produced papers allegedly given him by Alger Hiss, a respected State Department official who had been at Dumbarton Oaks, at Yalta, and at San Francisco, it seemed that the Soviet plot ran everywhere. Political maneuvers for partisan advantage became intertwined with security measures. Liberals, who suspected that the Hiss case was a contemporary parallel of the "Dreyfus affair" intended to destroy the remaining architects of the New Deal and Fair Deal as well as to catch Communists, undertook to defend Hiss on the assumption that he could not be guilty because he *must* not be. When he was convicted of perjury, they were rendered speechless and virtually powerless for a season. The indictment or conviction of other officials increased the fear of the American public. When it was found that a number of atomic scientists, as Communists, or in the name of world science, or with a cosmic naïveté about the best means to keep the peace of the world, had handed over secrets to the Russians, it seemed that no one could be trusted.

It was in this period of unbridled suspicion that the Yalta conference commitments, known by 1946 to be more numerous than originally supposed, were wrenched out of historical perspective and blamed for most of the evils in world politics since February, 1945. As a result, Yalta's historical significance has been confused, its decisions exaggerated, and its effect on the course of subsequent events distorted. Above all, the historical context in which Yalta occurred was overlooked. Forgotten was the fact that the Soviet Union had borne the main brunt of the German attack in 1941 and 1942, while Britain and the United States were trying to hold on in the Pacific and were gathering their forces for a return to Europe. Forgotten were wartime fears in the West that Russia might succumb or that she might decide to let the western Allies and Germany fight a costly war of attrition. Forgotten also was the fact that in the years 1942–45 co-ordination of Anglo-American and Russian pressure against Germany had brought victory in Europe. As a result of this forgetfulness, all Soviet gains at Yalta seemed uncalled for or part of a conspiracy to aid Russia. Yalta became a symbol for betrayal and a shibboleth for the opponents of Roosevelt and of international co-operation.

Each year after 1945 thus brought increased demands for "the whole truth" about Yalta. The defeat of Chiang Kai-shek focused attention on the part the Yalta Far Eastern concessions supposedly played in his downfall. The beginning of the war in Korea raised the question of whether or not Yalta had been responsible for Communist influence in that country. The recall of MacArthur led his supporters to assert that his advice, had it been sought in 1945, would have prevented concessions to the Russians. The year 1955 saw the publication by the State Department of documents on the Crimea conference. These were followed by Department of Defense releases. Neither set of documents backed the thesis of "betrayal and sellout" presented so often in the halls of Congress and during the political campaigns of 1952.

NO BETRAYAL AT YALTA

The State Department and military advisers who drew up the briefing papers and memoranda for President Roosevelt's use at Yalta and the officials who accompanied him to the conference did not mislead him into making wrongful concessions to the Russians. On nearly every concession made at the Crimea conference State Department advisers were more anti-Russian than Roosevelt or Churchill. Secretary of State Stettinius and his staff stood firmly against the exaggerated Soviet demands and no one did more than Ambassador Harriman to warn the President against them. Papers written by Hiss before and during the Yalta conference opposed the Russian demand for unlimited veto power in the Security Council of the proposed U.N. and contested the Soviet claim to special representation in the U.N. It is clear from the Hiss notes on the conference and from Charles Bohlen's [State Department adviser and translator at Yalta] testimony before the Senate Foreign Relations Committee in 1953 that Hiss's role was confined almost exclusively to United Nations questions. The published record of everything that Hiss wrote and said on the subject fully reflects a concern for safeguarding American interests. Roosevelt's final approval of the extra seats for the Russians took Hiss by surprise and found him saying a few minutes before the President's approval that the Americans had not agreed to the Russian request. It is an extreme and unfounded application of the principle of guilt by association to argue that Hiss's presence at Yalta and San Francisco in some way tainted those conferences with perjury and subversion.

Yet, concessions were made to the Russians at Yalta, and the most significant thus far have been those concerning the Far East. For a variety of reasons these Far East concessions have given rise to the most pronounced denunciations of the Yalta conference. Among these reasons are the following: (1) attacks against Yalta by a coalition of proponents of Chiang Kai-shek, opponents of Roosevelt and Marshall, and the champions of MacArthur, (2) an uninformed assumption that it was Yalta that caused the downfall of Chiang Kai-shek, (3) a general prejudice against "secret diplomacy" among the American people and the fact that the agreements were reached privately by Roosevelt and Stalin, (4) the weakening of American and Japanese defenses which the concessions represented, and (5) a conviction that Roosevelt had no moral right to grant Chinese territory to the Russians.

Bohlen's arguments that Churchill was not present at the discussions on the Far East because the United States was largely responsible for that theater of the war and that China was excluded because Russia was then unwilling to be connected openly with arrangements dealing with the Far East are cogent but not conclusive. The fact that the agreement was quickly reached regarding territory belonging to neither of the conferees is hard to reconcile with Wilsonian ideals of "open covenants openly arrived at" and with the spirit of the Atlantic Charter and the Cairo Declaration.

But the suggestion that Roosevelt's promise to seek Chiang Kai-shek's agreement to concessions in the Far East brought the downfall of Nationalist China has been effectively denied by Harriman and Bohlen, and is not borne out by the facts of twentieth-century Chinese development. The willingness of Chiang to carry out these concessions in return for Russian recognition of his government has already been noted. Arguments that the United States did not properly back Chiang Kai-shek against Mao Tse-tung and that Marshall and his advisers weakened the Nationalists in insisting on compromises with the Chinese Communists should not be charged against the negotiators at Yalta, whatever their foundation in fact. Actually, in 1945 the Generalissimo thought he had a good arrangement with Stalin and for a time after the war his armies seemed to be strongly situated in parts of northern China. Overextension of supply lines, failure to get firm possession of the liberated territory, overconfidence, poor leadership, inflation, refusal to reform Kuomintang corruption, failure to satisfy the land hunger of the Chinese peasant, and, above all, the failure of Stalin to keep his promises to Chiang Kai-shek are the chief explanations for the Nationalist debacle of 1946–50. Strategically, the grant of the Kuriles and Southern Sakhalin to a potential enemy of the United States was unsound. In case of a future war between the United States and the U.S.S.R. the American position would be definitely weakened. But few Americans thought of such a war in 1945.

The moral aspects of the concessions have worried liberal supporters of Roosevelt and angered his opponents. To those who had observed the spread of late nineteenth- and early twentieth-century imperialism, concessions to the Soviet Union at the expense of China smelled of an ancient evil. The names Dairen, Port Arthur, and the South Manchurian Railway reminded the West of the Treaty of Shimonoseki, the Russo-Japanese struggle for power in Korea and Manchuria in 1904–1905, and the steady march of Japan toward control of the Far East. The 1945 grant of concessions which the czar's representatives had once won from a defenseless China smacked of a return to the breakup of China. In the disillusionment which came after 1946 many people forgot that the territory Russia gained in 1945 had not been in China's control since 1905. Within a few weeks after the war ended, the Russians held the various ports and possessions which had been promised them, without the Nationalists ever being in contact with the territory involved. Later, Stalin returned part of these areas to the technical control of the Chinese Communists, who in turn made concessions to the Russians.

Despite these extenuating arguments, and the explanations presented earlier, there is no real defense on *moral* grounds of the Far Eastern concessions to the Soviet Union. It is the one point at which Roosevelt openly went back to the type of arrangement which he and other western leaders had previously condemned. Morality and reality were in conflict; reality won. Defenders of the Far Eastern concessions can only justify them in terms of (1) the need of Russian aid against Japan to shorten the war in the Far East and save American lives, or (2) the need to prolong wartime co-operation with the U.S.S.R. into the postwar era.

WAS RUSSIAN AID NEEDED IN THE FAR EAST?

Many critics of the Yalta conference have insisted that Russian participation was not needed. One group points to possession of the A-bomb and overwhelming naval and air superiority in the Pacific to prove that the United States at the beginning of February, 1945, needed no assistance to defeat Japan.

Knowledge of the A-bomb at Yalta

Major General Leslie R. Groves, military head of the atomic bomb project, at the end of December, 1944, notified General Marshall, Secretary Stimson, and President Roosevelt that one atomic bomb, possessing enormous destructive power, would be ready for use about the first of August, 1945, that one more would be ready toward the end of 1945, and that others would follow, apparently at shortened intervals thereafter. Colonel William S. Considine, who was assigned to the Manhattan atomic project in 1944–45, testified in 1951 that he informed Secretary Stettinius at Yalta that a successful bomb would in fact be constructed, that it would be ready about the first of August, and that such a bomb would wreck a large-sized city. These facts might well have made the military and political advisers of the President far more sanguine about their prospects of an early victory than they were. However, in the absence of an actual explosion of a bomb, there was some ground for military advisers, who had to fight until the end of the year with one bomb, to proceed on the basis that the bomb would be a bonus and not the weapon which would bring early victory.

Furthermore, the military advisers of the President were less positive concerning the value of the A-bomb than was the head of the Manhattan project. Of these the least hopeful was Admiral Leahy, Chief of Staff to the President. Leahy has frankly admitted that although General Groves in September, 1944, had made the most convincing report on the possibilities of the atomic bomb he had heard up until that time, he still did not have "much confidence in the practicability of the project." Less than a week before the actual dropping of the bomb on Hiroshima, Leahy told King George VI that he did not think it would be as effective as expected. "It sounds," he added, "like a professor's dream to me." President Truman in his memoirs has confirmed the admiral's skepticism on the subject. So far as Leahy was concerned, the development of the bomb did not affect the question of Russian aid one way or the other. His faith in 1944 and in 1945 lay in the navy; he was convinced that the fleet could defeat the Japanese without ground force help.

The Navy Argument

Fleet Admiral Ernest J. King has written that he, Leahy, Fleet Admiral Chester W. Nimitz, and other naval officers felt that the defeat of Japan could have been accomplished by sea and air power alone, without the necessity of the actual invasion of the Japanese home islands by ground forces. According to King, he and Leahy reluctantly acquiesced in the decision to attack the home islands, feeling "that in the end sea power would accomplish the defeat of Japan." Yet, on June 21, 1951, Admiral King wrote Senator William Knowland that at the time of the Yalta conference he was "agreeable" to the entry of the U.S.S.R. into the war against Japan. "Our contention," he continued, "was that blockade and

bombardment could bring about Japanese capitulation, and that in connection with this course of action, engagement of the Japanese armies in
Manchuria would hasten that capitulation." This throws great light on
the Far Eastern concessions. No one doubted at Yalta that the Japanese
would be ultimately defeated, nor that a blockade might gradually starve
the Japanese islands into submission. But Americans in the spring of
1945 had no desire to leave millions of soldiers, sailors, and airmen under
arms, waiting for the ultimate surrender of the Japanese, eighteen months
or more in the future.

The Air Force Story

Some critics have declared that air intelligence experts knew that Japan
was finished and that if General Henry H. Arnold had been well enough
to attend the Yalta conference, he could have made the President aware
of this fact and thus have prevented concessions to Stalin. Such a statement apparently assumes that the air force was then engaged in massive
operations of such a type that air bombardment could have ended the war
in the Pacific quickly without ground action. This hopeful thesis has been
refuted by the arguments of General Laurence S. Kuter, who represented
General Arnold at Yalta:

> By March 9, 1945, only 22 small-scale B-29 strikes had been flown
> against Japan from the Marianas. Although the size of these strikes was
> steadily growing, the average number of airplanes to reach Japan from
> the Marianas at the time of the Yalta conference was eighty. The Yalta
> conference ended exactly one month before the first of the effective
> medium-altitude fire-bomb strikes on Japanese cities had been delivered.
> . . . It was sixty-five days before the first five-hundred-airplane strike
> could be delivered. . . .

The bad reputation now attached to Yalta, Kuter concluded in 1955, has
arisen from subsequent political experience with Russia, and "to some extent from misinformation generated by partisan oratory and nourished by
shaky memories."

The Army Wanted Help

While it was believed that American naval and air forces had gained
superiority in the Pacific by February, 1945, military planners forecast
that the war against Japan would likely last eighteen months after the
defeat of Germany, with possible casualties, according to Secretary of
War Stimson, of at least 500,000 and possibly as many as a million men.
The first months of the 1945 campaigns had produced constantly mounting totals of dead and wounded. As has been noted (Chapter I), casualties at Iwo Jima and Okinawa confirmed the trend. In the spring General MacArthur himself favored Russian action in support of his offensives
against the Japanese home islands. This notwithstanding, in October,
1955, General MacArthur declared that he was not consulted about con-

cessions to the Russians and that he considered them fantastic. This argument is irrelevant. It is not the responsibility of the soldier to make political arrangements; rather it is to state what is necessary to accomplish his mission. MacArthur had only to notify Marshall of his needs, and the Chief of Staff had only to inform Roosevelt of army requirements in the Pacific. After that it was the President's duty to provide that aid on the best terms he could obtain. Had he refused to seek Soviet aid against Japan, he would almost certainly have been criticized by military commanders in 1945 instead of after his death.

It is interesting to note two contemporary reactions of Pacific veterans to the August, 1945, entry of the Russians into the war. General Robert L. Eichelberger, commander of the Eighth Army, declared: "Whether Japan surrenders in the near future or decides to fight on in a suicide finish, the entrance of Russia into the Pacific War has hastened the end of World War II." And the way the common soldier felt was revealed by the comment of Sergeant Hubert Eldridge of Kentucky, who told reporters: "I've been in the army four and a half years. Maybe those bombs and those Russians will help me get out now." The hope of getting home alive and quickly, clearly expressed in this statement, was the collective wish of the American soldiers in the Pacific; and that wish was one of the political realities that shaped the Yalta agreements.

What Would the Russians Have Done Without Concessions?

But the western Allies need not have promised the Russians anything, say the critics; Stalin would have fought Japan without concessions. Without Russian documents, one can not say positively what the Soviet Union would have done. Stalin had made a deal with an enemy in 1939; in 1945, he might conceivably have remained true to his 1941 treaty of neutrality with Japan, or even have converted it into a pact of alliance, if the Japanese had offered him concessions which he could not obtain from China with American help. Various roads were open to Stalin in the spring and summer of 1945. He might have made a deal with Japan in return for concessions in Manchuria and Korea; he might have remained neutral in the Far East until the United States suffered heavy casualties and then entered at peak strength into the Pacific war. Either of these policies would have enabled the Red Army to dominate Europe, while the United States and Britain withdrew their forces from Germany and Italy to the Pacific. Finally, Stalin might have attacked Japan without any agreement regarding the future terms of peace.

In view of the Russian ability to take what they wanted in 1945 without Allied agreement, in view of the additional aid the Allies needed in Europe and the Pacific, and in view of what Chiang Kai-shek was willing to give in August, 1945, for what he thought to be recognition by the Soviet government, one must conclude that the Far Eastern concessions at Yalta did not seem excessive in February, 1945. Even today it is difficult to avoid the conclusion that if Stalin had not received them from Roosevelt and Churchill he would have sought them—or even greater gains—from someone else or have taken them without Allied or Chinese consent. The terms of the Yalta agreements concerning the Far East were in the nature of a Roosevelt-Stalin contract and constituted not only concessions to Stalin but also restraining limitations. It was not Roosevelt's fault that Stalin later broke the contract.

THE MEANING OF YALTA

"It is a mistake," wrote Winston Churchill to Foreign Secretary Eden one month before the Yalta conference, "to try to write out on little pieces of paper what the vast emotions of an outraged and quivering world will be either immediately after the struggle is over or when the inevitable cold fit follows the hot." "These awe-inspiring tides of feeling," he added, "dominate most people's minds, and independent figures tend to become not only lonely but futile." The Prime Minister, with the prescience he so often showed, in these words pointed clearly to the problems which faced the Allies when they came to talk of the final victory and the beginnings of peace. The thirst for vengeance, the rapidly shifting desires of the public, and the unique difficulties of the democratic leader were thus graphically stated.

Churchill was aware that a responsible leader cannot escape the consequences of his acts. To mobilize the full support of the British and American people for war against Germany and Japan, he and Roosevelt had encouraged strong feelings against the aggressors. In order to maximize the war effort against the Axis states, Roosevelt and Churchill had often followed the rule of expediency in their dealings with the Soviet Union and other associated powers. Both leaders, perhaps mindful of the sneers of critics in the twenties at Wilson's World War I idealism, had tended to make their pleas at the level of self-preservation. Public demands for stern justice had been both acknowledged and spurred by the 1943 demand, which was never withdrawn, for unconditional surrender. At Yalta the free world still wanted punishment and reparation for Lidice, Rotterdam, Coventry, Nanking, Shanghai, Bataan, and Pearl Harbor. The story of the Malmedy massacre was still being circulated to troops in the field in Europe at the time of the Crimea conference. The full horrors of Buchenwald and Dachau were not yet known, but their stench was abroad.

Criticism of the actions of the Big Three at Yalta thus becomes in part an indictment of long-established Western assumptions about popular democracy. Roosevelt and Churchill were restricted in their actions at Yalta by the patterns of thought and action which their people demanded and which they themselves had laid down. As practical political leaders, they dared not go too far beyond what their followers would accept. One finds both a partial criticism and a partial explanation of the Yalta negotiations in one of the main theses of Walter Lippmann's thoughtful book, *Essays in the Public Philosophy*. "When the world wars came," Lippmann has written, "the people of the liberal democracies could not be aroused to the exertions and sacrifices of the struggle until

they had been frightened by the opening disasters, had been incited
to passionate hatred, and had become intoxicated with unlimited hope."
The enemy had to be portrayed as evil incarnate, and the people told
that when this particular opponent had been forced to unconditional surrender, "they would re-enter the golden age." Lippmann contends that
the people of the western democracies have shown a compulsion to error
which arises out of a time lag in democratic opinion and have compelled
their governments "to be too late with too little, or too long with too
much, too pacifist in peace and too bellicose in war, too neutralist or appeasing in negotiation or too intransigent."

The meaning of Yalta cannot be grasped unless the conditions under
which the conference leaders worked are remembered. In February, 1945,
the Allied peoples generally agreed that Germany and Japan must be
severely punished and cured of aggressive tendencies. Agreement was
widespread that Germany and Japan must be effectively disarmed and
their heavy industries restricted in order to prevent them from making
war in the future. The western powers generally acknowledged that the
U.S.S.R. had suffered terribly in the war and should receive compensation
from the common enemies. Thoughts of the postwar era were pervaded
by a desire to counterbalance the power of Germany and Japan by the
force of the "world policemen" who had co-operated to win the war.
Roosevelt certainly hoped, and probably believed until the last weeks
before his death, that he could sit down at a table with Stalin and
Churchill and work out solutions to the problems of the world. The Big
Three tended, as a result, to give smaller states little opportunity to shape
their own futures. The President strongly believed that Soviet expansive
tendencies would be allayed when the U.S.S.R. won security on its
European and Asian frontiers.

Other assumptions likewise encouraged Roosevelt to overestimate the
possibilities of postwar co-operation with the Soviet Union. Knowledge
that Russia had been severely damaged in the early years of the war
with Germany led him to surmise that the U.S.S.R. might require a generation to recover. Some Washington officials believed that the Soviet
Union would be dependent upon postwar economic aid for her recovery,
and that for this reason Stalin could be counted upon to maintain good
relations with the United States. In short, one must remember both the
war-born opportunism and the hopes and fears of 1945: concessions which
would shorten the war and save lives would be acceptable to the
people of the West; the formation of a workable United Nations organization held hope for the correction of any basic errors which might have
been made in the various peace arrangements; and, more realistically, it
was feared that the Soviet Union might become the center of opposition
to the West unless bound as closely as possible to its wartime allies.

All these factors powerfully asserted themselves when the Big Three
met in the Crimean palace of the czar in February, 1945. But yet another factor loomed large in the conference at Yalta. The disintegration
of Germany meant that the force which had dominated central Europe
since 1938 was gone and that its place in central-eastern Europe would

be taken by the Soviet Union. A disarmed Italy and a weakened France could not be expected to balance the enormous power of the Red Army. Britain, seriously drained of her capital wealth by the heavy exactions of the war and lacking the manpower reserves to challenge a potential enemy of Russia's strength, could not hope to redress the balance of Europe as she had for two centuries. The people of the United States viewed their exertions in Europe as temporary and hoped for their early termination; they were in no state of psychological readiness to take up Britain's traditional role. The approaching defeat of Japan threatened to create a power vacuum in the Far East like that which Hitler's defeat would leave in Europe. Thus concessions at Yalta inevitably reflected the powerful position of the Soviet Union in Europe and its potential power in the Far East. Personal diplomacy at Yalta came to grips with the basic realities of a new balance of power in the world at large, and the freedom of action of the individual statesman was greatly restricted by these impersonal forces. Therein lies the overriding fact about the conference; without its comprehension, the meaning of Yalta is sure to be missed.

Several courses were open to the western leaders at Yalta in dealing with the new set of power relationships. It was possible to make minimum concessions to Stalin and hope for Russian co-operation and goodwill; it was possible to break off discussions at the first sign of demands which would ratify the new power relationships or create a greater imbalance in world politics than already existed; and it was possible to state certain moral positions in indignant and ringing Wilsonian phrases. Roosevelt and Churchill selected the first course, believing and hoping that it would bring victory and at the same time save the peace. They gained something by forcing the Russians to put their promises on record; but they could not make Stalin keep his word. The United States and Great Britain have at least the moral right and, technically, the legal right to use Soviet violations as the basis for repudiation of Allied concessions at Yalta, for it was the Soviet breach of contract that started the "Cold War."

After 1952 Eisenhower and Dulles faced the same alternatives which confronted Roosevelt and Stettinius in 1945: the Russians must be lived with, or they must be fought. There were elements of kinship between Roosevelt's belief that he could achieve real peace by sitting down with Churchill and Stalin and Eisenhower's attempt in 1955 to settle world problems in conferences at "the summit." And there were even clearer similarities between the "spirit of Geneva" of 1955 and the spirit of Yalta a decade earlier. Both were predicated upon the necessity of co-existence and both assumed a mutual desire for co-operation. In 1955, as in 1945, American efforts to co-operate "bumped, very hard indeed, against the great stone face of Communism." Thus the Geneva conferences of 1955 may in another day be as violently and as generally attacked as Yalta was assailed after 1946. If so, the result will be neither sound history nor wise politics.

The vitality of a democratic society certainly demands constant and well-informed criticism of leadership. But neither the free world nor the

United States can be made strong by irrational denunciations of its leaders and cries of treason which grow out of frustration and fear. It was from these manifestations of national immaturity that the myth of the Yalta "betrayal" arose. The western world justifiably looks today to the United States for rational leadership and an infusion of confidence, not for mass hysteria and symptoms of a national inferiority complex. The country which constantly tears at its vitals and heedlessly destroys the reputations of its loyal public servants cannot give the sane and courageous guidance so desperately needed to calm the fears and solve the problems of a troubled world. In its reflections on Yalta, as in its conduct in world affairs, the United States can scarcely do better than adopt for its guidance the words of Washington: "Let us raise a standard to which the wise and honest can repair."

Additional Reading

Winston Churchill, *Triumph and Tragedy* (1953).
Herbert Feis, *Churchill, Roosevelt, Stalin* (1957).
———, *Between War and Peace: The Potsdam Conference* (1960).
———, *Japan Subdued: the Atom Bomb and the End of the War in the Pacific* (1961).
George F. Kennan, *Russia and the West under Lenin and Stalin* (1961).
W. L. Neumann, *Making the Peace, 1941–1945* (1950).
E. J. Rozek, *Allied Wartime Diplomacy: A Pattern in Poland* (1958).
R. E. Sherwood, *Roosevelt and Hopkins* (1948).

19 *ORIGINS OF THE COLD WAR*

American foreign policy has undergone a veritable "revolution" since 1945. In startling contrast to the post-World War I period, this time the American people and government undertook long-term economic and military responsibilities in Europe and the Far East. It seemed that valuable lessons had been absorbed from the unfortunate results of American withdrawal after 1919.

During World War II, the willingness of the American people to join a world collective security organization, the United Nations Organization, indicated the shift toward a more responsible postwar foreign policy. It was hoped that creation of the U.N.O. and continuation of Anglo-American-Soviet cooperation after the war would ensure a peaceful and stable world community. A large reservoir of goodwill and admiration existed in America for the Russian people, the result of their heroic resistance to the Nazi invaders, and the American government redoubled efforts to remove Soviet suspicions and insure postwar harmony. But all proved of little avail, and both President Roosevelt and his successor Harry S. Truman experienced increasing difficulties in dealing with the Soviets during the final months of the war. 1946 was the year of transition. As signs of Soviet unilateral policies and apparent violations of wartime agreements multiplied, American attitudes began to harden. The creation of puppet Communist regimes in Poland and in the Balkan states, refusal to cooperate in a unified policy for occupied Germany, and Soviet pressures on Turkey and Iran convinced the Truman administration that all hope for postwar collaboration and friendship was gone.

The challenge, as American policy-makers viewed it, was accepted early in 1947 and the policy of "containment" was adopted to check Soviet imperialism. In January, Bizonia was formed from the American and British zones in Germany, which with the subsequent adhesion of the French zone created the basis for the West German Republic; in March, the Truman Doctrine of military aid to states threatened with aggression was proclaimed; economic aid to war-racked Western Europe was offered via the Marshall Plan in June; and by the end of the year discussions were underway which culminated in 1949 in the signing of the North Atlantic Treaty of defensive military alliance.

The Cold War was underway with a vengeance. Soviet responses to American moves took a variety of forms: the largely spurious Molotov Plan for economic aid to the satellites; the formation of the Cominform, successor to the old Comintern, to tighten Moscow control over foreign Communist parties and governments; and the military "defensive" alliance known as the Warsaw Pact. In the years since, the Cold War has spread to envelop the Far East, Near East, and Africa. The following documents and readings center on the origins of this global struggle and on the question of responsibility for its inauguration. Most scholars have accepted the popular and official American view that Russian intransigence and unilateralism were alone to blame for termination of wartime cooperation and the beginning of postwar tensions and conflicts. A minority, however, has viewed the United States as equally, or even primarily, responsible for initiation of the Cold War.

DOCUMENTS

1. The Truman Doctrine and Containment of Russia

President Truman's address to Congress on March 12, 1947, initiated what was subsequently christened the policy of "containment." Although the President specifically asked authorization for military aid only to Greece and Turkey, he proclaimed a readiness to aid nations anywhere which were threatened by "armed minorities or by outside pressures." In the July issue that year of *Foreign Affairs*, George F. Kennan, one of the State Department policy planners, enunciated the new approach in an anonymous article on "The Sources of Soviet Conduct." It would be American policy to check Russian threats by a counter application of power wherever and whenever required. In addition to halting Soviet imperialism, containment would put Russia under great pressure and in time would encourage major changes, whether evolutionary or by violence, within the Soviet empire.

Greek-Turkish Aid Program: Message of the President to the Congress, March 12, 1947

The gravity of the situation which confronts the world today necessitates my appearance before a joint session of the Congress.

The foreign policy and the national security of this country are involved.

One aspect of the present situation, which I wish to present to you at this time for your consideration and decision, concerns Greece and Turkey.

The United States has received from the Greek Government an urgent appeal for financial and economic assistance. Preliminary reports from the American Economic Mission now in Greece and reports from the American Ambassador in Greece corroborate the statement of the Greek Government that assistance is imperative if Greece is to survive as a free nation.

I do not believe that the American people and the Congress wish to turn a deaf ear to the appeal of the Greek Government. . . .

When forces of liberation entered Greece they found that the retreating Germans had destroyed virtually all the railways, roads, port facilities, communications, and merchant marine. More than a thousand villages had been burned. Eighty-five percent of the children were tubercular. Livestock, poultry, and draft animals had almost disappeared. Inflation had wiped out practically all savings.

As a result of these tragic conditions, a militant minority, exploiting human want and misery, was able to create political chaos which, until now, has made economic recovery impossible.

Greece is today without funds to finance the importation of those goods which are essential to bare subsistence. Under these circumstances the people of Greece cannot make progress in solving their problems of reconstruction. Greece is in desperate need of financial and economic assistance to enable it to resume purchases of food, clothing, fuel, and seeds. These are indispensable for the subsistence of its people and are obtainable only from abroad. Greece must have help to import the goods necessary to restore internal order and security so essential for economic and political recovery.

The Greek Government has also asked for the assistance of experienced American administrators, economists, and technicians to insure that the financial and other aid given to Greece shall be used effectively in creating a stable and self-sustaining economy and in improving its public administration.

The very existence of the Greek state is today threatened by the terrorist activities of several thousand armed men, led by Communists, who defy the Government's authority at a number of points, particularly along the northern boundaries. . . .

Meanwhile, the Greek Government is unable to cope with the situation. The Greek Army is small and poorly equipped. It needs supplies and equipment if it is to restore authority to the Government throughout Greek territory.

Greece must have assistance if it is to become a self-supporting and self-respecting democracy.

The United States must supply that assistance. We have already extended to Greece certain types of relief and economic aid, but these are inadequate.

There is no other country to which democratic Greece can turn. . . .

The British Government, which has been helping Greece, can give no further financial or economic aid after March 31. Great Britain finds itself under the necessity of reducing or liquidating its commitments in several parts of the world, including Greece.

We have considered how the United Nations might assist in this crisis. But the situation is an urgent one requiring immediate action, and the United Nations and its related organizations are not in a position to extend help of the kind that is required. . . .

No government is perfect. One of the chief virtues of a democracy, however, is that its defects are always visible and under democratic processes can be pointed out and corrected. The Government of Greece is not perfect. Nevertheless it represents 85 percent of the members of the Greek Parliament who were chosen in an election last year. Foreign observers, including 692 Americans, considered this election to be a fair expression of the views of the Greek people. . . .

Greece's neighbor, Turkey, also deserves our attention.

The future of Turkey as an independent and economically sound state is clearly no less important to the freedom-loving peoples of the world than the future of Greece. The circumstances in which Turkey finds itself today are considerably different from those of Greece. Turkey

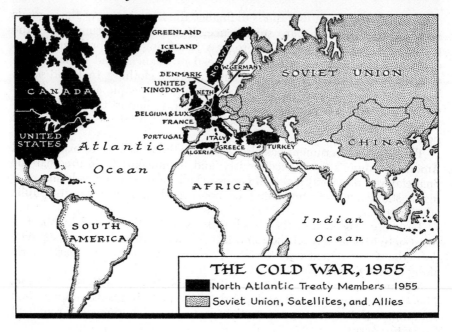

THE COLD WAR, 1955
North Atlantic Treaty Members 1955
Soviet Union, Satellites, and Allies

has been spared the disasters that have beset Greece. And during the war the United States and Great Britain furnished Turkey with material aid.

Nevertheless, Turkey now needs our support.

Since the war Turkey has sought additional financial assistance from Great Britain and the United States for the purpose of effecting that modernization necessary for the maintenance of its national integrity.

That integrity is essential to the preservation of order in the Middle East.

The British Government has informed us that, owing to its own difficulties, it can no longer extend financial or economic aid to Turkey.

As in the case of Greece, if Turkey is to have the assistance it needs, the United States must supply it. We are the only country able to provide that help.

I am fully aware of the broad implications involved if the United States extends assistance to Greece and Turkey, and I shall discuss these implications with you at this time. . . .

To insure the peaceful development of nations, free from coercion, the United States has taken a leading part in establishing the United Nations. The United Nations is designed to make possible lasting freedom and independence for all its members. We shall not realize our objectives, however, unless we are willing to help free peoples to maintain their free institutions and their national integrity against aggressive movements that seek to impose upon them totalitarian regimes. This is no more than a frank recognition that totalitarian regimes imposed upon free peoples, by direct or indirect aggression, undermine the foundations of international peace and hence the security of the United States.

The peoples of a number of countries of the world have recently had totalitarian regimes forced upon them against their will. The Government of the United States has made frequent protests against coercion and intimidation, in violation of the Yalta Agreement, in Poland, Rumania, and Bulgaria. I must also state that in a number of other countries there have been similar developments.

At the present moment in world history nearly every nation must choose between alternative ways of life. The choice is too often not a free one. . . .

I believe that it must be the policy of the United States to support free peoples who are resisting attempted subjugation by armed minorities or by outside pressures.

I believe that we must assist free peoples to work out their own destinies in their own way.

I believe that our help should be primarily through economic and financial aid which is essential to economic stability and orderly political processes.

The world is not static, and the *status quo* is not sacred. But we cannot allow changes in the *status quo* in violation of the Charter of the United Nations by such methods as coercion, or by such subterfuge as political infiltration. In helping free and independent nations to maintain their freedom, the United States will be giving effect to the principles of the Charter of the United Nations.

It is necessary only to glance at a map to realize that the survival and integrity of the Greek nation are of grave importance in a much wider situation. If Greece should fall under the control of an armed minority, the effect upon its neighbor, Turkey, would be immediate and serious. Confusion and disorder might well spread throughout the entire Middle East.

Moreover, the disappearance of Greece as an independent state would have a profound effect upon those countries in Europe whose peoples are struggling against great difficulties to maintain their freedoms and their independence while they repair the damages of war. . . .

Should we fail to aid Greece and Turkey in this fateful hour, the effect will be far-reaching to the West as well as to the East.

We must take immediate and resolute action.

I therefore ask the Congress to provide authority for assistance to Greece and Turkey in the amount of $400,000,000 for the period ending June 30, 1948. . . .

In addition to funds, I ask Congress to authorize the detail of American civilian and military personnel to Greece and Turkey, at the request of those countries, to assist in the tasks of reconstruction, and for the purpose of supervising the use of such financial and material assistance as may be furnished. I recommend that authority also be provided for the instruction and training of selected Greek and Turkish personnel. . . .

If further funds, or further authority, should be needed for purposes indicated in this message, I shall not hesitate to bring the situation before the Congress. On this subject the Executive and Legislative branches of the Government must work together.

This is a serious course upon which we embark.

I would not recommend it except that the alternative is much more serious. . . .

The seeds of totalitarian regimes are nurtured by misery and want. They spread and grow in the evil soil of poverty and strife. They reach their full growth when the hope of a people for a better life has died.

We must keep that hope alive.

The free peoples of the world look to us for support in maintaining their freedoms.

If we falter in our leadership, we may endanger the peace of the world —and we shall surely endanger the welfare of our Nation. . . .

2. The Marshall Plan

The offer of economic aid to facilitate European recovery from war damages launched a highly successful American policy based not on charity but on principles of enlightened self-interest. By 1952, when Marshall Plan aid ended and was succeeded by a Mutual Defense program, over $12 billions had been expended with the bulk concentrated on Great Britain, France, and Italy. The results were on the whole highly gratifying, for Communist inroads were checked and eventually the basis laid for a booming prosperity in Western Europe.

European Recovery Program: Remarks by the Secretary of State George C. Marshall at Harvard University, June 5, 1947

. . . In considering the requirements for the rehabilitation of Europe, the physical loss of life, the visible destruction of cities, factories, mines, and railroads was correctly estimated, but it has become obvious during recent months that this visible destruction was probably less serious than the dislocation of the entire fabric of European economy. For the past 10 years conditions have been highly abnormal. The feverish preparation for war and the more feverish maintenance of the war effort engulfed all aspects of national economies. Machinery has fallen into disrepair or is entirely obsolete. Under the arbitrary and destructive Nazi rule, virtually every possible enterprise was geared into the German war machine. Long-standing commercial ties, private institutions, banks, insurance companies, and shipping companies disappeared, through loss of capital, absorption through nationalization, or by simple destruction. In many countries, confidence in the local currency has been severely shaken. The breakdown of the business structure of Europe during the war was complete. Recovery has been seriously retarded by the fact that two years after the close of hostilities a peace settlement with Germany and Austria has not been agreed upon. But even given a more prompt solution of these difficult problems, the rehabilitation of the economic structure of Europe quite evidently will require a much longer time and greater effort than had been foreseen.

There is a phase of this matter which is both interesting and serious. The farmer has always produced the foodstuffs to exchange with the city dweller for the other necessities of life. This division of labor is the basis of modern civilization. At the present time it is threatened with breakdown. The town and city industries are not producing adequate goods to exchange with the food-producing farmer. Raw materials and fuel are in short supply. Machinery is lacking or worn out. The farmer or the peasant cannot find the goods for sale which he desires to purchase. So the sale of his farm produce for money which he cannot use seems to him an unprofitable transaction. He, therefore, has withdrawn many fields from crop cultivation and is using them for grazing. He feeds more grain to stock and finds for himself and his family an ample supply of food, however short he may be on clothing and the other ordinary gadgets of civilization. Meanwhile people in the cities are short of food and fuel. So the governments are forced to use their foreign money and credits to procure these necessities abroad. This process exhausts funds which are urgently needed for reconstruction. Thus a very serious situation is rapidly developing which bodes no good for the world. The modern system of the division of labor upon which the exchange of products is based is in danger of breaking down.

The truth of the matter is that Europe's requirements for the next three or four years of foreign food and other essential products—principally from America—are so much greater than her present ability to pay that she must have substantial additional help or face economic, social, and political deterioration of a very grave character.

The remedy lies in breaking the vicious circle and restoring the confidence of the European people in the economic future of their own countries and of Europe as a whole. The manufacturer and the farmer throughout wide areas must be able and willing to exchange their products for currencies, the continuing value of which is not open to question.

Aside from the demoralizing effect on the world at large and the possibilities of disturbances arising as a result of the desperation of the people concerned, the consequences to the economy of the United States should be apparent to all. It is logical that the United States should do whatever it is able to do to assist in the return of normal economic health in the world, without which there can be no political stability and no assured peace. Our policy is directed not against any country or doctrine but against hunger, poverty, desperation, and chaos. Its purpose should be the revival of a working economy in the world so as to permit the emergence of political and social conditions in which free institutions can exist. Such assistance, I am convinced, must not be on a piecemeal basis as various crises develop. Any assistance that this Government may render in the future should provide a cure rather than a mere palliative. Any government that is willing to assist in the task of recovery will find full cooperation, I am sure, on the part of the United States Government. Any government which maneuvers to block the recovery of other countries cannot expect help from us. Furthermore, governments, political parties, or groups which seek to perpetuate human misery in order to profit therefrom politically or otherwise will encounter the opposition of the United States.

It is already evident that, before the United States Government can proceed much further in its efforts to alleviate the situation and help start the European world on its way to recovery, there must be some agreement among the countries of Europe as to the requirements of the situation and the part those countries themselves will take in order to give proper effect to whatever action might be undertaken by this Government. It would be neither fitting nor efficacious for this Government to undertake to draw up unilaterally a program designed to place Europe on its feet economically. This is the business of the Europeans. The initiative, I think, must come from Europe. The role of this country should consist of friendly aid in the drafting of a European program and of later support of such a program so far as it may be practical for us to do so. The program should be a joint one, agreed to by a number of, if not all, European nations.

An essential part of any successful action on the part of the United States is an understanding on the part of the people of America of the character of the problem and the remedies to be applied. Political passion and prejudice should have no part. With foresight, and a willingness on the part of our people to face up to the vast responsibility which history has clearly placed upon our country, the difficulties I have outlined can and will be overcome.

3. The North Atlantic Treaty Organization

The "revolution" in American foreign policy was completed with the signing of the North Atlantic Pact in 1949. The United States thus engaged in the second binding military alliance of its history and the only one to be concluded in a period of nominal peace. The original membership of 12 has since been expanded to 15, with the inclusion of Greece, Turkey, and West Germany.

North Atlantic Treaty, April 4, 1949

Preamble

The Parties to this Treaty[1] reaffirm their faith in the purposes and principles of the Charter of the United Nations and their desire to live in peace with all peoples and all governments.

They are determined to safeguard the freedom, common heritage and civilization of their peoples, founded on the principles of democracy, individual liberty and the rule of law.

[1] Belgium, Canada, Denmark, France, Iceland, Italy, Luxembourg, Netherlands, Norway, Portugal, the United Kingdom, and the United States.

They seek to promote stability and well-being in the North Atlantic area.

They are resolved to unite their efforts for collective defense and for the preservation of peace and security.

They therefore agree to this North Atlantic Treaty:

Article 3. In order more effectively to achieve the objectives of this Treaty, the Parties, separately and jointly, by means of continuous and effective self-help and mutual aid, will maintain and develop their individual and collective capacity to resist armed attack.

Article 4. The Parties will consult together whenever, in the opinion of any of them, the territorial integrity, political independence or security of any of the Parties is threatened.

Article 5. The Parties agree that an armed attack against one or more of them in Europe or North America shall be considered an attack against them all; and consequently they agree that, if such an armed attack occurs, each of them, in exercise of the right of individual or collective self-defense recognized by Article 51 of the Charter of the United Nations, will assist the Party or Parties so attacked by taking forthwith, individually and in concert with the other Parties, such action as it deems necessary, including the use of armed force, to restore and maintain the security of the North Atlantic area.

Any such armed attack and all measures taken as a result thereof shall immediately be reported to the Security Council. Such measures shall be terminated when the Security Council has taken the measures necessary to restore and maintain international peace and security.

Article 6. For the purpose of Article 5 an armed attack on one or more of the Parties is deemed to include an armed attack on the territory of any of the Parties in Europe or North America, on the Algerian departments of France, on the occupation forces of any Party in Europe, on the islands under the jurisdiction of any Party in the North Atlantic area north of the Tropic of Cancer or on the vessels or aircraft in this area of any of the Parties.

Article 7. This Treaty does not affect, and shall not be interpreted as affecting, in any way the rights and obligations under the Charter of the Parties which are members of the United Nations, or the primary responsibility of the Security Council for the maintenance of international peace and security.

Article 9. The Parties hereby establish a council, on which each of them shall be represented, to consider matters concerning the implementation of this Treaty. The council shall be so organized as to be able to meet promptly at any time. The council shall set up such subsidiary bodies as may be necessary; in particular it shall establish immediately a defense committee which shall recommend measures for the implementation of Articles 3 and 5.

Article 10. The Parties may, by unanimous agreement, invite any other European state in a position to further the principles of this Treaty and to contribute to the security of the North Atlantic area to accede to this Treaty. . . .

Article 11. This Treaty shall be ratified and its provisions carried out by the Parties in accordance with their respective constitutional processes. . . .

Article 12. After the Treaty has been in force for ten years, or at any time thereafter, the Parties shall, if any of them so requests, consult together for the purpose of reviewing the Treaty. . . .

Article 13. After the Treaty has been in force for twenty years, any Party may cease to be a party one year after its notice of denunciation has been given to the Government of the United States of America, which will inform the Governments of the other Parties of the deposit of each notice of denunciation. . . .

READINGS

1. Containment: A Response to Soviet Imperialism

John Spanier, a political scientist interested in Cold War problems, shares the view that Soviet intransigence and expansionism compelled the United States to embark on a counter policy of military and economic containment. Russian actions after 1945 shattered American hopes for postwar harmony and tranquillity. Yet months of slow reassessment ensued before America accepted the challenge and, in the form of the Truman Doctrine, took a firm stand in behalf of the security of the free world.

The Beginning of the Cold War

JOHN SPANIER

Soviet Postwar Expansion

The American dream of postwar peace and Big Three cooperation was to be shattered as the Soviet Union expanded into Eastern and Central Europe, imposing its control upon Poland, Hungary, Bulgaria, Romania, and Albania. (Yugoslavia was already under the Communist control of Marshal Tito, and Czechoslovakia was living under the shadow of the

John Spanier, *American Foreign Policy Since World War II* (New York: Frederick A. Praeger, Publisher, 1962, revised edition), 19–27, 28–31, 32, 33. Reprinted with permission.

Red Army.) In each of these nations of Eastern Europe where the Russians had their troops, they unilaterally established pro-Soviet coalition governments. The key post in these regimes—the ministry of the interior, which usually controlled the police—was in the hands of the Communists. With this decisive lever of power in their grasp, it was an easy matter to extend their domination and subvert the independence of these countries. Thus, as the war drew to a close, it became clear that the words of the Yalta Declaration, in which the Russians had committed themselves to free elections and democratic governments in Eastern Europe, meant quite different things to the Russians than to Americans. To the Russians, "democratic governments" meant Communist governments, and "free elections" meant elections from which parties not favorable to the Communists were barred. The peace treaties with the former German satellite states (Hungary, Bulgaria, Romania), which were painfully negotiated by the victors in a series of Foreign Ministers' conferences during 1945 and 1946, could not reverse the tight Soviet grip on what were by now Russian satellite states. Democratic principles could not be extended beyond Western power. Russian dominance in the Balkans and Poland was, in short, firmly established, and Russian power now lapped the shores of the Aegean, the Straits of Constantinople, and—through its close relationship with Yugoslavia—the Adriatic.

Greece, Turkey, and Iran were the first states beyond the confines of the Red Army to feel the resulting expansionist pressure of the Soviet Union. In the period from the end of the war to early 1947, the Russians attempted to effect a major breakthrough into the Middle East. Every would-be world conqueror—Napoleon, Kaiser Wilhelm II, and Hitler, to mention only a few of the more recent ones—has tried to become master of this area. Napoleon called the Middle East the key to the world, and well he might, for the area links Europe, Africa, and Asia. The power that dominates the Middle East is in an excellent position to expand into North Africa and South Asia, and thereby gain control of the World-Island.

The pressure on Iran began in early 1946 when the Russians refused to withdraw their troops from that country. These troops had been there since late 1941, when Russia and Britain had invaded Iran in order to forestall increased Nazi influence and to use Iran as a corridor for the transportation of military aid shipped by the West to the Persian Gulf for transit to Russia. The Russians had occupied northern Iran, the British the central and southern sections. The Tripartite Treaty of Alliance signed in early 1942 by Iran, Britain, and Russia specified that within six months of the cessation of hostilities all troops would be withdrawn; the Allies also pledged themselves to respect Iran's sovereignty and territorial and political independence.

The final date set for evacuation from Iran was March 2, 1946. British and United States troops—the latter had arrived after America's entry into the war, to help move the lend-lease supplies to Russia—had already left. Only the Soviet troops still remained. Indeed, the Russians were sending in more troops and tanks. Their goal: to reduce Iran to a Soviet satellite.

The Russians had, in fact, begun their campaign in late 1944, when they demanded exclusive mineral and oil rights in northern Iran and offered to supply the Iranians with experts to help administer their government. When the Iranian Government rejected these demands, the Russians had organized a revolt by the Communist-controlled Tudeh Party in the north. The revolt began openly in November, 1945, and the Red Army prevented the Iranian Army from quelling it. The Tudeh Party, renamed the Democratic Party, then formed a government in Azerbaijan. The Russian game was clear: to force the Iranian Government to recognize the Soviet puppet regime in Azerbaijan, which would then send "elected representatives" to the legislature in Teheran. These would then exert pressure on the government to grant Russia the economic and political control it wanted in Iran. The result would have been the conversion of Iran into a Soviet satellite. It was imperative, therefore, that Soviet troops be forced to withdraw. Not until then could the national government and troops attempt to cope with the Communist government in the north.

During this period, the Soviet Union also put pressure on Turkey. Indeed, the Russians had begun to do this as early as June, 1945, when they suddenly demanded the cession of several Turkish districts lying on the Turkish-Russian frontier, the revision of the Montreux Convention governing the Dardenelles Straits in favor of a joint Russo-Turkish administration, Turkey's abandonment of her ties with Britain and the conclusion of a treaty with the Soviet Union similar to those which Russia had concluded with its Balkan satellites, and finally, the lease to the Soviet Union of bases for naval and land forces in the Straits for its "joint defense." In August, 1946, the Soviet Union renewed its demand, in a note to the United States and Britain, for a new administration of the Straits. In effect, this would have turned Turkey, like Iran, into a Soviet satellite.

In Greece, too, Communist pressure was exerted on the government through wide-scale guerrilla warfare, which began in the fall of 1946. Civil war in Greece was actually nothing new. During the war, the Communist and anti-Communist guerrillas fighting the Germans had spent much of their energy battling each other. When the British landed in Greece and the Germans withdrew from the country, the Communists had attempted to take over the capital city of Athens. Only after several weeks of bitter street fighting and the landing of British reinforcements was the Communist control of Athens dislodged and a truce signed in January, 1945. Just over a year later—in March, 1946—the Greeks held a general election in which right-wing forces captured the majority of votes.

The Greek situation did not improve, however. The country was exhausted from the Italian and German invasions, the four years of occupation, and the Germans' scorched-earth policy as they retreated. Moreover, Greece had always been dependent upon imports that were paid for by exports; but her traditional market in Central Europe was now closed. While the masses lived at a bare subsistence level, the black market flourished. The inability of any government to deal with this situation aroused a good deal of social discontent. And the large 100,000-man army which Greece needed to protect her from her Communist neighbors (Albania, Yugoslavia, and Bulgaria) had brought the country to near-bankruptcy. If Britain had not helped finance—as well as train and equip —the army and kept troops in the country to stabilize the situation, Greece would in all probability have collapsed. It was in these circumstances that in August, 1946, the Communists began to squeeze Greece by renewing the guerrilla warfare in the north, where the guerrilla forces could be kept well supplied by Greece's Communist neighbors.

In all these situations, the American Government was suddenly confronted with the need for action to support Britain, the traditional guardian of this area, against encroachment. In the case of Iran, the United States and Britain delivered firm statements which strongly implied that the two countries would use force to defend Iran. The Soviet response in late March, 1946, was the announcement that the Red Army would be withdrawn during the next five to six weeks. In the Turkish case, the United States sent a naval task force into the Mediterranean immediately after the receipt of the Soviet note on August 7. Twelve days later, the United States replied to the note by rejecting the Russian demand to share sole responsibility for the defense of the Straits with Turkey. Britain sent a similar reply. The Greek situation had not yet come to a head, and the need for American action could be postponed for a while longer. But it should be pointed out that the Administration's actions in Iran and Turkey were merely swift reactions to immediate crises. They were not the product of an over-all American strategy. Such a coherent strategy could only arise from a new assessment of Soviet foreign policy.

The Strategy of Containment

A period of eighteen months passed before the United States undertook that reassessment—from the surrender of Japan on September 2, 1945, until the announcement of the Truman Doctrine on March 12, 1947. Perhaps such a re-evaluation could not have been made any more quickly. Public opinion in a democratic country does not normally shift drastically overnight. It would have been too much to expect the American public to change suddenly from an attitude of friendliness toward the Soviet Union —inspired largely by the picture of Russian wartime bravery and endurance and by hopes for peaceful postwar cooperation—to a hostile mood. The American "reservoir of goodwill" for the Soviet Union could not be emptied that quickly. Moreover, the desire for peace was too strong. The United States wished only to be left alone to preoccupy itself once more with domestic affairs. The end of the war signaled the end of power politics and the restoration of normal peacetime harmony among nations. In response to this expectation, the public demanded a speedy demobilization. The armed forces were thus reduced to completely inadequate levels of strength. In May, 1945, at the end of the war with Germany, the United States had an army of 3.5 million men organized into 68 divisions in Europe, supported by 149 air groups. Our allies supplied another 47 divisions. By March, 1946, only ten months later, the United States had only 400,000 troops left, mainly new recruits; the homeland reserve was six battalions. Further reductions in Army strength followed. Air Force and Navy cuts duplicated this same pattern.

The Eightieth Congress, which convened in Washington in January, 1947, represented this postwar mood of withdrawal well. The Senate was divided into 51 Republicans and 45 Democrats, and the House into 245 Republicans and 118 Democrats. House Speaker Joseph Martin stated Republican intentions in his opening address to his colleagues: a reduction in government expenditures to allow for a 20 per cent income tax reduction. The Congress thereupon cut the President's budget from $41 billion to $31.5 billion. The Secretary of War denounced the cut and warned that the United States might have to withdraw its troops from Germany and Japan; and the Secretary of the Navy announced that the cut would render the Navy impotent. This deliberate and unilateral disarmament could not have failed to encourage Russian intransigence in Europe and increased Soviet pressure in southeast Europe and the Middle East. As this pressure increased in intensity and scope, however, American policy toward the Soviet Union began to be re-evaluated.

Three positions became clear during this period. At one extreme stood that old realist Winston Churchill. At the end of the European war, he had counseled against the withdrawal of American troops. He had insisted that they stay, together with British troops, in order to force the Soviet Union to live up to its Yalta obligations regarding free elections in Eastern Europe and the withdrawal of the Red Army from Eastern Germany. The United States had rejected Churchill's plea. In early 1946, at Fulton, Missouri, Churchill took his case directly to the American public. The Soviet Union, he asserted, was an expansionist state. "From Stettin in the Baltic to Trieste in the Adriatic, an iron curtain has descended across the continent. Behind that line lie all the capitals of the ancient states of Central and Eastern Europe. Warsaw, Berlin, Prague, Vienna, Budapest, Belgrade, Bucharest, and Sofia, all the famous cities and populations around them lie in the Soviet sphere and all are subject in one form or another, not only to Soviet influence but to a very high and increasing measure of control from Moscow." Churchill did not believe that the Russians wanted war: "What they desire is the fruits of war and the indefinite expansion of their power and doctrines." This could be prevented only by the opposing power of the British Commonwealth and the United States. Churchill, in short, said bluntly that the cold war had begun, that Americans must recognize this fact and give up their dreams of Big Three unity in the United Nations. International organization was no substitute for the balance of power. "Our difficulties and dangers will not be removed by closing our eyes to them. They will not be removed by mere waiting to see what happens; nor will they be relieved by a policy of appeasement." An alliance of the English-speaking peoples was the prerequisite for American and British security and world peace.

At the other extreme stood Secretary of Commerce Henry Wallace, who felt it was precisely the kind of aggressive attitude expressed by Churchill that was to blame for Soviet hostility. The United States and Britain had no more business in Eastern Europe than had the Soviet

Union in Latin America; to each, the respective area was vital for national security. Western interference in nations bordering on Russia was bound to arouse Soviet suspicion, just as Soviet intervention in countries neighboring on the United States would. "We may not like what Russia does in Eastern Europe," said Wallace. "Her type of land reform, industrial expropriation, and suspension of basic liberties offends the great majority of the people of the United States. But whether we like it or not, the Russians will try to socialize their sphere of influence just as we try to democratize our sphere of influence (including Japan and Western Germany)." The tough attitude that Churchill and other "reactionaries" at home and abroad demanded was precisely the wrong policy; it would only increase international tension. "We must not let British balance-of-power manipulations determine whether and when the United States gets into a war . . . 'getting tough' never bought anything real and lasting— whether for schoolyard bullies or world powers. The tougher we get, the tougher the Russians will get." Only mutual trust would allow the United States and Russia to live together peacefully, and such trust could not be created by an unfriendly American attitude and policy.

The American Government and public wavered between these two positions. The Administration recognized that Big Three cooperation had ended, and it realized that the time when the United States needed to demonstrate goodwill toward the Soviet Union in order to overcome the latter's suspicions had passed. No further concessions would be made to preserve the surface friendship with the Soviet Union. We had tried to gain Russia's amity by being a friend; it was now up to her leaders to demonstrate a similarly friendly attitude toward us as well. Paper agreements, written in such general terms that they actually hid divergent purposes, were no longer regarded as demonstrating such friendship. Something more than paper agreements was needed: Russian words would have to be matched by Russian deeds.

The American Secretary of State, James Byrnes, called this new line the "policy of firmness and patience." This phrase meant that the United States would take a firm position whenever the Soviet Union became intransigent, and that we would not compromise simply in order to reach a quick agreement. This change in official American attitude toward the Soviet Union was not, however, a fundamental one. A firm line was to be followed only on concrete issues. The assumption was that if the United States took a tougher bargaining position and no longer seemed in a hurry to resolve particular points of tension, the Soviet rulers would see the pointlessness of their obduracy and agree to fair compromise solutions of their differences with the United States and the West. In short, American firmness would make the Russians "reasonable." For they were regarded as "unreasonable" merely on particular issues; that this "unreasonableness" might stem from the very nature of the Communist regime had not yet occurred to American policy-makers. They did not yet agree with Churchill's position that the Soviet government was ideologically hostile to the West and that it would continue to expand until capitalism had been destroyed. The new American position, as one political analyst has aptly summed it up, "meant to most of its exponents that the Soviet Union had to be induced by firmness to play the game in the American way. There was no consistent official suggestion that the United States should begin to play a different game." The prerequisite for such a suggestion was that American policy-makers recognize the revolutionary nature of the Soviet regime.

This recognition came with increasing speed as the Greek crisis reached a peak. By early 1947, it was obvious that the United States would have to play a different game. It was George Kennan, the Foreign Service's foremost expert on the Soviet Union, who first presented the basis of what was to be a new American policy. Kennan's analysis began with a detailed presentation of the Communist outlook on world affairs. In the Soviet leaders' pattern of thought, he said, Russia had no community of interest with the capitalist states; indeed, they saw their relationship with the Western powers in terms of an innate antagonism. Communist ideology had taught them "that the outside world was hostile and that it was their duty eventually to overthrow the political forces beyond their borders. The powerful hands of Russian history and tradition reached up to sustain them in this feeling. Finally, their own aggressive intransigence with respect to the outside world began to find its own reaction. . . . It is an undeniable privilege for every man to prove himself right in the thesis that the world is his enemy; for if he reiterates it frequently enough and makes it the background for his conduct, he is bound to be right." According to Kennan, this Soviet hostility was a constant factor; it would continue until the capitalist world had been destroyed: "Basically, the antagonism remains. It is postulated. And from it flow many of the phenomena which we find disturbing in the Kremlin's conduct of foreign policy: the secretiveness, the lack of frankness, the duplicity, the war suspiciousness, and the basic unfriendliness of purpose." Kennan did suggest, however, that Soviet tactics might change, depending upon circumstances: "And when that happens, there will always be Americans who will leap forward with gleeful announcements 'that the Russians have changed,' and some who will even take credit for having brought about such 'changes.' But we should not be misled by tactical maneuvers. These characteristics of Soviet policy, like the postulates from which they flow, are basic to the *internal* nature of Soviet power, and will be with us . . . until the nature of Soviet power is changed. [Italics added.]" Until that moment, he said, Soviet strategy and objectives would remain the same.

The struggle would thus be a long one. Kennan stressed that Soviet hostility did not mean that the Russians would embark upon a do-or-die program to overthrow capitalism by a fixed date. They had no timetable for conquest. . . .

How could the United States counter such a policy—a policy that was always pushing, seeking weak spots, attempting to fill power vacuums? Kennan's answer was that American policy would have to be one of "long-term, patient, but firm and vigilant containment." The United States would find Soviet diplomacy both easier and more difficult to deal with than that of dictators such as Napoleon or Hitler. "On the one hand, it [Soviet policy] is more sensitive to contrary force, more ready to yield on individual sectors of the diplomatic front when that force is felt to be too strong, and thus more rational in the logic and rhetoric of power. On the other hand, it cannot be easily defeated or discouraged by a single victory on the part of its opponents. And the patient persistence by which it is animated means that *it can be effectively countered not by sporadic acts which represent the momentary whims of democratic opinion, but only by intelligent long-range policies on the part of Russia's adversaries— policies no less steady in their purpose, and no less variegated and re- sourceful in their application, than those of the Soviet Union itself.* [Italics added.]" Kennan thus envisaged containment as *the* test of American democracy, with our very survival as the stake. If the United States failed to meet the strict requirements of this test, it would suffer the same fate as previous civilizations, becoming no more than a name in history books.

On the other hand, if American society rose to the challenge, it could ensure its future. For containment could contribute to changes within the Soviet Union which might bring about a moderation of its revolutionary aims. The United States, Kennan emphasized, "has it in its power to in- crease enormously the strains under which Soviet policy must operate, to force upon the Kremlin a far greater degree of moderation and circum- spection than it has had to observe in recent years, and in this way to promote tendencies which must eventually find their outlet in either the breakup or the gradual mellowing of Soviet power. For no mystical, messianic movement—and particularly not that of the Kremlin—can face frustration indefinitely without eventually adjusting itself in one way or another to the logic of that state of affairs." Kennan's theory was thus not so new. He was, in effect, asserting the old thesis that within an authori- tarian or totalitarian society there are certain strains and stresses, and that these give rise to frustrations which can only be relieved by being channeled into an aggressive and expansionist foreign policy. Kennan's remedy was to prevent this expansion, thereby aggravating the internal tensions in such a way that they would either destroy the Soviet System or force the Soviet leaders to placate the domestic dissatisfaction. Assum- ing that the Soviet leaders preferred to remain in power and that they would therefore be compelled to adopt the second course, they would have no alternative but to moderate their foreign policy. For a relaxation of international tensions was the prerequisite for coping with their domestic problems. Thus, the Kremlin would have no choice but to sur- render its revolutionary aims and arrange a *modus vivendi* with the West- ern powers—above all, with the United States.

The Truman Doctrine

Whether the United States could meet this Soviet challenge became a pressing question when, on the afternoon of February 21, 1947, the First Secretary of the British Embassy in Washington visited the State Department and handed American officials two notes from His Majesty's Government. One concerned Greece, the other Turkey. In effect, they both stated the same thing: that Britain could no longer meet its traditional responsibilities in those two countries. Since both were on the verge of collapse, the import of the British notes was clear: that a Russian breakthrough could be prevented only by an all-out American commitment.

February 21 was thus a historic day. On that day, Great Britain, the only remaining power in Europe, acknowledged her exhaustion. She had fought Philip II of Spain, Louis XIV of France, Kaiser Wilhelm II and Adolf Hitler of Germany. She had preserved the balance of power which protected the United States for so long that it seemed almost natural for her to continue to do so. But her ability to protect that balance had steadily declined in the twentieth century. Twice she had needed American help. Each time, however, she had fought the longer battle; on neither occasion had the United States entered the war until it became clear that Germany and its allies were too strong for her and that we would have to help her in safeguarding our own security. Now, all of a sudden, there was no power to protect the United States but the United States itself; no one stood between this country and the present threat to its security. All the other major powers of the world had collapsed—except the Soviet Union, which was the second most powerful nation in the world and was wedded to an expansionist ideology. The cold fact of a bipolar world suddenly faced the United States. The country could no longer shirk the responsibilities of its tremendous power.

The immediate crisis suddenly confronting the United States had its locale in the eastern Mediterranean. Direct Soviet pressure on Iran and Turkey had temporarily been successfully resisted. The Russians had now turned to outflanking these two nations by concentrating their attention on Greece. If Greece collapsed—and all reports from that hapless country indicated that it would fall within a few weeks—it would only be a question of time until Turkey and Iran would crumble before Soviet power. But the fall of Greece would not only affect its neighbors to the east; it would also lead to an increase of Communist pressure on Italy. Italy would then be faced with two Communist states to its east—Yugoslavia and Greece—and with the largest Communist party in Western Europe in its own midst. And to the northwest of Italy lay France, with the second largest Communist party in the West. Thus, the security of all of Western Europe would be endangered as well. The immediate danger, however, remained in the eastern Mediterranean, and the Soviet desire for control over this area was underlined by its demands that the city of Trieste at the head of the Adriatic be yielded to Yugoslavia and that Italy's former colonies of Tripolitania and Eritrea in North Africa be placed under Soviet trusteeship.

The United States had no choice but to act in this situation. The results of inaction were only too clear: the collapse of Europe's flank in the eastern Mediterranean, the establishment of Communist dominance in the Middle East, and a Soviet breakthrough into South Asia and North Africa. The psychological impact upon Europe of such a tremendous

Soviet victory over the West would have been disastrous. For Europeans already psychologically demoralized by their sufferings and fall from power and prestige, this would have been the final blow. In short, what was at stake in Greece was America's survival itself.

President Truman was quick to recognize this stark fact. On March 12, 1947, he went before a joint session of Congress and delivered a speech which must rank as one of the most important in American history. The President first outlined the situation in Greece: her lack of natural resources; the cruel German occupation, resulting in widespread destruction; her inability to import the goods she needed for bare subsistence, let alone reconstruction; the Communist efforts to exploit these conditions by spreading political chaos and hindering any economic recovery; and the guerrilla warfare in northern Greece, where the Communist forces were receiving aid from Yugoslavia, Albania, and Bulgaria.

Then Truman came to the heart of his speech. Here he spelled out what was to become known as the Truman Doctrine. The United States, he emphasized, could survive only in a world in which freedom flourished. . . .

Truman asked Congress to appropriate $400 million for economic aid and military supplies for both countries, and to authorize the dispatch of American civilian and military personnel in order to help the two nations in their tasks of reconstruction and provide their armies with appropriate instruction and training. Truman ended on a grave note:

. . . I am confident that the Congress will face these responsibilities squarely.

The Congress and the American people did. History had once more shown that when a great and democratic people is given decisive and courageous leadership, the people will respond quickly and wisely. Under Truman's leadership, the American public had made a decisive commitment. The United States was now a full participant in the international arena. There could no longer be any retreat. The survival of freedom was dependent solely upon the United States. The only question was how responsibly and honorably this country would bear its new burden of world leadership.

2. American Responsibility for the Cold War

In the following selection, D. F. Fleming expresses a minority dissent among scholars in attributing the origins of the Cold War in large measure to allegedly misguided American policy and especially to the Truman Doctrine. Under the influence of Winston Churchill and others, Truman launched a dangerous and unwise policy of military alliances against Russia and a holy crusade against communism. Whatever the merits of Fleming's interpretation, the sensitive reader can appreciate the compelling earnestness of the author's plea for "co-survival." A political scientist at Vanderbilt University, Fleming has written extensively on American relations with the League of Nations and other international organizations.

The Cold War and Its Origins

D. F. FLEMING

Preface

This book is an account of the great continuing conflict of the twentieth century, the struggle which will determine whether our civilization is to disappear in the nuclear flames of a final war of annihilation or find essential unity in one family of organized nations.

The record here attempted was begun in 1947, when it seemed more than probable that we would go on into a third world war within one lifetime. It is the writer's effort to try to forestall what he has never doubted would be the end of both the American dream and Western civilization. . . .

It is my profound belief that nothing is so revolutionary as these world wars and that there is no rational alternative to relying chiefly on the irresistible force of evolution to modify communism, and all other systems, to bring them into closer harmony with the universal aspirations for a good life which all men share. I have never doubted that we can compete successfully with communism, if we place our main reliance on non-military methods.

However, after World War II our leaders quickly swung all the way over from our isolationist refusal to accept any responsibility in the world and came close to assuming military responsibility for everything everywhere. We heavily and positively over-compensated for our negative failure after 1918.

We do not seem able to learn the lesson of each succeeding world crisis until it is too late. During World War II we repented of our tragic failure to lead the League of Nations and we took our place at the head of a new league.

The lesson of World War I, that we cannot resign from the world, was learned at a sadly late date but once again the mandate of a world war was disregarded. The lesson of World War II was that the losing side must not plunge the world into another world war in order to restore or improve its position. We had just permitted Germany to do that, with calamitous consequences.

Nevertheless, after 1945 we ourselves at once assumed the position of a loser. Though we were the mightiest nation which had ever stood upon this planet, and though our undamaged strength had increased prodigiously as a result of World War II, we said that we had "lost" East Europe and China, and we rebelled against these two main consequences of the war.

Knowing that world wars can grow out of great myths like this, I was appalled to see the United States move promptly into a new balance of

D. F. Fleming, *The Cold War and Its Origins, 1917–1960* (Garden City, N. Y.: Doubleday & Company, Inc., 1961), Vol. I, pp. xi–xiii, 334–337, 348–357, 436–450, 474–476. Reprinted with permission.

power conflict, while the embers of the last one were still hot, certain that the terribly wounded Soviet Union was out to take over the world.

This was done, also, in the light of the deadly flashes at Hiroshima and Nagasaki, which revealed clearly and with finality that another world war would complete the lethal progression of our time toward mutual extermination.

Since August 6, 1945, this process has advanced with relentless speed. Our decision that the Soviets should never possess an A-bomb if international control could prevent it; their prompt acquisition of the weapon; our drive for the H-bomb, with Russian success almost simultaneous; their plunge to leadership in intercontinental jet bombers and global guided missiles—these and other miracles of destruction tumbling on each other's heels leave us little time to make peace.

Yet for fifteen years after 1945 peace was not made and we proceeded doggedly along the same old cycle of international rivalry, crisis after crisis, and ever mounting arms burdens—just as if the most destructive weapon of war was still the machine-gun, and as if we were still in the springtime of 1914, ignorant of the enormous steps toward destroying civilization soon to be made in the two world wars.

Of course we say to ourselves that because it would be so horrible and so senseless it will not happen. Our Civil Defense Administrator has told us that in a surprise attack the Soviets could kill above 40,000,000 Americans, merely with bombers, and if the best possible shelters had been constructed. Yet soon thousands of ICBM's must be expected to stand triggered in the northern forests on both sides. It has been estimated, too, that we could mount a surprise thermonuclear attack on the Soviet Union which would cause deaths in the order of several hundred millions, depending on which way the winds blew.

It is an easy retreat from reality to say that no ruler of a great power would ever be mad or frightened enough to give the order, and no small nation turbulent or rebellious enough to touch off catastrophe. But humane men reasoned in the same way in early 1914, as well as in 1938, and no man can be safe until peace is made, and until some curbs are put upon the power of governments to assert their sovereign wills against each other once too often.

Yet we Americans are currently trying hard to devise new rules for victory, or at least stalemate, in "limited" nuclear wars, without using the city and nation killers. We strive assiduously to produce "clean" H-bombs and whole families of little ones, in an attempt to restore some shadow of rational possibility to the institution of war, and to the threat of its use as an instrument of diplomacy. These efforts may ease us into the final nuclear holocaust, but they can never take us back into the ages when major wars could be survived. The only way of escape lies forward; toward the elimination of great power wars. The inexorable procession of "ultimate" weapons leaves us no choice but to master them before they destroy us. . . .

It was under the shadow of this infinite and constantly darkening peril that this book was written. That is why I have sought at every stage to present the other side, how it looks to "the enemy," in the belief that this is essential to the avoidance of the final grand smash.

Of course this has been a difficult undertaking in a time when nearly all of the great organs of public opinion management have been massed to stress the iniquity and wickedness of our opponents. Yet it is only by striving constantly to see the other side that we can hope to survive, in the age of push-button ICBM's and beyond. . . .

Rising Tension: November 1945–July 1946

During the last weeks of 1945 long speeches began to be made in the United States Senate revealing the deepest aversion to the Soviet Union and a corresponding desire to deal with her sternly.

Stop Appeasing Russia. Senator Burton K. Wheeler, of Montana, led off, on November 27, with a speech filling twenty-three pages in the *Congressional Record*, less a moderate amount of interruption. Wheeler was one of the many isolationists who were catapulted into the war by Pearl Harbor. Now that the war was over they were ready to say "I told you so" with a vengeance. Wheeler declared that Truman had "inherited an almost insoluble situation—one which some of us foresaw was the inevitable consequence of policies pursued before Pearl Harbor." Now, "something terrible is happening to America and the world. . . . We confront the greatest crisis in human history."

Before explaining what the catastrophe was, Wheeler proclaimed triumphantly that the entire world was out of control. He read quotations describing bad conditions all over the globe. Then he launched into a long assault upon the Soviet Union, defining the issue as not communism, but "power—sheer, naked and unadulterated power." He listed all the territories annexed by Russia, from Finnish Karelia to Bessarabia. Then he called the roll of the satellite countries dominated by the Soviets, from Finland all the way around to the Far East.

Why had all this happened? "The only reason why, to this moment, Russia has had a free hand to liquidate all potential opposition, both among organized patriotic resistance groups and among the disorganized helplessly miserable masses, is because we have been willing not only to shield her and keep the facts from the American people but also because, by our abject appeasement for the sake of a specious unity, we have deliberately played her game for her."

Being a very able lawyer, Wheeler had chosen his point of attack shrewdly. The great bulk of the American people knew that Allied appeasement of the Fascist dictators had been an abysmal failure. Americans also hate being suckers, especially a second time. If therefore they could be convinced that they were starting down the slippery path of appeasement again, or already sliding rapidly down it, they would be certain to react sharply. It would, moreover, be relatively easy to make that charge stick. The great backlog of pre-war distrust and fear of Communist Russia could be stirred to red heat without too much effort.

Proceeding, Wheeler charged that "our appeasement, our betrayal of principles, our abandonment of human beings to a fate worse than death have made Europe and Asia a veritable chamber of horrors." He inserted dozens of quotations, many dealing with the raping of German women by Russian troops, to show how horrible conditions were, and asserted that "we dare not look for one moment longer with the blurred vision of hate, of revenge, of fear, upon an enemy whose predicament now threatens the greatest human catastrophe in history.

After further pages of material to create sympathy for Germany, and charging that "every step" which Russia had taken since the San Francisco Conference showed that she intended "to go her way for power, power and more power," he declared that "we must quit appeasing Russia and let her know once and for all that we did not fight this war to let her enslave the people of Europe."

The charge that Russia controlled Eastern Europe merely because we appeased her was, of course, without foundation. She was there because the pre-war Allied effort to turn Hitler to the East had backfired. Far from wanting to prevent her entry into East Europe we had been keenly afraid she might stop on her own borders, but myriads of Americans would forget their history and bristle at the idea of appeasing the Reds.

Russia a World Aggressor. On December 4 Senator James O. Eastland, of Mississippi, took up the cudgels in favor of Germany. He quoted five long rape stories from the Patterson press, *The Washington Times* and *The New York Daily News*, before asserting that "even communistic periodicals are admitting that ten to fifteen million Germans will die of starvation this winter."

Germany had served both as a neutralizing agent and a barrier between the Oriental hordes and the West for 2000 years. Now "we find in Czechoslovakia savage, barbarian Mongolian hordes stalking the streets of western civilization as conquerors" and thinking of engulfing Western Europe. We could not permit Germany to become a satellite of Russia. Germany was the keystone of Europe. We must hold Western Europe. He shuddered to think what a union of Russia and Germany under the banner of communism would mean. The American people "must realize that Russia is a predatory, aggressor nation, and that today she follows the same fateful road of conquest and aggression with which Adolph Hitler set the world on fire."

This speech came close to justifying the Nazi racial theories and very near to saying that we had backed the wrong horse in supporting the savage Russians against the civilized Germans. It implied also, as had Wheeler, that we should change sides and back the Germans against the Reds. Before long many Americans would be planning to arm Germany again. But the really pregnant part of Eastland's speech was the charge that Russia was another aggressor, just as bad as Hitler.

This was another analogy that would be widely accepted without examination, as it was repeated over and over again in coming months. Together the cry "No More Appeasement" and the slogan "Another

Aggressor" made a potent combination. The moral was perfectly plain. If another aggressor is on the march we must stop this thing now. Delay only makes matters worse. . . .

Eden's Appraisal. Contemporaneous with Eastland's charge that Russia was an aggressor, just as dangerous as Hitler, Anthony Eden discussed Russia's motives in the House of Commons, on November 22, 1945. Chiding the Russians for thinking that any plans for the organization of Western Europe must be aimed at them, he avowed his full belief that Russia's arrangements in East Europe were directed against a German resurgence. They were not aimed at Britain. He was "convinced it is the literal truth. We know that Russian arrangements are not aimed against us."

This was the testimony of one of the most responsible of all British statesmen. He knew, as did any student of the war, that Russian policy in East Europe was dominated by the most powerful and poignant defensive purposes and emotions. But the immensely powerful anti-Russian and anti-Communist influences in the United States, both lay and clerical, gave no recognition to history. Russia in East Europe was a brutal, barbaric aggressor, obviously out to conquer the world.

Atomic World Power. Opportunely, too, the atomic bomb had provided a weapon with which we could stop this new menace. It enabled us to defend the United States against Russian "aggression," easily, surely and cheaply. Senator Edwin Johnson, of Colorado, leading member of the Military Affairs Committee, explained it to the Senate on November 28. We had the blueprints for a new plane with a flying range of 10,000 miles. "Therefore, with the strategic location of airfields from the Philippines to Alaska, on the coast of Asia, from Alaska to the Azores in the South Atlantic, we can drop, on a moment's notice, atomic bombs on any spot on the earth's surface and return to our base."

We dared not contemplate a defense program of lesser scope, Johnson said. Would the world like it? He thought most of it would, but no matter: "With vision and guts and plenty of atomic bombs, ultra-modern planes, and strategically located air-bases the United States can outlaw wars of aggression. . . ." The courage to do it was also the price of survival.

And the United Nations? "The world organization which I am thinking of is one designed to stop war with the atomic bomb in the hands of the United States as the club behind the door, to be used only when a bandit nation goes berserk."

Evidently there was still such a nation loose in the world. Johnson strongly opposed the talk of inevitable war with Russia, but he admonished her: "Don't make the fatal mistake of pushing us around. We won't take it."

Senator Johnson meant well by the world. He did not mean to hurt anyone. All he asked was the power to atom bomb "on a moment's notice" any nation which misbehaved. The Russians would have nothing to worry about so long as they conducted themselves properly, according to his standards. . . .

Churchill's Fulton Speech

Preliminary Conference. The same could hardly be said of Winston Churchill's famous speech at Westminster College, Fulton, Missouri—in President Truman's home state—on March 5, 1946. During several weeks spent in Florida he carefully matured his blast, after flying to Washington on February 10 for a conference with President Truman which was reported to concern his speech. That the content of the speech was discussed hardly admits of doubt, since it was to be a world-shaking event.

As the momentous day approached, Churchill returned from Florida to Washington and the President journeyed with him to Fulton to present him to his audience and to bless the occasion. . . .

The Address. The urgency of the occasion was soon evident. In the grand prose cadences which had thrilled so many millions of Americans during the war, Churchill declared that "Opportunity is here now, clear and shining, for both our countries. To reject it or ignore it or fritter it away will bring upon us all the long reproaches of the aftertime." Constancy of mind was essential and persistency of purpose.

What for? "Our over-all strategic concept" was to protect the myriad cottages or apartment homes of the wage earners "from the two gaunt marauders—war and tyranny." The Missouri folk had not been conscious that these two monsters were about to attack them until Churchill described "the frightful disturbance in which the ordinary family is plunged when the curse of war swoops down upon the bread-winner and those for whom he works and contrives."

It was evident that the situation was serious, for Churchill went on to urge that the UN "must immediately begin to be equipped with an international armed force" and a certain number of air squadrons. He asserted that it would be "criminal madness" to cast the atomic bomb adrift "in this still agitated and ununited world." No one would be able to sleep so soundly if some Communist, or Neo-Fascist state had invented the bomb. God had willed that this should not be.

Then he came to the second danger which threatened "the cottage home," tyranny, the "police governments" of Eastern Europe. It was "not our duty at this time, when difficulties are so numerous, to interfere forcibly in the internal affairs of countries whom we have not conquered in war," but we must "never cease to proclaim in fearless tones the great principles of freedom. . . ."

The inference was clear that we could not go to war to drive the Communists out of Eastern Europe *at this time,* but we must keep the matter in mind and we must keep on insisting that "the people of any country have the right and should have the power" to exercise all the rights of Englishmen and to enjoy all of the governmental processes and freedoms of the Anglo-Saxon world, which Churchill enumerated in full.

Then "at this sad and breathless moment" he came to "the crux of what I have travelled here to say"—no prevention of war or successful UN without an alliance of the English-speaking peoples, continuance of the Joint Chiefs of Staff, joint use of all naval and air force bases all over the world, doubling our mobility.

Otherwise, "The Dark Ages may return, the Stone Age." "Beware, I say: Time may be short. Do not let us take the course of letting events drift along until it is too late." A shadow had fallen. Nobody knew "what Soviet Russia and its Communist international organization intends to do in the future, or what are the limits if any to their expansive and proselytizing tendencies." From Stettin to Trieste there was "an iron curtain." He saw enormous and wrongful inroads into Germany.

Turkey and Persia were profoundly alarmed. And in front of the iron curtain "Communist Fifth Columns" were everywhere, "a growing challenge and peril to civilization." In the Far East there was anxiety, especially in Manchuria.

Having built up this picture of a terrible juggernaut operating all over the world which had to be tamed, Churchill then repulsed "the idea that a new war is inevitable, still more that it is imminent." He did not believe that Russia desired war, only "the fruits of war and the indefinite expansion of their power and doctrines." Therefore "while time remains" he demanded the "establishment of conditions of freedom and democracy as rapidly as possible in all countries." Since nothing except overwhelming force could rapidly eliminate communism from East Europe and Russia herself, he did not explain how this was to be done. . . .

Then he drew on the great prestige which he had won before 1930. The last time he "saw it all coming and cried aloud," but "no one paid any attention." Surely we "must not let that happen again." There must be "a good understanding," that is, a showdown, with Russia "now, in 1946."

The old warrior and world strategist was off again, and with a terrifying start. He had waged war on the Reds in Russia to the limit of British tolerance during 1919 and 1920. Then throughout the twenties he had preached the menace of the Red revolution, never losing an opportunity to refer to the Bolshevik leaders "as murderers and ministers of hell."

Forced to welcome their aid in 1941 to save Britain, he had incessantly attempted the impossible feat of using them to beat Germany while denying them the fruits of victory. Now he would mobilize the might of the United States to achieve what he had never been able to do before.

A Master Stroke. If, too, there is a Third World War, Churchill's Missouri speech will be the primary document in explaining its origins. His was the first full-length picture of a Red Russia out to conquer the world. Backed by the immense authority of his war record, and by the charm of his great personality, it pre-conditioned many millions of listeners for a giant new *cordon sanitaire* around Russia, for a developing world crusade to smash world communism in the name of Anglo-Saxon democracy. In print Churchill's battle cry became the bible of every warmonger in the world. It said all they had wanted to say and with his great name behind it, it could be used endlessly with great effect.

At Fulton, Churchill also prevailed over Roosevelt and Hull, the great American leaders who had checkmated him in all the later stages of the war, preventing him from creating a gulf between East and West. At Fulton he did it. Had Roosevelt lived, Churchill would never have dared to propose that he come to the United States and issue a call for a world alliance to encircle the Soviet Union and establish Western democracy in Eurasia. If he had ventured to make such a speech in the United States he would have been sharply disavowed. But with Roosevelt dead he was able not only to do that, but to carry President Truman along in his baggage.

Whether the idea of the speech originated with Churchill or Truman is not yet known. In the light of Truman's strongly hardened determination to quit "babying" the Soviets, he was probably the originator. It seems a little odd that in his *Memoirs* there is only one casual reference to an event of such outstanding importance, one of the chief landmarks of the Cold War. . . .

Brooks Atkinson wrote from Moscow describing "the outburst of fury" which Churchill's speech had loosed. It had enormously raised the pitch of political feeling in Russia. The Russian people were kept aware generally of threats to their security, but here was something specific. Like all other peoples, the Russians did not want war. "They have had a bellyfull of carnage. They have not had time enough yet to recover from the deep poignant suffering of the fierce war years, when they lost more lives than both the British and Americans." They would therefore be slow to believe in the possibility of war again, without a bombshell such as Churchill's speech. It "had the effect of electrifying and depressing everyone" and it fell squarely into the familiar pattern of Soviet beliefs—capitalistic hostility, encirclement and the violent imperialism of a dying capitalist economy leading to war—this time against the Soviet Union.

In other words, few things could have convinced the Russian people of the reality of great danger ahead so effectively as Churchill's speech did. He could and did do it better and more easily than any other living person, binding the Soviet peoples to their leaders as nothing else could. . . .

Our Firm But Moderate Policy of Making Peace Condemned. The extent of the push which Churchill gave toward irreconcilable conflict stands out sharply by comparing his speech with those of Byrnes and Vandenberg a few days before. Reporting on the London UN sessions Vandenberg filled four columns with praise of UN, listing the credit items on the ledger of the London meetings. Then he asked "What is Russia up to now?" He named the places all around the world where she was pressing for advantage, and asserted his belief that the two great rival ideologies could "live together in reasonable harmony if the United States speaks as plainly upon all occasions as Russia does; if the United States just as vigorously sustains its own purposes as Russia does. . . ." The situation called for "patience and good will but not for vacillation." . . .

On February 28 Byrnes made a speech which also indicated a tougher line toward Russia. Still he stressed that there had always been ideological differences in the world, and that "in this world there is room for many people with varying views and many governments with varying systems." The United States wished "to maintain friendly relations with all nations and exclusive arrangements with no nation." "We will gang up against no state," Byrnes declared. "We will do nothing to break the world into exclusive blocs or spheres of influence." Only an "inexcusable tragedy of errors could cause serious conflict between this country and Russia."

This was the policy which Byrnes and Vandenberg had enunciated a few days before Churchill spoke. Neither had given the slightest indication of belief that an irreconcilable conflict existed, or that Russia had to be hemmed in and overawed with overwhelming power. Neither had suggested that democracy had to be enforced everywhere. Both had given every indication that they expected to make peace, though with difficulty.

It was this sensible attitude which Churchill contradicted completely. He taught that all civilization was in imminent peril of destruction by Russia. The time was terribly short and our lives and fortunes could be saved only by a swift mobilization of overwhelming power against her. He desired to gang up with a vengeance.

Toughness Prescribed. It was this policy which, backed by President Truman, prevailed. Byrnes had already felt strong presidential disapproval for the agreements with Russia which he had made at Moscow. Truman had been influenced by his military and Congressional advisers, Admiral William D. Leahy, Senators Connally and Vandenberg, all of whom thought Byrnes had not been tough enough. This was the view of British Foreign Secretary Bevin, who had "rather openly accused him of weakness and appeasement." Now after the supreme demand for toughness at Fulton our policy steadily hardened. Churchill's speech "marked the critical point where relations between the West and the East turned for the worse." . . .

Moderation Advised. The *démarche* at Fulton, Missouri, launched the United States openly upon a policy of dealing with Russia as an incorrigible menace. On March 10, Cordell Hull revealed his deep alarm over the turn in events. We who are living, he said, must not allow the human race to commit suicide through selfishness, impatience and provocation. Addressing all the members of the United Nations, Hull offered a five-point program for overcoming what he termed the spirit of impatience. He urged each government to: (1) examine with sympathy and patience the views of others; (2) ascertain the true facts; (3) avoid the assumption of adamant positions; (4) refrain from exaggerating and over-emphasizing one's own claims; and (5) refrain from making an appeal to prejudice.

This was the voice of true statesmanship. Of course it needed to be heard in Moscow. Yet the voice of reason and moderation, of firmness and patience, could no longer have much effect in the West. There the implacable Truman-Churchill spirit had seized control. It was their policy of alliance against Russia and restraining communism by military means which was to rule for many a day—until its bankruptcy was demonstrated, as it would be, or another global war came. . . .

Atomic Ultimatum. The practical certainty that such a war could not be ended did not deter some Americans from wanting to start it. Thus George H. Earle, former American Minister to Bulgaria, returned to make "America realize what a frightful menace we have in Russia." It was "the greatest danger that ever threatened America." Civilization's outlook was "the blackest in history." He urged that Russia be given an ultimatum to "get back to her own territory and if they refused I would use the atomic bomb on them while we have it and before they get it." He asserted that "If Russia had the atomic bomb there would be few Americans alive today."

Truman's Baylor Speech. On March 6, 1947, President Truman made a speech at Baylor University on foreign economic policy which was a virtual declaration of irreconcilable conflict against both communism and democratic socialism. He explained that freedom was more important than peace and that freedom of worship and speech were dependent on freedom of enterprise. Something "deeper than a desire to protect the profits of ownership" was involved.

Freedom of enterprise was limited when governments conducted foreign trade or when the governments planned the economy. In the latter case "Governments make all the important choices and he (the trader) adjusts himself to them as best he can."

This, said the President, "was the pattern of the seventeenth and eighteenth centuries" and "Unless we act, and act decisively, it will be the pattern of the next century. . . . If this trend is not reversed the Government of the United States will be under pressure, sooner or later, to use these same devices to fight for markets and for raw materials." It would find itself in the business of "telling every trader what he could buy or sell, and how much, and when, and where." This was "not the American way" and "not the way of peace." The implication was plain that state trading (in the U.S.S.R. and its satellites) and government control of trade (in Britain and much of West Europe) led to war.

This was serious enough, but even more ominous were the assumptions that "the whole world should adopt the American system" and that "the American system could survive in America only if it became a world system."

The Baylor speech was closely studied by every European government as a challenge by the strongest economic unit ever developed on earth, one which had just grown to gargantuan size on government orders. During the four war years, 1942 to 1946 inclusive, the American Government had poured 306 billion dollars into the coffers of American business, taking all the responsibility, building hundreds of new plants for business to operate, guaranteeing unlimited markets and immense profits.

The result of this exhibition of "free enterprise" was the growth of the great American corporations to such power that at the end of the war our Federal Trade Commission reported that the 62 largest manufacturing corporations had accumulated liquid capital sufficient "to purchase the assets of nearly 90 per cent of all the other manufacturing corporations in the United States." Many of these tremendous economic giants were more powerful than the entire national economies of dozens of nations, but the Baylor speech declared that they must not have the competition of state owned or state planned economies. If American freedom of worship and speech was to survive, the regimented economies of the world had to go.

Coming from a government which controlled three-fourths of the world's invested capital, and more than half of its industry, the Baylor speech was a statement which would give all other governments pause. It indicated how easy it would be for the world's economic colossus to decide that all other economic systems were un-American and threats to American freedom. It indicated that the representatives of American capitalism who had come into key posts in Washington after Roosevelt's death held the same view about the world that Lenin and other Communist zealots had. The world could not accommodate diverse systems. It must be one or the other: communism or free enterprise capitalism.

The Occasion for the Doctrine

Paralysis in Britain. The apparently well founded hopes for peace at the end of the year were suddenly upset by a great snow storm which whirled into a high pressure area above northern Russia and descended on the British Isles, late in January 1947, covering them from three to twenty feet deep with snow which promptly froze into ice after one day of thaw.

Britain was paralyzed. Her tired miners, mainly older men, could not get into their deep, narrow, hard-to-work coal seams. The scanty supplies above ground could be moved only with slow, heroic efforts. It was several weeks before anything like normal circulation could be restored to Britain's economic veins, and by then $800,000,000 of desperately needed export production had been lost and the world had seen clearly that Britain was too weak to resume her former role as a great power. Up to that time the illusion had persisted that the power which had dominated the world for more than a century before 1914, and which had recovered after 1918, would take her place as a fairly strong third in the new galaxy of great powers. Actually, this was impossible. Another huge bite had been taken from her overseas assets. Now they were overbalanced by far larger debts owed to all the dominions—even $4,000,000,000 to India, now emerging into independence. What was left could not support a great navy and 1,400,000 troops scattered around the world, particularly if the British people at home were to have a decent standard of living. . . .

British Failure in Greece. The parlous state of affairs in Greece had been known to our government for several months. The British had explained to Secretary Byrnes in the previous summer that they would have to cut their losses in Greece. Since the end of the war the British had poured $760,000,000 worth of supplies into Greece, without doing more than keep the country alive. Nothing was left over for reconstruction. This was due to three reasons: the thorough ruination of Greece by the Germans and Italians; the antagonisms and demoralization left by the civil war a year earlier; and the inability of the corrupt Rightist government to suppress a large scale communist-led guerrilla movement which ruled the mountains and controlled most of the country outside the big cities. The government turned Rightist bands loose in the country, and they did their best to crush the Left, but the net result was to drive to the hills many embittered men who were not communists. The majority of the rebels were "not communists."

The rebels also received aid from communist ruled Bulgaria, Yugoslavia and Albania, Greece's northern neighbors. Besides arms, munitions and medical help the rebels were permitted to retreat over the border when hard pressed, to rest and be re-outfitted, particularly in Yugoslavia. The Western powers had tried to stop this aid through the United Nations, by sending a commission to investigate, which was still in Greece in March 1947, along with an official American economic mission headed by Paul Porter, but there was not much chance of success by this method against the opposition of Russia and her satellites.

The Greek Problem Presented to Us. This was the general situation when on February 24, 1947, the British Ambassador orally informed Under Secretary of State Dean Acheson, that the British Government would evacuate its army and cease to look after Greece on March 31. . . .

The Preparation of the Doctrine. The first meeting of State Department experts with Under Secretary of State Dean Acheson left some concerned by the responsibility of challenging the Soviet Union, others elated by the prospect, and some filled with awe. Acheson was to lead in the epochal turning point, since Secretary of State George Marshall was being intensively briefed for the approaching Moscow Conference on the future of Germany and would shortly leave for the Conference.

At a meeting with the Congressional leaders of both parties, on February 27, Acheson left them all deeply impressed by his account of the persistent efforts of the Soviet Union to encircle Turkey, thus laying three continents open to Soviet domination, and Germany—through the communists in France, Italy, Austria and Hungary. The Soviet Union was "aggressive and expanding" and Russia and the United States were "divided by an unbridgeable ideological chasm." Not since Rome and Carthage had there been such a polarization of power and it was up to us to block the Soviets in Greece and Turkey.

None of the leaders of Congress questioned the assumption of protectorates over Greece and Turkey. Senator Vandenberg, supported by others, insisted that the President should explain the new policy in a message to the Congress and a radio address to the people, in the broad context which Acheson had made, and he reiterated this request later. The radio address was dropped only at the last minute, but on April 27 Acheson had an off-the-record conference with about twenty leading newspaper men, and other briefing sessions prepared the way for public support of the program. A Cabinet committee prepared "a program of communication with leaders throughout the country, particularly business people." . . .

On the same afternoon [February 28] a large meeting of State, War and Navy officials was held in which the view was unanimous that the new policy should be presented to the public in terms of "assistance to free governments everywhere" that needed help against Communist aggression or subversion. This view came from all parts of the assembly, which also wanted the world strategic situation to be explained to the people.

A paper written up after this discussion became the basic document for the President's address and it contained the statement that it should be "the policy of the United States to support free peoples who are resisting attempted subjugation by armed minorities or by outside pressures." . . .

Truman's Long Held Purpose. The President himself was ready to seize the occasion to quarantine Soviet communism. On March 23, 1947, an authoritative article was published in the *New York Times* by Arthur Krock, who stated that the Truman Doctrine had been in the President's mind a long time. . . .

In his article of March 23 Krock stated that after inquiry he had reached the conclusion that Moscow had better disabuse itself of the growing impression that Mr. Truman merely adopted the view of his counsellors. On the contrary, the President began to abandon hope of achieving peace and security by "a continued policy of appeasement and official treatment of Russia as a government friendly to the United States," as long ago as the London Conference of Foreign Ministers in September 1945. "He made up his mind then that, when a fitting opportunity arose and one which Congress and the people would recognize as such, he would proclaim the new doctrine. On several occasions he thought the time had come, but some of his important advisers talked him out of it." When the British note of February 24, 1947, announcing withdrawal from Greece, came it pointed to a situation which the President found suited to his "long held purpose." It only remained to put "Mr. Truman's now-matured policy" before the world suitably. The alternative of limiting the message to the immediate task in hand was rejected and Clark Clifford, "who must at first hand have heard the doctrine in its long period of oral formulation," was set to drafting "the global anti-Communist policy." The President insisted that the important word *must,* instead of "should," be inserted in the master-key paragraph of the message, to make it read: "I believe that it *must* be the policy of the United States to support free peoples who are resisting attempted subjugation by armed minorities or by outside pressure." When it was finally finished Mr. Truman "rehearsed its delivery several times with apparently growing satisfaction." It said what he wanted to say. . . .

In his *Memoirs* (II, 105) Mr. Truman relates that the first draft of the message presented by the State Department "was not at all to my liking." In spite of all the high purpose recorded above by its draftsman, Joseph E. Jones, it was full of "all sorts of background data and statistical figures," sounding like "an investment prospectus." So Truman sent it back asking for more emphasis on general policy and it was rewritten for that purpose, but it still seemed to him "half-hearted." Therefore in "the key sentence" he scratched out "should" and wrote "must" and did the same thing in several other places. He "wanted no hedging in this speech."

George Kennan's Dissent. From this concordance of agreement that the Soviet Union and communism must be publicly quarantined there was one strong and surprising dissent. From our embassy in Moscow George F. Kennan had sent long messages urging a stiffening of our responses to Russia in the post-war period. In March 1947 he was in Washington, already designated by Marshall as head of a new policy planning staff. At the moment he was occupied with lectures to the War College and he had no part in formulating the Truman Doctrine, though he knew it was in preparation.

On the afternoon of March 6 he came over to see how things were going and was shown the third draft, before the message had gone to the White House and been sharply stiffened. In its milder form the message disturbed Kennan deeply. "To say that he found objections to it is to put it mildly," said Joseph M. Jones. "He objected strongly both to the tone of the message and to the specific action proposed." He favored economic aid to Greece, but wanted to keep the military aid small. He was opposed to aid of any kind to Turkey, whereas the others regarded the defense of the Straits as the most vital consideration involved, though the Turkish end was softpedalled in the message.

It was the tone and ideological content of the message to which Kennan most objected, "the portraying of two opposing ways of life, and the open-end commitment to aid free peoples." Moreover, he felt so strongly that he voiced his objections to a number of people in the Department including finally Acheson, but "It was too late."

This first reaction by Kennan to the Truman-Churchill Doctrine of a global quarantine of the Soviet Union and communism would have astonished the world had it been known soon after 1947, for his famous article on "The Sources of Soviet Conduct," in the July 1947 issue of *Foreign Affairs* (which will be discussed later), caused him to be widely regarded as the father of the containment doctrine. Yet in the light of the revelation just quoted it would seem that Kennan was rationalizing and softening the doctrine rather than fathering or inventing it. On the contrary, his initial reaction was that the proclamation of a head-on collision between two ways of life and two great powers was much too sweeping, and that it was dangerous. . . .

Did the Republicans Require Conversion? It has often been said that a planetary declaration of conflict with communism and the Soviet Union was necessary to pry from the famous 80th Congress Republican majorities the $400,000,000 desired as a first instalment for Greece and Turkey. This Congress, which had just taken its seat in January, was undoubtedly bent on reducing the budget and taxes. For two months they had been debating whether to cut the President's 37 billion budget by 6 billion or somewhat less. They would not like a big appropriation for foreign aid.

Nor was helping the corrupt Greek Government an easy thing to sell to Congress. On February 23 Stewart Alsop cabled from Athens that the main characteristic of this government seemed to be "its total impotence." Most of the Greek politicians had "no higher ambition than to taste the profitable delights of a free economy at American expense." Senator Vandenberg was reported to have told the President that if he expected to get the money he would have to "scare hell out of the country"—an apt description of the technique which was employed. This motive may also have determined in part Vandenberg's requirement that the President lay it all down in global terms in both a Congressional message and a radio address. . . .

The Truman Doctrine and Its Reception

The President read the message to a joint session of the two Houses of Congress on March 12, in an even monotone. He received light applause at three points. For the most part the Congress listened grimly and silently. On the same morning the *New York Times* had predicted that Truman would "ring down the curtain on one epoch in America's foreign policy." As he read, there could be no doubt that this was the case. . . .

We could not "realize our objectives," unless we were "willing to help free people to maintain their free institutions and their national integrity against aggressive movements that seek to impose upon them totalitarian regimes." This had happened, in spite of our frequent protests and in violation of the Yalta Agreement, in Poland, Bulgaria, Rumania and other countries. The time had come when "nearly every nation must choose between alternative ways of life," one distinguished by free institutions and the other by terror and oppression. He believed "that *it must be the policy of the United States to support free peoples who are resisting attempted subjugation by armed minorities or by outside pressure.*" [Italics added.]

"If Greece should fall under the control of an armed minority," confusion and disorder might spread east throughout the entire Middle East and west through the countries of Europe. He therefore asked for four hundred million dollars for Greece and Turkey and authority to detail civilian and military personnel to them.

All Revolution Forbidden. No pronouncement could have been more sweeping. Wherever a communist rebellion developed the United States would suppress it. Wherever the Soviet Union attempted to push outward, at any point around its vast circumference, the United States would resist. The United States would become the world's anti-communist, anti-Russian policeman.

This, too, was not the full extent of the Doctrine, for its all inclusive language also forbade every kind of revolution, democratic or otherwise. It would be difficult to find a revolution anywhere which had not been the work of an armed minority. The people might later come to the support of the fighting rebels, but revolutions were notoriously made by comparatively small groups of determined armed men. According to the new doctrine this could not happen, if for no other reason because some communists would almost inevitably be mixed up in the revolution, or an alarmed government would allege they were. The President went on to say that the status quo was not sacred, but he had made it so. So far as the United States was concerned the method by which this nation was born was outlawed. There would be no more revolutions thereafter, in spite of the fact that many hundreds of millions of people lived a miserable existence under the misrule of a few. Revolution was finished. All of these peoples would have to stay put. If their rulers should decide to alleviate their condition somewhat, well and good, but they could not be coerced or subjected to "such subterfuges as political infiltration." . . .

Encirclement of the Soviet Union Proclaimed. The wheel had come to full circle with a vengeance. The isolationist United States, desiring only to be let alone, had become the world's policeman. Wherever public order was disturbed, we would be there. Wherever the Soviet Government or communism attempted an advance the United States would combat it. The most gigantic land power on the face of the globe, living on the opposite side of the earth from the United States, was to be fenced in at all points. Thus far and no farther! In the two previous balance of power struggles Germany had complained constantly that she was being encircled, but not one of her opponents ever dreamed of admitting that she was. Now Mr. Truman had proclaimed from one of the world's greatest rostrums the most gigantic encirclement ever conceived in the mind of man. . . .

Europe Amazed and Alarmed. From Paris Harold Callender wrote that the ablest diplomatic officials in Europe, of French and other nationalities, regarded Truman's message as certain to compel a showdown between the Soviet Union and the Western world. They read it "with amazement, since they expected nothing so stern or forthright." It was "a revolution in United States foreign policy more notable even than American participation in the United Nations." To a "striking extent professional diplomatic quarters, and other non-Communist or anti-Communist quarters, echoed in only slightly attenuated form the Moscow charge of a new and expanding American imperialism." French journals commented uneasily on the pessimism of our attitude and on the sharpening of the issue.

In London "rumbles of protest and ironical cheers from Labor M.P.s punctuated each effort by speakers in the House of Commons to describe President Truman's program of American aid for Greece and Turkey as a step toward world freedom and democracy." The *Daily Herald,* official Labor party newspaper, said: "Our first reaction to President Truman's speech on Wednesday was one of uneasiness. Our second thoughts are no happier."

There was no spontaneous enthusiasm in Britain. Mr. Churchill spoke only for a minority. Most people were distinctly disturbed, especially because the United States was tending toward individual rather than collective action in international affairs. . . .

Censure in Britain. On April 7 the Cooperative Party of Great Britain, one of the major arms of the Labor Party, and representing about 7,500,-000 working people, "approved by a large majority" a resolution condemning Truman's program of aid to Greece and Turkey as "a menace to world peace and the negation of the democratic principles for the preservation of peace for which the grave sacrifices of the last war were made." The party executive opposed the resolution, but the delegates insisted on its passage. They felt that "this attempt to by-pass the United Nations Organization will seriously impair the authority of the organization and destroy the confidence and hopes of free peoples everywhere."

Simultaneously a poll of 83 diplomats, representing 38 countries, showed 82 per cent of them regretting as a matter of principle that the United States did not come before the UN with the Greek and Turkish problems. In France General Charles de Gaulle urged the unity of Western Europe, to provide a balance between the world's "two enormous masses, both expanding."

The Continent Shocked by the "Either-Or" Challenge. On March 30 Mallory Browne made a close survey of European opinion from London for the *New York Times.* In Britain he thought a vast majority welcomed the Truman Doctrine as evidence that the United States had come of age and would not withdraw into isolation again, but there was fear that Truman's "blunt challenge to Soviet Russia" might lead to a war in which Britain would be the first and worst victim. Many were afraid that another war would wipe out their island. In France and a number of other continental countries it appeared that "doubts prevailed over hopes." In Italy the enthusiasm of the favorable opinion was tempered by widespread fear that it meant war. The Czechs were equally fearful. In the Low Countries and Scandinavia, where some of the most politically mature peoples in the world live, most people appeared to have been "shocked by the strong language Truman used," and decidedly nervous over the consequences. Even the conservatives tended "to ask whether it was wise." From all the diversity of opinion one overwhelming impression emerged, that the United States had embarked on a course which would bring "either real peace or the annihilation of atomic war."

This contemporary judgment inescapably raises the question whether there was anything in the world situation in March 1947 which compelled the United States to stake the future of all humanity upon one world-shaking defiance of the Soviet Union. . . .

Was the Truman Doctrine a Declaration of War?

Formally and legally it was not. This could be asserted with a perfectly straight face, and with ample legal documentation. The Soviet Union was not mentioned, nor the Turkish Straits. We had a right to aid any friendly government that we wished to help. Turkey felt pressed and there was a crisis in Greece. We had as much right to proclaim an anti-communist crusade—or holding operation—as the Russian controlled press had to proclaim the inevitability of Western capitalism's collapse and the wickedness of Western "imperialism."

All this is incontrovertible and, given both our deep vexation over the communist organization of East Europe and the geopolitical argument, some action on our part in Greece was foreordained. Greece would not be allowed to fall into the Soviet orbit. Some anti-communist connotation was also advisable to secure quick congressional approval.

These considerations still leave the question whether it was wise and statesmanlike to issue a global declaration setting limits both to communist expansion and Soviet expansion. It can readily be argued that this was the straightforward thing to do, to draw a line around both. Yet strategically it was a rash and unenforceable commitment. The Soviet Union already occupied the Heartland of Eurasia to its full limits, and all of our sea and air power, plus the A-bomb could not indefinitely prevent her from pushing out if she chose. Worse still, an open direct proclamation of encirclement was one of the best means of causing her to choose to push out.

The global containment Doctrine committed the United States to standing guard, not only at the Straits but all around the vast perimeter of the Soviet Union and its satellites. It pledged the prestige and resources of the United States, and especially the prestige of Mr. Truman, at virtually all points on the earth which mattered, either militarily or politically, leaving the initiative to the Russians and to local communist movements. Wherever either chose to fight we would accept the battlefield, no matter how remote or unfavorable. This was clearly a self-defeating policy, one fitted to squander our resources on the way to an immeasurable, unmanageable war.

Turning Point. The defenders of the Truman Doctrine announced with satisfaction that it was the end of an era, the period of "appeasement," and the beginning of a new era of firm containment. However, a full appraisal indicated that a much more fateful turn had been made, the turn from a post-war period to a pre-war atmosphere. The Truman Doctrine and the X article both ignored the problem of settling the Second World War, giving the impression that no settlement could be reached, that it was to be hereafter a matter of pressure and counter pressure. Less than two years after the bombs stopped falling in Europe American diplomacy came close to abdicating. Its arguing powers were exhausted. Stronger measures would have to be taken.

In this sense the Truman Doctrine was an effective declaration of war, one which had formed in Mr. Truman's mind in the autumn of 1945, almost before the fumes of Hiroshima had drifted around the earth. It gave notice to both sides, and to innumerable millions of people all over the world who wanted no fresh conflict, that a new global struggle was joined. It started trains of fear and hatred and action in many millions of minds, centering around Washington and Moscow, which ran for many years. . . .

It is easy enough to declare cold war, draw lines and hurl thunderbolts. It requires statesmanship to make peace and draw the nations nearer together. . . .

There can be no real understanding of the Cold War unless chronology is kept in mind. What came first? What was action and what reaction? The later event could not be the cause of the earlier.

Especially is it necessary to consider what followed the Truman Doctrine. Not everything which came after it was an effect of the Doctrine, but its effects upon Soviet policy and action were bound to be profound.

There does not seem to be evidence of any sudden turn of Soviet policy to hostility toward the United States or toward the West after World War II. Frederick C. Barghoorn, a student of Soviet policy who works constantly with Russian language sources, speaks of "the gradual process by which the Politburo openly reverted to its pre-war line, and transferred the symbols of the 'reaction,' 'aggression,' and 'imperialism' from Germany and Japan to Britain and America." . . .

It was not until Andrei Zhdanov's speech of September 1947 that a postwar division of the world into two camps was proclaimed in Russia, "the anti-democratic and imperialist camp on the one side, and the anti-imperialist and democratic on the other." Attacking the Marshall Plan as a device for "the enslavement of Europe," Zhdanov accused the United States of seeking world domination. Because her "monopolists" feared the success of communism they had launched a world-wide crusade against communism, he charged.

This was undoubtedly political warfare, but it can hardly be considered remarkable after the enunciation of the Truman Doctrine, Kennan's elaboration of the American containment drive and the Marshall Plan—altogether the greatest peace time political-economic offensive on record. An offensive of this character was bound to bring replies, both ideological and actual.

Additional Reading

Norman A. Graebner, *Cold War Diplomacy, 1945–1960* (1962).
George F. Kennan, *American Diplomacy, 1900–1950* (1951).
Walter Lippmann, *The Cold War: A Study in U.S. Foreign Policy* (1947).
John Lukacs, *A History of the Cold War* (1961).
Joseph P. Morray, *From Yalta to Disarmament: Cold War Debate* (1961).
Harry B. Price, *The Marshall Plan and Its Meaning* (1955).
Hugh Seton-Watson, *Neither War nor Peace: The Struggle for Power in the Postwar World* (1960).
John L. Snell, *Wartime Origins of the East-West Dilemma over Germany* (1959).
———, "The Cold War: Four Contemporary Appraisals," *American Historical Review*, LXVIII (1962), 69–75.

20 THE KOREAN WAR AND AMERICAN FOREIGN POLICY: Asia First or Europe?

The years of the Truman administration were probably the most creative in the history of American foreign relations. In bold and imaginative response to the Communist challenge, new policies were designed and put into effect: Truman Doctrine, Marshall Plan, N.A.T.O., and Point Four technical assistance to "backward" nations. The American people in approving these measures revealed that they had at last matured and were prepared to assume the burdens and responsibilities as *the* great non-communist world power.

But it was a reluctant assumption of responsibility for many Americans. During World War II, it had been expected that after crushing the Axis powers and the institution of a new collective security organization, the United States could return to something close to prewar normality. Instead, the enormous costs and strains of the Cold War appeared destined to last into the indefinite future. Quite a few "conservatives" were also increasingly frustrated at the continued political predominancy of the Democratic party and certain social changes that were underway at home. A combination of unfortunate developments ignited this mixture of frustration and uneasiness into a fire-storm of public hysteria and hunts for scapegoats to blame for the national plight. Nationalist China fell by 1949 and was supplanted by a Communist regime allied to Moscow; Russia exploded its first atomic bomb in mid-1949, three to five years before expected by Western experts; the Korean War, begun in June, 1950, to halt the Red North Korean invasion, fluctuated dismayingly and without promise of speedy or complete victory; and at home, investigating committees unearthed evidence of considerable past Communist infiltration into government and of the loss of some military secrets.

The results were charges that America had been the victim of 20 years of Democratic blunder, plunder, and perhaps treason at home and abroad. Great public debates raged as to whether it was correct to continue to concentrate on the Communist menace primarily in Europe or to meet the challenges in the Far East by full involvement if necessary. The late Senator Joseph McCarthy, Republican from Wisconsin, used his subcommittee to launch a series of charges of treason and a "great conspiracy" to explain current ills. While he was by no means the only laborer in the vineyard of the domestic search for Communist infiltrators, McCarthy's name was attached as a label for the period 1950–1954. By the latter year, the hysteria was subsiding and American foreign policy remained essentially as before. Yet a considerable, if inestimable, damage had probably been wrought to the morale of the foreign service and in an increasing inflexibility of policy in the Far East.

The readings focus on the Korean War and General Douglas MacArthur's strategy differences with the Truman administration. The great public debate ignited by MacArthur's dismissal by Truman essentially involved whether

611

basic American strategy in the Cold War should concentrate on the Soviet menace in Europe or should emphasize the Far East as the immediate area of concern. Many critics of administration commitments in Europe were apparently the "new isolationists of the 1950's," as Norman A. Graebner describes them, for at the same time they advocated vigorous military measures in Asia which probably would have led to a major war with Red China.

DOCUMENTS

A Limited War in Korea

In the following two documents, President Truman explained to the American people why he acted on his executive authority in June, 1950, to defend invaded South Korea; and why, in April, 1951, he declined to enlarge the Korean War and decided to recall General Douglas MacArthur from command of the American forces there. The primacy of the Soviet threat in Europe and the dangers of a major diversionary war in Asia required efforts to limit the war in Korea.

Initial Measures Taken by the United States in the Korean Crisis: Statement by the President, June 27, 1950

In Korea, the Government forces, which were armed to prevent border raids and to preserve internal security, were attacked by invading forces from North Korea. The Security Council of the United Nations called upon the invading troops to cease hostilities and to withdraw to the 38th Parallel. This they have not done but, on the contrary, have pressed the attack. The Security Council called upon all members of the United Nations to render every assistance to the United Nations in the execution of this resolution. In these circumstances, I have ordered United States air and sea [and subsequently land] forces to give the Korean Government troops cover and support.

The attack upon Korea makes it plain beyond all doubt that communism has passed beyond the use of subversion to conquer independent nations and will now use armed invasion and war. It has defied the orders of the Security Council of the United Nations issued to preserve international peace and security. In these circumstances, the occupation of Formosa by Communist forces would be a direct threat to the security of the Pacific area and to United States forces performing their lawful and necessary functions in that area.

Accordingly, I have ordered the Seventh Fleet to prevent any attack on Formosa. As a corollary of this action, I am calling upon the Chinese Government on Formosa to cease all air and sea operations against the Mainland. The Seventh Fleet will see that this is done. The determination of the future status of Formosa must await the restoration of security in the Pacific, a peace settlement with Japan, or consideration by the United Nations.

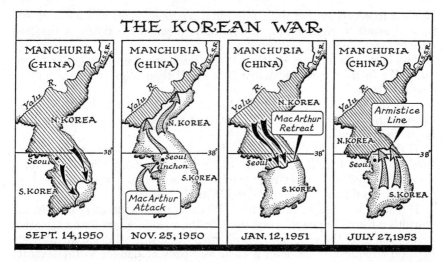

THE KOREAN WAR

MANCHURIA (CHINA)	MANCHURIA (CHINA)	MANCHURIA (CHINA)	MANCHURIA (CHINA)
SEPT. 14,1950	NOV. 25,1950	JAN. 12,1951	JULY 27,1953

I have also directed that United States forces in the Philippines be strengthened and that military assistance to the Philippine Government be accelerated. . . .

I know that all members of the United Nations will consider carefully the consequences of this latest aggression in Korea in defiance of the Charter of the United Nations. A return to the rule of force in international affairs would have far-reaching effects. The United States will continue to uphold the rule of law.

I have instructed Ambassador Austin, as the representative of the United States to the Security Council, to report these steps to the Council.

United States Policy in the Korean Conflict
Address by the President, April 11, 1951

I want to talk plainly to you tonight about what we are doing in Korea and about our policy in the Far East.

In the simplest terms, what we are doing in Korea is this: We are trying to prevent a third world war.

I think most people in this country recognized that fact last June. And they warmly supported the decision of the Government to help the Republic of Korea against the Communist aggressors. Now, many persons, even some who applauded our decision to defend Korea, have forgotten the basic reason for our action.

It is right for us to be in Korea. It was right last June. It is right today.

I want to remind you why this is true.

The Communist Threat to Freedom

The Communists in the Kremlin are engaged in a monstrous conspiracy to stamp out freedom all over the world. If they were to succeed, the United States would be numbered among their principal victims. It must be clear to everyone that the United States cannot—and will not—sit idly by and await foreign conquest. The only question is: When is the best time to meet the threat and how?

The best time to meet the threat is in the beginning. It is easier to put out a fire in the beginning when it is small than after it has become a roaring blaze.

And the best way to meet the threat of aggression is for the peace-loving nations to act together. If they don't act together, they are likely to be picked off, one by one.

If they had followed the right policies in the 1930's—if the free countries had acted together, to crush the aggression of the dictators, and if they had acted in the beginning, when the aggression was small—there probably would have been no World War II.

If history has taught us anything, it is that aggression anywhere in the world is a threat to peace everywhere in the world. When that aggression is supported by the cruel and selfish rulers of a powerful nation who are bent on conquest, it becomes a clear and present danger to the security and independence of every free nation.

This is a lesson that most people in this country have learned thoroughly. This is the basic reason why we joined in creating the United Nations. And since the end of World War II we have been putting that lesson into practice—we have been working with other free nations to check the aggressive designs of the Soviet Union before they can result in a third world war.

That is what we did in Greece, when that nation was threatened by the aggression of international communism.

The attack against Greece could have led to general war. But this country came to the aid of Greece. The United Nations supported Greek resistance. With our help, the determination and efforts of the Greek people defeated the attack on the spot.

Another big Communist threat to peace was the Berlin blockade. That too could have led to war. But again it was settled because free men would not back down in an emergency.

The Communist Plan for Conquest

The aggression against Korea is the boldest and most dangerous move the Communists have yet made.

The attack on Korea was part of a greater plan for conquering all of Asia. . . .

They want to control all Asia from the Kremlin.

This plan of conquest is in flat contradiction to what we believe. We believe that Korea belongs to the Koreans, that India belongs to the Indians—that all the nations of Asia should be free to work out their affairs in their own way. This is the basis of peace in the Far East and everywhere else.

The whole Communist imperialism is back of the attack on peace in the Far East. It was the Soviet Union that trained and equipped the

North Koreans for aggression. The Chinese Communists massed 44 well-trained and well-equipped divisions on the Korean frontier. These were the troops they threw into battle when the North Korean Communists were beaten.

Stopping Short of General War

The question we have had to face is whether the Communist plan of conquest can be stopped without general war. Our Government and other countries associated with us in the United Nations believe that the best chance of stopping it without general war is to meet the attack in Korea and defeat it there.

That is what we have been doing. It is a difficult and bitter task.

But so far it has been successful.

So far, we have prevented World War III.

So far, by fighting a limited war in Korea, we have prevented aggression from succeeding and bringing on a general war. And the ability of the whole free world to resist Communist aggression has been greatly improved.

We have taught the enemy a lesson. He has found out that aggression is not cheap or easy. Moreover, men all over the world who want to remain free have been given new courage and new hope. They know now that the champions of freedom can stand up and fight and that they will stand up and fight.

Our resolute stand in Korea is helping the forces of freedom now fighting in Indochina and other countries in that part of the world. It has already slowed down the timetable of conquest.

In Korea itself, there are signs that the enemy is building up his ground forces for a new mass offensive. We also know that there have been large increases in the enemy's available air forces.

If a new attack comes, I feel confident it will be turned back. The United Nations fighting forces are tough and able and well equipped. They are fighting for a just cause. They are proving to all the world that the principle of collective security will work. We are proud of all these forces for the magnificent job they have done against heavy odds. We pray that their efforts may succeed, for upon their success may hinge the peace of the world.

The Communist side must now choose its course of action. The Communist rulers may press the attack against us. They may take further action which will spread the conflict. They have that choice, and with it the awful responsibility for what may follow. The Communists also have the choice of a peaceful settlement which could lead to a general relaxation of tensions in the Far East. The decision is theirs, because the forces of the United Nations will strive to limit the conflict if possible.

We do not want to see the conflict in Korea extended. We are trying to prevent a world war—not to start one. The best way to do that is to make it plain that we and the other free countries will continue to resist the attack.

The Best Course to Follow

But you may ask: Why can't we take other steps to punish the aggressor? Why don't we bomb Manchuria and China itself? Why don't we assist Chinese Nationalist troops to land on the mainland of China?

If we were to do these things we would be running a very grave risk of starting a general war. If that were to happen, we would have brought about the exact situation we are trying to prevent.

If we were to do these things, we would become entangled in a vast conflict on the continent of Asia and our task would become immeasurably more difficult all over the world.

What would suit the ambitions of the Kremlin better than for our military forces to be committed to a full-scale war with Red China?

It may well be that, in spite of our best efforts, the Communists may spread the war. But it would be wrong—tragically wrong—for us to take the initiative in extending the war.

The dangers are great. Make no mistake about it. Behind the North Koreans and Chinese Communists in the front lines stand additional millions of Chinese soldiers. And behind the Chinese stand the tanks, the planes, the submarines, the soldiers, and the scheming rulers of the Soviet Union.

Our aim is to avoid the spread of the conflict.

The course we have been following is the one best calculated to avoid an all-out war. It is the course consistent with our obligation to do all we can to maintain international peace and security. Our experience in Greece and Berlin shows that it is the most effective course of action we can follow.

First of all, it is clear that our efforts in Korea can blunt the will of the Chinese Communists to continue the struggle. The United Nations forces have put up a tremendous fight in Korea and have inflicted very heavy casualties on the enemy. Our forces are stronger now than they have been before. These are plain facts which may discourage the Chinese Communists from continuing their attack.

Second, the free world as a whole is growing in military strength every day. In the United States, in Western Europe, and throughout the world, free men are alert to the Soviet threat and are building their defenses. This may discourage the Communist rulers from continuing the war in Korea—and from undertaking new acts of aggression elsewhere.

If the Communist authorities realize that they cannot defeat us in Korea, if they realize it would be foolhardy to widen the hostilities beyond Korea, then they may recognize the folly of continuing their aggression. A peaceful settlement may then be possible. The door is always open.

Then we may achieve a settlement in Korea which will not compromise the principles and purposes of the United Nations.

I have thought long and hard about this question of extending the war in Asia. I have discussed it many times with the ablest military advisers in the country. I believe with all my heart that the course we are following is the best course.

I believe that we must try to limit the war to Korea for these vital reasons: to make sure that the precious lives of our fighting men are not wasted; to see that the security of our country and the free world is not needlessly jeopardized; and to prevent a third world war.

Avoiding Confusion over U.S. Policy

A number of events have made it evident that General MacArthur did not agree with that policy. I have therefore considered it essential to relieve General MacArthur so that there would be no doubt or confusion as to the real purpose and aim of our policy.

It was with the deepest personal regret that I found myself compelled to take this action. General MacArthur is one of our greatest military commanders. But the cause of world peace is more important than any individual.

The change in commands in the Far East means no change whatever in the policy of the United States. We will carry on the fight in Korea with vigor and determination in an effort to bring the war to a speedy and successful conclusion. . . .

We are ready, at any time, to negotiate for a restoration of peace in the area. But we will not engage in appeasement. We are only interested in real peace.

Real peace can be achieved through a settlement based on the following factors:

One: the fighting must stop.

Two: concrete steps must be taken to insure that the fighting will not break out again.

Three: there must be an end to the aggression.

A settlement founded upon these elements would open the way for the unification of Korea and the withdrawal of all foreign forces.

In the meantime, I want to be clear about our military objective. We are fighting to resist an outrageous aggression in Korea. We are trying to keep the Korean conflict from spreading to other areas. But at the same time we must conduct our military activities so as to insure the security of our forces. This is essential if they are to continue the fight until the enemy abandons its ruthless attempt to destroy the Republic of Korea.

That is our military objective—to repel attack and to restore peace.

In the hard fighting in Korea, we are proving that collective action among nations is not only a high principle but a workable means of resisting aggression. Defeat of aggression in Korea may be the turning point in the world's search for a practical way of achieving peace and security.

The struggle of the United Nations in Korea is a struggle for peace.

The free nations have united their strength in an effort to prevent a third world war.

That war can come if the Communist rulers want it to come. But this Nation and its allies will not be responsible for its coming.

We do not want to widen the conflict. We will use every effort to pre-vent that disaster. And in so doing we know that we are following the great principles of peace, freedom, and justice.

READINGS

1. "Asia First" Strategy

When South Korea was invaded on June 25, 1950, President Truman acted solely on his executive authority and ordered American forces to join in the defense. Subsequently, the Security Council of the United Nations called for collective resistance to the North Korean invasion, but the bulk of non-Korean troops committed were to come from the United States. Under General MacArthur's command the U.N. forces in Korea rallied and by October entered Communist North Korea in order to unify the entire peninsula. As troops neared the Yalu River and the Manchurian frontier, Red Chinese "volunteers" suddenly entered the fray in late November, 1950, and drove MacArthur's forces below the 38th parallel before they rallied and returned approximately to that line. General MacArthur understandably was frustrated by the administration's refusal to allow him to expand the scope of the war by bombing Chinese bases and supply routes to North Korea. Put simply, he advocated an "Asia First" strategy to do whatever was necessary to win full victory in Korea, while the Truman administration insisted that the main Soviet threat was in Europe and refused to risk involvement in a mainland full-fledged war with Red China. MacArthur's attempts to appeal his case to the American people caused his recall from command on April 11, 1951. The following selection in defense of MacArthur is by Major General (Ret.) Charles Willoughby, formerly an intelligence officer on MacArthur's Staff.

The Chinese Communist War

C. A. WILLOUGHBY & J. CHAMBERLAIN

. . . When General MacArthur succeeded in the spectacular landing at Inchon, in September 1950, the fate of the North Koreans was sealed—but the Chinese Reds chose to wait until the end of October, *i.e.*, at least six weeks, before they started crossing the Yalu. Why did they fail to come to the assistance of the North Koreans immediately? For the simple reason that after Inchon, they had to face the probability that the Yalu bridges and their adjacent bases would be bombed, which would have jeopardized successful intervention.

So for six weeks all they did was to hint that if UN troops crossed the 38th Parallel, they might enter the war. Communist supporters and dupes promptly yielded to this blackmail. The Korean War would have termi-nated if the U.S. had issued a warning to the effect that any entry of the Chinese Communists into Korea would be considered an act of hostility.

They would have stayed on the other side of the Yalu. Instead—through a weak policy and for fear of Russian intervention—information must have been relayed to the other side, guaranteeing that those bridges would enjoy sanctuary and their bases left intact. And so, Ho Shai-Lai concluded, the Communists were not only assured that there was no real intention to win—but they were also guaranteed against the risk of losing. No better assurance could have been furnished. They marched on that assurance. . . .

General MacArthur reiterated that he "planned the air-interdiction of the Yalu bridges and expected to slow down the Reds through this measure." As it turned out, the General was expressly forbidden all-out air bombardment, on Washington orders, and half a dozen American divisions were consequently exposed to the full onslaught of overwhelming numbers. Was this a calculated sacrifice to some obscure diplomatic motivation?

The withdrawals of the Eighth Army were made with consummate skill. MacArthur himself regarded the whole operation as one of his best . . . if not the best! He felt that the hard decisions he had made and the skill displayed by his field commanders in their implementation had saved not only the Eighth Army but Korea itself and, with it, our future hopes for the Far East. MacArthur was well aware that the entire situation would be misunderstood and misrepresented but merely said dryly: "I've always been able to take care of the enemy in my front—but have never been able to protect myself from shafts from the rear."

After the entry of China into the war, the American Army was compelled to take odds never before encountered in the entire military history of the nation. There is nothing even remotely comparable in recent wars. However, the impact of the disaster school of war reporting on public opinion in the fall of 1950 was such that it must now be driven home forcefully that the frightening stories of the time represent a distortion of history. We fought harder in Korea than in Europe, and, given the circumstances, just as successfully. A brief parallel shows this vividly, for the Allied campaign in Italy had some similarities to that in Korea. Topography and road net were similar. The Italian front was approximately 100 miles as compared with 140 miles in Korea. In Italy, however, the Allies employed two armies, the American Fifth and the British Eighth with thirty-one first-class divisions to fight against a variable twenty to twenty-seven Italo-German divisions somewhat battered and usually half the Allied troop strength. Italy was a strategic sideshow. Nothing vital was at stake. The war could not conceivably be won there. One need not strain one's imagination to guess what thirty-one Anglo-American divisions, instead of only nine, would have done to the Chinese in Korea, at any stage of the war.

Nevertheless the Allied high command, the Joint Chiefs of Staff, the American and British "brass" in Italy threw in a great superiority of means. It is a point of historical importance that the same "brass," still powerful in Washington during 1950 and 1951, apparently changed the basis of their military calculations between the Anzio and the Yalu. It is impossible to understand on a professional basis how the General Staff in Washington could placidly accept the staggering odds piled on the Eighth Army in Korea. Instead of a pat on the back for our teen-age draftees of a few months' training who were fighting rather forlornly in an alien land, an inexplicable wave of defeatist reports engulfed the Eighth Army with wide repercussions at home and abroad. Here is a cross section of some characteristic comments of the period:

> The flight of our troops before Chinese peasant soldiers was the most shameful disgrace suffered by American arms since the first Battle of Bull Run in 1861. . . .
>
> It was America's worst licking since the battle of the Bulge and maybe even Pearl Harbor. Barring a military miracle, the Army might have to be evacuated in a new Dunkerque, from being lost in a new Bataan. . . .

An explosion of white-hot wrath was spontaneous throughout the rank and file of the Eighth Army. Petitions were circulated by enlisted men of the 2d Division, demanding a retraction and denouncing these reports as "vicious lies and slander upon thousands of American war dead."

A cold statistical comparison of dead, wounded, and missing with battle-action losses of World War II is a complete refutation of the deadly nonsense which was fed to an anxious and bewildered public. A reference to the Tenth Army in the Ryukus during World War II is enlightening, since some of the divisions involved in the three months' fight for Okinawa also appeared in the Yalu operations, viz., the 1st Marine and the 7th Infantry Division.

COMPARISON OF LOSSES

TENTH ARMY (RYUKUS) AND EIGHTH ARMY (YALU)

Ryukus Operations	*1945*	*Yalu Operations*	*1950*
XXIVth Corps	34,736	Eighth Army	7,337
7th Division	10,893	2d Division	4,131
27th Division	5,224	1st Cav. Div.	443
77th Division	7,126	24th Division	146
96th Division	10,247	25th Division	1,606
Corps Troops	1,246	Other U.N.	1,011
III Amph. Corps.	26,724	Xth Corps	5,638
1st Mar. Div.	13,002	1st Mar. Div.	2,891
2d Mar. Div.	95	3d Division	650
6th Mar. Div.	12,815	7th Division	2,097
Corps Troops	812		
Tact. Air Force	520		
Tenth Army Troops	1,015		
Army Garrisons	2,636		
Total	65,631		12,975

On the average, individual divisions on Okinawa sustained from *two to five times the losses incurred in the withdrawal from the Yalu* five years later. The Eighth Army in 1950 took on extraordinary numerical odds, facing from twenty-four to thirty-nine Chinese divisions; the Tenth Army in the Ryukus was involved with only one Japanese corps of three divisions. Bastogne in Belgium was not unlike Anju in Korea, and Anzio in Italy was not unlike Inchon.

In the Bulge operations in 1944, the 108th Division, directly in the line of advance of the German penetration, lost 8,490 men of its total strength of 14,032 in a period of fourteen days.

In the Anzio campaign in the spring of 1943, American losses for the four-month period amounted to an aggregate of 43,000. Casualties of the 3d Division alone were 3,131 during an eight-day period. That same division was in the Hamhung-Wonson withdrawal in Korea eight years later: it lost 650 men.

The evacuation of the X Corps from the port of Hungnam, with the 1st Marine, 3d and 7th Divisions fighting heroic rear-guard actions that stopped three Chinese corps in their tracks, was exposed to unwarranted comments. This remarkably smooth and efficient amphibious operation was loudly proclaimed "a second Dunkerque." The absurdity of this classification is self-evident:

	Ships Total	Ships Sunk	Personnel Evacuated	Equipment Salvaged
Dunkerque	841	163	338,000	—
Hungnam	163	—	205,000	350,000 tons 17,500 vehicles

About Dunkerque, Churchill said:

> More than 300,000 British and French troops scrambled for boats and ships of the rescue fleet. An estimated 2,000 men were lost at sea, as well as over 200 ships and most of the Army equipment, including 120,-000 vehicles, 2,700 artillery pieces and 90,000 rifles. Our armies at home were almost unarmed except for rifles. There were hardly five hundred field guns of any sort and hardly 200 tanks in the whole country. Months must pass before our factories could make good even the munitions lost in Dunkerque. . . .

Compare this tragic description of real disaster with the terse radio from General Almond, commander of the American X Corps, on December 24:

> The Xth Corps, reinforced, has completed evacuation by air and sea from Hungnam at 14:36 Hrs. 350,000 tons of supplies and equipment have been withdrawn. Nothing has been left to the enemy. 105,000 troops, including S. Korean units and approximately 100,000 refugees, have been evacuated to safety in South Korea. Structures of possible military value to the enemy have been destroyed. The enemy paid heavily for his attempt to interfere with our operations. The losses of our forces were comparatively light.

When General MacArthur, during his visit with General Almond at Yonpo Airport (near Hamhung) on December 8, asked, "How long can the X Corps maintain its position in this area with Hungnam Port as the base of supply?" General Almond replied:

For as long as you desire; the X Corps is now established in a tactically strong position with a secure base and line of supply by sea; we can stay here as a threat to the enemy's flank and should do so, unless there are no other troops available to support the Eighth Army from the U.S.

But higher authority had decreed that sufficient forces should not be sent from the United States and General MacArthur had to bow to the inevitable. He was forced to use the X Corps to strengthen the badly used Eighth Army in the south instead of maintaining it as a dagger in the enemy's flank at Hungnam and Hamhung.

MacArthur stabilized his lines early in January at a position midway in South Korea. General Walker had been killed in an accident and the Eighth Army was now under command of Gen. Matthew B. Ridgway. MacArthur flew to Korea on January 20, nullified any suggestion that the enemy might drive our forces into the sea, and issued orders for the counteroffensive.

His field strategy had involved breaking contact with the enemy and a rapid withdrawal to lengthen and expose the latter's supply lines. What resulted was a pyramiding of logistic difficulties for the Reds and an almost astronomical increase in the destructiveness of our air power. Soon the balance was restored between the opposing forces. MacArthur's objective was again to be the enemy's supply lines.

For psychological as well as other reasons MacArthur proposed by constant thrusts to regain the Seoul line for a base of operation from which to clear North Korea of enemy forces. This could be accomplished through the air destruction of enemy concentration and installations, the closing of major lines of enemy supply and communication through the sowing of defensive fields of suitable radioactive materials available as by-products of atomic manufacture, and simultaneous amphibious landings at the upper ends of both coasts of North Korea. For these amphibious landings, he would employ the new divisions just ordered to the Far East and picked veteran troops from Formosa which had been offered. It was to be Inchon again—only on a larger scale!

In frequent visits to the front, General MacArthur made his own lucid appraisal of the chronology of the fighting and accurately forecast the slow deterioration and eventual defeat of the Chinese hordes:

February 13: I am entirely satisfied with the situation at the front. The enemy has suffered a tactical reverse. His losses are amongst the bloodiest in modern times.

February 20: The enemy is finding it an entirely different problem fighting 350 miles from his base than when he had sanctuary in his immediate rear. He is paying now for the illusion so falsely but effectively propagandized that he had defeated our Eighth Army decisively. I note that Marshal Stalin has just predicted the annihilation of our forces in Korea—but his Comrades will have to do lots better than they have yet done, to prove him a prophet.

March 24: It is increasingly evident that the heavy destruction of the enemy's lines of supply, caused by our round-the-clock air and naval bombardment, left his troops in forward areas deficient in requirements.

The enemy's human-wave tactics have failed. He is showing less stamina than our own troops under the rigours of climate, terrain and battle. Of even greater significance has been the revelation that this new enemy, Red China, of such exaggerated and vaunted military power, lacks the industrial capacity essential to modern war.

Expansion of our operations to the enemy coastal areas and interior bases would doom Red China to imminent military collapse. These basic facts established, there should be no insuperable difficulty in arriving at decisions on the Korean problem if the issues are resolved on their own merits. . . .

To the very moment of General MacArthur's dismissal, Washington was informed of the fluctuating situation in Korea and the enormous potential of victory inherent in the last two months. As early as March, a blueprint was drawn: expansion of our operations to the enemy coastal and interior bases; the threat of aerial reprisal—a concept which was new to Truman but has since become a commonplace item, under Eisenhower, as a deterrent for war. MacArthur personified this threat. Somehow MacArthur had to be eliminated. The enemy made one last convulsive, bloody effort to discredit him in the field and so to convince the Western world that the fiction of military power that they and their stooges had established was real.

The enemy staged an abortive offensive in April. The Eighth Army anticipated it by fifteen days and was ready; our troops "rolled with the punch" and then counterattacked with brilliant success. The Reds tried again in May—and for the last time. They suffered crippling losses. Of twenty-one Chinese divisions which started the attack, sixteen lost half or more of their effectives and were *hors de combat;* the XII, XV, XXVII, and LX Corps had disappeared; only one corps, the XX was able to continue in action. It must be realized that the Chinese Third and Fourth Armies were the best they had; the seventy to eighty divisions, stuck in Korea and literally consumed in this holocaust, were the best divisions they had; in all of China, from Tibet to Siberia, there remained about 120 second-rate divisions of variable quality, from fair to poor—and the Korean drain was endless, relentless, and killing.

The Chinese recognized the implications: just short of collapse, they called for a truce for the sole purpose of physical recovery, and they obtained it through the crafty, superbly timed intervention of the Soviets in the gullible and lukewarm United Nations. President Truman added the final touch by relieving his ablest field commander on the eve of another victory. The effect of these incongruous measures coalesced to eliminate the one man in the Far East whom communism had reason to fear. Truman had played right into the Communists' evil hands. . . .

MacArthur recognized the symptoms of weakness of the Reds, drew common-sense conclusions, and pressed for a military decision through attack on the Chinese sanctuary. He recommended to Washington that he be permitted air-bombardment in due course of military installations north of the Yalu then actively employed against us, naval blockade of the coast of China to cut off enemy supplies, and renewed his request for the utilization of Nationalist Chinese troops available on Formosa. These recommendations were actually approved by the Joint Chiefs of Staff, but somewhere between the offices of the Secretary of Defense, Gen. George C. Marshall, the Secretary of State Dean G. Acheson, and President Truman, they were pigeonholed; and we took the course leading to the stalemate of positional warfare, by all odds the most costly and least productive method of waging war.

To his staff, General MacArthur said:

> The overriding deficiency incident to the conduct of the war in Korea by the United Nations lies in its lack of will for victory. Underlying the whole problem has always been the indeterminate question as to whether or not the Soviet contemplates the conquest of the world by military means rather than by those of more peaceful persuasion.
>
> If it intends to use force, the time and place will be at its own initiative and could not fail to be influenced by the fact that in the atomic area, the lead of the United States is being steadily diminished with the passage of time. So likewise is the great industrial potential of the United States as compared with the Communist world.
>
> In short, it has always been my own belief that any action we might take to resolve the Korean problem could not in itself be a controlling factor in the precipitation of a world conflict. It is quite probable that the Soviet masses are just as eager for peace as are our own people. They probably suffer the delusion that there are aggressive intentions against them on the part of the capitalist world and that they would welcome an imaginative approach which would allay this false impression. . . .

On January 14, 1951, President Truman sent a personal message to General MacArthur finishing with these words: "The entire nation is grateful for your splendid leadership in the difficult struggle in Korea and for the superb performance of your forces under most difficult circumstances." Less than three months later, on the eve of another victory, he suddenly, without warning, relieved MacArthur of his command in a most savage and brutal way. The peremptory order did not permit him even to bid good-by to his troops. Superbly trained, they carried on under other generals, one of whom, James A. Van Fleet, was fully as certain as MacArthur himself that victory over the Chinese Communists could have been had if the politicians had simply given the soldiers the word.

The Dismissal

As far as MacArthur's own knowledge of its circumstances is concerned, his dismissal is still shrouded in considerable mystery. His first information of it came over the public radio. But in summarizing, ex post facto, the possible reasons for it, MacArthur has listed three things which members of the Truman Administration seized upon to prepare a case for ridding themselves of their foremost general.

> The decision [said MacArthur] was arbitrary. I warned of the dangers of Formosa falling under Communist control. This was said to be contrary to existing policy. The Secretary of State has since declared that it was long-standing policy of the United States.

The second reason given was my readiness to meet the enemy commander to discuss terms. This identical proposal was received enthusiastically when made by the Soviets.

The third reason was my reply to a Congressman. There is a law that no member of the Armed Forces shall be restricted from communicating with members of Congress.

In retrospect, it must seem that all of the Administration's "reasons" masked something deeper. General Bradley, presumably speaking for the Joint Chiefs of Staff, said on one occasion that MacArthur "was not in sympathy with the decision to try to limit the conflict in Korea. The J.C.S. had decided to try to avoid a third war." Yet MacArthur desired only to destroy the enemy where he had chosen to attack, in Korea. His proposals to bomb the Yalu bridges, to avail himself of the right of "hot pursuit" of enemy aircraft, and to utilize his own air and naval forces to carry the war to the enemy's supply and communications, were hardly a prescription for a third *world* war. They were merely the prescription for ending the war he had been ordered to fight. In no case was he in favor of sending American troops to fight on Chinese soil. "Anybody who advocates that," so MacArthur said, "should have his head examined."

The first inkling of trouble with the Administration came when MacArthur made a reply to an inquiry by the Veterans of Foreign Wars about the strategic value of Formosa. The letter, written on August 27, 1950, is hardly startling, for its contents are today an accepted part of our Far Eastern strategy. But it constitutes an interesting footnote to history, by a military commander of the first rank who has spent many years in the Far East:

Any appraisal of Formosa's strategic potential, requires an appreciation of the changes wrought in the course of the past war. Prior thereto the Western strategic position of the United States lay on the littoral line of the Americas with an exposed island salient extending out through Hawaii, Midway, and Guam to the Philippines. That salient was not an outpost of strength but an avenue of weakness along which the enemy could and did attack us. The Pacific was a potential area of advance for any predatory force intent upon striking at the bordering land areas.

All of this was changed by our Pacific victory. Our strategic frontier then shifted to embrace the entire Pacific Ocean, which has become a vast moat to protect us as long as we hold it. Indeed it acts as a protective shield for all of the Americas and for all lands of the Pacific Ocean area. We control it to the shores of Asia by a chain of islands extending in an arc from the Aleutians to the Marianas held by us and our former allies. *From this island chain we can prevent any hostile movement into the Pacific.* Our line of defense is a natural one and can be maintained with a minimum of military effort and expense. It envisions no attack against anyone, nor does it provide the bastions essential for offensive operations, but properly maintained would be an invincible defense against aggression. If we hold this line we may have peace. If we lose it, war is inevitable.

The geographic location of Formosa is such that in the hands of a power unfriendly to the United States, it constitutes an enemy salient in the very center of this defense perimeter. There is on Formosa a concentration of operational air and naval bases which is potentially greater than any similar concentration on the Asiatic mainland. Our air supremacy at once would become doubtful. Formosa in the hands of a hostile power could be compared to an unsinkable aircraft carrier and submarine tender. Submarine blockade by the enemy would become a virtual certainty.

As a routine courtesy to journalists, copies of this letter were sent to the press some days before it was scheduled to be read at the Veterans of Foreign Wars annual convention in Chicago. To MacArthur, the letter seemed sheerest common sense about geographical factors as they relate to strategy. But the President, for reasons that are still inexplicable, took violent exception to the letter and ordered it withdrawn. MacArthur complied with the order. It was too late, however, to keep its contents from reaching the public; *Life* magazine and David Lawrence's *U.S. News and World Report,* for example, had already printed it and committed it to the mails. *Life,* in fact, had made it its editorial for the week.

Within twenty-four hours of the "withdrawal" that failed to withdraw the letter's contents, Truman summoned Louis Johnson, his Secretary of War, to discuss ways and means for the relief of MacArthur "as Korean commander." Johnson revealed this in testimony before the Joint Senate Investigating Committee on June 14, 1951. After discussion, however, the conclusion was reached not to do anything "at that time." MacArthur did not have the slightest suspicion of what was going on.

Considering that Formosa was a touchy subject with both State Department and White House, MacArthur's previous staff visit to Formosa and brief consultation with Chiang Kai-shek in 1950 must be considered a contributory cause to the smoldering hostility in Washington.

There was no real cause for resentment, however. MacArthur had no plenary power to arrive at political understandings. He was not an ambassador charged with negotiating for the State Department. On the other hand, it was well within his prerogatives as a regional commander in the Far East to visit adjacent strategic areas for purposes of obtaining firsthand impressions of their military and geographic potentials. When he could not go himself, he habitually sent senior staff officers or commanders. General Stratemeyer of the Air Force, accompanied by General Willoughby, made just such an exploratory staff journey to Hong Kong, Hai-phong, Bangkok, and Singapore.

MacArthur thus flew to Formosa. Washington was advised and made no objections. The General met Chiang and his principal civil and military staff. He attended a briefing of the map-room variety which outlined the Nationalist Chinese concept of the situation. He attended a ceremonial dinner—and then returned to Tokyo: *Tant de fruit pour une omelette?*

The Inchon victory followed MacArthur's temporary "reprieve" by Truman and Louis Johnson—and naturally nothing much could be done to push immediately for the removal of a commander who had just won a decisive battle. But on March 20 of the following year, when the fighting in Korea had reached the "accordion" stage, Washington plucked up its nerve. The occasion for moving decisively against MacArthur presented itself on the 20th when MacArthur wrote a mild enough answer to a letter from Joe Martin, leader of the House Republicans. It read:

> Dear Congressman Martin:
>
> I am most grateful for your note of the 8th forwarding me a copy of your address of February 12th. The letter I have read with much interest, and find that with the passage of years you have certainly lost none of your old-time punch.
>
> My views and recommendations with respect to the situation created by Red China's entry into war against us in Korea have been submitted to Washington in most complete detail. Generally these views are well known and clearly understood, as they follow the conventional pattern of meeting force with maximum counter-force as we have never failed to do in the past. Your view with respect to the utilization of the Chinese forces on Formosa is in conflict with neither logic nor this tradition.
>
> It seems strangely difficult for some to realize that here in Asia is where Communist conspirators have elected to make their play for global conquest, and that we have joined the issue thus raised on the battlefield; that here we fight Europe's war with arms while the diplomats there still fight it with words; that if we lose the war to Communism in Asia the fall of Europe is inevitable, win it and Europe most probably would avoid war and yet preserve freedom. As you point out, we must win. There is no substitute for victory.
>
> With renewed thanks and expressions of most cordial regard, I am
>
> Faithfully yours,
> Douglas MacArthur

MacArthur had been saying the same sort of thing for months, in both letters and statements. But this time it was "different" for one simple reason: Truman had decided to act. The Administration was making ready for its great "peace" play; Acheson was even then busy circulating peace proposals to the UN nations which had troops in Korea. It was at this point that MacArthur called upon the Chinese Communist commander in Korea to surrender—"or else." MacArthur offered the Chinese commander an opportunity to meet with him for a discussion in the field. He stressed the reserve strength which the United Nations could bring to bear upon the enemy if he insisted upon continuing the war.

MacArthur construed his own "peace" offer as (*a*) a smart stroke of psychological warfare and (*b*) an effort to back up the peace campaign that was being waged in the United Nations. To Truman, however, it was an impertinence. Two days after the Martin letter had been published, Truman conferred with Acheson, Bradley, Marshall, and Averell Harriman. The generals were uneasy at first about touching a soldier who was a popular idol, but Acheson and Truman carried the day. After sounding out the Joint Chiefs of Staff, who formulated some "military considerations" which made the firing of MacArthur desirable, Bradley was in a position to tell Truman that the high brass "concurred" with his decision to relieve MacArthur. Truman's own reasons for taking the step were subsequently summed up as (*a*) the letter about Formosa, (*b*) the Martin letter and (*c*) the offer to deal with the Chinese in the field.

As a fitting irony, Truman then turned over to the "European-minded" Marshall the job of drafting a dismissal message for the Presidential signature.

> I deeply regret [the message said] that it becomes my duty as President . . . to replace you as Supreme Commander. . . . You will turn over your commands, effective at once, to Lieut. Gen. Matthew B. Ridgway. . . . My reasons for your replacement will be made public concurrently with the delivery to you of the foregoing order, and are contained in the next following message.
>
> Harry S. Truman

It was originally planned to let Secretary of War Frank Pace, Jr., who was then in the Far East, deliver the dismissal note to MacArthur at the Tokyo Embassy. But the April 12 radio got there ahead of Pace. MacArthur and his wife were entertaining visitors at luncheon when Sid Huff, the General's aide, picked the dismissal notice from a news broadcast. With tears in his eyes he called Mrs. MacArthur from the table. She returned to break the news.

Not a flicker of emotion stirred MacArthur's face. When the General subsequently read the official confirmation, he turned to his wife and said serenely, "Jean, we're going home at last." To the press, Gen. Courtney Whitney said: "I have just left the General. He received the word magnificently. He never turned a hair. His soldierly qualities were never more pronounced. I think this has been his finest hour."

The Communists reveled in the news when they heard it. In a "Proclamation of the Japanese Communist Party concerning General MacArthur's Dismissal," they said:

> MacArthur's dismissal most plainly reveals that due to the strongly growing discrepancy and divergence of opinion amongst the imperialistic nations, a cornerstone of their war-provocative policy seeking world control has crumbled before the peace-loving masses composed of over a billion people.
>
> One of Premier Stalin's great predictions, that "all meddlers will no doubt meet with certain failure," has come true.
>
> It is also clear that as a result of this dismissal the separatist peace group [pro U.S.] is now in a state of confusion, and the Yoshida cabinet and their clique have lost their staunch supporter of the past several years.
>
> We now have an opportune moment. By taking advantage of the confusion, an all-out peace and antiwar preparation movement can be strengthened.
>
> In co-ordination with a poll of 40,000,000 [Japanese] voters on the general peace issue, efforts will be made to expose thoroughly the maladministration of the Yoshida cabinet, sweeping from local autonomy the Liberal party influence advocating a separate peace [with the U.S.] at the same time bringing about the downfall of the Yoshida cabinet.

The plain people of Japan, however, spoke with a different voice. The dismissal dominated news and editorial columns in Tokyo and other Japanese cities more completely than any world event since the surrender.

The initial reaction was shock and disappointment, regret and fear. The final phase was one of resolutions of national gratitude and sincere editorial tributes to MacArthur's efforts in behalf of Japan. Said *Mainichi Shimbun* (circulation 3,970,000):

> MacArthur's dismissal is the greatest shock since the end of the war. He dealt with the Japanese people not as a conqueror but a great reformer. He was a noble political missionary. What he gave us was not material aid and democratic reform alone—but a new way of life, the freedom and dignity of the individual. . . . We shall continue to love and trust him as one of the Americans who best understood Japan's position.

Said *Asahi Shimbun* (circulation 4,074,000):

> The removal is a great disappointment to the Japanese, especially when the peace settlement is so near. Japan's recovery must be attributed solely to his guidance. We feel as if we had lost a kind and loving father.

On the day of MacArthur's departure the 20-mile roadway to Haneda Airfield was lined by thousands of Japanese, of every social class, bearing American and Japanese flags. People wept as the General's car rolled past them. And *Mainichi Shimbun* provided the final commentary:

> We wanted your further help in nurturing our green democracy to fruition. We wanted your leadership at least until a signed peace treaty had given us a send-off into the world community.

The citizens of Kanagawa Prefecture, embracing the great port city of Yokohama, put into words what was latent in many Japanese hearts. On the base of a bronze bust which Japan's leading sculptor had been commissioned to create, the words foretold the judgment of history: "General Douglas MacArthur—Liberator of Japan."

The reaction of America to the General's homecoming was no less affecting than that of Japan to his departure. When he landed in San Francisco, he had spent twenty-five years on foreign service, longer than any officer or man of the U.S. Army. On Friday afternoon, in Japan, he had first heard the news of the dismissal. He was gone on Monday to receive at home the greatest welcome ever accorded an American. His staff thrilled to the echo of his closing words as he said farewell in the halls of Congress:

> I have just left your fighting sons in Korea. They have met all tests there and I can report to you without reservations, they are splendid in every way.
> It was my constant effort to preserve them and end this savage conflict honorably and with the least loss of time and a minimum sacrifice of life. Its growing bloodshed has caused me the deepest anguish and anxiety. Those gallant men will remain often in my thoughts and in my prayers always.
> I am closing my fifty-two years of military service. When I joined the Army, even before the turn of the century, it was the fulfillment of all my boyish hopes and dreams.
> The world has turned over many times since I took the oath on the

plain at West Point, and the hopes and dreams have long since vanished, but I still remember the refrain of one of the most popular barracks ballads of that day, which proclaimed, most proudly, that "Old soldiers never die. They just fade away."

And like the old soldier of that ballad, I now close my military career and just fade away—an old soldier who tried to do his duty as God gave him the light to see that duty.

Goodbye.

2. MacArthur's Recall, A Necessary Reassertion of Civilian Authority

The defense of the administration was that the main enemy was Soviet Russia and that the area of principal threat was in Western Europe. MacArthur's recommendations would thus have led to war in a secondary area and would have opened the way for a possible Soviet thrust in Europe. Dismissal of MacArthur came because his insubordination required a reassertion of civilian control of foreign policy and the military.

Truman Versus MacArthur: Achilles Rebound

JOHN W. SPANIER

Prior to the North Korean attack in June 1950, the Administration's foreign policy was based upon the fundamental assumption that the Soviet Union presented the chief threat to American security; Moscow's leaders were committed to the elimination of all non-Communist nations. George Kennan compared Soviet expansion to

> a fluid stream which moves constantly, wherever it is permitted to move, toward a given goal. Its main concern is to make sure that it has filled every nook and cranny available to it in the basin of world power. But if it finds unassailable barriers in its path, it accepts these philosophically and accommodates itself to them. The main thing is that there should always be pressure, unceasing constant pressure, toward the desired goal. There is no trace of any feeling in Soviet psychology that the goal must be reached at any given time.

The American task was, therefore, to erect "unassailable barriers" in the path of Soviet power to contain its further spread. The Truman Doctrine, the Marshall Plan, the Berlin Airlift, NATO, were all part of this policy.

The principal aim of this "long-term, patient but firm and vigilant containment of Russia's expansive tendencies" was not the destruction of the Soviet Union and its satellites, but the creation of a balance of power to effect this "containment." The objective of this policy was to deter the Kremlin from attempting to achieve world domination by resort to total war, lead it instead to the negotiating table, and to settle the principal cold war issues. A second characteristic of containment was its

Reprinted by permission of the publishers from John W. Spanier, *The Truman-MacArthur Controversy and the Korean War.* Cambridge, Mass.: The Belknap Press of Harvard University Press. Copyright, 1959, by The President and Fellows of Harvard College. Pp. 257–277.

assumption that such a "situation of strength" could be attained by the United States only in association with its principal NATO allies. American independence and security had traditionally required a balance of power in the interior of Europe to check any nation which possessed ambitions to conquer the sea-bordering states as a prerequisite to first eliminating England and then proceeding to world conquest. Consequently, the collapse of NATO could not be tolerated.

The military heart of this containment policy was the almost complete reliance upon strategic air power to deter or win World War III. The Western armies stationed in Europe were not sufficiently large to prevent the Russian army from reaching the English Channel. The NATO army was primarily a "plate-glass" which would set off the burglar alarm and send the United States Strategic Air Command flying toward its Soviet targets. The assumption was that the only kind of war possible was a total war which would begin the moment the Soviet Union struck a surprise blow at either the United States or America's "first line of defense" in Western Europe.

It was this reliance upon a strategy of total war which had been responsible for the Joint Chiefs' recommendation to withdraw American troops from South Korea and for Secretary Acheson's and General MacArthur's exclusion of the Republic from the Pacific defense perimeter. For in an all-out war South Korea would indeed be neither strategically vital to the United States nor defensible; its fate would be determined by the results of the conflict fought in other theaters. The limited war with which the North Koreans faced the President and his advisers on June 25, 1950, therefore presented the Administration with an agonizing dilemma.

On the one hand, the Communist invasion of South Korea struck at the basic presuppositions of American policy. If the primary purpose of containment was to prevent further Soviet expansion, American inaction in the face of Soviet aggression could only encourage further such acts in the future. The appetites of dictators were insatiable; one meal only whetted their palates and increased their hunger. If the aim of containment was also to hold together the Western powers, American refusal to rescue a friend in distress would disintegrate NATO. Our European allies would have believed that in a similar crisis they would be abandoned in a similar manner; consequently, they would have dismissed American treaty pledges as valueless, turned to neutralism for safety, isolated the United States, and deprived the Strategic Air Command of a large measure of its deterrent power.

On the other hand, the limited Soviet challenge in Korea did not fit our strategic doctrine. South Korea was certainly not "worth" the price of total war; massive retaliation upon Moscow was not the answer to the shrewd Russian exploitation of the government's one-sided concentration upon air-atomic striking power. A more limited response was needed. Fortunately, the United States had several undermanned and "undertrained" divisions in near-by Japan. Ironically, therefore, the Administration was compelled to fight a limited war to preserve its total-war policy; it was forced to respond by less than total means to a Soviet satellite in order

to prevent the disintegration of a policy predicated upon massive retaliation as the principal means of deterring or winning a total war with the
Soviet Union.

The price for American unpreparedness to fight a less than total war
was strategic improvisation. Administration officials, still deeply imbued
with the belief that the main contest would be with the Soviet Union
and fought over the possession of Western Europe, thought of the Korean
War only as a strategic diversion cleverly planned by the Kremlin as a
means to weaken American power and divert it from Europe. Thus, while
the government's political and military leaders knew that the limited
Soviet attack in Korea left the United States with no alternative but to
respond to it, they were determined that the fighting in the "far-off"
Asian peninsula be kept as limited as possible. The Korean War was a
necessary war: to teach the Soviet leaders that aggression would not
pay; to hold together the Western alliance; and to preserve the military
basis of containment. Nevertheless, it remained a "peripheral" war.

During the first stage of the conflict the objective was the restoration
of the Republic of Korea to its prewar status. General MacArthur's magnificent amphibious operation at Inchon transformed the character of the
war; his military victory changed it from a defensive war seeking only to
re-establish the *status quo* to an offensive war attempting to affect a
permanent change in the *status quo*. The North Koreans had been defeated, the military situation favored the fulfillment of an American goal
of several years' standing: the unification of the whole of Korea. The
Administration thereupon shifted its emphasis from containing the expansion of Soviet power to the forceful liberation of a Soviet satellite.

At the same time, the Administration abandoned the two assumptions
upon which it had based its strategy in previous clashes with the Soviet
Union: first, that the United States had to limit its efforts to contain
Soviet expansionist moves to the restoration of the *status quo;* and second,
that if the United States managed to re-establish the old equilibrium, the
Russian leaders broke off the engagement and accepted the pre-crisis
situation. After Inchon, however, the United States government made
no attempt, as it had, for instance, after its successful resistance in Berlin,
to negotiate an end to the hostilities through diplomatic channels. The
Administration offered the Soviets only the total elimination of their
satellite; in accordance with its own conclusion that it was dangerous to
extend its reaction to Russian moves beyond the re-establishment of the
status quo, the government must have expected the rejection of its demand for North Korea's unconditional surrender. Secretary Acheson had
himself stated that governments do not negotiate their own survival.
American insistence upon the military unification of Korea thus assured
the continuation of hostilities.

This objective was officially proclaimed on October 7, 1950. Prior to
that day the aim of the campaign had been only the restoration of the
status quo: since a non-Communist South Korea had existed before the
outbreak of the Korean War, the threat to Communist China of a liberated Republic of Korea was no greater than that before June 25, 1950.

But on October 7, as American-led forces surged northwards toward the Manchurian border, the threat to Communist China's industrial center became one of far greater magnitude. But the Administration believed that it was politically safe to drive into North Korea and free the Soviet satellite from Communist domination. The Chinese Communists were believed to be Chinese first and Communist second; moreover, they were allegedly already involved in such an intense struggle with the Soviet Union to prevent the latter from detaching Northern China, Manchuria, and Sinkiang, that Peking's anxious eyes were turned to the Northern provinces, not to Korea; China's traditional enemy was Russia, not the United States.

The resulting attempt of the Democrats to practice in October and November 1950 what the Republicans were only to preach two years later, led Communist China to intervene in order to redress the balance. The rapid change in the resulting military situation quickly led the Administration to deny its revisionist objective and revert once more to its *status quo* guise. The continued division of Korea was inherent in the Administration's rejection of MacArthur's military proposals to counter China's intervention.

One of the reasons for this rejection was the Administration's concern lest the Soviet Union might precipitate World War III. The government insisted that the United States must not offer the Russians any pretext for intervention. "Every decision I made in connection with the Korean conflict," the President wrote later, "had this one aim in mind: to prevent a third world war and the terrible destruction it would bring to the civilized world. This means that we should not do anything that would provide the excuse to the Soviets and plunge the free nations into full-scale all-out war . . . The points that appeared most critical [in the middle of December 1950] were Berlin, Western Germany, Indo-China, Yugoslavia, and Iran. In each of these areas a minor incident could easily be created which would give the Russians an excuse for open intervention . . . and the Kremlin might not be bluffing and might have decided that the time was in fact ripe for a general war with the United States." In the Administration's opinion, MacArthur's strategy to bomb Communist China, blockade her ports, and sanction Chinese Nationalist attacks upon the mainland would provide the Kremlin with just such an excuse.

But even if the Soviet Union should remain a spectator, the United States could not extend the war; it had to avoid becoming engaged in a "war of attrition" with Chinese manpower. Korea would "bleed us dry" and make it impossible to build a strong military defense in Europe. A large-scale commitment of American power in Asia would not only expose Europe to Soviet armies; it might incite such an attack at a moment of maximum American weakness on the continent. Nothing, General Bradley asserted, would delight the Kremlin more than the "enlargement of the war in Korea to include Red China . . . It would necessarily tie down additional forces, especially our sea power and air power, while the Soviet Union would not be obliged to put a single man into the conflict . . . A 'limited war' with Red China would increase the risk we are taking by engaging too much of our power in an area that is not the critical strategic prize. Red China is not the powerful nation seeking to dominate the world . . ." It was for this reason that MacArthur's strategy would involve us in the wrong war, at the wrong place, at the wrong time, and with the wrong enemy. The President stressed the same point: ". . . I never allowed myself to forget that America's principal enemies were sitting in the Kremlin, or that we could not afford to squander our reawakening strength as long as that [of] the enemy was not committed in the field but only pulling the strings behind the scenes." The United States had, therefore, to conserve its strength to check the main danger— Soviet Russia which *was* "the powerful nation seeking to dominate the world"—and not waste its power in a peripheral area.

This view was shared by Britain and France. America's chief allies were reluctant to see American power directed to the Far East before Europe was secure against Russian assault; they had no desire to risk the outbreak of World War III so soon after the second had ended for an area that was to them of minor strategic significance; and they hoped that their friendly attitude would hasten the split between the Chinese Communists and the Kremlin, as well as identify at least Britain and France with the new trends in Asia, social progress and national independence. Thus, if the United States decided to carry the war to Communist China, it would have to "go it alone." But the premise of creating "situations of strengths" and balancing Soviet might or winning a total war was NATO's unity and combined strength. It "is of transcendent importance," Secretary Acheson stressed, "that in our policies in all parts of the world, where danger may be created, we work absolutely in hand with our allies."

For these reasons, American policy-makers were willing to settle the war on the 38th Parallel. The Communists had attempted to erase the parallel and expand their power by incorporating South Korea into the Communist bloc; neither the north Koreans nor the Chinese Communists had achieved this objective. The Communists had also hoped to destroy the Western alliance and isolate the United States; in this too they had failed. NATO had been preserved and greatly strengthened by the new rearmament program and the addition of four American divisions. And Korea's primary purpose, to put the Communists on notice that the Western Powers would not tolerate Communist expansion by military force, had been achieved. The wisest course was thus to end this strategic diversion, to conclude this peripheral war, and once again concentrate on the main task: the strengthening of air-atomic striking power to deter the Soviet Union from precipitating total war and the building of a "situation of strength" in Western Europe.

MacArthur's fundamental charge against the Administration was that its restrictions kept him from achieving "victory" in the field. Inherent in this accusation was MacArthur's repudiation of the Administration's basic assumptions, above all the supposition that the Soviet Union might be ready and willing to fight a total war, and that the United States, therefore, must not provide an eager Kremlin with any excuse for attack.

MacArthur contended that the Administration divorced theory from practice. In theory, American foreign policy was based upon the assumption that the United States held sufficient power, above all air-atomic striking power, to deter the Soviet Union from launching an all-out war; in practice, American policy-makers acted upon the assumption that a limited extension of the war would hand the Soviets an excuse for precipitating World War III. On the one hand, the Kremlin was allegedly reluctant to engage in global hostilities with the United States because of America's greater retaliatory strength, inherent primarily in the destructive power of the Strategic Air Command; on the other hand, the Kremlin regarded our purported deterrent power with so little respect that it would deliberately risk total war rather than suffer a limited defeat of Communist China (a limited defeat would preclude the unconditional surrender and overthrow of Peking, and leave it weakened but nevertheless in control of the Chinese mainland).

MacArthur failed to see any consistency between the Administration's rationale of its foreign policy, based upon the atomic impact of massive retaliation, and its failure to act upon its own premise. If it were true that the United States held the atomic balance—as he believed and the Administration professed—then his recommendations for air attacks and a naval blockade of Communist China could be safely executed. SAC would continue to deter the Soviet Union and ensure that the limited hostilities, although somewhat extended, would remain confined to the Chinese-Korean theater; our superior strategic air power would provide the umbrella under which this expanded limited war could be fought. It was sheer fantasy, MacArthur charged, to suppose that American air attacks upon Manchuria would provide an eager Kremlin the opportunity to enter the battle. The Soviet Union possessed far inferior retaliatory power (the Russians did not begin to develop their long-range air force until 1954); why should it, therefore, be allowed to handcuff American strength? The United States possessed the superior atomic sanction; why should it not take advantage of this greater power? MacArthur pointed to the paradox that the side with the smaller strategic strength had paralyzed the will to act of the side which possessed the more effective striking force. The Administration's fear to act upon his recommendations to attack across the Yalu and the resultant impasse on the Korean battlefield was not a military stalemate, but a stalemate between the Soviet leaders *militarily incapable* of destroying the center of free world power and American policy-makers *psychologically reluctant* to exploit the advantage of the very atomic balance which they claimed was the primary safeguard of peace.

If the Russian leaders were really militarily capable of winning a total war and were merely seeking a convenient pretext to launch World War III, they would hardly need the United States to furnish the excuse; they were perfectly capable of manufacturing their own. If they were, however, restrained by American air power, they would rather tolerate a limited defeat of their chief ally than risk suicide. North Korea was no more "worth" the cost of an all-out conflict to the Soviet Union than

South Korea had been to the United States; nor was Communist China's position in North Korea "worth" that price as long as American objectives remained confined to the Korean peninsula.

MacArthur also dissented from the Administration's assumption that even if an attack upon Communist China would not precipitate World War III, this country must not become engaged in a "war of attrition" lest this course would weaken NATO and provoke a Soviet attack. The General denied that the Korean War was a Russian maneuver to draw American strength away from Europe and dissipate it against Chinese manpower, a strategic diversion which must be ended as soon as possible at minimum cost to the central effort to strengthen our total-war deterrent.

Not only was the "real" challenge against the enemy's number-one team in Europe hypothetical, for it was "Russia's policy . . . not to sacrifice its own troops but to use those of friends," but:

> Mr. Truman failed abysmally to comprehend the Soviet Strategy in the latter's continuing and relentless effort to control the world . . . He failed to understand that the global panorama has long encompassed three great areas of potential struggle: In the center, Europe; on the flanks, Asia to the north and Africa to the south. Mr. Truman apparently thought of the center as the area of supreme interest and potential struggle, believing that if it could be held safely all else would fall into place . . .
>
> What the Soviets sought were the economic frontiers of the world— Asia to the north, Africa to the south—frontiers which possessed such a mighty reservoir of the world's potential wealth in raw resources. The center represented little in economic advance, the flanks everything. The Soviet strategy was merely to defend in Europe but to advance by way of the flanks; to cause the free world to concentrate its resources at the center to the neglect of the vital ends.

Korea was, therefore, the right war at the right place at the right time, and above all else, with the right enemy. For Communist China was Soviet Russia's chief ally and most powerful friend in Asia. Therefore, a defeat inflicted upon Communist China, however limited that defeat might be, would affect both Soviet strength in Asia and the global balance of power between the Western and Communist blocs. The defeat of the Chinese Communists in Korea would strengthen the friendship and support of the Asian peoples, particularly the Japanese and Filipinos, for the United States; the loss of American prestige in an acceptance of the stalemate would alienate their sympathies. Conversely, Communist China's status would be recognized as "the military colossus of the East"; America's fear to demonstrate its superior strength would make our friends feel less secure and drive the neutral nations deeper into neutralism; for they would feel more threatened as a result of Peking's unchallenged recognition as a strong and menacing neighbor and therefore look upon the Communist states with a more friendly, if also a more apprehensive, eye. The destruction of Communist China's industrial complex, military depots, and communication network would gravely weaken Sino-

Soviet offensive strength in the Far East and deter Moscow and Peking from initiating any further aggressive adventures; confining hostilities to the Korean peninsula and concluding the war on the basis of the *status quo* would leave Sino-Soviet power intact and encourage it to exploit the West's weakness and lack of determination in other areas. Indeed, if the war in Korea were "lost"—by MacArthur's definition—the Western democracies would have suffered such a first-class political and psychological defeat that the Soviets could not but be emboldened to new efforts to undermine Western Europe. But to drive the Chinese Communists out of Korea in accordance with his strategy, MacArthur asserted, would demonstrate to the Western nations that even the Sino-Soviet alliance shrank from certain risky steps; victory would raise Europe's self-confidence by showing the limits of Communist power and the superior strength of the United States. It is for this reason that MacArthur insisted that Korea was *the* test of NATO and that Europe's first line of defense was not in Germany but in Korea.

His war in Korea was not, therefore, a sideshow; it was at the center of the world-wide struggle. The war, to be sure, contained its risks, but this was inherent in the nature of international politics and the original decision to fight in Korea; the conflict also presented a great opportunity to inflict a limited yet severe defeat upon the Sino-Soviet bloc, demonstrate American determination and power, raise Western resolution and self-assurance, and forestall the disaffection of friendly Asian nations. This opportunity outweighed all the risks, particularly since these risks were minimized by the deterrent power of America's superior atomic air-striking power.

MacArthur also emphasized that an alliance could act decisively only if its members were agreed on the nature of the danger facing them. If they were not animated by such a common realization, they not only did not add to the security of the United States; they detracted from it by restraining the United States from taking the steps necessary to safeguard its interests. The argument that the Administration could not accept his recommendations because it could not afford to isolate itself in the face of the Soviet threat toward Europe, was invalid; it was not the existence of the alliance which would deter the enemy's aggression, but the resolution which bound it together in concrete instances which called for vigorous action. When such determination and will-power were lacking, the United States must protect its own interests. The Administration's unwillingness to risk the loss of its allies allowed American policy to be dictated by the weaker members of the alliance. Under these circumstances, the achievement of allied unity became self-defeating; for the price of continued cooperation was the substance of action. In MacArthur's opinion, this price was too high and was paid upon the false assumption that unilateral action by the United States in Asia would undermine NATO, isolate this country, and encourage a Soviet attack in Europe. MacArthur believed that this prejudged the issue because it presumed that the United States was more dependent for its security upon its European allies than they upon the United States.

Since he was unwilling to accept formal unity for inaction or half-hearted effort, MacArthur advised that in order to forestall the disastrous effects he foresaw from an acceptance of a Korean stalemate, the United States "go it alone." European reluctance to become involved in major hostilities in the Far East ought not to prevent the Administration from taking actions which were in America's interest; the Administration could not give global scope to an alliance whose conflict of interests in areas outside of Europe paralyzed it.

The United States was sufficiently strong to fight the Korean War by herself; she had to act unilaterally if necessary, and pursue alone those policies which aimed at the preservation of a favorable balance of power. The United States must not allow this balance to be overturned by subordinating her strategy to allied fears; for in the final analysis, the security of Europe depended upon this country's ability to maintain this equilibrium. After the North Korean invasion, the United States had not first asked its allies whether they would approve of American intervention; the American government had acted in accordance with the dictates of national security. Allied consent had subsequently been extended, but it had not been a precondition for action. The Administration ought now to act upon its own precedent.

Communist China's appearance on the battlefield thus brought into the open the almost total disagreement between the Administration and its Commander in Chief, Far East, a disagreement which had, of course, never lain far below the surface and had irritated the relationship between Washington and Tokyo from the beginning of the war. Since shortly after the outbreak of hostilities, MacArthur had openly advocated that the United States maximize its commitment to Chiang Kai-shek and take a strong stand against Communist China; and his repeated "military" criticisms of the Administration's preoccupation with Europe and alleged neglect of American interests in the Far East were hardly new.

But these frequent and vigorous challenges of Administration policy after China's intervention were, however, incompatible with the President's continuing civilian supremacy and authority as chief diplomat and Commander in Chief to formulate and implement the policies the Chief Executive considered necessary to ensure the nation's self preservation. MacArthur embarrassed the Administration by giving the world the impression that the United States spoke with two voices—one civilian, one military—on foreign policy; he confused our allies and increased their reluctance to follow American policy because they feared that the government could not control him; and his March 24 statement actually forestalled the execution of Presidential policy. This situation was intolerable and left Mr. Truman no choice but to dismiss his field commander. But the price the President paid included, among other things, the adoption of a stronger anti-Mao and pro-Chiang policy along the lines advocated by the "old soldier" who refused to fade away.

The Administration's political weakness and vulnerability in Congress was a further cause for the Truman-MacArthur controversy; the President's lack of strength was particularly noticeable in the Senate. The reason for this was that in early 1950 the leadership of the Republican party in Congress on matters of foreign policy returned from the liberal eastern wing of the party to the traditional and predominantly middle-western conservatives, who constitute the majority of Republicans in Congress. These conservative Republicans rejected "bipartisan" cooperation. They believed that partisanship in foreign policy was politically expedient; "me-tooism" in international affairs, as in domestic affairs, resulted in defeat at the polls. Policies stamped with the Administration trade-mark were credited by the electorate to the party in power, and not to the "loyal" opposition which had supported them. In addition, Taft Republicans were convinced that the Democratic party, aided by the "heretical" eastern wing of their own party, were destroying the foundations of the American political and economic system, and that this process could be halted only by the restoration to power of the heirs and custodians of the "true" Republican tradition with its belief in a strong legislature, a balanced budget, and a minimum of government intervention in business. Thus partisanship in foreign policy was also an ideological necessity.

The conservative Republicans focused their criticisms upon the New Dealers. The latter's crimes were many: they had fathered "Socialism" and the Welfare State in America; they had involved the United States in World War II; they had "sold out" China and Eastern Europe at the wartime conferences with Stalin; and they had allowed Communist agents and "sympathizers" to infiltrate the American government. In short, the New Dealers were responsible for altering the traditional libertarian American system, entangling the United States in the complications of the international world, and aiding, either unwittingly or deliberately, the forces of World Communism. This conspiratorial interpretation of American domestic and foreign politics could not have been advanced at a more appropriate moment in American postwar history. Popular frustration with the cold war was widespread.

Republican mid-term election successes appeared to prove to orthodox party strategists that opposition *per se* was good politics, and that their pre-election estimate that attacks upon foreign policy were politically profitable was correct. As a result, after November 7, 1950, they no longer confined their broadsides to Yalta, Teheran, and Potsdam; Alger Hiss and other cases of espionage; the Administration's "loss" of China and responsibility for the war in Korea; they now attacked the whole scope of American foreign policy, particularly the European policy. General MacArthur's close link to this group, among whom such leaders as Taft, Wherry, Bridges, and Knowland were largely oriented toward Asia, lent it great prestige and strengthened its criticisms.

These attacks had even before June 25, 1950, imposed an increasing inflexibility upon American Far Eastern policy; they had prevented the Administration from initiating its Mao Tse-tito policy and forestalled the complete abandonment of Chiang Kai-shek. The Administration's protection of Formosa after the outbreak of North Korean aggression satisfied the opposition only temporarily. As the war progressed, their assaults became increasingly vociferous in their demands for a stronger anti-Mao and pro-Chiang policy; and their electoral gains, together with Communist China's intervention, added to the pressure exerted upon the Administration to adopt General MacArthur's proposal to extend the war and hit across the Yalu River.

These attacks were not, however, powerful enough to achieve this aim; but they were sufficiently strong to place American diplomacy in a domestic political straightjacket which foreclosed negotiations as a means to end hostilities, brought the Administration to endorse a large-scale military-aid program for Chiang, to announce a rather doubtful enthusiasm for his regime, and even to issue a call for a revolution within Communist China. Thus, in May and June 1951, during the Senate inquiry into MacArthur's dismissal, the extraordinary and ridiculous situation arose in which, on the one hand, the Administration was defending its limitation of the war and its dismissal of General MacArthur for advocating the opposite course, and at the same time renouncing its acceptance of the *status quo* and the implicit recognition of Peking's existence which this implied, and presenting the key issue as the survival of the Chinese Communist regime itself. Since regimes do not, however, negotiate about their own survival, this issue could only have been settled by the total war with Communist China—and perhaps with the Soviet Union —which the Administration had already rejected as too dangerous a course. Thus, if the government's call for an internal revolt within Communist China had been taken seriously by Peking, it would have committed the United States to an interminable war with no possibility of ending it through negotiations or a cease-fire.

Walter Lippmann subsequently wrote that the situation had been so serious that President Truman

> was not able to make peace, because politically he was too weak at home. He was not able to make war because the risks were too great. This dilemma of Truman's was resolved by the election of Eisenhower . . . President Eisenhower signed an armistice which accepted the partition of Korea and a peace without victory because, being himself the victorious commander in World War II and a Republican, he could not be attacked as an appeaser. President Truman and Secretary Acheson, on the other hand, never seemed able to afford to make peace on the only terms which the Chinese would agree to, on the terms, that is to say, which Eisenhower did agree to. The Democrats were too vulnerable to attack from the political followers of General MacArthur and of the then powerful Senator McCarthy, and indeed to attack from the whole right wing of the Republican party.

Thus the separation of powers exaggerated the peculiar American tendency to define foreign policy objectives in abstract and ideological terms; for to gain congressional and popular support for their policies, presidents must oversell their policies. This they do, not by presenting the key issues as enlightened—yet nevertheless, "selfish"—national interests, but as the highest moral principles and aims.

Whereas interests can, however, be compromised, principles cannot.

Their integrity, indeed their survival, can be guaranteed only by the total destruction of the enemy and the complete elimination of the evil which threatens to contaminate, if not to abolish, them. Anything less than the full application of "righteous power," and the achievement of complete victory, creates an embarrassing discrepancy between expectation and reality, and leaves in its wake widespread disillusionment.

The Administration's political weakness was evident, however, not only in its acceptance of much of its critics' policy and its apparent inability to sign an armistice on or near the 38th Parallel, but also in its failure to take effective measures to restrict MacArthur's discretionary powers. Nowhere was this more vividly demonstrated than in North Korea after the first signs of Chinese Communist intervention. MacArthur believed that boldness and a show of force would convince Peking that Korea's fate had already been settled; any hesitation would be interpreted as weakness and an invitation to full-scale intervention. The Administration proposed that only South Korean troops be sent into the area along the Manchurian frontier and northeastern provinces bordering the Soviet Union; by this means it expected to reassure Peking that American troops would not invade Manchuria. But MacArthur advanced the proper "purely military" considerations which he claimed necessitated his advance to the Yalu, and the government surrendered meekly. The reason it later advanced for its laxness was the American tradition granting generals great latitude in determining the tactical means to gain their objectives. This was primarily a rationalization; American policy-makers could hardly have been blind to the interrelationship of tactical means on the one hand and strategic concepts and political consequences on the other. A more reasonable explanation would attribute their paralysis to the Administration's fear of being accused of "softness" toward Communism, its uncertainty that MacArthur could not again carry off a "tremendous gamble" as at Inchon, its field commander's heightened prestige since that brilliant victory and Republican mid-term victories.

This is not to say that MacArthur's determination to launch his "end of the war" offensive, or the Administration's failure to stop him, were responsible for Communist China's full-scale intervention. The key decision determining the intervention was probably the crossing of the parallel; this is not, however, to excuse Washington's relaxation of political control as MacArthur advanced into North Korea. In seeking allied support for the crossing of the parallel, the Administration had given assurances that it would direct its military operations in North Korea with circumspection, that it would conduct itself with caution and avoid all acts which might provoke either Russia or China. MacArthur's operations, in the view of the allies, hardly supported this understanding; in their opinion, MacArthur's "belligerent" statements, together with his advance to the Yalu, gave Peking reasonable grounds for suspicion of American intentions and at least a partial justification for its intervention. Consequently, London and Paris refused to sanction an extension of the war beyond the Yalu, and slowed down and later eviscerated the Administration's condemnation of Communist

China. This one incident, they believed, had shown both MacArthur's liberal—perhaps more appropriately, unwarranted—interpretation of his
orders, and the Administration's inability to exert effective control over
him. Thus Truman's domestic weakness was one of the principal causes
for the lack of allied confidence and insistence upon restraint.

The intensity of the executive-legislative battle not only allowed Mac-
Arthur to inject himself into this conflict and exploit his strong legislative
support, but made it incumbent upon the Administration to invoke the
Joint Chiefs' public support for its policies. Thus, ironically, the President's main reason for dismissing MacArthur, the necessity to preserve
the principle of civilian control of the military, had to rely for its defense
almost completely upon General Bradley and his three colleagues. The
Joint Chiefs, widely regarded as a strictly professional and disinterested
body, could command senatorial attention, for they combined the roles of
World War II heroes and technical experts; consequently, they bore the
chief burden of explaining to the inquiring senators the relationship of
military strategy to political objectives, the respective contribution of
Europe and Asia to our national security, and the value and role of
allies in American policy. Secretary Acheson, despite the articulate, organized, and persuasive presentation of his testimony, could command
no such reception; his Congressional audience received him in a more
hostile and skeptical mood.

If the Administration's political vulnerability left the Joint Chiefs little
choice but to lend their glamor to the government's policies, it also squan-
dered much of their wartime prestige and reputation for political
neutrality. Senator Taft's announcement, shortly after General Mac-
Arthur's dismissal, that he no longer possessed any confidence in General
Bradley's professional judgment—as if "purely military" evaluations were
ever without political implications!—is symptomatic of this change of
attitude. Apparently the Senator believed that Bradley's opinions were
warped by a purported pro-Democratic bias. Taft's criticism, however,
even if it were true—and all the evidence belies it—would hardly be
germane; for he is not disputing the fact that military men speak for or
against national issues of a highly controversial nature in public, but the
fact that General Bradley agreed with the President's policy, and disagreed with his, Senator Taft's, views. His point was not that a criticism
of his and former President Hoover's almost exclusive reliance on air and
sea power for the defense of the American Gibraltar should have been the
task of the military's civilian superiors; his point was that General Bradley
had found his strategy wanting. His concern was not, therefore, with
the problem that partisan alignment of generals implied for the future
of civilian supremacy; he was merely incensed that there were also "Democratic Generals," like the chairman of the Joint Chiefs, not just "Republican Generals," like MacArthur.

Nonetheless, the Senator's hostility to General Bradley does draw attention to the manner in which the separation of powers between
the President and Congress draws military leaders into political conflict. The danger in this is not that military officers belong, as Senator

Taft seemed to believe, to one or the other of the two principal parties. The real threat lies elsewhere; that the generals' independent judgment lends itself to exploitation by both parties; and that this will signal, as Walter Lippmann has written, "the beginning of an altogether intolerable thing in a republic: namely a schism within the armed forces between the generals of the Democratic Party and the generals of the Republican Party"; and that the result will considerably weaken civilian control and presidential direction of foreign policy.

Our study of the Truman-MacArthur controversy has shown that the preservation of civilian control is not merely a simple matter of maintaining a number of appropriate constitutional and institutional safeguards. Indeed, the word "control" is in itself somewhat vague, for it implies that to avert a threat from the professionals of the sword restraints need be applied only to them; this is not necessarily true. At a time of high international tension, such as 1950–1951, during which the population and their elected officials are intensely preoccupied with security, the dominance of the military and "military" attitudes among civilians both in and out of government may become overriding. This is particularly true if such a period of crisis should last a relatively long time, or be followed rapidly by successive crises. Under such circumstances, American democracy may be transformed into a "garrison state" in which all power is concentrated in the Executive, authority flows downward, and democratic liberties are merely memories. This state of affairs, as Louis Smith has emphasized, may come "not by willful usurpation by the military but by successive adaptations for defense having the support of public opinion. It may be ushered in, not by conspiracy, but by plebiscite. It may come into power, not over the wreckage of the civil organs traditionally expected to repress it, but with their respective support."

This points to what is thus the principal as well as the most easily perceptible factor determining the effectiveness of civilian control: the quality of the nation's civilian leadership, that is, the ability of the politically responsible officials to recognize threats to their supremacy and their courage to act in order to preserve their control, no matter how unpopular their steps.

> Only to the extent that civilian leaders are committed to democratic values and procedures and the necessity for a civilian point of view can the requisite supremacy be maintained. Their intelligence and understanding, their clarity of purpose and direction, and their courage and confidence in the face of various anxieties and exigencies of a "cold war" and even full-scale war itself seem to be crucial . . . civilian apathy and ignorance may as effectively subvert civilian supremacy as a deliberate attempt by the military to augment their supremacy.

Another factor of key importance during a period of war is a field commander who is not violently opposed to the policies he is expected to execute, at least not so violently that he will refuse to restrict his objections to constitutionally authorized channels. No government can allow a military officer to challenge its whole foreign policy publicly; such toleration would undermine its authority to determine the nation's policy, divide the domestic support it needs, and alienate the allies it desires.

This need for a field commander more in sympathy with official strategy becomes even more urgent in view of the latitude the United States has traditionally granted its military officers. Since it is not customary for an Administration to issue specific orders to a military executive thousands of miles away, the latter can, owing to poor judgment or deliberate design, make decisions whose political and strategic consequences may well prevent the achievement of the government's objectives, if not undermine them. Necessity may, therefore, compel a re-examination of the tradition of military freedom lest it excuse us into disaster. In limited warfare not only military strategy, but on occasions even military tactics, have important political repercussions.

Imposing such restrictions on the man in the field will require a change in the traditional American attitude that war is a purely military instrument. The military, as well as their civilian superiors, will have to recognize that Clausewitz' definition of war as a political tool means that military operations are not only subordinate to political aims, but that there is no such thing as an autonomous sphere in which military operations are conducted in a strictly military manner unencumbered by "outside interference." None of the other generals who directed the Korean War, with the sole exception of General Ridgway, understood war in any broader sense than their own narrow professional definition. James Van Fleet, Mark Clark, Turner Joy, all took MacArthur literally and echoed his calls for a military victory; after all, was MacArthur not voicing merely the obvious?

Not until military men as a whole accept the need for close political direction will they be less likely to issue public statements voicing their displeasure at the "political interference" with their conduct of a limited war; indeed, until they abandon their notion that war is a military tool they will find it difficult wholly to accept the concept of limited warfare. Military men seem sometimes to forget that they are servants of the state and that they will not be judged by the nature of the policies they implement, only by how well they implement these policies. Their civilian superiors are responsible for the actual formulation of political strategy, not they. It is not their function to take their disagreements into the public forum for national debate.

Indeed, unless the soldier observes more carefully the limitations imposed upon him by his professional obligations and responsibilities, he will in fact be helping to undermine the control his civilian superiors exercise over him. For the separation of powers provides, as one writer has aptly phrased it, "a perpetual invitation, if not an irresistible force, drawing military leaders into political conflicts." In these circumstances, it will be a rare political opposition that will resist taking the field commander's criticisms (or the criticisms of one or more members of the Joint Chiefs) to the nation in order to capture political power by exploiting the American public's temperamental inability or unwillingness to fight anything less than total war. As it is, the institutional and psychological jealousies between the President and Congress, the irresponsible opposition which profits politically from Administration weaknesses and failures, the weak party discipline, and the possibility of a mid-term upset, seriously limit even a strong chief executive's degree of "peacetime" diplomatic freedom and ability to carry on his own foreign policy without succumbing, at least to some degree, to his opponent's program. The link between the opposition party and the general in the field, particularly a popular general, will intensify this tendency.

But basically the problem of preserving effective civilian control and minimizing the possibilities of the soldier–opposition party liaison is a question of how rapidly the American people adjust their traditional approach to foreign policy under the pressures and tensions of the cold war: how quickly they learn that they cannot at one moment preoccupy themselves with domestic affairs to the almost complete neglect of foreign policy, and at the next moment, when the enemy menace has become clear, focus all their attention and energies upon his utter destruction; how soon they accept the constantly recurring limited challenges, even limited wars, without the kind of intense and desperate frustration which might spill over either into total war or isolation. The process of learning is necessarily a slow one. "Taken as a whole," Robert Osgood has said, "the American record in foreign policy since 1945 is a remarkable adaptation to novel and challenging circumstances." Nevertheless, this record "does not show a real adjustment, either in its underlying conceptions of force and politics or in its concrete policies, to the imperatives of a strategy capable of resisting limited aggression by limited means. Such adaptation is bound to be encumbered by the weight of traditional habits of mind resisting the pressure of unprecedented events."

The time of such adaptation can, however, be shortened in the armed forces through education. Officers should receive a broader training than they have in the past so that they become aware of the wider context in which military policies have to be decided. Some civilians may fear that military men with a fuller understanding of the political and economic conditions that affect military strategy will be able to present their military points of view more effectively and thereby undermine civilian authority. In fact, such officers, precisely because they are aware of the broader framework of policy, are least likely to threaten civilian supremacy. The MacArthur case, to be sure, might prove otherwise; but the MacArthurs, who are willing to challenge their governments openly in an effort to change official policy to one more in accordance with their own political predilections, are a rarity. The Mark Clarks, Van Fleets, and Turner Joys, with their strong belief that war is a nonpolitical instrument and that wars can only be won if the politicians and diplomats do not "interfere" in them are not a rarity. It is for them that Clausewitz wrote that "the art of war in its highest point of view becomes a policy, but, of course, a policy which fights battles instead of writing notes. According to this view, it is an unpermissible and even harmful distinction, according to which a great military event or the plan for such an event should admit a *purely military judgment;* indeed, it is an unreasonable procedure to consult professional soldiers on the plan of war, that they may give a *purely military opinion* . . . [For] war is an instrument of policy; it must necessarily bear the character of policy; it must measure with policy's measure. The conduct of war, in its great outlines, is, therefore, policy itself, which takes up the sword in place of the pen, but does not on that account cease to think according to its own laws." The traditional American belief in the separation of military and nonmilitary factors may not have been harmful during a period of isolation; it cannot, unless revised, fail to be harmful, even disastrous, at a time of global involvement.

Additional Reading

Herbert Agar, *The Price of Power: America Since 1945* (1955).

Eric F. Goldman, *The Crucial Decade and After: America, 1945–1960* (1961 ed.).

Norman A. Graebner, *The New Isolationism* (1956).

Trumbull Higgins, *Korea and the Fall of MacArthur* (1960).

Walter Johnson, *1600 Pennsylvania Avenue: Presidents and the People, 1929–1959* (1960).

G. F. Kennan, *Realities of American Foreign Policy* (1954).

Harry S. Truman, *Memoirs* (2 vols., 1956).

Allen S. Whiting, *China Crosses the Yalu* (1960).

21 *CURRENTS IN AMERICAN FOREIGN POLICY SINCE 1952*

The readings in this chapter do not focus on a specific historical problem but were selected to illustrate the main thrust and tenor of the Eisenhower-Dulles era and the early years of the Kennedy administration. The Republicans triumphed in the 1952 presidential election by concentrating on a growing public unhappiness with the Korean War in particular and the Cold War in general, plus the issues of domestic corruption and alleged Communist infiltration in government. Secretary of State John Foster Dulles, until his retirement and death in 1959, played an unusually large role in shaping American foreign policies and an attempt was made under his guidance to effect a new departure promising dramatic successes at lower costs. Yet by the end of the Eisenhower period, most scholars and observers were agreed that the Republicans had been compelled to continue the essentials of the Truman-Acheson containment policy. The administration of President John F. Kennedy, succeeding in 1961, has not achieved any major changes in containment either, but in contrast to the Eisenhower administration it has greatly increased military spending for conventional and strategic nuclear weapons and has launched a new economic aid program for Latin America.

1. Dynamic Liberation and the New Look

The Republican platform in 1952 in effect promised to reverse the containment policy, allegedly immoral because it accepted the status quo and left millions of people in the satellite countries behind the Iron Curtain, and to seize the initiative with a new dynamic policy capable of putting Russia on the defensive and slowly pushing back Soviet power. In his pre-confirmation testimony before the Senate committee, the moralistic Dulles spoke of substituting "Peaceful Liberation" for containment. Subsequently, a new approach to Soviet aggressive thrusts on the periphery of the "free world" was announced. Instead of meeting attacks wherever they occurred and perhaps having American power drained by a number of Koreas in the future, the United States would reserve the right to retaliate instantly and massively with its atomic-hydrogen forces directly at the heart of Communist power in Soviet Russia. This approach led to a "New Look" in military policy: in contrast to the previous emphasis on balanced military forces armed both with conventional and atomic weapons, the new policy stressed expenditures on the atomic deterrent, or as a Secretary of Defense put it, the getting of a "bigger bang for the buck."

647

Senate Hearings on Dulles' Appointment to the State Department

Communist Enslavement of Free Peoples

. . . The CHAIRMAN. I am particularly interested in something I read recently, to the effect that you stated you were not in favor of the policy of containment. I think you advocated a more dynamic or positive policy.

Can you tell us more specifically what you have in mind? This, of course, is subject always to your own objections, if you think the question goes beyond a matter of qualifications.

Mr. DULLES. There are a number of policy matters which I would prefer to discuss with the committee in executive session, but I have no objection to saying in open session what I have said before: namely, that we shall never have a secure peace or a happy world so long as Soviet communism dominates one-third of all of the peoples that there are, and is in the process of trying at least to extend its rule to many others.

These people who are enslaved are people who deserve to be free, and who, from our own selfish standpoint, ought to be free because if they are the servile instruments of aggressive despotism, they will eventually be welded into a force which will be highly dangerous to ourselves and to all of the free world.

Communist Defection

Therefore, we must always have in mind the liberation of these captive peoples. Now, liberation does not mean a war of liberation. Liberation can be accomplished by processes short of war. We have, as one example, not an ideal example, but it illustrates my point, the defection of Yugoslavia, under Tito from the domination of Soviet communism.

Well, that rule of Tito is not one which we admire, and it has many aspects of despotism, itself; but at least it illustrates that it is possible to disintegrate this present monolithic structure which, as I say, represents approximately one-third of all the people that there are in the world.

Soviet Russian-Chinese Alliance

The present tie between China and Moscow is an unholy arrangement which is contrary to the traditions, the hopes, the aspirations of the Chinese people. Certainly we cannot tolerate a continuance of that, or a welding of the 450 million people of China into the servile instruments of Soviet aggression.

Policy of Containment

Therefore, a policy which only aims at containing Russia where it now is, is, in itself, an unsound policy; but it is a policy which is bound to fail because a purely defensive policy never wins against an aggressive policy.

If our only policy is to stay where we are, we will be driven back. It is only by keeping alive the hope of liberation, by taking advantage of that wherever opportunity arises, that we will end this terrible peril which dominates the world, which imposes upon us such terrible sacrifices and so great fears for the future. But all of this can be done and must be done in ways which will not provoke a general war, or in ways which will not provoke an insurrection which would be crushed with bloody violence, such as was the case, for example, when the Russians instigated the Polish revolt, under General Bor, and merely sat by and watched them when the Germans exterminated those who were revolting.

Peaceful Liberation

It must be and can be a peaceful process, but those who do not believe that results can be accomplished by moral pressures, by the weight of propaganda, just do not know what they are talking about.

I ask you to recall the fact that Soviet communism, itself, has spread from controlling 200 million people some 7 years ago to controlling 800 million people today, and it has done that by methods of political warfare, psychological warfare and propaganda, and it has not actually used the Red Army as an open aggressive force in accomplishing that.

Surely what they can accomplish, we can accomplish.

Surely if they can use moral and psychological force, we can use it; and, to take a negative defeatist attitude is not an approach which is conducive to our own welfare, or in conformity with our own historical ideas. . . .

Speech of John Foster Dulles before the Council on Foreign Relations, January 12, 1954

It is now nearly a year since the Eisenhower administration took office. During that year I have often spoken of various parts of our foreign policies. Tonight I should like to present an overall view of those policies which relate to our security.

First of all, let us recognize that many of the preceding foreign policies were good. Aid to Greece and Turkey had checked the Communist drive to the Mediterranean. The European Recovery Program had helped the peoples of Western Europe to pull out of the postwar morass. The Western powers were steadfast in Berlin and overcame the blockade with their airlift. As a loyal member of the United Nations, we had reacted with force to repel the Communist attack in Korea. When that effort exposed our military weakness, we rebuilt rapidly our military establishment. We also sought a quick buildup of armed strength in Western Europe.

These were the acts of a nation which saw the danger of Soviet communism; which realized that its own safety was tied up with that of others; which was capable of responding boldly and promptly to emergencies. These are precious values to be acclaimed. Also, we can pay tribute to congressional bipartisanship which puts the nation above politics.

But we need to recall that what we did was in the main emergency action, imposed on us by our enemies.

Let me illustrate.

1. We did not send our army into Korea because we judged in advance that it was sound military strategy to commit our Army to fight land battles in Asia. Our decision had been to pull out of Korea. It was Soviet-inspired action that pulled us back.

2. We did not decide in advance that it was wise to grant billions annually as foreign economic aid. We adopted that policy in response to the Communist efforts to sabotage the free economies of Western Europe.

3. We did not build up our military establishment at a rate which involved huge budget deficits, a depreciating currency, and a feverish economy because this seemed, in advance, a good policy. Indeed, we decided otherwise until the Soviet military threat was clearly revealed.

We live in a world where emergencies are always possible, and our survival may depend upon our capacity to meet emergencies. Let us pray that we shall always have that capacity. But, having said that, it is necessary also to say that emergency measures—however good for the emergency—do not necessarily make good permanent policies. Emergency measures are costly; they are superficial; and they imply that the enemy has the initiative. They cannot be depended on to serve our long-time interests.

The Need for Long-Range Policies

This "long time" factor is of critical importance.

The Soviet Communists are planning for what they call "an entire historical era," and we should do the same. They seek, through many types of maneuvers, gradually to divide and weaken the free nations by overextending them in efforts which, as Lenin put it, are "beyond their strength, so that they come to practical bankruptcy." Then, said Lenin, "our victory is assured." Then, said Stalin, will be "the moment for the decisive blow."

In the face of this strategy, measures cannot be judged adequate merely because they ward off an immediate danger. It is essential to do this, but it is also essential to do so without exhausting ourselves.

When the Eisenhower administration applied this test, we felt that some transformations were needed.

It is not sound military strategy permanently to commit U.S. land forces to Asia to a degree that leaves us no strategic reserves.

It is not sound economics, or good foreign policy to support permanently other countries; for in the long run, that creates as much ill will as good will.

Also, it is not sound to become permanently committed to military expenditures so vast that they lead to "practical bankruptcy."

Change was imperative to assure the stamina needed for permanent security. But it was equally imperative that change should be accompanied by understanding of our true purposes. Sudden and spectacular change had to be avoided. Otherwise, there might have been a panic among our friends and miscalculated aggression by our enemies. We can, I believe, make a good report in these respects.

We need allies and collective security. Our purpose is to make these relations more effective, less costly. This can be done by placing more reliance on deterrent power and less dependence on local defensive power.

This is accepted practice so far as local communities are concerned. We keep locks on our doors, but we do not have an armed guard in every home. We rely principally on a community security system so well equipped to punish any who break in and steal that, in fact, would-be aggressors are generally deterred. That is the modern way of getting maximum protection at a bearable cost.

What the Eisenhower administration seeks is a similar international security system. We want, for ourselves and the other free nations, a maximum deterrent at a bearable cost.

Local defense will always be important. But there is no local defense which alone will contain the mighty landpower of the Communist world. Local defenses must be reinforced by the further deterrent of massive retaliatory power. A potential aggressor must know that he cannot always prescribe battle conditions that suit him. Otherwise, for example, a potential aggressor, who is glutted with manpower, might be tempted to attack in confidence that resistance would be confined to manpower. He might be tempted to attack in places where his superiority was decisive.

The way to deter aggression is for the free community to be willing and able to respond vigorously at places and with means of its own choosing.

So long as our basic policy concepts were unclear, our military leaders could not be selective in building our military power. If an enemy could pick his time and place and method of warfare—and if our policy was to remain the traditional one of meeting aggression by direct and local opposition—then we needed to be ready to fight in the Arctic and in the Tropics; in Asia, the Near East, and in Europe; by sea, by land, and by air; with old weapons and with new weapons.

The total cost of our security efforts, at home and abroad, was over $50 billion per annum, and involved, for 1953, a projected budgetary deficit of $9 billion; and $11 billion for 1954. This was on top of taxes comparable to wartime taxes; and the dollar was depreciating in effective value. Our allies were similarly weighed down. This could not be continued for long without grave budgetary, economic, and social consequences.

But before military planning could be changed, the President and his advisers, as represented by the National Security Council, had to take some basic policy decisions. This has been done. The basic decision was to depend primarily upon a great capacity to retaliate, instantly, by means and at places of our choosing. Now the Department of Defense and the Joint Chiefs of Staff can shape our military establishment to fit what is *our* policy, instead of having to try to be ready to meet the enemy's many choices. That permits of a selection of military means instead of a multi-plication of means. As a result, it is now possible to get, and share, more basic security at less cost. . . .

2. Criticisms of Eisenhower's Foreign Policies

Long before the end of Eisenhower's second term it was obvious that (1) the chief diplomatic contribution of the Eisenhower period was merely the further extension of defensive alliances around the globe to contain Communist expan-sion; and (2) that the tragic aftermath of the 1956 Hungarian Revolution had revealed the bankruptcy of "liberation" policies. The United States had to a degree encouraged this type of revolt against Communist masters but when it occurred feared to intervene lest World War III be precipitated. A "balance of terror" in the new weapons had been reached between the United States and Soviet Russia which precluded dramatic changes in favor of either side.

In October of 1957, Soviet Russia scored a technological and psychological triumph in launching the first earth satellite (Sputnik) and thereafter indicated that it possessed a decisive lead over the United States in the ballistics mis-siles field. When the American Defense Secretary in 1959 admitted that if Russia built to capacity it might have a 3 to 1 missile lead over the United States by the early 1960's, a number of alarmed critics, Democrats and Re-publicans, began to speak of imminent national danger and to urge heavy defense spending to overcome the "missile gap." Subsequently, revised intel-ligence estimates of actual Soviet production and increased American pro-curement largely eliminated the alleged gap.

In the following selection, Democratic Senator J. William Fulbright of Arkansas, Chairman of the Senate Foreign Relations Committee, criticized the Eisenhower administration for a general failure to respond creatively to foreign policy challenges.

Speech by Senator Fulbright,
March 5, 1960

Mr. FULBRIGHT. Mr. President, the Congress of the United States has been in session for 2 months. During that period we have heard the President in his report on the state of the Union assure the American people that all is right with the world, and that our freedoms and our place in the world are secure.

We have received his budget message and been assured again that all is well—indeed, very good, because we look forward to a budget surplus, albeit we must do without new schools and better missiles. . . .

We have debated the state of our defenses and argued whether by 1962 the Soviet superiority in missiles would be 3 to 1 or maybe only 2 to 1. . . .

Where do we stand today?

A nation with a gross national product that will soon hit a peacetime high of $500 billion and with a per capita income of over $2,500—nearly

double that of any other nation—is debating the extent to which our
Armed Forces may be inferior to those of the Soviet Union.

If there is confusion about the facts, some things are clear. It is humiliating that the debate should have to occur. Its occurrence is evidence of
our failures. It is a revelation of our lack of foresight of possessing great
riches yet failing to use them to make ourselves, and keep ourselves, the
world's strongest power, although to do less is to invite national extinction.

Mr. Khrushchev, having outrun us, is not one to let our grass grow
under his feet. "It would be naive to think," he has said, "that we are
going to sit with arms folded" while the Americans "make every effort to
raise their rocketry from the state it is now in and reach a better position."
But before considering this let us place the problem in perspective.

Men have anciently yearned for a universal commonwealth. Now we
have it of sorts. But it is a commonwealth of fear kept going by a precarious balance of terror, a chilling oscillation between negotiation and
incineration.

We endure in an era of total crisis. The great truths are denied. Black
becomes white, the horizontal vertical. Whole states—as Estonia, Latvia,
Lithuania and lately Tibet—sink from sight. Whole countries—as Hungary—languish behind bars. An ancient culture such as China's is shattered and remade overnight into the largest anthill slave state men have
ever known. . . .

We have never faced an antagonist quite like this one. The Soviet
Union swiftly leaped from the oxcart to the moon. It rose from a second-
rate underdeveloped country to loom menacingly over the world.

Master of complex technologies, primitive and advanced, her soldiers
march with black bread in their hands and the awful secrets of nuclear
fission in their minds. Their leaders are obsessed by a dedicated sense of
mission to dominate all mankind. . . .

Elsewhere, a colossal specter rises in the Far East. It commands the
world's largest labor force. At this time 100 million people—a group exceeding half of our total population—are building the world's greatest
network of hydroelectric stations, irrigation canals, and dams. Red China
is attempting within one generation an enterprise greater than any undertaken by man: that of catching up, in this short time, with the most advanced industrialized nations. Many experts believe she will become a
major industrial power during the late 1960's.

China's vast population grows. Soon 1 in 3, or 1 in 4, of all men will
be Chinese. Awesomely industrious, tough, inured to hardship, China's
millions are as the fingers of the hand manipulated by their determined
and ruthless masters. They direct a revolution unparalleled in its dimen-
sions which in its pitilessness, has swiftly destroyed a culture ancient
when Christ was born.

We may expect that within foreseeable time the fingers will become a
clenched fist prepared to smash all that stands in the path of China's
domination of the Asian reaches, their resources, and the nearly three-
quarters of a billion people who inhabit them.

Returning to the Soviet Union we find that Mr. Khrushchev even as he

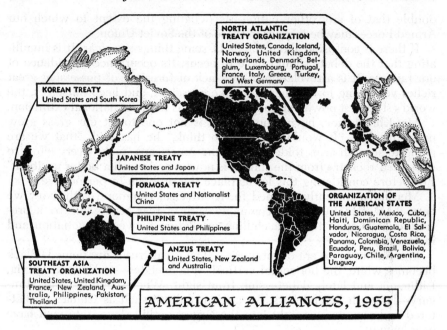

NORTH ATLANTIC TREATY ORGANIZATION
United States, Canada, Iceland, Norway, United Kingdom, Netherlands, Denmark, Belgium, Luxembourg, Portugal, France, Italy, Greece, Turkey, and West Germany

KOREAN TREATY
United States and South Korea

JAPANESE TREATY
United States and Japan

FORMOSA TREATY
United States and Nationalist China

PHILIPPINE TREATY
United States and Philippines

ANZUS TREATY
United States, New Zealand and Australia

ORGANIZATION OF THE AMERICAN STATES
United States, Mexico, Cuba, Haiti, Dominican Republic, Honduras, Guatemala, El Salvador, Nicaragua, Costa Rica, Panama, Colombia, Venezuela, Ecuador, Peru, Brazil, Bolivia, Paraguay, Chile, Argentina, Uruguay

SOUTHEAST ASIA TREATY ORGANIZATION
United States, United Kingdom, France, New Zealand, Australia, Philippines, Pakistan, Thailand

AMERICAN ALLIANCES, 1955

bade goodby to his American hosts,* repeated what he has often said: Communism would take us over. Given communism's unrelenting objective—world domination—this goal is logical. We must be the first to go by one means or another. For when the free world's shield is broken those whom it shelters become defenseless.

We have been warned, but have we heard? If we should perish it will not be for lack of warning but for lack of the will to survive.

In this context there is something new under the sun. It is a newness illuminated by the fact that the sun itself is no longer inviolate and unattainable. For the first time a would-be conqueror could win the world; win it in perhaps 30 minutes. He might succeed where others, from Genghis Khan to Hitler, had failed.

How almost overwhelming, then, must be the temptation to such a one to act? How nearly irresistible the compulsion to use his ocean-spanning, catastrophic weapons? How intoxicating the vision that, winning, the world would be one state to do his bidding with its people as his puppets, its continents as his provinces, and its seas as his lakes?

How must the aspirant conqueror be moved when he contrasts the position of his country and ours at the end of the war—only 15 years ago —and today? For among nations, as among individuals, what ultimately counts is not being but becoming.

At the war's end we were, incomparably, the world's strongest power, commanding the mightiest fighting force ever assembled, and a monopoly of atomic weapons. Our wartime casualties had been small, our homeland was untouched, our farms and factories had hugely expanded. The world's

* Khrushchev toured the United States in September 1959.

gold flowed to us. The world's trade fell to us as former rivals were removed from competition. We stood upon the heights of power, prestige, riches. We had arrived.

What of the Soviet Union in 1945? She did not announce her casualties lest they reveal her grave weakness. But they were on the order of 20 million people. She suffered an enormous loss of houses, factories, power-plants, domestic animals. Many thought that for years to come her energies would be absorbed by domestic reconstruction.

But she quickly repaired her war damages. Then she built a giant heavy industry, created new cities, opened vast new lands to cultivation. Above all she advanced education in a mighty surge of passionate and determined effort. . . .

Forty-four years ago communism was confined to a rented room in Zurich, Switzerland. Today it dominates one-third of the earth containing 40 percent of the population and a third of the industrial power. . . .

Surprisingly to the West, the Soviet Union exploded an atomic bomb only 4 years after the war's end. Four years later she exploded a hydrogen bomb. Now abreast of us in this field she forged ahead of us in the conquest of space as she launched man's first satellite and was first to the moon.

She maintains vast armies, and a navy second to ours. No power has ever had, in peacetime, so many submarines. They number 450; two-thirds of them long-range ocean patrol types. In 1956 alone Soviet shipyards built 100 submarines, or one every third or fourth day during the year. This is as many submarines as we have in our entire fleet.

In addition the Soviet Union is mounting a worldwide trade offensive aimed primarily at us. Hence the challenge to us is total. It involves the military, the political, the intellectual, and the industrial. The measures of our antagonist cannot be countered by half-measures or by halfhearted competition.

If, Mr. Khrushchev must reason, his country has come so far so fast, how much will it forge ahead of us in the future unless we greatly step up our pace in education, weapons, foreign aid, and foreign trade? But how shall we excel in these fields if we are more concerned with keeping up with the Joneses than surpassing the challenges of Khrushchevs?

How shall others appraise us—to consider only one phase of the struggle—in the light of Dr. Wernher von Braun's remarks about the conquest of space?

Last year he said the Russians disregarded our efforts. "The Russians appear so sure of their technological leadership," he observed, "and their ability to retain the initiative that they do not even consider the possibility someone else might beat them to the moon."

They were right. They got there first.

Only the other day Dr. von Braun said we cannot overtake the Soviet Union in the space race "for several years." It is "still moving faster than us," and he would "not be surprised" if it placed the first man in orbit this year.

President Eisenhower denies we are in a space race. But ordinary men believe we are in the race and are behind the pacesetter. Mr. Eisenhower also denies that our prestige has been lowered by our poor showing in space.

Here he is contradicted by an administration member, Mr. George V. Allen, head of the U.S. Information Agency. He says that the effect of Sputnik I was to "plunge the U.S. scientific prestige far below that of the Soviet Union" in critical India, Italy, Turkey, and elsewhere.

Many, in a world dominated by science, regard us as occupying a second-rate position in science. How long will it be before they fatally downgrade us to the status of second-rate power?

Mr. Eisenhower is also in sharp conflict with critics of our defenses. He treats them contemptuously. He was not disturbed, he said, "because anyone with a parochial viewpoint says the bosses know nothing about it."

Generals are not to reason why. Their Commander in Chief complains that "too many generals have all sorts of ideas." . . .

Yet this is the somber reality. Mr. Eisenhower, by virtue of his powers as President of the United States and Commander in Chief of its Armed Forces is the only man alive whose decisions about our armaments, if faulty, could cause the free world to be lost in an afternoon.

But he has dubbed those who disagree with his judgments as "noisy extremists"; men unpatriotic because they have "the tendency to disparage our country," while they are also dishonest because their asser tions are "spurious"; that is, they are fake.

The group so condemned includes such distinguished soldiers as former Army Chiefs of Staff Generals Ridgway and Taylor, Gen. James M. Gavin, former Chief of Army Research and Development, and General Power, present Chief of the Strategic Air Command; such distinguished journalists as Joseph Alsop and Walter Lippmann, and such research organizations as the Rand Corp. and the Rockefeller Bros. Fund. . . .

Perhaps more disturbing is the President's assertion to a press conference that he knows more than "almost anyone" about military matters. This is dangerous because the President's attitudes foreclose discussion while precluding reason; deter military men, fearful of their careers, from speaking up; encourage the dominance of yes-men, and tend to drive superior men from the service. Such men are repelled by assumptions of omniscience this side of heaven. . . .

These men believe that our survival is imperiled; that we are not doing enough to assure our security to the greatest degree possible; that we should do more; and if it costs more to do more we ought to pay for it in the spirit of "damn the torpedoes, go ahead."

But let there be no mistake about this. If we are to have peace we must have a high degree of discipline at home. We must understand—and the President is the only man among us who can bring this forcibly to the Nation—that waging peace in our times is a task of formidable proportions second only to waging war.

The successful waging of peace requires a vigorous national administration, an informed people, and a mature people who know that you cannot be adult without being willing to pay for what you want. It is only in heaven that you can eat your cake and have it too.

This is the melancholy pass to which we have come. It is like the common story of the rich, miserly recluse found starving in a garret. There has never been a time when we did not have the resources of men, money, and access to knowledge that might have given us a wide lead over any aggressor and made attack upon us suicidal. Yet we have apparently believed we could not afford to spend enough to secure our liberties.

Let us again hear from *Life* magazine, a longtime, devoted supporter of this administration. In its issue of February 15, 1960, *Life* says editorially:

> President Eisenhower's defense budget is dangerously deficient. He has great military experience and deep confidence his $41 billion program is adequate. But harsh facts argue it isn't.
>
> The harshest fact is that by the President's own intelligence estimates, the Soviets by 1963 will have twice as many ICBM's as we—enough by SAC Commander Thomas Power's warning, to wipe out all our bases and retaliatory planes in one salvo.
>
> In order to do all that needs to be done we are convinced that the United States must spend on defense, at the very least, $2 billion more than it is now planning.

3. Kennedy: A More Vigorous Foreign Policy

A few days after taking office, President John F. Kennedy outlined to Congress and the nation the more energetic policies he intended to pursue in defense and foreign affairs. The "New Frontier" in military policy was in essence a return to the Truman program of maintaining adequate conventional as well as nuclear arms; in foreign policy, it meant a de-emphasis on military pacts as the way to halt the spread of Communism and a renewed program of economic aid to underdeveloped countries via governmental grants and loans, in conjunction with the cooperation of the prosperous countries of Western Europe.

President Kennedy's 1961 State of the Union Message

. . . But all these problems pale when placed beside those which confront us around the world. No man entering upon this office, regardless of his party, regardless of his previous service in Washington, could fail to be staggered upon learning—even in this brief 10-day period—the harsh enormity of the trials through which we must pass in the next four years. Each day the crises multiply. Each day their solution grows more difficult. Each day we draw nearer the hour of maximum danger, as weapons spread and hostile forces grow stronger. I feel I must inform the Congress that our analyses over the last 10 days make it clear that—in each of these principal areas of crises—the tide of events has been running out and time has not been our friend.

In Asia, the relentless pressures of the Chinese Communists menace the security of the entire area—from the borders of India and South Viet Nam to the jungles of Laos, struggling to protect its newly won independence. We seek in Laos what we seek in all Asia, and, indeed, in all the world— freedom for the people and independence for their government. This Nation shall persevere in our pursuit of these objectives. . . .

In Latin America, Communist agents seeking to exploit that region's peaceful revolution of hope have established a base on Cuba, only 90 miles from our shores. Our objection with Cuba is not over the people's drive for a better life. Our objection is to their domination by foreign and domestic tyrannies. Cuban social and economic reform should be encouraged. Questions of economic and trade policy can always be negotiated. But Communist domination in this hemisphere can never be negotiated. . . .

Our greatest challenge is still the world that lies beyond the cold war— but the first great obstacle is still our relations with the Soviet Union and Communist China. We must never be lulled into believing that either power has yielded its ambitions for world domination—ambitions which they forcefully restated only a short time ago. On the contrary, our task is to convince them that aggression and subversion will not be profitable routes to pursue those ends. Open and peaceful competition—for prestige, for markets, for scientific achievement, even for men's minds—is something else again. For if freedom and communism were to compete for man's allegiance in a world at peace, I would look to the future with ever increasing confidence.

To meet this array of challenges—to fulfill the role we cannot avoid on the world scene—we must reexamine and revise our whole arsenal of tools.

One must not overshadow the other. On the Presidential coat of arms, the American eagle holds in his right talon the olive branch, while in his left is held a bundle of arrows. We intend to give equal attention to both.

First, we must strengthen our military tools. We are moving into a period of uncertain risk and great commitment in which both the military and diplomatic possibilities require a free world force so powerful as to make any aggression clearly futile. Yet in the past, lack of a consistent, coherent military strategy, the absence of basic assumptions about our national requirements and the faulty estimates and duplication arising from interservice rivalries have all made it difficult to assess accurately how adequate—or inadequate—our defenses really are.

I have, therefore, instructed the Secretary of Defense to reappraise our entire defense strategy—our ability to fulfill our commitments—the effectiveness, vulnerability, and dispersal of our strategic bases, forces, and warning systems—the efficiency and economy of our operation and organization—the elimination of obsolete bases and installations—and the adequacy, modernization, and mobility of our present conventional and nuclear forces and weapons systems in the light of present and future dangers. I have asked for preliminary conclusions by the end of February —and I shall then recommend whatever legislative, budgetary, or executive action is needed in the light of these conclusions.

In the meantime, I have asked the Defense Secretary to initiate immediately three new steps clearly needed now:

(a) I have directed prompt action to increase our airlift capacity. Obtaining additional air transport mobility—and obtaining it now—will better assure the ability of our conventional forces to respond, with discrimination and speed, to any problem at any spot on the globe at any moment's notice. In particular it will enable us to meet any deliberate effort to avoid or divert our forces by starting limited wars in widely scattered parts of the globe.

(b) I have directed prompt action to step up our Polaris submarine program. Using unobligated shipbuilding funds now (to let contracts originally scheduled for the next fiscal year) will build and place on station—at least 9 months earlier than planned—substantially more units of a crucial deterrent—a fleet that will never attack first, but possess sufficient powers of retaliation, concealed beneath the seas, to discourage any aggressor from launching an attack on our security.

(c) I have directed prompt action to accelerate our entire missile program. . . . If we are to keep the peace, we need an invulnerable missile force powerful enough to deter any aggressor from even threatening an attack he would know could not destroy enough of our own force to prevent his own destruction. For as I said upon taking the oath of office: "Only when our arms are sufficient beyond doubt can we be certain beyond doubt that they will never be employed."

Secondly, we must improve our economic tools. Our role is essential and unavoidable in the construction of a sound and expanding economy for the entire non-Communist world, helping other nations build the strength to meet their own problems, to satisfy their own aspirations, and to surmount their own dangers. The problems in achieving this goal are towering and unprecedented—the response must be towering and unprecedented as well, much as lend-lease and the Marshall plan were in earlier years, which brought such fruitful results.

(a) I intend to ask the Congress for authority to establish a new and more effective program for assisting the economic, educational, and social development of other countries and continents. That program must stimulate and take more effectively into account the contributions of our allies, and provide central policy direction for all our own programs that now so often overlap, conflict, or diffuse our energies, and resources. Such a program, compared to past programs, will require—

more flexibility for short-run emergencies;

more commitment to long-term development;

new attention to education at all levels;

greater emphasis on the recipient nations' role, their effort and their purpose, with greater social justice for their own people, with broader distribution and participation of their people, and more efficient public administration and more efficient tax systems of their own.

and orderly planning for national and regional development instead of a piecemeal approach. . . .

(c) To our sister Republics to the south, we have pledged a new alliance for progress—alianza para progreso. Our goal is a free and prosperous Latin America, realizing for all its states and their citizens a degree of economic and social progress that matches their historic contributions of culture, intellect, and liberty. To start this Nation's role at this time in that alliance of neighbors, I am recommending the following:

That the Congress appropriate in full the $500 million fund pledged by the Act of Bogotá, to be used not as an instrument of the cold war, but as a first step in the sound development of the Americas.

That a new Inter-Departmental Task Force be established under the leadership of the Department of State, to coordinate at the highest level all policies and programs of concern to the Americas.

That our delegates to the OAS, working with those of other members, strengthen that body as an instrument to preserve the peace and to prevent foreign domination anywhere in the hemisphere.

That, in cooperation with other nations, we launch a new hemispheric attack on illiteracy and inadequate educational opportunities at all levels; and, finally,

That a food-for-peace mission be sent immediately to Latin America to explore ways in which our vast food abundance can be used to help end hunger and malnutrition in certain areas of suffering in our own hemisphere.

(d) This administration is expanding its new food-for-peace program in every possible way. The product of our abundance must be more effectively used to relieve hunger and help economic growth in all corners of the globe. I have asked the director of this program to recommend additional ways in which these surpluses can advance the interests of world peace—including the establishment of world food reserves.

(e) An even more valuable national asset is our reservoir of dedicated men and women—not only on our college campuses but in every age group—who have indicated their desire to contribute their skills, their efforts, and a part of their lives to the fight for world order. We can mobilize this talent through the formation of a National Peace Corps, enlisting the services of all those with the desire and capacity to help foreign lands meet their urgent needs for trained personnel.

(f) Finally, while our attention is centered on the development of the non-Communist world, we must never forget our hopes for the ultimate freedom and welfare of the eastern European peoples. In order to be prepared to help reestablish historic ties of friendship, I am asking the Congress for increased discretion to use economic tools in this area whenever this is found to be clearly in the national interest. This will require amendment of the Mutual Defense Assistance Control Act along the lines I proposed as a member of the Senate, and upon which the Senate voted last summer. Meanwhile, I hope to explore with the Polish Government the possibility of using our frozen Polish funds on projects of peace that will demonstrate our abiding friendship and interest in the people of Poland.

Third, we must sharpen our political and diplomatic tools—the means of cooperation and agreement on which an enforceable world order must ultimately rest.

(*a*) I have already taken steps to coordinate and expand our disarmament effort—to increase our programs of research and study—and to make arms control a central goal of our national policy under my personal direction. The deadly arms race, and the huge resources it absorbs, have too long overshadowed all else we must do. We must prevent that arms race from spreading to new nations, to new nuclear powers, and to the reaches of outer space. We must make certain that our negotiators are better informed and better prepared—to formulate workable proposals of our own and to make sound judgments about the proposals of others.

I have asked the other governments concerned to agree to a reasonable delay in the talks on a nuclear test ban—and it is our intention to resume negotiations prepared to reach a final agreement with any nation, that is equally willing to agree to an effective and enforceable treaty.

(*b*) We must increase our support of the United Nations as an instrument to end the cold war instead of an arena in which to fight it. . . .

(*c*) Finally, this administration intends to explore promptly all possible areas of cooperation with the Soviet Union and other nations "to invoke the wonders of science instead of its terrors." Specifically, I now invite all nations—including the Soviet Union—to join with us in developing a weather prediction program, in a new communications satellite program, and in preparation for probing the distant planets of Mars and Venus, probes which may someday unlock the deepest secrets of the universe.

Today this country is ahead in the science and technology of space, while the Soviet Union is ahead in the capacity to lift large vehicles into orbit. Both nations would help themselves as well as other nations by removing these endeavors from the bitter and wasteful competition of the cold war. The United States would be willing to join with the Soviet Union and the scientists of all nations in a greater effort to make the fruits of this new knowledge available to all—and, beyond that, in an effort to extend farm technology to hungry nations—to wipe out disease— to increase exchanges of scientists and their knowledge—and to make our own laboratories available to technicians of other lands who lack the facilities to pursue their own work. Where nature makes natural allies of us all, we can demonstrate that beneficial relations are possible even with those with whom we most deeply disagree—and this must someday be the basis of world peace and world law. . . .

4. Cuba: the "Eyeball to Eyeball" Confrontation

The revolutionary regime of Fidel Castro in Cuba increasingly manifested Marxian Communist overtones in 1960 and continued its violent denunciation of alleged Yankee imperialism in the Western Hemisphere. The harassment caused President Eisenhower to break diplomatic relations with Cuba in January, 1961. President Kennedy continued his anti-Castro policy, although the attempted invasion of Cuba at the Bay of Pigs by Cuban exile forces in April, 1961 was a fiasco. When Soviet Russia not only underwrote Cuba financially and sent numerous technicians to help stabilize its chaotic economy, but also sought to establish a missile base there, President Kennedy met the challenge firmly. In October, 1962, he offered Khrushchev the alternative of a withdrawal or an armed confrontation. After a brief hesitation, Khrushchev agreed to remove the missiles and bombers.

The Castro regime remained, however, and Republican critics early in 1963 charged that Kennedy had failed to ensure by land inspection that the threat had been completely removed, and that inadequate measures had been taken to eliminate Castroism from the Caribbean.

The Soviet Threat to the Americas: Address by President Kennedy, October 22, 1962

Good evening, my fellow citizens. This Government, as promised, has maintained the closest surveillance of the Soviet military buildup on the island of Cuba. Within the past week unmistakable evidence has established the fact that a series of offensive missile sites is now in preparation on that imprisoned island. The purpose of these bases can be none other than to provide a nuclear strike capability against the Western Hemisphere. . . .

The characteristics of these new missile sites indicate two distinct types of installations. Several of them include medium-range ballistic missiles capable of carrying a nuclear warhead for a distance of more than 1,000 nautical miles. Each of these missiles, in short, is capable of striking Washington, D.C., the Panama Canal, Cape Canaveral, Mexico City, or any other city in the southeastern part of the United States, in Central America, or in the Caribbean area.

Additional sites not yet completed appear to be designed for intermediate-range ballistic missiles capable of traveling more than twice as far—and thus capable of striking most of the major cities in the Western Hemisphere, ranging as far north as Hudson Bay, Canada, and as far south as Lima, Peru. In addition, jet bombers, capable of carrying nuclear weapons, are now being uncrated and assembled in Cuba, while the necessary air bases are being prepared.

This urgent transformation of Cuba into an important strategic base—by the presence of these large, long-range, and clearly offensive weapons of sudden mass destruction—constitutes an explicit threat to the peace and security of all the Americas, in flagrant and deliberate defiance of the Rio Pact of 1947, the traditions of this nation and hemisphere, the Joint Resolution of the 87th Congress, the Charter of the United Nations, and my own public warnings to the Soviets on September 4 and 13.

Soviet Contradictions Cited

This action also contradicts the repeated assurances of Soviet spokesmen, both publicly and privately delivered, that the arms buildup in Cuba would retain its original defensive character and that the Soviet Union had no need or desire to station strategic missiles on the territory of any other nation.

The size of this undertaking makes clear that it has been planned for some months. Yet only last month, after I had made clear the distinction between any introduction of ground-to-ground missiles and the existence of defensive antiaircraft missiles, the Soviet Government publicly stated on September 11 that, and I quote, "The armaments and military equipment sent to Cuba are designed exclusively for defensive purposes," and, and I quote the Soviet Government, "There is no need for the Soviet Government to shift its weapons for a retaliatory blow to any other country, for instance Cuba," and that, and I quote the Government, "The Soviet Union has so powerful rockets to carry these nuclear warheads that there is no need to search for sites for them beyond the boundaries of the Soviet Union." That statement was false.

Only last Thursday, as evidence of this rapid offensive buildup was already in my hand, Soviet Foreign Minister Gromyko told me in my office that he was instructed to make it clear once again, as he said his Government had already done, that Soviet assistance to Cuba, and I quote, "pursued solely the purpose of contributing to the defense capabilities of Cuba," that, and I quote him, "training by Soviet specialists of Cuban nationals in handling defensive armaments was by no means offensive," and that "if it were otherwise," Mr. Gromyko went on, "the Soviet Government would never become involved in rendering such assistance." That statement also was false.

No Room for Deception

Neither the United States of America nor the world community of nations can tolerate deliberate deception and offensive threats on the part of any nation, large or small. We no longer live in a world where only the actual firing of weapons represents a sufficient challenge to a nation's security to constitute maximum peril. Nuclear weapons are so destructive and ballistic missiles are so swift that any substantially increased possibility of their use or any sudden change in their deployment may well be regarded as a definite threat to peace.

For many years both the Soviet Union and the United States, recognizing this fact, have deployed strategic nuclear weapons with great care, never upsetting the precarious *status quo* which insured that these weapons would not be used in the absence of some vital challenge. Our own strategic missiles have never been transferred to the territory of any other nation under a cloak of secrecy and deception; and our history, unlike that of the Soviets since the end of World War II, demonstrates that we have no desire to dominate or conquer any other nation or impose our system upon its people. Nevertheless, American citizens have become adjusted to living daily on the bull's eye of Soviet missiles located inside the U.S.S.R. or in submarines.

In that sense missiles in Cuba add to an already clear and present danger—although it should be noted the nations of Latin America have never previously been subjected to a potential nuclear threat.

But this secret, swift, and extraordinary buildup of Communist missiles —in an area well known to have a special and historical relationship to the United States and the nations of the Western Hemisphere, in violation of Soviet assurances, and in defiance of American and hemispheric policy—this sudden, clandestine decision to station strategic weapons for the first time outside of Soviet soil—is a deliberately provocative and unjustified change in the *status quo* which cannot be accepted by this country if our courage and our commitments are ever to be trusted again by either friend or foe.

The 1930's taught us a clear lesson: Aggressive conduct, if allowed to grow unchecked and unchallenged, ultimately leads to war. This nation is opposed to war. We are also true to our word. Our unswerving objective, therefore, must be to prevent the use of these missiles against this or any other country and to secure their withdrawal or elimination from the Western Hemisphere.

Our policy has been one of patience and restraint, as befits a peaceful and powerful nation, which leads a worldwide alliance. We have been determined not to be diverted from our central concerns by mere irritants and fanatics. But now further action is required—and it is underway; and these actions may only be the beginning. We will not prematurely or unnecessarily risk the costs of worldwide nuclear war in which even the fruits of victory would be ashes in our mouth—but neither will we shrink from that risk at any time it must be faced.

Initial Steps Proposed

Acting, therefore, in the defense of our own security and of the entire Western Hemisphere, and under the authority entrusted to me by the Constitution as endorsed by the resolution of the Congress, I have directed that the following *initial* steps be taken immediately:

First: To halt this offensive buildup, a strict quarantine on all offensive military equipment under shipment to Cuba is being initiated. All ships of any kind bound for Cuba from whatever nation or port will, if found to contain cargoes of offensive weapons, be turned back. This quarantine will be extended, if needed, to other types of cargo and carriers. We are not at this time, however, denying the necessities of life as the Soviets attempted to do in their Berlin blockade of 1948.

Second: I have directed the continued and increased close surveillance of Cuba and its military buildup. The Foreign Ministers of the OAS [Organization of American States] in their communique of October 3 rejected secrecy on such matters in this hemisphere. Should these offensive military preparations continue, thus increasing the threat to the hemisphere, further action will be justified. I have directed the Armed Forces to prepare for any eventualities; and I trust that, in the interest of both the Cuban people and the Soviet technicians at the sites, the hazards to all concerned of continuing this threat will be recognized.

Third: It shall be the policy of this nation to regard any nuclear missile launched from Cuba against any nation in the Western Hemisphere as an attack by the Soviet Union on the United States, requiring a full retaliatory response upon the Soviet Union.

Fourth: As a necessary military precaution I have reinforced our base at Guantanamo, evacuated today the dependents of our personnel there, and ordered additional military units to be on a standby alert basis.

Fifth: We are calling tonight for an immediate meeting of the Organ of Consultation, under the Organization of American States, to consider this threat to hemispheric security and to invoke articles 6 and 8 of the Rio Treaty in support of all necessary action. The United Nations Charter allows for regional security arrangements—and the nations of this hemisphere decided long ago against the military presence of outside powers. Our other allies around the world have also been alerted.

Sixth: Under the Charter of the United Nations, we are asking tonight that an emergency meeting of the Security Council be convoked without delay to take action against this latest Soviet threat to world peace. Our resolution will call for the prompt dismantling and withdrawal of all offensive weapons in Cuba, under the supervision of U.N. observers, before the quarantine can be lifted.

Seventh and finally: I call upon Chairman Khrushchev to halt and eliminate this clandestine, reckless, and provocative threat to world peace and to stable relations between our two nations. I call upon him further to abandon this course of world domination and to join in an historic effort to end the perilous arms race and transform the history of man. He has an opportunity now to move the world back from the abyss of destruction—by returning to his Government's own words that it had no need to station missiles outside its own territory, and withdrawing these weapons from Cuba—by refraining from any action which will widen or deepen the present crisis—and then by participating in a search for peaceful and permanent solutions.

This nation is prepared to present its case against the Soviet threat to peace, and our own proposals for a peaceful world, at any time and in any forum—in the OAS, in the United Nations, or in any other meeting that could be useful—without limiting our freedom of action.

U.S. Wishes Peace with U.S.S.R.

We have in the past made strenuous efforts to limit the spread of nuclear weapons. We have proposed the elimination of all arms and military bases in a fair and effective disarmament treaty. We are prepared to discuss new proposals for the removal of tensions on both sides—including the possibilities of a genuinely independent Cuba, free to determine its own destiny. We have no wish to war with the Soviet Union, for we are a peaceful people who desire to live in peace with all other peoples.

But it is difficult to settle or even discuss these problems in an atmosphere of intimidation. That is why this latest Soviet threat—or any other threat which is made either independently or in response to our actions this week—must and will be met with determination. Any hostile move anywhere in the world against the safety and freedom of peoples to whom we are committed—including in particular the brave people of West Berlin—will be met by whatever action is needed. . . .

U.S. Chooses Difficult Path

My fellow citizens, let no one doubt that this is a difficult and dangerous effort on which we have set out. No one can foresee precisely what course it will take or what costs or casualties will be incurred. Many months of sacrifice and self-discipline lie ahead—months in which both our patience and our will will be tested, months in which many threats and denunciations will keep us aware of our dangers. But the greatest danger of all would be to do nothing.

The path we have chosen for the present is full of hazards, as all paths are; but it is the one most consistent with our character and courage as a nation and our commitments around the world. The cost of freedom is always high—but Americans have always paid it. And one path we shall never choose, and that is the path of surrender or submission.

Our goal is not the victory of might but the vindication of right—not peace at the expense of freedom, but both peace *and* freedom, here in this hemisphere and, we hope, around the world. God willing, that goal will be achieved.

A Republican Criticism of Kennedy's Cuban Policy: Speech of Senator Kenneth B. Keating of New York, February 25, 1963

It would be unfortunate if the debate on Cuba degenerated into a name calling, political brawl.

What the United States does or refrains from doing in regard to the Soviet base in Cuba may determine the peace and security of the whole world. We must consider this issue as Americans, not as Republicans or Democrats. And our goal must be to find solutions, not to develop campaign fodder for the coming elections.

Let it be conceded that the mistakes in Cuba go back many years to periods of Republican as well as Democratic administrations and that both parties bear a heavy responsibility for the tragic conditions which now exist in Cuba. Let it also be conceded that there are men and women in both parties equally dedicated to the task of ridding this hemisphere of its first Communist military base. . . .

My own judgment is that Cuba is now the No. 1 testing ground in the struggle between international communism and the free world. This is not because of any fear of an invasion of the United States from Cuba, as some have said in an effort to belittle concern with the problem of Cuba. Did anyone fear an invasion of the United States from South Korea if it fell to the Chinese Reds? Does anyone now fear an invasion of the United States from South Vietnam if it should fall to the Communists? We have recognized in these areas and in such places as Greece and Turkey and

Lebanon as well as in Berlin, that you cannot appease a tyrant, that the appetite of the Communists is insatiable, and that the only way to prevent the Communists from swallowing up the world piece by piece is to make sure they get indigestion every time they reveal their hunger pains. . . .

No two situations are entirely alike and there are elements in the Cuban situation which certainly are unique. The Soviet takeover of Cuba was accomplished not by an invasion but by subversion. Obviously, this is a more difficult tactic to detect and forestall, but its consequences are no less grave or menacing. Hitler had his Quislings, and the Communists have their Castros not only in Cuba, but in many areas of the world. We cannot blind ourselves to conquest by subversion or covert aggression, anymore than we can to conquest by overt and naked aggression. The same loss of freedom and expansion of communism is involved in both cases and neither can be tolerated without imperiling world peace. If we condone what has happened in Cuba, how can we possibly prevent the same pattern from repeating itself in British Guiana, after it achieves independence, or in Venezuela or Brazil or Mexico, or in any other country in which Communist agents are busily at work?

It seems to me that the first ingredient of any effective policy with regard to Cuba is that we recognize the nature of the threat. There is no possibility of success in efforts to eliminate the Soviets and their military equipment from this hemisphere if we downgrade the implications of the Cuban takeover. Our allies cannot be expected to join in the kind of concerted action which is necessary to deal with this situation, if important figures in our own country portray the problem merely as an irritant or a nuisance, and indicate a readiness to accept the status quo. Our leaders must make clear, not only to all Americans, but to the whole world, that the Soviet takeover in Cuba presents, at the very least, the same threat to the peace, security, and freedom of the world as the attempted Red takeovers of South Korea, South Vietnam, and the Congo.

We have acted boldly and with great determination in all of those areas, and there is no reason for us to respond with any less vigor to a threat in our own hemisphere just off our own shores. I believe that our partners in the struggle against international communism would fully understand our concern with the Soviet base in Cuba if our views were effectively articulated and skillfully conveyed. . . .

The dissatisfaction and uncertainty which are evident throughout the Nation today with regard to what is going on in Cuba and what it really means do not stem from congressional statements on the subject. The real cause for the crisis of confidence, the credibility gap, that exists widely throughout the Nation, lies in the complete failure of our Government leaders to articulate a clear and firm policy toward the Soviet takeover in Cuba. . . .

The present crisis of confidence with respect to Cuba can be traced directly to an increasing disillusionment with the zigzag policy of improvisation which has characterized the executive branch's pronouncements on this subject. At times, the improvisation has been good, as it was last October, when our Government acknowledged that strategic missile systems were in Cuba, and responded with determination and boldness. At other times, such as the Bay of Pigs, our improvisation was disastrous. In the long run, this policy has inevitably tended to undermine national confidence. . . .

When the President finally confronted the Nation with the Soviet missile threat in Cuba, the entire country united behind him and applauded his firm action in forcing withdrawal of the missiles and Ilyushin bombers. The country stood 100 percent behind the President's policies in this crisis and the Soviets backed down. . . .

Unfortunately, we failed to press our advantage and were unwilling to insist on on-site inspection to make certain that the Soviets were living up to their agreement. As a result of this improvisation of policy, there is doubt again as to just what the Soviets are doing in Cuba. . . .

What we have lacked most in Cuba is a long-term, consistent, and effective policy for ridding this hemisphere of Soviet conquest. When such a policy is enunciated, it will not lack support from either side of the aisle in this Chamber, or from any segment of the American people. Until that time, however, disunity and national concern are unavoidable. . . .

5. Kennedy Counters De Gaulle's Challenge to Western Unity

Western Europe by 1963 had outgrown its earlier dependence on the United States. Thanks in large part to the Marshall Plan, the nations of Western Europe were experiencing a phenomenal economic prosperity and with it a resurgence of national pride and confidence. A natural result was an increasing demand for equality and partnership with the United States in directing the affairs of the NATO alliance. President Charles de Gaulle of France especially had challenged the predominant American leadership. After his overture for an Anglo-American-French directorate of the Western alliance was rebuffed in 1959, de Gaulle began to pursue his own vision of a continental European association of "fatherlands," which would counterbalance the Anglo-American influence within NATO and eventually, perhaps, comprise a third force between America and Russia. French cooperation with NATO was reduced, de Gaulle insisted on building a French national nuclear force, and the British application for membership in the European Common Market was vetoed in early 1963. Doubts also were raised by de Gaulle of American readiness to risk destruction of its own cities in a nuclear war in order to defend Western Europe.

President Kennedy acted vigorously to meet the challenge. Fearful lest France disrupt NATO and block a larger European union, Kennedy chose July 4, 1962 to deliver an address at Independence Hall, Philadelphia, in which he strongly advocated further European unity and American interdependence. He seemed thereby to presage a future Atlantic Confederacy which would join Western Europe and America in closer economic and political bonds. A year later he undertook a goodwill tour of West Germany, Great Britain and Italy, obviously in order to counter de Gaulle's divisive tactics and to reassert American leadership. His address at Frankfurt, West Germany answered doubts about the reliability of the American commitment by asserting a readiness to defend Europe even at the risk of all-out nuclear warfare if events should ever necessitate.

The Goal of an Atlantic Partnership: Address by
President Kennedy, July 4, 1962

It is high honor for any citizen of the great Republic to speak at this hall of independence on this day of independence. . . .

Because our system is designed to encourage both differences and dissent—because its checks and balances are designed to preserve the rights of the individual and the locality against preeminent central authority—you and I both recognize how dependent we are, one upon the other, for the successful operation of our unique and happy form of government. Our system and our freedom permit the legislative to be pitted upon occasions against the Executive, the State against the Federal Government, the city against the countryside, the party against party, interest against interest, all in competition or in contention one with another. Our task—your task in the statehouse and my task in the White House—is to weave from all these tangled threads a fabric of law and progress. Others may confine themselves to debate, discussion, and that ultimate luxury—free advice. Our responsibility is one of decision, for to govern is to choose.

Thus, in a very real sense you and I are the executors of the testament handed down by those who gathered in this historic hall 186 years ago today. For they gathered to affix their names to a document which was above all else a document not of rhetoric but a bold decision. It was, it is true, a document of protest, but protests had been made before. It set forth their grievances with eloquence, but such eloquence had been heard before. But what distinguished this paper from all the others was the final, irrevocable decision that it took to assert the independence of free States in place of colonies and to commit to that goal their lives, their fortunes, and their sacred honor.

Today, 186 years later, that Declaration—whose yellowing parchment and fading, almost illegible lines I saw in the past week in the National Archives in Washington—is still a revolutionary document. To read it today is to hear a trumpet call. For that Declaration unleashed not merely a revolution against the British but a revolution in human affairs. Its authors were highly conscious of its worldwide implications, and George Washington declared that liberty and self-government were, in his words, "finally staked on the experiment intrusted to the hands of the American people."

This prophecy has been borne out for 186 years. This doctrine of national independence has shaken the globe, and it remains the most powerful force anywhere in the world today. There are those struggling to eke out a bare existence in a barren land who have never heard of free enterprise but who cherish the idea of independence. There are those who are grappling with overpowering problems of illiteracy and ill health and who are ill equipped to hold free elections, but they are determined to hold fast to their national independence. Even those unwilling or unable to take part in any struggle between East and West are strongly on the side of their own national independence. If there is a single issue in the world today which divides the world, it is independence—the independence of Berlin or Laos or Viet-Nam, the longing for independence behind the Iron Curtain, the peaceful transition to independence in those newly emerging areas whose troubles some hope to exploit.

The theory of independence—as old as man himself—was not invented in this hall, but it was in this hall that the theory became a practice—that the word went out to all the world that "The God who gave us life, gave us liberty at the same time."

And today this nation—conceived in revolution, nurtured in liberty, matured in independence—has no intention of abdicating its leadership in the worldwide movement for independence to any nation or society committed to systematic human suppression.

Spirit of European Unity

As apt and applicable as this historic Declaration of Independence is today, we would do well to honor that other historic document drafted in this hall—the Constitution of the United States—for it stressed not independence but interdependence, not the individual liberty of one but the indivisible liberty of all.

In most of the old colonial world the struggle for independence is coming to an end. Even in areas behind the Curtain, that which Jefferson called "the disease of liberty" still appears to be infectious. With the passing of ancient empires, today less than 2 percent of the world's population lives in territories officially termed "dependent." As this effort for independence, inspired by the spirit of the American Declaration of Independence, now approaches a successful close, a great new effort—for interdependence—is transforming the world about us. And the spirit of that new effort is the same spirit which gave birth to the American Constitution.

That spirit is today most clearly seen across the Atlantic Ocean. The nations of Western Europe, long divided by feuds more bitter than any which existed among the Thirteen Colonies, are joining together, seeking, as our forefathers sought, to find freedom in diversity and unity in strength.

The United States looks on this vast new enterprise with hope and admiration. We do not regard a strong and united Europe as a rival but as a partner. To aid its progress has been the basic objective of our foreign policy for 17 years. We believe that a united Europe will be capable of playing a greater role in the common defense, of responding more generously to the needs of poorer nations, of joining with the United States and others in lowering trade barriers, resolving problems of currency and commodities, and developing coordinated policies in all other economic, diplomatic, and political areas. We see in such a Europe a partner with whom we could deal on a basis of full equality in all the great and burdensome tasks of building and defending a community of free nations.

It would be premature at this time to do more than to indicate the high regard with which we view the formation of this partnership. The first order of business is for our European friends to go forward in forming the more perfect union which will some day make this partnership possible.

U.S. Ready for a "Declaration of Interdependence"

A great new edifice is not built overnight. It was 11 years from the Declaration of Independence to the writing of the Constitution. The construction of workable Federal institutions required still another generation. The greatest works of our nation's founders lay not in documents and declarations but in creative, determined action. The building of the new house of Europe has followed this same practical and purposeful course. Building the Atlantic partnership will not be cheaply or easily finished.

But I will say here and now on this day of independence that the United States will be ready for a "Declaration of Interdependence," that we will be prepared to discuss with a United Europe the ways and means of forming a concrete Atlantic partnership, a mutually beneficial partnership between the new union now emerging in Europe and the old American Union founded here 175 years ago.

All this will not be completed in a year, but let the world know it is our goal.

In urging the adoption of the United States Constitution, Alexander Hamilton told his fellow New Yorkers to "think continentally." Today Americans must learn to think intercontinentally.

Acting on our own by ourselves, we cannot establish justice throughout the world. We cannot insure its domestic tranquillity, or provide for its common defense, or promote its general welfare, or secure the blessings of liberty to ourselves and our posterity. But joined with other free nations, we can do all this and more. We can assist the developing nations to throw off the yoke of poverty. We can balance our worldwide trade and payments at the highest possible level of growth. We can mount a deterrent powerful enough to deter any aggression, and ultimately we can help achieve a world of law and free choice, banishing the world of war and coercion.

For the Atlantic partnership of which I speak would not look inward only, preoccupied with its own welfare and advancement. It must look outward to cooperate with all nations in meeting their common concern. It would serve as a nucleus for the eventual union of all free men—those who are now free and those who are avowing that some day they will be free. . . .

Kennedy's Speech at Frankfurt, West Germany, June 25, 1963

. . . We are partners for peace, not in a narrow bilateral context, but in a framework of Atlantic partnership. The ocean divides us less than the Mediterranean divided Greece and Rome. Our constitution is old and yours is young—and our culture is young and yours is old—but in our commitment we can and must speak and act with one voice. Our roles are distinct but complementary—and our goals are the same: Peace and freedom for all men, for all time, in a world of abundance, in a world of justice.

That is why our nations are working together to strengthen NATO, to expand trade, to assist the developing countries, to align our monetary policies and to build the Atlantic Community. I would not diminish the miracle of West Germany's economic achievements. But the true German miracle has been your rejection of the past for the future—your reconciliation with France, your participation in the building of Europe, your leading role in NATO, and your growing support for constructive undertakings throughout the world.

Your economic institutions, your constitutional guarantees, your confidence in civilian authority, are all harmonious with the ideals of older democracies. And they form a firm pillar of the democratic European community. . . .

The future of the West lies in Atlantic partnership—a system of cooperation, interdependence and harmony whose people can jointly meet their burdens and opportunities throughout the world. Some say this is only a dream, but I do not agree. A generation of achievement—the Marshall Plan, NATO, the Schuman Plan, and the Common Market—urges us up the path to greater unity.

There will be difficulties and delays, and doubts and discouragement. There will be differences of approach and opinion. But we have the will and the means to serve three related goals—the heritage of our countries, the unity of our continents and the interdependence of the Western alliance.

Some say that the United States will neither hold to these purposes nor abide by its pledges—that we will revert to a narrow nationalism. But such doubts fly in the face of history. For 18 years the United States has stood its watch for freedom all around the globe. The firmness of American will, and the effectiveness of American strength, have been shown in support of free men and free governments, in Asia, in Africa, in the Americas; and above all, here in Europe we have undertaken, and sustained in honor, relations of mutual trust and obligation with more than 40 allies. We are proud of this record, which more than answers doubts. But, in addition, these proved commitments to the common freedom and safety are assured, in the future as in the past, by one great fundamental fact—that they are deeply rooted in America's own self-interest. Our commitment to Europe is indispensable—in our interest as well as yours.

It is not in our interest to try to dominate the European councils of decision. If that were our objective, we would prefer to see Europe divided and weak, enabling the United States to deal with each fragment individually. Instead we have and now look forward to a Europe united and strong—speaking with a common voice—acting with a common will—a world power capable of meeting world problems as a full and equal partner.

This is in the interest of us all. For war in Europe, as we learned twice in 40 years, destroys peace in America. A threat to the freedom of Europe is a threat to the freedom of America. That is why no administration in Washington can fail to respond to such a threat—not merely from good will but from necessity. And that is why we look forward to a united Europe in an Atlantic partnership—an entity of interdependent parts, sharing equally both burdens and decisions, and linked together in the task of defense as well as the arts of peace.

This is no fantasy. It will be achieved by concrete steps to solve the problems that face us all: military, economic and political. Partnership is not a posture but a process—a continuous process—a continuous process that grows stronger each year as we devote ourselves to common tasks.

The first task of the Atlantic Community was to assure its common defense. That defense was and still is indivisible. The United States will risk its cities to defend yours because we need your freedom to protect ours. Hundreds of thousands of our soldiers serve with yours on this continent, as tangible evidence of this pledge. Those who would doubt our pledge or deny this indivisibility—those who would separate Europe from America or split one ally from another—would only give aid and comfort to the men who make themselves our adversaries and welcome any Western disarray.

The purpose of our common military effort is not war but peace—not the destruction of nations but the protection of freedom. The forces that West Germany contributes to this effort are second to none among the Western European nations. Your nation is in the first line of this defense—and your divisions, side by side with our own, are a source of strength to us all.

These conventional forces are essential, and they are backed by the sanction of thousands of the most modern weapons here on European soil and thousands more, only minutes away, in posts around the world. Together our nations have developed for the forward defense of free Europe a deterrent far surpassing the present or prospective force of any hostile power.

Nevertheless, it is natural that America's nuclear position has raised questions within the alliance. I believe we must confront these questions—not by turning the clock backward to separate nuclear deterrents—but by developing a more closely unified Atlantic deterrent, with genuine European participation.

How this can best be done—and it is not easy—in some ways more difficult to split the atom politically than it was physically—but how this can best be done is under discussion with those who may wish to join in this effort. The proposal before us now is for a new Atlantic force. Such a force would bring strength instead of division. It would belong to all members, not one, with all participating on a basis of full equality. And as Europe moves towards unity, its role and responsibility, here as elsewhere, would and must increase accordingly. Meanwhile, there is much to do. We must work more closely together on strategy, training and planning.

European officers from NATO are being assigned to Strategic Air Command headquarters in Omaha, Neb. Modern weapons are being deployed here in western Europe. And America's strategic deterrent—the most powerful in history—will continue to be at the service of the whole alliance.

Second: Our partnership is not military alone. Economic unity is also imperative—not only among the nations of Europe, but across the wide Atlantic. Indeed, economic cooperation is needed throughout the entire free world. By opening our markets to the developing countries of Africa, Asia and Latin America, by contributing our capital and skills, by stabilizing basic prices, we can help assure them of a favorable climate for freedom and growth. This is the Atlantic responsibility. For the Atlantic nations themselves helped to awaken these peoples. Our merchants and our traders ploughed up their soils—and their societies as well—in search of minerals and oil and rubber and coffee. Now we must help them gain full membership in the 20th century, closing the gap between the rich and the poor.

Another great economic challenge is in the coming round of trade negotiations. Those deliberations are much more important than a technical discussion of trade and commerce. They are an opportunity to build common industrial and agricultural policies across the Atlantic. They are an opportunity to open up new sources of demand, to give new impetus to growth, and make more jobs and prosperity, for our expanding populations. They are an opportunity to recognize the trading needs and aspirations of other free countries, including Japan.

In short, these negotiations are a test of our unity. While each nation must naturally look out for its own interests, each nation must also look out for the common interest—the need to reduce the imbalance between developed and underdeveloped nations—and the need to stimulate the Atlantic economy to higher levels of production rather than stifle it by higher levels of protection.

We must not return to the nineteen-thirties when we exported to each other our own stagnation. We must not return to the discredited view that trade favors some nations at the expense of others. Let no one think that the United States—with only a fraction of its economy dependent on trade and only a small part of that with western Europe—is seeking trade expansion in order to dump its goods on this continent.

Trade expansion will help us all. The experience of the Common Market—like the experience of the German Zollverein—shows an increased rise in business activity and general prosperity resulting for all participants in such trade agreements, with no member profiting at the expense of another. As they say on my own Cape Cod, "A rising tide lifts all the boats." And a partnership, by definition, serves both partners, without domination or unfair advantage. Together we have been partners in adversity—let us also be partners in prosperity.

Beyond development and trade is monetary policy. Here again our interests run together. Indeed there is no field in which the wider interests of all more clearly outweigh the narrow interest of one. We have lived by that principle, as bankers to freedom, for a generation. Now that other nations—including West Germany—have found new economic strength, it is time for common efforts here, too. The great free nations of the world must take control of our monetary problems if these problems are not to take control of us.

And third and finally, our partisanship depends on common political purpose. Against the hazards of division and lassitude, no lesser force will serve. History tells us that disunity and relaxation are the great internal dangers of an alliance. Thucydides reported that the Peloponnesians and their allies were mighty in battle but handicapped by their policy-making body—in which, he related "each presses its own end . . . which generally results in no action at all . . . they devote more time to the prosecution of their own purposes than to the consideration of the general welfare— each supposes that no harm will come of his own neglect, that it is the business of another to do this and that—and so, as each separately enter- tains the same illusion, the common cause imperceptibly decays."

Is this also to be the story of the grand alliance? Welded in a moment of imminent danger, will it disintegrate into complacency, with each member pressing its own ends to the neglect of the common cause? This must not be the case. Our old dangers are not gone beyond return, and any division among us would bring them back in doubled strength.

Our defenses are now strong—but they must be made stronger. Our economic goals are now clear—but we must get on with that performance. And the greatest of our necessities, the most notable of our omissions, is progress toward unity of political purpose.

For we live in a world in which our own united strength will and must be our first reliance. As I have said before, and will say again, we work toward the day where there may be real peace between us and the Communists. And we will not be second in that effort. But that day is not yet here.

We in the United States and Canada see 200 million people, and here on the European side of the Atlantic alliance 300 million people. The strength and unity of this half-billion human beings are and will continue to be the anchor of all freedom, for all nations. Let us from time to time pledge ourselves again to our common purposes. But let us go on, from words to actions, to intensify our efforts for still greater unity among us, to build new associations and institutions on those already established. Lofty words cannot construct an alliance or maintain it—only concrete deeds can do that.

The great present task of construction is here on this continent where the effort for a unified free Europe is under way. It is not for Americans to prescribe to Europeans how this effort should be carried forward. Nor do I believe that there is any one right course or any single final pattern. It is Europeans who are building Europe.

Yet the reunion of Europe, as Europeans shape it—bringing a perma- nent end to the civil wars that have repeatedly wracked the world—will continue to have the determined support of the United States. For that reunion is a necessary step in strengthening the community of freedom.

It would strengthen our alliance for defense. And it would be in our national interest as well as yours.

It is only a fully cohesive Europe that can protect us all against fragmentation of our alliance. Only such a Europe will permit full reciprocity of treatment across the ocean, in facing the Atlantic agenda. With only such a Europe can we have a full give-and-take between equals, and equal sharing of responsibilities, and an equal level of sacrifice. I repeat again—so that there may be no misunderstanding—the choice of paths to the unity of Europe is a choice which Europe must make. But as you continue this great effort, undeterred by either difficulty or delay, you should know that this new European greatness will be not an object of fear, but a source of strength, for the United States of America.

There are other political tasks before us. We must all learn to practice more completely the art of consultation on matters stretching well beyond the immediate military and economic questions.

Together, for example, we must explore the possibilities of leashing the tensions of the cold war and reducing the dangers of the arms race. Together we must work to strengthen the spirit of those Europeans who are not now free, to re-establish their old ties to freedom in the West, so that their desire for liberty and their sense of nationhood and their sense of belonging to the Western community over hundreds of years, will survive for future expression.

We ask those who would be our adversaries to understand that in our relations with them we will not bargain one nation's interest against another, and that the commitment to the cause of freedom is common to us all.

All of us in the West must be faithful to our conviction that peace in Europe can never be complete until everywhere in Europe, and that includes Germany, men can choose, in peace and freedom, how their countries shall be governed, and choose, without threat to any neighbor, reunification with their countrymen.

I preach no easy liberation and I make no empty promises, but my countrymen, since our country was founded, believe strongly in the proposition that all men shall be free and all free men shall have this right of choice.

As we look steadily eastward in the hope and purpose of new freedom, we must look—and evermore closely—to our trans-Atlantic ties. The Atlantic Community will not soon become a single overarching superstate. But practical steps toward stronger common purpose are well within our means. As we widen our common effort in defense, and our three-fold cooperation in economics, we shall inevitably strengthen our political ties as well. Just as your current efforts for unity in Europe will produce a stronger voice in the dialogue between us, so in America our current battle for the liberty and prosperity of all our citizens can only deepen the meaning of our common historic purposes. In the far future there may be a great new union for us all. But for the present, there is plenty for all to do in building new and enduring connections.

In short, the words of Thucydides are a warning, not a prediction. We have it in us, as 18 years have shown, to build our defenses, to strengthen our economies, and to tighten our political bonds, both in good weather and bad. We can move forward with the confidence that is born of success and the skill that is born of experience. And as we move, let us take heart from the certainty that we are united not only by danger and necessity, but by hope and purpose as well.

For we know now that freedom is more than the rejection of tyranny— that prosperity is more than an escape from want—that partnership is more than a sharing of power. These are, above all, great human adventures. They must have meaning and conviction and purpose—and because they do, in your country and in mine, in all the nations of the alliance, we are called to a great new mission.

It is not a mission of self-defense alone—for that is a means, not an end. It is not a mission of arbitrary power—for we reject the idea of one nation dominating another. The mission is to create a new social order, founded on liberty and justice, in which men are the masters of their fate, in which states are the servants of their citizens, and in which all men and women can share a better life for themselves and their children. That is the object of our common policy.

To realize this vision, we must seek a world of peace—a world in which peoples dwell together in mutual respect and work together in mutual regard—a world in which peace is not a mere interlude between wars, but an incentive to the creative energies of humanity. We will not find such a peace today, or tomorrow. The obstacles to hope are large and menacing. Yet the goals of a peaceful world—today and tomorrow—must shape our decisions and inspire our purposes.

So we are all idealists. We are all visionaries. Let it not be said of this Atlantic generation that we left ideals and visions to the past, nor purpose and determination to our adversaries. We have come too far, we have sacrificed too much, to disdain the future now. And we shall ever remember what Goethe told us—that the "highest wisdom, the best that mankind ever knew" was the realization that "he only earns his freedom and existence who daily conquers them anew."

Additional Reading

John R. Beal, *John Foster Dulles* (1959).
Marquis Childs, *Eisenhower: Captive Hero* (1958).
David J. Dallin, *Soviet Foreign Policy after Stalin* (1961).
Robert J. Donovan, *Eisenhower: the Inside Story* (1956).
Roscoe Drummond and G. Coblentz, *Duel at the Brink: John Foster Dulles' Command of American Power* (1960).
G. F. Kennan, *Russia, the Atom and the West* (1958).
Hans Morgenthau, "John Foster Dulles," in Norman Graebner, ed., *An Uncertain Tradition: American Secretaries of State in the Twentieth Century* (1961), 289–308.
Hugh Seton-Watson, *Neither War nor Peace* (1960).